CRACK THE CORE EXAM

6th (2019) Edition

VOLUME 1

PROMETHEUS LIONHART, M.D.

Crack the Core Exam - Vol 1 -

Sixth Ed. - Version 1.0

Disclaimer:

Readers are advised - this book is **NOT to be used for clinical decision making**. Human error does occur, and it is your responsibility to double check all facts provided. To the fullest extent of the law, the Author assumes no responsibility for any injury and/or damage to persons or property arising out of or related to any use of the material contained in this book.

ISBN: 9781730848933

Imprint: Independently published. — Prometheus Lionhart (*Earth Dimension C-137)*

Cover design, texts, and illustrations: copyright © 2018 by Prometheus Lionhart

Additional Art Provided by: armandsketch/shutterstock.com , Vector Tradition SM/shutterstock.com, Galitsyn/shutterstock.com, and licensed via adobe

No Slave Labor (Resident or Fellow) was used in the creation of this text

All Chapters Were Written and Illustrated By
PROMETHEUS LIONHART, M.D

VOLUME 1:

VOLUME 2:
—Topics: Neuro, MSK, Nukes, Mammo, Strategy

WAR MACHINE
—Topics: Physics, Non Interpretive Skills, BioStats

Legal Stuff

Readers are advised - **this book is NOT to be used for clinical decision making**. Human error does occur, and it is your responsibility to double check all facts provided. To the fullest extent of the law, the Author assumes no responsibility for any injury and/or damage to persons or property arising out of or related to any use of the material contained in this book.

Are There Recalls In This Book? ABSOLUTELY NOT.

The Author has made a considerable effort (it's the outright purpose of the text), to speculate how questions might be asked. A PhD in biochemistry can fail a med school biochemistry test or biochem section on the USMLE, in spite of clearly knowing more biochem than a medical student. This is because they are not used to medicine style questions. The aim of this text is to explore the likely style of board questions and include material likely to be covered, informed by the ABR's study guide.

Throughout the text the author will attempt to fathom the manner of questioning and include the corresponding high yield material. A correct estimation will be wholly coincidental.

Humor / Profanity Warning

I use profanity in this book. I make "grown up" jokes. Now is not the time to be recreationally outraged - I'm just trying to make the book readable and fun. Probably not a good idea to read the book out loud to small children or elderly members of your church / temple / mosque.

I also talk a mess of shit about different medical specialties. I do this because Radiologists are tribal, and stroking that urge tends to calm people. Probably not a good idea to read the book out loud to members of your family that are in specialties other than Radiology. The truth is I respect all the other sub-specialties of medicine (even family medicine) - those are dirty jobs but someone needs to do them. I just wasn't strong enough to dedicate my life to poop, pus, and note-writing. I'm glad someone was.

"Maybe people that create things aren't concerned with your delicate sensibilities"
- RICK AND MORTY – SEASON 2 EPISODE 8

What Makes This Book Unique?

The impetus for this book was not to write a reference text or standard review book, but instead, a strategy manual for solving multiple choice questions for Radiology. The Author wishes to convey that the multiple choice test is different than oral boards in that you can't ask the same kinds of open-ended essay-type questions. *"What's your differential?"*

Questioning the contents of one's differential was the only real question on oral boards. Now that simple question becomes nearly impossible to format into a multiple choice test. Instead, the focus for training for such a test should be on things that can be asked. For example, anatomy facts - what is it? ... OR... trivia facts - what is the most common location, or age, or association, or syndrome? ... OR... What's the next step in management? Think back to medical school USMLE style, that is what you are dealing with once again. In this book, the Author tried to cover all the material that could be asked (reasonably), and then approximate how questions might be asked about the various topics. Throughout the book, the author will intimate, "this could be asked like this," and "this fact lends itself well to a question." Included in the second volume of the set is a strategy chapter focusing on high yield "buzzwords" that lend well to certain questions.

This is NOT a reference book.
This book is NOT designed for patient care.
This book is designed for studying specifically for multiple choice tests, case conference, and view-box pimping/quizing.

I FIGHT FOR THE USERS

-TRON 1982

1 THE ART OF WAR

PROMETHEUS
LIONHART, M.D.

The art of war is of vital importance… It is a matter of life and death, a road either to safety or to ruin. Hence it is a subject of inquiry which can on no account be neglected. - Sun Tzu

My idea for this first chapter is to provide some guidance on how to "wage war." I'm going to share with you my philosophy on training and performing optimally under pressure. Specifically, I want to give you some ideas on how to deal with test anxiety, fear of failure, motivation, and self mastery.

June / November is Coming

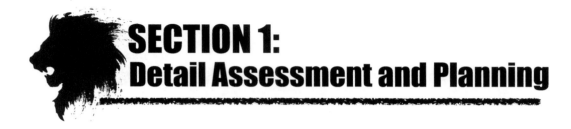

SECTION 1:
Detail Assessment and Planning

Before we get started with the "when" and "how" of the exam you need to have a clear understanding of the *"what."* Let us begin with the most important topic - *"passing."*

The official stance is that everyone can theoretically pass the examination - which sounds good if you are simply testing for safety and competence. The problem occurs when you bring in professional statisticians and test metric experts (which all professional exams do). These people insist on creating a normalized curve to validate the exam. An examination with 100% pass rate is statistically invalid (it wasn't sensitive enough to detect the "dangerous radiology trainees").

If they passed everyone they would totally invalidate their own exam. They would risk public perception perceiving the exam as a cash grab disguised as a formality. If they failed more than 20 or 25% they would have a full revolt to deal with (lead by Program Directors who want you reading nodule followups not studying for a repeat exam). They can't set a hard number or they risk one of these two scenarios. So, like every other standardized exam you've ever taken, it's curved. They may not "curve" the exam in the traditional sense, but questions will be removed until the statistics provide an acceptable yield of passing and failing scores. This is standard operating procedure on any exam of this magnitude.

Which leads me to my second point. Frequently I am asked *"what do I need to score to pass ?"* You can't think about this as a raw score. You can't say I got 9/10 correct so I passed. What if everyone else got 10/10 right ? You just got the lowest score in the country. If anyone is gonna fail it's you - despite getting 90% of the questions right. You need to think about it as your score relative to the rest of the room. Historically around 10% of people fail, and 1-2% of people condition physics. So, if you score in the 15th percentile or higher you are probably safe.

Another common question is, *"how many subjects can I condition ?"* On the old oral boards there was a certain number of subjects that you could condition (fail) without having to retake the entire exam. You would just have to come back in a few weeks and be tested on that subject (or subjects) to meet criteria for a pass. The original official statement on the CORE exam was something similar, that you could fail up to five categories. However, when no one ever conditioned anything other than physics after 5-6 years people started to notice that was probably bullshit. Now there has been an official statement that only physics can be conditioned. Your clinical totals are lumped into a raw score and then compared to a predetermined minimal score (that is later adjusted to fail around 10% of people).

You may be thinking to yourself *"That doesn't sound hard. I've never been that low on anything."* There is no greater danger than underestimating your opponent. You have never competed at this level before. Your shelf exam scores , USMLE, etc… don't mean shit because you were competing against Family Medicine , Peds, Psych, etc…. This time you are competing against Radiology Residents only. Yes, it is less competitive compared to the "glory days" but Radiology still has a lot of smart people in it. Smart enough to realize how to avoid the worst parts of medicine anyway. Plus, you are dealing with an extremely motivated group. Most reasonable people are terrified to fail this exam and will therefore be putting considerable effort into passing.

But Prometheus!? I heard someone say *"all you need to do is take call to pass."*

Yes… someone did famously say that. Everyone has an agenda in this life. My agenda is to help you pass this exam. Other people… perhaps they want you to take call for them. Or perhaps they just want to make sure you are "safe" and "protect the public." Those people (if they are reading) can prove their virtuous motives by writing questions that are fair, clinically relevant, and follow topics on the official provided study guide. If your motivations are truly genuine consider writing a fair test, free of trickery, on bread and butter topics would make board review books unnecessary.

I prefer teaching clinical radiology anyway (RadiologyRonin.com)

- - -

Let us switch gears and discuss the structure of the exam. The exam is a multiple choice test consisting of around 600 questions. The punishment is administered over two days, the first is typically longer than the second (7.5 hours and 6 hours respectively). They give you 30 mins "break time" but that is built into the exam.

The CORE Exam covers 18 categories *(sometimes 17 - in Chicago)*. The categories include: breast, cardiac, gastrointestinal, interventional, musculoskeletal, neuroradiology, nuclear, pediatric, reproductive/endocrinology, thoracic, genitourinary, vascular, computed tomography, magnetic resonance, radiography/fluoroscopy, ultrasound, physics, and safety. This book is outlined to cover the above sections, with the modalities of CT, MRI, Radiography, Fluoroscopy, and Ultrasound integrated into the system based chapters as one would reasonably expect.

On the exam, Physics questions are integrated into each category with no distinct physics examination administered. However, the physics section is still considered a virtual section, and you can fail / condition it. In fact, the physics portion is actually the overall largest section.

Useless trivia from a portion of the RadioIsotope Safety Exam (RISE), one of the requirements for Authorized User Eligibility Status, is also included within the Exam.

SECTION 2:
Waging War

In the previous section, I tried to introduce the idea that the exam should not be viewed as a test on which a certain "minimum score" is required to pass. Instead, I want you to look at the exam as a contest in which you must finish in the top 85% to achieve victory.

I'm not trying to scare you. I'm just trying to help you understand that you must take this exam serious. It's tough and smart people fail it every year.

Over the next 6-12 months, when you are out partying and horsing around - remember that someone else out there at the same time is working hard. Someone is learning, getting smarter, and preparing to win.

Life is a struggle. Everybody fights - and that doesn't mean getting punched in the face. That means not hitting the snooze button, managing your personal relationships, dealing with disability, trying to do the right thing for your children - etc… etc… and everyone gets asked the same question - *"Can I move on, or am I going to give up on my dreams ?"*

Transform a threat into a challenge. A life free of struggle is a life void of meaning. We are born for battle. Battle against the beasts of the jungle. Battle against the rival tribes. And… yes… battle against each other on the glorious field of multiple choice questions.

I encourage you to embrace this as a great opportunity to harness your will. Thank all the Gods of War for providing you with this chance to prove your greatness.

SECTION 3:
Attack by Stratagem

"Victorious warriors win first and then go to war."

Let's talk about specifics. I will now share with you my 3 Promethean Laws for success on this exam and in life.

 LAW 1 – **You must do anything your opponents are willing to do.**

Example: If everyone is using my books, then you must also. If everyone is using a particular q-bank (or banks) then you must also. If everyone is studying a certain amount per day then you must also.

 LAW 2 – You must do things your opponent is NOT willing to do.

Example – Setting your alarm at 2 am to study while everyone else is asleep. Listening to lectures while driving to work, while in the shower, while pooping.

Example – Finding ways to maximize your study time. Specific ideas (things that I do) include the application of *"conscious labor"* to improve efficacy in specific tasks. Example – I never take a shower for longer than 3 mins. I turn the water on and get in (while it's freezing cold) – I play the game of enduring the cold shower as it heats up. This may sound crazy but it is a method for callusing the mind. It helps me remember my priorities. I want to win the exam more than I want to enjoy a warm shower. Warm showers don't help me win the exam. Less extreme examples would be never touching the snooze button. Not watching any tv, movies, news, comics, etc… until victory is achieved. This is not punishment – and should not looked at as such. These are habits of the ultra-successful. People who are competing for Olympic gold medals tend to know dick about anything other than their sport. I remember seeing an interview with a female gold medalist (I don't recall the sport) but the reporter ask her who she was supporting in the presidential election and she didn't even know who was running. She acted embarrassed and people watching that probably thought to themselves "Dumb jock! Doesn't even know who is running for President!" The people thinking that will never understand what it's like to achieve an elite level of success at anything. Knowing political trivia doesn't help her win at gymnastics (or whatever) and time spent on anything other than her craft is wasted. While you are wasting time on current events the enemy is training and you can't allow them to work when you are not (see Law 1). Minimize distractions - Maximize productivity.

LAW 2 - continued…

Example – Doing things to improve your mental conditioning. Like a runner might swim to help cross train muscles that are also useful to running. This is where the habits of the "Sly Man" are useful (I'll tell you more about the "Sly Man" later in the chapter). Improving your focus through forcing yourself to be present in the moment. Not allowing yourself to be distracted by anxiety, fear or regret. Present in the moment. Looking for ways to improve. Etc…

LAW 3 – Performance on "Game Day" must equal performance in practice

Let us take a few minutes and discuss *"test anxiety."*

"Anxiety" is a dishonest word though isn't it?
Let's use a more accurate word. **FEAR**

No… I'm not afraid. I'm way too macho to be afraid of things. There is a difference between being afraid, and being a coward. Only crazy people don't experience fear. It's ok to be afraid. If you let that fear dominate your decision making… that is when you run into problems.

The inability to control fear is the root cause of the *"text anxiety"* problem. Fear more than anything else keeps people from achieving their full potential in sports, life, in business - in everything.

Fear of what?? Fear of failure right? Nope... That is not it. That is not what you are afraid of. It's not failing. It is the fear of a perceived threat to your ego, your self esteem. The fear of looking bad and getting embarrassed in front of your peers. The fear of being exposed as a fraud. Not really smart enough to be a Radiologist.

> Notice that all these feeling of dread of anxiety are focused on the future - the consequences which result after you have failed. This problematic focus on the future will become important as we proceed with this discussion.

Agree?

Now… lets talk about how to conquer fear and channel all that psychogenic energy into a powerful motivated force.

SECTION 4:
Weaknesses and Strengths

I want to spend a little bit of time discussing some strategies for controlling fear, and obliterating the negative effects of anxiety on your game day performance.

Controlling fear involves two things: (1) choice, and (2) strategy.

The "choice" is the conscious decision to confront your fear. Once you have made the decision to confront it, you can then begin to implement a "strategy". The strategy that I am going to suggest is to not consider this as an effort to eliminate fear. Fear is normal. Only crazy people don't have fear. The goal is to increase courage.

 Mechanism 1: Generating Courage Through Purpose

One powerful mechanism to increase courage is to have a goal or purpose that is worthy. For example, a mother may run into a burning building to save her child. Does she do this because she is no longer afraid of fire? Or does she do it because her purpose as a mother out weighs the fear and allows her to generate extreme courage?

Purpose ⟶ Courage

 Mechanism 2: The Perspective of the Joker

Another mechanism for overcoming fear is to begin to view the world from a certain point of view. A point of view similar to that of the Court Jester.

The point of view of the Jester (or Joker) is to view not just the various social institutions, but all formations of the natural world as games. You must be careful of the word "game." When people use the word "game" they often mean "frivolous." There can be important games.

Imagine that you were playing a game of Super Mario Brothers. What if you believed that if you fell into a cavern or were bit by one of those plant things (or a turtle) that you would actually die ? Do you think this would make you better at the game ? You'd be terrible at it. You wouldn't be able to relax, you would second guess every movement, and ultimately your performance would be awful. All because you believed this game was real and the dangers within it were real.

Games are best played as games.

Mechanism 2: The Perspective of the Joker - continued...

Hopefully you can begin to understand the benefits of this strategy. In viewing stressful challenges as games you can remove the effects of fear. This is not the only benefit though. The sincerity that exists in the nature of play - the act of doing things simply for themselves actually improves your performance.

Games are best played as games.

 Mechanism 3: "The Art of Not Giving a Fuck".

In discussing the perspective of the Joker people will often become upset and insist the consequences of failure are very real. That the fear of failure is justified.

Remember that your fear lives in just one place - your head.

Confront the fear rationally. Are you afraid of being embarrassed? I can only be embarrassed if the people I think I've embarrassed myself in front of have my respect. If I don't respect you - your opinion means nothing to me. As the Lebowski says "that's just like your opinion man." I refer to this as *"The Art of Not Giving a Fuck"*.

Someone worth respecting would understand the difficulty of the task and not judge you poorly for failure. The only people who never fail are the people who don't try.

Remember, the Joker sees the whole world as game playing. That's why, when people take their games seriously - the people who make a lot of stern and pious expressions - the Joker can't help but laugh. It's hard to not laugh when you see people pretending that what they do is so very serious. As Bill Hicks would say "It's Just a Ride"

I also hear this a lot. If I fail the test I'll lose my fellowship. First of all you don't need one – the necessity of a fellowship is a lie propagated by the institution that wants you as a slave for an extra year. Even if you really want to do one – you wont lose it . They won't even know you failed, and passing is not required even to be accredited at hospitals and work as an Attending. Probably some of your Attendings are international grads who haven't even sat for the CORE exam yet – I know some of mine were. Plus, they don't give a shit - they just want you as a slave. If they "take" your fellowship away they might have to do your work - and that would defeat the entire purpose of having fellows.

There is nothing really on the line other than your ego. Our minds project a backdrop of fear onto our reality. That is the default setting.

SECTION 5:
Variations and Adaptability

I have many hobbies. Disco Dance, Ping Pong, Sunbathe.

But my primary hobby is trying to be the best version of myself.   I am obsessed with maximizing my potential as a human being. Since this is a competition, I thought it might be helpful to share with you some of my ideas on this topic.

I'll start off by saying that I can't necessarily help you be "the best." What we are talking about here is being "the best you." I like to imagine that people are born as various shaped and sized canisters. Not all of these canisters will hold the same amount of liquid. My Dad used to say "all men were NOT created equal." It's just a fact that some people are better at certain things than others. Some people have greater potential than others. We can't all be Tony Stark. The point is to try and be the best version of yourself. The best you. You want to fill that canister all the way up to the brim. Don't be the half full bottle, thats only half a life.

 Method 1: Mental Optimization - The Sly Man

I'm sure you are wondering… why is he so "sly" ?

The Sly Man is the second aspect of the Joker - the deeper aspect. This concept is based on Gurdjieff's idea of "the Sly Man" – sometimes referred to as "The Forth Way."

The idea is that when you play you are doing things only for the purpose of doing them. For example, when you listen to music you aren't trying to get to the end of the song, or count the notes, or derive meaning in the lyrics. You are listening to the music only for the purpose of listening. The other thing that happens as you play, or dance, or listen to music is that you become present (mentally) for the process. This in itself is a method to increase focus, and energy in daily life. This is a method for minimizing day-dreaming and absent mindedness. This is the way of the Sly Man.

Study only for the purpose of studying. Avoid the mentality of "getting through the material." Try and read the material the same way you would if you were reading a novel for pleasure. If done correctly you will find your studying endurance and recall ability improve.

Method 2: Mental Optimization - The Self Remembering Exercise:

Most people exist in a state of semi-hypnotic "waking sleep." Studying or performing like this is not ideal. The *"Self Remembering Exercise"* is a tool to increase your ability to harness this power and increase your focus. People who really dive deep into this stuff will make a big deal about how "self remembering" and "being present" are not the same thing. For the focused goal of maximizing performance on the exam, I will just say that either will serve the same purpose.

How this works is that in the morning (or prior to entering the study hall, or exam room) you must spend 5-10 mins being present in the moment. Close you eyes and repeat to yourself "I am here in this place." Generate the sense of being present in the current moment. Concentrate only on your breathing once you achieve the state of being present.

Why waste time doing this? Meditation makes my penis soft!

I agree, it's not alpha and typically I only endorse alpha male (or female) behavior…but this thing really works. Remember how I said that all your feeling of dread of anxiety are focused on the future - the consequences which result after you have failed ? If you center your mind on the present, all that shit melts away. It is really just that simple. Anytime you feel anxiety and dread building inside yourself perform the self remembering exercise. Eyes closed - say "I am here in this place" , build a sense of presence in the current moment, focus on your breathing, and then return to the exam / practice room and proceed to kick ass. Repeat as needed.

 Method 3: Mental Optimization - The Accountability Mirror

This is a mechanism I learned from David Goggins. Goggins is the fucking man - if you don't know about him, he's worth a google. He is a man that understands the power of true fucking will power.

The accountability mirror works like this. In the morning you put sticky notes of the things you want to accomplish in that day on the mirror. Not just individual tasks but how you handle yourself and behave. At the end of the day when you are getting ready for bed, brushing your teeth (or tooth - if you are from West Virginia), you have to look in that mirror and answer for your progress. You either accomplished your goals or you didn't. You have to look at it and face it down. The only way you can improve outcomes is to be 100% honest about the effort that you put in and the outcomes that resulted. Hearing "you did great!" even when you didn't isn't helping. Be honest with yourself. Make the changes you need to make and get better.

Method 4: Physical Optimization - Sunlight

I know that nerds burn easily when exposed to the sun. Plus the Radiologist walks in shadow and moves in silence (to guard against extraterrestrial violence).

Seriously - you only need like 5 mins a day. Your pineal gland demands it. I don't care if it's freezing cold outside – get your ass out there and look at the sun for 5 mins. Be mindful in the moment and play the standing outside in the sun game.

 ## Method 5: Physical Optimization - Sleep

I have trained myself to sleep 4 hours a night by mapping and understanding my REM cycles. People will say they *"can't do that."* People use the phrase *"can't do that"* when they really mean *"I don't want to do that because it will hurt too much."* Callous your mind.

This takes some effort and practice. If I get 3.5 hours sleep I feel terrible. I don't really care about "feeling terrible." A warrior does not complain of physical discomfort. The problem is I can't concentrate. I also feel this way with 4.5 hours sleep. At 4 hours though… the Lion roars.

The trick is to map your sleep patterns. There are apps that can do this. Alternatively, you can go full retard and buy a *"sleep shepherd,"* which is my endorsement if you really want an accurate map plus the added benefits of binaural beats.

Take two weeks and create a sleep journal. What you are looking for is how long it takes you to go through two REM cycles. Then you can plot your bed time and wake up time to maximize productivity. If you do this right you can potentially get 4 extra hours a day to study.

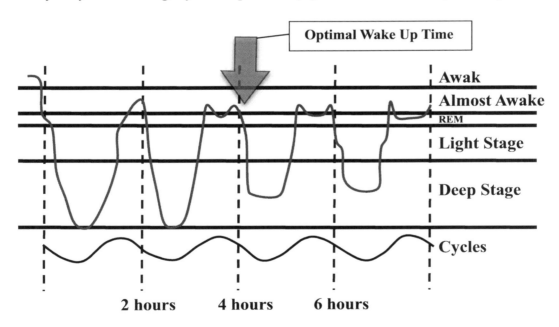

Method 5: Physical Optimization - Sleep - Continued

Sleep Induction: Another component to getting the most out of your sleep is the ability to fall asleep rapidly. All that time you might be spending staring at the ceiling is time wasted. I recommend the use of a *"sleep induction mat."* It's basically a porcupine. This is most helpful if you have a "busy mind" - full of distracting thoughts.

How this works: It's a bunch of sharp (dull) plastic points. You take your shirt off and lay on them. It hurts. The pain distracts you from all the random shit you might be thinking about. Practice the self remembering exercise. In about 5 mins you will notice that it doesn't hurt anymore. That is because your body is releasing a low level of endorphins. Sit up - roll the thing up - and go to sleep.   Some people will tell you that it takes 30 mins to work. That's horse-shit. 5 mins tops.

 Method 6: Physical Optimization - Diet

The human body is designed to operate perfectly… in a world that existed 10,000 years ago. Despite what the primitive "rat brain" may tell you, sugar is the devil. Foosball, school, girls, and Ben Franklin are also the devil - but that is unrelated to this discussion.

Avoiding highs and lows is key to optimal function. Avoiding IBS cramps and constant shitting is also ideal. I'm not going to endorse a particular diet by brand name. I'll just say there is a lot of data showing that a Ketogenic diet (or something similar) helps to maximize mental function.

 Method 7: Physical Optimization - Movement

You need 15 mins a day of movement. This can be actual alpha male gym stuff, or beta male yoga – but any form of movement works and is necessary to maximize your mental health.

SECTION 6:
Use of Energy

Let's switch gears and talk about specifics on how to plan a strategy and use resources.

When to Begin Studying:

Frat Answer: Most people put in a 6 month training camp. They will typically being aggressive studying starting in late December or early January in preparation for the June exam.

I think the amount of time necessary to pass depends on how strong you are as a multiple choice test taker, how much studying you did in the first 2 years of training, the amount/quality of teaching at your training institution, and your own ability to retain trivia.

My recommendation would be between 9 and 6 months. Any longer than 9 months and you risk forgetting the trivia you learned at the beginning of your training camp. I like the analogy of a bucket with a hole in the bottom. You pour water (knowledge) in the bucket and it slowly drips out the bottom. You want the bucket to be filled to the brim the morning of the exam.

- 9 Months = The upper limit of trivia retention

- 6 Months = Average

- 3 Month = You better be a trivia machine

- Less than 3 Months = Go ahead and register for the repeat exam.

What to do Prior to Starting to Study:

You need to come up with a game plan. The specifics of this plan is not something I can help you create because each one of you has unique social circumstances and backgrounds. Some of you have kids. Some of you have jealous wives / husbands. Some of you have program directors who will not give you one minute off service to study but will still throw you in the pillory if you fail.

Whatever your social situation you need 3 things:

(1) Somewhere quiet to study that is free of distractions.

(2) Time in this ideal study environment

(3) Resources to study (books, questions, videos, and Google).

The Ideal Study Environment:

There is a person inside you that does not want to study. This person doesn't care that you will be humiliated if you fail. This person believes in nothing Lebowski. He/She only wants to eat, read celebrity gossip, watch internet porn, and sleep.

When it comes to successful preparation this person is your greatest enemy. For me at least, it seems that dealing with this person (your inner hungry, sleepy, porn crazed, Justin Bieber fan) is like dealing with a meth addict. Don't leave the meth lying around where he/she can see it. If he/she gets ahold of it… the study session is over.

What is "the meth" ? It varies from person to person. It most cases it's your fucking phone.

Do NOT bring your phone into the study environment. If you must bring your phone (for child care reasons, etc…) then put it on a shelf on the other side of the room.

Other Tips:

- Don't show up hungry. Eat prior to going into the study environment. Avoid sugar as it will make you crash.

- Caffeine is your friend. If your religion forbids the use of caffeine - dig around in your sacred text for loop holes. Most major religions allow you to ask for forgiveness later. The best time to ask for forgiveness is after you pass the exam.

- *How much caffeine ?* There is at least one paper that showed that small hourly doses of caffeine (0.3mg per kg of body weight [approx 20 mg per hour] is optimal). Caffeine tablets – cut can help you keep this accurate. Stay away from energy drinks and all that bullshit – you want to keep the dose steady. Consider keto coffee (bullet proof coffee) or other coffee brands with high fat content to help improve bioavailability.

- No music in the environment. This feeds the lazy person inside you and is a distraction. I will listen to music prior to studying. Like a pro wrestler walk out song . The first 31 seconds of "Welcome to the Jungle" is my current suggestion. Ideally you sit down at your desk right when Axl Rose says "Cha!"

- No "Study Buddies." You need to be alone in this room. Your inner lazy person will try and small talk with your study partner's inner lazy person. It will start out innocent with you asking them a legit questions about radiology / physics. 30 seconds later you will be chatting about Kardashians.

- If you must study in a public location, you should make it clear to your classmates that you don't want to be interrupted - snarl at them. You should also bring ear plugs for when they start talking to each other.

How Many Hours Per Day Should You Study:

You need about 2-3 hours on weekdays, and 8-12 hours a day on the weekends. This is the minimum. The real answer would be "however much would kill you, minus one second."

For me, studying early in the morning is superior to the evening. After work you are tired, your family is the most needy, and you are the most distractible. Most days when I left work as a Resident I was angry about something. Usually one or more of my asshole Attendings having no regard for my need to study. All that hate (although motivating) was also distracting. It's hard to study when you are trying to plot revenge.

I understand some people are just not wired for early morning studying, but it is ideal if you can make yourself do it.

Along those lines…*Sleep is for pussies*. See prior discussion on optimizing your sleep.

Stealing an hour during the day.

Most programs have a noon and / or morning lecture. At this point in your training you know when these are useful and when they are a waste of time. I would have zero remorse about ditching a low yield lecture to study. If you feel bad for even one second just think about what will happen to you if you fail. If you do decide to ditch a lecture make it count. Have your hiding place / study environment picked out. Have your goals for what you want to get through clear. The more productive that hour is the less bad you will feel about doing it.

Resources:

Essentials: Crack the Core Vol 1, Crack the Core Vol 2, Physics War Machine, Crack the Core Case Companion.

Highly Recommended: TitanRadiology.com / RadiologyRonin.com - Board Review Course and Clinical Mastery. ** Ronin will be taking over in early 2019.

Supplemental: Google Images - No single book can match the power of the internet.

Q Banks: Last year I released a Q Bank via TitanRadiology. I'm hoping to improve and expand the question bank this year with the new RadiologyRonin.com platform (launching in early 2019). Obviously that is going to be the one I'll endorse. Regardless, my opinion is that more questions are better. I would do as many practice questions as possible which will likely mean using multiple commercial q banks.

How To Use the Resources:

Everyone is starting from a different place depending on your individual background and interests.   Having said that nearly everyone has 5 tasks to accomplish:

(1) *Fill in the large holes.* Everyone sucks at something. There are probably 3-4 sections (maybe more) that you feel particularly weak in.

(2) *Accumulation of Random Trivia.* Even if you think you are strong in a certain subject there is almost certainly a laundry list of trivia that you don't have available for recall.

(3) *Physics.* Nearly everyone starts out knowing almost zero physics.

(4) *Non-Interpretive Skills.* This is another topic that pretty much no one has any exposure to.

(5) *Biostats.* You will have to review the basics on this as well.

Suggested Strategy for the Clinical Portions:

(1) Make a list of the subjects you suck the most at.

(2) Read the corresponding sections / chapters in Crack. Read them slowly. Google image anything you've never seen before.

(3) Watch the corresponding videos to these chapters on RadiologyRonin.

(4) Start at the beginning of Crack Vol 1 and work your way to the end of Vol 2. Don't skip the Chapters you read already - this is your second time through those. Annotate and mark up the books. I've purposefully provided lots of room for extra notes. Also, the paper is not glossy for a reason - I did this so you can write in the books without smearing shit everywhere.

(5) Start back at the beginning of Crack Vol 1. This time we are going to add practice questions. Pick a Q Bank, they are all pretty similar (mine is best obviously). Read a chapter in Crack (example Peds) then do the corresponding Peds questions. Make notes in the book as needed. Work your way all the way through the book. This process can be supplemented with the corresponding Ronin Videos.

(6) Start to switch over to 90% questions - 10% reading. Now is the time to read the Case Companion. You should be doing 150 + questions a day. Go ahead and make them random, that will simulate the exam.

Practice Questions:

Practice questions do two things for you. (1) They help expose holes in your knowledge. (2) They help you practice your timing and discipline.

I think it's important to backload questions until you have a foundation. There is no point in doing practice physics questions if you have never read a page of physics. It's a total waste. Clinical radiology is the same way. Don't mess with questions until you have read the chapter in Crack at least once.

Once you have entered "phase 2" - which would correspond with step 6 above. It's time to start doing questions with a timer. Average one minute per question. Practice your disciplined approach (reading the entire question, reading all the choices, never change your answer). You should be doing more and more questions every week leading up to the exam - revising the material as needed.

In the volume 2 strategy chapter I discuss the *"Genius Neuron."* He (She) is your closest friend and you must learn to trust his/her advice.

Learning Physics / Non-Interpretive Skills:

There are two strategies. Both are equally valid depending on your personality.

Strategy 1: Learn it all at once. Blocking out 6-8 weeks of your study schedule and just hit physics every day.

Strategy 2: Ration it in with the clinical reading. For example if you study for two hours, 1 hour in physics, 1 hour in clinical.

Regardless of which strategy you pick you should follow the same steps:

(1) Read the *War Machine* cover to cover once. RadiologyRonin videos may help solidify topics. If necessary google topics that remain confusing.

(2) Start over and read each chapter - then do corresponding questions.

(3) Continue to do practice questions to keep the material fresh.

(4) Reviewing the ABR's NIS source document will still be necessary (make sure you are using the most up to date version). Read the War Machine's discussion first - it will likely make the document more digestible.

The Last Month:

(1) Most (90%) of your time should be spent on timed practice questions.

(2) The other 10% you should spend preparing your high yield review. You should start by putting together a list of all the random trivia that you will forget immediately after the exam. This is a list of all the numbers, half-lives, photon energies, etc.. The back of the *War Machine* has a good start on this but you will likely want to add to it.

The Last Week:

(1) Continue doing practice questions.

(2) Study your high yield numbers / trivia every day. Try and concentrate it to 1-2 pages of stuff you are having trouble remembering.

(3) Review Biostats, and skim the ABR's Non-Interpretive Skills study guide.

The Morning of the Exam:

Look at your highest yield notes (the 1-2 pages of trivia you have boiled down). Read it over and over and over again until they make you get rid of all your notes.

When You Sit Down To Take The Exam:

(1) Check to make sure your markers work. If you got a dud fix it now. You don't want "dead marker rage" to make you drop a question mid exam.

(2) Scribble down all the formulas and numbers you can remember on one of the dry erase boards. Six hours into the exam that information won't be in your short-term memory any more.

(3) Give yourself a vigorous scalp massage - like 30 seconds. This increases blood flow to the brain and reduces stress. Seriously, it really works. I learned this from Ivan Vasylchuk (Ukrainian Sambist, Merited Master of Sport, World Champion, and Winner of the SportAccord World Combat Games).

**Don't forget to do this on the second day of the exam also.

The Night Between Exam Days:

Anticipate the subjects that haven't been tested yet and review your notes on those. Avoid drinking or socializing. This is war. The people in the hotel lobby aren't your friends, those are the people trying to push you into the bottom 15%. You can be friends with them after you pass. Plus, arguing over who missed what will only increase your anxiety.

- Avoid alcohol - even if you are "sure you failed." A strong performance day 2 can resurrect you. In general, most people feel like they did terrible after day 1. Remember, it is all about how you did relative to you cohort.

- Study 2-3 hours.

- Don't eat anything that will give you diarrhea.

- 15 minutes on the treadmill can be tremendously helpful to reduce stress.

- Get 6-8 hours sleep.

SECTION 7:
Weaponize Your Will

This last section is a discussion on how to weaponize your will power and stay motivated for the duration of the training camp.

Attack by Fire

10-15% of people will fail this exam. You must beat those people to pass.

No one has the right to beat you. I don't care where you trained. I don't care where you came from. No one has the right to beat you. When doubt seeks in you can go two roads. You can go to the left or you can go to the right. You may hear people say "failure is not an option." This is silly, failure is always an option. Failure is the most readily available option – but it's not the only option - it is a choice. You can choose to fail or you can choose to succeed.

Self doubt and negative thoughts are the road to failure. I want to tell you this – as someone who prides himself on both physical and mental toughness – it is normal to feel that way sometimes. The vast majority of people reading this book are perpetual winners in life, and those kinds of people hate to admit weakness to others and to themselves.

You are not your accomplishments. You are not your failures. You are you.

Recognizing that about yourself gives you the power to overcome negative thought through the awesome power of hard work. Earn your victory. Deserve to win - the Gods of War will look favorably upon you. Don't hold back. Go 100% the entire time. You may hear people say – "you look tired, you look exhausted." The worst feeling in the world is losing and knowing that it was because you were lazy and didn't put in the work. I'd much rather get beat knowing I did everything I could to be prepared. "You look tired, you look exhausted," - yeah… you bet your ass I'm tired, that is the whole fucking point. My goal is always to be exhausted at the end of each day. You want to feel like you got hit by a fucking freight train. That's the feeling I like. That's how I know I'm giving my best effort.

I train hard, I work hard, I fight hard, and I fight for victory.

In any competition, I want only one thing and that is to leave with my hand raised, at the top of the podium, with the gold medal – and I make no apologies for that. You shouldn't either.

Tactical Dispositions - *"Snarl More"*

Prior to entering the study environment - find a mirror and make the ugliest face you can.

Not a silly face. Not a sad face. A snarl.

A good snarl can give you what the Bible calls a psychological edge.

Maneuvering the Army

Most people go through their lives trying to avoid pain. This is a mistake. You are competing in a high stakes contest. Pain is your friend. If you can endure more time in the study room relative to your opponents then you have an edge (Law 2). Once you understand this you won't avoid pain anymore. Look for pain. Invite him in and have dinner with him.

You don't look for me pain…. I look for you.

Vacuity and Substance

Many of you have probably had fairly normal lives with loving families and friends. I imagine that could be a source of motivation. When you feel that you are too tired to study, or can't motivate yourself to enter the study environment, think about them. Think about how much better things will be for them once you are making a real salary.

Rise and Grind.

Illusion and Reality

For others, perhaps you have traveled a different path. Not everyone has enjoyed a life filled with good times and noodle salad. Some of us were born in the dark, molded by it.
Now, you are after something. It could be revenge. It could be money. Or…. it could be something else.

Vengeance is a powerful motivator. Think of all the people who have tried to stop you. Think of all the people who have mistreated you. Visualize their stupid ugly faces smirking and smiling when they hear you failed the exam. Let it boil you blood. Now picture those same people making a face like they smelled a fart when they hear you passed the exam. You will find that you aren't tired anymore. You are ready to train.

As a resident I went as far as putting a picture of one of my tormentors in my shoe. That way every step I took I was walking on this persons face.

30

SELF AFFIRMATION

-A TOOL TO WEAPONIZE YOUR WILL-

I have an oath that I read to myself -especially when I'm tired, as a tool to harness my will. I encourage you to modify the oath to make it yours. Hang it somewhere you can see it daily. Perhaps beside a picture of the person you hate the most in this world. Or… if you are less of a Sith and more of a Jedi - hang it beside a photo of the people you love.

MY NAME IS (your name here) AND THIS IS MY OATH

IN SOUND MIND I MAKE THIS OATH.

I DECLARE THAT I AM NOT PERFECT.

I KNOW THAT THERE WILL BE CHALLENGES TO OVERCOME, BUT I SWEAR ON THE POWERS OF THIS UNIVERSE THAT I WILL FIGHT WITH ALL MY HEART, ALL MY STRENGTH, AND ALL MY SOUL TO OVERCOME.

I WILL OUTWORK ALL HUMAN BEINGS THAT STAND IN FRONT OF ME. NO ONE WILL TRY AS HARD AS ME. THEY DO NOT HAVE MY HEART OR UNRELENTING DESIRE.

I DECLARE THAT I WILL PERSIST WHEN OTHERS GIVE UP.

I WILL ALWAYS BE HUNGRY FOR MORE. EVEN WHEN THINGS SEEM IMPOSSIBLE, I WILL NOT GIVE UP.

TODAY I AM GOING TO WAR.

NO ONE HAS THE RIGHT TO TAKE MY DREAMS FROM ME.

I WILL SACRIFICE UNTIL I REACH THE TOP. NO TEMPTATION WITH SWAY ME. I CRAVE ONLY THE BLOOD OF THE ENEMY.

MY HEART IS ON FIRE. NO MATTER HOW LOUD MY BODY SCREAMS, I WILL WILL SCREAM LOUDER.

I AM FOCUSED. I AM PREPARED FOR BATTLE.

COME AT ME, I DARE YOU. I AM PREPARED FOR WAR.

Despite these words, this page is intentionally blank.

2 Pediatrics

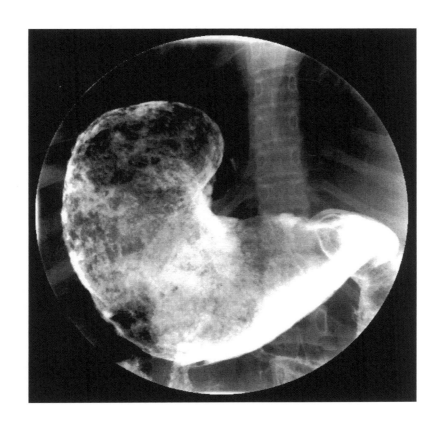

PROMETHEUS
LIONHART, M.D.

SECTION 1:
Skull & Scalp

Craniosynostosis

"Craniosynostosis" is a fancy word for premature fusion of one or several of the cranial sutures. The consequence of this premature fusion is a weird looking head and face (with resulting difficulty getting a date to the prom). Besides looking like a gremlin (or a cone-headed extraterrestrial forced to live as a typical suburban human), these kids can also have increased intracranial pressure, visual impairment, and deafness.

There are different named types depending on the suture involved – thus it's worth spending a moment reviewing the names and locations of the normal sutures.

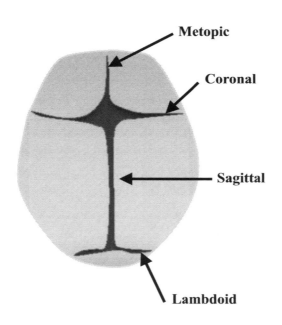

	Bones Involved	Fusion Direction	Fusion Order
Metopic (frontal)	Frontal	Front to Back	First (9-24 months)
Coronal	Frontal & Parietal	Lateral to Medial	Second
Lambdoid	Parietal & Occipital	Lateral to Medial	Third
Sagittal	Parietal	Back to Front	Fourth

Craniosynostosis Continued...

Pathology / Sub-type Trivia:

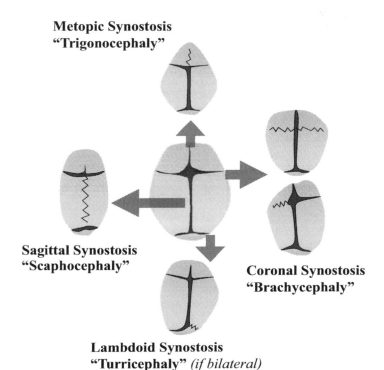

Metopic Synostosis "Trigonocephaly"

Sagittal Synostosis "Scaphocephaly"

Coronal Synostosis "Brachycephaly"

Lambdoid Synostosis "Turricephaly" *(if bilateral)*

"Plagiocephaly"
Potential Source of Fuckery

This word basically means "flat."

You will see it used to describe unilateral coronal synostosis as *"anterior plagiocephaly."*

You will see it used to describe unilateral lambdoid synostosis as *"posterior plagiocephaly."*

The problem is that many people use the word "plagiocephaly" to describe the specific entity of *"deformational plagiocephaly"* - which is just benign positional molding, not a pathologic early closure. On the following page, I'll go into more detail on this. Just know you may be required to read the question writer's mind when the word is used to differentiate between the benign and pathologic entities.

Metopic (frontal)	Trigonocephaly	• Eyes are close together (*hypotelorism*) • Ethmoid sinuses underdeveloped • Medial part of the orbit slants up	"Quizzical Eye" appearance
Coronal	Brachycephaly	• Unilateral subtype is more common. • Unilateral type causes the ipsilateral orbit to elevate, and contralateral frontal bone to protrude "frontal bossing" • Bilateral form is Rare - should make you think <u>syndromes</u> (*Borat's brother Bilo**).	"Harlequin Eye" * if unilateral.
Lambdoid	Turricephaly *(if bilateral)*	• Tall Cranium (oxycephaly, acrocephaly) • See Next Page for Unilateral Discussion	Least Common Form
Sagittal	Scaphocephaly or Dolichocephalic	• Long, Narrow Head. • Looks like an upside-down boat. • Usually the kids have a normal IQ • Usually the kids do NOT have hydrocephalus • Associated with Marfans *(both are tall and skinny).*	Most Common Form

*For the purpose of this text, Borat's brother Bilo is presumed to have syndromic mental retardation / developmental delay. Not iatrogenic encephalopathy related to the intracranial placement of a red haired woman's tooth - as therapy for demon induced epilepsy - which is suggested in some reports.

⚖️ **THIS *vs* THAT: Posterior Plagiocephaly *vs* True Unilateral Lambdoid Synostosis**

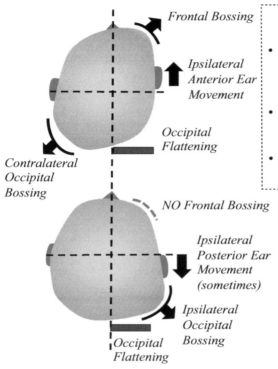

Frontal Bossing

Ipsilateral Anterior Ear Movement

Occipital Flattening

Contralateral Occipital Bossing

NO Frontal Bossing

Ipsilateral Posterior Ear Movement (sometimes)

Ipsilateral Occipital Bossing

Occipital Flattening

Deformational Posterior Plagiocephaly

- Infants that sleep on the same side every night develop a flat spot on the preferred dependent area of the head (occipital flattening).

- It is managed conservatively (sleep on the other side for a bit).

- Note the contralateral Occipital and ipsilateral Frontal Bossing.

Unilateral Lambdoid Synostosis

- This is rare.

- Note the Occipital Bossing is on the same side, and the Frontal Bossing doesn't occur.

- The ear doesn't always shift, but when it does it is usually posterior.

- The management is often surgical.

↩ **NEXT STEP:**

Outside of the jungle (or the year 1987), the diagnosis of synostosis is going to be made with CT + 3D. If asked what test to order I would say <u>CT with 3D recons.</u> Having said that, they could show you a skull plain film (from 1987) and ask you to make the diagnosis on that.

If the test writer was feeling particularly cruel and bitter he/she could show the diagnosis with ultrasound. In that case, remember that a normal open suture will appear as an uninterrupted hypoechoic fibrous gap between hyperechoic cranial bones (Bright – Dark – Bright, Bone – Suture - Bone).

Although certain MR gradient sequences can be used, MRI has traditionally been considered unreliable in identifying sutures individually.

Trivia For the purpose of multiple choice, there are numerous random bone buzzwords that are supposed to elicit the reflexive diagnosis **NF-1** in your brain when you hear / read them.

The more common ones include:
- Absence / Dysplasia of the Greater Sphenoid Wing,
- Tbial Pseudoarthrosis,
- Scoliosis, and
- Lateral Thoracic Meningocele.

I'd like to add *"bone defect in the region of the lambdoid suture"* or the *"asterion defect"* to that list of reflex generators.

It's rare and poorly described - therefore potentially high yield.

<u>Trivia</u> Craniosynostosis Syndromes:

Most of the time (85%) premature closure is a primary (isolated) event, although it can occur as the result of a syndrome (15%). The two syndromes worth having vague familiarity with are Apert's and Crouzon's.

	Apert's	• Brachycephaly (usually) • Fused Fingers (syndactyly) - "sock hand"
	Crouzon's	• Brachycephaly (usually) • 1st Arch structures (maxilla and mandible hypoplasia). • Associated with patent ductus arteriosus and aortic coarctation. • Short central long bones (humerus, femur) - "rhizomelia" • Chiari I malformations 3: ~70% of cases

⚖ THIS *vs* **THAT**: Skull Markings

Convolutional Markings	Copper Beaten	Luckenschadel - *"Lacunar"*
Normal gyral impressions on the inner table of the skull. You see them primarily during normal rapid brain growth (age 3-7). Usually mild and favors the posterior skull. If you see them along the more anterior skull then you should think about a "copper beaten" skull from the increased intracranial pressure.	The same thing as convolutional markings (the normal gyral impressions), just a shit ton more of them. You also see them along the anterior portions of the skull not just the posterior. Think about things that cause **increased intracranial pressure.** Classic examples: • Craniosynostosis • Obstructive Hydrocephalus	Oval, round, and finger shaped defects (craters) within the inner surface of the skull Different than Copper Beaten in that: (A) They aren't gyriform. (B) They aren't related to increased ICP. (C) They are usually present at birth. Instead they are the result of defective bone matrix. Classic Association: • **Chiari II malformation** / Neural Tube Defects.

Wormian Bones

In technical terms, there are a bunch of extra squiggles around the lambdoid sutures. "Intrasutural Bones" they call them.

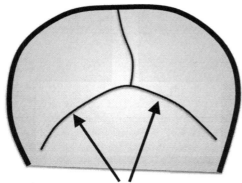

Normal Lambdoid Sutures

There is a massive differential, but I would just remember these "**PORK-CHOP**"

Pyknodysostosis
Osteogenesis Imperfecta
Rickets
Kinky Hair Syndrome
(Menke's / Fucked Copper Metabolism)

Cleidocranial Dysostosis
Hypothyroidism / **H**ypophosphatasia
One too many 21st chromosomes (*Downs*)
Primary Acro-osteolysis *(Hajdu-Cheney)*

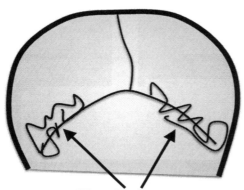

Wormian Bones
-Extra Squiggles-

Parietal Foramina

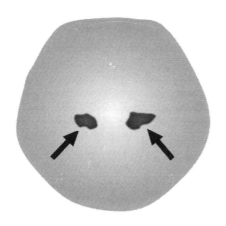

These paired, mostly round, defects in the parietal bones represent <u>benign congenital defects.</u> The underlying cause is a delayed or incomplete ossification in the underlying parietal bones.

They can get big and confluent across the midline. Supposedly, (at least for the big ones - > 5mm) they are associations with cortical and venous anomalies.

Dermoid / Epidermoid of the Skull

In the context of the skull, you can think about these things as occurring from the congenital misplacement of cells from the scalp into the bony calvarium.

The result is a growing lump of tissue (keratin debris, skin glands, etc…) creating a bone defect with benign appearing sclerotic borders.

There are a few differences between the two subtypes that could be potentially testable (contrasted masterfully in the chart).

Although, I suspect a *"what is it ?"* type question is more likely. As such, look through some google image examples to prepare yourself for that contingency.

	Epidermoid	Dermoid
Histology	Only Skin (Squamous Epithelium)	Skin + Other Stuff Like Hair Follicles, Sweat Glands Etc..
Age of Onset	Present between age 20-40	Typically have an earlier presentation
Location	Parietal Region is Most Common (*"behind the ears"*)	Tend to be midline. *The skin ones tend to be around the orbits.*
		Associated with Encephaloceles - especially when midline
CT	CSF Density	- More Heterogeneous, - Calcifications (internal or peripheral) may be present
MRI	T1 Variable, T2 Bright, NO Enhancement	T1 Bright, T2 Bright, +/- Wall Enhancement

Congenital Dermal Sinus

Usually when people talk about these things they are referring to the spina bifida style midline lumbosacral region defects. However, we are going to stay focused on the skull / face. The two classic locations for dermal communications with the dura are the occiput and the nose. Both of which are classically midline, and can be associated with a dermoid cyst. For gamesmanship, consider a sinus tract anytime you see a cyst in these locations.

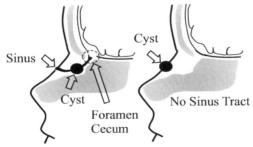

Dural communication will require communication through the foramen cecum.

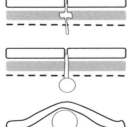

Sinus tracts may or may not have associated dermal or intraosseous cysts.

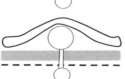

Cysts may or may not have sinus tracts.

⚖️ THIS *vs* THAT: Scalp Trauma

There are 3 scalp hematoma subtypes. Because the subtypes are fairly similar, there is a high likelihood a sadistic multiple choice writer will attempt to confuse you on the subtle differences - so let's do a quick review.

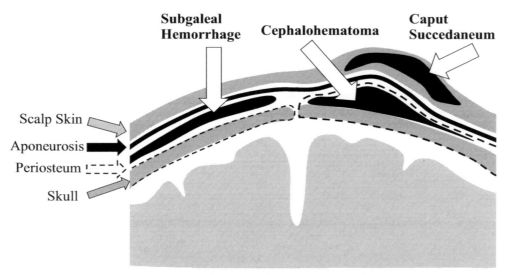

	Subgaleal Hemorrhage	**Cephalohematoma**	**Caput Succedaneum**
Location	Deep to the Aponeurosis *(between aponeurosis and periosteum)*	Under the Periosteum *(skin of the bone)*	Subcutaneous Hemorrhage *(superficial to the aponeurosis)*
Suture Relationship	NOT limited by suture lines	Limited by suture lines *(won't cross sutures)*	NOT limited by suture lines
Trivia	Covers a much larger area than a cephalohematoma	Outer border may calcify as a rim and leave a deformity - sorta like a myositis ossificans.	
Complications	Potentially life-threatening - rapid blood loss. Often not seen until 12-72 hours post delivery.	Usually requires no intervention *(resolves within a few weeks)* Can get super infected (E.Coli). Abscess would require drainage. Can cause skull osteomyelitis.	Requires no intervention *(resolves within a few days)*
Cause	Vacuum Extraction	Instrument or Vacuum Extraction	Prolonged Delivery

Skull Fractures

Accidental (and non-accidental) head trauma is supposedly (allegedly, allegedly) the most common cause of morbidity and mortality in children. As you might imagine, the pediatric skull can fracture just like the adult skull - with linear and comminuted patterns. For the purpose of multiple choice, I think we should focus on the fracture patterns that are more unique to the pediatric population: Diastatic, Depressed, and "Ping-Pong"

- *Diastatic Fracture:* This is a fracture along / involving the suture. When they intersect it is usually fairly obvious. It can get tricky when the fracture is confined to the suture itself. The most common victim of this sneaky fracture is usually the Lambdoid, followed by the Resident reading the case on night float …with Attending backup (asleep in bed). *How does one know there is traumatic injury to a suture ?* Classically, it will widen. This is most likely to be shown in the axial or coronal plane so you can appreciate the asymmetry (> 1 mm asymmetry relative to the other side).

- *Depressed Fracture:* This is a fracture with inward displacement of the bone. *How much inward displacement do you need to call it "depressed" ?* Most people will say "equal or greater to the thickness of the skull." Some people will use the word *"compound"* to describe a depressed fracture that also has an associated scalp laceration. Those same people may (or may not) add the word *"penetrating"* to describe a compound fracture with an associated dural tear.
Will any of those people be writing the questions ? The dark side clouds everything. Impossible to see the future is.

- *Ping Pong Fracture*: This is actually another subtype of depressed fracture but is unique in that it is a <u>greenstick</u> or "<u>buckle</u>" type of fracture. Other potentially testable differences include:

  - *Outcomes:* Ping Pong fractures typically have a favorable / benign clinical outcome (depressed fractures have high morbidity).

  - *Etiology:* Diastatic and depressed fracture types usually require a significant wack on the head. Where as "ping pong" fractures often occur in the setting of birth trauma (Mom's pelvic bones +/- forceps).

  - *Imaging Appearance:* Ping Pong fractures are hard as fuck to see. To show this on a test you'd have to have CT 3D recons demonstrating a smooth inward deformity. You could never see that shit on a plain film. I can't imagine anyone being a big enough asshole to ask you to do that. Hmmm…. probably.

NEXT STEP: Depressed Fx	

Unlike linear fractures (which usually heal without complication), depressed fractures often require surgery. Some general indications for surgery would include:

- Depression of the fragments > 5mm (supposedly fragments more than 5mm below the inner table are associated with dural tears),

- Epidural bleed

- Superinfection (abscess, osteomyelitis)

- "Form" (cosmetic correction to avoid looking like a gargoyle),

- "Function" (if the frontal sinus is involved, sometimes they need to obliterate the thing to avoid mucocele formation).

THIS *vs* THAT:

Fracture	Normal Suture
> 3mm	< 2mm
Wide Center	Equal Width
"Darker"	"Lighter"
Straight Line, with Angular Turns	Squiggly Line, with Curves

Leptomeningeal Cyst - *"Growing Skull Fracture"*

A favorite of board examiners since the Cretaceous Period.

Typical Pathogenesis:

- Step 1: You fracture your noggin, 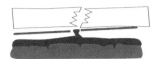 AND tear the underlying dura.

- Step 2: Leptomeninges herniate through the torn dura into the fracture site.

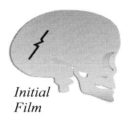 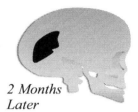

Initial Film   *2 Months Later*

- Step 3: Over time (a few months) CSF pulsations progressively widen the fracture site and prohibit normal healing.

- Step 4: You know you shouldn't, but you just can't resist the urge to poke your own brain through the now cavernous cranial defect.

- Step 5: The poking triggers a powerful hallucinogenic experience. You have a telepathic conversation with a room filled with self transforming elf machines. You are overwhelmed with tremendous curiosity about exactly what/who they are and what they might be trying to show you.

- Step 6: You develop epilepsy from poking your brain too much. Or was it not enough? - you can't remember

Sinus Pericranii

A rare disorder that can be shown as a focal skull defect with an associated vascular malformation. The underlying pathology is a low flow vascular malformation - which is a communication between a dural venous sinus (usually the superior sagittal) and an extra cranial venous structure via the emissary veins.

Most likely way to show this:

(1) MRI - with some type of vascular sequence - post contrast or MRA/TOF.

(2) CT showing the skull defect - wanting a next step (ultrasound or MRI to demonstrate the vascular component).

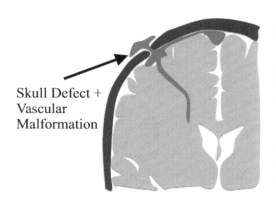

Skull Defect + Vascular Malformation

<u>N</u>on-<u>A</u>ccidental <u>T</u>rauma (Abusive Head Trauma)

Although car wrecks and falls account for the majority of skull fractures in children, there still remains the timeless truth — some people just can't take screaming kids.

For the purpose of multiple choice, the follow clues should make your spider-sense tingle.

- Inconsistent History:
  "My 7 month old wrecked his bike"

- Subdural Hematoma

- Retinal hemorrhage

- DAI / Parenchymal Contusion

- Cerebral Edema, Stroke
  (less specific but still worrisome)

- Depressed Skull Fx, or Fracture Crossing Suture Line
  (less specific but still worrisome)

 GAMESMANSHIP:

Subdurals have a stronger association with NAT relative to epidurals. Think about vigorous shaking (trying to get that last drop of ketchup out of the bottle) tearing bridging cortical veins.

"Look High, Look Low"
- Sneaky Ways to Suggest NAT -

- Look High: Thrombosed (hyperdense) cortical vein at the vertex

- Look Low: Retroclival hematoma (thin hyperdense sliver in the pre-pontine region)

- Look Lower: Edema within the cervical soft tissues

⚖ **THIS** *vs* **THAT:**

Retroclival Hematoma	
Epidural	Subdural
Below the Tectorial Membrane	Above the Tectorial Membrane

⚖ **THIS** *vs* **THAT:**

Extra Axial Fluid	
Chronic Subdural (CSF Density)	Prominent CSF Spaces
Medial Displacement of Bridging Vein *(sometimes smashed and not well seen)*	Cortical veins are adjacent to the inner table
Usually Unilateral. If Bilateral Usually Asymmetric in Size.	Usually Symmetric

More on NAT later in the chapter.

SECTION 2:
Pediatric Brain - Select Topics

Disclaimer: Brain tumors , cord tumors, and a bunch of other random Peds Neuro pathologies are discussed in detail within the Neuro chapter found in volume 2. The same is true for congenital heart, certain GU, GYN, and MSK topics - found within their dedicated chapters. If you find yourself saying *"Hey! What about that thing? This asshole is seriously not going to talk about that?"* Relax, I split things up to reduce redundancy and cluster things for improved retention.

———

Enlarged extra-axial fluid spaces:

Extra-axial fluid spaces are considered enlarged if they are greater than 5 mm. **BESSI** is the name people throw around for "**b**enign **e**nlargement of the **s**ubarachnoid **s**pace in **i**nfancy." The etiology is supposed to be immature villa (that's why you grow out of it).

BESSI Trivia:

- It's the most common cause of macrocephaly,
- Typically presents around month 2 or 3, and has a strong male predominance.
- Typically resolves after 2 years with no treatment,
- There is an increased risk of subdural bleed - either spontaneous or with a minor trauma. This subdural is usually isolated (all the same blood age), which helps differentiate it from non-accidental trauma, where the bleeds are often of different ages.

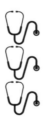 *Trivia* - Pre-mature kids getting tortured on ECMO often get enlarged extra-axial spaces. This isn't really the same thing as BESSI but rather more related to fluid changes / stress.

> **THIS vs THAT:**
> **BESSI vs Subdural Hygroma**
>
> ***BESSI*** - Cortical veins are adjacent to the inner table - they are usually seen secondary to enlargement of the subarachnoid spaces (positive cortical vein sign)
>
> ***Subdural*** - Cortical veins are displaced away from the inner table - they are often not seen secondary to compression.

Enlarged symmetric subarachnoid spaces <u>favoring the anterior aspect of the brain</u> (spaces along the posterior aspect of the brain are typically normal).

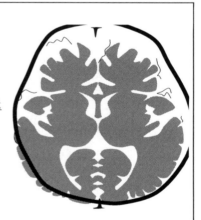

Brain parenchyma is normal and there is either normal ventricle size or very mild communicating hydrocephalus. Communicating meaning that all 4 ventricles are big.

Periventricular Leukomalacia (Hypoxic-Ischemic Encephalopathy of the Newborn)

This is the result of an ischemic / hemorrhagic injury, typically from a hypoxic insult during birthing. The kids who are at the greatest risk are premature and little (less than 1500 g). The testable stigmata is cerebral palsy - which supposedly develops in 50%. The pathology favors the watershed areas (characteristically the white matter dorsal and lateral to the lateral ventricles).

The milder finding can be very subtle. Here are some tricks:

(1) *Use PreTest Probability:* The kid is described as premature or low birth weight.

(2) *Brighter than the Choroid:* The choroid plexus is an excellent internal control. The normal white matter should always be less bright (less hyperechoic) when compared to the choroid.

(3) *"Blush" and "Flaring"* : These are two potential distractors that need to be differentiated from legit grade 1 PVL. *"Blush"* describes the physiologic brightness of the posterosuperior periventricular white matter - this should be less bright than choroid, and have a more symmetric look. *"Flaring"* is similar to blush, but a more hedgy term. It's the word you use if you aren't sure if it's real PVL or just the normal brightness often seen in premature infants white matter. The distinction is that *"flaring"* should go away in a week. Grade 1 PVL persists > 7 days.

The later findings are more obvious with the development of cavitary periventricular cysts. The degree of severity is described by the size and distribution of these cysts. These things take a while to develop - some people say up to 4 weeks. So, if they show you a day 1 newborn with cystic PVL they are leading you to conclude that the vascular insult occurred at least 2 weeks prior to birth (not during birth - which is often the case).

 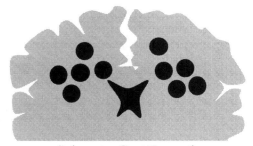

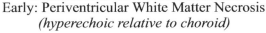

Early: Periventricular White Matter Necrosis
(hyperechoic relative to choroid)
          Subacute: Cyst Formation

Trivia

The most severe grade (4), which has subcortical cysts, is actually more common in full term infants rather than preterms.

Germinal Matrix Hemorrhage

I like to think about the germinal matrix as an embryologic seed that sprouts out various development cells during brain development. Just like a seed needs water to grow, the germinal matrix is highly vascular. It's also very friably and susceptible to stress.

An important thing to understand is that the germinal matrix is an embryology entity. So it only exists in premature infants. As the fetus matures the thing regresses and disappears.

By 32 weeks, germinal matrix is only present at the caudothalamic groove.
By 36 weeks, you basically can't have it (if no GM, then no GM hemorrhage).

Take home point - **No GM Hemorrhage in a full term infant.**

The scenario will always call the kid a premature infant (probably earlier than 30 weeks). The earlier they are born the more common it is.

Up to 40% occur in the first 5 hours, and most have occurred by day 4 (90%).

Grading system (1-4) - *quick and dirty* -

1. Little bit of blood at the caudothalamic groove

2. Blood in the ventricles but no dilation

3. Blood in the ventricles with dilation

4. Blood in the brain parenchyma.

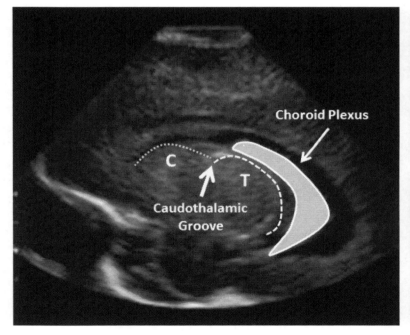

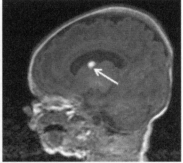

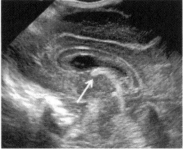

Grade 1 GM Hemorrhage
-Blood in the CT Groove

SECTION 3:
Pediatric Head & Neck - Select Topics

Disclaimer: *All of the temporal bone pathology you would commonly associate with Peds is also discussed in detail in the Neuro chapter - found in Volume 2. This is also true for the classic orbital pathologies of childhood (Retinoblastoma etc...)*

Choanal Atresia – This results from a membrane that separates the nasal cavity from its normal communication with the oral cavity. It is usually unilateral but can be bilateral. It will not surprisingly be symptomatic immediately if bilateral. Classic stories are *"can't pass NG tube,"* and *"respiratory distress while feeding"* (neonates have to breath through their noses). You will also sometimes hear a history of *"a continuous stream of snot draining from one or both nostrils."*

CHARGE
Coloboma,
Heart defect,
Atresia (Choanal)
Retarded growth,
Genitourinary
abnormalities
Ear anomalies

There are two different types: bony (90%), and membranous (10%). The appearance is a unilateral or bilateral posterior nasal narrowing, with thickening of the vomer.

Trivia: There are many syndromic associations including <u>CHARGE</u>, Crouzons, DiGeorge, Treacher Collins, and Fetal Alcohol Syndrome. CHARGE is the one people mention the most in articles.

Congenital Piriform Aperture Stenosis

This results from abnormal development of the medial nasal eminences, and subsequent **failure of formation of the primary palate. You can see this in isolation or with choanal atresia.** The piriform aperture of the nasal cavity (bony inlet of the nose) is stenotic (as the name suggests), and the palate is narrow. The classic picture is the associated **central maxillary "MEGA-incisor."** Midline defects of the brain (corpus callosum agenesis, and holoprosencephaly) are associated — as my Grandma always said *"face predicts brain"*.

The big thing to know is the **high association with hypothalamic-pituitary-adrenal axis dysfunction.**

Next Step - You have to image the brain

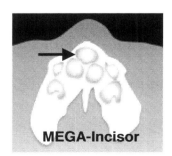

MEGA-Incisor

Ectopic Thyroid:

Thyroid topics will be covered again in the endocrine chapter. I do want to mention one or two now for completeness.

To understand ectopic thyroid trivia you need to remember that the thyroid starts (embryology wise) at the back of the tongue. It then descends downward to a location that would be considered normal. The "pyramidal lobe" actually represents a persistence of the inferior portion of the thyroglossal duct - that is why this thing is so variable in appearance. Sometimes this process gets all fucked up and the thyroid either stays at the back of the tongue (lingual thyroid) or ends up half way down the neck or even in the chest (ectopic thyroid).

Trivia to know:
- Most "developed" countries test for low thyroid at birth (Guthrie Test). That will trigger a workup for either ectopic tissue or enzyme deficiencies.
- Nukes (I-123 or Tc-MIBI) is superior to ultrasound for diagnosing ectopic tissue. This is by far the most likely way to show this on a multiple choice exam. I guess CT would be #2 - remember thyroid tissue is dense because of the iodine.
- Ultrasound does have a preoperative role in any MIDLINE neck mass - with the point of that ultrasound being to confirm that you have a normal thyroid in a normal place. If you resect a midline mass (which turns out to be the kids only thyroid tissue) you can expect an expensive well rehearsed didactic lecture on pediatric neck pathology from an "Expert Witness" sporting a $500 haircut.
- Lingual thyroid (back of the tongue) is the most common location of ectopic thyroid tissue

Thyroglossal Duct Cyst:

As we discussed previously, thyroid related pathology can occur anywhere between the foramen cecum (the base of the tongue) and the thyroid gland. In this situation we are talking about the duct (which is the embryological thyroid interstate highway to the neck) failing to involute fully. What you get is a left over cyst - hence the name. The classic locations are (1) at the base of the tongue, and (2) midline anterior to the hyoid. Now textbooks will make a big deal about these things becoming slightly lateral below the hyoid. Do NOT get hung up on that. For the purpose of multiple choice remember these guys are <u>midline</u>. <u>Midline</u> is the buzzword.

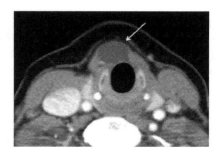

Things to know:
- Classic Buzzword / Scenario = **<u>Midline</u> Cyst in the Neck of a Kid.**
- *Next step* once you find one = confirm normal thyroid location and/ or look for ectopic tissue (Ultrasound +/-Tc-MIBI, or I-123).
- They are cystic (it's not called a "Duct Solid")
- Enhancing nodule within the cyst = CANCER (usually papillary)
- They can get infected.

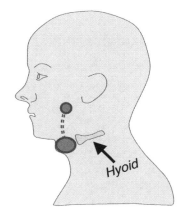

Hyoid

Branchial Cleft Cyst (BCC)

Another cystic embryologic remnant. There are a bunch of types (and subtypes… and sub-subtypes) and you can lose your fucking mind trying to remember all of them - don't do that. Just remember that by far the **most common is a 2nd Branchial Cleft Cyst** (95%). The **angle of the mandible** is a classic location. They can get infected, but are often asymptomatic. Extension of the cyst between the ICA and ECA (**notch sign**) just above the carotid bifurcation is pathognomonic.

How can this be asked on multiple choice:

- *What is it ?* - Most likely on CT or MRI. Ultrasound would be tough, unless they clearly labeled the area "lateral neck" or oriented you in some other way.

- *Location Fuckery.* They could (and this would be super mean) ask you the relationship of a type 2 based on other neck anatomy. So - posterior and lateral to the submandibular gland or lateral to the carotid space, or anterior to the sternocleidomastoid. How I would handle that? Just remember it's going to be lateral to everything. **Lateral is the buzzword.**

- *Mimic* - They could try and trick you into calling a necrotic level 2 lymph node a BCC. Thyroid cancer (*history of radiation exposure*) and nasopharyngeal cancer (*history of HPV*) can occur in "early adulthood." If you have a "new" BCC in an 18 year old - it's probably a necrotic node. *Next Step* = Find the cancer +/- biopsy the mother fucker.

- I say LATERAL cyst in the neck, you say branchial cleft cyst

- I say MIDLINE cyst in the neck, you say thyroglossal duct cyst

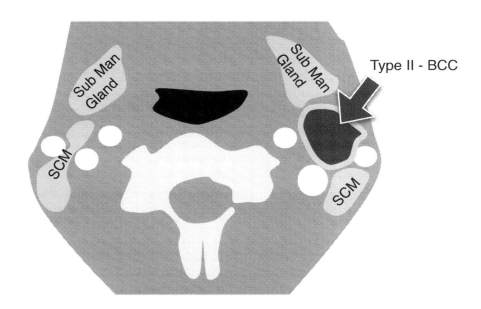

49

Jugular Vein Pathology

There are two jugular vein issues that occur in kids that I should probably mention.

Septic Thrombophlebitis - i.e. clotted jugular vein. You see this classically in the setting of a recent pharyngeal infection (or recent ENT surgery).

How can this be asked on multiple choice:

- *What is it ?* - Showing the clotted vein with the appropriate clinical history.

- *"Lemierre's Syndrome"* - Seeing if you know that it has a fancy syndrome name.

- *Next Step?* Looking in the lungs for *septic emboli*. This could also be done in the reverse. Show you the septic emboli, give you a history of ENT procedure (or recent infection), and have you ask for the US of the neck veins.

- *USMLE Step 1 Association Trivia* = **Fusobacterium necrophorum** is the bacteria that causes the septic emboli. As this bacteria sounds like a Marvel Comic villain the likelihood of it being asked increases by at least 5x.

Phlebectasia - Idiopathic dilated jugular vein.

How can this be asked on multiple choice:

- *What is it ?* - Showing the dilated vein.

- *Trivia* - It is NOT related to a stenosis. There are no other signs of venous congestion.

- *Trivia* - It gets worse with the Valsalva maneuver - *"neck mass that enlarges with valsalva."*

Phlebectasia - Dilated Jugular Vein

Hemangioma of Infancy

These things are actually the most common congenital lesions in the head and neck. Just like any hemangioma they contain vascular spaces with varying sizes and shapes. Most people consider them a "tumor" more than a vascular malformation.

Things to know:
- *How they look* = Super T2 bright, with a bunch of flow voids. Diffusely vascular on doppler.
- *Phases* = Typically they show up around 6 months of age, grow for a bit, then plateau, then involute (6-10 years). Usually they require no treatment.
- *Indications for Treatment* = Large size / Rapid growth with mass effect on the airway or adjacent vascular structures. Fucking with the kids eye movement or eyelid opening.
- *Treatment* = Typically medical = Beta blocker (propranolol)
- *Associations* = PHACES Syndrome (discussed later in the chapter)

> **Vocabulary Trivia -**
> **THIS vs THAT:**
>
> **Infantile Hemangiomas** = NOT present at birth. Show up around 6 months of age. Nearly always involute.
>
> **Congenital Hemangiomas** = Present at birth. May (RICH) or may not (NICH) involute.

Cystic Hygroma (Lymphangioma)

This is another cystic lesion of the neck, which is most likely to be shown as an OB ultrasound (but can occur in the Peds setting as well). The classic look / location is a cystic mass hanging off the back of the neck on OB US (or in the posterior triangle if CT/MRI).

Trivia:

- *Associations:* **Turners** (most common association). **Downs** (second most common association). **Aortic Coarctation** (most common CV abnormality), Fetal Hydrops (bad bad bad outcomes).

- *Septations* = Worse Outcome

- T2 Bright (like a hemangioma). Does NOT enhance (hemangiomas typically do).

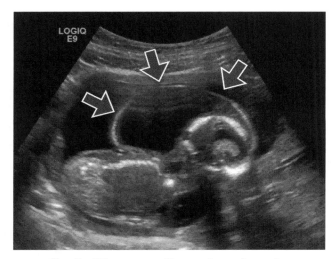
Cystic Hygroma (Lymphangioma)

Fibromatosis Coli ("Congenital Torticollis")

This is a benign "mass" of the **sternocleidomastoid** in neonates who present with **torticollis** (chin points towards the opposite side - or you could say they look away from the lesion) . It's really just a benign inflammation that makes the muscle look crazy big.

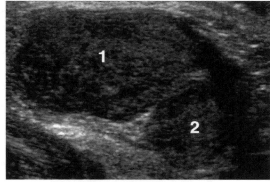

Ultrasound can look scary, until you realize it's just the enlarged SCM. Ultrasound is still the best imaging test. Sometimes it looks like there are two of them, but that's because the SCM has two heads. It goes away on its own, sometimes they do passive physical therapy or try and botox them.

- This Dragon has Two Heads -

- Most common cause of a neck "mass" in infancy
- Classic scenario is a 4 week old with a palpable neck mass and torticollis toward the affected side
- Best imaging test = US.
- Things that make you think it's not FC: mass is outside the SCM, or internal calcifications – in which case you should think to yourself ... nice try Mother fuckers– that's a neuroblastoma.

 Gamesmanship:

So... there can be significant fuckery with the "direction" things curve or people look depending on how the question is ask. What do I mean ?

If you made the mistake of just memorizing the word "towards" in association with fibromatosis coli you might get tricked if the options were: A - Patient looks towards the involved side. B - Patient looks toward the uninvolved side. You'd run into the same problem with the word "away."

Now, that might seem obvious once I spell it out like that but I'm pretty sure at least a few of you were making a flashcard that had only the word "towards" on it. You have to assume the test writer has the worst intentions for you. Don't provide them with any opportunity to trick you.

Rhabdomyosarcoma

Although technically rare as fuck, this is the most common mass in the masticator space of a kid. Having said that if you see it in the head/neck region is almost always in the orbit. In fact, its the *most common extra-occular orbital malignancy in children* (dermoid is most common benign orbital mass in child). The most classic scenario would be an 8 year old with painless proptosis and no signs of infection.

What do sarcomas look like?

I'll talk about this more in the MSK chapter, but in general I'll just say they look mean as cat shit (enhancing, solid, areas of necrosis, etc..).

SECTION 4:
Airway

Croup

This is the most common cause of acute upper airway obstruction in young children. The peak incidence is between 6 months and 3 years (average 1 year). They have a **barky "croupy" cough**. It's viral. The thing to realize is that the lateral and frontal neck x-ray is done not to diagnosis croup, but to exclude something else. Having said that, the so-called *"steeple sign"* – with loss of the normal lateral convexities of the subglottic trachea is your buzzword, and if it's shown, that will be the finding. Questions are still more likely to center around facts (age and etiology). **The culprit is often parainfluenza virus.**

Epiglottitis

In contrast to the self-limited croup, this one can kill you. It's mediated by H. Influenza and the classic age is 3.5 years old (there is a recent increase in teenagers - so don't be fooled by that age). The lateral x-ray will show marked swelling of the epiglottis *(thumb sign)*. A fake out is the "omega epiglottis" which is caused by oblique imaging. You can look for thickening of the aryepiglottic folds to distinguish.

Trivia: Death by asphyxiation is from the aryepiglotic folds (not the epiglottis)

Exudative Tracheitis

This is an uncommon but serious (possibly deadly) situation that is found in slightly older kids. It's caused by an exudative infection of the trachea (sorta like diptheria). It's usually from Staph A. and affects kids between 6-10. The buzzword is *linear soft tissue filling defect within the airway*.

Croup	Epiglottitis	Exudative Tracheitis
6 months – 3 years (peak 1 year)	Classic = 3.5 years, but now seen with teenagers too	6-10 years
Steeple Sign: loss of the normal shoulders (lateral convexities) of the subglottic trachea	**Thumb Sign:** marked enlargement of epiglottis	Linear soft tissue filling defect (a membrane) seen within the airway
Viral (*Most Common - parainfluenza*)	H-Flu	Staph. A

Retropharyngeal Cellulitis and Abscess

Discussed in detail in the Neuro chapter of Volume 2 (page 145). I'll just say quickly that you do see this most commonly in young kids (age 6 months -12 months). If they don't show it on CT, they could show it with a lateral x-ray demonstrating **massive retropharyngeal soft tissue thickening**. For the real world, you can get pseudothickening when the neck is not truly lateral. To tell the difference between positioning and the real thing, a repeat with an extended neck is the next step.

Subglottic Hemangioma

Hemangiomas are the most common soft tissue mass in the trachea, and they are most commonly located in the subglottic region. In croup there is symmetric narrowing with loss of shoulders on both sides (Steeple Sign). In contradistinction, subglottic hemangiomas have loss of just one of the sides.

Trivia
- Tends to favor the left side
- 50% are associated with cutaneous hemangiomas
- 7% have the PHACES syndrome

More on hemangiomas later in the chapter.

PHACES
P- Posterior fossa *(Dandy Walker)*
H- Hemangiomas
A- Arterial anomalies
C- Coarctation of aorta, cardiac defects
E- Eye abnormalities
S- Subglottic hemangiomas

- Gamesmanship -
Frontal and Lateral Neck Radiographs

For the frontal, there are two main things to think about.

(1) Croup and
(2) Subglottic Hemangioma

You can tell them apart by the shouldering.

If you can't tell…. try and let the history bias you. Cough? Fever? Think Croup.

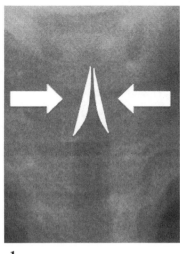 

1   2

For the lateral, there are 4 main things to think about:

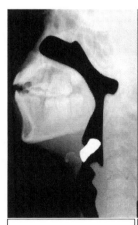 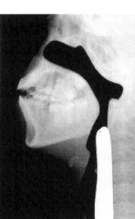 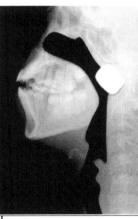 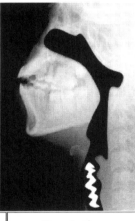

Epiglottitis	Retropharyngeal Abscess	Tonsils (adenoids)	Exudative Tracheitis
Looks like a thumb If the ordering suspects the diagnosis, do NOT bring this kid to x-ray. Have them do a portable.	Too wide (*> 6mm at C2, or > 22mm at C6*) **Next Step = CT** *don't forget to look in the mediastinum for*	Not seen till about 3-6 months, and not big till around 1-2 years. Too big when they encroach the airway	Linear Filling Defect It's usually staph

SECTION 5:
Chest

Before we proceed with the trivia I need to make sure you know / can do two things for me.

1) Know how to tell if a neonatal chest is **hyper-inflated or not**. Don't get hung up on this low vs normal - that's a bunch of bologna. Just think (a) Hyper-inflated, or (b) NOT Hyper-inflated.

The easiest way to do this is to just count ribs. More than 6 Anterior, or 8 Posterior as they intersect the diaphragm is too much. As a quick review, remember that the anterior ribs (grey) are the ones with a more sloping course as the move medially, where as the posterior ribs (black) have a horizontal course.

Other helpful signs suggesting hyperinflation:
- Flattening of the diaphragms
- Ribs take on a more horizontal appearance
- Some increased lucency under the heart

2) Know what "**Granular**" looks like. Know what "**Streaky**" or "**Ropy**" looks like. My good friends at Amazon are not capable of printing a clear picture of these so I want you to stop reading and
   A. Go to google images
   B. Search "*Granular neonatal chest x-ray.*" Look at a bunch of examples. Maybe even download a few of them for review.
   C. Search "*Streaky Perihilar neonatal chest x-ray.*" Look at a bunch of examples. Maybe even download a few of them for review.
   D. Search "*Ropy neonatal chest x-ray.*" Look at a bunch of examples. Maybe even download a few of them for review.

Random Pearl: We are going to talk about the presence of a pleural effusion as a discriminator. One pearl is to *look for an accentuated (thick) minor fissure* on the right. If you see that shit, kid probably has an effusion. Confirm by staring with fierce intensity at the lung bases to look for obliteration of the costophrenic sulcus.

As we proceed forward with the trivia, pay close attention to lung volumes, and the words "granular", "streaky", and "ropy."

High Volumes
+ Perihilar Streaky

➡️

Alphabet - MNoP
Meconium Aspiration
Non GB Neonatal
Pneumonia

You will find that you can divide the big 5 in half by doing something like this:

Not High (low or normal) Volumes
+ Granular

➡️

SSD
Group B Pneumonia

———

Meconium Aspiration

This typically occurs secondary to stress (hypoxia), and is *more common in term or post-mature babies (the question stem could say "post term" delivery)*. The pathophysiology is all secondary to chemical aspiration.

Trivia:
- The buzzword "ropy appearance" of asymmetric lung densities
- Hyperinflation with alternative areas of atelectasis
- Pneumothorax in 20-40% of cases

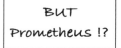
BUT Prometheus !?

How can it have hyperinflation?? Aren't the lungs full of sticky shit (literally) ??? The poop in the lungs act like miniature ball-valves ("floaters" I call them), causing <u>air trapping</u> - hence the increased lung volumes.

Reality vs Multiple Choice: *"Meconium Staining" on the amniotic fluid is common (like 15% of all births), but development of "aspiration syndrome" is rare with only 5% of those 15% actually have aspiration symptoms. Having said that, if the question header bothers to include "Green colored amniotic fluid" or "Meconium staining" in the question header they are giving you a major hint. Don't overthink a hint like this. If they ask "What color was George Washington's white horse?" the answer is NOT brown.*

Transient Tachypnea of the Newborn (TTN)

The classic clinical scenario is a history of c-section (vagina squeezes the fluid out of lungs normally). Other classic scenario histories include "diabetic mother" and/or "maternal sedation." Findings are going to start at 6 hours, peak at one day, and be done by 3 days. You are going to see coarse interstitial marking and fluid in the fissures.

Trivia:
- Classic histories: C-Section, Maternal Sedation, Maternal Diabetes
- Onset: Peaks at day 1, Resolved by Day 3
- Lung Volumes – Normal to Increased

Surfactant-Deficient Disease (SDD)

This is also called hyaline membrane disease, or RDS. It's a disease of pre-mature kids. The idea is that they are born without surfactant (the stuff that makes your lungs stretchy and keeps alveolar surfaces open). It's serious business and is the most common cause of death in premature newborns. You get **low lung volumes and bilateral granular opacities** (just like B-hemolytic pneumonia). But, unlike B-hemolytic pneumonia you **do NOT get pleural effusions**. As a piece of useful clinical knowledge, a normal plain film at 6 hours excludes SDD.

Surfactant Replacement Therapy

They can spray this crap in the kid's lungs, and it makes a huge difference (decreased death rate etc…). Lung volumes get better, and granular opacities will clear centrally after treatment. The post treatment look of bleb-like lucencies can mimic PIE.

Trivia:
•Increased Risk of Pulmonary Hemorrhage
•Increased Risk of PDA

Neonatal Pneumonia (Beta-Hemolytic Strep - or "GBS")

This is the most common type of pneumonia in newborns. It's acquired during exit of the dirty birth canal. Premature infants are at greater risk relative to term infants. It has some different looks when compared to other pneumonias (why I discuss it separately).

Trivia:
•It often has low lung volumes (other pneumonias have high)
•Granular Opacities is a buzzword (for this and SDD)
•Often (25%) has pleural effusion (SDD will not)
•LESS likely to have pleural effusion compared to the non Beta hemolytic version (25% vs 75%)

Neonatal Pneumonia (not Beta-Hemolytic Strep - "Non GB" or "Non GBS")

Lots of causes. Typical look is patchy, asymmetric perihilar densities, effusions, and hyperinflation. Will look similar to surfactant deficient disease but will be full term. Effusions are also much more likely (they are rare in SDD).

Persistent Pulmonary HTN

Also called "persistent fetal circulation". Normally, the high pulmonary pressures seen in utero (that cause blood to shunt around the lungs) decrease as soon as the baby takes his/her first breath. Dr. Goljan (Step 1 wizard) calls this a "miracle," and used this basic physiology to deny evolution. When high pressures persist in the lungs it can be primary (the work of Satan), or secondary from hypoxia (meconium aspiration, pneumonia, etc…). The CXR is going to show the cause of the pulmonary HTN (pneumonia), rather than the HTN itself.

Solving Cases Using Buzzwords

When I say *"Post Term Baby,"*
You Say *Meconium Aspiration*

When I say *"C-Section,"*
You say *Transient Tachypnea*

When I say *"Maternal Sedation"*
You say *Transient Tachypnea*

When I say *"Premature"*
You say *RDS*

How this could work:

*Blah Blah Blah , **Post Term Delivery** of a beautiful baby girl. What is the diagnosis?*

(A) RDS
(B) Transient Tachypnea
(C) Meconium Aspiration

Solving Cases Using Lung Volumes:

High *(flat diaphragms)*:

- Meconium Aspiration

- Transient Tachypnea

- Non BH Neonatal Pneumonia

Low:

- Surfactant Deficiency (no pleural effusion)

- Beta-Hemolytic Pneumonia (gets pleural effusions)

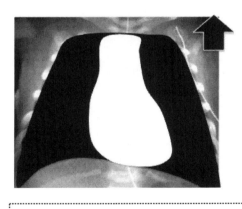

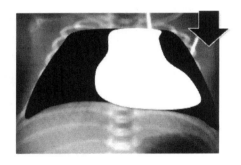

How this could work:

*Blah Blah Blah , **This Picture** of a beautiful baby girl. What is the diagnosis?*

(A) RDS
(B) Transient Tachypnea
(C) Meconium Aspiration

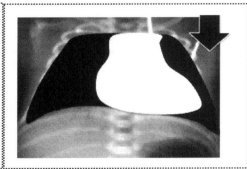

- Life in the NICU (just as glamorous as it sounds) -

Pulmonary Interstitial Emphysema (PIE)

When you have surfactant deficiency and they put you on a ventilator (which pulverizes your lungs with PEEP), you can end up with air escaping the alveoli and ending up in the interstitium and lymphatics. On CXR it looks like **linear lucencies (buzzword)**. It's a warning sign for impending Pneumothorax. Most cases of PIE occur in the first week of time (bronchopulmonary dysplasia – which looks similar – occurs in patients older than 2-3 weeks). **Surfactant therapy can also mimic PIE.** The treatment is to switch ventilation methods and/or place them PIE side down.

A total zebra is the progression of PIE to a large cystic mass. The thing can even cause mediastinal mass effect.

Trivia:
- Consequence of ventilation
- Usually occurs in the first week of life
- Buzzword = Linear Lucencies
- Warning Sign for Impending Pneumothorax
- Treatment is to put the affected side down

Chronic Lung Disease - CLD / (Bronchopulmonary Dysplasia - BPD)

This is the kid born premature (with resulting surfactant deficiency), who ends up being tortured in ventilator purgatory. His/her tiny little lungs take a ferocious ass whipping from positive pressure ventilation and oxygen toxicity — "barotrauma" they call it. This beating essentially turns the lungs into scar, inhibiting their ability to grow correctly. That is why people call this "a disease of lung growth impairment."

- *Classic Vignette:* Prolonged ventilation in a tiny (<1000 grams), premature kid (<32 weeks)

- *Classic Look:* Alternating regions of fibrosis (coarse reticular opacities), and hyper-aeration (cystic lucencies).

- *Buzzword:* **"Band like opacities"**

- ***Classic This vs That:* CLD vs PIE.** They both have cystic lucencies. The difference (as is often the case in peds) is TIME.

PIE = First week of life, **CLD** = After 3 to 4 weeks' postnatal age

-Congenital Chest-

Pulmonary Hypoplasia

This can be primary or secondary. Secondary causes seem to lend themselves more readily to multiple choice questions. Secondary causes can be from decreased hemi-thoracic volume, decreased vascular supply, or decreased fluid. The most common is the decreased thoracic volume, typically from a space occupying mass such as a **congenital diaphragmatic hernia** (with bowel in the chest), but sometimes from a neuroblastoma or sequestration. Decreased fluid, refers to the **Potter Sequence** (no kidneys -> no pee -> no fluid -> hypoplastic lungs).

Bronchopulmonary Sequestration *(no communication with airway)*

These are grouped into intralobar and extralobar with the distinction being which has a pleural covering. The venous drainage is different (intra to pulmonary veins, extra to systemic veins). **You can NOT tell the difference radiographically.** The *practical difference is age of presentation*; intralobar presents in adolescence or adulthood with recurrent pneumonias, extralobar presents in infancy with respiratory compromise.

• **Intralobar:** Much more common (75%). Presents in adolescence or adulthood as recurrent pneumonias (bacteria migrates in from pores of Kohn). **Most commonly in the left lower lobe** posterior segment (2/3s). Uncommon in the upper lobes. In contradistinction from extralobar sequestration, it is rarely associated with other developmental abnormalities. *Pathology books love to say "NO pleural cover" - but you can't see that shit on CT or MR.*

• **Extralobar:** Less common of the two (25%). Presents in infancy with respiratory compromise (primarily because of the associated anomalies - Congenital cystic adenomatoid malformation (CCAM), congenital diaphragmatic hernia, vertebral anomalies, congenital heart disease, pulmonary hypoplasia). It rarely gets infected since it has its own pleural covering. These are sometimes described as part of a bronchopulmonary foregut malformation, and may actually have (rarely) a patent channel to the stomach, or distal esophagus. *Pathology books love to say "has a pleural cover" - but you can't see that shit on CT or MR.*

Intralobar	Extralobar
More Common	Less Common
Presents in Adolescence	Presents in Infancy
Recurrent Infections	Associated Congenital Anomalies
No Pleural Cover	Has its own pleural cover
Pulmonary Venous Drainage	Systemic Venous Drainage

Gamesmanship: I say recurrent pneumonia in same area, you say intralobar sequestration.

Bronchogenic Cysts

Typically an incidental finding. They are generally solitary and unilocular. They typically do NOT communicate with the airway, so if they have gas in them you should worry about infection.

Congenital Cystic Adenomatoid Malformation (CCAM)

- (Other Aliases Include - **CPAM***)*

As the name suggests it's a malformation of adenomatoid stuff that replaces normal lung. Most of the time it only affects one lobe. There is no lobar preference (unlike CLE which favors the left upper lobe). There are cystic and solid types (type 1 cystic, type 3 solid, type 2 in the middle). There is a crop of knuckle heads who want to call these things CPAMs and have 5 types, which I'm sure is evidence based and will really make an impact in the way these things are treated. CCAMs communicate with the airway, and therefore fill with air. Most of these things (like 90%) will spontaneously decrease in size in the third trimester. The treatment (at least in the USA) is to cut these things out, because of the iddy bitty theoretical risk of malignant transformation (pleuropulmonary blastoma, rhabdomyosarcoma).

Q: *What if you see a systemic arterial feeder (one coming off the aorta) going to the CCAM ?*
A: Then it's not a CCAM, it's a Sequestration. — mumble to yourself "nice try assholes"

Congenital Lobar Emphysema (CLE)

The idea behind this one is that you have bronchial pathology (maybe atresia depending on what you read), that leads to a ball-valve anomaly and progressive air trapping. On CXR, it looks like a lucent, hyper-expanded lobe.

Trivia:
- It's not actually emphysema – just air trapping secondary to bronchial anomaly
- It prefers the left upper lobe (40%)
- Treatment is lobectomy

Gamesmanship
- The classic way this is shown in case conference or case books is with a series of CXRs. The first one has an opacity in the lung (the affected lung clears fluid slower than normal lung). The next x-ray will show the opacity resolved. The following x-ray will show it getting more and more lucent. Until it's actually pushing the heart over.

Congenital Diaphragmatic Hernia (CDHs)

Most commonly they are **B**ochdalek type. **B** is in the **B**ack – they are typically posterior and to the left. The appearance on CXR is usually pretty obvious.

Trivia:
- Usually in the Back , and on the left (Bochdalek)
- If it's on the right - there is an association with GBS Pneumonia
- Mortality Rate is related to the degree of pulmonary Hypoplasia
- Most have Congenital Heart Disease
- Essentially all are malrotated

Gamesmanship
- One trick is to show the NG tube curving into the chest.

🔥 Locational Strategy 🔥

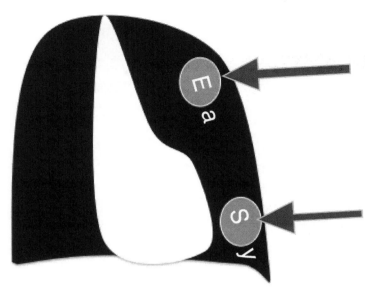

Left Upper Lobe:

Think **Congenital Lobar Emphysema (CLE)** first

But, remember CCAM has no lobar prevalence, so it can be anywhere

Left Lower Lobe:

Think **Sequestration** First

Congenital Diaphragmatic Hernia (CDHs) favors this side too

Case 1. Newborn with congenital heart disease

A. Intralobar Sequestration
B. Extralobar Sequestration
C. Congenital Lobar Emphysema

Case 2. 10 year old with recurrent pneumonia

A. Intralobar Sequestration
B. Extralobar Sequestration
C. Congenital Lobar Emphysema

**Intralobar is seen older kids,
**Extralobar is seen in infants with co-morbids
** CLE is in the upper lobe

-Special Situations in Peds Chests-

Viral – In all ages this is way more common than bacterial infection. Peribronchial edema is the buzzword for the CXR finding. "Dirty" or "Busy" Hilum. You also end up with debris and mucus in the airway which causes two things (1) hyperinflation and (2) subsegmental atelectasis. **Respiratory Syncytial Virus (RSV)** - This will cause the typical non-specific viral pattern as well. However, there is the classic testable predilection to cause a segmental or lobar atelectasis — particularly in the right upper lobe.

Round Pneumonia – Kids get round pneumonia. They love to show this, and try to trick you into thinking it's a mass. Younger than 8 you are thinking round pneumonia, round pneumonia, round pneumonia – with S. Pneumonia being the culprit. The PhD trivia is that these occur because you don't have good collateral ventilation pathways. Round pneumonia is usually solitary, and likes the posterior lower lobes. Take home message: *No CT to exclude cancer , just get a follow up x-ray.*

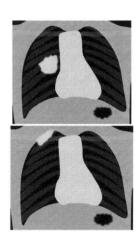

Neonatal atypical peripheral atelectasis (NAPA) - It is best to think about this as a cousin or uncle of Round Pneumonia (they are in the same family). It is essentially the same thing except it is peripheral. The classic look is a round, pleural based "mass" in the apex of the lung. Similarly to the "round pneumonia" this is a transient finding and will resolve as the primary process improves.

Lipoid Pneumonia - Classic history is a parent giving their newborn a teaspoonful of olive oil daily to cultivate *"a spirit of bravado and manliness."* Although this seems like a pretty solid plan, and I can't fault their intentions – it's more likely to result in chronic fat aspiration. Hot Sauce is probably a better option. Most people will tell you that bronchoalveolar lavage is considered the diagnostic method of choice. CXR nonspecific - it is just airspace opacities. CT is much more likely to be the modality used on the exam. The classic finding is low attenuation (-30 to -100 HU) within the consolidated areas reflecting fat content.

Bronchial Foreign Body:

The key concept is that it causes **air trapping**. The lung may look more lucent (from air trapping) on the affected side. You **put the affected side down and it will remain lucent** (from air trapping). Another random piece of trivia is that under fluoro the mediastinum will shift AWAY from the affected side on expiration.

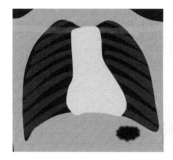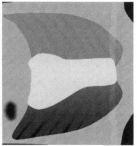

Bottom Lung is
Black = Air Trapping

Key Point: A normal inspiratory CXR is meaningless. Don't forget that the crayon / green bean is going to be radiolucent. You need expiratory films to elicit air trapping. Normally, the bottom lung is gonna turn white (move less air). If there is air trapping the bottom lung will stay black.

Swyer James – This is the classic unilateral lucent lung. It typically occurs after a viral lung infection in childhood resulting in post infectious obliterative bronchiolitis. The size of the affected lobe is smaller than a normal lobe (it's not hyper-expanded).

Papillomatosis - Perinatal HPV can cause these soft tissue masses within the airway and lungs. It's also seen in adults who smoke. *"Multiple lung nodules which demonstrate cavitation"* is the classic scenario. Some testable trivia includes the 2% risk of squamous cell cancer, and that manipulation can lead to dissemination. The appearance of cysts and nodules can look like LCH (discussed more in the thoracic chapter), although the trachea is also involved.

Sickle Cell / Acute Chest – Kids with sickle cell can get "Acute chest." Acute chest actually occurs more in kids than adults (usually between age 2-4). This is the leading cause of death in sickle cell patients. Some people think the pathology is as such: you infarct a rib -> that hurts a lot, so you don't breath deep -> atelectasis and infection. Others think you get pulmonary microvascular occlusion and infarction. Regardless, if you see opacities in the CXR of a kid with sickle cell, you should think of this.

Gamesmanship (how do you know it's sickle cell?)
- Kid with Big Heart
- Kid with bone infarcts (look at the humeral heads)
- Kid with H shaped vertebra (look on lateral)

Cystic Fibrosis- So the sodium pump doesn't work and they end up with thick secretions and poor pulmonary clearance. The real damage is done by recurrent infections.

Things to know:
- Bronchiectasis (begins cylindrical and progresses to varicoid)
- It has an **apical predominance** (lower lobes are less affected)
- Hyperinflation
- They get Pulmonary Arterial Hypertension
- Mucus plugging (finger in glove sign)
- Men are infertile (vas deferens is missing)

CF Related Trickery
• Fatty Replaced Pancreas on CT
• Abdominal Films with Constipation
• Biliary Cirrhosis (from blockage of intrahepatic bile ducts), and resulting portal HTN

Primary Ciliary Dyskinesia – The motile part of the cilia doesn't work. They can't clear their lungs and get recurrent infections. These guys have lots of bronchiectasis just like CF. BUT, this time it's lower lobe predominant (CF was upper lobe).

Things to know:
- Bronchiectasis (**lower lobes**)
- 50% will have Kartageners (situs inversus). So, 50% will not
- Men are infertile (sperm tails don't work)
- Women are sub-fertile (cilia needed to push eggs around)

THIS vs THAT:	
Cystic Fibrosis	**Primary Ciliary Dyskinesia**
Upper Lobe Predominant - Brochiectasis	Lower Lobe Predominant - Brochiectasis
Infertile - Men are Missing the Vas Deferens	Infertile - Men's Sperm Don't Swim For Shit

-Primary Lung Tumors-

Pleuropulmonary Blastoma (PPB) – This is a primary intrathroacic malignancy. They can look a lot like CCAMs and even have different types (cystic, mixed, solid). These things are usually right sided, pleural based, and without chest wall invasion or calcifications. **No rib invasion** *(helps distinguish it from the Askin / Ewing Sarcoma of the Chest Wall - if they won't tell you the age),* No calcification. The more solid types can have mets to the brain and bones. The cystic type seem to occur more in kids less than a year old, and be more benign.

Things to know about PPBs:
- Big Fucking Mass (B.F.M.) in the chest of a 1-2 year old
- Shouldn't have an eaten-up rib (Askin tumors often do)
- 10% of the time they have a multilocular cystic nephroma.

-Catheters / Lines-

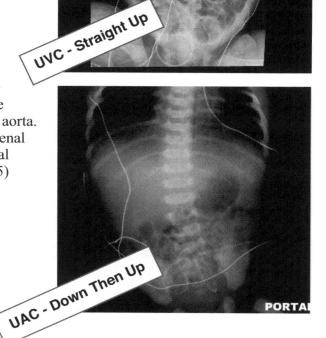

Umbilical Venous Catheter (UVC) –
A UVC passes from the umbilical vein to the left portal vein to the ductus venosus to a hepatic vein to the IVC. You don't want the thing to lodge in the portal vein because you can infarct the liver. The ideal spot is at the IVC – Right Atrium junction.

Development of a *"Cystic Liver Mass"* (Hematoma) can suggest UVC erosion into the liver.

Umbilical Artery Catheter (UAC) –
A UAC passes from the umbilicus, down to the umbilical artery, into an iliac artery then to the aorta. Positioning counts, as the major risk factor is renal arterial thrombosis. You want to avoid the renal arteries by going high (T8-T10), or low (L3-L5)

Things to know about UACs:
- It goes down first
- It should be placed either high (T8-T10) or low (L3-L5)
- Omphalocele is a contraindication

ECMO - Extracorporeal Membrane Oxygenation

Neonatologists primarily use this device to torture sick babies - hopefully into revealing the various government secrets they have stolen, or the location of their organization's underground lair. "Enhanced interrogation" or "temporizing measure of last resort," they call it - to get around the Geneva Conventions.

Oh you want to pretend you can't talk? Get the ECMO catheters!

Alternatively, it can be used as a last resort in neonatal sepsis, severe SSD, and meconium aspiration. Actually, in cases of meconium aspiration ECMO actually does work (sometimes).

Types:

There are two main types: (1) Veno-Arterial "V-A", and (2) Veno-Venous "V-V"

In both cases deoxygenated blood is removed from the right atrium and pumped into a box (artificial lung) to get infused with oxygen. The different is how it is returned.

In V-**A**, blood goes ***back to the Aorta*** (you can see why this would help rest the left ventricle). The catheter is usually placed at the origin of the innominate or "overlying the arch."

In V-**V** blood goes right back into the right atrium. In this situation even if the lungs were totally clogged with shit (meconium aspiration) and no oxygen exchange was happening it wouldn't matter because the blood that is being pumped (RA -> RV -> Pulmonary Artery) already has oxygen in it.

VenoArterial "V-A"	VenoVenous "V-V"
Catheter Position: RA + Aorta *(near the origin of the innominate artery)*	Catheter Position: RA + RA "Dual Lumen"
Heart + Lung Support	Lung Support
Carotid artery and Right Jugular Vein are "Sacrificed" to the Volcano God in the hopes of a plentiful harvest.	

ECMO - Extracorporeal Membrane Oxygenation - Continued

Things to Know:

- **Lung White Out = Normal.** Mechanism is variable depending on who you asked. The way I understand it is that the airway pressure suddenly drops off causing atelectasis, plus you have a change in circulation pattern that now mimics the fetal physiology (mom = artificial lung). Resulting oxygen tension changes lead to an edema like pattern. A multiple choice trick could be to try and make you say it is worsening airspace disease, or reflects the severity of the lung injury. Don't fall for that. It's an expected finding.

- Consequences of V-A. I mentioned on the prior page that they typically ligate the carotid when they place the Arterial catheter. No surprise that they will be at **increased risk for neurologic ischemic complications** as a result.

- **Crucial Complication = Hemorrhage.** The combination of anticoagulation (necessary in ECMO) and being sick as stink puts these kids at super high risk for head bleeds. This is why they will get screened for germinal matrix hemorrhage prior to being placed on ECMO and then routinely screened with head ultrasounds (expertly read by the second year resident on call).

Catheter Position Gamesmanship:

I think there are two likely ways a multiple choice question could be structured related to ECMO catheter position. The first would be to show you a series of daily radiographs with the latest one demonstrating migration of one or both catheters. Thats the easy way to do it.

The sneaky way would be to show you the catheter with the lucent distal end and the dot marker on the tip. This would be particularly evil as there are tons of different catheter brands and looks, but if I was going to try and trick you, this would be the way that I would do it.

In this case, the venous catheter looks falsely high from it's lucent tip, but that round metallic marker (near the black arrow) shows the tip in the RA.

The arterial catheter "overlies the region of the aortic arch," which is normal.

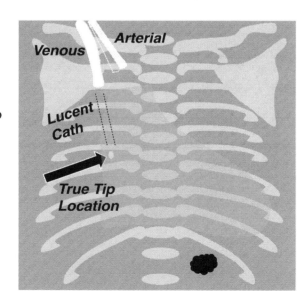

SECTION 6:
Mediastinal Masses

Anterior:

Normal Thymus: This is the most common mediastinal "mass." It's terribly embarrassing to call a normal thymus a mass, but can actually be tricky sometimes. It can be pretty big in kids less than 5 (especially in infants). Triangular shape of the thymus is sometimes called the "sail sign." Not to be confused with the other 20 sail signs in various parts of the body, or the spinnaker sail sign, which is when pneumomediastinum lifts up the thymus.

Thymic Rebound: In times of acute stress (pneumonia, radiation, chemotherapy, burns), the thymus will shrink. In the recovery phase it will rebound back to normal, and sometimes larger than before. During this rebound it **can be PET avid.**

Lymphoma: This is the **most common abnormal mediastinal mass in children** (older children and teenagers). Lymphoma vs Thymus can be tricky. Thymus is more in kids under 10, Lymphoma is seen more in kids over 10. When you get around age 10, you need to look for cervical lymph nodes to make you think lymphoma. If you see calcification, and the lesion has NOT been treated you may be dealing with a teratoma. Calcification is uncommon in an untreated lymphoma.

Complications: Compression of SVC, Compression of Pulmonary Veins, Pericardial Effusion, Airway Compression.

Germ Cell Tumor (GCT): On imaging, this is a large anterior mediastinal mass arising from or at least next to the thymus. It comes in three main flavors, each of which has a few pieces of trivia worth knowing:

1- Teratoma - Mostly Cystic, with **fat** and calcium

2 - Seminoma - Bulky and Lobulated. *"Straddles the midline"*

3 - NSGCT - Big and Ugly - Hemorrhage and Necrosis. Can get crazy and invade the lung.

I say, Extra Gonadal Germ Cell Tumor, You Say Klinefelter's Syndrome (47 XXY)

Klinefelter patients have the worst syndrome ever. They have small penises, they get male breast cancer, and as if things couldn't possibly get worse... they get germ cell tumors in their chest. In fact, **they are at 300x the risk of getting a GCT**. Pineal gland Germ Cells have also been reported in Klinefelter patients, giving them vertical gaze palsy. In that case, they can't even look up to the sky and say "Why God* ?! Why Me!? Why Klinefelter's!?"

**God, Allah, Mother Earth, Celestial Deity NOS*

Middle

Lymphadenopathy – Middle mediastinal lymphadenopathy is most often from granulomatous disease (TB or Fungal), or from lymphoma.

Duplication Cysts – These fall into three categories (a) bronchogenic, (b) enteric, (c) neuroenteric. The neuroenterics are traditionally posterior mediastinal.

Bronchogenic – water attenuation – close to the trachea or bronchus. Bronchogenic cysts tend to be middle mediastinal (esophageal cysts can be middle or posterior mediastinal).

Enteric – water attenuation close to the esophagus (lower in the mediastinum). Abutment of the esophagus is the key finding.

Posterior

Neuroblastoma – This is the most common posterior mediastinal mass in a child under 2. This is discussed in complete detail in the GU PEDs section. I'll just mention that compared to abdominal neuroblastoma, thoracic neuroblastoma has a better outcome. It may involve the ribs and vertebral bodies. Also, remember that Wilms usually mets (more than neuroblastoma) to the lungs, so if it's in the lungs don't forget about Wilms.

Ewing Sarcoma – *This is discussed in complete detail in the MSK PEDs section.* \

Askin Tumor (Primitive Neuroectodermal tumor of the chest wall):
This is now considered part of the Ewing Sarcoma spectrum, and is sometimes called an Ewing sarcoma of the chest wall. They tend to displace adjacent structures rather than invade early on (when they get big they can invade). They look heterogenous, and the solid parts will enhance.

Neuroenteric Cyst – By convention these are associated with vertebral anomalies (think scoliosis). The cyst does NOT communicate with CSF, is well demarcated, and is water density.

Extramedullary Hematopoiesis - This occurs in patients with myeloproliferative disorders or bone marrow infiltration (including sickle cell). Usually, this manifests as a big liver and big spleen. However, in a minority of cases you can get soft tissue density around the spine (paraspinal masses), which are bilateral, smooth, and sharply delineated.

Strategy - The Anterior Mediastinal Mass

Lymphoma - In a kid just assume it's Hodgkins (which means it's gonna involve the thymus). *Why assume Hodgkins ?* Hodgkins is 4x more common than NHL. Hodgkins involves the thymus 90% of the time.

Q: *How the hell do you tell a big ass normal thymus in a little baby vs a lymphoma?*
A: My main move is to go age. **Under 10 = Thymus, Over 10 = Lymphoma.**

Thymic Rebound - If the test writer is headed in this direction they MUST either (a) <u>bias you with a history</u> saying stuff like **"got off chemo"** or **"got off corticosteroids"** or (b) show you a series of axial CTs with the thing growing and maintaining normal morphology. I think "a" is much more likely.

The Funk: In general just think morphology / density:

- **Soft Tissue - Kinda Homogenous** = Think **Lymphoma or Hyperplasia**

- **Fat = Germ Cell Tumor** (*Why God!? Why Klinefelters!?*)

- **Water** = Congenital Stuff - Think **Lymphangiomas**

Strategy - The Posterior Mediastinal Mass

First Rule of Peds Multiple Choice Test Taking - **TIMING! AGE!**

Under 10 - Think **malignant**, Think **neuroblastoma.**

2nd Decade - Think **benign.**

If it's a round mass- Think about **Ganglioneuromas & Neurofibromas**

If it's cystic (and there is scoliosis) think **Neuroenteric Cyst**

If they show you coarse bone trabeculation - with an adjacent mass (or a **history of anemia**) - Think **Extramedullary Hematopoiesis**

Strategy - The B.F.M. "<u>B</u>ig <u>F</u>ucking <u>M</u>ass"

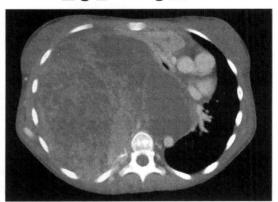

If you see a B.F.M. in the chest of a kid, you basically have two choices:

(1) **Askin Tumor (PNET / Ewings)** - *AGE 10+, look for an eaten up rib.
(2) **Pleuropulmonary Blastoma** *AGE is typically less than 2.

SECTION 7: Luminal GI

Esophageal Atresia /

TE fistula: This can occur in multiple subtypes, with the classic ways of showing it being a **frontal CXR with an NG tube stopped in the upper neck**, or a fluoro study (shown lateral) with a blind ending sac or communication with the tracheal tree.

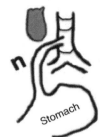

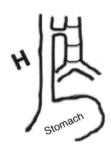

N-Type Fistula (85%)   **Esophageal Atresia NO Fistula (10%)**   **H-Type Atresia (1%)**

There are 5 main subtypes, only 3 of which are worth knowing (being familiar with) for the purpose of the exam.

Things to Know About Esophageal Atresia / TE Fistula:
• Most Important Thing To Know are the VACTERL associations (more on this later)
• The most common subtype is the N-Type (blind ended esophagus, with distal esophagus hooked up to trachea
• Excessive Air in the Stomach = H type (can also be with N type)
• No Air in the Stomach = Esophageal Atresia
• The presence of a right arch (4%) must be described prior to surgery (changes the approach).

VACTERL: This is extremely high yield. VACTERL is a way of remembering that certain associations are seen more commonly when together (when you see one, look for the others).

They occur with different frequency:	VACTERL association is diagnosed when 3 or more of the defined anomalies affect a patient.
V – Vertebral Anomalies (37%) **A** – Anal (imperforate anus) (63%) **C** – Cardiac (77%) **TE** – Tracheoesophageal Fistula or Esophageal Atresia (40%) **R** – Renal (72%) **L** – Limb (radial ray) – 58%	Therefore, keep investigating when 1-2 of these anomalies are found. The **heart** and **kidneys** are the **most commonly affected** organs in this association.

Trivia: If both limbs are involved, then both kidneys tend to be involved. If one limb is involved, then one kidney tends to be involved.

Esophageal Foreign Bodies: Kids love to stick things in their mouths (noses and ears). This can cause a lot of problems including direct compression of the airway, perforation, or even fistula to the trachea. Stuff stuck in the esophagus needs to be removed.

THIS *vs* THAT: Trachea vs Esophagus:

The esophagus is a dirty sock, it flexes to accommodate that big piece of steak you didn't even bother to chew. The trachea is rigid, like that math teacher I had in high school (who hated music… and colors), but unlike the math teacher it has a flexible membrane in the back.

The point of me mentioning this is to help you problem solve a *"where is the coin"* type question. The esophagus will accommodate the coin so it can be turned in any direction. The trachea is rigid and will force the coin to rotate into the posterior membrane — so it will be skinny in the AP direction.

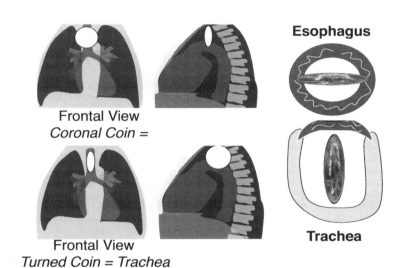

Frontal View
Coronal Coin =

Frontal View
Turned Coin = Trachea

Esophagus

Trachea

Additional trivia relates to swallowed batteries, magnets, and pennies

- **Swallowed Magnets** – One magnet is ok. Two or more magnets is a problem. The reason is that they can attract each other across intestinal walls leading to obstruction, necrosis, perforation, and a law suit. They need a surgical consult. Also… MRI is contraindicated.

- **Disc Batteries** – They look like coins, except they have two rings. The literature is not clear, but it appears that modern batteries rarely leak (leaking is bad – caustic chemicals, heavy metals etc..). So most people will watch the transit with serial x-rays. If it gets stuck, they go and get it. If you leave it in longer than a week or so, the risk of it leaking increases.

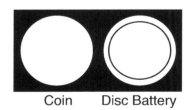

Coin   Disc Battery

- **Pennies** - Those minted prior to 1982 (copper pennies) are safe. Those **minted after 1982 contain mostly Zinc** which when combined with stomach acid **can cause gastric ulcerations**, and if absorbed in great enough quantity can cause zinc toxicosis (which is mainly pancreatic dysfunction / pancreatitis). The ulcers are the more likely thing to happen, so just remember that.

- S*o how the hell can you tell the date of a penny that is swallowed?* Either (a) the question stem will have to say something like - "2 year old child playing with father's collection of 1984 pennies", or the more likely (b) **showing you the penny with characteristic radiolucent holes** - from erosion.

Vascular Impressions

This is a very high yield topic for the purpose of multiple choice exams. Like my Grandma always said, you never get a second chance to make a first vascular impression.

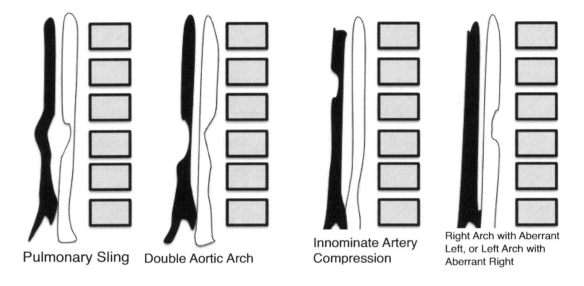

Pulmonary Sling   Double Aortic Arch   Innominate Artery Compression   Right Arch with Aberrant Left, or Left Arch with Aberrant Right

Pulmonary Sling:

- The **only variant that goes between the esophagus and the trachea**.
- Classic question is that this is **associated with trachea stenosis** (which is actually primary and not secondary to compression).
- High association with other cardiopulmonary and systemic anomalies: hypoplastic right lung, horseshoe lung, TE-fistula, imperforate anus, and complete tracheal rings.
- Treatment is controversial but typically involves surgical repositioning of the artery

Double Aortic Arch:

- Most Common **SYMPTOMATIC** vascular ring anomaly

Left Arch with Aberrant Right Subclavian Artery

- Most Common Aortic Arch Anomaly — not necessarily symptomatic.
- **"Dysphagia Lusoria"** - fancy Latin speak (therefore high yield) for trouble swallowing in the setting of this variant anatomy
- **"Diverticulum of Kommerell"** pouch like aneurysmal dilatation of the proximal portion of an aberrant right subclavian artery

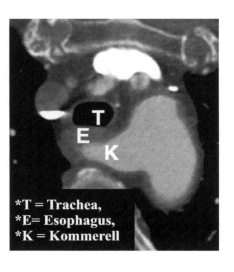

*T = Trachea,
*E= Esophagus,
*K = Kommerell

-Bowel Obstruction (in the neonate)-

Bowel obstruction in the neonate can be thought of as either high or low. Here are causes you should keep in your mind when you think the question stem is leading toward obstruction.

Why might you think the question is leading you toward obstruction? Anytime you are dealing with a neonate, and the history mentions **"vomiting,"** **"belly pain,"** or **"hasn't passed a stool yet."**

The following sections will walk through an algorithm, starting with plain films for diagnosis (and sometimes management).

High	Low
Midgut Volvulus / Malrotation	Hirschsprung Disease
Duodenal Atresia	Meconium Plug Syndrome
Duodenal Web	Ileal Atresia
Annular Pancreas	Meconium Ileus
Jejunal Atresia	Anal Atresia / Colonic Atresia

Sub Section 1: "Bubbles"

People who do peds radiology are obsessed with "bubbles" on baby grams. The idea is to develop a pattern-based approach to bowel obstruction in the newborn.

My preferred "bubble method" favors 8 possible patterns. This is a method originally developed by the brilliant (and devilishly handsome) Charles Maxfield at Duke.

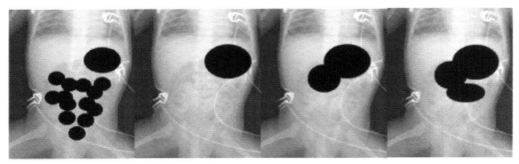

Normal **Single Bubble** **Double Bubble** **Triple Bubble**

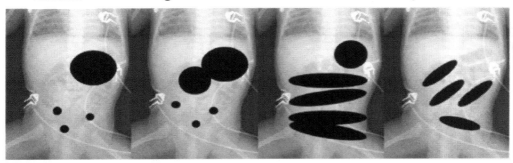

Single Bubble -plus distal gas **Double Bubble -plus distal gas** **Diffusely Dilated** **Diffusely Mildly Dilated**

Sub Section 1: "Bubbles" - Continued

Single Bubble

= Gastric (antral or pyloric) atresia.

Double Bubble = _Duodenal Atresia (highly specific)_. Some authors will say that UGI is not necessary because of how highly specific this is. The degree of distention will be more pronounced than with midgut volvulus (which is a more acute process). Thought to be secondary to failure to canalize during development (often an isolated atresia)

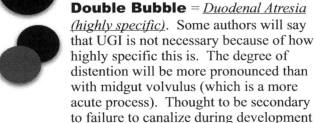

> **Duodenal Atresia Trivia:**
> • 30% have Downs
> • 40% have polyhydramnios and are premature
> • The "single atresia" - cannulation error
> • On multiple choice test the "double bubble" can be shown on 3rd trimester OB ultrasound, plain film, or on MRI.

Triple Bubble = Jejunal Atresia. When you call jejunal atresia, you often prompt search for additional atresias (colonic). Just remember that jejunal atresia is secondary to a vascular insult during development.

• _"Multiple Atresia" - vascular error._

Single Bubble with Distal Gas = Can mean nothing (lotta air swallowing). If the clinical history is bilious vomiting , this is ominous and can be midgut volvulus (surgical emergency). Next test would be emergent Upper GI.

Double Bubble with Distal Gas = Seeing distal gas excludes duodenal atresia. The DDx is a duodenal web, duodenal stenosis, or midgut volvulus. Next step would be upper GI.

Multiple Diffusely Dilated Loops = Suggestive of a low obstruction (ileum or colon). Next step is contrast enema. If the contrast enema is normal you need to follow with upper GI (to exclude an atypical look for midgut volvulus).

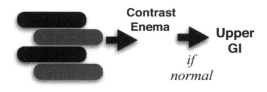

Mildly Dilated, Scattered Loops = "Sick Belly" – Can be seen with proximal or distal obstruction. Will need Upper GI and contrast enema.

Sub Section 2: Upper GI Patterns

Upper GI on kids is fair game in multiple choice tests, and real life. Often the answer of this test can equal a trip to the OR for kids, so it's no trivial endeavor.

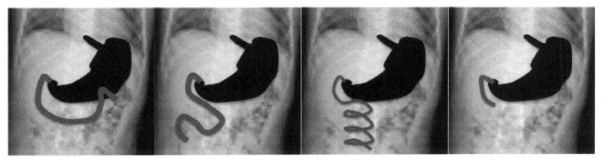

| Normal | Malrotation | Corkscrew Duodenum | Complete Duodenum Obstruction |

Malrotation – Normally, the developmental rotation of the gut places the ligament of Trietz to the left of the spine (at the level of the duodenal bulb). If mother nature fucks up and this doesn't happen, you end up with <u>the duodenum to the right of the midline</u> (spine). These patients are at increased risk for midgut volvulus and internal hernias. If you see the appearance of malrotation and the clinical history is bilious vomiting, then you must suspect midgut volvulus.

Trivia regarding Malrotation
   •Associated with Heterotaxy Syndromes. Associated with Omphaloceles.
   •Classically shown as the SMA to the right of the SMV (on US or CT).
   •False Positive on UGI – Distal Bowel Obstruction displacing the duodenum (because of ligamentous laxity).

Corkscrew Duodenum - This is diagnostic of midgut volvulus (surgical emergency). The appearance is an Aunt Minnie.

 Gamesmanship: *In an infant --*

I say "**Non-Bilious Vomiting**" --- You Say **Hypertrophic Pyloric Stenosis**

Next Step ? Ultrasound

I say "**Bilious Vomiting**" --- You Say **Mid Gut Volvulus** (*till proven otherwise*)

Next Step ? Upper GI

Ladd's Bands – In older children (or even adults) obstruction in the setting of malrotation will present as intermittent episodes of spontaneous duodenal obstruction. The cause is not midgut volvulus (a surgical emergency) but rather kinking from Ladd's Bands.

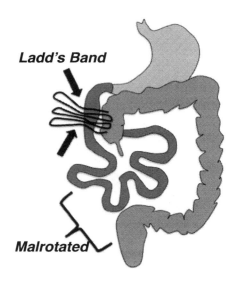

So what the hell is a "Ladd's Band" ? We are talking about a fibrous stalk of peritoneal tissues that fixes the cecum to the abdominal wall, and can obstruct the duodenum.

Complete Duodenal Obstruction – Strongly associated with midgut volvulus. If you were thinking duodenal atresia, look for distal air (any will do) to exclude that thought. Plus, as discussed above, you want to see a dilated duodenum (double bubble) for duodenal atresia.

Ladd's Procedure –

Procedure to prevent midgut volvulus. Traditionally, the Ladd's Bands are divided, and the appendix is taken out. The small bowel ends up on the right, and the large bowel ends up on the left. They are fixed in place by adhesions (just by opening the abdomen).

It is still possible to develop volvulus post Ladd's (but it's rare – 2-5%).

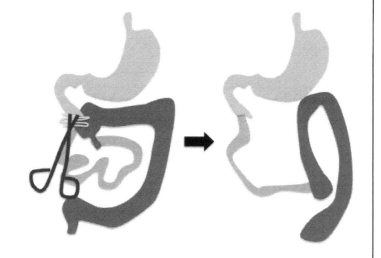

Ladds Procedure:
- Divide the Adhesive Ladds Bands
- Widen the Mesentery to a safe distance
- Take out the appendix (bill extra for that)

Partial Duodenal Obstruction – If the kid is vomiting this might be from extrinsic narrowing (Ladd band, annular pancreas), or intrinsic (duodenal web, duodenal stenosis). You can't tell.

Hypertrophic Pyloric Stenosis –

Thickening of the gastric pyloric musculature, which results in progressive obstruction. Step 1 buzzword is "non-bilious vomiting." Here is the most likely multiple choice trick; **this does NOT occur at birth or after 3 months.**

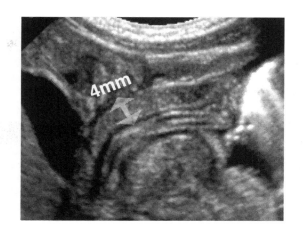

There is a specific age range of 2-12 weeks (peak at 3-6 weeks).

Criteria is 4mm and 14mm (4mm single wall, 14mm length).

The primary differential is pylorospasm (which will relax during exam). The most common pitfall during the exam is gastric over distention, which can lead to displacement of the antrum and pylorus – leading to false negative.

False positive can result from off axis measurement.

The phenomenon of *"paradoxical aciduria"* has been described, and is a common buzzword.

——

Gastric Volvulus- This comes in two flavors; organoaxial and mesenteroaxial.

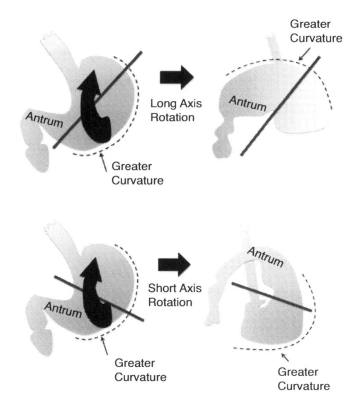

•*Organoaxial* – The greater curvature flips over the lesser curvature (rotation along the long axis). This is seen in old ladies with paraesophageal hernias.

•*Mesenteroaxial* – Twisting over the mesentery (rotation along short axis). The *antrum flips near the GE junction.* **Can cause ischemia** and needs to be fixed. Additionally this type causes obstruction. *This type is **more common in kids.***

Duodenal Web: This is best thought of as *"almost duodenal atresia."* The reason I say that is, just like duodenal atresia, this occurs from a failure to canalize, but instead of a total failure of canalization (like duodenal atresia) this bowel is only partially canalized, leaving behind a potentially obstructive web.

Trivia to know:
- Because the web is distal to ampulla of Vater - you get **bile-stained emesis**
- **Associated with** malrotation and **Downs syndrome**
- The **"wind sock"** deformity is seen more in older kids - where the web-like diaphragm has gotten stretched.

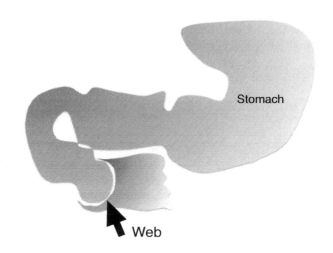

Stomach

Web

Annular Pancreas: Essentially an embryologic screw up (failure of ventral bud to rotate with the duodenum), that results in encasement of the duodenum.

In Kids = Think Duodenal Obstruction

In Adults = Think Pancreatitis

How it could be shown:

- On CT: Look for pancreatic tissue (same enhancement as the nearby normal pancreas) encircling the descending duodenum.

- On Fluoro: Look for an extrinsic narrowing of the duodenum. Obviously this is non-specific (typical barium - voodoo), use the location and clinical history to bias yourself.

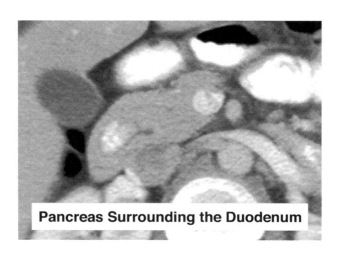

Pancreas Surrounding the Duodenum

Sub Section 3: "Low Obstruction" in a Neonate

Just like the upper GI and "bubble" plain film in sections 1 & 2, the lower obstruction can be approached with a pattern-based method. You basically have 4 choices: Normal, Short Microcolon, Long Microcolon, and a Caliber Change from micro to normal.

—

Normal:
- This is what normal looks like:

Short Microcolon -
- Think about <u>Colonic Atresia</u>

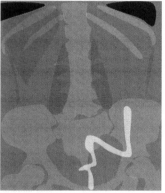

Long Microcolon - This can be seen with meconium ileus or distal ileal atresia.

•Meconium Ileus – **ONLY in patients with CF.** The pathology is the result of thick sticky meconium causing obstruction of the distal ileum. Contrast will reach ileal loops, and demonstrate multiple filling defects (meconium). This can be addressed with an enema.

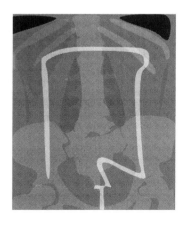

•Distal Ileal Atresia - This is the result of intrauterine vascular insult. **Contrast will NOT reach ileal loops**. This needs surgery.

Caliber Change – This can be seen with small left colon syndrome or Hirschsprungs

•Small Left Colon (Meconium Plug) Syndrome

– This is a transient functional colonic obstruction, that is self limited and relieved by contrast enema.

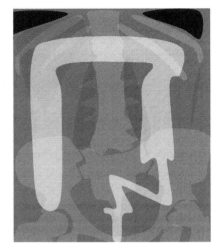

*Most Testable Fact:
It is **NOT associated with CF**.

*2nd Most Testable Fact:
It is seen in **infants of diabetic mothers** or if mom received magnesium sulfate for eclampsia.

•Hirschsprung Disease

– Failure of the ganglion cells to migrate and innervate the distal colon. Affected portions of the colon are small in caliber, whereas the normally innervated colon appears dilated.

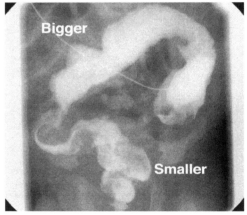

Trivia:
• It's 4:1 more common in boys.
• 10% association with Downs.
• Diagnosis is made by rectal biopsy.

How it can be Shown:
-Enema - **Rectum smaller than the Sigmoid**
  "Recto-sigmoid ratio < 1"
-Enema - **Rectum with "sawtooth pattern"**
  Represents bowel spasm

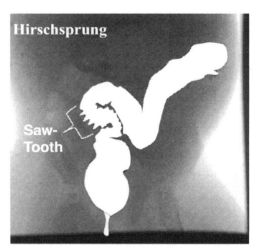

Presentation:
  (1) Newborn who fails to have BM > 48 hours (or classically > 72 hours)
  (2) "Forceful passage of meconium after rectal exam"
  (3) One month old who shows up "sick as stink" with NEC bowel

•Total Colonic Aganglionosis

- This is a super rare variant of Hirschsprungs, and **can mimic microcolon**. The piece of commonly asked trivia is that it can also involve the terminal ileum.

Meconium Peritonitis:

This is a potential complication of bowel atresia or <u>meconium ileus</u>. It has a very characteristic look. It's a **calcified mass in the mid abdomen**, traditionally shown on plain film. It is the result of a sterile peritoneal reaction to an in-utero bowel perforation.

Usually, the perforation seals off prior to birth and there is no leak.

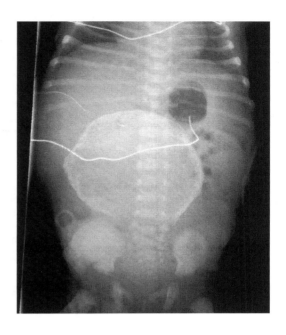

Imperforate or Ectopic Anus:

This can range from simple membranous anal atresia to an arrest of the colon as it descends through the puborectalis sling. The thing to know is fistula to genitourinary tract. Imperforate anus is also associated with a tethered cord (probably need a screening ultrasound).

- *I say "Baby with no asshole", you say "VACTERL"*
- *I say "Baby with no asshole", you say "Screening US for tethered cord"*

-Obstruction in an Older Child-

"My belly hurts" questions in an older child.

This scenario should make you think of 6 main things - the classic AA-II-MM or "AIM" differential - with appropriate credit given to the brilliant and under appreciated Aldrich Killian (A.I.M.s founder).

- Classic DDx "AIM" –
Appendicitis, **A**dhesions
Inguinal Hernia, **I**ntussusception
Midgut Volvulus, **M**eckels

Appendicitis – In children older than 4 this is the most common cause for bowel obstruction. If they show this in the PEDs section it's most likely to be on ultrasound. In that case you can expect a blind-ending tube, non-compressible, and bigger than 6 mm.

Inguinal Hernia: This is covered in more depth in the GI chapter. Big points are that **indirect hernias are more common in kids**, they are lateral to the inferior epigastric, and incarceration is the most common complication. Umbilical hernias are common in kids, but rarely incarcerate.

Trivia to know: This is the most common cause of obstruction in boy 1 month - 1 year.

Intussusception – The age range is 3 months – 3 years, before or after that you should think of lead points (90% between 3 months and 3 years don't have lead points). The normal mechanism is forward peristalsis resulting in invagination of proximal bowel (the intussusceptum) into lumen of the distal bowel (the intussuscipiens). They have to be bigger than 2.5 cm to matter (in most cases- these are enterocolic), those that are less than 2.0 cm are usually small bowel-small bowel and may reduce spontaneously within minutes. Just like an appendix, in the peds section, I would anticipate this shown on ultrasound as either the target sign or pseudo-kidney.

There are 3 main ways to ask questions about this: (1) *what is it ?*- these should be straight forward as targets or pseudo kidneys, (2) *lead points* - stuff like HSP (vasculitis), Meckle diverticulum, enteric duplication cysts, and (3) *reduction trivia.*

Reducing Intussusception Trivia:
• Contraindications: Free Air (check plain film). Peritonitis (based on exam)
• Recurrence: Usually within 72 hours
• Success Rates – 80-90% with air (Henoch-Schonlein purpura has a reduced success rate)
• Risk of Perforation – 0.5%
• Air causes less peritonitis (spillage of fecal material) than barium
• **Pressure should NOT exceed 120 mmHg**
• Needle decompression would be the next step if they perforate and get tension pneumoperitoneum

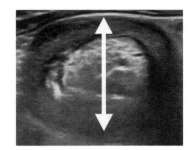

Not Every Target is an Ileocolic.
You want this this to be > **2.5 cm**

Meckels Diverticulum: This is a congenital diverticulum of the distal ileum. A piece of total trivia is that it is a persistent piece of the omphalomesenteric duct. Step 1 style, "rule of 2s" occurs in 2% of the population, has 2 types of heterotopic mucosa (gastric and pancreatic), located 2 feet from the IC valve, it's usually 2 inches long (and 2 cm in diameter), and usually has symptoms before the child is 2. If it has gastric mucosa (the ones that bleed typically do) it will take up Tc-Pertechnetate just like the stomach (hence the Meckel's scan).

High Yield Trivia (Regarding Complications)
• Can get diverticulitis in the Meckels (mimic appendicitis)
• GI Bleed from Gastric Mucosa (causes 30% of symptomatic cases)
• Can be a lead point for intussusception (seen with inverted diverticulum)
• Can Cause Obstruction

-Luminal GI - Special Topics-

Enteric Duplication Cysts – These are developmental anomalies (failure to canalize). They don't have to communicate with the GI lumen but can. They are most commonly in the ileal region (40%). They have been known to cause in utero bowel obstruction / perforation.

Strategy: A common way to show this is a cyst in the abdomen (on ultrasound). If you have a random cyst in the abdomen you need to ask yourself - *"does this have gut signature?"*

- Cyst with Gut Signature = Enteric Duplication Cyst
- Cyst without Gut Signature = Omental Cyst
- WTF is "Gut Signature ?" - It's alternating bands of hyper and hypo echoic signal - supposedly representing different layers of bowel.

Trivia to know: 30% of the time they are **associated with vertebral anomalies**.

Distal Intestinal Obstruction Syndrome – This is a cause of bowel obstruction in an older kid (20 year old) with cystic fibrosis. This is sometimes called the *"meconium ileus equivalent,"* because you end up with a distal obstruction (as the name implies) secondary to dried up thick stool. It more commonly involves the ileum / right colon. Kids who get this, are the ones who aren't compliant with their pancreatic enzymes.

Gastroschisis – Extra-abominal evisceration of neonatal bowel (sometimes stomach and liver) through a paraumbilical wall defect.

Trivia to know:
- It does NOT have a surrounding membrane (omphalocele does)
- It's **always on the RIGHT side.**
- Associated anomalies are rare (unlike omphalocele).
- Maternal Serum AFP will be elevated (higher than that of omphalocele)
- Outcome is usually good
- For some reason they get bad reflux after repair.

Omphalocele – This is a congenital midline defect, with herniation of gut at the base of the umbilical cord.

Trivia to know:
- It DOES have a surrounding membrane (gastroschisis does not)
- **Associated anomalies are common** (unlike gastroschisis)
- Trisomy 18 is the most common associated chromosomal anomaly
- Other associations: Cardiac (50%), Other GI, CNS, GU, Turners, Klinefelters, Beckwith-Wiedemann.
- Outcomes are not that good, because of associated syndromes.
- Umbilical Cord Cysts (Allantoic Cysts) are associated.

Mesenteric Adenitis - Self-limiting, usually viral inflammatory condition of mesenteric lymph nodes. It is a **classic clinical mimic of appendicitis**. The finding is a cluster of large right lower quadrant lymph nodes.

Necrotising Enterocolitis (NEC)

This is bad news. The general thinking is that you have an immature bowel mucosa (from being premature or having a heart problem), and you get translocated bugs through this immature bowel. It's best thought of as a combination of ischemic and infective pathology.

Who gets it?
- **Premature Kids** (90% within the first 10 days of life)
- Low Birth Weight Kids (< 1500 grams)
- **Cardiac Patients** (<u>sometimes occult</u>) – they can be full term
- Kids who had perinatal asphyxia
- **Hirschsprung Kids** that go home and come back – they **present around month 1.**

What does it look like?
- Pneumatosis – most definitive finding; Look for Portal Venous Gas Next
- Focal Dilated Bowel (especially in the right lower quadrant) – the terminal ileum / right colon is the region most affected by NEC
- Featureless small bowel , with separation (suggesting edema).
- Unchanging bowel gas pattern – this would be a dirty trick – showing several plain films from progressing days, with the bowel gas pattern remaining the same.

Pneumatosis vs Poop - The age old question.
- First question - has the kid been feed? No food = No poop.
- Second question - is it staying still? Poop will move, Pneumatosis will stay still.

Useless Trivia:
- Use of maternal breast milk is the only parameter associated with decreased incidence of NEC.

SECTION 8:
Solid Organ GI

-Pirates of the Pancreas-

CF - The pancreas is nearly always (90%) with CF patients. Inspissated secretions cause proximal duct obstruction leading to the two main changes in CF: (1) Fibrosis (decreased T1 and T2 signal) and the more common one (2) fatty replacement (increased T1).

Patients with CF diagnosed as adults tend to have more pancreas problems than those diagnosed as children. Those with residual pancreatic exocrine function can have bouts of recurrent acute pancreatitis. Small (1-3mm) pancreatic cysts are common.

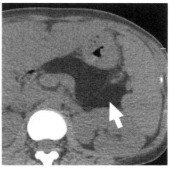

Complete Fatty Replacement

High Yield Trivia:
- **Complete fatty replacement** is the most common imaging finding in adult CF
- Enlarged with fatty replacement = **lipomatous pseudohypertrophy of the pancreas.**
- Fibrosing Colonopathy: Thick walled right colon as a complication of enzyme replacement therapy.

 Shwachman-Diamond Syndrome - The 2nd most common cause of pancreatic insufficiency in kids (CF #1). Basically, it's a kid with diarrhea, short stature, and eczema. Will also cause lipomatous pseudohypertrophy of the pancreas.

 Dorsal Pancreatic Agenesis - You only have a ventral bud (the dorsal bud forgets to form). Since the dorsal buds makes the tail, the appearance is that of a pancreas without a tail. All you need to know is that (1) this sets you up for diabetes *(most of your beta cells are in the tail)*, and (2) it's associated with polysplenia.

Pancreatitis – The most common cause of pancreatitis in peds is trauma (seat belt).

 NAT: Another critical point to make is that non-accidental trauma can present as pancreatitis. If the kid isn't old enough to ride a bike (handle bar injury) or didn't have a car wreck (seat belt injury) you need to think NAT.

Tumors of the Pediatric Pancreas:
Even at a large pediatric hospital its uncommon to see more than 1-2 of these a year. Obviously, they are still fair game for multiple choice. This is what I would know:

Solid and Papillary Epithelial Neoplasm (SPEN) - The most common pediatric solid tumor. It's found in female adolescents (usually asian, or black). The outcomes are pretty good after surgical resection. If you get shown a case in the peds setting this is probably it. I'll mention this thing again in the Adult GI chapter.

Otherwise, I would try and use age as a discriminator (if they are nice enough to give it to you).

Peds Pancreatic Mass
Age 1 = Pancreatoblastoma
Age 6 = Adenocarcinoma
Age 15 = SPEN

-Liver Masses-

Tumors: For Peds liver tumors I like to use an age-based system to figure it out. Mass in the liver, first think – what is the age? Then use the narrow DDx to figure it out.

 Age 0-3: With kids that are newborns you should think about 3 tumors:

Infantile Hepatic Hemangioma:

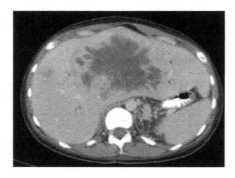

Often < 1. Associated with high output CHF, this is classically shown as a <u>large heart on CXR</u> plus a mass in the liver. The aorta above the hepatic branches of the celiac is often enlarged relative to the aorta below the celiac because of differential flow. Skin hemangiomas are present in 50%. **Endothelial growth factor is elevated**. These can be associated with Kasabach-Merritt Syndrome (the platelet eater).

How do they do? - Actually well. They tend to spontaneously involute without therapy over months-years - as they progressively calcify.

Hepatoblastoma:

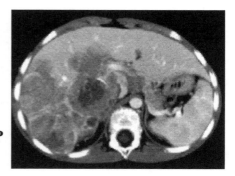

Most common primary liver tumor of childhood (< 5). The big thing to know is that it's associated with a bunch of syndromes – mainly hemi-hypertrophy, Wilms, Beckwith-Weidemann crowd. *Prematurity is a risk factor.* This is usually a well circumscribed solitary <u>right sided</u> mass, that may extend into the portal veins, hepatic veins, and IVC. <u>Calcifications are present 50% of the time.</u> **AFP is elevated.** Another piece of trivia is the hepatoblastoma **may cause a precocious puberty** from making bHCG.

I would know 3 things: (1) Associated with Wilms, (2) AFP, (3) Precocious Puberty

Mesenchymal Hamartoma:

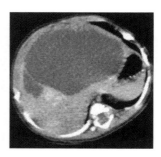

This is the predominately **cystic mass** (or multiple cysts), sometimes called a "developmental anomaly." Because it's a "developmental anomaly" it shouldn't surprise you that the **AFP is negative**. <u>Calcifications are UNCOMMON.</u> What is common is a large portal vein branch feeding the tumor.

 **Age > 5:**

HCC: This is actually the <u>second most common liver cancer in kids</u>. You'll see them in kids with cirrhosis (biliary atresia, Fanconi syndrome, glycogen storage disease). **AFP will be elevated.**

Fibrolamellar Subtype: This is typically seen in younger patients (<35) <u>without cirrhosis</u> and a normal AFP. The **buzzword is central scar**. The scar is similar to the one seen in FNH with a few differences. This scar does NOT enhance, and is T2 dark *(the FNH scar is T2 bright)*. As a point of trivia, this tumor is Gallium avid. This tumor **calcifies more often than conventional HCC.**

Undifferentiated Embryonal Sarcoma: This is the pissed off cousin of the mesenchymal hamartoma. It's also cystic, but the mass is much more aggressive. It will be a hypodense mass with septations and fibrous pseudocapsule. This mass has been known to rupture.

 **Any Age:**

Mets: Think about Wilms tumor or Neuroblastoma

Now, there are several other entities that can occur in the liver of young children / teenagers including; Hepatic Adenoma, Hemangiomas, Focal Nodular Hyperplasia, and Angio Sarcoma. The bulk of these are discussed in greater detail in the adult GI chapter.

-Congenital Biliary / Liver-

Choledochal cysts are congenital dilations of the bile ducts –classified into 5 types by some dude named Todani. The high yield trivia is <u>type 1 is focal dilation of the CBD and is by far the most common.</u> Type 2 and 3 are super rare. Type 2 is basically a diverticulum of the bile duct. Type 3 is a "choledochocele." Type 4 is both intra and extra hepatic. Type 5 is Caroli's, and is intrahepatic only. I'll hit this again in the GI chapter.

Caroli's is an AR disease associated with polycystic kidney disease and medullary sponge kidney. The hallmark is intrahepatic duct dilation, that is large and secular. Buzzword is **"central dot sign"** which corresponds to the portal vein surrounded by dilated bile ducts.

AR Polycystic Kidney Disease: This will be discussed in greater detail in the renal section, but kids with AR polycystic kidney disease will have cysts in the kidneys, and variable degrees of <u>fibrosis in the liver.</u> The degree of fibrosis is actually the opposite of cystic formation in the kidneys (bad kidneys ok liver, ok kidneys bad liver).

Hereditary Hemorrhagic Telangiectasia (Osler-Weber-Rendu):
Autosomal dominant disorder characterized by multiple AVMs in the liver and lungs. It leads to cirrhosis, and a massively dilated hepatic artery. The *lung AVMs set you up for brain abscess.*

Biliary Atresia: If you have prolonged newborn jaundice (> 2 weeks) you should think about two things (1) neonatal hepatitis, and (2) Biliary Atresia. It's critical to get this diagnosis right because they need corrective surgery (Kasai Procedure) prior to 3 months. Patients with biliary atresia really only have **atresia of the ducts outside the liver** (absence of extrahepatic ducts), in fact *they have proliferation of the intrahepatic ducts.* They will develop cirrhosis without treatment and not do well.

Trivia to Know about Biliary Atresia:
- Associations with Polysplenia, and Trisomy 18
- **Gallbladder may be absent** *(normal gallbladder – supports neonatal hepatitis)*
- Triangle Cord Sign – triangular echogenic structure by the portal vein – possibly remnant of the CBD.
- Hepatobiliary Scintigraphy with 99m Tc-IDA is the test of choice to distinguish (discussed in the Nukes Chapter).
- Alagille Syndrome: This is a total zebra. All you need to know is hereditary cholestasis, from paucity of intrahepatic bile ducts, and peripheral pulmonary stenosis. *The purpose of a liver biopsy in biliary atresia is to exclude this diagnosis.*

Gallstones: If you see a peds patient with gallstones think <u>sickle cell.</u>

- Spleen -

Infarcted Spleen – Just say sickle cell.

Polysplenia and Asplenia – *Heterotaxia syndromes* are clutch for multiple choice tests. The major game played on written tests is *"left side vs right side."*

So what the hell does that mean? I like to start in the lungs. The right side has two fissures (major and minor). The left side has just one fissure. So if I show you a CXR with two fissures on each side, (a left sided minor fissure), then the patient has two right sides. Thus the term "bilateral right sidedness."

What else is a right sided structure? The liver. So, these patients won't have a spleen (the spleen is a left sided structure).

The opposite is true. Since the spleen is on the left, a "bilateral left sided" patient will have polysplenia.

Heterotaxia Syndromes	
Right Sided	**Left Sided**
Two Fissures in Left Lung	One Fissure in Right Lung
Asplenia	Polysplenia
Increased Cardiac Malforations	Less Cardiac Malformations
Reversed Aorta/IVC	Azygos Continuation of the IVC

Aorta/IVC: This relationship is a little more confusing when you try to reason it out. The way I keep it straight is by remembering that the IVC is usually on the right. If you are "bilateral left" then you don't have a regular IVC — hence the azygos continuation. Then I just remember that the other one (flipped IVC/Aorta) is the other one.

Normal
IVC *(on the right)*
Aorta *(on the left)*

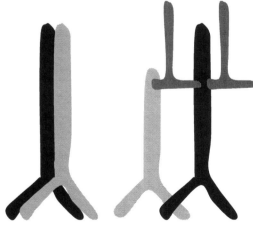

Reversed (Aorta/ ICV)
-Asplenia

Azygos Continuation
-Polysplenia

Right Isomerism	Left Isomerism

Heterotaxia Syndromes / Situs - Cont...

So on the prior page I used terms like "bilateral right sided" and "bilateral left sided" to help make the concept more digestible. I didn't make those words up. You will read that some places but I think to be ready for the full gauntlet of heterotaxia related fuckery you should also be ready for words that start with *"situs"* and end with *"isomerism."*

Situs Vocab: There are 3 vocab words that start with the word "Situs."

- **Situs Solitus** - Instead of just saying <u>normal</u>, you can be an asshole and say *"Situs Solitus."*
- **Situs Inversus Totalis** - Total <u>mirror image transposition</u> of the abdominal and thoracic stuff.
- **Situs Ambiguus** (Ambiguous) - This is a tricky way of saying <u>Heterotaxy</u>, of which you can have left or right "isomerism."

"Isomerism" - I guess some asshole really liked organic chemistry…. This is a fancy way of saying bilateral right or bilateral left - as explained on the prior page.

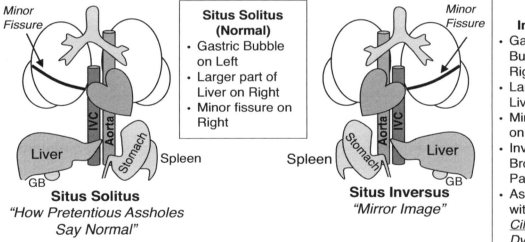

Situs Solitus (Normal)
- Gastric Bubble on Left
- Larger part of Liver on Right
- Minor fissure on Right

Situs Solitus
"How Pretentious Assholes Say Normal"

Situs Inversus
- Gastric Bubble on Right
- Larger part of Liver on Left
- Minor fissure on Left
- Inverted Bronchial Pattern
- Associated with *Primary Ciliary Dyskinesia*

Situs Inversus
"Mirror Image"

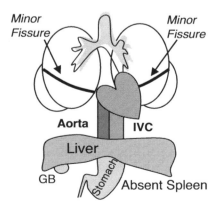

Visceral Heterotaxy with Thoracic Right Isomerism

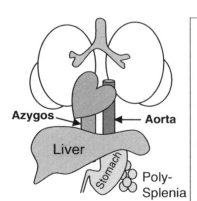

V.H. with T Left Isomerism
- Absent Minor Fissures
- Interrupted IVC
- Polysplenia
- *Biliary Atresia (10%)*

Visceral Heterotaxy with Thoracic Left Isomerism

- Top 4 Things for Peds GI -

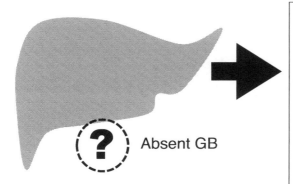

Absent GB

Biliary Atresia:
- Congenital liver fibrosis → cholangiopathy → neonatal jaundice (after 1 week of life)
- US: Bright band of tissue (triangular cord sign) near branching of common bile duct; small or absent gallbladder (fasting ~ 3 hours)
- Scintigraphic: No tracer excretion into bowel by 24 hours
- Biopsy to exclude = Zebra Alagille syndrome
- Treated with Kasai procedure

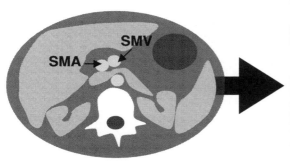
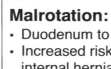

SMV - 2 o'clock position relative to SMA

Malrotation:
- Duodenum to the right of the midline
- Increased risk for mid gut volvulus, and internal hernia
- *"Bilious vomiting"*
- SMA to the right of the SMV

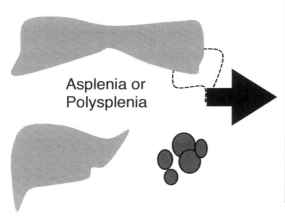

Asplenia or Polysplenia

Heterotaxia Syndromes	
Right Sided	**Left Sided**
Two Fissures in Left Lung	One Fissure in Right Lung
Asplenia	Polysplenia
Increased Cardiac Malforations	Less Cardiac Malformations
Reversed Aorta/IVC	Azygos Continuation of the IVC

VACTERL

- **V** – **V**ertebral Anomalies (37%)
- **A** – **A**nal (imperforate anus) (63%)
- **C** – **C**ardiac (77%)
- **TE** – **T**racheoesophageal Fistula or **E**sophageal Atresia (40%)
- **R** – **R**enal (72%)
- **L** – **L**imb (radial ray) – 58%

SECTION 9:
Congenital GU

Renal Agenesis – This comes in one of two flavors; (1) Both Kidneys Absent - this one is gonna be Potter sequence related, (2) One Kidney Absent - this one is gonna have reproductive associations.

Most likely way to test this: Show unilateral agenesis on prenatal US - as an absent renal artery (in view of the aorta) or oligohydramnios - with followup questions on associations. Or make it super obvious with a CT / MRI and ask association questions.

Unilateral Absence Association
- 70% of women with unilateral renal agenesis have associated genital anomalies (usually **unicornuate uterus, or a rudimentary horn**).
- 20% of men are missing the epididymis, and vas deferens on the same side they are missing the kidney. PLUS they have a seminal vesicle cyst on that side.

Potter Sequence: Insult (maybe ACE inhibitors) = kidneys don't form, if kidneys don't form you can't make piss, if you can't make piss you can't develop lungs (pulmonary hypoplasia).

Lying Down Adrenal or "Pancake Adrenal" Sign – describes the elongated appearance of the adrenal not normally molded by the adjacent kidney. It can be used to differentiate surgical absent vs congenitally absent.

Horseshoe Kidney – This is the most common fusion anomaly. The kidney gets hung up on the IMA. Questions are most likely to revolve around the complications / risks:

- *Complications from Position* - Easy to get smashed against vertebral body - kid shouldn't play football or wrestle.
- *Complications from Drainage Problems:* Stones, Infection, and Increased risk of Cancer (from chronic inflammation) - big ones are Wilms, TCC, and the Zebra **Renal Carcinoid.**
- *Association Syndrome Trivia* - Turner's Syndrome is the classic testable association.

Crossed Fused Renal Ectopia – One kidney comes across the midline and fuses with the other. Each kidney has its own orthotopic ureteral orifice to drain through. It's critically important to the patient to know that *"the Ectopic Kidney is Inferior."* The left kidney more commonly crosses over to the right. Complications include stones, infection, and hyponephrosis (50%).

The classic way to show this is two axial CTs. The first at the level of the kidneys hinting that one kidney may be absent. The second through the bladder (on a delayed phase) showing two opacified ureters.

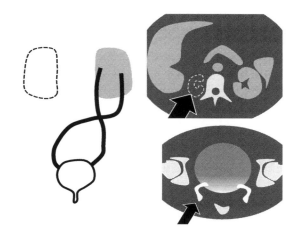

Congenital UPJ Obstruction

– This is the most common congenital anomaly of the GU tract in neonates. About 20% of the time, these are bilateral. Most (80%) of these are thought to be caused by intrinsic defects in the circular muscle bundle of the renal pelvis. Treatment is a pyeloplasty. A Radiologist can actually add value by **looking for vessels crossing the UPJ** prior to pyeloplasty, as this changes the management.

Q: 1970 called and they want to know how to tell the difference between a prominent extrarenal pelvis vs a congenital UPJ obstruction.
A:"Whitaker Test", which is a urodynamics study combined with an antegrade pyelogram.

Classic History: Teenager with flank pain after drinking "lots of fluids."

Classic Trivia: These do NOT have dilated ureters (NO HYDROURETER).

Autosomal Recessive Polycystic Kidney Disease (ARPKD)

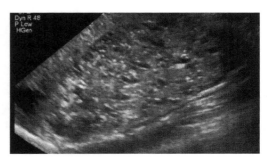

ARPKD: Big Bright, with Lost Corticomedullary Differentiation.

– These guys get HTN and renal failure. The liver involvement is different than the adult form (ADPKD). Instead of cysts they have abnormal bile ducts and fibrosis. This congenital hepatic fibrosis is ALWAYS present in ARPKD. The **ratio of liver and kidney disease is inverse**. The worse the liver is the better the kidneys do. The better the liver is the worse the kidneys are. Death is often from portal hypertension.

On ultrasound the kidneys are smoothly enlarged and diffusely echogenic, with a loss of corticomedullary differentiation. In utero you sometimes will not see urine in the bladder.

Neonatal Renal Vein Thrombosis – This is an associated condition of **maternal diabetes**. It is typically unilateral (usually left). The theory is that it starts peripherally and progresses toward the hilum. When acute, will cause renal enlargement. When chronic, will result in renal atrophy.

Neonatal Renal Artery Thrombosis – This occurs secondary to **umbilical artery catheters**. Unlike renal vein thrombosis it does NOT present with renal enlargement but instead severe hypertension.

Prune Belly (Eagle Barrett Syndrome)

This is a malformation triad which occurs in males. Classically shown on a babygram with a kid shaped like a pear (big wide belly).

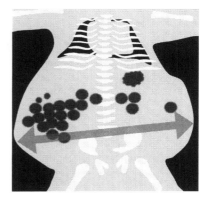

Triad:
* Deficiency of abdominal musculature
* Hydroureteronephrosis
* Cryptorchidism
(bladder distention interferes with descent of testes)

-Congenital Ureter and Urethra-

Congenital (primary) MEGAureter – This is a "wastebasket" term for an enlarged ureter which is intrinsic to the ureter (NOT the result of a distal obstruction). Causes include (1) distal adynamic segment (analogous to achalasia, or colonic Hirschsprungs), (2) reflux at the UVJ, (3) it just wants to be big (totally idiopathic). The distal adynamic type "obstructing primary megaureter," can have some hydro, but generally speaking an *absence of dilation of the collecting system* helps distinguish this from an actual obstruction.

Retrocaval Ureter (circumcaval)- This is actually a problem with the development of the IVC, which grows in a manner that pins the ureter. Most of the time it's asymptomatic, but can cause partial obstruction and recurrent UTI. IVP will show a "reverse J" or "fishhook" appearance of the ureter.

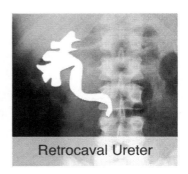

Retrocaval Ureter

Duplicated System – The main thing to know about duplicated systems is the so-called "**Weigert-Meyer Rule**" where the upper pole inserts inferior and medially. The upper pole is prone to ureterocele formation and obstruction. The lower pole is prone to reflux. Kidneys with duplicated systems tend to be larger than normal kidneys. In girls, a duplicated system can lead to incontinence (ureter may insert below the sphincter - sometimes into the vagina).

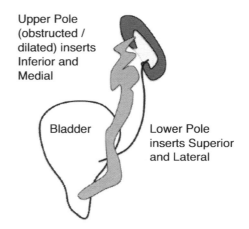

Upper Pole (obstructed / dilated) inserts Inferior and Medial

Bladder

Lower Pole inserts Superior and Lateral

- *Upper Pole Obstructs*
- *Lower Pole Refluxes*

Ureterocele – A cystic dilation of the intravesicular ureter, secondary to obstruction at the ureteral orifice. IVP (or US) will show the *"cobra head" sign*, with contrast surrounded by a lucent rim, protruding from the contrast filled bladder. This is associated with a duplicated system (specifically the upper pole).

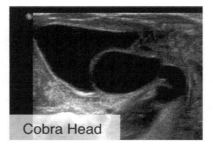

Cobra Head

Ectopic Ureter – The ureter inserts distal to the external sphincter in the vestibule. More common in females and associated with incontinence (not associated with incontinence in men). Ureteroceles are best demonstrated during the early filling phase of the VCUG.

Posterior Urethral Valves:

This is a fold in the posterior urethra that leads to outflow obstruction and eventual renal failure (if it's not fixed). It is the most common cause of urethral obstruction in male infants.

Now, this can be shown a variety of ways; it could be shown in the classic VCUG. The key finding on VCUG is an *abrupt caliber change between the dilated posterior urethra and normal caliber anterior urethra.*

Another, much sneakier way to show this is with a fetal MRI. The MRI would have to show hydro in the kidney and a "key-hole" bladder appearance.

"Peri-renal fluid collection" is a buzzword, and it's the result of forniceal rupture. Obviously that is non-specific and can be seen with any obstructive pathology.

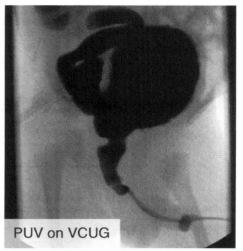

PUV on VCUG

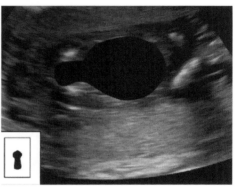

Strategy for *"Next Step"* types of Questions :

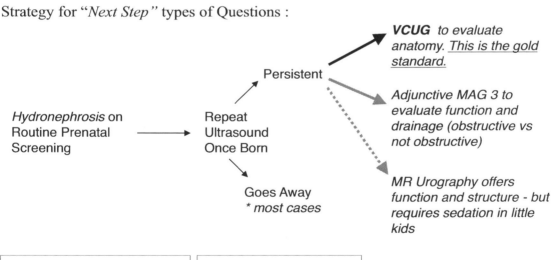

Hydronephrosis on Routine Prenatal Screening → Repeat Ultrasound Once Born

Persistent

Goes Away
* most cases

VCUG to evaluate anatomy. *This is the gold standard.*

Adjunctive MAG 3 to evaluate function and drainage (obstructive vs not obstructive)

MR Urography offers function and structure - but requires sedation in little kids

Non-*Obstructive* Causes of Hydro in Baby Boys	**Obstructive Causes of Hydro in Baby Boys**
-Vesicoureteral Reflux (VUR)	-PUV
-Primary Megaureter	-UPJ Obstruction
-Prune Belly = Zebra	-Ureteral Ectopia

Vesicoureteral Reflux (VUR) –

Normally, the ureter enters the bladder at an oblique angle so that a "valve" is developed. If the angle of insertion is abnormal (horizontal) reflux can develop. This can occur in the asymptomatic child, but is seen in 50% of children with UTIs. The recommendations for when the boy/girl with a UTI should get a VCUG to evaluate for VUR is in flux (not likely to be tested). Most of the time VUR resolves by age 5-6.

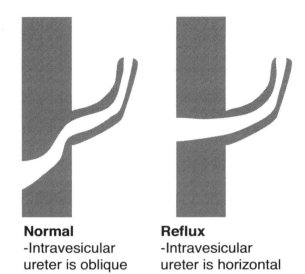

Normal
-Intravesicular ureter is oblique

Reflux
-Intravesicular ureter is horizontal

There is a grading system for VUR which goes 1-5.
- One is reflux halfway up the ureter,
- Two is reflux into a non-dilated collecting system, (calyces still pointy),
- Three you have dilation of the collecting system, and calyces get blunted
- Four the system gets mildly tortuous,
- Five the system is very tortuous.

A sneaky trick would be to show the echogenic mound near the UVJ, that results from injection of "deflux", which is a treatment urologist try. Essentially, they make a bubble with this proprietary compound in the soft tissues near the UVJ and it creates a valve (sorta). Anyway, they show it in a lot of case books and textbooks so just keep your eyes peeled.

Additional Pearl: Chronic reflux can lead to scarring. This **scarring can result in hypertension** and/or chronic renal failure.

Additional Pearl: If the reflux appears to be associated with a "hutch" diverticulum - people will use the vocabulary "Secondary" VUR rather than Primary VUR. The treatment in this case will be surgical.

"Hutch" Diverticula
- Occur at or adjacent (usually just above) the UVJ.
- Caused by congenital muscular defect
- Difficult to see on US — better seen with VCUG.
- They are "dynamic" and best seen on the voiding (micturition) phase
- If associated with VUR will often be surgically resected

Hutch

- Congenital Bladder -

The Urachus: The umbilical attachment to the bladder (started out being called the allantois, then called the Urachus). This usually atrophies into the umbilical ligament. Persistent canalization can occur along a spectrum (patent, sinus, diverticulum, cyst).

- *Trivia:* Most common complication of urachal remnant = infection

- *Trivia:* Urachal anomalies are twice as common in boys (relative to girls)

- *Trivia:* **The most important piece of trivia is that when these guys get cancer, it's** <u>**adenocarcinoma**</u> (90% of cases). To hint at this multiple choice test writers will often use the phrase "<u>midline bladder structure</u>"

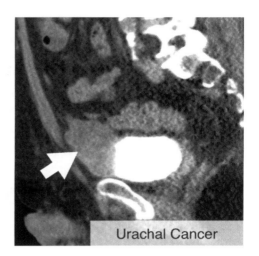

Urachal Cancer

Urachal Spectrum:

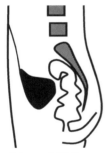  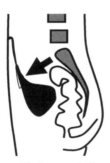  

| Normal Obliterated Urachus (only the ligament remains) | Patent Urachus | Vesicourachal Diverticulum | Urachal Cyst | Umbilical Urachal Sinus |

Bladder Exstrophy - This is a herniation of the urinary bladder through a hole in the anterior infra-umbilical abdominal wall.

What do you need to know?

- Increased incidence of <u>Malignancy</u> in the extruded bladder
- It's Adenocarcinoma - just like a Urachal Remnant would get
- Aunt Minnie "Manta Ray Sign" - with **unfused pubic bones**. This looks like a monster wide pubic symphysis on an AP pelvic radiograph.

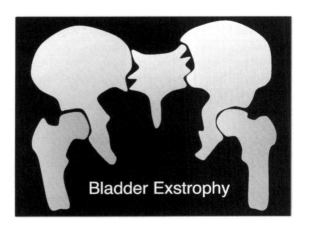

Bladder Exstrophy

Cloacal Malformation – GU and GI both drain into a common opening (like a bird). This only happens in females.

SECTION 10:
Solid Organ GU

When it comes to solid renal masses – an age-based strategy is the ticket.

Why an age-based strategy? If they give you the age of the patient, you can use this chart to eliminate distractors which don't fit. If you are lucky, you won't even have to look at the picture.

Neonate	Around Age 4	Teenager
Nephroblastomatosis	Wilms	RCC
Mesoblastic Nephroma	Wilms Variants	Lymphoma
	Lymphoma	
	Multilocular Cystic Nephroma	

Tumor / Mass	Rapid Review Trivia
Mesoblastic Nephroma	*"Solid Tumor of Infancy"* (you can be born with it)
Nephroblastomatosis	"Nephrogenic Rests" - left over embryologic crap that didn't go away Might turn into wilms (bilateral wilms especially) "Next Step" - f/u ultrasound till 7-8 years old Variable appearance
Wilms	90% + Renal Tumors *"Solid Tumor of Childhood"* - **Never born with it** Grows like a solid ball (will invade rather than incase) Met to the lung (most common)
Clear Cell - Wilms	Met to Bone
Rhabdoid - Wilms	Brain Tumors It fucks you up, it takes the money (it believes in nothing Lebowski)
Multi-Cystic Nephroma	Micheal Jackson Tumor (Young Boys, Middle Age Women) Big cysts that don't communicate Septal Enhancement Can't Tell it is not Cystic Wilms (next step = resection)
RCC	*"Solid Tumor of Adolescent"* Syndromes - VHL, TS
Renal Lymphoma	Non-Hodgkin Multifocal

- Solid Age 0-3

Nephroblastomatosis – These are persistent nephrogenic rests beyond 36 weeks. It's sorta normal (found in 1% of infants). But, it can be a precursor to Wilms so you follow it. When Wilms is bilateral, 99% of the time it had nephroblastomatosis first. It goes away on its own (normally). *It should NOT have necrosis – this makes you think Wilms*. It has a variable appearance, and is often described as "homogeneous." Although more commonly a focal homogeneous ball, the way it's always shown in case conferences and case books is as a hypodense rind.

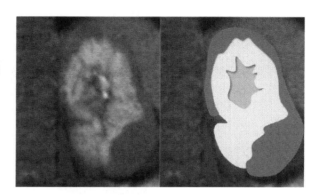

Nephroblastomatosis
-Hypodense Rind -

Ultrasound screening q 3 months till age 7-8 is the usual routine - to make sure it doesn't go Wilms on you.

Mesoblastic Nephroma - *"Solid renal tumor of infancy."* This is a fetal hamartoma, and generally benign. It is the most common neonatal renal tumor (80% diagnosed in the first month on life). Often involves the renal sinus. Antenatal ultrasound may have shown polyhydramnios.

Pearl: If it really looks like a Wilms, but they are just too young (< 1 year) then call it mesoblastic nephroma.

- Cystic Age 0-3

Multicystic Dysplastic Kidney - You have multiple tiny cysts forming in utereo. What you need to know is (1) that there is "no functioning renal tissue," (2) contralateral renal tract abnormalities occur like 50% of the time (most commonly <u>UPJ obstruction)</u>.

MCDK vs Bad Hydro?
• In hydronephrosis, the cystic spaces are seen to communicate.
• In difficult cases renal scintigraphy can be useful. MCDK will show no excretory function.

Pearl: MCDK has MACROscopic cysts that do NOT communicate

- Solid Around Age 4 🕐

Wilms

"Solid renal tumor of childhood." This is the most common solid renal tumor of childhood. This is NOT seen in a newborn. Repeat, you can NOT be born with this tumor. The average age is around 3. It typically spreads via direct invasion.

Associated Syndromes:

Overgrowth

- **Beckwith-Wiedemann** – Macroglossia (most common finding), Omphalocele, Hemihypertrophy, Cardiac, Big Organs.
- **Sotos** – Macrocephaly, Retarded (CNS stuff), Ugly Face

> I Say **Beckwith-Wiedemann**
>
> You Say,
> - **Wilms,**
> - **Omphalocele,**
> - **Hepatoblastoma**

Non-Overgrowth

- **WAGR** - Wilms, Aniridia, Genital, Growth Retardation
- **Drash** – Wilms, Pseudohermaphroditism, Progressive Glomerulonephritis

Wilms Nevers

- **NEVER Biopsy** suspected Wilms (you can seed the tract and up the stage)
- Wilms **NEVER occurs before 2 months of age** (Neuroblastoma can)

> **Wilms in a 1 year old ?**
> Think about associated syndromes. Wilms loves to pal around with:
> - **Hemihypertrophy,**
> - **Hypospadias,**
> - **Cryptorchidism**

Bilateral Wilms

- About **5-10%** will have bilateral disease (*"Synchronous Bilateral Wilms"*)

Wilms Variants *(look just like Wilms)*
- **Clear Cell** – likes to go to bones (lytic)
- **Rhabdoid** – "Terrible Prognosis" – Associated with aggressive Rhabdoid brain tumors

- Cystic Around Age 4

Multilocular Cystic Nephroma

"Non-communicating, fluid-filled locules, surrounded by thick fibrous capsule." By definition these things are characterized by the absence of a solid component or necrosis.

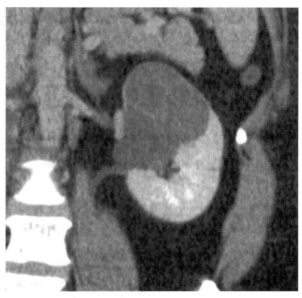

Buzzword is "<u>protrude into the renal pelvis</u>."

There is a classic bimodal occurrence (4 year old boys, and 40 year old women).

I like to think of this as the Michael Jackson lesion – it loves young boys and middle-aged women

Multilocular Cystic Nephroma
"Protruding into the renal pelvis"

- Solids in Teenager

Renal Lymphoma and RCC can occur in teenagers. Renal lymphoma can occur in 5 year olds as well. Both of these cancers are discussed in detail in the adult GU chapter.

- Other GU Masses / Cancers -

Rhabdomyosarcoma – This is the most common bladder cancer in humans less than 10 years of age. They are often infiltrative, and it's hard to tell where they originate from. **"Paratesticular Mass" is often a buzzword.** They can met to the lungs, bones, and nodes. The Botryoid variant produces a polypoid mass, which looks like a bunch of grapes. *I'll discuss this again in the testicle section on page 60.*

Neuroblastoma - Isn't a Renal Mass, but is frequently contrasted with Wilms so I want to discuss it in the renal section. It is the most common extra-cranial solid childhood malignancy. They typically occur in very young kids (you can be born with this). 95% of cases occur before age 10. They occur in the abdomen more than the thorax (adrenal 35%, retroperitoneum 30%, posterior mediastinum 20%, neck 5%).

Staging: Things that up the stage include crossing the midline, and contralateral positive nodes. These things make it Stage 3.

Better Prognosis Seen with – Diagnosis in Age < 1, Thoracic Primary, Stage 4S.

Associations:
- NF-1, Hirschsprungs, DiGeorge, Beckwith Wiedemann
- Most are sporadic

STAGE 4 <u>S</u> - HIGH YIELD

- Less than 1 year old
- Distal Mets are Confined to Skin, Liver, and Bone <u>Marrow</u>
- Excellent Prognosis.

**A common distractor is to say 4S goes to cortical bone. This is false! It's the marrow.

Random Trivia:
- Opsomyoclonus (dancing eyes, dancing feet) – paraneoplastic syndrome associated with neuroblastoma.
- "Raccoon Eyes" is a common way for orbital neuroblastoma mets to present
- MIBG is superior to Conventional Bone Scan for Neuroblastoma Bone Mets
- Neuroblastoma bone mets are on the "lucent metaphyseal band DDx"
- Sclerotic Bone mets are UNCOMMON
- Urine Catecholamines are always (95%) elevated

Neuroblastoma	**Wilms**
Age: usually less than 2 (can occur in utero)	Age: Usually around age 4 **(never before 2 months)**
Calcifies 90%	Calcifies Rarely (<10%)
Encases Vessels (doesn't invade)	Invades Vessels (doesn't encase)
Poorly Marginated	Well Circumscribed
Mets to Bones	Doesn't usually met to bones (unless clear cell Wilms variant). Prefers lung.

SECTION 11:
Adrenal

Neuroblastoma – *Discussed previously in the renal section*

Neonatal Adrenal Hemorrhage – This can occur in the setting of birth trauma or stress.

Trivia - Neonatal adrenal hemorrhage is associated with scrotal hemorrhage

THIS *vs* THAT: Hemorrhage *vs* Neuroblastoma:

- Ultrasound can usually tell the difference (**adrenal hemorrhage is anechoic and avascular,** neuroblastoma is echogenic and hyper-vascular).
- MRI could also be done to problem solve if necessary (**Adrenal Hemorrhage low T2 , Neuroblastoma high T2).**

 Gamesmanship - "Next Step" Adrenal mass of a neonate.

Neonates that are sick enough to be in the hospital hemorrhage their fucking adrenals all the time. An adrenal hemorrhage can look just like a mass on ultrasound. Yes, technically it should be anechoic and avascular - but maybe your tech sucks, or maybe you don't get shown a picture they just tell you it's a mass. The question writer is most likely going to try and trick you into worrying about a neuroblastoma (which is also going to be a mass in the adrenal).

Next Step? Sticking a needle in it, sedating the kid for MRI, or exposing him/her to the radiation of CT, PET, or MIBG are all going to go against the "image gently" propaganda being pushed at academic institutions. Plus it's unnecessary. As is true with most things in radiology, they either get better or they don't. Hemorrhage is going to resolve. The cancer is not. So **the first step is going to be followup ultrasound imaging**.

 Gamesmanship - History of "adrenal insufficiency" ?
Does that help you in the setting of a newborn adrenal mass?

Nope. Most cases are actually caused by a 21 alpha hydroxylase deficiency (congenital adrenal hyperplasia). Those tend to look different than hemorrhage or a mass- they are more "cerebriform." The problem is you can acquire adrenal insufficiency from neoplastic destruction (neuroblastoma) or regular good old fashioned hemorrhage.

More on Adrenals in the Endocrine Chapter.

SECTION 12:
Reproductive

Hydrometrocolpos –

Essentially the vagina won't drain the uterus. This condition is characterized on imaging by an expanded fluid-filled vaginal cavity with associated distention of the uterus.

You can see it presenting in infancy as a mass, or as a teenager with delayed menarche.

Causes include <u>imperforate hymen (most common)</u>, vaginal stenosis, lower vaginal atresia, and cervical stenosis.

For multiple choice trivia think about this as a "midline pelvic mass" , which can cause hydronephrosis (mass effect from distended uterus).

Trivia: Associated with Uterus Didelphys (which often ~75% has a transverse vaginal septum)

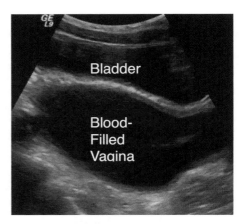

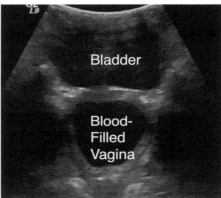

Ovary – A complete discussion of ovarian masses is found in the GYN chapter. I'll briefly cover some PEDs specific ovarian issues.

Torsion: In an adult, ovarian torsion is almost always due to a mass. In a child, torsion can occur with a normal ovary, secondary to excessive mobility of the ovary. As described in the GYN chapter you are going to see an enlarged (swollen) ovary, with peripheral follicles, with or without arterial flow. What is "enlarged" ? Unlike an adult you can't really use a fixed number to call the ovary enlarged (ovarian volumes in the peds setting are notoriously variable). The solution is to compare the ovary in question to the contralateral size. <u>Suspect torsion if the ovary is at least 3 times the size of the opposite "normal" ovary</u>. **Fluid-Debris Levels** within the displaced follicles is another described adolescent ovarian torsion finding.

Masses: About two-thirds of ovarian neoplasms are benign dermoids/teratomas (discussed in detail in the GYN chapter). The other one third are cancer. The cancers are usually germ cells (75%). Again, mural nodules and thick septations should clue you in that these might be cancer. Peritoneal implants, ascites, and lymphadenopathy, are all bad signs and would over-ride characteristics of the mass.

Random Scrotum Trivia

Hydrocele: Collection of serous fluid and is the most common cause of painless scrotal swelling. Congenital hydroceles result from a patent processus vaginalis that permits entry of peritoneal fluid into the scrotal sac.

Complicated Hydrocele (one with septations): This is either a hematocele vs pyocele. The distinction is clinical.

Varicocele: Most of these are idiopathic and found in adolescents and young adults. They are more frequent on the left. They are uncommon on the right, and if isolated (not bilateral) should stir suspicion for abdominal pathology (nutcracker syndrome, RCC, retroperitoneal fibrosis).

"Next Step" - Isolated right-sided varicocele = Abdomen CT.

HSP: This vasculitis is the most common cause of idiopathic scrotal edema (more on this in the vascular chapter).

Acute Pain in or around the Scrotum

The top three considerations in a child with acute scrotal pain are (1) torsion of the testicular appendage, (2) testicular torsion, and (3) epididymo-orchitis.

Epididymitis – The epididymal head is the most common part involved. Increased size and hyperemia are your ultrasound findings. This occurs in two peaks: under 2 and over 6. You can have infection of the epididymis alone or infection of the epididymis and testicle (isolated orchitis is rare).

Orchitis – Nearly always occurs as a progressed epididymitis. When *isolated the answer is mumps*.

Torsion of the Testicular Appendages – This is the most common cause of acute scrotal pain in age 7-14. The testicular appendage is some vestigial remnant of a mesonephric duct. Typical history is a sudden onset of pain, with a **Blue Dot Sign** on physical exam (looks like a blue dot). Enlargement of the testicular appendage to greater than 5 mm is considered by some as the best indicator of torsion

Torsion of the Testicle – Results from the testis and spermatic cord twisting within the serosal space leading to ischemia. The testable trivia is that it is caused by a *failure of the tunica vaginalis and testis to connect* or a **"Bell Clapper Deformity"**. This deformity is usually bilateral, so if you twist one they will often orchiopexy the other one. If it was 1950 you'd call in your nuclear medicine tech for scintigraphy. Now you just get a Doppler ultrasound. Findings will be absent or asymmetrically decreased flow, asymmetric enlargement, and slightly decreased echogenicity of the involved ball.

Extra-Testicular Mass:

Paratesticular Rhabdomyosarcoma: By far the most common extra-testicular mass in young men and the only one really worth mentioning. If you see a mass in the scrotum that is not for sure in the testicle this is it (unless the history is kick to the balls from a spiteful young lady - and you are dealing with a big fucking hematoma). If it's truly a mass - this is the answer.

Trivia:
- The most common location is actually the head/neck - specifically the orbit and nasopharynx.
- There is a bimodal peak (2-4, then 15-17).

Testicular Masses

Testicular Masses can be thought of as intratesticular or extratesticular. With regard to intratesticular masses, ultrasound can show you that there is indeed a mass but there are no imaging features that really help you tell which one is which. **If the mass is extratesticular , the most likely diagnosis is an embryonal rhabdomyosarcoma** from the spermatic cord or epididymis

Testicular Mircolithiasis – This appears as multiple small echogenic foci within the testes. Testicular microlithiasis is <u>usually an incidental finding</u> in scrotal US examinations performed for unrelated reasons. It <u>might have a relationship with Germ Cell Tumors (controversial)</u>. Follow-up in 6 months, then yearly is probably the recommendation (maybe - it's very controversial, and therefore unlikely to be asked).

Microlithiasis

Testicular Cancer:
The histologic breakdown is as follows:

- **Germ Cell** (90%)
    - Seminoma (40%) – seen more in the 4th decade
    - Non Seminoma (60%)
        - Teratoma, Yolk Sacs, Mixed Germ Cells, Etc…

- **Non Germ Cell** (10%)
    - Sertoli
    - Leydig

> **THIS vs THAT:**
> **Testicular Calcifications**
>
> Tiny (micro) = Seminoma
>
> BIG = Germ Cell Tumor

Testicular Masses Cont..

The two Germ Cell Tumors seen in the first decade of life are the yolk sac tumor, and the teratoma.

Yolk Sac Tumor: Heterogeneous Testicular Mass in < 2 year old = Yolk Sac Tumor. **AFP** is usually super elevated.

Teratoma – Pure testicular teratomas are only seen in young kids < 2. Mixed teratomas are seen in 25 year olds. Unlike ovarian teratoma, these guys often have aggressive biological behavior.

Choriocarcinoma: An aggressive, highly vascular tumor, seen more in the 2nd decade.

Sertoli Cell Tumors – These testicular tumors are usually bilateral and are visualized on US as "burned-out" tumors (dense echogenic foci that represent calcified scars). A subtype of Sertoli cell tumor associated with Peutz-Jeghers syndrome typically occurs in children. If they show you the <u>Peurtz-Jegher lips and bilateral scrotal masses, this is the answer</u>.

Testicular Lymphoma – Just be aware that lymphoma can "hide" in the testes because of the blood testes barrier. Immunosuppressed patients are at increased risk for developing extranodal/ testicular lymphoma. On US, the normal homogeneous echogenic testicular tissue is replaced focally or diffusely with hypoechoic vascular lymphomatous tissue. **Buzzword = multiple hypoechoic masses of the testicle.**

Not Really Reproductive But It Is Pelvic

Sacrococcygeal Teratoma – This is the most common tumor of the fetus or infant. These solid and/or cystic masses are typically large and found either on prenatal imaging or birth. Their largeness is a problem and can cause mass effect on the GI system, hip dislocation, and even nerve compression leading to incontinence. They are usually benign (80%), although those presenting in older infants tend to have a higher malignant potential. The location of the mass is either external to the pelvis (47%), internal to the pelvis (9%), or dumbelled both inside and outside (34%).

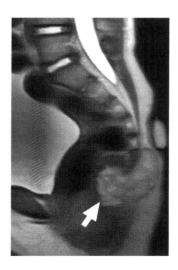

There is another classification that discusses involvement of the abdomen.

The easiest way to remember it is like this:
-Type 1 - Totally extra pelvic
-Type 2 - Barely pelvic, but not abdominal
-Type 3 - Some abdominal
-Type 4 - Totally inside abdomen ** *this one has the highest rate of malignancy.*

Trivia: They have to cut the coccyx off during resection. Incomplete resection of the coccyx is associated with a high recurrence rate.

SECTION 13:
MSK

Fracture: In general, little kids bend they don't break. You end up with lots of buckles and greensticks. For problem solving you can get a repeat in 7-10 days as periosteal reaction is expected in 7-10 days. Kids tend to heal completely, often with no sign of prior fracture.

Involvement of the Physis: The major concern is growth arrest, probably best asked by showing a **physeal bar** ("early" bony bridge crossing the growth plate). You can get bars from prior infection, but a history of trauma is gonna be the more classic way to ask it.

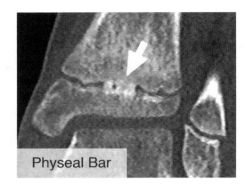

Physeal Bar

Salter-Harris Classification lends itself well to multiple choice:

Type 1 : S – Slipped

Complete physeal fracture, with or without displacement.

Type 2: A – Above (or "Away from the Joint")

Fracture involves the metaphysis. This is the most common type (75%).

Type 3: L – Lower
(3 is the backwards "E" for Epiphysis)

Fracture involves the epiphysis. These guys have a chance of growth arrest, and will often require surgery to maintain alignment

Type 4: T – Through

Fracture involves the metaphysis and epiphysis. These guys don't do as well, often end up with growth arrest, or focal fusion. They require anatomic reduction and often surgery.

Type 5: R – Ruined

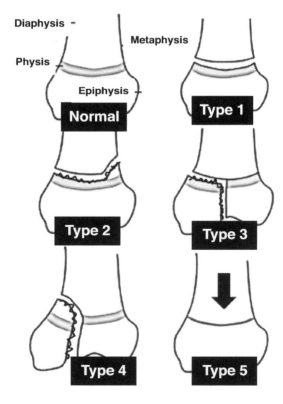

Compression of the growth plate. It occurs from axial loading injuries, and has a very poor prognosis. These are easy to miss, and often found when looking back at comparisons (hopefully ones your partner read). The buzzword is **"bony bridge across physis"**.

Toddler's Fracture: Oblique fracture of the midshaft of the tibia seen in a child just starting to walk (new stress on bone). If it's a spiral type you probably should query non-accidental trauma. The typical age is 9 months – 3 years.

Stress Fracture in Children: This is an injury which occurs after repetitive trauma, usually after new activity (walking). The most common site of fracture is the tibia – proximal posterior cortex. The tibial fracture is the so-called "toddler fracture" described above. Other classic stress fractures include the **calcaneal fracture – seen after the child has had a cast removed and returns to normal activity.**

- The Elbow -

My God... these peds elbows.

Every first year resident knows that elevation of the fat pad (sail sign) should make you think joint effusion and possible occult fracture. Don't forget that sometimes you can see a thin anterior pad, but you should never see the posterior pad (posterior is positive). I like to bias myself with statistics when I'm hunting for the peds elbow fracture. The most common fracture is going to be a supracondylar fracture (>60%), followed by lateral condyle (20%), and medial epicondyle (10%).

Radiocapitellar Line: This is a line through the center of the radius, which should intersect the middle of the capitellum on every view (regardless of position). If the radius is dislocated it will NOT pass through the center of the capitellum

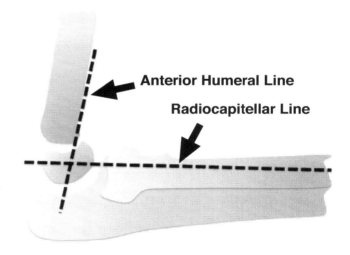

Anterior Humeral Line: This time you need a true lateral. A line along the anterior surface of humerus, should pass through the middle third of the capitellum. With a supracondylar fracture (the most common peds elbow fracture) you'll see this line pass through the anterior third.

Ossification Centers are a source of trickery.

Remember they occur in a set order (**CRITOE**),
- **C**apitellum (Age 1),
- **R**adius (Age 3),
- **I**nternal (medial epicondyle Age 5),
- **T**rochlea (Age 7),
- **O**lecranon(Age 9), and
- **E**xternal (lateral epicondyle Age 11).

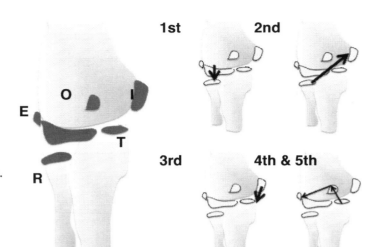

Zig Zag Search Pattern Hunting For the Next Center

-Elbow Tricks:

Lateral Condyle Fx: This is the **second most common distal humerus fracture** in kids. Some dude named Milch classified them. The thing to know is a fracture that passes through the capitello-trochlear groove is unstable (Milch II). Since it's really hard to tell this, **treatment is based on the displacement of the fracture fragment (> or < 2mm).**

Trochlea – can have multiple ossification centers, so it **can have a fragmented appearance.**

Medial Epicondyle Avulsion (Little League Elbow) – There are two major tricks with this one. (1) Because it's an extra-articular structure, its avulsions **will not necessarily result in a joint effusion.** (2) It **can get interposed** between the articular surface of the humerus and olecranon. Avulsed fragments can get stuck in the joint, even when there is no dislocation.

Anytime you see a dislocation – ask yourself
- Is the patient 5 years old ? And if so
- Where is the medial epicondyle ?

*The importance of **IT** (cr**IT**oe) –*
- You should never see the trochlea and not see the internal (medial epicondyle), if you do it's probably a displaced fragment

THIS vs **THAT:**	
Common Elbow Fractures	**Uncommon Elbow Fractures**
Lateral Condylar	*Lateral Epicondyle*
Medial Epicondyle	*Medial Condyle*

Nursemaids Elbow: When a child's arm is pulled on, the radial head may sublux into the annular ligament. X-rays typically don't help, unless you supinate the arm during lateral position (which often relocates the arm).

- Avulsion Injuries:

Kids tendons tend to be stronger than their bones, so avulsion injuries are more common (when compared to adults). The pelvis is the classic location to test this.

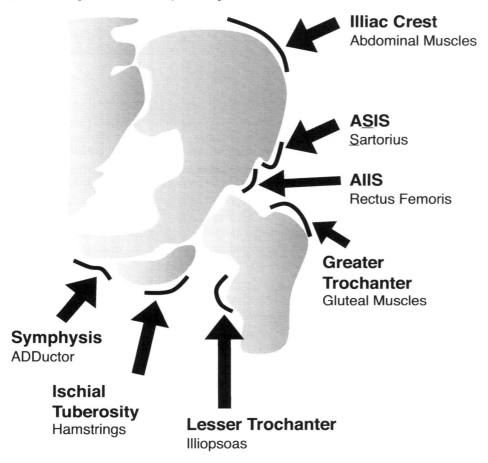

Illiac Crest
Abdominal Muscles

ASIS
Sartorius

AIIS
Rectus Femoris

Greater Trochanter
Gluteal Muscles

Symphysis
ADDuctor

Ischial Tuberosity
Hamstrings

Lesser Trochanter
Illiopsoas

- Chronic Fatigue Injuries:

Sinding-Larsen-Johansson – This is a chronic traction injury at the **insertion of the patellar tendon on the patella**. It's seen in active adolescents between age 10-14. **Kids with cerebral palsy** are prone to it.

Osgood-Schlatter – This is due to repeated micro trauma to the patellar tendon on its insertion at the tibial tuberosity. It's bilateral 25% of the time, and more common in boys.

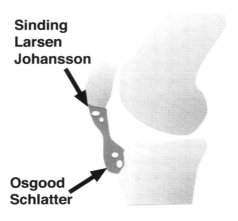

Sinding Larsen Johansson

Osgood Schlatter

- Periosteal Reaction in the Newborn -

Congenital Rubella: Bony changes are seen in 50% of cases, with the classic buzzword being **"celery stalk"** appearance, from generalized lucency of the metaphysis. This is usually seen in the first few weeks of life.

Syphilis: Bony changes are seen in 95% of cases. Bony changes do NOT occur until 6-8 weeks of life (Rubella changes are earlier). Metaphyseal lucent bands and periosteal reaction along long bones can be seen. The classic buzzword is **"Wimberger Sign"** or **destruction of the medial portion of the proximal metaphysis of the tibia.**

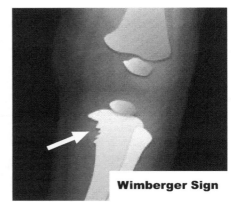

Wimberger Sign

Caffey Disease – Have you ever seen that giant multiple volume set of peds radiology books? Yeah, same guy. This thing is a self limiting disorder of soft tissue swelling, periosteal reaction, and irritability **seen within the first 6 months of life**. The **classic picture is the really hot mandible on bone scan**. The mandible is the most common location (clavicle, and ulna are the other classic sites). It's rare as hell, and probably not even real. There have been more sightings of Chupacabra in the last 50 years.

Prostaglandin Therapy – Prostaglandin E1 and E2 (often used to keep a PDA open) can cause a periosteal reaction. The classic trick is to show a chest x-ray with sternotomy wires (or other hints of congenital heart), and then periosteal reaction in the arm bones.

Neuroblastoma Mets – This is really the only childhood malignancy that occurs in newborns and mets to bones.

Physiologic Growth: So this is often called "Physiologic Periostitis of the Newborn" , which is totally false and wrong. It **does NOT happen in newborns**. *You see this around 3 months* of age, and it should resolve by six months. **Proximal involvement (femur) comes before distal involvement (tibia).** It **always involves the diaphysis**.

> *It is **NOT** physiologic periostitis if:*
> * *You see it before 1 month*
> * *You see it in the tibia before the femur*
> * *It does not involve the diaphysis.*

Abuse – Some people abuse drugs, some just can't stand screaming kids, some suffer both shortcomings. More on this later.

- Other "Aggressive Processes" in Kids -

Langerhans Cell Histiocytosis (LCH) – Also known as EG (eosinophilic granuloma). It's twice as common in boys. Skeletal manifestations are highly variable, but lets just talk about the classic ones:

- *Skull* – **Most common site.** Has **"beveled edge"** from uneven destruction of the inner and outer tables. If you see a round lucent lesion in the skull of a child think this (and neuroblastoma mets).

- *Ribs* – Multiple lucent lesions, with an expanded appearance

- *Spine* – **Vertebra plana**

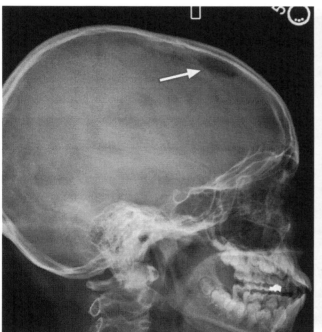
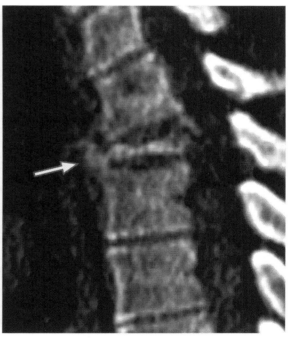

LCH - *Beveled Edge Skull Lesion*   **LCH** - *Vertebra Plana*

*I'll touch on this more in the MSK chapter.

Ewing Sarcoma and **Osteosarcoma** are also covered in depth in the MSK chapter

Osteomyelitis

It usually occurs in babies (30% of cases less than 2 years old). It's usually hematogenous (adults it directly spreads - typically from a diabetic ulcer).

There are some changes that occur over time, which are potentially testable.

Newborns - They have open growth plates and perforating vessels which travel from the metaphysis to the epiphysis. Infection typically starts in the metaphysis (it has the most blood supply because it is growing the fastest), and then can spread via these perforators to the epiphysis.

Kids - Later in childhood, the perforators regress and the avascular epiphyseal plate stops infection from crossing over. This creates a "septic tank" scenario, where infection tends to smolder. In fact, 75% of cases involve the metaphyses of long bones (femur most common).

Adults - When the growth plates fuse, the barrier of an avascular plate is no longer present, and infection can again cross over to the epiphysis to cause mayhem.

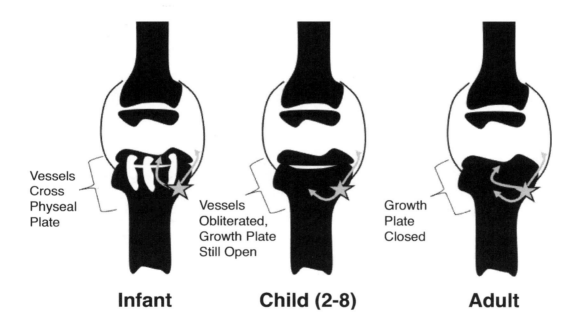

Vessels Cross Physeal Plate

Vessels Obliterated, Growth Plate Still Open

Growth Plate Closed

Infant   **Child (2-8)**   **Adult**

Trivia:
- Hematogenous spread more common in kids (direct spread in adult)
- Metaphysis most common location, with target changes as explained above
- Bony changes don't occur on x-ray for around 10 days.
- It's serious business and can rapidly destroy the cartilage if it spreads into the joint

**Discussed again in the MSK Chapter*

- Skeletal Dysplasia -

There is a bunch of vocabulary to learn regarding dysplasias:

English	Fancy Doctor Speak
Short Fingers	Brachydactyly
Too Many Fingers	Polydactyly
Two or More Fused Fingers ("Sock Hand" – I call it)	Syndactyly
Contractures of Fingers	Camptodactyly
Radially Angulated Fingers (Usually 5th)	Clinodactyly
Long, Spider-Like Fingers	Arachnodactyly
Limb is Absent	Amelia
Limb is mostly Absent	Meromelia
Hands / Feet (distal limbs) are Short	Acromelic
Forearm or Lower Leg are short (middle limbs)	Mesomelic
Femur or Humerus (proximal limbs) are short	Rhizomelic
Short All Over	Micromelic

 How I remember the lengths:
- **Mes**o is in the **M**iddle,
- **Acro** sounds like **Acro**megaly (they get big hands), and
- The other one is the other one (Rhizo).

There are tons of skeletal dysplasias and extensive knowledge of them is way way way way beyond the scope of the exam. Instead I'm going to mention 3 dwarfs, and a few other miscellaneous conditions.

- Dwarfs -
(or "Dwarves" If you are practicing radiology in middle earth):

Achondroplasia – This is the most common skeletal dysplasia, and is the mostly likely to be seen at the mall (or on television). It results from a fibroblast growth factor receptor problem (most dwarfisms do). It is a **rhizomelic** (short femur, short humerus) dwarf. They often have weird big heads, trident hands (3rd and 4th fingers are long), narrowing of the interpedicular distance, and the tombstone pelvis. Advanced paternal age is a risk factor. They make good actors, excellent rodeo clowns, and various parts of their bodies (if cooked properly) have magical powers.

Thanatophoric – This is the **most common lethal dwarfism**. They have **rhizomelic shortening** (humerus, femur). The femurs are sometimes called **telephone receivers**. They have short ribs and a long thorax, and small iliac bones. The **vertebral bones are flat** (platyspondyly), and the **skull can be cloverleaf shaped**.

Asphyxiating Thoracic Dystrophy (Jeune) – This is usually fatal as well. The big finding is the "Bell shaped thorax" with <u>short ribs</u>. 15% will have too many fingers (polydactyly). If they live, they have kidney problems (chronic nephritis). You can differentiate a dead Thanatophoric dwarf, from a dead Jeune dwarf by looking at their vertebral bodies. The Jeune bodies are normal (the thanatophorics are flat).

Additional Random Dwarf Trivia:
- **Ellis-Van Crevald** *is the dwarf with multiple fingers.*
- **Pseudoachondroplasia** *is this weird thing not present at birth, and spares the skull.*
- **Pyknodysostosis** *osteopetrosis, in a dwarf, with a wide angled jaw, & Acro-osteolysis.*

The Dwarf Blitz - 5 Things I Would Remember About Dwarfs

1. **The Vocab**: Rhizo (humerus, femur) vs Acro (hands, feet) vs Meso (forearm, tib/fib)
2. **Most dwarfs are Rhizomelic** - if forced to choose, always guess this
3. The pedicles are supposed to widen slightly as you descend the spinal column, **Achondroplasia** has the opposite - they narrow. If you see a <u>live</u> dwarf, with short femurs / humerus, and **narrowing of the pedicles** then this is the answer. *(technically thantophorics can get this too - but it's more classic for achondroplasia)*
4. Thanatophoric is your main dead dwarf. Usually the standout feature is the **telephone receiver femur** (and a crazy cloverleaf head)
5. **Jeune** is another dead dwarf - but the **short ribs** really stand out.

- Misc Conditions -

Osteogenesis Imperfecta – They have a collagen defect and make brittle bones. Depending on the severity it can be totally lethal or more mild. It's classically shown with a **totally lucent skull**, or **multiple fractures with hyperplastic callus**. Another classic trick is to show the legs with the **fibula longer than the tibia**. They have **wormian bones**, and often flat or beaked vertebral bodies. Other trivia is the blue sclera, hearing impairment (**otosclerosis**), and that they tend to suck at football.

Osteopetrosis – They have a defect in the way osteoclasts work, so you end up with disorganized bone that is sclerotic and weak (prone to fracture). There are a bunch of different types, with variable severity. The infantile type is lethal because it takes out your bone marrow. With less severe forms, you can have abnormal diminished osteoclastic activity that varies during skeletal growth, and results in alternating bands of sclerosis parallel to the growth plate. Most likely the way this will be shown is the "bone-in-bone" appearance in the vertebral body or carpals. Picture frame vertebrae is another buzzword. Alternatively, they can show you a diffusely sclerotic skeleton, with diffuse loss of the corticomedullary junction in the long tubular bones.

Pyknodysostosis - Osteopetrosis + Wormian Bones + Acro-Osteolysis. They also have *"wide (or obtuse) angled mandible"*, which apparently is a buzzword.

Klippel Feil – You get **congenital fusion of the cervical spine** (sorta like JRA). The cervical vertebral bodies will be tall and skinny. There is often a sprengel deformity (high riding scapula). Another common piece of trivia is to show the omovertebral bone – which is just some big stupid looking vertebral body.

Hunters / Hurlers / Morquio - All three of these are mucopolysaccharidoses. Findings include **oval shaped vertebral bodies with anterior beak**. The beak is actually mid in Morquio, and inferior in Hurlers. **Clavicles and ribs are often thick (narrow more medially) – like a canoe-paddle**. The pelvis shape is described as the opposite of achondroplasia – the iliac wings are tall and flaired. The hand x-ray is the most commonly shown in case books and gives you **wide metacarpal bones with proximal tapering**.

Few More Trivia Points on Morquio:
- They are dwarfs
- The most common cause of death is cervical myelopathy at C2
- The bony changes actually progress during the first few years of life

Neurofibromatosis – Just briefly remember that type 1 can cause **anterior tibial bowing**, and **pseudarthrosis at the distal fibula**.

This is an Aunt Minnie.

They often have scoliosis. Just think of the elephant man.

Gauchers – This is the most common lysosomal storage disease. It gives you a big spleen, and big liver among a few bone signs.

- *AVN of the Femoral Heads*
- *H-Shaped Vertebra*
- *Bone Infarcts (lots of them)*
- *Erlenmeyer Flask Shaped Femurs*

Caudal Regression Syndrome – This is a spectrum that includes sacral and/or coccyx agenesis. You see it with VACTERL and Currarino Triads Syndromes.

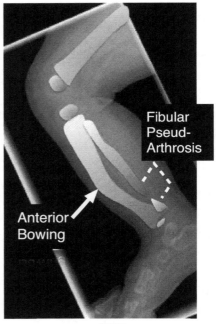

NF1

Scoliosis – Lateral curvature of the spine, which is usually idiopathic in girls. It can also be from vertebral segmentation problems. NF can cause it as well (that's a piece of trivia).

Radial Dysplasia- Absence or hypoplasia of the radius (usually with a missing thumb) is a differential case (VACTERL, Holt-Oram, Fanconi Anemia, <u>T</u>hrobocytopenia <u>A</u>bsent <u>R</u>adius). As a point of trivia TAR kids will have a thumb.

Hand Foot Syndrome - The classic history is hand or foot pain / swelling in an infant with sickle cell. This is a dactylitis, and felt to be related to ischemia. It will resolve on its own, after a few weeks. <u>Radiographs can show a periostitis two weeks after the pain goes away.</u>

Blounts *(tibia vara)*. Varus angulation occurring at the medial aspect of the proximal tibia *(varus bowing occurs at the metaphysis not the knee)*. This is often bilateral, and NOT often seen before age 2 *(two sides, not before two)*. Later in the disease progression the medial metaphysis will be depressed and an osseous outgrowth classically develops. You can see it in two different age groups; (a) early – which is around age 2 and (b) late – which is around age 12.

- Two Sides - Not Before Two
- Two Different Ages (2-3, 12)

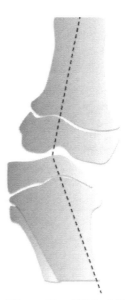

Blount's -Tibia VARA

- Feet -

Congenital foot is a complicated and confusing topic, about which I will avoid great detail because it is well beyond the scope of the exam. I am going to at least try and drop some knowledge which could be called upon in the darkest of hours to work these problems out.

Step 1: Vocabulary. Just knowing the lingo is very helpful for getting the diagnosis on multiple choice foot questions.

- Talipes = *Congenital ,*
- Pes = *Foot or Acquired*
- Equines = *"Plantar Flexed Ankle", Heel Cord is often tight, and the heel won't touch the floor*
- Calcaneus = *Opposite of Equines. The Calcaneus is actually angled up*
- Varus = *Forefoot in*
- Valgus = *Forefoot out*
- Cavus = *High Arch*
- Planus = *Opposite of Cavus – "bizarro cavus" - FLAT FOOT*
- Supination – *Inward rotation – "Sole of foot in" - holding s̲oup with the bottom of your foot*
- Pronation – *Outward rotation – "Sole of foot out"*

Step 2: Hindfoot Valgus vs Varus

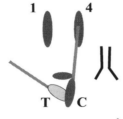

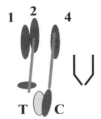

Normal

First look at the normal acute angle the talus and calcaneus make on a lateral view.

Hindfoot Valgus

Think about this as the talus sliding nose down off the calcaneus. This make the angle wider.

If the talus slides off you lose your longitudinal arch - which essentially characterizes hindfoot valgus.

Also, note that the nose down (nearly **vertical**) appearance of the talus . *"Too Many Toes"*

Hindfoot Varus

This is the opposite situation, in which you have a narrowing of the angle between the talus and calcaneus.

Notice the two bones lay nearly parallel - like two **"clubs"** laying on top of each other.

Step 3 - Knowing the two main disorders. The flat foot (valgus), and the club foot (varus).

Flat Foot (Pes Planus)- This can be congenital or acquired. The peds section will cover congenital and the adult MSK section will cover acquired. The congenital types can be grouped into flexible or rigid (the flexible types are more common in kids). The distinction can be made with plantar flexion views (flexible improves with stress). The ridged subtypes can be further subdivided into tarsal coalition and vertical talus. In any case you have a **hindfoot valgus.**

Tarsal Coalition – There are two main types (talus to the calcaneus, and talus to the navicular). They are pretty equal in incidence, and about 50% of the time are bilateral. You can have bony or fibrous/cartilaginous subtypes. The fibrous/cartilaginous types are more common than the bony types.

- **Talocalcaneal**– Occurs at the middle facet.
  Has the *"continuous C-sign"* produced from an *"absent middle facet"* on the lateral view. Talar beak (spur on the anterior talus - white arrow) is also seen in about 25% of cases.

- **Calcaneonavicular**– Occurs at the anterior facet.
  Has the *"anteater sign"* Where the *elongated anterior process of the calcaneus* resembles the blood thirsty nose of a ravenous ant eater. This is best seen on an oblique view.

- **Vertical Talus** (equinus hindfoot valgus) – This is sometimes called the *"rocker-bottom foot"* because the talus is in extreme plantar flexion with dorsal dislocation of the Navicular – resulting in a locked talus in plantar flexion. As a point of trivia this is often associated with myelomeningocele.

Club Foot (Talipes Equino Varus)- Translation – Congenital Plantar Flexed Ankle Forefoot. This is sorta why I lead with the vocab, all the congenital feet can be figured out based on the translated language. This thing is more common in boys, and bilateral about half the time. The toes are pointed down (equines), and the talocalcaneal angle is acute (varus).

Key features:
- Hindfoot varus (decreased talocalcaneal angle)
- Medial deviation and inversion of the forefoot
- Elevated Plantar Arch

Trivia: The most common surgical complication is over correction resulting in a "rocker bottom" flat foot deformity.

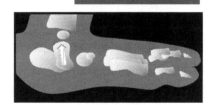

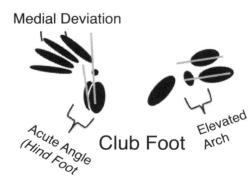

Medial Deviation

Acute Angle (Hind Foot) **Club Foot** Elevated Arch

- Hip Dysplasia -

Developmental Dysplasia of the Hip - This is seen more commonly in females, children born breech, and oligohydramnios. The physical exam buzzwords are asymmetric skin or gluteal folds, leg length discrepancy, palpable clunk, or delayed ambulation. It's bilateral about 1/3 of the time. Ultrasound is done to evaluate (after physical exam), and is excellent until the bones ossify (then you need x-rays). A common trick is to be careful making a measurement in the first week of life - the laxity immediately after birth (related to maternal estrogen) can screw up the measurements.

 Angles:

On ultrasound the **alpha angle, should be more than 60 degrees**. Anything less than that and your cup is not deep enough to hold your ball. The plain film equivalent in the **acetabular angle, which is the complimentary angle (and therefore should be less than 30).**

Getting them confused? Remember that the *"Alpha Angle is the Alpha Male"* - and therefore the bigger of the two angles. **But don't forget that DDH is more common in women (not alpha males).

The acetabular angle should decrease from 30 degrees at birth to 22 degrees at age 1. DDH is the classic cause of an increased angle, but neuromuscular disorder can also increase it.

The position of the femoral epiphysis (or where it will be) should be below Hilgenreiner's line "**H**", and medial to Perkin's Line "**P**". Shenton's Line "**S**" should be continuous.

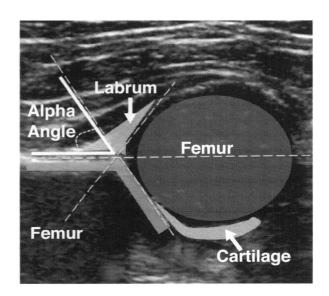

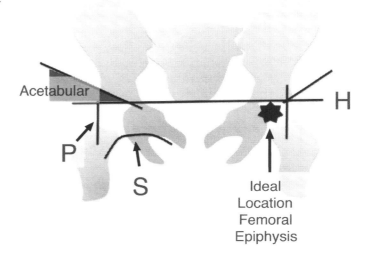

Proximal Focal Femoral Deficiency – This is a congenital zebra, which ranges from absent proximal femur to hypoplastic proximal femur. You get a varus deformity. This is a mimic of DDH, but DDH will have normal femur leg length.

Slipped Capital Femoral Epiphysis (SCFE) – This is **a type 1 Salter Harris**, through the proximal femoral physis. What makes this unique is that unlike most SH 1s, this guy has a bad prognosis if not fixed. The classic history is a **fat African American adolescent (age 12-15)** with hip pain. It's bilateral in 1/3 of cases (both hips don't usually present at same time). The **frog leg view is the money – this is always the answer on next step questions**.

Legg-Calve-Perthes – This is AVN of the proximal femoral epiphysis. It's seen more in boys than girls (4:1), and favors **white people around age 5-8**. These kids tend to be smaller than average for their age. This is **bilateral about 10% of the time (less than SCFE)**. The subchondral lucency (crescent sign) is best seen on a frog leg. Other early signs include an asymmetric small ossified femoral epiphysis. MRI has more sensitivity. The flat collapsed femoral head makes it obvious. Sterile joint effusions (transient synovitis) can be associated.

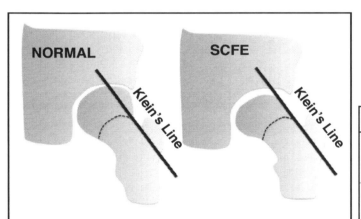

"Klein's Line" - Drawn along the edge of the femur and should normally intersect with lateral superior femoral epiphysis. This line is used to evaluate for SCFE. When the line doesn't cross the lateral epiphysis think SCFE.

***Testable Trivia** - Frog Leg View is more sensitive for this measurement

THIS vs THAT:	
Perthes	**SCFE**
Often Small White Kids	Overweight Black Kids
Age 5-8	Age 12-15
Bilateral 10%	Bilateral 30%

Septic Arthritis- This is serious business , and considered the most urgent cause of painful hip in a child. Wide joint space (lateral displacement of femoral head), should prompt an ultrasound, and that should prompt a joint tap. If you have low suspicion and don't want to tap the hip, You could pull on the leg under fluoro and try and get gas in the joint. This air arthrogram sign supposedly excludes a joint effusion (and therefore a septic joint) – depending on who you ask.

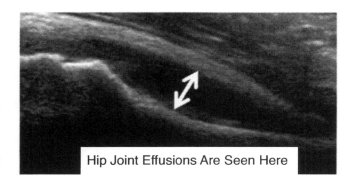
Hip Joint Effusions Are Seen Here

Transient Synovitis – This is a sterile (reactive) hip effusion that occurs in the setting of a systemic illness (usually viral URI or GI). As the name suggests this is "transient" and goes away in a few days. This is actually very common. Some sources will say its the most common hip disorder in growing children (peak age is around 5). The ED will be in a full panic and want you to tap it at 3 am.

THIS *vs* THAT: Transient Synovitis *vs* Septic Arthritis

Telling these apart is actually important for real life (not getting sued) since a septic hip will fucking destroy the kid's cartilage (usually if it's missed for more than 4 days).

Ortho (and in very rare situations a "smart" ED doc) will use a clinical parameter *"the Kocher Criteria"* to tell them apart. Criteria is 4 parts:

- Fever
- Inability to walk
- Elevated ESR (or CRP)
- WBC > 12K

- If 3/4 are positive = Septic
- If CRP is negative and the kid can bear weight it's NOT Septic
- CRP is the strongest independent risk factor for septic arthritis

Typical workup is going to be:
1. X-Ray Hip series (AP, Lateral, and Frog Leg) which is usually negative in real life but will probably show medial joint widening on the exam.
2. Ultrasound which will show an effusion.
3. Then a clinical decision based on Kocher Criteria (>2) and "Gut Instinct" to Aspirate
4. MRI would only be used if/when hip aspiration can't/hasn't been performed.

- Metabolic -

Rickets – Not enough vitamin D. Affects the most rapidly growing bones (mostly knees and wrists). Buzzwords **"fraying, cupping, and irregularity along the physeal margin. "** They are at increased risk for SCFE. "Rachitic rosary" appearance from expansion of the anterior rib ends at the costochondral junctions. As a pearl, **rickets is never seen in a newborn** (Mom's vitamin D is still doing its thing).

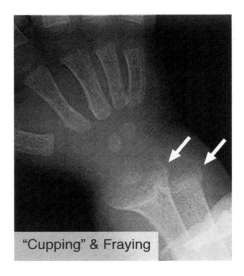

"Cupping" & Fraying

Hypophosphatasia - This looks like **Rickets in a newborn**. They will have frayed metaphyses and bowed long bones. The underlying pathology is deficient serum alkaline phosphatase. There is variability in severity with lethal perinatal / natal forms, and more mild adult forms.

Scurvy – Not enough vitamin C. This is rare as hell outside of a pirate ship in the 1400s. For the purpose of trivia (which multiple choice tests love) the following stuff is high yield:

- <u>Does NOT occur before 6 months of age</u> (maternal stores buffer)
    - Bleeding Disorders Common
    - Subperiosteal hemorrhage (lifts up the periosteum)
- Hemarthrosis
- "Scorbutic rosary" appearance from expansion of the costochondral junctions (very similar to rickets).

Lead Poisoning – This is most commonly seen in kids less than two who eat paint chips. The classic finding is a **wide sclerotic metaphyseal line (lead line),** in an area of rapid growth (knee). It will not spare the fibula (as a normal variant line might).

Lucent Metaphyseal Bands
– This is a classic peds DDx. - **LINE.**

- *Leukemia*
- *Infection (TORCH)*
- *Neuroblastoma Mets*
- *Endocrine (rickets, Scurvy)*

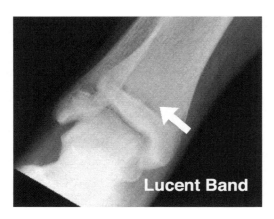

Lucent Band

- Non-Accidental Trauma (NAT) -

"Some People Just Can't Take Screaming Kids."

Any suspicious fracture should prompt a skeletal survey ("baby gram" does NOT count). Suspicious fractures would include highly specific fractures (metaphyseal corner fracture, posterior rib fractures) or fractures that don't make sense - toddler fracture in a non-ambulatory child.

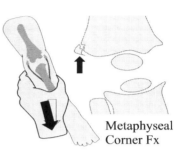

Metaphyseal
Corner Fx

- **Posterior Medial Rib Fracture:** In a child under the age of 3, this is pretty reliable. Supposedly this type of fracture can only be made from squeezing a child.

- **Metaphyseal Corner Fractures:** When this is present in a non-ambulatory patient (infant) it is HIGHLY specific. The only exception is obstetric trauma. After age 1, this becomes less specific.

- **Skull Fracture:** The general idea is anything other than a parietal bone fracture (which is supposedly seen more with an actual accident) is concerning.

- **Solid Organ and Lumen Injury -** Don't forget about this as a presentation for NAT. Duodenal hematoma and pancreatitis (from trauma) in an infant - should get you to say NAT. Just think *"belly trauma in a kid that is too young to fall on the handle bars of their bike"*.

Dating the Fracture:

- *Periosteal Reaction:* This means the fracture is less than a week old.
- *Complete healing:* This occurs in around 12 weeks.
- *Exceptions:* Metaphyseal, skull, and costochondral junction fractures will often heal without any periosteal reaction.

Child Abuse Mimics

Rickets and OI , can have multiple fractures at different sites and are the two most commonly described mimics.

Wormian bones and bone mineral density issues are clues that you are dealing with a mimic. They will have to show you one or the other (or both) if they are gonna get sneaky.

SECTION 14:
Pediatric Spine

- Spinal Cord on Ultrasound -

Normal Ultrasound Appearance / Anatomy Review:

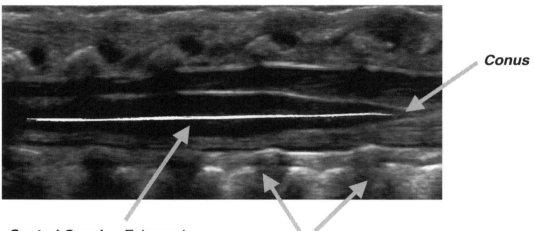

Conus

Central Canal — Echogenic

Vertebral Bodies - Shadowing

Central Canal - Easily identified as an echogenic line. Although that is sort of counter intuitive.

Why would a structure with fluid in it be echogenic? The reason is that you are actually seeing a "central echo complex" - which is the interface between the anterior median fissure and the myelinated ventral white matter commissure.

Remember that interfaces between things with large differences in impedance cause a lot of reflections (thus an echogenic line).

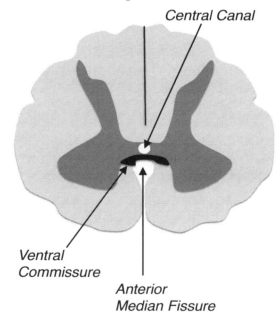

Central Canal

Ventral Commissure

Anterior Median Fissure

Trivia: Technically in a newborn the central canal is not even fluid filled (it's packed with glial fibrils), but that level of trivia is beyond the scope of the exam (probably).

Low lying cord / Tethered cord: Because the canal grows faster than the cord, a fixed attachment ("tethering") results in cord stretching and subsequent ischemia. This can be primary (isolated), or secondary (associated with myelomeningocele, filum terminale lipoma, or trauma). *The secondary types are more likely shown on MR (to showcase the associated mass - fluid collection), the primary types are more likely shown on US - as a straight counting game.*

Imaging Features: Low conus (**below L2**), and thickened filum terminale (> 2mm).

A common piece of trivia used as a distractor is that meningomyelocele is associated with Chiari malformations, lipomyelomeningocele is NOT.

High Yield Trivia

- <u>Anal Atresia</u> = High Risk For Occult Cord Problems (including tethering) – should get screened
- Low lying / tethered cords are closely linked with <u>Spina Bifida</u> (tufts of hair)
- Low Dimples (below the gluteal crease) **Do NOT** need screening,
    - These never extend intra-spinally. They might later become a pilonidal sinuses - but aren't ever gonna have shit to do with the cord.
- High Dimples (above the gluteal crease) **DO** need screening.

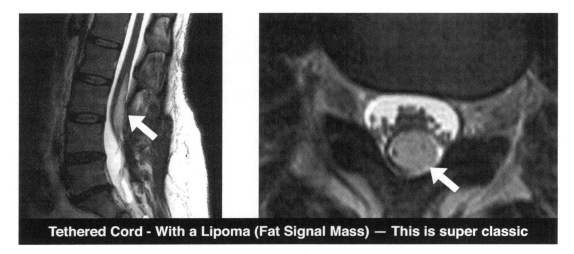

Tethered Cord - With a Lipoma (Fat Signal Mass) — This is super classic

---

For Screening Purposes:

Low dimples (below the butt crease) don't get screened, basically everything else does.

Most Likely Question Style: "Which of the following does NOT get screened ?"
(Answer = low dimple).

- Misc Variant Topics -

Terminal Ventricle (ventricularis terminalis):

This is a developmental variant. Normally, a large portion of the distal cord involutes in a late stage of spinal cord embryology. Sometimes this process is not uniform and you get stuck with a stupid looking cyst at the end of your cord. These things are usually small (around 4 mm), and cause no symptoms. Sometimes they can get very big (like this example) and cause some neurologic symptoms.

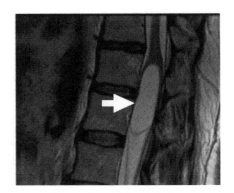

Terminal Ventricle

Pars Interarticularis Defects (Spondylolysis):

This is considered a fatigue or stress fracture, probably developing in childhood. It is a classic cause of back pain in an adolescent athlete. Although they are usually not symptomatic (only 25% are). The process represents a hole / break in the connecting bone between the superior and inferior articular facets. If there is forward "slippage" you can deploy the word **spondylolisthesis**.

Almost always (90% +) you see this at L5 (2nd most common at L4). They tend to have more spondylolisthesis and associated degenerative change at L4-L5 than L5-S1. They can be seen on the oblique plain film as a "collar on the scottie dog." The collar on the "scotty dog" appearance on an oblique plain film is probably the most common way they show this in case books and conferences. On the AP view this can be a cause of a sclerotic pedicle (the contralateral pedicle – from wiggle stress). On CT it is usually more obvious with the break clearly demonstrated.

**Pars Defects with anterolisthesis will have neuroforaminal stenosis, with spinal canal widening (when severe will have spinal canal stenosis as well). If the process is purely a degenerative spondylolisthesis (not much slippage), the resulting facet arthropathy will favor the canal with less severe effects on the neuro foramina.

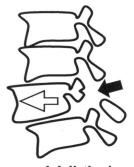

spondylolisthesis

Scotty Dog = Collar (represent the pars defect).

Anatomy trivia: the eye is the pedicle.

Spinal Dysraphism:

You can group these as open or closed (closed with and without a mass). Open means neural tissue exposed through a defect in bone and skin (spina bifida aperta). Closed means the defect is covered by skin (spina bifida occulta).

Open Spinal Dysraphisms: This is the result of a failure of the closure of the primary neural tube, with obvious exposure of the neural placode through a midline defect of the skin. You have a dorsal defect in the posterior elements. The **cord is going to be tethered.** There is an association with diastematomyelia and Chiari II malformations. Early surgery is the treatment / standard of care.

- *Myelocele*: This is the more rare type where the neural placode is flush with the skin.

- *Myelomeningocele:* This is the more common type (98%) where the neural placode protrudes above the skin. These are more common with Chiari II malformations.

Closed Spinal Dysraphisms with Subcutaneous Mass

- *Meningocele*: This is herniation of a CSF filled sac through a defect in the posterior elements (spina bifida). It is most typical in the lumbar or sacral regions. Although they can occur in the cervical spine. They may be anterior (usually pre-sarcral). An important point is **that neural tissue is NOT present in the sac.**

- *Lipomyelocele / Lipomyelomeningocele:* These are lipomas with a dural defect. On exam you are going to have a subcutaneous fatty mass above the gluteal crease. **These are 100% associated with tethered cord** (myelomeningocele may or may not).

- *Terminal Myelocystocele* – This is a herniation of a terminal syrinx into a posterior meningocele via a posterior spinal defect.

Closed Spinal Dysraphisms without Subcutaneous Mass

- *Intradural lipomas* – Most common in the thoracic spine along the dorsal aspect. They don't need to be (but can be) associated with posterior element defects.

- *Fibrolipoma of the filum terminale* – This is often an incidental finding "fatty filum". There will be a linear T1 bright structure in the filum terminale. The filum is not going to be unusually thickened and the conus will be normally located.

- *Tight filum terminale* – This is a thickened filum terminale (> 2 mm), with a low lying conus (below the inferior endplate of L2). You may have an associated terminal lipoma. The "**tethered cord syndrome**" is based on the clinical findings of low back pain and leg pain plus urinary bladder dysfunction. This is the result of stretching the cord with growth of the canal.

- *Dermal Sinus* – This is an epithelial lined tract that extends from the skin to deep soft tissues (sometimes the spinal canal, sometimes a dermoid or lipoma). These are T1 low signal (relative to the background high signal from fat).

Diastematomyelia – This describes a sagittal split in the spinal cord. They almost always occur between T9-S1, with normal cord both above and below the split. You can have two thecal sacs (or just one), and each hemi-cord has its own central canal and dorsal/ventral horns. Classification systems are based on the presence / absence of an osseous or fibrous spur and duplication or non-duplication of the thecal sac.

Caudal Regression: This is a spectrum of defects in the caudal region that ranges from partial agenesis of the coccyx to lumbosacral agenesis. The associations to know are VACTERL and Currarino triad. Think about this with maternal diabetes. "Blunted sharp" high terminating cord is classic, with a "shield sign" from the opposed iliac bones (no sacrum).

Fuckery - Note than the Meningocele of Currarino is **A**nterior. It's not posterior. A potential deployment of fuckery is to put "Posterior" Sacral Meningocele as a distractor for Currarino Triad.

Anyone who would do that is an Asshole (a structure which also happens to be posterior).

Currarino Triad:

Anterior Sacral Meningocele,

Anorectal malformation,

Sacrococcygeal osseous defect (scimitar sacrum).

3
GASTROINTESTINAL

PROMETHEUS LIONHART, M.D.

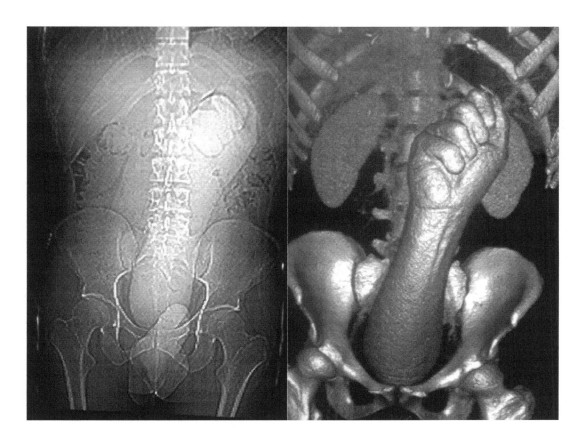

Between the time when the oceans drank Atlantis, and the rise of the sons of Aryas, there was an age undreamed of. And unto this, barium, was used to differentiate various luminal GI pathologies.

Let me tell you of the days of high adventure!

SECTION 1:
Luminal

- Esophagus -

Anatomy:

A Ring: The muscular ring above the vestibule.

B Ring: The mucosal ring **B**elow the vestibule. This is a thin constriction at the GE junction. Symptomatic dysphagia can occur if it narrows (historically defined at <13mm in diameter). **If it's narrowed (and symptomatic) you call it a Schatzki.** Just Say *"Shatz-'B'-Ring"*

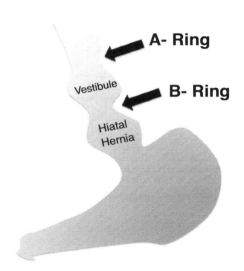

Z Line: Represents the squamocolumnar junction (boundary between esophageal and gastric epithelium). This doesn't necessarily correspond with the B-ring. This is an endoscopy finding, and is only rarely seen as a thin serrated line.

Mucosa should have thin, parallel uniform folds.

Anatomic Trivia

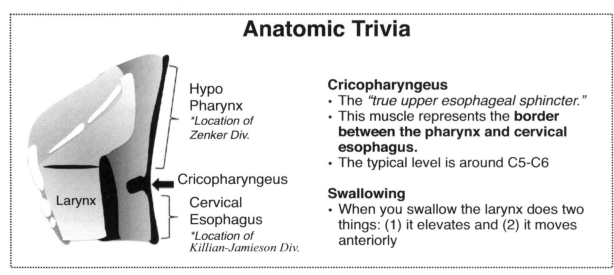

Cricopharyngeus
- The *"true upper esophageal sphincter."*
- This muscle represents the **border between the pharynx and cervical esophagus.**
- The typical level is around C5-C6

Swallowing
- When you swallow the larynx does two things: (1) it elevates and (2) it moves anteriorly

---

According to historical records, Left and Right Posterior Oblique positions were commonly used when performing a thoracic barium swallow exam. So which hand should the barium cup go in ??? The trick is to consider the potential for the barium filled cup to obscure the field of view as the patient is drinking. If the cup is placed in the more anterior hand this could happen… so don't do that.

Too Long Didn't Read: **L**PO = **L**eft Hand   **R**PO = **R**ight Hand

| **Left Posterior Oblique** | **Right Posterior Oblique** |

Pathology:

Reflux Esophagitis:

A common cause of fold thickening, which if left uncheck can cause some serious problems.

Behold the potential spectrum of unchecked aggression ->

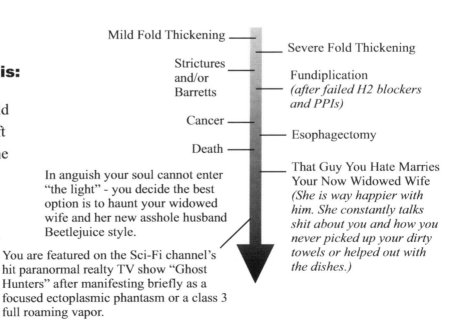

Mild Fold Thickening —
Severe Fold Thickening
Strictures and/or Barretts —
Fundiplication *(after failed H2 blockers and PPIs)*
Cancer —
Esophagectomy
Death —
That Guy You Hate Marries Your Now Widowed Wife *(She is way happier with him. She constantly talks shit about you and how you never picked up your dirty towels or helped out with the dishes.)*

In anguish your soul cannot enter "the light" - you decide the best option is to haunt your widowed wife and her new asshole husband Beetlejuice style.

You are featured on the Sci-Fi channel's hit paranormal realty TV show "Ghost Hunters" after manifesting briefly as a focused ectoplasmic phantasm or a class 3 full roaming vapor.

Barretts: This is a precursor to adenocarcinoma - that develops secondary to chronic reflux. The way this will be shown is a **high stricture with an associated hiatal hernia**.

Buzzword = **Reticular Mucosal Pattern**.

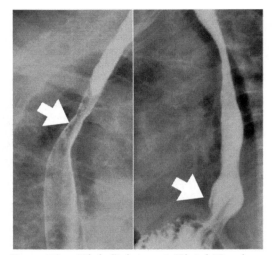

Barrett's - High Stricture + Hiatal Hernia

Feline Esophagus:

Often described as an Aunt Minnie

You have transient, fine transverse folds which course mid and lower esophagus.

It can be normal, but has a high association with reflux esophagitis..... *correlate clinically.*

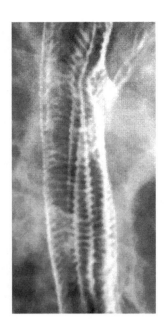

*Folds are Transient
(they go away with swallowing)

Cancer: On barium you want to see the words *"irregular contour"*, and *"abrupt (shouldered) edges."* I like to use stereotypes to remember the subtypes and associations:

Squamous: This is a black guy who drinks and smokes, and once tried to kill himself with an alkaloid ingestion (drank lye). The stricture/ulcer/mass is in the mid esophagus.

Adeno: This is a white guy, who is stressed out all the time. He has chronic reflux (history of PPI use). He had a scope years ago that showed Barretts, and he did nothing because he was too busy stressing out about stuff. The stricture/ulcer/mass is in the lower esophagus.

Critical Stage: T3 (Adventitia) vs T4 (invasion into adjacent structures) - obviously you need CT to do this. The earlier stages are distinguished by endoscopy - so not your problem and unlikely to be tested. T3 vs T4 is in the radiologists world - and therefore the most likely to be tested.

Herniation of the stomach comes in several flavors with the most common being the sliding type 1 (95%), and the rolling para-esophageal type 2. The distinction between the two is based on the position of the GE junction.

Small type 1s are often asymptomatic but do have an <u>association with reflux</u> if the function of the GE sphincter is impaired. The Para-E <u>type 2</u> has a reportedly <u>higher rate of incarceration.</u>

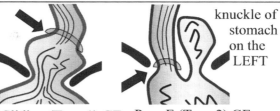

knuckle of stomach on the LEFT

Sliding (Type 1) GE Junction ABOVE the diaphragm — arrow.

Para-E (Type 2) GE Junction BELOW the diaphragm — arrow.

Fundoplication Blitz

What is this Fundoplication ? The gastric fundus is wrapped around the lower end of the esophagus and stitched in place, reinforcing the lower esophageal sphincter. The term "Nissen" - refers to a 360 degree wrap. Loose (< 360) wraps can also be done, and have French sounding names like "toupet," - these are less high yield.

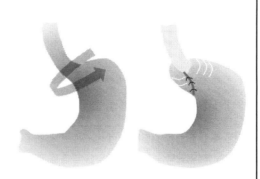

Early Complication: The early problem with these is esophageal obstruction (or narrowing). This occurs from either post op edema, or a wrap made too tight. You see this peak around week 2. *Barium will show total or near total obstruction of the esophagus.*

Failure: There are two main indications for the procedure (1) hiatal hernia, and (2) reflux. So failure is defined by recurrence of either of these. The most common reason for recurrent reflux is telescoping of the GE junction through the wrap - or a "slipped Nissen."

- *Most common reason for recurrent reflux ?*= slipped Nissen

- *Most common reason for slipped Nissen ?* = short esophagus

- *WTF is a "short esophagus" ?* The exact definition is elusive (and depends on the phase of the moon). For the purpose of multiple choice test I'd go with *"Hiatal Hernia that is fixed/non- reducible, and greater than 5cm"*

- *How can you tell if the wrap has slipped ?* Fundoplication wrap should have length of narrowed esophagus < 2cm (anything greater suggests a slipped wrap)

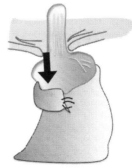

Wrap "Slipped" Down

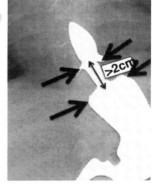

- Remember recurrent hernia (GE junction above the diaphragm) is not normal.

What is the treatment for a "short esophagus" ? Collis gastroplasty (lengthening + fundoplication).

Trivia: You cannot vomit after a fundoplication

Candidiasis: A hint in the question stem might be "HIV Patient" or "Transplant Patient" (someone who is immunocompromised). They could also tell you the patient has "achalasia" or "scleroderma" - because motility disorders are also at increased risk. The most common finding is discrete plaque-like lesions. Additional findings include: nodularity, granularity, and fold thickening as a result of mucosal inflammation and edema. When it is most severe, it looks more shaggy with an irregular luminal surface.

Glycogenic Acanthosis: This is a mimic of candidiasis, which has multiple elevated benign nodules in an **asymptomatic elderly patient**. It is essentially an epithelial collection of glycogen.

Ulcers:

- **Herpes Ulcer:** Small and multiple with a halo of edema (*Herpes has a Halo*)

- **CMV and HIV:** Large Flat Ulcer (*they look the same*)

Varices:

Linear often serpentine, filling defects causing a scalloped contour. The differential diagnosis for varices includes varicoid carcinoma (this is why you need them distended on the study).

THIS *vs* **THAT:**	
Uphill Varices	**Downhill Varices**
Caused by Portal Hypertension	Caused by SVC obstruction (catheter related, or tumor related)
Confined to Bottom Half of Esophagus	Confined to Top Half of Esophagus

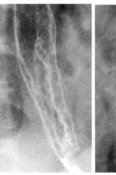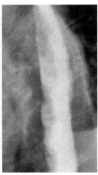

Varicoid appearance that flattens out with a large barium bolus - this dynamic appearance proves it's not a fixed varicoid looking cancer.

Esophageal (enteric) duplication cysts: If they show one of these it will be on CT (what? GI path not on barium?). Seriously, they would have to show this on CT. It is gonna be in the *posterior mediastinum*, and have an <u>ROI showing water density</u>. This is the only way you can show this.

Possible Ways This Could Be Tested:

- *What is it / What does it look like ?* - Water density cyst in the posterior mediastinum

- *Most common location ?* - The ileum (esophagus is #2).

- *How can they present ?* Either as an incidental in an adult, or if they are big enough - as an infant with dysphagia / breathing problems.

- *Malignant Risk ?* Nope - they are benign

Esophageal Diverticulum

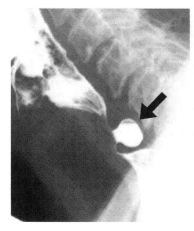
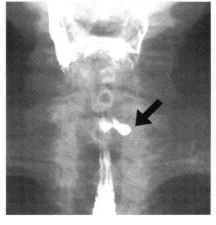
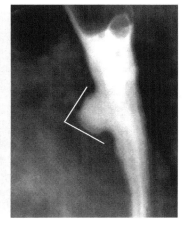

Zenker Diverticulum:
Pulsion Diverticulum in the back *(Z is in the back of the alphabet)*.

The question they always ask is: site of weakness = **Killian Dehiscence** or triangle.

Another sneaky point of trivia is that the diverticulum **arise from the hypopharynx** (not the cervical esophagus).

Killian-Jamieson Pulsion Diverticulum:

This one is **anterior and lateral**.

It protrudes through an area of weakness below the attachment of the cricopharyngeus muscle and lateral to the ligaments that help suspend the esophagus on the cricoid cartilage.

This one is **in the cervical esophagus.**

Traction Diverticulum:

Mid esophageal, and often <u>triangular</u> in shape.

These occur from scarring (think granulomatous disease or TB).

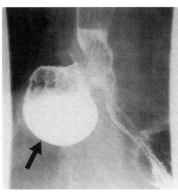

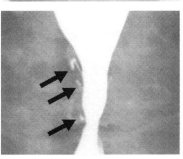

Epiphrenic Diverticula:

Located just above the diaphragm (**usually on the RIGHT**).
** The para-esophageal hernia is usually on the LEFT.

They are considered pulsion types (associated with motor abnormality).

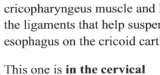

THIS vs THAT:	
Traction	**Pulsion**
Triangular	Round
Will Empty	Will **NOT** Empty (contains no muscle the walls)

Esophageal Pseudodiverticulosis:

This is an Aunt Minnie. What you have are dilated submucosal glands that cause multiple small out pouchings. **Usually due to chronic reflux esophagitis**.

There is controversy about the whole candida situation. Per the Mayo GI book, candida is often cultured but is not the causative factor.

Papilloma:

The most common benign mucosal lesion of the esophagus. It's basically just hyperplastic squamous epithelium.

Esophageal Web:

Most commonly located at the cervical esophagus (near the cricopharyngeus). This thing is basically a ring (you never see posterior only) caused by a thin mucosal membrane.

It's a **risk factor for** esophageal and hypopharyngeal **carcinoma**

Plummer –Vinson Syndrome: iron def anemia, dysphagia, thyroid issues, "spoon-shaped nails"

Normal Submucosal venous plexus (higher up and shallow)

Web - circumferential (anterior and posterior) in lower cervical region

Esophageal Pseudodiverticulosis:

Tons of little tiny out-pouchings which aren't really diverticula but instead dilated excretory mucosal ducts. There is a described association with esophageal strictures (90%), reflux, and candidiasis.

The appearance is fairly classic and is better demonstrated with a single phase of contrast (instead of the fancy double contrast).

Eosinophilic Esophagitis:

Classically a young man with a long history of dysphagia (also atopia and peripheral eosinophilia). Barium shows **concentric rings** (distinct look). They fail treatment on PPIs, but get better with steroids.

 Buzzword = **"Ringed Esophagus"**

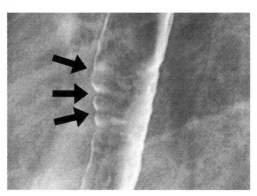

Eosinophilic Esophagitis - Rings

Esophageal Spasm:

Most of the time the exam is normal, but for the purpose of multiple choice I'd expect *"corksrew"* tertiary contractions favoring the distal esophagus.

The term *nutcracker esophagus* requires manometric findings (>180mmHg).

Dysphagia Lusoria – THIS IS HIGH YIELD. Syndrome refers to problems swallowing secondary to compression from an aberrant right subclavian artery (most patients with aberrant rights don't have symptoms).

** *Refer to page 74 for the chart on esophageal vascular impressions.*

The Dilated Esophagus

If you get shown a big dilated esophagus (full cheerios, mashed potatoes, and McDonald's french fries… or "freedom fries" as I call them), you will need to think about 3 things.

(1) **Achalasia:** A motor disorder where the distal 2/3 of the esophagus (smooth muscle part) doesn't have normal peristalsis (*"absent primary peristalsis"*), and the lower esophageal sphincter won't relax.

The esophagus will be dilated above a smooth stricture at the GE junction (**Bird's Beak**).

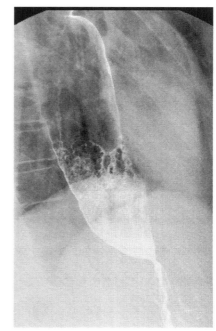

"Vigorous Achalasia" - An early / less severe form which classically has repetitive simultaneous non-propulsive contractions. It's more common in women, but the secondary cancer occurs more in men.

Things to know:

- Failure of the lower esophageal sphincter to relax
- Increased risk of Candida

"Chagas Disease" - More common in the jungle. The esophagus get paralyzed by some parasite transmitted by a fly. The appearance is identical to Achalasia - and some people even lump them together (others reserve the term "achalasia" for idiopathic types only). You'll simply need to read the mind of the test question writer to know what camp he/she falls into.

(2) **"Pseudoachalasia"** *(secondary achalasia)* has the appearance of achalasia, but is secondary to a cancer at the GE junction. The difference is that real Achalasia will eventually relax, the pseudo won't. They have to show you the mass - or hint at it, or straight up tell you that the GE junction didn't relax. Alternatively they could be sneaky and just list a bunch of cancer risk factors (smoking, drinking, chronic reflux) in the question stem. Next step would probably be CT (or full on upper GI).

(3) **Scleroderma:** Involves the esophagus 80% of the time. Again the lower 2/3 of the esophagus stops working normally. The LES is incompetent and you end up with chronic reflux, which can cause scarring, Barretts, and even cancer (Adeno). They will show you lung changes (most commonly **NSIP**), and the barium esophagus (or a small bowel series showing closely spaced valvulae conniventes – *hide bound*).

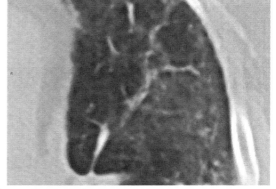

NSIP - Ground Glass with sub-pleural sparring

- Esophagus – High Yield Trivia -

Path	Trivia
Esophagitis	Fold Thickening. May have smooth stricture at GE junction if severe
Barretts	Buzzword: Reticulated Mucosal Pattern Classically shown as Hiatal Hernia + High Stricture
Medication Induced Esophagitis	Ulcers; Usually at the level of the arch or distal esophagus
Crohns Esophagitis	Ulcers ; can be confluent in severe disease
Candidia	Discrete plaque like lesions that are seen as linear or irregular filling defects that tend to be longitudinally oriented, separated by normal mucosa Buzzword: Shaggy – when severe Not always from AIDS, can also be from motility disorders such as achalasia and scleroderma
Glycogenic Acanthosis	Looks like Candidia, but in an asymptomatic old person
Herpes Ulcers	Multiple small, with Edema Halo (herpes has halo)
CMV / AIDS	Large Flat ulcers
Achalasia	Buzzword: Bird Beak, - smooth stricture at GE junction Path is failure of LES to relax (but it will slowly relax) Increased risk of Squamous Cell CA, and Candida
Pseudoachalsia	Cancer at the GE junction. Fixed Obstruction, will not relax
Scleroderma	Involves the Esophagus 80% of the time Looks a little like Achalasia (they will show you lung changes- NSIP) Sequelae of reflux: stricture, Barrets, cancer
Long Stricture	DDx: NG tube in too long, Radiation, Caustic Ingestion
Pseudodiverticulosis	Dilated submucosal glands, usually due to chronic reflux esophagitis. Esophageal stricture is seen in 90% of cases
Zenker Diverticula	Zenker in the back (above cricopharyngeus) From the hypopharynx
Killian-Jamieson	Lateral (below cricopharyngeus) From the cervical esophagus.

- Stomach -

Location Based Trivia

- **H Pylori** Gastritis – Usually in **Antrum**
- **Zollinger-Ellison** – Ulcerations in the stomach (**jejunal ulcer** is the buzzword). Duodenal bulb is actually the most common location for ulcers in ZE. Remember ZE is from gastrinoma - and might be a way to test MEN syndromes.
- **Crohns** – Uncommon in the stomach, but when it is, it likes the **antrum**
- **Menetrier's** – Usually in the **Fundus** (*classically spares the antrum*)
- **Lymphoma** – "**Crosses the Pylorus**" – classically described as doing so, although in reality adenocarcinoma does it more.

- Selective Polyposis Syndromes -

Gardner Syndrome	FAP (Hyperplastic Stomach Polyps , Adenomatous Bowel Polyps) + Desmoid Tumors, Osteomas, Papillary Thyroid Cancer
Turcots	FAP (Hyperplastic Stomach Polyps, Adenomatous Bowel Polyps) + Gliomas and Medulloblastomas
Hereditary nonpolyposis Syndrome (Lynch) - HNPCC	DNA Mismatch Repair They get cancer everywhere in everything
Peutz-Jeghers	Hamartoma Style! Mucocutaneous Pigmentation Small and Large Bowel CA, Pancreatic CA, and GYN CA
Cowden	Hamartoma Style! **BREAST CA**, Thyroid CA, Lhermitte-Duclos (*posterior fossa noncancerous brain tumor*)
Cronkhite-Canada	Hamartoma Style! Stomach, Small Bowel, Colon, Ectodermal Stuff (skin, hair, nails, yuck)
Juvenile Polyps	Hamartoma Style!
Zenker Diverticula	Zenker in the back (above cricopharyngeus)

GIST

This is the most common mesenchymal tumor of the GI tract (70% in stomach). Think about this in an old person (it's rare before age 40).

Some tricks to know:

- Lymph node enlargement is NOT a classic feature

- The malignant ones tend to be big angry mother fuckers (>10cm with ulceration - and possible perforation).

- The association with Carney's triad - Extra-Adrenal Pheochromocytoma, GIST, Pulmonary Chondroma (hamartoma)

- The association with NF-1

Carneys Triad
"**C**arney's **E**at **G**arbage"
Chondroma *(pulmonary)*   **E**xtra Adrenal Pheo   **G**IST

Stomach Ulcers - Benign vs Malignant
— 1960s style medicine - for the "exam of the future" -

Malignant	**Benign**
Width > Depth	Depth > Width
Located within Lumen	Project beyond the expected lumen
Nodular, Irregular Edges	Sharp Contour
Folds adjacent to ulcer	Folds radiate to ulcer
Aunt Minnie: Carmen Meniscus Sign	Aunt Minnie: Hampton's Line
Can be anywhere	Mostly on Lesser Curvature

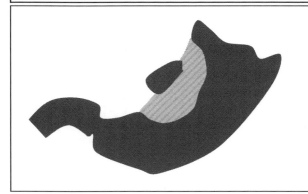

Carmen Meniscus

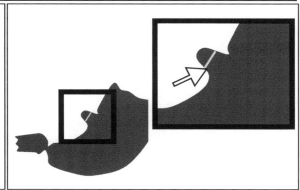

Hampton's Line

- Gastric Cancer -

It's Either Lymphoma (<5%) or Adenocarcinoma (95%).

Gastric adenocarcinoma is usually a disease of an old person (median age 70). H. Pylori is the most tested risk factor.

Trivia to know:

- Ulcerated carcinoma (or the "penetrating cancer") has the look of an advanced cancer

- Metastatic spread to the ovary is referred to as a **Krukenberg Tumor.**

- Gastroenterostomy performed for gastric ulcer disease (old school – prior to PPIs) have a 2x – 6x- increased risk for development of carcinoma within the gastric remnant.

- Step 1 trivia question: swollen left supraclavicular node = **Virchow Node.**

Ulcer Trivia:
Gastric Ulcers - They have 5% chance of being cancer.
Duodenal Ulcers - Are never cancer (on multiple choice)
Gastric Ulcers occurs from "altered mucosal resistance"
Duodenal Ulcers occur from "increased peptic acid"
Duodenal Ulcers are usually solitary, when not think ZE.

Gastric Lymphoma, can be primary (MALT), or secondary (systemic lymphoma). The stomach is the most common extranodal site for non-Hodgkin lymphoma. Even when extensive, it **rarely causes gastric outlet obstruction**. It was classically described as *"crossing the pylorus"*, although since gastric carcinoma is like 10x more common it is actually more likely to do that. Has multiple looks and can be big, little, ulcerative, polypoid, or look like target lesions. It can also look like Linitis Plastica.

Trivia: It can rupture with treatment (chemo).

Linitis Plastica: The leather bottle stomach. It's the result of a scirrhous adenocarcinoma, with diffuse infiltration. Can be from **breast** or lung mets.

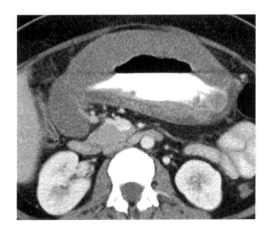

Lymphoma - Crossing the Pylorus

Gastric Cancer is "More Likely" Than Lymphoma to...
•More Likely to Cause Gastric Outlet Obstruction
•More Likely to be in the distal stomach
•More Likely to extend beyond the serosa and obliterate adjacent fat plains
•More Likely to be a focal mass (95% of primary gastric tumors are adenocarcinoma)

- Misc. Gastric Conditions -

Mets to the Stomach: This is actually very rare. *Melanoma is probably the most common* culprit, when it does occur.

Menetrier's Disease: Rare and has a French sounding name, so it's almost guaranteed to be on the test. It's an idiopathic gastropathy, with rugal thickening that classically involves the fundus and spares the antrum. Bimodal age distribution (childhood form thought to be CMV related). They end up with low albumin, from loss into gastric lumen.

Essential Trivia: Involves the fundus, and spares the antrum.

Ram's Horn Deformity *(Pseudo Billroth 1)* Tapering of the antrum causes the stomach to look like a Ram's Horn. This is a differential case, and can be seen with Scarring via peptic ulcers, Granulomatous Disease (Crohns, Sarcoid, TB, Syphilis), or Scirrhous Carcinoma.

Essential Trivia: **The stomach is the most common GI tract location for sarcoid.**

Gastric Volvulus

Two Flavors:

• *Organoaxial* – the greater curvature flips over the lesser curvature. This is seen in old ladies with paraesophageal hernias. It's way more common.

• *Mesenteroaxial* – twisting over the mesentery. Can cause ischemia and needs to be fixed. Additionally this type causes obstruction. This type is more common in kids.

Organoaxial

Mesenteroaxial

Gastric Diverticulum: The way they always ask this is by trying to get you to call it an adrenal mass (it's most commonly in the posterior fundus). Find the normal adrenal.

Gastric Varices: This gets mentioned in the pancreas section, but I just want to hammer home that test writers love to ask **splenic vein thrombus causing isolated gastric varices.** Some sneaky ways they can ask this is by saying "pancreatic cancer" or "Pancreatitis" causes gastric varices. Which is true.... because they are associated with splenic vein thrombus. So, just watch out for that.

Areae Gastricae: This is a **normal** fine reticular pattern seen on double contrast. Multiple choice writers have been known to ask when does this "enlarge"? The answer is that it enlarges in elderly and patient's with H. Pylori. Also it can focally enlarge next to an ulcer. It becomes obliterated by cancer or atrophic gastritis.

Chronic Aspirin Therapy: "Multiple gastric ulcers" is the buzzword. Obviously this is non-specific, but some sources say it occurs in 80% of patient's with chronic aspirin use. As a point of trivia, aspirin does NOT cause duodenal ulcers. If you see multiple duodenal ulcers (most duodenal ulcers are solitary) you should think Zollinger-Ellison.

- Upper GI Surgical Complications -

Bilio-pancreatic (afferent) limb

Gastro-Jejunal (efferent) or "Roux"limb

Billroth 1	**Billroth 2**	**Roux-en-Y**

Pylorus is removed and the proximal stomach is sewed directly to the duodenum.

Done for Gastric CA, Pyloric Dysfunction, or Ulcers.

Less Post Op Gastritis (relative to Billroth 2)

Partial gastrectomy, but this time the stomach is attached to the jejunum.

Done for Gastric CA, or Ulcers.

Risks:

- Dumping syndrome - slightly
- Afferent loop syndrome
- Increased risk of gastric CA 10-20 year after surgery

Stomach is divided to make a "pouch." This gastric pouch is attached to the jejunum. The excluded stomach attaches to the duodenum as per normal. The jejunum is attached to the other jejunum to form the bottom of the Y.

Done for weight loss (usually). Can also be performed for gastric cancer as an alternative to Billroth if the primary lesion has directly invaded the duodenum or head of the pancreas.

Supposedly these have less reflux, and less risk of recurrent gastric CA.

They are at increased risk for gallstones, and they have all that internal hernia shit.

Afferent Loop Syndrome: An uncommon complication post billroth 2. The most common cause is obstruction (adhesions, tumor, intestinal hernia) of the afferent. The acute form may have a closed loop obstruction. The result of this afferent obstruction is the build up of biliary, pancreatic, and intestinal secretions resulting in afferent limb dilation. The back pressure from all this back up dilates the gallbladder, and causes pancreatitis. A much less common cause is if the stomach preferentially drains into the afferent loop.

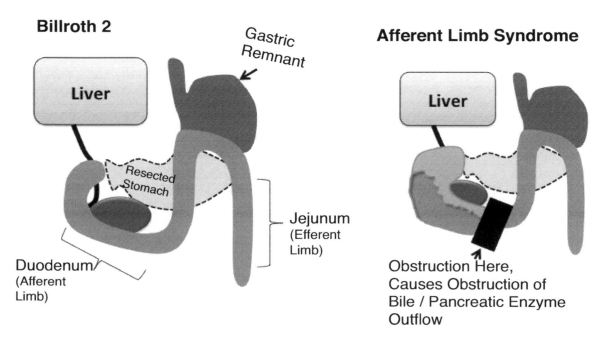

Jejunogastric Intussusception: This is a rare complication of gastroenterostomy. The Jejunum herniates back into the stomach (usually the efferent limb) and can cause gastric obstruction. High mortality is present with the acute form.

Bile Reflex Gastritis: Fold thickening and filling defects seen in the stomach after Billroth I or II are likely the result of bile acid reflux.

Gastro-Gastric Fistula: This is seen in Roux-en-Y patients who gain weight years later. The anastomotic breakdown is a chronic process, and often is not painful.

Cancer: With regard to these old peptic ulcer surgeries (Billroths), there is a 3-6 times increased risk of getting adenocarcinoma in the gastric remnant (like 15 years after the surgery).

Dumping Syndrome: Different than the "dumping syndrome" associated with late night Taco Bell. This type of dumping is related to rapid transit of undigested food from the stomach. Tc Gastric Emptying study is an option to diagnose this. The therapy is typically conversion of Billroth to Roux-en-Y (and avoiding delicious carbs).

Small Bowel -

Introduction, the Lost Art, and Historical Perspective:

In the modern age a legitimate working knowledge of the barium fluoroscopic examination is exceedingly rare. Ever since the late Cretaceous period, when the Oort cloud of comets rained down upon the dinosaurs of the Yucatan Peninsula legitimate expertise in the field has been essentially extinct. Now all that remains of this ancient practice is a collection of pretenders who spend their days in the swamps of fuckery deploying the phrase *"of course I know what I'm looking at"* as subterfuge.

Understanding that this barbaric ancient practice still represents "fair game" on the modern boards, I set out on a journey to re-discover the lost knowledge. This journey took me across the globe, into the most primitive corners of the world - as these were the only locations the modality is still commonly practiced. I was searching for any ancient relic that I could use to construct a high yield summary. My journey was a treacherous one, necessitating significant risk to gain favor with the natives. I barely survived several bouts of malaria and one (five) bouts of gonorrhea in my quest to discover the ancient methods of fluoroscopic interpretation. Eventually, as is often the case in life - my persistence was rewarded. I was confident I had finally unearthed a legitimate method of interpretation that I could use to complete the section on bowel fold patterns.

The method I discovered is as ancient as the practice of barium driven fluoroscopic imaging. Originally described in the scrolls of Xuthal (a city-state of ancient Valusia) during the Hyborian Age. The knowledge contained in the scrolls details the chronicle of a low born son of a village blacksmith whom after the destruction of the Aquilonian fortress of Venarium, was struck by wanderlust and began a journey. According to his chronicle - this 20 year journey saw him encounter skulking monsters, evil wizards, tavern wenches, and beautiful princesses.

It was during his travels he learned many things, including the ancient 3 step method of the small bowel follow through - the details of which I will now discuss.

STEP 1 - Evaluate the Folds

Thin (< 3mm) Straight Folds with Dilation			• Mechanical Obstruction • Paralytic Ileus • Scleroderma • Sprue
Thick Straight Folds > 3mm	Segmental Distribution		• Ischemia • Radiation • Hemorrhage • Adjacent Inflammation
Thick Straight Folds > 3mm	Diffuse Distribution		• Low Protein • Venous Congestion • Cirrhosis
Thick Folds with Nodularity	Segmental Distribution		• Crohns • Infection • Lymphoma • Mets
Thick Folds with Nodularity	Diffuse Distribution		• Whipples • Lymphoid Hyperplasia • Lymphoma • Mets • Intestinal Lymphangiectasia

STEP 2a - Evaluate for Loop Separation with or without Tethering

Loop Seperation	**Without Tethering**		• Ascites, • Wall Thickening (Crohns, Lymphoma), • Adenopathy • Mesenteric Tumors
Loop Seperation	**With Tethering**		Tethering looks like someone is pinching and pulling the loops towards the displacing mass. • Carcinoid

A pearl is that an extrinsic processes will spare the mucosa, intrinsic process will alter the mucosa.

STEP 2b - If Nodules are Present Evaluate the Distribution and Secondary Findings To Help Narrow the Differential.		
"Sand Like Nodules"	Diffuse micronodules in the jejunum.	• **Whipples** (Tropheryma whipplei) • **Pseudo-Whipples** (MAC Infection)
Uniform 2-4mm Nodules		• **Lymphoid Hyperplasia**
Nodules of Larger or Varying Sizes		• **Cancer** - think Mets (Melanoma)
"Cobblestoning"		• Raised islands of mucosa separated by linear streaks running perpendicular to the lumen of the bowel. • These streaks represent ulceration. • This findings (especially when combined with areas of stricture, and loop separation from fat proliferation) should make you think **Crohns**

STEP 3: Trademark Features:

After comparing this 3 main features - many multiple choice distractors can be eliminated. If necessary specific features of each disease can be compared - with that discussion to follow.

Ribbon Bowel		Bowel is featureless, atrophic, and has fold thickening (ribbon-like). **Graft vs Host**

STEP 3: Trademark Features - Continued:

Hidebound Bowel	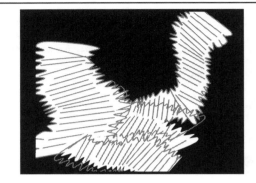	Narrow separation of normal folds with mild bowel dilation. **Scleroderma**
Moulage sign (tube of wax)	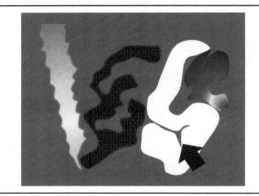	Dilated jejunal loop with complete loss of jejunal folds - opacified like a "tube of wax" **Celiac**
Fold Reversal		Jejunum loses folds to look more like the normal Ileum, Ileum gains folds (in the right lower quadrant) to look more like normal Jejunum **Celiac**
A Fucking Worm	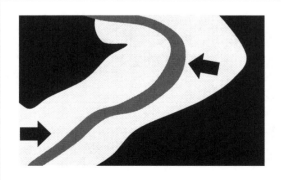	Thread Like Defect in the Barium Column **Ascaris Suum** (asshole demon worm)

- Selected Small Bowel Path -

The Target Sign:

•**Single Target:** GIST, Primary Adenocarcinoma, Lymphoma, Ectopic Pancreatic Rest, Met (Melanoma).

•**Multiple Target:** Lymphoma, Met (Melanoma)

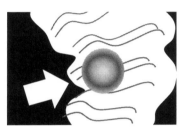

Clover Leaf Sign:

This is an Aunt Minnie for Healed Peptic Ulcer of the Duodenal Bulb.

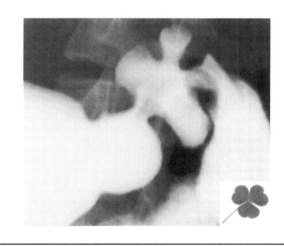

Whipples: Rare infection (Tropheryma Whipplei)

Just like a stripper - it prefers white men in their 50s. The bug infiltrates the lamina propria with large macrophages infected by intracellular whipple bacilli leading to marked swelling of intestinal villi and thickened irregular mucosal folds primarily in duodenum and proximal jejunum. The buzzword is "sand like nodules" referring to diffuse micronodules in the jejunum. Jejunal mucosal folds are thickened. This is another cause of low density (near fat) enlarged lymph nodes.

Pseudo-Whipples: Also an infection - but this time MAI (instead of T. Whipplei). This is seen in AIDS patients with CD4<100. The imaging findings of nodules in the jejunum and retroperitoneal nodes are similar to Whipples (hence the name). The distinction between the two is not done with imaging but instead via an acid fast stain (MAC is positive).

Intestinal Lymphangiectasia: Lymphangiectasia results from obstruction to the flow of lymph from the small intestine into the mesentery. This results in dilation of the intestinal and serosal lymphatic channels. This can be primary from lymphatic hypoplasia, or secondary from obstruction of the thoracic duct (or any place in between).

Celiac Sprue: Small bowel malabsorption of gluten.

High yield points:

- Can cause malabsorption of iron, and lead to iron deficiency anemia.

- Associated with Idiopathic Pulmonary Hemosiderosis (Lane Hamilton Syndrome)

- Increased Risk of bowel wall **lymphoma**

- Gold standard is biopsy (*surprisingly not barium*)

- Dermatitis Herpetiformis – some skin thing (remember that from step 1)

Findings (CT / Barium)

- **Fold Reversal** is the Buzzword (Jejunum like Ileum, Ileum like Jejunum)

- Moulage Sign – dilated bowel with effaced folds (tube with wax poured in it)

- Cavitary Lymph Nodes (low density)

- Splenic Atrophy

Graft vs Host: Buzzword = **Ribbon bowel.** It occurs in patients after bone marrow transplant. It's less common with modern anti-rejection drugs. Skin, Liver, and GI tract get hit. Small bowel is usually the most severely affected. Bowel is featureless, atrophic, and has fold thickening (ribbon-like).

SMA Syndrome: This is an obstruction of the 3rd portion of the duodenum by the SMA (it pinches the duodenum in the midline). It is seen in **patients who have recently lost a lot of weight.**

Meckel's Diverticulum / Diverticulitis: This is a congenital true diverticulum of the distal ileum. A piece of total trivia is that it is a persistent piece of the omphalomesenteric duct. Step 1 style, "rule of 2s" occurs in 2% of the population, has 2 types of heterotopic mucosa (gastric and pancreatic), located 2 feet from the IC valve, it's usually 2 inches long (and 2 cm in diameter), and usually has symptoms before the child is 2. If it has gastric mucosa (the ones that bleed typically do) it will take up Tc-Pertechnetate just like the stomach (hence the Meckel's scan).

High Yield Meckel's Trivia (Regarding Complications)

- Can get diverticulitis in the Meckels (mimic appendix)
- GI Bleed from Gastric Mucosa (causes 30% of symptomatic cases)
- Can be a lead point for intussusception (seen with inverted diverticulum)
- Can cause Obstruction

Duodenal Inflammatory Disease: You can have fold thickening of the duodenum from adjacent inflammatory processes of the pancreas or gallbladder. You can also have thickening and fistula formation with Crohn's (usually when the colon is the primary site). Primary duodenal Crohns can happen, but is super rare. **Chronic dialysis patients may get severely thickened duodenal folds** which can mimic the appearance of pancreatitis on barium.

Jejunal Diverticulosis: Less common than colonic diverticulosis, but does occur. They occur along the mesenteric border. Important **association is bacterial overgrowth and malabsorption.** They could show this with CT, but more likely will show it with barium (if they show it at all).

- Small Bowel Cancer -

Adenocarcinoma: Most common in the proximal small bowel (<u>usually duodenum</u>). Increased incidence with celiac disease and regional enteritis. Focal circumferential bowel wall thickening in proximal small bowel is characteristic on CT. The duodenal web does NOT increase the risk.

Lymphoma: It's usually the non-Hodgkin flavor. Patients with celiac, Crohns, AIDS, and SLE are higher risk. It can look like anything (infiltrative, polypoid, multiple nodules etc....). **Key piece of trivia is they usually do NOT obstruct, even with massive circumferential involvement**. The Hodgkin subtype is more likely to cause a desmoplastic reaction.

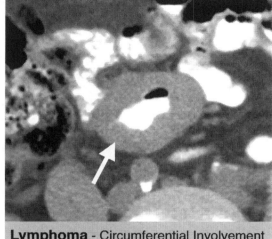

Lymphoma - Circumferential Involvement

Carcinoid: This has an **Aunt Minnie look with a mass + desmoplastic stranding.** "Starburst" appearance of the mesenteric mass with calcifications. This tumor most commonly occurs in young adults. The <u>primary tumor is often not seen</u>. That calcified crap you are seeing is the desmoplastic reaction. Liver mets are often hyper vascular. Step 1 style, you don't get carcinoid syndrome (flushing, diarrhea) until you met to the liver. The **most common primary location is the distal ileum** *(older literature says appendix)*. The appendix, has the best prognosis of all GI primary sites. Systemic serotonin degrades the heart valves (right sided), and classically causes tricuspid regurgitation - *more on this in the cardiac chapter*. MIBG or Octreotide scans can assist with diagnosis and staging - *more on this in the nuclear medicine chapter.*

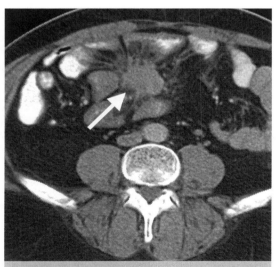

Carcinoid - *Sunburst Desmoplastic Rx*

Mets: This is usually **melanoma** (which hits the small bowel in 50% of fatal cases). You can also get hematogenous seeding of the small bowel with breast, lung, and Kaposi sarcoma. Melanoma will classically have multiple targets.

- Hernias -

Inguinal Hernias: - the most common type of abdominal wall hernia. M>F (7:1)

Direct	Indirect
Less common	More Common
Medial to inferior epigastric artery	Lateral to inferior epigastric artery
Defect in Hesselbach's Triangle	Failure of processus vaginalis to close
NOT covered by internal spermatic fascia	Covered by internal spermatic fascia

Femoral: Likely to obstruct. Seen in old ladies. They are medial to the femoral vein, and posterior to the inguinal ligament (usually on the right).

Obturator Hernia: Another old lady hernia. Often seen in patients with increased intra-abdominal pressure (Ascites, COPD – chronic cougher). Usually asymptomatic – but can strangulate.

Lumbar Hernia: Can be superior (Grynfeltt-Lesshaft) through the superior lumbar triangle, or inferior (Petit) through the inferior lumbar triangle. Superior is more common than inferior. Otherwise, they are very similar and usually discussed together. Causes are congenital or acquired (post-surgery).

Spigelian Hernia: The question is probably the location along the Semilunar line *("S" for "S")* through the transversus abdominis aponeurosis close to the level of the arcuate line.

Littre Hernia: Hernia with a Meckel Diverticulum in it.

Amyand Hernia: Hernia with the appendix in it.

Richter Hernia: Contains only one wall of bowel and therefore **does not obstruct**. This are actually at higher risk for strangulation.

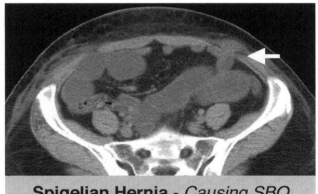

Spigelian Hernia - *Causing SBO*

Richter - *Only one wall herniates*

- Hernias Post Laparoscopic Roux-en-Y Gastric Bypass -

Factors that promote internal hernia after gastric bypass: (1) Laproscopic over Open – supposedly creates fewer adhesion, so you have more mobility (2) Degree of weight loss ; more weight loss = less protective, space occupying mesenteric fat.

There are 3 potential sites.

(1) At the defect in the transverse mesocolon, through which the Roux-Loop Passes (if it's done in the retrocolic position).
(2) At the mesenteric defect at the enteroenterostomy
(3) Behind the Roux limb mesentery placed in a retrocolic or antecolic position (**retrocolic Petersen** and **antecolic Petersen** type). ** This is the one they will likely ask because it has an eponym with it.

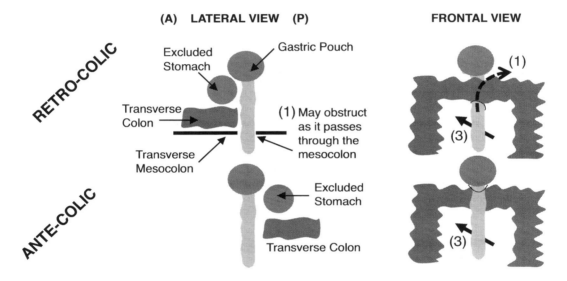

Internal Hernia: These can be sneaky. The most common manifestation is closed loop obstruction (often with strangulation). There are 9 different subtypes, of which I refuse to cover. I will touch on the most common, and the general concept.

General Concept: This is a herniation of viscera through the peritoneum or mesentery. The herniation takes place through a known anatomic foramina or recess, or one that has been created post operatively.

Paraduodenal (right or left): This is by far the most common type of internal hernia. They can occur in 5 different areas, but it's much simpler to think of them as left or right. Actually, **75% of the time they are on the left**. The exact location is the duodenojejunal junction ("fossa of Landzert"). Here is the trick; the herniated small bowel can become trapped in a **"sac of bowel"** between the pancreas and stomach to the left of the ligament of Treitz.   The sac characteristically contains the IMV and the left colic artery.

The right-sided PDHs are located just behind the SMA and just below the transverse segment of the duodenum, at the "Fossa of Waldeyer." The classic setting for right-sided PDHs is non-rotated small bowel, with normally rotated large bowel.

- Large Bowel / Rectum

THIS *vs* THAT: Crohns Disease *vs* Ulcerative Colitis:

Crohns Disease: Typically seen in a young adult (15-30), but has a second smaller peak later 60-70. Discontinuous involvement of the entire GI tract (mouth -> asshole). Stomach, usually involves antrum (Ram's Horn Deformity). Duodenal involvement is rare, and NEVER occurs without antral involvement. Small bowel is involved 80% of the time, with the terminal ileum almost always involved (Marked Narrowing = String Sign). After surgery the "neo-terminal ileum" will frequently be involved. The colon involvement is usually right sided, and often spares the rectum / sigmoid. Complications include fistulae, abscess, gallstones, fatty liver, and sacroiliitis.

Crohns Buzzwords	
Squaring of the folds	An early manifestation from obstructive lymphedema
Skip lesions	Discontinuous involvement of the bowel
Proud loops	Separation of the loops caused by infiltration of the mesentery, increase in mesenteric fat and enlarged lymph nodes
Cobblestoning	Irregular appearance to bowel wall caused by longitudinal and transverse ulcers separated by areas of edema
Pseudopolyps	Islands of hyperplastic mucosa
Filiform	Post-inflammatory polyps – long and worm-like
Pseudodiverticula	Found on anti-mesenteric side. From bulging area of normal wall opposite side of scarring from disease
String-sign	Marked narrowing of terminal ileum from a combination of edema, spasm, and fibrosis

Ulcerative Colitis:

Just like Crohns, it typically occurs in a "young adult" (age 15-40), with a second peak at 60-70. Favors the male gender. It **involves the rectum 95% of the time, and has retrograde progression.** Terminal ileum is involved 5-10% of the time via backwash ileitis (wide open appearance). It is continuous and does not "skip" like Crohns. It is associated with Colon Cancer, Primary Sclerosing Cholangitis, and Arthritis (similar to Ankylosing Spondylitis).

On Barium, it is said that the colon is ahaustral, with a diffuse granular appearing mucosa. "Lead Pipe" is the buzzword (shortened from fibrosis).

Here is a key clinical point: UC has an increased risk of cancer (probably higher than Crohns), and it doesn't classically have enlarged lymph nodes (like Crohns does), so if you see a big lymph node in an UC patient (especially one with long standing disease), you have to think that it might be cancer.

More Common In : Crohns vs UC	
Path	**More Common IN**
Gallstones	Crohns
Primary Sclerosing Cholangitis	Ulcerative Colits
Hepatic Abscess	Crohns
Pancreatitis	Crohns

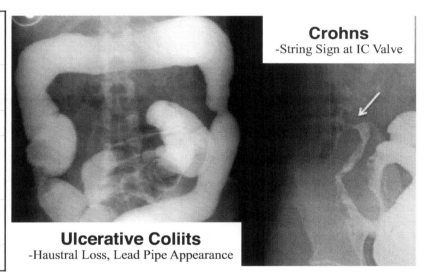

Crohns
-String Sign at IC Valve

Ulcerative Coliits
-Haustral Loss, Lead Pipe Appearance

THIS *vs* THAT:	
Crohns	**UC**
Slightly less common in the USA	Slightly more common in the USA
Discontinuous "Skips"	Continuous
Terminal Ileum – *String Sign*	Rectum
Ileocecal Valve "Stenosed"	Ileocecal Valve "Open"
Mesenteric Fat Increased *"creeping fat"*	Perirectal fat Increased
Lymph nodes are usually enlarged	Lymph nodes are NOT usually enlarged
Makes Fistulae	Doesn't Usually Make Fistulae

Misc Large Bowel Pathology

Toxic Megacolon: Ulcerative colitis, and to a lesser degree Crohns, is the primary cause. C-Diff can also cause it. Gaseous dilation distends the transverse colon (on upright films), and the right and left colon on supine films. **Lack of haustra** and pseudopolyps are also seen. Some people say the presence of normal hausta excludes the diagnosis. **Don't do a barium enema** because of the risk of perforation. Another piece of trivia is that peritonitis can occur without perforation.

Behcets: Ulcers of the penis and mouth. Can also affect GI tract (and **looks like Crohns**) – *most commonly affects the ileocecal region*. It is also a cause of **pulmonary artery aneurysms** (test writers like to ask that).

Diverticulosis / Diverticulitis: Some trivia worth knowing is that diverticulosis actually bleeds more than diverticulitis. Right-sided is less common (but is seen in young Asians). Fistula formation is actually most common with diverticulitis, and can occur to anything around it (another piece of bowel, the bladder, etc..).

Epiploic Appendagitis / Omental Infarct:

Epiploic appendages along the serosal surface of the colon can torse, **most commonly on the left**. There is not typically concentric bowel wall thickening (unlike diverticulitis).

Omental infarction is typically a larger mass with a more oval shape and central low density. It is **more commonly on the right** (*ROI – right omental infarct*). Both entities are self-limiting.

Appendicitis

The classic pathways are: obstruction (fecalith or reactive lymphoid tissue) -> mucinous fluid builds up increasing pressure -> venous supply is compressed -> necrosis starts -> wall breaks down -> bacteria get into wall -> inflammation causes vague pain (umbilicus) -> inflamed appendix gets larger and touches parietal peritoneum (pain shifts to RLQ).

It occurs in an adolescent or young adult (or any age). The measurement of 6 mm was originally described with data from ultrasound compression, but people still generally use it for CT as well. Secondary signs of inflammation are probably more reliable for CT.

Appendix Mucocele – Mucinous cystadenomas are the most common mucinous tumor of the appendix. They produce mucin and can really dilate up and get big. They look similar to cystadenocarcinomas and can perforate leading to pseudomyxoma peritonei. On ultrasound the presence of an "**onion sign**" – layering within a cystic mass - is a suggestive feature of a mucocele.

Colonic Volvulus: Comes in several flavors:

- *Sigmoid:* Most common adult form. Seen in the nursing home patient (chronic constipation is a predisposing factor). Buzzword is coffee bean sign (or inverted 3 sign). Another less common buzzword is Frimann Dahl's sign – which refers to 3 dense lines converging towards the site of obstruction. Points to the RUQ. Recurrence rate after decompression = 50%.

THIS vs THAT: Volvulus	
Sigmoid	**Cecal**
Old Person	Younger Person
Points to the RUQ	Points to the LUQ

- *Cecal:* Seen in a younger person (20-40). Associated with people with a "long mesentery." More often points to the LUQ. Much less common than sigmoid.

- *Cecal Bascule:* Anterior folding of the cecum, **without twisting**. A lot of surgical text books dispute this thing even being real (they think it's a focal ileus). The finding is supposedly dilation of the cecum in an ectopic position in the middle abdomen, without a mesenteric twist.

Colonic Pseudo-Obstruction *(Colonic Ileus, Ogilvie Syndrome):* Usually seen after serious medical conditions and in nursing home patients. It can persist for years, or progress to bowel necrosis and perforation. The classic look is marked diffuse dilation of the large bowel, without a discrete transition point.

Diversion Colitis: Bacterial overgrowth in a blind loop through which stool does not pass (any surgery that does this).

Colitis Cystica: This cystic dilation of the mucous glands comes in two flavors: Superficial or Profunda (Deep).

Superficial: The superficial kind consists of cysts that are small in the entire colon. It's associated with vitamin deficiencies and tropical sprue. Can also be seen in terminal leukemia, uremia, thyroid toxicosis, and mercury poisoning.

Profunda: These cysts may be large and are seen in the pelvic colon and rectum.

 Rectal Cavernous Hemangioma: Obviously very rare. Just know it's associated with a few syndromes; Klippel-Trenaunay-Weber, and Blue Rubber Bleb. They might show you a ton of phleboliths down there.

Gossypiboma: This isn't really a GI pathology but it's an abscess mimic. It's a retained cotton product or surgical sponge and it can elicit an inflammatory response.

- Infections -

Entamoeba Histolytica:

Parasite that causes bloody diarrhea. Can cause liver abscess, spleen abscess, or even brain abscess. Within the colon it is one of the causes of toxic megacolon. They are typically "flask-shaped ulcers" on endoscopy. With regard to barium, the buzzword is *"coned cecum"* referring to a change in the normal bulbous appearance of the cecum, to that of a cone. It affects the cecum and ascending colon most commonly and unlike many other GI infections, **spares the terminal ileum**.

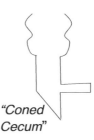

"Coned Cecum"

Colonic TB:

Typically involves the terminal ileum, and is another cause of the "**coned cecum**" appearance. Causes both ulcers and areas of narrowing. Two other signs: (1) *Fleischner sign* – enlarged gaping IC valve, and (2) *Stierlin sign* – narrowing of the TI.

Colonic CMV:

Seen in patients who are immunosuppressed. Causes deep ulcerations – which can lead to perforation. Step 1 question = Cowdry Type A intranuclear inclusion bodies

Infections that like the Duodenum (and proximal small bowel)	Infections that like the Terminal Ileum
Giardia	TB
Strongyloides	Yersinia

C-Diff:

Classically seen after antibiotic therapy, the toxin leads to a super high WBC count. CT findings of the *"accordion sign"* with contrast trapped inside mucosal folds is always described in review books and is fair game for multiple choice. The barium findings include thumb printing, ulceration, and irregularity. Of course it can cause toxic megacolon as mentioned on the prior page.

Neutropenic Colitis (Typhlitis):

Infection **limited to the cecum** occurring in severe neutropenia.

- Colon Cancer -

Adenocarcinoma: Common cause of cancer death (#2 overall). Cancers on the right tend to bleed (present with bloody stools, anemia). Cancers on the left tend to obstruct. **Apple core** is a buzzword.

Squamous Cell Carcinoma – Occasionally arises in the anus *(think HPV)*.

Lipomas: The second most common tumor in the colon.

Adenoma – The most common benign tumor of the colon and rectum. The *villous adenoma has the largest risk for malignancy.*

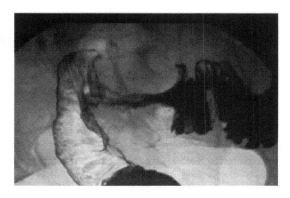

Apple Core Lesion - Cancer

McKittrick-Wheelock Syndrome:

This is a <u>villous adenoma</u> that causes a mucous diarrhea leading to severe fluid and electrolyte depletion.

The clinical scenario would be something like "80 year old lady with diarrhea, hyponatremia, hypokalemia, hypochloremia… and this" and they show you a mass in the rectum / bowel.

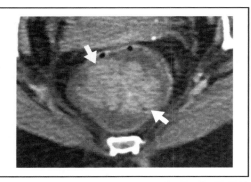

Rectal Cancer:
"Cancer of the Prison Wallet"

Trivia:
- Nearly always (98%) adenocarcinoma
- If the path says Squamous - the cause was HPV *(use your imagination on how it got there).*
- Total mesorectal excision is standard surgical method
- Lower rectal cancer (0-5 cm from the anorectal angle), have the highest recurrence rate.
- MRI is used to stage - and you really only need T2 weight imaging - contrast doesn't matter
- Stage T3 - called when tumor breaks out of the rectum and into the perirectal fat. This is the critical stage that changes management (they will get chemo/rads prior to surgery).

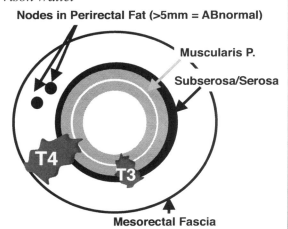

Nodes in Perirectal Fat (>5mm = ABnormal)

Muscularis P.

Subserosa/Serosa

T4

T3

Mesorectal Fascia

SECTION 2:
Peritoneal Cavity

Pseudomyxoma Peritonei: This is a gelatinous ascites that results from either (a) ruptured mucocele (usually appendix), or intraperitoneal spread of a mucinous neoplasm (ovary, colon, appendix, and pancreas). It's usually the appendix (least common is the pancreas). The buzzword is "**scalloped appearance of the liver.**" Recurrent bowel obstructions are common.

Peritoneal Carcinomatosis: The main thing to know regarding peritoneal implants is that the natural flow of ascites dictates the location of implants. This is why the **retrovesical space is the most common spot**, since it's the most dependent part of the peritoneal cavity.

Omental Seeding/Caking: The omental surface can get implanted by cancer and become thick (like a mass). The catch-phrase is "posterior displacement of the bowel from the anterior abdominal wall."

Primary Peritoneal Mesothelioma: This is super rare. People think about mesothelioma involving the pleura (and it does 75% of the time), but the other 25% of the time it involves the peritoneal surface. The thing to know is that it occurs 30-40 years after the initial asbestosis exposure.

Cystic Peritoneal Mesothelioma: This is the even more rare benign mesothelioma, that is NOT associated with prior asbestos exposure. It usually involves a women of child-bearing age (30s).

Mesenteric Lymphoma: This is usually non-Hodgkin lymphoma, which supposedly involves the mesentery 50% of the time. The **buzzword is "sandwich sign."** The typical appearance is a lobulated confluent soft tissue mass encasing the mesenteric vessels "sandwiching them."

Barium Gone Bad

Complications of barium use are rare, but can be very serious. They come in two main flavors: (1) Peritonitis, and (2) Intravasation.

Barium Peritonitis: This is why you use water soluble contrast anytime you are worried about leak. The pathology is an attack of the peritoneal barium by the leukocytes which creates a monster inflammatory reaction (often with massive ascites and sometimes hypovolemia and resulting shock). If no "real doctor" is available, you should give IV fluids to reduce the risk of hypovolemic shock. The long term sequela of barium peritonitis is the development of granulomas and adhesions (causing obstructions and an eventual lawsuit).

Barium Intravasation: This is super rare, but can happen. If barium ends up in the systemic circulation it kills via pulmonary embolism about 50% of the time. Risk is increased in patients with inflammatory bowel or diverticulitis (altered mucosa).

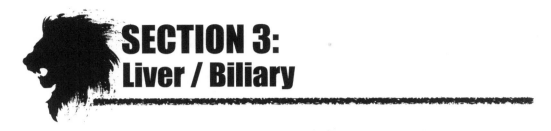

SECTION 3:
Liver / Biliary

Bare Area: The liver is covered by visceral peritoneum except at the porta hepatis, bare area, and the gallbladder fossa. An injury to the "bare area" can result in a retroperitoneal bleed.

Couinaud System: Functional division of the liver into multiple segments. *"Functional"* is the key word. Each segment will have its own biliary drainage, inflow, and outflow.

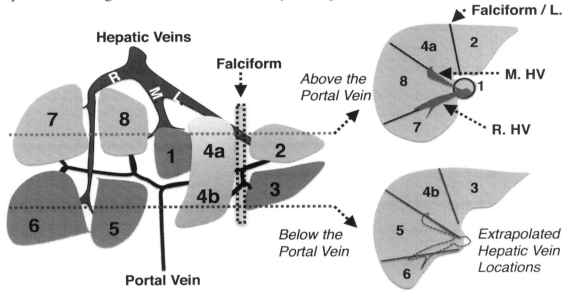

Couinaud System Testable Trivia:
- Right Hepatic Vein Divides 7/8, and 6/5
- Middle Hepatic Vein Divides 4a/8, 4b/5
- Left Hepatic Vein / Fissure for the Ligamentum Teres (falciform) divides 4a/2, 4b/3
- The Portal Vein Divides the Liver into Upper and Lower Segments
- The Caudate Lobe (Segment 1) is unique in that it drains directly to the IVC.

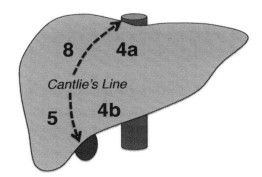

"Cantlie's Line" *divides the liver into a functional left and right hepatic lobes.*
This line runs from the IVC to the middle of the gallbladder fossa.

Caudate Lobe: The caudate lobe (segment 1) has a direct connection to the IVC through it's own hepatic veins, which do not communicate with the primary hepatic veins. Additionally, the caudate is supplied by branches of both the right and left portal veins – which matters because the caudate may be spared or hypertrophied as the result of various pathologies such as Budd Chiari, etc… (as discussed later in the chapter).

Additional Anatomic Trivia:

Trivia: Along the same lines of anatomy explaining pathology, the intra-hepatic course of the right portal vein is longer than the left, which is why it is more susceptible to fibrosis *(this is why the right liver shrinks, and the left liver grows in cirrhotic morphology).*

Trivia: Most common vascular variant = Replaced right hepatic (origin from the SMA)

Trivia: Most common biliary variant = Right posterior segmental into the left hepatic duct.

Normal MRI Signal Characteristics: I like to think of the spleen as a bag of water/blood (T2 bright, T1 dark). The pancreas is the "brightest T1 structure in the body" because it has enzymes. The liver also has enzymes and is similar to the pancreas (T1 Brighter, T2 darker), just not as bright as the pancreas

Fetal Circulation: The fetal circulation anatomy is high yield anatomic trivia.

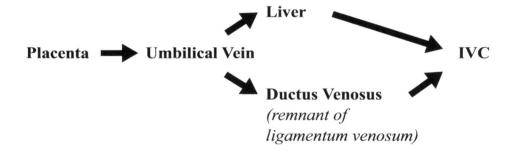

Classic Ultrasound Anatomy:

There are 4 high yield looks, that are classically tested with regard to ultrasound anatomy. In years past, these were said to have been shown by oral boards examiners (likely the same dinosaurs writing the exam).

Trivia: Pancreas should be more echogenic than liver

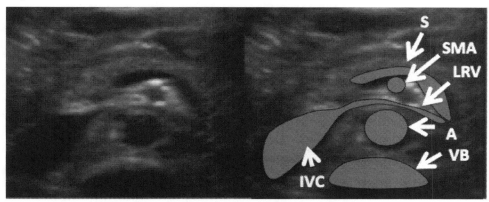

S = Splenic Vein, SMA = SMA, LRV = Left Renal Vein,
A= Aorta, VB = Vertebral Body, IVC = IVC

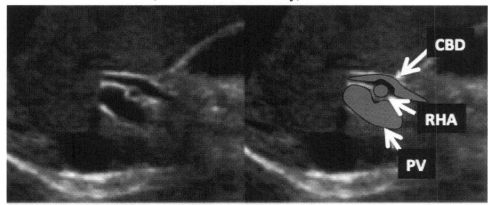

RHA - Right Hepatic Artery, CBD = Common Bile Duct, PV = Portal Vein

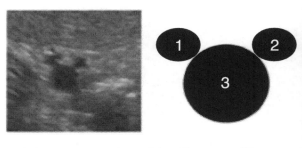

Mickey Mouse Sign: (1) Bile Duct, (2) Hepatic Artery, (3) Portal Vein

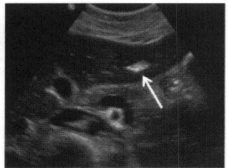

Fat in the Falciform Ligament / Ligamentum Teres

Promethean Dialogue on the Liver -

A discourse on the liver, cirrhosis, portal HTN, and the development of HCC

My idea is that by leading with a discussion of normal physiology, and the changes that occur with diffuse liver injury, that a lot of the processes and changes that occur with cirrhosis will make more sense (and be easier to remember). If you are in a rush to cram for the test just skip this discussion and move on to the charts. If you have more time, I think understanding the physiology is worthwhile.

Hepatocyte injury can occur from a variety of causes including viruses, alcohol, toxins (*alfatoxins i.e. peanut fungus*), and nonalcoholic fatty liver disease. These injuries result in increased liver cell turnover, to which the body reacts by forming regenerative nodules. The formation of regenerative nodules is an attempt by the liver not just to replace the damaged hepatocytes but also to compensate for lost liver function. In addition to activation of hepatocytes, stellate cells living in the space of Disse become active and proliferate changing into a *myofibroblast –like cell* that produces collagen. This collagen deposition causes fibrosis.

The development of fibrosis first puts the squeeze on the right portal vein (which _usually_ has a longer intrahepatic course). This causes atrophy of segments 6 and 7, and compensatory hypertrophy of the caudate, segments 2 and 3. Because these changes, some people will try and use a caudate / right lobe ratio (*C/RL >0.75 is 99% specific*) to call cirrhosis.

Another consequences of the Longer Right Portal Vein Course is that Hepatic Abscess (often from ascending hematogenous sources) nearly always (75%+) involves the right hepatic lobe.

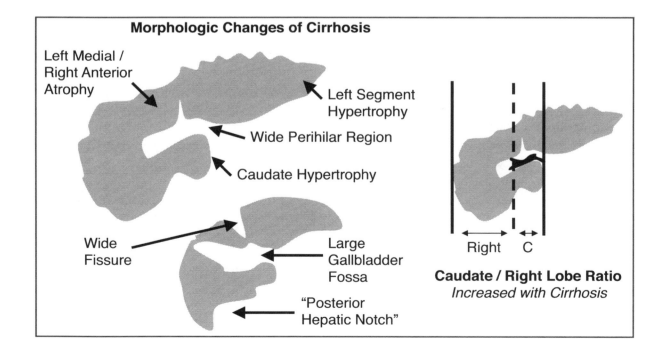
Morphologic Changes of Cirrhosis

Left Medial / Right Anterior Atrophy

Left Segment Hypertrophy

Wide Perihilar Region

Caudate Hypertrophy

Wide Fissure

Large Gallbladder Fossa

"Posterior Hepatic Notch"

Right   C

Caudate / Right Lobe Ratio
Increased with Cirrhosis

All this squeezing can lead to portal hypertension. Portal hypertension is usually the result of increased hepatic resistance from pre-hepatic (*portal vein thrombosis, tumor compression*), hepatic (*cirrhosis, schistosomiasis*) and post hepatic (*Budd-Chiari*) causes. Obviously, most cases are hepatic with schistosomiasis being the most common cause world-wide, and EtOH cirrhosis being the most common cause in the US. Once portal venous pressure exceeds hepatic venous pressure by 6-8 mmHg – portal hypertension has occurred (*variceal bleeding + ascites around > 12*). In reaction to this increased resistance offered by the liver, collaterals will form to decompress the liver by carrying blood away from it. These tend to be esophageal and gastric varices. As a point of trivia, in pre-hepatic portal hypertension, collaterals will form above the diaphragm and in the hepatogastric ligaments to bypass the obstruction.

The liver has a dual blood supply (70% portal, 30% hepatic artery) with compensatory relationships between the two inflows; arterial flow increases as portal flow decreases. This helps explain the relationship between these two vessels with regard to Doppler US. As fibrosis leads to portal hypertension, velocity in the hepatic artery increases.

Another phenomenon related to this "hepatic arterial buffer response" is the **THAD**. These **T**ransient **H**epatic **A**ttenuation **D**ifferences are typically seen in the arterial / early portal phase - NOT on the equilibrium / delayed phases (hence the word "transient"). The easiest way to think about them is that they are focal "arterial buffer responses." In other words, in that tiny little spot right there the liver feels like there isn't enough portal flow, so it responses by increasing the arterial flow. This can happen for several reasons:

- **Cirrhosis:** A bunch of scar / fibrosis deforms the hepatic sinusoids compressing the tiny little portal veins (think about arteries and veins in the neck or groin - pressure will compress the vein first) - people call this "shunting." This is most typical in the subcapsular region.

- **Clot:** Venous blood flow could be compromised from a clot in a portal vein branch (these enhancement patterns are typically larger, wedge shaped, and extend towards the periphery).

- **Mass** (B9 or Malignant): This can occur from two primary mechanisms. 1 - You could have the direct mass effect from the mass smashing the veins. 2 - The tumor could be recruiting / up-regulating arterial flow (VEGF etc…).

- **Abscess / Infection:** Also probably a mixed mechanism. Some direct mass effect, but also some element of "hyperemia" - causing a "siphon effect." For clarity we aren't just talking liver abscess here, cholecystitis cause also have this region effect.

The perfusion related changes you see with cirrhosis aren't just local, you can also have global patterns. Since the fibrosis blockade takes place at the level of the central lobular vein (into sinusoids), flow remains adequate for the central zones of the liver, but not for the peripheral zones. The arterial response produces enhancement of the peripheral subcapsular hepatic parenchyma with relative hypodensity of the central perihilar area. The consequent CT pattern is referred to as the "central–peripheral" phenomenon.

Sometimes you will see reversal of flow (hepatofugal – *directed away from the liver*). As an aside, apparently "fugal" is latin for "flee." So the blood is fleeing the liver, or running away from it. Reversed flow in the portal system is seen in cirrhosis between 5-25% of the time.

| BUT Prometheus !? | *Why does the portal vein reverse flow instead of just clotting off in the setting of high resistance to inflow?* |

The answer has to do with the unique dual hepatic blood supply (70% P / 30% A). As mentioned above, in cirrhosis, the principal area of obstruction to blood flow is believed to be in the outflow vessels (the hepatic venules and distal sinusoids). The outflow obstruction also partially shits on the hepatic artery, causing increased resistance as well. So why doesn't the artery clot or reverse ? The difference is that the portal system can decompress through the creation of collaterals, and the artery cannot. So the artery does something else, it opens up tiny little connections to the portal system. The enlargement of these tiny communications has been referred to as "parasitizing the portosystemic decompressive apparatus." If the resistance is high enough, hepatic artery inflow will be shunted into - and can precipitate hepatofugal flow in the portal vein. So, in patients with hepatofugal flow in the main portal vein or intrahepatic portal vein branches, the shunted blood comes from the hepatic artery. This is the long answer for why cirrhotic changes can lead to THADs, and why these cirrhosis related THADs tend to be subcapsular.

With increased resistance in the liver to the portal circulation, you also start to have colonic venous stasis (worse on the right). This can lead to *"Portal Hypertensive Colopathy,"* which is basically an edematous bowel that mimics colitis. Why is it worse on the right? The short answer is that collateral pathways develop more on the left (splenorenal shunt, short gastrics, esophageal varices), and decompress that side. The trivia question is that it does resolve after transplant. The same process can affect the stomach *"Portal Hypertensive Gastropathy" causing a thickened gastric wall on CT, as well as cause upper GI bleeding in the absence of varices.*

Earlier I mentioned that hepatocytes react to injury by turning into regenerative nodules. This is how multi-focal HCC starts. Regenerative nodules -> Dysplastic nodules (increased size and cellularity) -> HCC. As this process takes place, the nodule changes from preferring to drink portal blood to only wanting to drink arterial blood. This helps explain why HCC has arterial enhancement and rapid washout. The transformation also follows a progression from T2 dark (regenerative) -> T2 bright (HCC). A buzzword is *"nodule within nodule"* where a central bright T2 nodule has a T2 dark border. This is concerning for transformation to HCC.

Regenerative	Dysplastic	HCC
Contains Iron	Contains Fat, Glycoprotein	
T1 Dark, T2 Dark	T1 Bright, T2 Dark	T2 Bright
Does NOT Enhance	Usually Does NOT Enhance	Does Enhance

Another thing that happens with hepatocarcinogenesis is the decrease in a thing called the OATP bile uptake transporter. This is the transporter that moves biliary contrast agents (example = Eovist) into the cells. It's the reason normal liver cells look bright on the delayed phase when using a hepatocyte specific agent. It's also the reason FNHs look super bright on delayed images as they are basically hypertrophied hepatocytes. As hepatocytes become cancer they lose function in this transporter and become dark on the delayed phase. The exception (highly testable) is the well differentiated HCC which retains OATP function and is therefore bright on the 20 min delayed Eovist sequence.

There is one last concept that I wanted to "squeeze" in. The squeezing that causes portal hypertension also squeezes out most benign liver lesions (cysts, hemangiomas). So, lesions in a cirrhotic liver should be treated with more suspicion.

—

Hepatic Contrast Phase Timing & Window

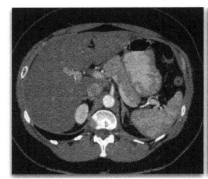 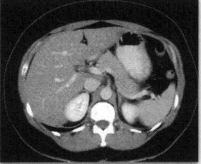 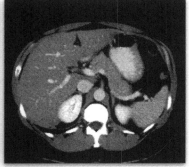

Arterial Phase
- 25-30 seconds after injection

Portal Venous Phase
- 70 seconds

"Liver Window"
Center: 100 Width: 200

- MR Contrast - Hepatobiliary Considerations -

I want to clarify a few issues that can be confusing (and may also be testable).

How they work: Gadolinium (which is super toxic) is bound to some type of chelation agent to keep it from killing the patient. The shape and function of the chelation agent determine the class and brand name. The paramagnetic qualities of gadolinium cause a local shortening of the T1 relaxation time on neighboring molecules (remember short T1 time = bright image).

Types of Agents: I want you to think about MRI contrast in two main flavors:
(1) Extracellular and (2) Hepatocyte Specific.

Extracellular: These are nonspecific agents that are best thought of as Iodine contrast for CT. They stay outside the cell and are blood flow dependent (just like CT contrast). The imaging features in lesions will be the same as CT - although the reason they look bright is obviously different - CT contrast increases the density (attenuation), MR contrast shortens the T1 time locally – which makes T1 brighter. The classic imaging set up is a late hepatic arterial phase (15-30 seconds), portal venous phase (70 seconds), and a hepatic venous or interstitial phase (90 seconds – 5 mins) - just like CT.

Classic Example of a Non-Specific Extracellular Agent = Gd-DTPA (Magnevist)

Hepatocyte Specific: Certain chelates are excreted via the bile salt pathway. In other words, they are taken up by normal hepatocytes and excreted into the bile. This gives you great contrast between normal hepatocytes and things that aren't normal hepatocytes (cancer). The 20 min delay is the imaging sequence that should give you a homogenous bright liver (dark holes are things that don't contain normal liver cells / couldn't drink the contrast). The problem is that it's pretty non-specific with a handful of benign things still taking it up (classical example is FNH), and at least one bad thing taking it up (well-differentiated HCC). Plus, a handful of benign things won't take it up (cysts, etc..). There are at least three good reasons to use this kind of agent: (1) it's great for proving an FNH is an FNH - as most lesions won't hold onto the Gd at 20 mins, (2) it's great for looking for bile leaks, and (3) once you've established a baseline MRI (characterized all those benign lesions) it's excellent for picking up new mets (findings black holes on a white background is easy).

Classic Example of a Hepatocyte Specific Agent = Gd-EOB-DTPA (Eovist).

Is Eovist a pure Hepatocyte Specific Agent ? Nope – It also acts like a non-specific extracellular agent early on (although less intense). About 55% is excreted into the bile – and gives a nice intense look at 20 mins.

What about Gd-BOPTA (Multihance) ? This is mostly an extra-cellular agent, but has a small amount (5%) of biliary excretion. The implication is that you can use Multihance to look for a bile leak you just have to wait longer (45mins-3 hours) for the Gd to accumulate.

What about Manganese instead of Gd ? This is the old school way to do biliary imaging. It works the same as Gd – by causing T1 shortening.

- Liver Masses -

Hemangioma: This is the most common benign liver neoplasm. Favors women 5:1. They may enlarge with pregnancy. On US will be bright (unless it's in a fatty liver, than can be relatively dark). On US, flow can be seen in vessels adjacent to the lesion but NOT in the lesion. On CT and MRI tends to match the aorta in signal and have "peripheral nodular discontinuous enhancement". Should totally fill in by 15 mins. Atypical hemangioma can have the "reverse target sign."

Trivia: A hemangioma can change its sonographic appearance during the course of a single examination. No other hepatic lesion is known to do this.

Hemangioma US Pearls:
- Need to core for biopsy, FNA does not get enough tissue (only blood)
- Hyperechoic (65%)
- Enhanced thru transmission is common
- NO Doppler flow inside the lesion itself
- Atypical appearance – hyperechoic periphery, with hypoechoic center (reverse target)
- Calcifications are extremely rare

Focal Nodular Hyperplasia (FNH): This is the second most common benign liver neoplasm. Believed to start in utero as an AVM. It is NOT related to OCP use. It is composed of normal hepatocytes, abnormally arranged ducts, and Kupffer cells (reticuloendothelial cells). May show spoke wheel on US Doppler. On CT, should be "homogenous" on arterial phase. Can be a **"Stealth" lesion** on MRI – T1 and T2 isointense. Can have a central scar. Scar will demonstrate delayed enhancement (like scars do). *Biopsy Trivia: You have to hit the scar, otherwise path results will say normal hepatocytes.* Sulfur Colloid is always the multiple choice test question (reality is that it's only hot 30-40%). Unlike hepatic adenomas, they are not related to the use of birth control pills, although as a point of confusing trivia and possibly poor multiple choice test question writing, birth control pills may promote their growth.

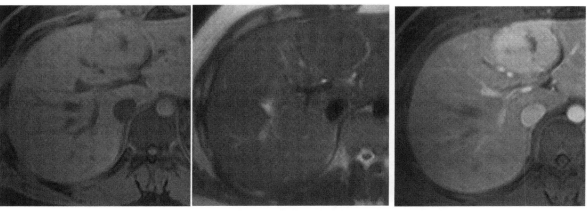

| T1 - Stealth | T2 - Stealth | Arterial Homogenous Enhancement
-Also has a Central Scar |

Hepatic Adenoma: Usually a solitary lesion seen in a female on OCPs. Alternatively could be seen in a man on anabolic steroids. When it's multiple you should think about glycogen storage disease (von Gierke) or liver adenomatosis. No imaging methods can reliably differentiate hepatic adenoma from hepatocellular carcinoma. Rarely, they *may degenerate into HCC* after a long period of stability. They *often regress after OCPs are stopped*. Their propensity to bleed sometimes makes them a surgical lesion if they won't regress.

 Gamesmanship: Signal Drop Out with in and out of phase can be used to show fat

Trivia:
    Q: Most common location for hepatic adenoma (75%)
    A: Right Lobe liver

Management: You stop the OCPs and re-image, they should get smaller. Smaller than 5cm, watch them. Larger than 5cm they often resect because (1) they can bleed and (2) they can rarely turn into cancer.

—

HCC: Occurs typically in the setting of cirrhosis and chronic liver disease; Hep B, Hep C, hemochromatosis, glycogen storage disease, Alpha 1 antitrypsin. AFP elevated in 80-95%. Will often invade the portal vein, although invasion of the hepatic vein is considered a more "specific finding."

"Doubling Time" – the classic Multiple Choice Question. This is actually incredibly stupid to ask because there are 3 described patterns of growth (slow, fast, and medium). To make it an even worse question, different papers say different stuff. Some say: Short is 150 days, Medium to 150-300, and Long is >300. I guess the answer is 300 – because it's in the middle. Others define medium at around 100 days. A paper in Radiology (*May 2008 Radiology, 247, 311-330*) says 18-605 days. The real answer would be to say follow up in 3-4.5 months.

Other Random Trivia: HCCs like to explode and cause spontaneous hepatic bleeds.

Fibrolamellar Subtype of HCC: This is typically seen in a younger patients (<35) without cirrhosis and a normal AFP. The buzzword is central scar. The scar is similar to the one seen in FNH with a few differences. This scar does NOT enhance, and is T2 dark (usually). As a point of trivia, this tumor is Gallium avid. This tumor calcifies more often than conventional HCC.

THIS vs THAT: Classic HCC vs Fibrolamellar HCC	
HCC	**FL HCC**
Cirrhosis	No Cirrhosis
Older (50s-60s)	Young (30s)
Rarely Calcifies	Calcifies Sometimes
Elevated AFP	Normal AFP

THIS vs THAT: Central Scars of FNH and Fibrolamellar HCC	
FNH	**FL HCC**
T2 Bright	T2 Dark (usually)
Enhances on Delays	Does NOT enhance
Mass is Sulfur Colloid Avid (sometimes)	Mass is Gallium Avid

Cholangiocarcinoma: Where HCC is a cancer of the hepatocyte, cholangiocarcinoma is a cancer of the bile duct. Cholangiocarcinoma believes in nothing Lebowski. It fucks you up, it takes the money (prognosis is poor).

Who gets it? The most classic multiple choice scenario would be an 80 year old man, with primary sclerosing cholangitis - **PSC** *(main risk factor in the West)*, recurrent pyogenic **"oriental" cholangitis** (main risk factor in the East), Caroli Disease, Hepatitis, HIV, history of cholangitis, and fucking Liver Worms (Clonorchis). Oh who also had a semi-voluntary cerebral angiogram performed by a Nazi with a cleft asshole (in 1930s Germany, Thorotrast was the preferred angiographic contrast agent).

Gamesmanship - They could tell you the dude has ulcerative colitis, as a way to infer that he also has PSC.

Buzzword = "Painless Jaundice." (just like pancreatic head CA)

THIS *vs* THAT:
- HCC = Invades the Portal Vein
- Cholangiocarcinoma = Encases the Portal Vein

What does it look like? It is variable and the described subtypes overlap. The easiest way to conceptualize this thing is as a <u>scar generating cancer</u>. **Fibrosis (scar)** is the main thing you are seeing - either primarily as a mass that *enhances on delayed imaging* (just like scar in the heart), or secondarily through the desmoplastic pulling of the scar (example *capsular retraction* and *ductal dilation*). The dilation of ducts is most likely to be shown as unilateral and peripheral, although if the lesion is central the entire system can obstruct.

Classic Features:
- Delayed Enhancement
- Peripheral Biliary Dilation
- Liver Capsular Retraction
- NO tumor capsule

Klatskin Tumor: Cholangiocarcinoma that occurs at the bifurcation of the right and left hepatic ducts. It's usually small but still causes biliary obstruction ("shouldering / abrupt tapering" on MRCP). These things are mean as cat shit. It is a "named" subtype, so that increases the likelihood of it showing up on a multiple choice exam.

Staging Pearls: There are like 3-4 major systems, each one has rules on the subtype (intrahepatic, extrahepatic, hilar/Klatskin), and honestly resectability is incredibly variable depending on how much of a gun slinger the surgeons at your institution are. This combination of factors makes specifics nearly untestable (under "fair" conditions). Having said that, here are some potentially testable pearls:

- Proximal extent of involvement is a key factor for surgical candidacy (more = bad).
- Atrophy of a lobe implies biliary +/- vascular involvement of that lobe (imaging often underestimates disease burden).
- Typically combinations of bilateral involvement (veins on the right, ducts on the left - vice versa, etc.. etc… etc…) is bad news.

Hepatic Angiosarcoma: This used to be the go to for thorotrast questions. Even though everyone who got thorotrast died 30 years ago, a few dinosaurs writing multiple choice test questions still might ask it. Hepatic Angiosarcoma is very rare, although technically the most common primary sarcoma of the liver. It is associated with toxic exposure - arsenic use (latent period is about 25years), Polyvinyl chloride exposure, Radiation, and yes... thorotrast. Additional trivia, is that you can see it in Hemochromatosis and NF patients.

It's usually multifocal, and has a propensity to bleed.

—

Biliary Cystadenoma Uncommon benign cystic neoplasm of the liver. Usually seen in middle aged women. Can sometimes present with pain, or even jaundice. They can be unilocular or multilocular and there are no reliable methods for distinguishing from biliary cystadenocarcinoma (which is unfortunate).

—

Mets to the Liver: If you see mets in the liver, first think colon. Calcified mets are usually the result of a mucinous neoplasm (colon, ovary, pancreas).

With regard to ultrasound: Hyperechoic mets are often hypervascular (renal, melanoma, carcinoid, choriocarcinoma, thyroid, islet cell). Hypoechoic mets are often hypovascular (colon, lung, pancreas).

"Too Small To Characterize" - even in the setting of breast cancer (with no definite hepatic mets) tiny hypodensities have famously been shown to be benign 90-95% of the time.

—

Lymphoma: Hodgkins lymphoma involves the liver 60% of the time (Non Hodgkins is around 50%), and may be hypoechoic.

—

Kaposi Sarcoma: Seen in patients with AIDS. Causes diffuse periportal hypoechoic infiltration. Looks similar to biliary duct dilation.

Benign Liver Masses

	Ultrasound	CT	MR	Trivia	
Hemangioma	Hyperechoic with increased through transmission	Peripheral Nodular Discontinuous Enhancement	T2 Bright	Rare in Cirrhotics	Kasabach-Merritt; the sequestration of platelets from giant cavernous hemangioma
FNH	Spoke Wheel	Homogenous Arterial Enhancement	"Stealth Lesion - Iso on T1 and T2"	Central Scar	Bright on Delayed Eovist (Gd-EOB-DTPA)
Hepatic Adenoma	Variable	Variable	Fat Containing on In/Out Phase	OCP use, Glycogen Storage Disease	Can explode and bleed
Hepatic Angiomyolipoma	Hyperechoic	Gross Fat	T1/T2 Bright	Unlike renal AML, 50% don't have fat	Tuberous Sclerosis

- Congenital Liver -

Cystic Kidney Disease (both AD and AR): Patient's with AD polycystic kidney disease will also have cysts in the liver. This is in contrast to the AR form in which the liver tends to have fibrosis.

 **Hereditary Hemorrhagic Telangiectasia (Osler-Weber-Rendu)** Autosomal dominant disorder characterized by multiple AVMs in the liver and lungs. It leads to cirrhosis and a *massively dilated hepatic artery*.

Trivia: The lung AVMs set you up for brain abscess.

- Liver Infections -

Infection of the liver can be thought of as either viral, abscess (pyogenic or amoebic), fungal, parasitic, or granulomatous. As previously mentioned, the long intra-hepatic course of the right portal vein results in most hematogenous infection favoring the right hepatic lobe.

Viral: Hepatitis which is chronic in B and C, and acute with the rest. A point of trivia is that **HCC in the setting of hepatitis can occur in the acute form of Hep B** (as well as chronic). Obviously, chronic hep C increases risk for HCC. On ultrasound the "starry sky" appearance can be seen. Although, this is non-specific and basically just the result of liver edema making the fat surrounding the portal triads look brighter than normal.

Pyogenic: These can mimic cysts. For the purpose of multiple choice, *a single abscess is Klebsiella, and multiple are E. Coli.* The presence of gas is highly suggestive of pyogenic abscess.

"Double Target" sign with central low density, rim enhancement, surrounded by more low density is the classic sign of a liver abscess on CT.

Next Step Amebic Abscess: A special situation (potentially testable) is the amebic abscess in the left lobe. Those needs to be emergently drained (they can rupture into the pericardium).

🐝 Infection Buzzwords 🐝	
Viral Hepatitis	Starry Sky (US)
Pyogenic Abscess	Double Target (CT)
Candida	Bull's Eye (US) ⬤
Amoebic Abscess	"Extra Hepatic Extension"
Hydatid Disease	Water Lily, Sand Storm CT US
Schistosomiasis	Tortoise Shell

- Diffuse Liver Processes -

Fatty Liver: Very common in America. Can be focal (next to gallbladder or ligamentum teres), can be diffuse, or can be diffuse with sparing. You can call it a few different ways.

For CT: If it's a non-contrast study, 40 HU is a slam dunk. If it's contrasted, some people say you can NEVER call it. Others say it's ok if (a) it's a good portal venous phase (b) the HU is less than 100, and (c) it's 25 H.U. less than the spleen.

On US: If the liver is brighter than the right kidney you can call it. Hepatosteatosis is a fat liver. NASH (hepatitis from a fat liver) has abnormal LFTs.

On MRI: Two standard deviation difference between in and out of phase imaging. Remember the drop out is on the out of phase images (india ink ones - done at T.E 2.2 ms - assuming 1.5T).

Fuckery: This signal drop out assumes there is more water than fat in the liver. As such, the degree of <u>signal loss is maximum when the fat infiltration is 50%</u> (exactly 1:1 signal loss). When the percentage of fat grows larger than 50% you will actually see a less significant signal loss on out of phase imaging, relative to that maximum 50%.

What causes it? McDonalds, Burger King, and Taco Bell. Additional causes include chemotherapy (breast cancer), steroids, cystic fibrosis.

Hemochromatosis: Iron overload. They can show this two main ways:

(1) The first is just liver and spleen being T1 and T2 dark.
(2) The second (and more likely) way this will be shown is *in and out of phase changes the opposite of those seen in hepatic steatosis*. **Low signal on <u>in phase</u>, and high signal on out of phase. ("Iron on In-phase")**

Watch out now — this is the opposite of the fat drop out
**FAT - Drop out on OUT of phase (india ink one - T.E. 2.2 ms) - 1.5 T
**IRON - Drop out on IN phase (non india ink one - T.E. 4.4 ms) - 1.5 T

The second main piece of trivia is to tell *primary vs secondary.*

Primary is the inherited type, caused by more GI uptake, with resulting iron overload. The key point is the pancreas is involved and the spleen is spared.

Secondary is the result of either chronic inflammation or multiple transfusions. The body reacts by trying the "Eat the Iron," with the reticuloendothelial system. The key point is the pancreas is spared and the spleen is not.

"Primary = Pancreas" , "Secondary = Spleen"

Hemochromatosis	
Primary	**Secondary**
Genetic - increased absorption	Acquired - chronic illness, and multiple transfusions
Liver, **Pancreas**	Liver, **Spleen**
Heart, Thyroid, Pituitary	

Budd Chiari Syndrome: Classic multiple choice scenario is a pregnant woman, but can occur in any situation where you are hypercoagulable (*most common cause is idiopathic*). The result of hepatic vein thrombosis.

The characteristic findings of Budd-Chiari syndrome include hepatic venous outflow obstruction, intrahepatic and systemic collateral veins, and large regenerative (hyperplastic) nodules in a dysmorphic liver. The caudate lobe is often massively enlarged (spared from separate drainage into the IVC). In the acute phase, the liver will show the *classic "flip-flop pattern"* on portal phase with low attenuation central, and high peripherally. The liver has been described as "nutmeg" with an inhomogeneous mottled appearance, and delayed enhancement of the periphery of the liver.

Who gets a "Nutmeg Liver" ???
- Budd Chiari
- Hepatic Veno-occlusive disease
- Right Heart Failure (Hepatic Congestion)
- Constrictive Pericarditis

Arterial: Central Enhancement Peripheral Minimal Portal V: Central Washout Peripheral Enhancement

Regenerative (hyperplastic) nodules can be difficult to distinguish from multifocal hepatocellular carcinoma. They are bright on T1 and typically dark or iso on T2. Multiple big (>10cm) and small (<4cm) nodules in the setting of Budd-Chiari suggest a benign process. T2 dark also helps (HCC is usually T2 bright).

Presentation can be acute or chronic. Acute from thrombus into the hepatic vein or IVC. These guys will present with **rapid onset ascites**. Chronic from fibrosis of the intrahepatic veins, presumably from inflammation.

Who gets massive caudate lobe hypertrophy???
- Budd Chiari
- Primary Sclerosing Cholangitis
- Primary Biliary Cirrhosis

Hepatic Veno-occlusive Disease: This is a form of Budd Chiari that occurs from occlusion of the small hepatic venules. It is endemic in Jamaica (from Alkaloid bush tea). In the US it's typically the result of XRT and chemotherapy. The main hepatic veins and IVC will be patent, but portal waveforms will be abnormal (slow, reversed, or to-and fro).

—

Passive Congestion: Passive hepatic congestion is caused by stasis of blood within the liver due to compromise of hepatic drainage. It is a common complication of congestive heart failure and constrictive pericarditis. It is essentially the result of elevated CVP transmitted from the right atrium to the hepatic veins.

Findings include:
- Refluxed contrast into the hepatic veins
- Increased portal venous pulsatility
- Nutmeg liver

- Misc Liver Conditions -

Portal Vein Thrombosis: Occurs in hypercoaguable states (cancer, dehydration, etc...). Can lead to *cavernous transformation*, with the development of a bunch of serpiginous vessels in the porta hepatis which may reconstitute the right and left portal veins. This takes like 12 months to happen (*it proves portal vein is chronically occluded*).

Pseudo Cirrhosis: Treated breast cancer mets to the liver can cause contour changes that mimic cirrhosis. Specifically, multifocal liver retraction and enlargement of the caudate has been described. Why this is specific for breast cancer is not currently known, as other mets to the liver don't produce this reaction.

Cryptogenic Cirrhosis: Essentially cirrhosis of unknown cause. Most of these cases are probably the result of nonalcoholic fatty liver disease.

Liver Transplant: The liver has great ability to regenerate and may double in size in as little as 3 weeks, making it ideal for partial donation. Hepatitis C is the most common disease requiring transplantation (followed by EtOH liver disease and cryptogenic cirrhosis). In adults, right lobes (segments 5-8) are most commonly implants. This is the opposite of pediatric transplants, which usually donates segments 2-3. The modern surgery has four connections (IVC, artery, portal vein, CBD).

Contraindications include, extrahepatic malignancy, advanced cardiac disease, advanced pulmonary disease, or active substance abuse, Portal HTN is NOT a true contraindication although it does increase the difficulty of the surgery and increase mortality.

Normal Transplant US
- Normal Doppler should have a RAPID systolic upstroke
  - Diastolic -> Systolic in less than 80msec (0.08 seconds)
- Resistive Index is Normally between 0.5 – 0.7
- Hepatic Artery Peak Velocity should be < 200 cm/sec

Syndrome of Impending Thrombosis
3-10 days post transplant
(1st) Initial Normal Waveform
(2nd) No diastolic flow
(3rd) Dampening Systolic flow
Tardus Parvus
RI < 0.5
(4th) Loss of Hepatic Waveform

As mentioned before, the normal liver gets 70% blood flow from the portal vein, making it the key player. In the transplanted liver, the *hepatic artery is the king* and is the primary source of blood flow for the bile ducts (which undergo necrosis with hepatic artery failure). Hepatic artery thrombosis comes in two flavors: early (< 15 days), and later (years). The late form is associated with chronic rejection and sepsis.

Trivia: Tardus Parvus is more likely secondary to stenosis than thrombosis

- Biliary -

Jaundice: You always think about common duct stone, but the most common etiology is actually from a benign stricture (post traumatic from surgery or biliary intervention).

Bacterial Cholangitis: Hepatic abscess can develop secondary to cholangitis, usually as the result of stasis (so think stones). The triad of jaundice, fever, and right upper quadrant pain is the step 1 question.

Primary Sclerosing Cholangitis (PSC): Chronic cholestatic liver disease of unknown etiology characterized by progressive inflammation which leads to multifocal strictures of the intra and /or extrahepatic bile ducts. The disease often results in cirrhosis, and is **strongly associated with cholangiocarcinoma**. The buzzword for the **cirrhotic pattern is "central regenerative hypertrophy"**. It is associated with inflammatory bowel disease (Ulcerative Colitis 80%, Crohn's 20%). It is an indication for transplant, with a post transplant recurrence of about 20%.

> Dilated intrahepatic bile ducts is very rare in all forms of cirrhosis
>
> EXCEPT
>
> Primary Sclerosing Cholangitis

 PSC Buzzwords:
- "Withered Tree" - The appearance on MRCP, from abrupt narrowing of the branches
- "Beaded Appearance" - Strictures + Focal Dilations

AIDS Cholangiopathy: Infection of the biliary epithelium (*classically Cryptosporidium*) can cause ductal disease in patients with AIDS. The appearance mimics PSC with intrahepatic and/or extrahepatic multifocal strictures.

The classic association/finding is <u>papillary stenosis</u> (which occurs 60% of the time).

THIS *vs* THAT: AIDS Cholangiopathy *vs* Primary Sclerosing Cholangitis	
AIDS	**PSC**
Focal Strictures of the extrahepatic duct > 2cm	Extrahepatic strictures rarely > 5mm
Absent saccular deformities of the ducts	Has saccular deformities of the ducts
Associated Papillary Stenosis	

182

Oriental Cholangitis *(Recurrent pyogenic cholangitis):* Common in Southeast Asia (hence the culturally insensitive name). They always show it as **dilated ducts that are full of pigmented stones.**

🐝 **Buzzword:** "straight rigid intrahepatic ducts."

The cause of the disease is not known, but it may be associated with clonorchiasis, ascariasis, and nutritional deficiency. These guys don't do as well with endoscopic decompression and often need surgical decompression.

> The anatomically longer, flatter left biliary system tends to make the disease burden <u>left dominant</u> *(the opposite of hematogenous processes which favor the right lobe).*

Remember this is a major risk factor for cholangiocarcinoma in the East.

Primary Biliary Cirrhosis: An autoimmune disease that results in the destruction of small & medium bile ducts *(intra not extra).* It primarily affects **middle-aged women**, who are often asymptomatic. In the early disease, normal bile ducts help distinguish it from PSC. In later stages, there is irregular dilation of the intrahepatic ducts, with **normal extrahepatic ducts.** There is increased risk of HCC. If caught early it has an excellent prognosis and responds to medical therapy with ursodeoxycholic acid. The step 1 trivia is "**antimitochondrial antibodies (AMA)**" which are present 95% of the time.

Long Common Channel:
An anatomic variant in which the common bile and pancreatic duct fuse prematurely at the level of the pancreatic head (prior to the sphincter of Oddi complex).

The testable consequence is the <u>increased incidence of pancreatitis</u> - as reflux of enzymes is more common.

There is also an association with Type 1 choledochocysts.

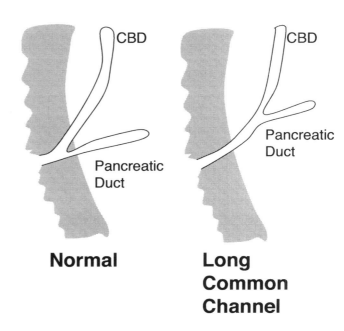

Normal

Long Common Channel

Choledochal Cysts / Caroli's: Choledochal cysts are congenital dilation of the bile ducts –classified into 5 types by some dude named Todani.

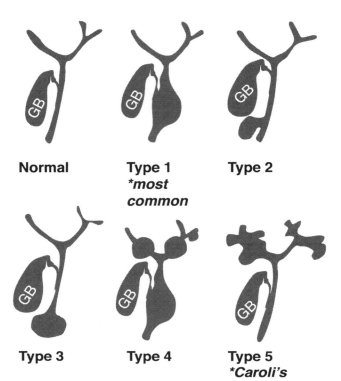

The high yield trivia is type 1 is focal dilation of the CBD and is by far the most common.

Type 2 and 3 are super rare. Type 2 is basically a diverticulum of the bile duct.

Type 3 is a "choledochocele."

Type 4 is both intra and extra.

Type 5 is Caroli's, and is intrahepatic only.

Caroli's is an AR disease *associated with polycystic kidney disease and medullary sponge kidney*. The hallmark is intrahepatic duct dilation, that is large and saccular. **Buzzword is "central dot sign"** which corresponds to the portal vein surrounded by dilated bile ducts.

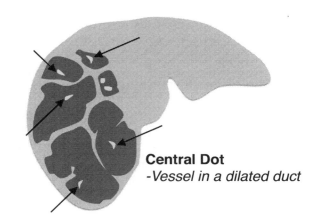

Central Dot
-*Vessel in a dilated duct*

Complications
- **Cholangiocarcinoma**
- *Cirrhosis*
- *Cholangitis*
- *Intraductal Stones*

 Gamesmanship: If they give you imaging of dilated biliary ducts and a history of repeated cholangitis, think choledocal cyst. These things get stones in them and can be recurrently infected.

- Ductal High Yield Summary -

Caroli's
-*Communicates with the ducts*
-*Type 5 Cyst*
-*Central Dot Sign (on CT, MR, US)*
-*Associated with Polycystic Kidney,*
Medullary Sponge Kidney,
Cholangiocarcinoma

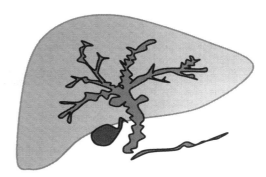

Primary Sclerosing Cholangitis
-*40 year old Male with U.C.*
-*Withering Tree*
-*Beading*
-*Mild Dilation*
-*Strongly Associated with Ulcerative*
Colitis & Cholangiocarcinoma

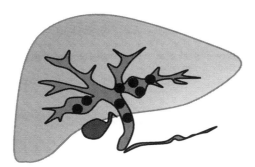

**Oriental Cholangiohepatitis
(Recurrent Pyogenic)**
-*Associations with clonorchiasis,*
ascariasis
-*Lots of Stones*
-*Favors the left ductal system*
- *Strongly Associated with*
Cholangiocarcinoma

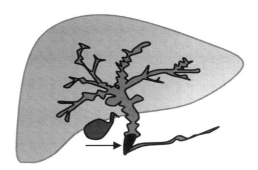

AIDS Cholangiopathy
-*Related to* Cryptosporidium or
cytomegalovirus.
-*Segmental Strictures (looks like PSC)*
-*Ducts look like PSC + Papillary*
Stenosis
- *Associated with Cholangiocarcinoma*

Association:	**Cholangiocarcinoma vs B9 Strictures:**
If you can't remember what the association is, and it's ductal pathology, always guess Cholangiocarcinoma.	• CA Strictures tends to be long, with "shouldering." • B9 strictures tend to be abrupt and short.

SECTION 4: Gallbladder

Normal Gallbladder

The normal gallbladder is found inferior to the interlobar fissure between the right and left lobe. The size varies depending on the last meal, but is supposed to be < 4 x < 10cm. The wall thickness should be < 3mm. The lumen should be anechoic.

Variants / Congenital

Phrygian cap: A phrygian cap is seen when the GB folds on itself. It means nothing.

Intrahepatic Gallbladder: Variations in gallbladder location are rare, but the intrahepatic gallbladder is probably the most frequently recognized variant. Most are found right above the interlobar fissure.

Duplicated Gallbladder: It can happen.

Duct of Luschka: An accessory cystic duct. This can cause a big problem (persistent bile leak) after cholecystectomy. There are several subtypes which is not likely to be tested.

Accessory Subvesicular
(most common)

Hepaticocystic

Pathology

GB Wall Thickening (> 3mm): Very non-specific. Can occur from biliary (Cholecystitis, AIDS, PSC…) or non-biliary causes (hepatitis, heart failure, cirrhosis, etc.…).

Gallstones: Gallstones are found in 10% of asymptomatic patients/ Most (75%) are cholesterol, the other 25% are pigmented. They cast shadows.

Reasons a stone might not cast a shadow
- It's not a stone
- It's a stone, but < 3mm in size
- The sonographer is an amateur (Bush league psyche-out stuff. Laughable, man)

-Gallbladder Shadowing-

(1) Gallbladder full of stones
   Clean shadowing.

(2) Porcelain Gallbladder
   Variable shadowing

(3) Emphysematous Cholecystitis
   Dirty shadowing.

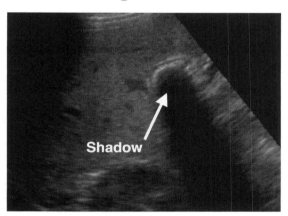

Shadow

Mirizzi Syndrome: This occurs when the common hepatic duct is obstructed secondary to an impacted cystic duct stone. The stone can eventually erode into the CHD or GI tract.

Key point is the increased co-incidence of *gallbladder CA (5x more risk)* with Mirizzi.

Another key piece of trivia is that Mirizzi **occurs more in people with a low cystic duct insertion (normal variant),** allowing for a more parallel course and closer proximity to the CHD.

Mirizzi
-Cystic Duct Stone Obstructing CBD

Adenomyomatosis: Results from hyperplasia of the wall with formation of intramural mucosal diverticula (Rokitansky-Aschoff sinuses) which penetrate into the wall of the gallbladder. These diverticula become filled with cholesterol crystals – which manifest from the unique acoustic signature as comet-tail artifact (highly specific for adenomyomatosis).

Comes in 3 flavors: Generalized (diffuse), Segmental (annular), and Fundal (localized or adenomyoma). The Localized form can't be differentiated from GB cancer.

 Gamesmanship: Don't be tricked into selecting *"Adenomyosis"* as a distractor. That shit is in the uterus. Remember the larger word is in the smaller organ. Or, you can think about the two Ms in **M**yo**M**at - turned inward sorta looks like a gallbladder.

Porcelain Gallbladder:

- Extensive wall calcification.
- The key point is increased risk of GB Cancer.
- These are surgically removed.

Gallbladder Polyps:

These can be cholesterol (by far the most common), or non cholesterol (adenomas, papillomas). Cholesterol polpys aren't real polyps, but instead are essentially enlarged papillary fronds full of lipid filled macrophages, that are attached to the wall by a stalk.

The non-cholesterol subtypes are almost always solitary and are typically larger. The larger polyps may have Doppler flow. They are NOT mobile and do NOT shadow. *Once they get to be 1 cm, people start taking them out.*

THIS vs **THAT**: Gallbladder Polyps	
Benign	**Malignant**
< 5mm *these are nearly always cholesterol polyps	> 1cm *between 5mm-10mm usually get followed for growth
Pedunculated	Sessile
Multiple	Solitary
Comet Tail Artifact on Ultrasound (seen in cholesterol polyps)	Enhancement on CT/ MRI greater than the adjacent gallbladder wall. Flow on Doppler.

Gallbladder Cancer:

- Classic vignette would be an elderly women with nonspecific RUQ pain, weight loss, anorexia and a long standing history of gallstones, PSC, or large gallbladder polyps.
- Most GB cancers are associated with gallstones (found in 85% of cases)
- Mirizzi syndrome has a well described increased risk of GB cancer
- Other risk factors include smoldering inflammatory processes (PSC, Chronic Cholecystitis, Porcelain Gallbladder), and large polyps ("large" = bigger than 1cm)
- Unless the cancer is in the fundus (which can cause biliary obstruction) they often present late and have horrible outcomes with 80% found with direct tumor invasion of the liver or portal nodes at the time of diagnosis.

SECTION 5:
Hepatic Doppler

Brief introduction to terminology.

- *"Duplex"* means color.
- *"Spectral"* means color with a waveform.

- Concept of Arterial Resistance -

Some organs require continuous flow (brain), whereas others do not (muscles). The body is smart enough to understand this, and will make alterations in resistance / flow to preserve energy. When an organ needs to be "on," its arteriolar bed dilates, and the waveform becomes low resistance. This allows the organ to be appropriately perfused. When an organ goes to "power save" mode, its arterioles constrict, the waveform switches to high resistance, and blood flow is diverted to other more vital organs.

To help quantify this low resistance high resistance thing, we use this **"Resistive Index (RI)"** - which is defined **as V1-V2 / V1.**

Just remember that things that need blood all the time, will have continuous diastolic flow – and thus a low resistance wave form.

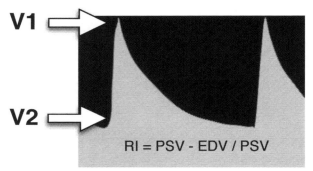

RI = PSV - EDV / PSV

What is this "Tardus Parvus" ?

Tardus: Refers to a slowed systolic upstroke. This can be measured by acceleration time, the time from end diastole to the first systolic peak. An acceleration time > 0.07 sec correlates with >50% stenosis of the renal artery

Parvus: Refers to decreased systolic velocity. This can be measured by calculating the acceleration index, the change in velocity from end diastole to the first systolic peak.

An acceleration index < 3.0 m/sec-correlates with >50% stenosis of the renal artery

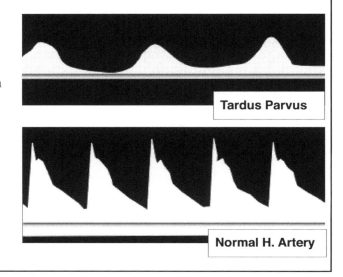

Tardus Parvus

Normal H. Artery

- Understanding Stenosis -

The vocabulary of "Upstream vs Downstream" is somewhat confusing. Try and remember, that the flow of blood defines the direction.

- Upstream = Blood that has NOT yet passed through the stenosis
- Downstream = Blood that has passed through the area of stenosis

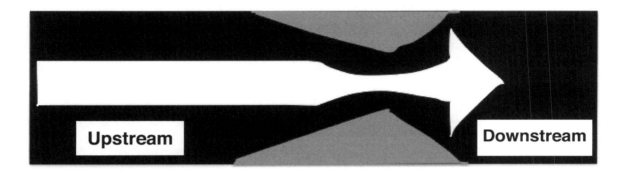

So there are direct and indirect signs of stenosis.

<u>Direct Signs:</u> The direct signs are those found at the stenosis itself and they include elevated peak systolic velocity and spectral broadening (immediate post stenotic).

<u>Indirect Signs:</u> The indirect signs are going to be tardus parvus (downstream) – with time to peak (systolic acceleration) > 70msec. The RI downstream will be low (< 0.5) because the liver is starved for blood. The RI upstream will be elevated (> 0.7) because that blood needs to overcome the area of stenosis.

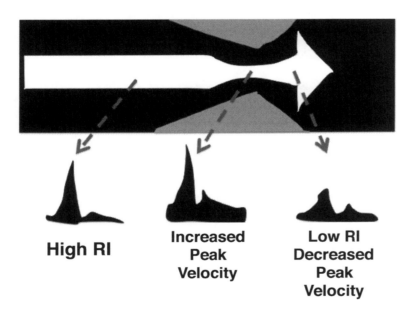

High RI   **Increased Peak Velocity**   **Low RI Decreased Peak Velocity**

- Hepatic Veins -

Flow in the hepatic veins is complex, with alternating forward and backward flow. The bulk of the flow should be forward "antegrade" (liver -> heart). Things that mess with the waveform are going to be pressure changes in the right heart which are transmitted to the hepatic veins (CHF, Tricuspid Regurg) or compression of the veins directly (cirrhosis).

Anything that increases right atrial pressure (atrial contraction) will cause the wave to slope upward. "A" represents atrial contraction.

Anything that decreases right atrial pressure will cause the wave to slope downward.

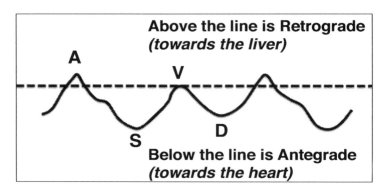

Above the line is Retrograde *(towards the liver)*

Below the line is Antegrade *(towards the heart)*

Abnormal Hepatic Vein Waveforms can manifest in one of three main categories:

(1) More Pulsatile

(2) Less Pulsatile

(3) Absent = Budd Chiari

Increased HV Pulsatility	Decreased HV Pulsatility
Tricuspid Regurg	**Cirrhosis**
Right Sided CHF	Hepatic Venous Outflow Obstruction (any cause)

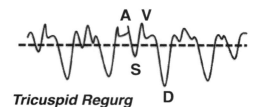
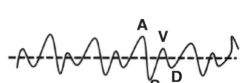

- Portal Vein -

Flow in the portal vein should always be towards the liver (antegrade). You can see some normal cardiac variability from hepatic venous pulsatility transmitted through the hepatic sinusoids. Velocity in the normal portal vein is between 20-40 cm/s. The waveform should be a gentle undulation , always remaining above the baseline.

You have three main patterns:

(1) Normal

(2) Pulsatile

(3) Reversed

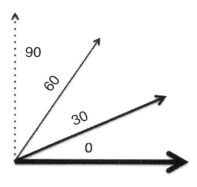

NORMAL

PULSATILE

REVERSED

Causes of Portal Vein Pulsatility: **Right-sided CHF, Tricuspid Regurg, Cirrhosis** with Vascular AP shunting.

Causes of Portal Vein Reversed Flow: The big one is **Portal HTN** (any cause).

Absent Flow: This could be considered a fourth pattern. It's seen in thrombosis, tumor invasion, and stagnant flow from terrible portal HTN.

Slow Flow: Velocities less than 15 cm/s. Portal HTN is the most common cause. Additional causes are grouped by location:

- Pre – Portal Vein Thrombosis
- Intra – Cirrhosis (any cause)
- Post – Right-sided Heart Failure, Tricuspid Regurg, Budd-Chiari

 Final Doppler Trivia:

An ultra-common quiz question is to ask **"what should the Doppler angle be?"** Now even though ultrasound physics is covered in more detail in the dedicated section of the War Machine this is a high yield enough point to warrant repetition. **The answer is "less than 60. "**

Why? Doppler strength follows the cosine of the angle. For example, Cos 90 = 0, Cos 60 = 0.5, Cos 0 = 1.0 - the doppler strength follows the Cos.

SECTION 6: Pancreas

Trivia regarding the pancreas can be broadly clustered into: Solid Lesions, Cystic Lesions, Pancreatitis, and Misc Trivia (mostly developmental stuff).

> **Classic US Trivia:** The Pancreatic Echogenicity should be GREATER than the normal liver.

- Misc Pancreas Trivia -

Anatomy: The pancreas is a retroperitoneal structure (the tail may be intraperitoneal).

Cystic Fibrosis: The pancreas is involved in 85-90% of CF patients. Inspissated secretions cause proximal duct obstruction leading to the two main changes in CF:
(1) Fibrosis (decreased T1 and T2 signal)
(2) Fatty replacement (increased T1) - the more common of the two

Patients with CF, who are diagnosed as adults, tend to have more pancreas problems than those diagnosed as children. Just remember that those with residual pancreatic exocrine function tend to have bouts of recurrent acute pancreatitis (they keep getting clogged up with thick secretions). Small (1-3 mm) pancreatic cysts are common.

High Yield Trivia:
- *Complete fatty replacement* is the most common imaging finding in adult CF
- Markedly enlarged with fatty replacement has been termed lipomatous **pseudohypertrophy of the pancreas**. *This is a buzzword.
- *Fibrosing Colonopathy:* Wall thickening of the proximal colon as a complication of enzyme replacement therapy.

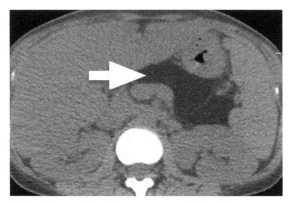

CF - Fatty Replacement of the Pancreas

Shwachman-Diamond Syndrome: The 2nd most common cause of pancreatic insufficiency in kids (CF #1). Basically, it's a kid with diarrhea, short stature (metaphyseal chondroplasia), and eczema. *Will also cause lipomatous pseudohypertrophy of the pancreas.*

Pancreatic Lipomatosis:

Most common pathologic condition involving the pancreas. The most common cause in childhood is CF (in adults it's Burger King).

Additional causes worth knowing are Cushing Syndrome, Chronic Steroid Use, Hyperlipidemia, and Shwachman-Diamond Syndrome.

THIS vs THAT: Pancreatic Agenesis vs Pancreatic-Lipomatosis	
Agenesis	**Lipomatosis**
Does NOT have a duct	Does have a duct

Dorsal Pancreatic Agenesis: - All you need to know is that (1) this sets you up for diabetes *(most of your beta cells are in the tail)*, and (2) it's associated with polysplenia.

Annular Pancreas: Essentially an embryologic screw up *(failure of ventral bud to rotate with the duodenum),* that results in encasement of the duodenum. Results in a rare cause of duodenal obstruction (10%), that typically presents as duodenal obstruction in children and pancreatitis in adults. Can also be associated with other vague symptoms (post-prandial fullness, "symptoms of peptic ulcer disease", etc…).

- Remember in adults this can present with pancreatitis (the ones that present earlier - in kids - are the ones that obstruct).
- On imaging, look for an annular duct encircling the descending duodenum.

Pancreatic Trauma: The pancreas sits in front of the vertebral body, so it's susceptible to getting smashed in blunt trauma. Basically, **the only thing that matters is integrity of the duct.** If the duct is damaged, they need to go to the OR. The most common delayed complication is pancreatic fistula (10-20%), followed by abscess formation. Signs of injury can be subtle, and may include focal pancreatic enlargement or adjacent stranding/fluid.

Imaging Pearls:
- Remember it can be subtle with just focal enlargement of the pancreas
- If you see low attenuation fluid separating two portions of the enhancing pancreatic parenchyma this is a laceration, NOT contusion.
- The presence of fluid surrounding the pancreas is not specific, it could be from injury or just aggressive hydration — on the test they will have to show you the liver and IVC to prove it's aggressive fluid resuscitation.

High Yield: Traumatic Pancreatitis in a kid too young to ride a bike = NAT.

Suspected Pancreatic Duct Injury? - Next Step - MRCP or ERCP

- Pancreatitis -

Acute Pancreatitis:

Etiology: By far the most common causes are gallstones and EtOH which combined make up 80% of the cases in the real world. However, for the purpose of multiple choice tests, a bite from the native scorpion of the island of Trinidad and Tobago is more likely to be the etiology. Additional causes include ERCP (*which usually results in a mild course*), medications (*classically valproic acid*), trauma (*the most common cause in a child*), pancreatic cancer, infectious (*post viral in children*), hypercalcemia, hyperlipidemia, autoimmune pancreatitis, pancreatic divisum, groove (para-duodenal) pancreatitis, tropic pancreatitis, and parasite induced.

Clinical Outcomes: Prognosis can be estimated with the "Balthazar Score." Essentially, you can think about pancreatitis as "mild" *(no necrosis)* or "severe" *(having necrosis)*. Patients with necrosis don't start doing terrible until they get infected, then the mortality is like 50-70%.

Key Point: Outcomes are directly correlated with the degree of pancreatic necrosis.

Severe Pancreatitis: Severe acute pancreatitis has a biphasic course. With the first two weeks being a pro-inflammatory phase. This is a sterile response in which infection rarely occurs. The third and fourth weeks transition to an anti-inflammatory period in which the risk of translocated intestinal flora and the subsequent development of infection increases.

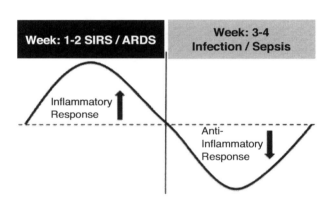

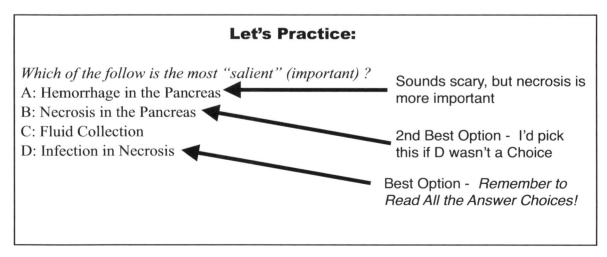

Let's Practice:

Which of the follow is the most "salient" (important) ?
A: Hemorrhage in the Pancreas — Sounds scary, but necrosis is more important
B: Necrosis in the Pancreas
C: Fluid Collection — 2nd Best Option - I'd pick this if D wasn't a Choice
D: Infection in Necrosis — Best Option - *Remember to Read All the Answer Choices!*

VOCAB - Radiologist LOVE to Argue over Words — *therefore high yield*

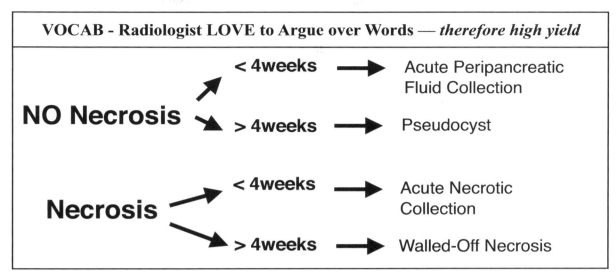

NO Necrosis
- < 4weeks → Acute Peripancreatic Fluid Collection
- > 4weeks → Pseudocyst

Necrosis
- < 4weeks → Acute Necrotic Collection
- > 4weeks → Walled-Off Necrosis

Vascular Complications:
- Splenic Vein and Portal Vein Thrombosis
  - *Isolated gastric varices can be seen secondary to splenic vein occlusion*
- Pseudo-aneurysm of the GDA and Splenic Artery

Non-Vascular Complications:
- Abscess, Infection, etc… as discussed
- Gas, as a characteristic sign of an infected fluid collection, is detected in only 20% of cases of pancreatic abscesses.

Random Imaging Pearl:
- On Ultrasound, an inflamed pancreas will be *hypoechoic* (edematous) when compared to the liver (opposite of normal).

- Pancreatic Divisum –

Anatomy Refresher: There are two ducts, a major (Wirsung), and a minor (Santorini). Under "normal" conditions the major duct will drain in the inferior of the two duodenal papilla (major papilla). The minor duct will drain into the superior of the two duodenal papilla (minor papilla). The way I remember this is that "Santorini drains Superior", and "Santorini is Small," i.e. the minor duct.

Pancreatic Divisum is the most common anatomic variant of the human pancreas, and occurs when the main portion of the pancreas is drained by the minor or accessory papilla. The clinical relevance is an increased risk of pancreatitis.

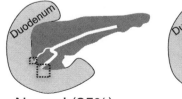

Normal (85%)
-Bifid System with Rudimentary Dorsal Duct-

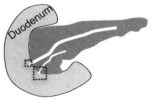

Divisum (~15%)

- Chronic Pancreatitis -

CP represents the end result of prolonged inflammatory change leading to irreversible fibrosis of the gland. Acute pancreatitis and chronic pancreatitis are thought of as different disease processes, and most cases of acute pancreatitis do not result in chronic disease. So, acute doesn't have to lead to chronic (and usually doesn't), but chronic can still have recurrent acute.

Etiology: Same as acute pancreatitis, the **most common causes are chronic alcohol abuse and cholelithiasis which together result in about 90% of the cases. (EtOH is #1)**

Imaging Findings: Findings can be thought of as early or late:

Early:
- Loss of T1 signal *(pancreas is normally the brightest T1 structure in the body)*
- Delayed Enhancement
- Dilated Side Branches

Late:
- Commonly small, uniformly atrophic – but can have focal enlargement
- Pseudocyst formation (30%)
- **Dilation and beading of the pancreatic duct with calcifications**
  ** *most characteristic finding of CP.*

THIS vs THAT: Chronic Pancreatitis Duct Dilation vs Pancreatic Malignancy Duct Dilation	
CP	**Cancer**
Dilation is Irregular	Dilation is uniform *(usually)*
Duct is < 50% of the AP gland diameter	Duct is > 50% of the AP gland diameter *(obstructive atrophy)*

Complications: Pancreatic cancer *(20 years of CP = 6% risk of Cancer)* is the most crucial complication in CP and is the biggest diagnostic challenge because focal enlargement of the gland induced by a fibrotic inflammatory pseudotumor may be indistinguishable from pancreatic carcinoma.

Uncommon Types and Causes of Pancreatitis

Autoimmune Pancreatitis	Associated with elevated IgG4	Absence of Attack Symptoms	Responds to steroids	Sausage Shaped Pancreas, capsule like delayed rim enhancement around gland (like a scar). **No duct dilation. No calcifications.**
Groove Pancreatitis	Looks like a pancreatic head Cancer - but with little or no biliary obstruction.	Less likely to cause obstructive jaundice (relative to pancreatic CA)	Duodenal stenosis and /or strictures of the CBD in 50% of the cases	Soft tissue within the pancreaticoduodenal groove, with or without delayed enhancement
Tropic Pancreatitis	Young Age at onset, associated with malnutrition	Increased risk of adenocarcinoma		Multiple large calculi within a dilated pancreatic duct
Hereditary Pancreatitis	Young Age at Onset	Increased risk of adenocarcinoma	SPINK-1 gene	Similar to Tropic Pancreatitis
Ascaris Induced	Most commonly implicated parasite in pancreatitis			Worm may be seen within the bile ducts

When I Say - Autoimmune Pancreatitis

I Say Autoimmune Pancreatitis	You Say IgG4
I Say IgG4	Autoimmune Pancreatitis Retroperitoneal Fibrosis Sclerosing Cholangitis Inflammatory Pseudotumor Riedel's Thyroiditis

THIS vs THAT:
Autoimmune Pancreatitis vs Chronic Pancreatitis

Autoimmune Pancreatitis	Chronic Pancreatitis
No ductal dilation	Ductal Dilation
No calcifications	Ductal Calcifications

- Cystic Pancreatic Lesions -

Pseudocyst: When you see a cystic lesion in the pancreas, by far the *most common cause is going to be an inflammatory pseudocyst,* either from acute pancreatitis or chronic pancreatitis.

Simple Cysts: True epithelial lined cysts are rare, and tend to occur with syndromes such as VHL, Polycystic Kidney Disease, and Cystic Fibrosis.

Serous Cystadenoma (Grandma)*:* The former term "microcystic adenoma" helps me think of a little old lady, which is appropriate for a lesion primarily found in elderly ladies. The lesion is benign, and classically described as a heterogeneous, mixed-density lesion made up of multiple small cysts, which resembles a sponge. They are more commonly (70%) located in the pancreatic head (*mucinous is almost always in the body or tail*). An additional key distinction is that it does NOT communicate with the pancreatic duct (*IPMNs do*). About 20% of the time they will have the classic central scar, with or without central calcifications (*mucinous calcifications are peripheral*).

Rarely, they can be unilocular. When you see a unilocular cyst with a lobulated contour located in the head of the pancreas, you should think about this more rare unilocular macrocystic serous cystadenoma subtype.

Trivia: Serous Cystadenoma is associated with Von Hippel Lindau
Memory Aid: "GRANDMA Serous is the HEAD of the household"

Mucinous Cystic Neoplasm (Mother)*:* This pre-malignant lesion is "always" found in women, usually in their 50s. All are considered pre-malignant and need to come out. They are found in the body and tail (*serous was more common in the head*). There is generally no communication with the pancreatic duct (*IPMNs will communicate*). Peripheral calcifications are seen in about 25% of cases (*serous was more central*). They are typically unilocular. When mutlilocular, individual cystic spaces tend to be larger than 2 cm in diameter (*serous spaces are typically smaller than 2 cm*).

Memory Aid: "MUCINOUS in the MOTHER"

Solid Pseudopapillary Tumor of the Pancreas - (Daughter)*:* Very rare, low grade malignant tumor that occurs almost exclusively in young (30s) females (usually Asian or Black). It is typically large at presentation, has a predilection for the tail, and has a "thick capsule." Similar to a hemangioma it may demonstrate progressive fill-in of the solid portions.

IPMN – <u>I</u>ntraductal <u>P</u>apillary <u>M</u>ucinous <u>N</u>eoplasm: These guys are mucin-producing tumors that arise from the duct epithelium. They can be either side branch, main branch, or both.

Side Branch *"The pulmonary nodule of the pancreas"*	Main Branch	Features Concerning For Malignancy
•Common and usually meaningless •Typically appear as a small cystic mass, often in the head or uncinate process •If large amounts of mucin are produced it may result in main duct enlargement •Lesions less than 3cm, are usually benign	•Produces diffuse dilation of the main duct •Atrophy of the gland and dystrophic calcifications may be seen — *mimicking Chronic Pancreatitis* •**Have a much higher % of malignancy compared to side branch** •All Main Ducts are considered malignant, and resection should be considered	•Main duct >10 mm (some sources say 1.5 cm) •Diffuse or multifocal involvement •Enhancing nodules •Solid hypovascular mass

- Cystic Pancreatic Lesion Summary -

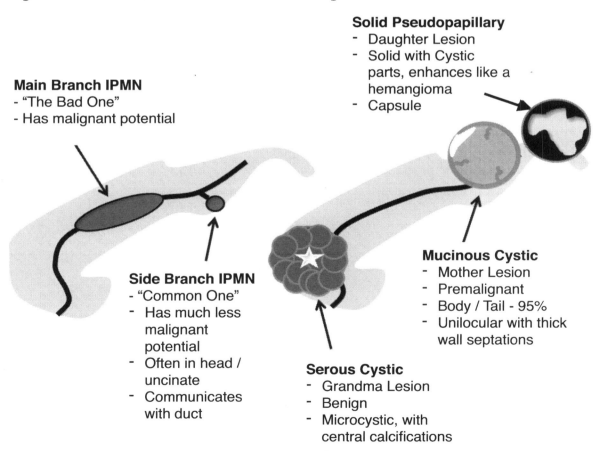

Solid Pseudopapillary
- Daughter Lesion
- Solid with Cystic parts, enhances like a hemangioma
- Capsule

Main Branch IPMN
- "The Bad One"
- Has malignant potential

Side Branch IPMN
- "Common One"
- Has much less malignant potential
- Often in head / uncinate
- Communicates with duct

Mucinous Cystic
- Mother Lesion
- Premalignant
- Body / Tail - 95%
- Unilocular with thick wall septations

Serous Cystic
- Grandma Lesion
- Benign
- Microcystic, with central calcifications

- Solid Pancreatic Lesions -

Pancreatic Cancer basically comes in two flavors. (1) Ductal Adenocarcinoma – *which is hypovascular* and (2) Islet Cell / Neuroendocrine *which is hypervascular.*

Ductal Adenocarcinoma: In the setting of a multiple choice test, the finding of an enlarged gallbladder with painless jaundice is highly suspicious for pancreatic adenocarcinoma, especially when combined with migratory thrombophlebitis (*Trousseau's syndrome*). The peak incidence is in the 7th or 8th decade. The strongest risk factor is smoking.

Approximately two-thirds of these cancers arise from the pancreatic head. On ultrasound, obstruction of both the common bile duct and the pancreatic duct is referred to as the "double duct sign". On CT, the findings are typically a hypovascular mass which is poorly demarcated and low attenuation compared to the more brightly enhancing background parenchyma.

The key to staging is assessment of the <u>SMA and celiac axis,</u> which if involved make the patient's cancer unresectable. Involvement of the GDA is ok, because it comes out with the whipple.

Additional Trivia Points about Pancreatic Adenocarcinoma:
- Tumor Marker = CA 19-9
- Hereditary Syndromes with Pancreatic CA:
    o HNPCC, BRCA Mutation, Ataxia-Telangiectasia, Peutz-Jeghers
- Small Bowel Follow Through: Reverse impression on the duodenum "Frostburg's Inverted 3 Sign" or a "Wide Duodenal Sweep." *They would have to actually find a case of the inverted 3 to show it, but could ask it in words. The "Wide Duodenal Sweep" could actually be shown.*

Periampullary Tumor: Defined as originating within 2cm of the major papilla. It can be difficult to differentiate from a conventional pancreatic adenocarcinoma as both obstruct the bile duct, and present as a mass in the pancreatic head. Basically, all you need to know about them is they can try and treat them with a Whipple and they have a better prognosis than pancreatic adenocarcinoma.

Trivia: There is an increased incidence of ampullary carcinoma in Gardner's Syndrome.

Islet Cell / Neuroendocrine:

Neuroendocrine tumors are uncommon tumors of the pancreas. Typically hypervascular, with brisk enhancement during arterial or pancreatic phase. They can be thought of as non-functional or functional, and then subsequently further divided based on the hormone they make. The can be associated with both MEN 1 and Von Hippel Lindau.

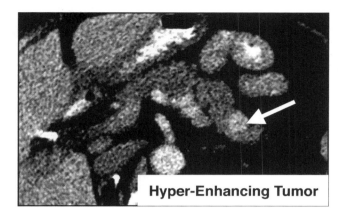

Hyper-Enhancing Tumor

Insulinoma: The most common type (about 75%). They are almost always benign (90%), solitary, and small (< 2cm).

Gastrinoma: The second most common type overall, but <u>most common type associated with MEN 1</u>. They are malignant like 30-60%. They can cause increased gastric acid output and ulcer formation - Zollinger-Ellison syndrome.

 The Buzzword is Jejunal Ulcer = Zollinger-Ellison

Non-Functional: The 3rd most common type, usually malignant (80%), and are usually large and metastatic at the time of diagnosis.

I say "non-functional,"
you say Large with Calcification

- Gastrinoma Triangle -

The anatomical region where most (90%) of gastrinomas arise.

Boundaries

- Superior: Junction of the cystic and common bile ducts
- Inferior: Start of the third portion of the duodenum
- Medial: Start of the body of the pancreas

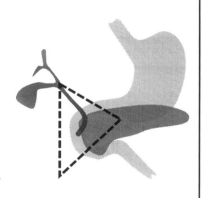

Intrapancreatic Accessory Spleen

It is possible to have a pancreatic mass that is actually just a piece of spleen. The typical scenario is that of post traumatic splenosis. Look for the question stem to say something like *"history of trauma."* Another hint may be the absence of a normal spleen.

Imaging Findings:
-Follows spleen on all image sequences (dark on T1, and bright on T2 - relative to the liver).
-It will restrict diffusion (just like the spleen).
-The classic give away, and most likely way it will be shown is as a <u>tiger striped mass on arterial phase</u> (tiger striped like the spleen on arterial phase).

Trivia: Nuclear medicine tests - (1) Heat Treated RBCs, and (2) Sulfur Colloid can be used to prove the mass is spleen (they both take up tracer — just like a spleen).

SECTION 7:
Surgical

The Whipple Procedure:

The standard Whipple procedure involves resection of the pancreatic head, duodenum, gastric antrum, and almost always the gallbladder. A jejunal loop is brought up to the right upper quadrant for gastrojejunal, choledochojejunal or hepaticojejunal, and pancreatojejunal anastomosis.

An alternative method used by some surgeons is to perform a pancreatoduodenectomy and preserve the pylorus when possible. There is debate in the surgery literature with regard to which method should be the standard. In this pylorus-preserving pancreatoduodenectomy, the stomach is left intact and the proximal duodenum is used for a duodenojejunal anastomosis.

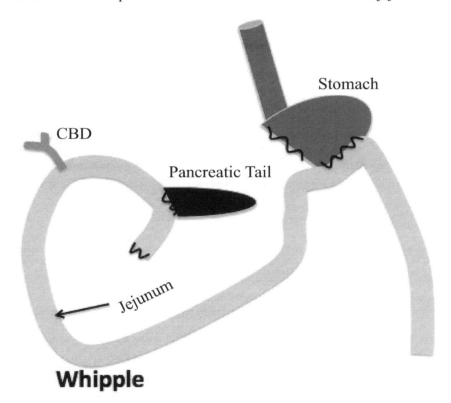

Whipple

Complications:

Delayed gastric emptying (*need for NG tube longer than 1- day*) and pancreatic fistula (*amylase through the surgical drain >50 ml for longer than 7-10 days*), are both clinical diagnoses and are the most common complications after pancreatoduodenectomy. Wound infection is the third most common complication, occurring in 5%–20% of patients.

- Transplant -

Pancreas transplant (usually with a renal transplant) is an established therapy for severe type 1 diabetes – which is often complicated by renal failure. The vascular anatomy regarding this transplant is quite complicated and beyond the scope of this text. Just know that the pancreas transplant receives arterial inflow from two sources: the donor SMA, (*which supplies the head via the inferior pancreaticoduodenal artery*) and the donor splenic artery, (*which supplies the body and tail*). The venous drainage is via both the donor portal vein and the recipient SMV. Exocrine drainage is via the bowel (*in older transplants via the bladder*).

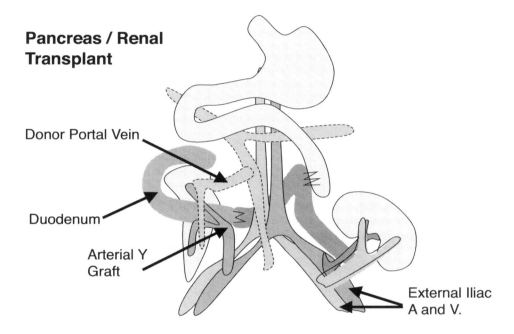

Pancreas / Renal Transplant

Donor Portal Vein

Duodenum

Arterial Y Graft

External Iliac A and V.

The number one cause of graft failure is acute rejection. The number two cause of graft failure is donor splenic vein thrombosis. Donor splenic vein thrombosis usually occurs within the first 6 weeks of transplant. Venous thrombosis is much more common than arterial thrombosis in the transplant pancreas, especially when compared to other transplants because the vessels are smaller and the clot frequently forms within and propagates from the tied-off stump vessels.

Both venous thrombosis and acute rejection can appear as reversed diastolic flow. Arterial thrombosis is also less of a problem because of the dual supply to the pancreas (via the Y graft). A point of trivia is that the resistive indices are not of value in the pancreas, because the organ lacks a capsule. The graft is also susceptible to pancreatitis, which is common < 4 weeks after transplant and usually mild. Increased rates of pancreatitis were seen with the older bladder drained subtype.

 "Shrinking Transplant" is a buzzword for chronic rejection, where the graft progressively gets smaller in size.

SECTION 8:
Spleen

Normal Trivia

By the age of 15 the spleen reaches its normal adult size. The spleen contains both "red pulp" and "white pulp" which contribute to its tiger striped appearance during arterial phase imaging. The red pulp is filled with blood (a lot of blood), and can contain up to one liter of blood at any time. The spleen is usually about 20 HU less dense than the liver, and slightly more echogenic than the liver (equal to the left kidney). The splenic artery (which usually arises from the celiac trunk) is essentially an end vessel, with minimal collaterals. Occlusion of the splenic artery will therefore result in splenic infarction.

Pathology involving the spleen can be categorized as either congenital, acquired (as the sequela of trauma or portal hypertension), or related to a "mass." A general rule is that most things in the spleen are benign with exception of lymphoma or the rare primary angiosarcoma.

Normal Spleen on MRI:

The spleen is basically a big watery lymph node. It restricts diffusion (like a lymph node).

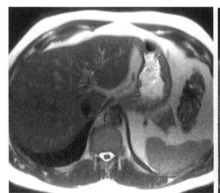 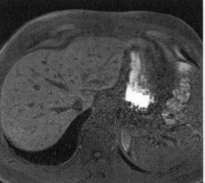 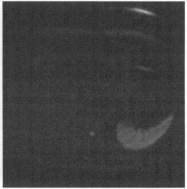

It's Bright on T2
-Relative to the liver

It's Dark on T1
-Relative to the liver

Just like a lymph node it
will restrict diffusion

Heterotaxy Syndromes: Super High Yield - please see discussion on page 92

Accessory Spleens: These are very common; we see them all the time. Some random trivia that might be testable includes the fact that sulfur colloid could be used to differentiate a splenule from an enlarged pathologic lymph node. Additionally, in the scenario where a patient is post splenectomy for something like ITP or autoimmune hemolytic anemia, an accessory spleen could hypertrophy and present as a mass. Hypertrophy of an accessory spleen can also result in a recurrence of the original hematologic disease process.

Wandering Spleen: A normal spleen that "wanders" off and is in an unexpected location. Because of the laxity in the peritoneal ligaments holding the spleen, a wandering spleen is associated with abnormalities of intestinal rotation. The other key piece of trivia is that unusual locations set the spleen up for torsion and subsequent infarction. A chronic partial torsion can actually lead to splenomegaly or gastric varices.

Trauma: The spleen is the most common solid organ injured in trauma. This combined with the fact that the spleen contains a unit or so of blood means splenic trauma can be life threatening. Remember the trauma scan is done in portal venous phase (70 second), otherwise you'd have to tell if that tiger-striped, arterial-phase spleen is lacerated.

Splenosis: This occurs post trauma where a smashed spleen implants and then recruits blood supply. The implants are usually multiple and grow into spherical nodules typically in the peritoneal cavity of the upper abdomen (*but can be anywhere*). It's more common than you think and has been reported in 40-60% of trauma. Again, Tc Sulfur colloid (or heat-treated RBC) can confirm that the implants are spleen and not ovarian mets or some other terrible thing.

Gamna Gandy Bodies (Siderotic Nodule):
These are small foci of hemorrhage in the splenic parenchyma that are usually associated with portal hypertension. They are T2 dark.

Gradient is the most sensitive sequence.

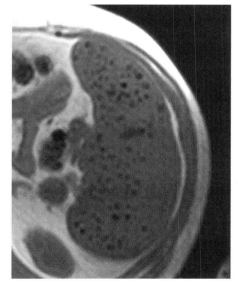

Gamna Gandy Bodies

Sarcoidosis: Sarcoid is a disease of unknown etiology that results in noncaseating granulomas which form in various tissues of the body (*complete discussion in the chest section of this text*). The spleen is involved in 50% - 80% of patients. Splenomegaly is usually the only sign. However, aggregates of granulomatous splenic tissue in some patients may appear on CT as numerous discrete 1-2cm hypodense nodules. Rarely, it can cause a massive splenomegaly and possibly rupture. Don't forget that the gastric antrum is the most common site in the GI tract.

Peliosis: This is a rare condition characterized by multiple blood filled cyst-like spaces in a solid organ (*usually the liver – peliosis hepatitis*). When you see it in the spleen it is usually also in the liver (isolated spleen is extremely rare). The etiology is not known, but for the purpose of multiple choice tests it occurs in women on OCPs, men on anabolic steroids, **people with AIDS, renal transplant patients** (up to 20%) , and patients with Hodgkin lymphoma. It's usually asymptomatic but can explode spontaneously.

-Splenic Vascular Abnormalities-

Splenic artery aneurysm is the most common visceral arterial aneurysm. Pseudoaneurysm can occur in the setting of trauma and pancreatitis. The incidence is higher in women of child bearing age who have had two or more pregnancies (*4x more likely to get them, 3x more likely to rupture*). It's usually saccular and in the mid-to-distal artery. They usually fix them when they get around 2-3cm.

Colossal fuck up to avoid: Don't call them a hypervascular pancreatic islet cell mass and biopsy them.

Splenic vein thrombosis frequently occurs as the result of pancreatitis. Can also occur in the setting of diverticulitis or Crohn's. Can lead to isolated gastric varices.

Infarction can occur from a number of conditions. On a multiple choice test the answer is sickle cell. The imaging features are classically a wedge-shaped, peripheral, low attenuation defect.

- Splenic Infections -

Most common radiologically detected splenic infection is histoplasmosis (with multiple round calcifications). Splenic TB can have a similar appearance (but much less common in the US). Another possible cause of calcified granuloma in the spleen in brucellosis, but these are usually solitary and 2 cm or larger. They may have a low density center, encircled by calcification giving the lesion a "bull's eye" appearance.

In the immunocompetent patient, **splenic abscess** is usually due to an aerobic organism. **Salmonella is the classic bug** – which develops in the setting of underlying splenic damage (trauma or sickle cell). In immunocompromised patients, unusual organisms such as fungi, TB, MAI, and PCP can occur and usually present as multiple micro-abscesses. Occasionally, fungal infections may show a "bulls-eye" appearance on ultrasound.

- Splenic Size - Too Big vs Too Small -

It's good to have a differential for a big spleen and a small spleen.

Small Spleen	Big Spleen
Sickle Cell	Passive Congestion (heart failure, portal HTN, splenic vein thrombosis)
Post Radiation	Lymphoma
Post Thorotrast	Leukemia
Malabsorption Syndromes (ulcerative colitis > crohns)	Gauchers

 **Felty's Syndrome** – abnormality of granulocytes, with a triad of: (1) Splenomegaly, (2) Rheumatoid Arthritis, (3) Neutropenia

- Benign Masses of the Spleen -

Cysts:

Post traumatic cysts (pseudocysts) are the most common cystic lesion in the spleen. They can occur secondary to infarction, infection, hemorrhage, or extension from a pancreatic pseudocyst. As a point of trivia they are "pseudo" cysts because they have no epithelial lining. They may have a thick wall or prominent calcifications peripherally.

Epidermoid cysts are the second most common cystic lesion in the spleen. They are congenital in origin. As a point of absolutely worthless trivia, they are "true" cysts and have an epithelial lining. They typically grow slowly and are usually around 10cm at the time of discovery. They can cause symptoms if they are large enough. They are solitary 80% of the time, and have peripheral calcifications 25% of the time.

Hydatid or Echinococcal cysts are the third most common cystic lesion in the spleen (most common worldwide). They are caused by the parasite Echinococcus Granulosus. Hydatid cysts consist of a spherical "mother cyst" that usually contains smaller "daughter cysts." Internal septations and debris are often referred to as "hydatid sand." The "water lily sign" is seen when there is detachment of the endocyst membrane resulting in floating membranes within the pericysts (looks like a water lily). This was classically described on CXR in pulmonary echinococcal disease.

Hemangioma is the most common benign neoplasm in the spleen. This dude is usually smooth and well marginated demonstrating contrast uptake and delayed washout. *The classic peripheral nodular discontinuous enhancement seen in hepatic lesions may not occur,* especially if the tumor is smaller than 2 cm.

Lymphangiomas are rare entities in the spleen but can occur. Most occur in childhood. They may be solitary or multiple, although most occur in a subcapsular location. Diffuse lymphangiomas may occur (lymphangiomatosis).

Hamartomas are also rare in the spleen, but can occur. Typically this is an incidental finding. Most are hypodense or isodense and show moderate heterogeneous enhancement. They can be hyperdense if there is hemosiderin deposition.

 Littoral Cell Angioma is a zebra that shows up occasionally in books and possibly on multiple choice tests. Clinical hypersplenism is almost always present. Usually presents as multiple small foci which are hypoattenuating on late portal phase. MR shows hemosiderin (low T1 & T2).

- Malignant Masses of the Spleen -

Most things that occur in the spleen are benign. Other than lymphoma (discussed below) it is highly unlikely that you will encounter a primary malignancy of the spleen (*but if you do it's likely to be vascular*). For the purposes of academic discussion (and possible multiple choice trivia), angiosarcoma is the most common.

Angiosarcoma: It is aggressive and has a poor prognosis. On CT it can manifest as a poorly defined area of heterogeneity or low density in an enlarged spleen. They can contain necrosis and get big enough to rupture *(spontaneous rupture occurs like 30% of the time)*. Contrast enhancement is usually poor. Yes, these can occur from prior thorotrast exposure.

Lymphoma is the most common malignant tumor of the spleen, and is usually seen as a manifestation of systemic disease. *Splenomegaly is the most common finding* (and maybe the only finding in low-grade disease). Although both Hodgkins and Non-Hodgkins types can involve the spleen, Hodgkins type and high-grade lymphomas can show discrete nodules of tumor. With regard to imaging, they are low density on CT, T1 dark, and are PET hot.

Metastatic disease to the spleen is rare. When it does occur, it occurs via common things (Breast, Lung, Melanoma).

Trivia: Melanoma is the most common primary neoplasm to met to the spleen.

This page is for notes and scribbles.

4
URINARY

PROMETHEUS LIONHART, M.D.

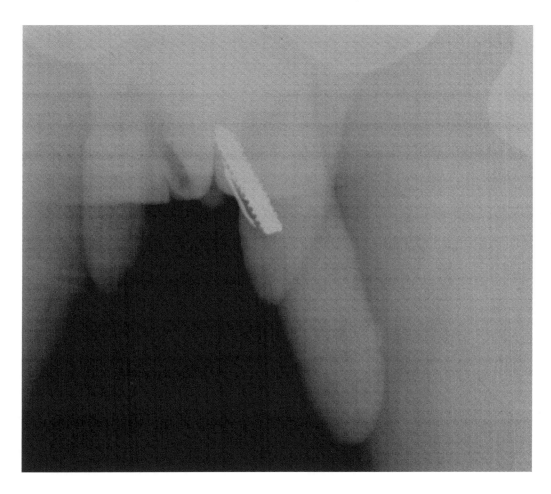

SECTION 1:
Anatomy / Congenital

Normal Anatomy:

The normal adult kidney is shaped like a bean, with a smooth (often lobulated) outer border. The kidney is surrounded by a thick capsule outlined by echogenic perirenal fat. This echogenic fat is contiguous with the renal sinus, filling the middle of the kidney. The cortex extends centrally into the middle of the kidney, separated by slightly less echogenic medullary pyramids. The normal kidney should be between 9 cm and 15 cm in length.

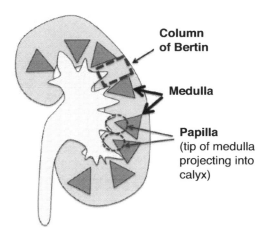

Column of Bertin

Medulla

Papilla
(tip of medulla projecting into calyx)

The echogenicity of the kidney should be equal to or slightly less than the liver and spleen. If the renal echogenicity is greater than the liver, this indicates some impaired renal function (medical renal disease). Liver echogenicity significantly greater than the kidney indicates a fatty liver.

Variant Anatomy

Fetal Lobulation – The fetal kidneys are subdivided into lobes that are separated with grooves. Sometimes this lobulation persists into adult life. The question is always:

Fetal Lobulation vs Scarring:

•**Lobulation** = Renal surface indentations overlie the space between the pyramids

•**Scarring** = Renal surface indentations overlie the medullary pyramids.

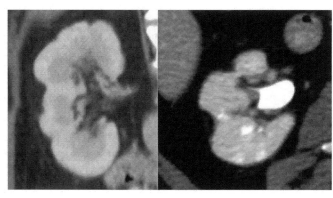

Fetal Lobulation
-Indentations Between Pyramids

Renal Scarring
-Indentations Over Pyramids

Dromedary Hump

– Focal bulge on the left kidney, which forms as the result of adaptation to the adjacent spleen.

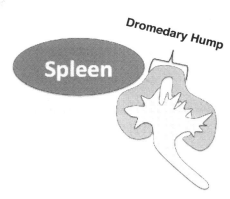

Prominent (or hypertrophied) Column of Bertin

– Normal variant in which hypertrophied cortical tissue located between the pyramids results in splaying of the sinus. Other than the hypertrophy it looks totally normal. It will enhance the same as adjacent parenchyma.

Most likely to be shown on ultrasound, - looks like a big echogenic cortex. On CT or MR it would be too easy.

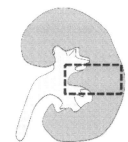

Prominent Column of Bertin

Renal Agenesis

– Congenital absence of one or both kidneys. If it's unilateral this can be asymptomatic. If it's bilateral think about the "Potter Sequence." When it's unilateral (it's usually sporadic), for the purpose of multiple choice think about associated GYN anomalies in women (70% of women with unilateral renal agenesis have associated genital anomalies - **unicornuate uterus**). With regard to men, **20% with renal agenesis have absence of the ipsilateral epididymis and vas deferens or have an ipsilateral seminal vesicle cyst.**

Associations: Ipsilateral seminal vesicle cysts, absent ipsilateral ureter, absent ipsilateral hemitrigone and absent ipsilateral vas deferens.

- **Potter Sequence:** Insult (maybe ACE inhibitors) = kidneys don't form, if kidneys don't form you can't make piss, if you can't make piss you can't develop lungs (pulmonary hypoplasia).
- **Mayer-Rokitansky-Kuster-Hauser:** – Mullerian duct anomalies including absence or atresia of the uterus. Associated with unilateral renal agenesis.
- **Lying Down Adrenal or "Pancake Adrenal" Sign:** – describes the elongated appearance of the adrenal not normally molded by the adjacent kidney. It can be used to differentiate surgically absent vs congenitally absent.

Horseshoe Kidney & Crossed Fused Renal Ectopia

Discussed in the Peds chapter (page 94).

SECTION 2: Renal Mases

- Renal Cell Carcinoma -

The most common primary renal malignancy. RCC till proven otherwise: (a) Enhances with contrast (> 15 HU), (b) calcifications in a fatty mass. Risk factors include tobacco use, syndromes like VHL, chronic dialysis (> 3years), family history. These dudes make hypervascular mets. They are ALWAYS lytic when they met to the bones.

> **Timing**
> Nephrogram phase (80 seconds) = Most sensitive for detection of RCC

- *Pseudoenhancement:* A less than 10 HU increase in attenuation is considered within the technical limits of the study and is not considered to represent enhancement. More rare once a cyst is larger than 1.5 cm.

- *Can RCC have fat in it?* - Oh yeah, for sure -especially clear cell. This leads to the potential sneaky situation of a fat containing lesion in the liver (which can be a RCC met). Now to make this work they'd have to tell you the patient had RCC - or show you one. A helpful hint is that RCCs with macroscopic fat nearly always have some calcification/ossification - if they don't it's probably an AML.

Subtypes:

- **Clear Cell** – Most common subtype. This is the one that is associated with VHL. It is typically more aggressive than papillary, and will enhance equal to the cortex on corticomedullary phase.
- **Papillary** – This is the second most common type. It is usually less aggressive than clear cell (more rare subtypes can be very aggressive). They are less vascular and will not enhance equal to the cortex on corticomedullary phase. They also are in the classic T2 dark differential (along with lipid poor AML and hemorrhagic cyst).
- **Medullary** – Associated with Sickle Cell Trait. It's highly aggressive, and usually large and already metastasized at the time of diagnosis. Patient's are usually younger.
- **Chromophobe** – All you need to know is that it's associated with Birt Hogg Dube.

Conventional RCC Staging:
Stage 1: Limited to Kidney and < 7 cm
Stage 2: Limited to Kidney but > 7 cm
Stage 3: Still inside Gerota's Fascia
A: Renal Vein Invaded
B: IVC below diaphragm
C: IVC above diaphragm
Stage 4: Beyond Gerota's Fasica
Ipsilateral Adrenal

Subtype	Syndrome / Association
Clear Cell	Von Hippel-Lindau
Papillary	Hereditary papillary renal carcinoma
Chromophobe	Birt Hogg Dube
Medullary	Sickle Cell Trait

Renal Lymphoma: This can literally look like anything. Having said that the most common appearance is bilaterally, enlarged kidneys, with small, low attenuation cortically based solid nodules or masses. A solitary mass is seen in about 1/4 of the cases.

Trivia: Out of all the renal masses - lymphoma is the most likely to preserve the normal reniform shape.

Renal Leukemia: The kidney is the most common visceral organ involved. Typically the kidneys are smooth and enlarged. Hypodense lesions are cortically based only, with little if any involvement of the medulla.

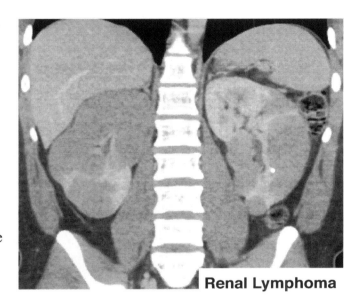

Renal Lymphoma

Angiomyolipoma (AML): This is the most common benign tumor of the kidney. Almost all (95%) of them have macroscopic fat, and this is the defining feature. They are usually incidental (in the real world).

The things to know about them are:
(1) They are associated with Tubular Sclerosis
(2) They can bleed if they get big enough (> 4cm). It's controversial if they grow or bleed more in pregnancy (if they ask you, I guess you should say yes – because that's the old knowledge but some modern papers are saying not for sure).
(3) They should never have calcifications (that's probably a RCC).
(4) They can be lipid poor (about 5% are), and those are T2 dark.

Gamesmanship: Traditional Spectral Fat Sat or In and Out of Phase (India Ink) can be used to suggest an AML. Just remember, rarely RCCs can have fat:

Fat with Calcifications = RCC,   Fat with No Calcifications = Probably AML

Oncocytoma - This is the second most common benign tumor (after AML). It looks a lot like a RCC, but has a **central scar** 33% of the time (and 100% of the time on multiple choice). There will be no malignant features (such as vessel infiltration). They cannot be distinguished from RCC on imaging and must be treated as RCC till proven otherwise.

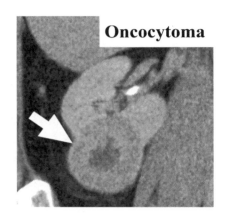

Oncocytoma

If they want to ask about an Oncocytoma they can show it 3 ways: (1) Solid Mass with central scar - CT or MRI, (2) "Spoke wheel" vascular pattern on US, (3) Hotter than the surrounding renal cortex - on PET CT.

Gamesmanship: I have encountered two types of GU radiologists in my life. The first type is the practical type - he/she doesn't EVER even mention oncocytoma, because enhancing renal masses have to come out. Even if you biopsy it and get oncocytes, it doesn't matter because RCCs can have oncocytic features.

The second type is more of your classic academic type. To try and sound impressive this person will often include this (and other rare entities) in the differential. Another common psychopathology in these types is excessive word nazism ("don't say that, say this"). I'm fairly certain you have met this person - there is usually one in every section.

> **The PET Trick:**
>
> RCC is typically COLDER than surrounding renal parenchyma on PET,
>
> Oncocytoma is typically HOTTER than surrounding renal parenchyma on PET,

So if you are shown an enhancing renal mass with a central scar, how do you decide if it's a RCC or an oncocytoma? The way to figure it out is simple - just read the mind of the person who wrote the question. If it's a practical type then all enhancing renal masses are RCC till proven otherwise. If it's the academic type then central scar = oncocytoma. You may also think… which of these two people is more likely to volunteer to write board questions?

Trivia: A syndrome associated with bilateral oncocytomas is <u>Birt Hogg Dube</u> (they also get chromophobe RCC).

Multilocular Cystic Nephroma -

"Non-communicating, fluid-filled locules, surrounded by thick fibrous capsule." By definition these things are characterized by the absence of a solid component or necrosis.

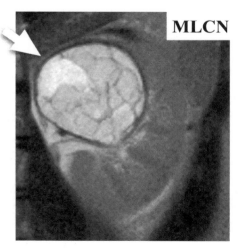

MLCN

 Buzzword: "protrudes into the renal pelvis."

The question is likely the bimodal occurrence (4 year old boys, and 40 year old women).

I like to think of this as the *Michael Jackson lesion – it loves young boys and middle aged women.*

SECTION 3:
Cystic Disease

Bosniak Cyst Classification:

- Class 1: Simple – less than 15 HU with no enhancement
- Class 2: Hyperdense (< 3 cm). Thin calcifications, Thin septations
- Class 2F: Hyperdense (> 3 cm). Minimally thickened calcifications (5% chance cancer)
- Class 3: Thick Septations, Mural Nodule (50% chance cancer)
- Class 4: Any enhancement (>15 HU)

Class 1:
-Simple Anechoic
- 0% chance of CA

Class 2:
-Hyperdense (<3cm)
-Thin Calcifications
-Thin Septations
- 0% chance of CA

Class 2F:
-Hyperdense (>3cm)
-Thin Calcifications
- < 5% chance of CA

Class 3:
-Thick Calcifications
-Mural Nodule
-50% chance of CA

Class 4:
-Any Enhancement
-100% chance of CA

Hyperdense cysts: Basically, if the mass is _greater than 70 HU_ and homogenous, it's benign (hemorrhagic or proteinaceous cyst) 99.9% of the time.

Autosomal Dominant Polycystic Kidney Disease (ADPKD) – Kidneys get progressively larger and lose function (you get dialysis by the 5th decade). Hyperdense contents & calcified wall are frequently seen due to prior hemorrhage. What you need to know is: (1) it's **A**utosomal **D**ominant "**AD**ult", (2) They get cysts in the liver 70% of the time, (3) they get seminal vesicle cysts (some sources say 60%), and (4) they get Berry Aneurysms. As mentioned before, they don't have an intrinsic risk of cancer, but do get cancer once they are on dialysis.

Autosomal Recessive Polycystic Kidney Disease (ARPKD) – These guys get HTN and renal failure. The liver involvement is different than the adult form. Instead of cysts they have abnormal bile ducts and fibrosis. This **congenital hepatic fibrosis is ALWAYS present in ARPKD**. The ratio of liver and kidney disease is inversely related. _The worse the liver is the better the kidneys do. The better the liver is, the worse the kidneys do._ On ultrasound the kidneys are smoothly enlarged and diffusely echogenic, with a loss of corticomedullary differentiation.

Lithium Nephropathy —Occurs in patients who take lithium long term. Can lead to diabetes insipidus and renal insufficiency. The kidneys are normal to small in volume with multiple (innumerable) tiny cysts, usually 2-5 mm in diameters. These "microcysts" are distinguishable from larger cysts associated with acquired cystic disease of uremia. They are probably going to show this on MRI with the history of bipolar disorder.

—

Uremic Cystic Kidney Disease – About 40% of patients with end stage renal disease develop cysts. This rises with duration of dialysis and is seen in about 90% in patients after 5 year of dialysis. The thing to know is: **Increased risk of malignancy with dialysis (3-6x).**

Trivia: The cysts will regress after renal transplant.

Von Hippel Lindau – Autosomal dominant multi-system disorder. 50-75% have renal cysts. 25-50% develop RCC (clear cell).

- Pancreas: Cysts, Serous Microcystic Adenomas, Neuroendocrine (islet cell) tumor
- Adrenal: Pheochromocytoma (often multiple)
- CNS: Hemangioblastoma of the cerebellum, brain stem, and spinal cord

ADPKD	Cysts in Liver	Kidneys are BIG
VHL	Cysts in Pancreas	
Acquired (Uremic)		Kidneys are small

Tuberous Sclerosis – Autosomal dominant multi-system disorder. You have hamartomas everywhere (brain, lung, heart, skin, kidneys). The renal findings are multiple bilateral angiomyolipomas. They also have renal cysts, and occasionally RCC (same rate as general population, but in younger patient population). With regard to other organ systems:

- Lung – LAM – thin walled cysts and chylothorax
- Cardiac – Rhabdomyosarcoma (typically involve cardiac septum)
- Brain – Giant Cell Astrocytoma, Cortical and subcortical tubers, subependymal nodules
- Renal – AMLs, RCC (in younger patients)

T2 Dark Renal Cyst

Cysts are supposed to be T2 bright. If you see the "T2 Dark Cyst" then you are dealing with the classic differential of:

(1) Lipid Poor AML
- A small percentage of AMLs are lipid poor in the general population.
- For the purpose of multiple choice - If you see a lipid poor AML (especially if you see a bunch of them) you need to think about Tuberous Sclerosis - about 30% of their AMLs are lipid poor.

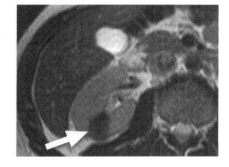

(2) Hemorrhagic Cyst
- These will likely be T1 bright

(3) Papillary Subtype RCC
- Remember that clear cells (the most common sub-type) are T2 HYPER Intense.
- Both Clear Cell and Papillary will enhance, - but the clear cell enhances more avidly (equal to cortex on cortico-medullary phase).

Multicystic Dysplastic Kidney:

This is a peds thing (and is discussed in that chapter). Quick refresher - this is the situation where you have multiple tiny cysts forming in utero from some type of insult.

What you should know:
- *"No functioning renal tissue,"* - shown with MAG 3 exam.
- Contralateral renal tract abnormalities occur like 50% of the time. Typically you think of reflux (VUR) and UPJ Obstructions

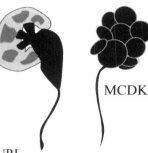

MCDK

UPJ Obstruction Contralateral Kidney

THIS *vs* **THAT: MCDK vs Bad Hydro**

- In hydronephrosis, the cystic spaces are seen to communicate.
- In difficult cases renal scintigraphy can be useful. MCDK will show no excretory function.

THIS *vs* **THAT: Peripelvic Cyst vs Parapelvic Cyst**

Para (beside): Originates from parenchyma, may compress the collecting system. These look a lot like the cortical cysts that you see all the time, but instead of bulging out - they bulge in.

Para

Peri (around): Originates from renal sinus, mimics hydro. If you didn't have a pyelogram (delayed) phase - might be tricky to tell apart.

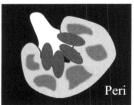

Peri

SECTION 4: Infection

Pyelonephritis – This is a clinical diagnosis. However you do end up diagnosing it. It's associated with stones. The most common organism is E. Coli. In acute bacterial nephritis, alternating bands of hypo and hyperattenuation (striated nephrogram) are seen. These wedge shaped areas are related to decreased perfusion. Perinephric stranding is also commonly seen.

Striated Nephrogram DDx:

- Acute ureteral obstruction
- Acute pyelonephritis
- Medullary sponge kidney
- Acute renal vein thrombosis
- Radiation nephritis
- Acutely following renal contusion
- Hypotension (bilateral)
- Infantile polycystic kidney (bilateral)

Abscess – Pyelo may be complicated by abscess, which can present on CT as round or geographic low attenuation collections that do not enhance centrally, but do have an enhancing rim. Bigger than 3cm and these guys might visit the IR section for drainage.

Chronic Pyelonephritis – Sort of a controversial entity. It is not clear whether the condition is an active chronic infection, arises from multiple recurrent infections, or represents stable changes from a remote single infection. The imaging findings are characterized by renal scarring, atrophy and cortical thinning, with hypertrophy of residual normal tissue. Basically, you have a small deformed kidney, with a bunch of wedge defects, and some hypertrophied areas.

Emphysematous Pyelonephritis – This is a life threatening necrotizing infection characterized by gas formation within or surrounding the kidney. What you need to know (1) it's really bad, (2) diabetics almost exclusively get it, (3) echogenic foci with dirty shadowing on ultrasound,

Emphysematous Pyelitis – This is less bad relative to emphysematous pyelonephritis. The gas is localized to the collecting system. It's more common in women, diabetics, and people with urinary obstruction. Radiographic finding is gas outlining the ureters and dilated calices.

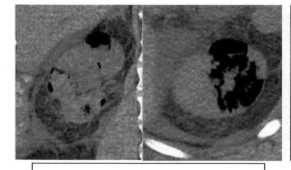

Emphysematous Pyelonephritis

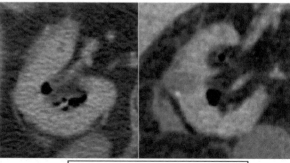

Emphysematous Pyelitis

Pyonephrosis – An infected or obstructed collecting system (which is frequently enlarged). Can be from a variety of causes; stones, tumor, sloughed papilla secondary to pyelonephritis. Can totally jack your renal function if left untreated. Fluid-Fluid level in the collecting system can be seen on US. CT has trouble telling the difference between hydro and pyonephrosis.

Xanthogranulomatous Pyelonephritis (XGP) – chronic
destructive granulomatous process that is basically always seen with a staghorn stone acting as a nidus for recurrent infection. You can have an associated psoas abscess with minimal perirenal infection. It's an Aunt Minnie, with a very characteristic "Bear Paw" appearance on CT. The kidney is not functional, and sometimes nephrectomy is done to treat it.

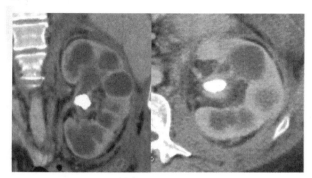

Xanthogranulomatous Pyelonephritis - *Bear Paw*

Papillary Necrosis:

This is ischemic necrosis of the renal papillae, most commonly involving the medullary pyramids.

<u>Diabetes is the most common cause</u>.

Other important causes include: pyelonephritis (especially in kids), sickle cell, TB, analgesic use, and cirrhosis.

Filling defects might be seen in the calyx.

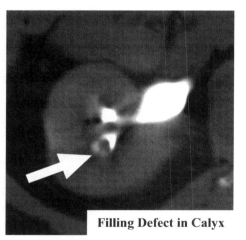

Filling Defect in Calyx

The appearance of a necrotic cavity in the papillae with linear streaks of contrast inside the calyx has been called a *"lobster claw sign."*

 Trivia: 50% of sickle cell patients develop papillary necrosis

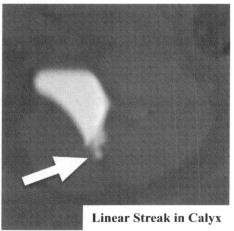

Linear Streak in Calyx

TB- The most common extra-pulmonary site of infection is the urinary tract. There are features of papillary necrosis and parenchymal destruction. You can have extensive calcification. Basically you end up with a shrunken, calcified kidney ("putty kidney.") This end stage appearance is essentially an auto-nephrectomy. The "Kerr Kink" is a sign of renal TB with scarring leading to a sharp kink at the pelvi-ureteric junction.

HIV Nephropathy – This is the most common cause of renal impairment in AIDS (CD4 < 200) patients. Although the kidneys can be normal in size, they are classically enlarged, and bright (echogenic). Some sources will go as far as saying that normal echotexture excludes the disease (this entity is essentially always is bright). Loss of the renal sinus fat appearance has also been described (it's edema in the fat, rather than loss of the actual fat).

Just think - **BIG** and **BRIGHT** kidney in HIV positive patient who is clinically in nephrotic syndrome (massive proteinura).

 Gamesmanship: To show you the kidney is big (longer than 12 cm) they will have to put calibers on the kidney. Calibers on anything should be a clue that the size being displayed is relevant.

Final diagnosis is going to be via biopsy of the big bright kidney.

Disseminated PCP in HIV patients can result in punctate (primarily cortical) calcifications.

Contrast Induced Nephropathy (CIN)
An Infectious Propaganda

The more you read about this the more you realize it's probably complete (or at least near complete) bullshit. Unfortunately a number of academics (mostly nephrologists) have made a career on this and can be pretty defensive when the subject is brought into question. For example, just the other day I had the following interaction with one such member of the nephrology community.

Nephrologist: Hey! Do you believe in the plague of Contrast Induced Nephropathy ?

Prometheus: I don't know. There seems to be some controversy in the literature…

Nephrologist: Don't jerk me around ! It's a simple question! A baby could answer it!

Prometheus: I guess so…

Nephrologist: Oh, you made a wise choice, my friend! If you had said no, I would have bitten your ear off ! I would have come at you like a tornado made of arms and teeth. And – and fingernails.

*Adapted from SNL transcript 1/10/98

———

In your abundant free time, read this paper and become enlightened. I will warn you, don't let the nephrologists catch you reading it.

Davenport, Matthew S., et al. "The challenges in assessing contrast-induced nephropathy: where are we now?." American Journal of Roentgenology 202.4 (2014): 784-789.

———

For the Exam — Trivia to know:
- Allergic reactions are a NOT considered a risk factor for CIN.
- "Risk Factors" for CIN include pre-existing renal insufficiency, diabetes mellitus (even more so with pre-existing renal insufficiency), cardiovascular disease with CHF, dehydration, and myeloma.
- Hydration via IV with 0.9% normal saline 6-12 hours before and continuing 4-12 hours after contrast administration supposedly decreases the incidence of CIN in patients with chronic renal insufficiency (true mechanism is diluting Cr levels). Oral hydration has been shown to not work as well.

SECTION 5:
Calcifications

Nephrolithiasis (kidney stones)

There are several different stone types. The most likely testable trivia for each is:

- *Calcium Oxalate* – By far the most common type (75%)
- *Struvite Stone* – More common in women and associated with UTI
- *Uric Acid* – "Unseen" on x-ray.
- *Cystine* – Rare and associated with congenital disorders of metabolism
- *Indinavir* – Stones in HIV patients which are **the ONLY stones NOT seen on CT.**

Treatment Trivia: There are two pieces of trivia that matter with regard to treatment.

Size Matters:
- Stones measuring 5 mm or smaller have a high likelihood of spontaneously passing.
- Stones measuring 1 cm or larger have a high likelihood of NOT passing spontaneously.

Composition (Uric Acid vs Not Uric Acid):
- Uric acid stones very rarely will require any kind of invasive intervention (lithotripsy, etc…). The reason is they are very pH dependent. Big Fat People and/or diabetics tend to have more acidic urine (from all that Mountain Dew) which leads to an increase in uric acid stones. They can be treated with medical therapy (potassium citrate or sodium bicarbonate) to increase the pH and melt the stones. You can't melt a calcium stone by messing with the pH.

Diagnosis of Uric Acid Stones:

Since identification of a uric acid stone is going to change management that makes it a target for trivia on multiple choice. There are 2 things that I would know:

(1) Uric Acid Stones tend to have lower attenuation (< 500 HU).
(2) Uric Acid Stones will have little if any change in H.U. with dual energy CT. The reason is they are composed of "light elements." The larger atoms (Calcium, Phosphorous, Magnesium, and Sulfur) tend to have a larger change - which is the basis of dual energy CT (80 kv, and 140 kv) identification of stone composition.

Trivia: Non Uric Acid Stones will have higher HU at 80 kVp relative to 140 kVp.
Trivia: Uric Acid Stones will be very similar at 80 kVp relative to 140 kVp. *If they do show a small change it will be the opposite - with a slightly higher HU at 140 kVp.
Trivia: Calcium stones are going to show the biggest HU change between high and low energies. In general, low/high energy ratios are going to be around 1.1 for uric acid, 1.25 for cystine, and > 1.25 for calcium.

 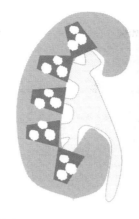 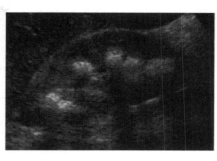

Cortical Nephrocalcinosis

This is typically the sequela of **cortical necrosis,** which can be seen after an acute drop in blood pressure (shock, postpartum, burn patients, etc...).

It starts out as a hypodense non-enhancing rim that later develops thin calcifications.

Mimic is disseminated PCP.

Medullary Nephrocalcinosis

Hyperechoic renal papilla / pyramids which may or may not shadow.

Causes:

- *Hyperparathyroidism* - Most people will say this is the most common.

- Medullary Sponge Kidney - Some people will say this is the most common.

- Lasix - Common cause in children.

- Renal Tubular Acidosis (distal subtype - type 1)

Trivia: RTA and Hyper PTH - tend to cause a more dense calcification that medullary sponge.

———

Medullary Sponge Kidney

A congenital cause of medullary nephrocalcinosis (usually asymmetric). The underlying mechanism is a cystic dilation of the collecting tubules of the kidney - so the testable association with Ehlers-Danlos makes sense. The association with Carolis also sorta makes sense. The association with Beckwith-Wiedemann doesn't really make sense (and therefore is the most likely to be tested).

Think about medullary sponge kidney with unilateral less dense medullary nephrocalcinosis.

SECTION 6:
Perfusion / Vascular

Page Kidney

– This is a subcapsular hematoma which causes renal compression and complex fuckery with the renin-angiotensin system. The result is hypertension.

The capsule is the real issue here. That capsule is tough and won't expand so the hematoma puts the squeeze on the "meat" of the kidney. You could never get a "page pancreas" because the pancreas has no capsule. This is the same reason why resistive indices are worthless in a pancreas (no capsule) but sometimes useful in a kidney (which has a capsule).

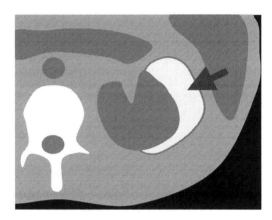

Subcapsular Hematoma + HTN = Page

Classic Clinical History: Hypertension post biopsy, lithotripsy, or trauma.

THIS vs **THAT** Delayed vs Persistent Nephrogram

Delayed Nephrogram – One kidney enhances and the other doesn't (or does to a lesser degree). Basically this is happening from pressure on the kidney, either extrinsic from a Page kidney situation, or intrinsic from an obstructing stone.

Persistent Nephrogram – This is seen with hypotension/shock and ATN. They can show this two ways, the first would be on a plain film of the abdomen (with dense kidneys), the second would be on CT. The tip offs are going to be that they tell you the time (3 hours etc…) and it's gonna be bilateral.

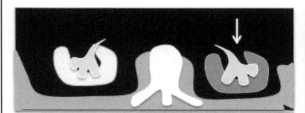

Delayed Nephrogram

3 Hours

Persistent Nephrogram

Renal Infarct

So wedge shaped hypodensities in the kidney can be seen with lots of stuff (infarct, tumor, infection, etc…). Renal infarcts are most easily identified on post contrast imaging in the cortical phase. If the entire renal artery is out, well then it won't enhance (duh).

Two tricks that they could pull are the:

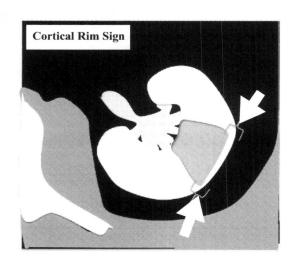

(1) *"Cortical Rim Sign"* – which is absent immediately after the insult, but is seen 8 hours to days later. You have a dual blood supply, which allows the cortex to stay perfused.

(2) *"Flip Flop Enhancement"* can be seen where a region of hypodensity / poor enhancement on early phases becomes relatively hyperdense on delayed imaging.

Renal Vein Thrombosis

Numerous causes; including dehydration, indwelling umbilical venous catheters (most common in neonates), and nephrotic syndrome (most common in adults). This can mimic a renal stone; presenting with flank pain, an enlarged kidney, and a delayed nephrogram.

On Doppler they are going to show you Reversed arterial diastolic flow and absent venous flow. *This is discussed again in the subsequent transplant section.*

SECTION 7:
Transplant

Renal transplant is the best treatment for end stage renal disease, and the quality of life is significantly better than that of a long term dialysis patient. The transplanted kidney is most commonly placed in the extraperitoneal iliac fossa so that the allograft can be anastomosed with the iliac vasculature and urinary bladder.

Normal: A transplant kidney is just like a native kidney. It should have low resistance (it's always "on"). The upstroke should be brisk, and the flow in diastole forward (remember it's always "on").

- Understanding Renal RIs -

There are two major points to know first when thinking about RIs. The first is *the kidney has a capsule*, and that capsule is unforgiving (it believes in nothing Lebowski). The second is a *sick kidney is a swollen kidney*.

Now lets look at this formula:
$$RI = \frac{\text{Peak Systolic - End Diastolic "lowest diastolic"}}{\text{Peak Systolic}}$$

If the meat (parenchyma) of the kidney is sick and swollen, but can't expand because it is wrapped in a tight unforgiving capsule you can imagine the blood vessels going through that kidney are going to get the squeeze.

You can also probably imagine that the passive diastolic flow would be more impaired (compared to the active systolic flow) by this squeeze.

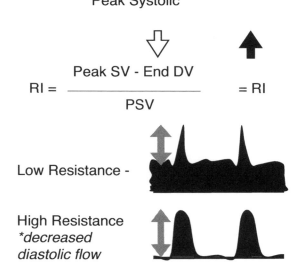

$$RI = \frac{\text{Peak SV - End DV}}{\text{PSV}} = RI$$

Low Resistance -

High Resistance
*decreased diastolic flow

If the meat of the kidney becomes "sick" from whatever the cause might be (*rejection, infection, inflammation,* etc…) it swells increasing resistance.

The higher the RI the sicker the kidney. This is why RIs are useful, and this is why an upward trend in RI is worrisome. The RI isn't really specific. "Sick" can mean lots of stuff. It does tell you something is wrong, especially if there is an upward trend.

RI's should stay below 0.7, higher than that should trigger you to think something is wrong.

You can think of complications in 3 main flavors
(a) Urologic, (b) Cancer, (c) Vascular

- Urologic Complications -

Urinoma – This is usually found in the first 2 weeks post op. Urine leak or urinoma will appear as an anechoic fluid collection with no septations, that is rapidly increasing in size. MAG 3 nuclear medicine scan can be used to demonstrate this (or the cheaper ultrasound).

Hematoma – Common immediately post op. Usually resolves spontaneously. Large hematoma can produce hydro. Acute hematoma will be echogenic, and this will progressively become less echogenic (with older hematomas more anechoic and septated).

Lymphocele – Lymphoceles typically occur **1-2 months after transplant**. They are caused by leakage of lymph from surgical disruption of lymphatics. The fluid collection is usually medial to the transplant (between the graft and the bladder). They are actually the <u>most common fluid collection to cause transplant hydronephrosis</u>.

 Buzzword = Ipsilateral lower extremity edema from femoral vein compression.

Acute Rejection / ATN - Up to 20% of transplant patients will have some early rejection. Both ATN and Acute rejection tend to occur in the first week or so. On ultrasound the pyramids become prominent, the transplant itself gets bigger, and the RIs go up. ATN vs Acute Rejection is best distinguished on MAG-3; ATN has normal perfusion and Rejection does not (both will have delayed excretion).

Chronic Rejection – This occurs one year post transplant. The kidney may enlarge, and you can lose corticomedullary differentiation. The RIs will elevate (> 0.7), which is nonspecific.

Calculous Disease – Compared with the general population, transplant kidneys are at increased risk of stone formation.

- Cancer in the Transplant -

The prolonged immunosuppression therapy that renal transplant patients are on places them at significantly (100x) increased risk of developing cancer.

RCC – Increased risk, with most of the cancers (90%) actually occurring in the native kidney. Etiology is not totally understood; maybe it's the immunosuppression or the fact that many transplant patients were on dialysis (a known risk factor) that leads to the cancer risk. In reality it doesn't matter, and is probably both.

Post Transplant Lymphoproliferative Disorder (PTLD) – This is an uncommon complication of organ transplant, associated with B-Cell proliferation. It is most common in the first year post transplant, and often involves multiple organs. The treatment is to back off the immunosuppression.

Cyclophosphamide – As a point of trivia, significant exposure to cyclophosphamide (less common now with the development of cyclosporin A) is associated with increased risk of urothelial cancer.

Vascular Complications -

Renal Vein Thrombosis - Typically seen <u>**within the first week**</u>. Typically the kidney is swollen. Instead of showing you the Doppler of the renal vein (which would show no flow), they will most likely show you the artery, which classically has <u>**reversed diastolic flow**</u>.

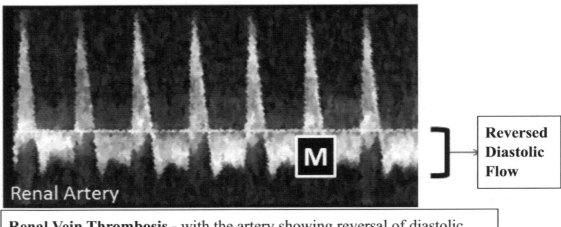

> **Renal Vein Thrombosis** - with the artery showing reversal of diastolic flow. Some people call this the "reverse M sign."

Renal Artery Thrombosis – *Usually* seen <u>**within the first month**</u>. Typically caused by kinking, hypercoagulation, or hyperacute rejection. Delayed (late) thrombosis is often due to stenosis.

Renal Artery Stenosis – Typically seen <u>**within the first year**</u> after transplant (usually weeks to months). Easily the <u>**most common vascular complication of transplant**</u>. This usually occurs at the anastomosis (especially end-to-end types). The clinical / scenario buzzword is going to be <u>"refractory hypertension."</u> Criteria include:
- PSV > 200-300 cm/s.
- PSV ratio > 2.0 (Stenotic Part vs Non Stenotic Part)
- Tardus Parvus: Measured at the Main Renal Artery Hilum (NOT at the arcuates)
- Anastomotic Jetting

Arteriovenous Fistula (AVF) – These occur secondary to biopsy. They occur about 20% of the time post biopsy, but are usually small and asymptomatic. They will likely show it with **tissue vibration artifact** (perivascular, mosaic color assignment due to tissue vibration), with high arterial velocity, and pulsatile flow in the vein.

Pseudoaneurysm – These also occur secondary to biopsy, but are less common.   They can also occur in the setting of graft infection, or anastomotic dehiscence. They will most likely show you the classic "yin-yang" color picture. Alternatively, they could show Doppler with biphasic flow at the neck of the pseudoaneurysm.

Renal Transplant Vascular Complications

Renal VEIN Thrombosis	Renal ARTERY Thrombosis	Renal ARTERY Stenosis	AV Fistula
Within the FIRST WEEK	Very Early (more common) or Late	Within the first year (can be early or late)	After a biopsy
Clinical is usually "decreased urine output" and "tender over graft"	The early kind is from hyperacute rejection, embolism, surgical fuck up (clamp injury / kink). The late type is usually secondary to stenosis.	Clinical = Refractory Hypertension.	Clinical is usually "gross hematuria
Flow in the vein is gone. **Reversed diastolic arterial flow.**	Flow in the artery and vein is gone.	PSV > 200 cm/s or 2-2.5 fold increase from the "normal" vessel	Vein with have turbulent "arterial" flow.
Grey Scale = Enlarged Kidney	Grey Scale = Infarct	Usually at the level of the surgical anastomosis	Tissue vibration artifact.
		PTA (angioplasty) is usually the initial treatment of choice - for significant RAS. Some institutions will favor surgery if the anastomosis is involved.	

Renal Transplant Non-Vascular Complications

Week 1	Weeks 1-4	Months 1-6	After 6 Months
Urinoma	Lymphocele	Lymphocele	Chronic Rejection
Hematoma		Drug Toxicity	RCC
			Lymphoma
			PTLD

SECTION 8:
Trauma

Obviously the kidney can get injured in trauma (seen in about 10%). Injury can be graded based on the presence of hematoma -> laceration -> involvement of the vein, artery, or UPJ obstruction.

 Gamesmanship: A good "Next Step" type question in the setting of renal trauma (or pelvic fracture) would be to prompt you to get delayed imaging - this is helpful to demonstrate a urine leak.

Terminology:

- **"Fractured Kidney"** - A laceration, which extends the full depth of the renal parenchyma. By definition the laceration *must connect two cortical surfaces* - so think about it going all the way through.

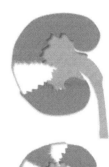

- **"Shattered Kidney"** - This is a more severe form of a fractured kidney. A kidney with 3 or more fragments - this is the most severe form of renal fracture.

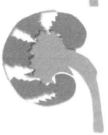

Renal Trauma - Rapid Pearls

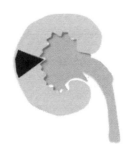

Wedge Shaped Perfusion Abnormality - Think Segmental Artery Injury

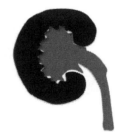

Diffuse NonPerfusion— Think Devascularized Kidney

Persistent Nephrogram — Think Renal Vein Injury / Thrombosis

SECTION 9:
Ureter

Developmental Ureteral Anomalies: Discussed in the Peds chapter (page 94).

Ureter Infection / Inflammation:

Stones – Stones tend to lodge in 3 spots: UPJ, UVJ, pelvic brim.

Ureteral Wall Calcifications – Wall calcifications should make you think about two things: (1) TB, (2) Schistosomiasis (worms).

Ureteritis cystica - Numerous tiny subepithelial fluid-filled cysts within the wall of the ureter. The condition is the result of chronic inflammation (from stones and/or chronic infection). Typically this is seen in diabetics with recurrent UTI. There may be an increased risk of cancer.

Ureteral pseudodiverticulosis – This is similar to ureteritis cystica in that both conditions are the result of chronic inflammation (stones, infection). Instead of being cystic filling defects, these guys are multiple small outpouchings. They are bilateral 75% of the time, and favor the upper and middle third. There is an association with malignancy.

Malakoplakia *("The Accursed")* – Former Lord of the Dark Elves of Svartalfheim and rare chronic granulomatous condition, this pathology can create soft tissue nodularity / plaques in the bladder and ureters (bladder more often). It is seen in the setting of chronic UTIs (highly associated with E.Coli), **often in female immunocompromised patients**. There is also a more remote association with the Casket of Ancient Winters. Since malakoplakia most frequently manifests as a mucosal mass involving the ureter or bladder, the most common renal finding is obstruction secondary to a lesion in the lower tract. Step 1 buzzword = Michaelis-Gutmann Bodies.

The most easily tested piece of trivia is this: Malakoplakia is **NOT premalignant**, and usually gets better with antibiotics.

Leukoplakia – This is essentially squamous metaplasia secondary to chronic irritation (stones or infections). The bladder is more commonly involved than the ureter. Imaging findings are unlikely to be shown, but would be mural filling defects.

The most easily tested piece of trivia is this: Leukoplakia is considered premalignant and the cancer is squamous cell.

> **Leukoplakia = Premalignant**
> **Malakoplakia = NOT Premalignant**

Trivia: Leukoplakia is associated with squamous cell carcinoma NOT transitional cell

Retroperitoneal Fibrosis

This condition is characterized by proliferation of aberrant fibro-inflammatory tissue, which typically surrounds the aorta, IVC, iliac vessels, and frequently traps and obstructs the ureters. It is idiopathic 75% of the time. Other causes include prior radiation, medications (methyldopa, ergotamine, methysergide), inflammatory causes (pancreatitis, pyelonephritis, inflammatory aneurysm), and malignancy (desmoplastic reaction, lymphoma).

Things (trivia) to know:
- Mostly (75 %) idiopathic AKA "Ormond Disease"
- Associated with IgG4 disorders (autoimmune pancreatitis, Riedel's thyroiditis, inflammatory pseudotumor)
- Classically shown with medial deviation of ureters
- It's more common in men
- Malignancy associated RP fibrosis occurs about 10% of the time (some people advocate using PET to find a primary)
- The Fibrosis will be Gallium avid, and PET hot in its early stages and cold in its late stages (mirroring its inflammatory stages). Metabolically active RP fibrosis will show increased FDG and Gallium uptake, regardless of a benign or malignant underlying cause

Subepithelial Renal Pelvis Hematoma:

This tends to occur in patients on long-term anticoagulation or a history of hemophilia. You are going to have a thickened upper tract wall - which is a classic **mimic for TCC**.

 Gamesmanship: I would expect pre and post contrast images so that you can make the classic findings of **hyperdense clot on the pre-contrast that does NOT enhance**. Although a non-contrast alone (showing blood in the urinary pelvis) with the history of hemophilia should also be enough to seal the deal.

THIS vs THAT: Deviation of the Ureters

Lateral Deviation of the Ureters	Medial Deviation "Waisting" of the Ureters
Retroperitoneal Adenopathy	Retroperitoneal Fibrosis
Aortic Aneurysm	Retrocaval Ureter (right side)
	Pelvic Lipomatosis
Psoas Hypertrophy *(proximal ureter)*	Psoas Hypertrophy *(distal ureter)*

SECTION 10:
Lower Tract Cancer

Transitional Cell Carcinoma – This histologic subtype makes up a very large majority (90%) of the collecting system cancers. Imaging buzzword is "goblet" or "champagne glass sign" on CT IVP.

High Yield Statistical Trivia

- Ureter is the least common location for TCC of the urinary tract
- TCC of the renal pelvis is 2x -3x times more common than ureter
- TCC of the bladder is 100x times more common than ureter
- In the ureter 75% of the TCCs are in the bottom 1/3
- If you have upper tract TCC there is a 40% chance of developing a bladder TCC
- If you have bladder TCC there is a 4% chance of developing a Renal Pelvis or Ureteral TCC
- Ureteral TCC is bilateral 5%

RISK FACTORS
• Smoking
• Azo Dye
• Cyclophosphamide
• Aristolochic acid (Balkan Nephropathy – see below)
• Horseshoe Kidney
• Stones
• Ureteral Pseudodiverticulosis
• Hereditary Non-Polyposis Colon Cancer (type 2)

Balkan Nephropathy – This is some zebra degenerative nephropathy endemic to the Balkan States. The only reason I mention it is that it has a super high rate of renal pelvis and upper ureter TCCs. It's thought to be secondary to eating aristolochic acid (AA) in seeds of the Aristolochia clematitis plant (herb).

Squamous cell - This is much less common than TCC (in the US anyway). The major predisposing factor is schistosomiasis (they both start with an "S").

Hematogenous Metastasis – Mets to the ureters are rare but can occur (GI, Prostate, Renal, Breast). They typically infiltrate the periureteral soft tissues and demonstrate transmural involvement.

Fibroepithelial Polyp - This is a benign entity presents as a filling defect in the renal pelvis or proximal ureter - which mimics a TCC (blood clot or radiolucent stone). The diagnosis is typically made post nephrectomy - since the assumption is nearly always TCC.

Gamesmanship: For the purpose of multiple choice (and real life), renal pelvis filling defects should always be assumed to be either clot, calcium (stone), or cancer. The only way I can think that a polyp question could be ask would be something like "which features would make a polyp more likely?" It has to be a trivia question, they couldn't (in good conscious) expect you to pick polyp over TCC with imaging alone — even if the findings and demographics were perfect - that would be teaching a terrible clinical message.

THIS vs THAT:	
Polp	**TCC**
Younger (30-40)	Older (60-70)
Smooth / Oblong	Irregular
Mobile	Fixed

SECTION 11:
Bladder

Normal Anatomy: Normal bladder is an extraperitoneal structure, with 4 layers. The dome of the bladder has a peritoneal cover. It's lined with transitional urothelium.

- Developmental Anomalies -

Prune Belly (Eagle Barrett) This is discussed in the Peds chapter (page 95).

Urachus : This is also discussed in the Peds chapter (page 99). I will briefly mention that the primary concern is the development of a midline <u>adenocarcinoma</u>. Most of the time the presence of a midline mass makes it obvious although calcification within any urachal soft tissue should make you think cancer.

Bladder Diverticula – These are more common in boys, and can be seen in a few situations. Most bladder diverticula can also be acquired secondary to chronic outlet obstruction (big prostate). There are a few syndromes (Ehlers Danlos is the big testable one) that you see them in as well.

"Hutch Diverticulum:" Also discussed in the Peds chapter (page 98).

Quick refresher on some key points.
- NOT associated with posterior urethral valves or neurogenic bladder.
- Hutch Diverticula is associated with ipsilateral reflux - and referred to as "secondary reflux"
- Bladder Diverticula typically arise from the lateral walls or near the ureteral orifices
- Diverticula at the anterior / superior bladder are more likely to be urachal diverticula
- Most Diverticula are acquired (not congenital)
- Ureters more commonly deviate medially adjacent to a diverticula

Bladder Ears – "Transitory extraperitoneal herniation of the bladder" if you want to sound smart. This is not a diverticulum. Instead, it's transient lateral protrusion of the bladder into the inguinal canal. It's very common to see, and likely doesn't mean crap. However, some sources say an inguinal hernia may be present 20% of the time. Smooth walls, and usually wide necks can help distinguish them from diverticula.

- Bladder Cancer -

Rhabdomyosarcoma – This is the most common bladder cancer in humans less than 10 years of age. They are often infiltrative, and it's hard to tell where they originate. "Paratesticular Mass" is often a buzzword. They can met to the lungs, bones, and nodes. The Botryoid variant produces a polypoid mass, which looks like a bunch of grapes.

Transitional Cell Carcinoma – As stated above, the bladder is the most common site, and this is by far the most common subtype. All the risk factors, are the same as above. If anyone asks "superficial papillary" is the most common TCC bladder subtype.

Squamous Cell Carcinoma – When I say Squamous Cell Bladder, you say Schistosomiasis. This is convenient because they both start with an "S." The classic picture is a heavily calcified bladder and distal ureters (usually shown on plain film, but could also be on CT). Another common association with squamous cell cancer of the bladder in the presence of a longstanding Suprapubic catheter. This also starts with an "S."

Adenocarcinoma of the Bladder – This is a common trick question. When I say Adenocarcinoma of the Bladder, you say Urachus. 90% of urachal cancers are located midline at the bladder dome. Bladder Exstrophy is also associated with an increased risk of adenocarcinoma.

Leiomyoma ("bladder fibroid") – Benign tumor (not cancer - even though the section is bladder cancer). It's often incidentally discovered (most common at the trigone).

Testable Trivia:

- Most common benign bladder tumor.
- Looks like a fibroid (smooth, solid, homogeneous)
- Young/Middle Age People (usually)
- Clinical Buzzword "urinary hesitancy" or "dribbling"

Bladder Cancer			
Transitional Cell	**Squamous Cell**	**Adenocarcinoma**	**Rhabdomyosarcoma**
Typical (Most Common)	Schistosomiasis	Urachal Remnant	Peds
	Suprapubic catheter	Bladder Exstrophy	

- Diversion Surgery -

After radical cystectomy for bladder cancer there are several urinary diversion procedures that can be done. People generally group these into incontinent and continent procedures. There are a ton of these (over 50 have been described). I just want to touch on the big points, and focus on complications (the most testable subject matter). The general idea is that a piece of bowel is made into either a conduit or reservoir, and then the ureters are attached to it.

Early Complications:

•*Alteration in bowel function:* **Adynamic ileus is the most common early complication**, occurring in almost 25% of cases. In about 3% of cases you can get SBO, usually from adhesions near the enteroenteric anastomosis.

•*Urinary Leakage:* This occurs in about 5% of cases, and usually at the ureteral-reservoir anastomosis. A urinoma can develop when the leaked urine is not collected by urinary drains.

•*Fistula:* This is uncommon and seen more in patients who have had pelvic radiation.

Late Complications (> 30 days)

•*Urinary infection:* This can be early or late.

•*Stones:* Remember to look on the non-contrast study.

•*Parastomal Herniation:* This occurs about 15% of the time with ileal conduits. Obesity is a contributing factor. Most don't matter, but 10% will need a surgical fix.

•*Urinary stricture:* The **left side is higher risk than the right**, secondary to the angulation (it's brought through or under the mesentery).

•*Tumor Recurrence:* The more advanced the original disease, the higher the risk for recurrence. The incidence is between 3-15%, and can present as a soft tissue mass at the ureter, bladder, or pelvic lymph node.

- Psoas Hitch -

The "psoas hitch" procedure results in an Aunt Minnie appearance of the bladder, making it uniquely testable.

This procedure is done in the situation where you have had an injury or pathology (stricture, cancer, etc...) involving a long segment of the distal ureter. Normally you would just cut that shit out and re-implant into the bladder. But what if the left over portion of the ureter is too short? The solution is to stretch the ipsilateral portion of the bladder towards the short ureter and sew it ("hitch it") to the psoas muscle. That way you can get away with a short ureter, because you stretched the bladder to bridge the gap.

Key Points:

- *Why it's done?* Used for people with long segment distal ureter injury / disease
- *Aunt Minnie Appearance* on CT IVP or Plain Film IVP (with contrast filling the bladder).

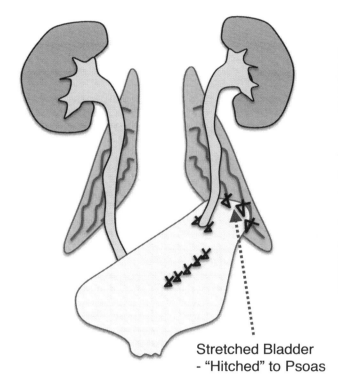

Stretched Bladder
- "Hitched" to Psoas

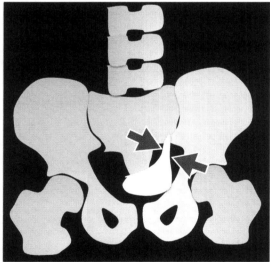

Aunt Minnie Appearance of the Hitched Bladder filled with contrast on a delayed IVP.

The "hitched" side has an upward projection towards the psoas muscle.

- "Acquired" — Infectious / Inflammation -

Emphysematous Cystitis – Gas forming organism in the wall of the bladder. More than half the time it's a diabetic patient. It's usually from E. Coli. It's gonna be very obvious on plain film and CT. Ultrasound would be sneaky, and you'd see dirty shadowing.

TB – The upper GU tract is more commonly effected, with secondary involvement of the bladder. Can eventually lead to a thick contracted bladder. Calcifications might be present.

Schistosomiasis – Common in the third world. Eggs are deposited in the bladder wall which leads to chronic inflammation. Things to know: the entire bladder will calcify (often shown on plain film or CT), and you get squamous cell cancer.

Fistula – This occurs basically in 3 conditions; (1) diverticulitis, (2) Crohns, (3) Cancer. This is more common in men, although women are at significantly increased risk after hysterectomy (the uterus protects the bladder).

Fistula - Most Common Etiology
• Colovesicial Fistula = Diverticular Disease
• Ileovesical Fistula = Crohns
• Rectovesical Fistula = Neoplasm or Trauma

Neurogenic Bladder – This comes in two flavors: (a) small contracted bladder, (b) atonic large bladder. The buzzword / classic sign is *"pine cone" bladder*, because of its appearance. It can lead to urine stasis, and that stasis can predispose to bladder CA, **stones**, and infection.

Acquired Bladder Diverticula - As mentioned above, these can be acquired mainly via outlet obstruction (just think big prostate). They are most common at the UVJ. They can lead to stasis, and that stasis can predispose to bladder CA, stones, and infection.

Bladder Stones – These guys show up in two scenarios: (1) they are born as kidney stones and drop into the bladder (2) they develop in the bladder secondary to stasis (outlet obstruction, or **neurogenic bladder**). They can cause chronic irritation and are a known risk factor for both TCC and SCC.

"Pear Shaped Bladder" – This is more of a sign than a pathology. Think two things (1) pelvic lipomatosis, and (2) hematoma.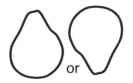

- Bladder Trauma -

What they want you to know is; extra versus intra peritoneal rupture. CT Cystography (contrast distending bladder) is the best test.

Extraperitoneal – This one is **more common (80-90%)**. Almost always associated with pelvic fracture. This can be managed medically.

- If there is a pelvic fracture, then the chance of a bladder rupture is 10%.
- If there is a bladder rupture, there is almost always a pelvic fracture
- Molar Tooth Sign: Contrast surrounding the bladder, in the prevesicle space of Retzius. This indicates extraperitoneal bladder rupture.

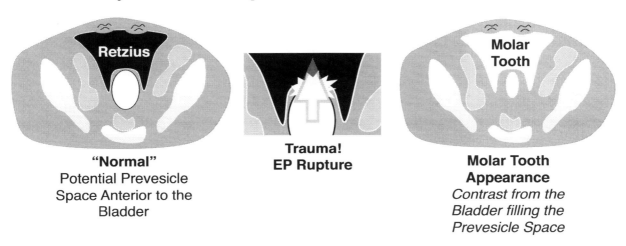

"Normal"
Potential Prevesicle
Space Anterior to the
Bladder

Trauma!
EP Rupture

Molar Tooth
Appearance
*Contrast from the
Bladder filling the
Prevesicle Space*

Intraperitoneal - This one is less common. A direct blow to a full bladder, basically pops the balloon and blows the top off (bladder dome is the weakest part). The dude will have contrast outlining bowel loops and in the paracolic gutters. This requires surgery.

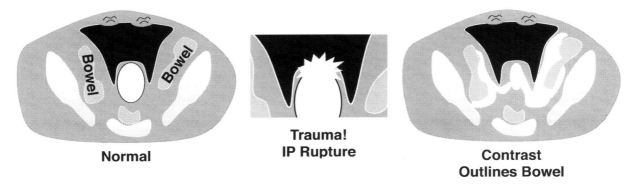

Normal

Trauma!
IP Rupture

Contrast
Outlines Bowel

"Pseudo Azotemia" (Pseudo Renal Failure) - If the bladder is ruptured the creatinine in urine can be absorbed via the peritoneal lining. This will massively elevate the creatinine making it seem like the patient is in acute renal failure. The kidneys are normal.

SECTION 12:
Urethra

- Male -

Normal Anatomy (most commonly seen on a RUG), is high yield. Here are the basics:

- The length is highly variable with most texts using the following graded scale:
  (itty bitty -> teeny tiny -> tiny -> small -> medium -> large -> extra large -> Lionhart sized).

- Anatomists divide the thing into two main parts - anterior and posterior. The anterior part is made up of the penile urethra + the bulbar urethra. The posterior part is made up of the membranous and prostatic urethra.

- The most anterior portion of the urethra is termed the fossa navicularis which has a Latin / French sound to it, so it is probably testable.

- The "Verumontanum" (another fancy sounding term) is an ovoid mound that lies in the posterior wall of the prostatic urethra. An additional testable piece of trivia is that in the center of this thing is the prostatic utricle (which is an embryologic "mullerian" remnant).

- The anterior part fills with a retrograde study (RUG). The posterior part fills with an antegrade study (voiding urethrography). "Dynamic Urethrography" is the term used when these studies are combined. You can fill the whole thing with a RUG - but that requires pressure to overcome the normal spasms of this cruel and unusual procedure.

- There are two methods for identifying the bulbar-membranous junction (which is important for delineating pathology - anterior vs posterior). The first is to find the "cone" shaped appearance of the proximal bulbar urethra. The cone will taper into the membranous portion. The second (used if you can't opacify the urethra) is to draw a line connecting the inferior margins of the obturator foramina.

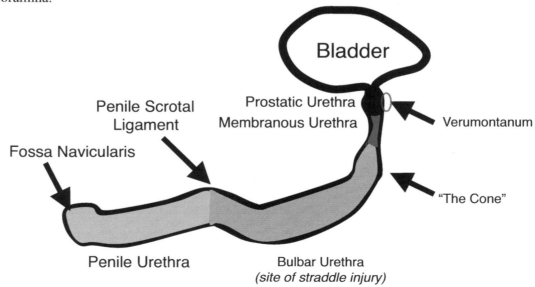

Trauma:

Trauma + Blood in the meatus = "Next Step" RUG.

Anterior Injury - Classic = Crashed your bicycle (or tricycle). i.e. = <u>Straddle Injury</u>. Unicycle wreck is less often associated with urethral injury (because of the lack of cross bar) but is often associated with various juggling, fire eating, and sword swallowing injury patterns - as well as mania, and histrionic personality disorder.

Posterior Injury - Classic = Crashed your Ferrari. Testable trivia = Often associated with a <u>pelvic fracture and bladder injury</u>. I speculate that crashing ones Ferrari is also associated with sudden and severe atrophy of the penis.

1970s Classification System - Fair Game for the "Exam of Future."

Type 1	Type 2	Type 3 (most common)	Type 4	Type 5
"STRETCHED"	Membraneous Urethra Tear	Membraneous + Bulbar Urethra Tear	Bladder Base injury extending into Prostatic Urethra	Bulbous Urethra "Anterior"
Posterior	Posterior	Anterior + Posterior	Posterior	Anterior
Urethra is intact and normal on RUG	ABOVE an INTACT UG Diaphram	UG Diaphragm is ruptured.		
	Extraperitoneal contrast is present	Extraperitoneal contrast is present		Straddle Injury
	No perineum contrast (intact UG diaphragm prevents this)	Perineum contrast (UG diaphragm is torn). Contrast in the scrotum.		
	Associated with Incontinance	Associated with Incontinance	Associated with Incontinance	

- Urethral Strictures -

THIS vs THAT: The Bicycle Crossbar Injury vs The Injury From a Woman of Questionable Moral Standard

Straddle Injury: The most common external cause of traumatic stricture is this type of mechanism. The physiology is compression of the urethra against the inferior edge of the pubic symphysis. **The bulbous urethra is the site of injury** (this is the most likely question).

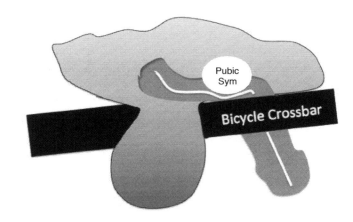

Gonococcal Urethral Stricture: This tends to be a **long irregular stricture** (the straddle stricture was short). It occurs in the **distal bulbous urethra**.

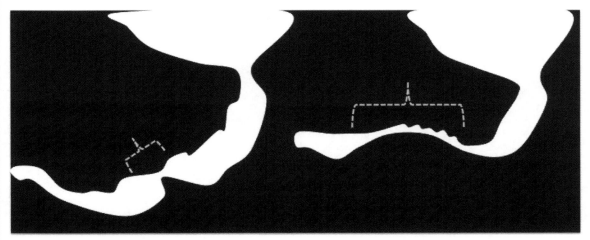

Straddle Injury
Short Segment - Bulbous Urethra

Gonococcal
Long Segment & Irregular- Bulbous Urethra

Other Male Urethral Pathologies:

Pancreatic Transplant: This has been known to cause urethral injury, if the drainage is to the bladder (the old way of doing it). Extravasation from urethral injury is said to occur in about 5% of cases and is secondary to pancreatic enzymes jacking the urethra.

Condyloma Acuminatum – Multiple small filling defects seen on a RUG should make you think this. Although, instrumentation including a retrograde urethrography is actually not recommended because of the possibility of retrograde seeding.

Urethrorectal Fistula: This may occur post radiation, and is classically described with brachytherapy (occurs in 1% of patients).

Urethral Diverticulum: In a man, this is almost always the result of long term foley placement.

Cancer: Malignant tumors of the male urethra are rare. When they do occur, **80% are squamous cell cancers** (the *exception is that prostatic urethra actually has transitional cell 90% of the time*).

Urethral Diverticulum Cancer: Cancer in a urethral diverticulum is nearly **ALWAYS adenocarcinoma** (rather than squamous cell).

Female Urethra:

Female Urethral Diverticulum: Urethral diverticulum is way more common in females. They are usually the result of repeated infection of the periurethral glands (classic **history is "repeated urinary tract infections"**).

In case books and conferences this is **classically shown as a Sagittal MRI**. It often coexists with stress urinary incontinence (60%) and urinary infection.

 The **buzzword is "saddle-bag"** configuration, which supposedly is how you tell it from the urethra.

Stones can also develop in these things. All this infection and irritation leads to increased **risk of cancer**, and the very common **high yield factoid is this is most commonly adenocarcinoma (60%).**

- GU Cancer Blitz ! -

Renal Cancer: *(Adenocarcinoma)*

- -Subtypes:
- Clear Cell - Most Common (Enhances More)
- Papillary - 2nd Most Common (Enhances Less)
- Medullary - Buzzword for Sickle Cell Trait
- Chromophobe - Buzzword for Burt Hogg Dube

- -Syndrome:
- Von Hippel Lindau - Multiple Clear Cells

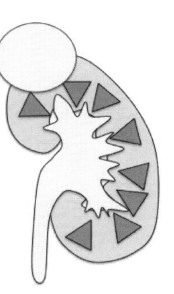

Ureteral Cancer *(Transitional Cell)*

- -Location - *think about where you get the most stasis*
- *Renal Pelvis - Twice as common as Ureter*
- *Distal Third of Ureter - Most common site*
- *Middle is 2nd, and Proximal is Third*

- Relationship to Bladder CA
- *Bladder CA is way more common (like 100x more).*
- *So if you have bladder CA you don't need upper tract CA. Since upper tract CA is not all that common, if you smoked enough Marlboro Reds to get renal pelvis CA, you probably smoked enough to get multifocal disease including the bladder.*

Bottom Line:
> *Bladder can be isolated*
> *Ureteral CA usually also has bladder CA*

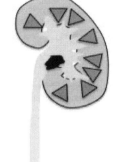

Bladder Cancer

Transitional Cell CA
-The normal kind
-Much more common than the ureter (like 100x)

Squamous Cell CA
-With lots of calcifications
-In the setting of schistosomiasis
- Chronic suprapubic catheter

Adenocarcinoma
-Midline CA (Urachus)
-Bladder Exstrophy

Urethral Cancer

Bladder

Urethral Diverticulum
-Adenocarcinoma

Prostatic Urethra
-Transitional Cell (90%)
-Think about it like a Bladder CA

Bulbar / Penile Urethra
-Squamous Cell CA (80%)

Blank for Scribbles and Notes

5
REPRODUCTIVE

PROMETHEUS LIONHART, M.D.

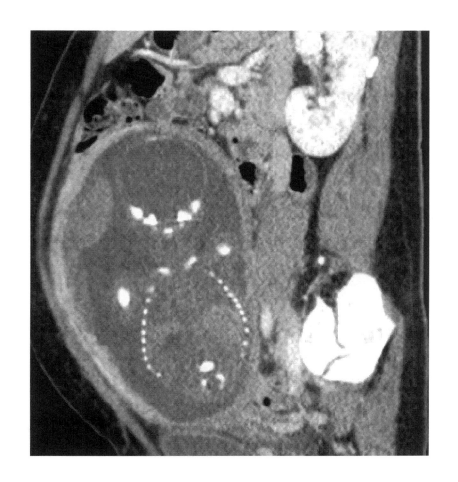

SECTION 1:
Congenital

The Uterus – Changes During Life

- *Neonate* - Uterus is larger than you would think for a baby (maternal / placental hormones are still working). If you look close, the shape is a little weird with the <u>cervix often larger than the fundus.</u>

- *Prepuberty* - The shape of the uterus changes - becoming more <u>tube-like</u>, with the <u>cervix and uterus the same size.</u>

- *Puberty* - The shape of the uterus changes again, now looking more like an adult (<u>pear-like</u>) - with the <u>fundus larger than the cervix.</u> In puberty, the uterus starts to have a visible endometrium - with phases that vary during the cycle.

The Ovaries – Changes During Life

Just like with the uterus, infants tend to have larger ovaries (volume around 1 cc), which then decrease and remain around or less than 1 cc until about age 6. The ovaries then gradually increase to normal adult size as puberty approaches and occurs.

Turner Syndrome – The XO kids. Besides often having aortic coarctations, and horseshoe kidneys they will have a <u>pre-puberty uterus</u> and <u>streaky ovaries.</u>

Embryology:

The quick and dirty of it is that the mullerian ducts make the uterus and upper 2/3 of the vagina. The urogenital sinus grows up to meet the mullerian ducts and makes the bottom 1/3 of the vagina. Wolffian ducts are the boy parts, and should regress completely in girls.

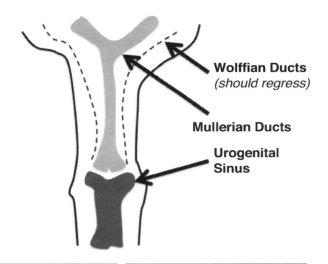

Wolffian Ducts
(should regress)

Mullerian Ducts

Urogenital Sinus

Mullerian Ducts	**Wolffian Ducts**	**Urogenital Sinus**
Uterus	Vas Deferens	Prostate
Fallopian Tubes	Seminal Vesicles	Lower 1/3 of the Vagina
Upper 2/3 of the Vagina	Epididymis	

My idea for teaching this somewhat confusing topic is to tap into the thought process of embryology to help understand why anomalies happen, and why they happen together. The embryology I'm about to discuss is not strict and doesn't use all the fancy French / Latin words. It's more concept related…

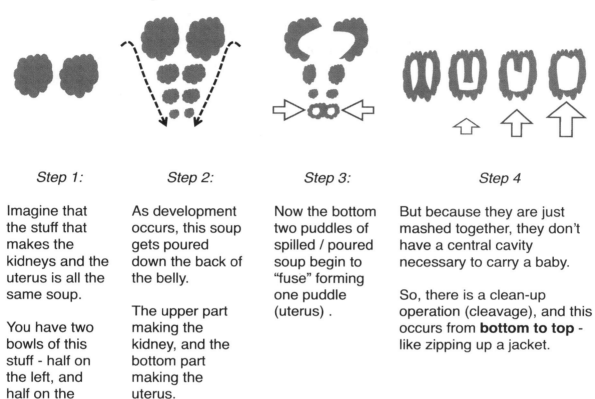

Step 1:	Step 2:	Step 3:	Step 4
Imagine that the stuff that makes the kidneys and the uterus is all the same soup. You have two bowls of this stuff - half on the left, and half on the right.	As development occurs, this soup gets poured down the back of the belly. The upper part making the kidney, and the bottom part making the uterus.	Now the bottom two puddles of spilled / poured soup begin to "fuse" forming one puddle (uterus) .	But because they are just mashed together, they don't have a central cavity necessary to carry a baby. So, there is a clean-up operation (cleavage), and this occurs from **bottom to top** - like zipping up a jacket.

So there are 3 main ways this whole process can get screwed up.

(1) You can only have soup on one side. This is a **"failure to form"** As you can imagine, if you don't have the soup on one side you don't have a kidney on that side. You also don't have half of your uterus. This is why a unilateral absent kidney is associated with Unicornuate Uterus (+/- rudimentary horn).

(2) As the soup gets poured down it can **fail to fuse** completely. This can be on the spectrum of mostly not fused - basically separate (Uterus Didelphys) or mostly fused except the top part - so it looks like a heart (Bicornuate). Because the Bicornuate and Didelphys are related pathologies - they both get vaginal septa (Didelphys more often than Bicornuate - easily remembered because it's a more severe fusion anomaly).

(3) The clean up operation can be done sloppy ("**failure to cleave**"). The classic example of this is a "Septate uterus," where a septum remains between the two uterine cavities.

"Failure to Form"

- **Mullerian Agenesis** (Mayer-Rokitansky-Kuster-Hauser syndrome): Has three features: (1) vaginal atresia, (2) absent or rudimentary uterus (unicornuate or bicornuate) and (3) normal ovaries. The key piece of trivia is that the **kidneys have issues** (agenesis, ectopia) in about half the cases.

- **Unicornuate Uterus** – There are 4 subtypes (basically +/- rudimentary horn, +/- endometrial tissue). Obviously, endometrial tissue in a non-communicating horn is going to cause pelvic pain. Also, Endometrial tissue in a rudimentary horn (communicating or not) – increases the risk of miscarriage and uterine rupture. **40% of these chicks will have renal issues (usually renal agenesis) ipsilateral to the rudimentary horn**.

> **Vocab**
> *(in case you don't speak French or whatever)*
>
> **Cornus = Uterus**
> **Collis = Cervical**

"Failure to Fuse"

- **Uterus Didelphys** – This is a complete uterine duplication (two cervices, two uteri, and two upper 1/3 vagina). A vaginal septum is present 75% of the time. If the patient does not have vaginal obstruction this is usually asymptomatic.

- **Bicornuate** – This comes in two flavors (one cervix "unicollis", or two cervix "bicollis"). There will be separation of the uterus by a deep myometrial cleft - makes it look "heart shaped". Vaginal septum is seen around 25% of the time (less than didelphys). Although they can have an increased risk of fetal loss, it's much less of an issue compared to Septate. Fertility isn't as much of a "size thing" as it is a blood supply thing. Remember you can have 8 babies in your belly at once and have them live… live long enough to take part in your reality show.

- **T- Shaped** – This is the **DES related anomaly**. It is historical trivia, and therefore extremely high yield for the "exam of the future." DES was a synthetic estrogen given to prevent miscarriage in the 1940s. The daughters of patients who took this drug ended up with vaginal clear cell carcinoma, and uterine anomalies – classically the "T-Shaped Uterus."

"Failure to Cleave"

- **Septate** – This one has two endometrial canals separated by a fibrous (or muscular) septum. Fibrous vs Muscular can be determined with MRI and this distinction changes surgical management (different approaches). There is an increased risk of infertility and recurrent spontaneous abortion. The septum has a shitty blood supply, and if there is implantation on it - it will fail early. They can resect the septum - which improves outcomes.

- **Arcuate Uterus** – Mild smooth concavity of the uterine fundus (instead of normal straight or convex) This is not really a malformation, but more of a <u>normal variant</u>. It is **NOT associated with infertility or obstetric complications**.

THIS vs THAT: Bicornuate vs Septate

Bicornuate

- *"Heart Shaped"* - Fundal contour is <u>less</u> than 5 mm above the tubal ostia

- No significant infertility issues

- Resection of the "septum" results in poor outcomes

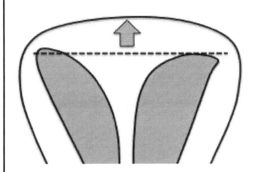

Septate

- Fundal contour is **Normal**; <u>more</u> than 5 mm above the tubal ostia

- Legit infertility issues - implantation fails on the septum (it's a blood supply thing)

- Resection of the septum can help

Hysterosalpingogram (HSG)

If you haven't seen (or done one) before - this is a procedure that involves cannulation of the cervix and injecting contrast under fluoro to evaluate the cavity of the uterus.

Testable Trivia:
- HSGs are performed on days 7-10 of menstrual cycle, (after menstrual bleeding complete - i.e. "off the rag")
- Contraindications: infection (PID), active bleeding ("rag week"), pregnancy, and contrast allergy.
- Bicornuate vs Septate is tough on HSG - you need MRI or 3D Ultrasound to evaluate the outer fundal contour.

0-7 "Rag Week," 7-14 Proliferative, 14-28 Secretory
*Day 14 Ovulation

SECTION 2:
Acquired

Salpingitis Isthmica Nodosa (SIN):

This is a nodular scarring of the fallopian tubes that produces an Aunt Minnie Appearance. As trivia, it usually involves the proximal 2/3 of the tube. This is of unknown etiology, but likely post inflammatory / infectious (i.e. being a woman of questionable moral standard / "free spirit"). It's strongly **associated with infertility and ectopic pregnancy** and that is likely the question.

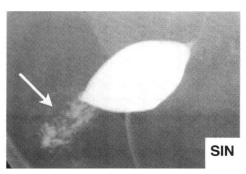

SIN

- Nodular diverticula of the fallopian tubes
- No dominant channel

Uterine AVM – These can be congenital or acquired, with acquired types being way more common. They can be serious business and you can totally bleed to death from them. The typical ways to acquire them include: **previous dilation and curettage,** therapeutic abortion, caesarean section, or just multiple pregnancies. Doppler ultrasound is going to show: serpiginous and/or tubular anechoic structures within the myometrium with **high velocity color Doppler flow.**

Intrauterine Adhesions (Ashermans) – This is scarring in the uterus, that occurs secondary to injury: prior dilation and curettage, surgery, pregnancy, or infection (classic GU TB). This is typically shown on HSG, with either (a) non filling of the uterus, or (b) multiple irregular linear filling defects (lacunar pattern), with inability to appropriately distend the endometrial canal. MRI would show a bunch of T2 dark bands. Clinically, this results in infertility.

Endometritis – This is in the spectrum of PID. You often see it 2-5 days after delivery, especially in women with prolonged labor or premature rupture. You are going to have fluid and a thickened endometrial cavity. You can have gas in the cavity (not specific in a postpartum women). It can progress to pyometrium, which is when you have expansion with pus.

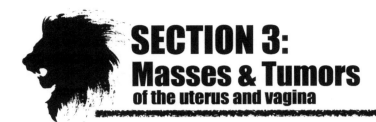

SECTION 3:
Masses & Tumors
of the uterus and vagina

Fibroids (Uterine Leiomyoma): These benign smooth muscle tumors are the most common uterine mass. They are more common in women of African ancestry. They like estrogen and are most common in reproductive age (rare in prepubertal females). Because of this estrogen relationship they tend to grow rapidly during pregnancy, and involute with menopause. Their location is classically described as submucosal (least common), intramural (most common), or subserosal.

Typical Appearance: The general rule is they **can look like anything**. Having said that, they are usually hypoechoic on ultrasound, often with peripheral blood flow and shadowing in the so called "Venetian Blind" pattern. On CT, they often have peripheral calcifications ("popcorn" as seen on plain film). On MRI, **T1 dark** (to intermediate), **T2 dark**, and variable enhancement. The fibroids with higher T2 signal are said to respond better to IR treatment. A variant subtype is the lipoleiomyoma, which is fat containing.

- *Degeneration:* 4 types of degeneration are generally described. *What they have in common is a lack of / paucity of enhancement (fibroids normally enhance avidly).*

- *Hyaline – This is the most common type.* The fibroid outgrows its blood supply, and you end up getting the accumulation of proteinaceous tissue. They are T2 dark, and do not enhance post Gd.

- *Red (Carneous)* – This one **occurs during pregnancy.** This is caused by venous thrombosis. The classic imaging finding is a **peripheral rim of T1 high signal**. The T2 signal is variable.

- *Myxoid* – Uncommon type of degeneration. This is suggested by T1 dark, **T2 bright** and minimal gradual enhancement.

- *Cystic* – Uncommon type

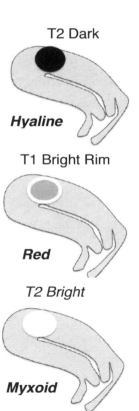

T2 Dark

Hyaline

T1 Bright Rim

Red

T2 Bright

Myxoid

Uterine Leiomyosarcoma – The risk of malignant transformation to a leiomyosarcoma is super low (0.1%). These look like a fibroid, but rapidly enlarge. Areas of necrosis are often seen.

Adenomyosis - This is endometrial tissue that has migrated into the myometrium. You see it **most commonly in multiparous women of reproductive age, especially if they've had a history of uterine procedures** (Caesarian section, dilatation and curettage).

Although there are several types, adenomyosis is usually generalized, favoring large portions of the uterus (especially the **posterior wall**), but **sparing the cervix**. It classically causes marked enlargement of the uterus, with preservation of the overall contour.

They can show it with Ultrasound or MRI. Ultrasound is less specific with findings including a heterogeneous uterus (hyperechoic adenomyosis, with hypoechoic muscular hypertrophy), or just enlargement of the posterior wall. MRI is the way better test with the most classic feature being **thickening of the junctional zone of the uterus to more than 12 mm** (normal is < 5 mm). The thickening can be either focal or diffuse. Additionally, the findings of small high T2 signal regions corresponding to regions of cystic change is a classic finding.

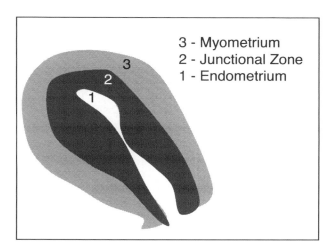

3 - Myometrium
2 - Junctional Zone
1 - Endometrium

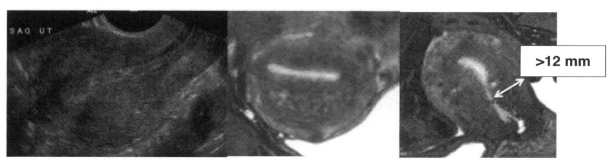

>12 mm

Adenomyosis of the Uterus
- Note the T2 Bright Cystic Foci and thick junctional zone

- Thick Endometrium -

Remember the stripe is measured without including any fluid in the canal. Focal or generalized thickening in post menopausal women greater than 5mm should get sampled. Premenopausal endometriums can get very thick - up to 20mm can be normal.

Trivia:
- *Estrogen secreting tumors* – Granulosa Cell tumors of the ovary will thicken the endometrium.
- *Hereditary Non-Polyposis Colon Cancer (HNPCC)* – have a 30-50x increased risk of endometrial cancer

---

Postmenopausal Bleeding:
Is it from atrophy or cancer?

•Endometrium less than 5 mm = Probably Atrophy

•Endometrium > 4-5 mm = Maybe cancer and gets a biopsy

Tamoxifen Changes – This is a SERM (acts like estrogen in the pelvis, blocks the estrogen effects on the breast). It's used for breast cancer, but **increases the risk of endometrial cancer**. It will cause subendometrial cysts, **and the development of endometrial polyps** (30%). Normally, post menopausal endometrial tissue shouldn't be thicker than 4mm, but on Tamoxifen the endometrium is often thick (some papers say the mean is 12 mm at 5 years). When do you biopsy? Clear guidelines on this are illusive (if forced to guess I'd pick 8 or 10 mm). The only thing that seems consistent is that routine screening is NOT advised. If you are wondering if a polyp is hiding you can get a sonohysterogram (ultrasound after instillation of saline).

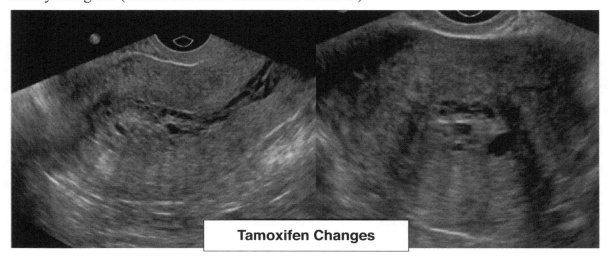
Tamoxifen Changes

Endometrial Fluid – In premenopausal women this is a common finding. In postmenopausal women it means either cervical stenosis or an obstructing mass (**usually cervical stenosis**).

- Endometrial Cancer -

Basically all uterine cancers are adenocarcinoma (90%+). The only possible exception for the purpose of multiple choice would be the rare "leiomyosarcoma" - which looks like a giant fucking fibroid.

Typical Scenario: A postmenopausal patient (60s) with bleeding.

"Work Up" First step is going to be an ultrasound. If the endometrium is too thick (most people say 4- 5mm) then it gets a biopsy. Almost always this will be stage 1 disease, and no further imaging will be done. If there is concern that it's more than stage 1 – that is when you would get MRI (CT is shit for the uterus and would never be the right answer).

- First Step Postmenopausal Bleeder = Ultrasound

- Too Thick ? = Biopsy

- Extent of Disease = MRI

Appearance on MRI:

- *T1 Iso*

- *T2 Mildly Hyper*

- *T1+C Homogenous, but less enhancement compared to adjacent myometrium (it's dark).*

- *DWI Will show restricted diffusion. This sequence is good for "Drop mets" into the vagina, and for lymph node detection.*

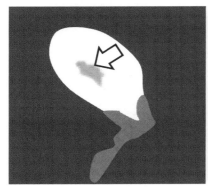 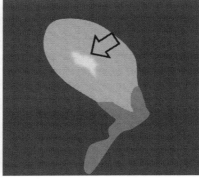 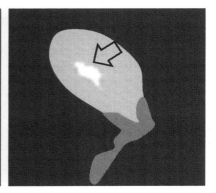

T1+C: *Tumor Enhances Less than Adjacent Myometrium*   ***T2 :*** *Tumor is Mildly Bright*   ***DWI :*** *Tumor Restricts*

- Endometrial Cancer - Continued

Critical Stage *(most testable stage) – Stage 1 to Stage 2*

- Stage 2 disease is defined as cervical stroma invasion. This is supposedly high risk for lymph node mets.

- The diagnostic key is the post contrast imaging (obtained 2-3 mins after injection). If the cervical mucosa enhances normally, you have excluded stromal invasion.

- Stage 2 is probably going to change management by adding pre-op radiation to the cervix, plus a change from TAH to radical hysterectomy (obviously this varies from center to center).

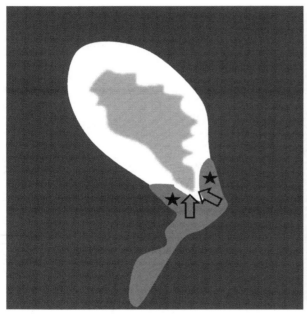

Stage 1:
T1+C: Normal Dark Cervical Stroma (star).
Enhancement of the Cervical Mucosa
(arrows) Excludes Invasion.

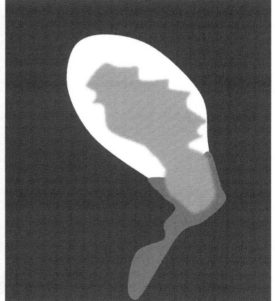

Stage 2:
T1+C: Tumor Invasion of the Cervix

Other Possible Trivia:

- Moving from stage 1A (<50% myometrium) to stage 1B (>50% of the myometrium) also increases the risk of lymph node disease.

- Some sites will do lymph node sample at stage 1A, and radical lymph node dissection at stage 1B.

- Cervical Cancer -

It's **usually squamous cell**, related to **HPV** (like 90%). The big thing to know is parametrial invasion (stage IIb). Stage IIa or below is treated with surgery. **Once you have parametrial invasion (stage IIb),** or involvement of the lower 1/3 of the vagina it's gonna get chemo/ radiation. In other words, management changes so that is the most likely test question.

Cervical Cancer Staging Pearls		
Stage II A	Spread beyond the cervix, but NO parametrial invasion	Surgery
Stage II B	Parametrial involvement but NOT extension to pelvic side wall.	Chemo/ Radiation

How can I tell If there is Parametrial Invasion ?
I don't even know what the hell the "parametrium" is....

What is this parametrium ? The parametrium is a fibrous band that separates the supravaginal cervix from the bladder. It extends between the layers of the broad ligament.

Why is it so important ? The uterine artery runs inside the parametrium, hence the need for chemo - once invaded.

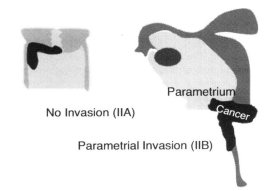

No Invasion (IIA)

Parametrium

Cancer

Parametrial Invasion (IIB)

How do you tell if it's invaded ? Normally the cervix has a T2 dark ring. That thing should be intact. If the tumor goes through that thing, you gotta call it invaded.

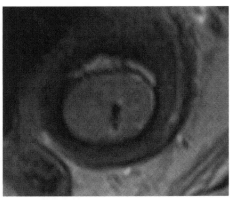

T2 Dark Ring Intact
(No Parametrial invasion)

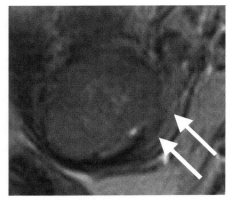

T2 Dark Ring Disrupted - arrow
(Parametrial invasion)

- Vagina -

Could also be referred to as the *"Petal-soft Fold of Womanhood," "Pearl of Passion,"* or *"Door of Femininity"* - if the question writer is a fan of Romance Novels.

Solid Vaginal Masses:

An uninvited solid vaginal mass is usually a bad thing. It can be secondary (cervical or uterine carcinoma protruding into the vagina), or primary such as a clear cell adenocarcinoma or rhabdomyosarcoma.

Leiomyoma – Rare in the vagina, but can occur (most commonly in the anterior wall).

Squamous Cell Carcinoma – The most common cancer of the vagina (85%). This is associated with HPV. This is just like the cervix.

Clear Cell Adenocarcinoma - This is the zebra cancer seen in women whose mothers took DES (a synthetic estrogen thought to prevent miscarriage). That plus "T-Shaped Uterus" is probably all you need to know.

Vaginal Rhabdomyosarcoma - This is the most common tumor of the vagina in children. There is a bimodal age distribution in ages (2-6, and 14-18). They usually come off the anterior wall near the cervix. It can occur in the uterus, but typically invades it secondarily. Think about this when you see a solid T2 bright enhancing mass in the vagina / lower uterus in a child.

Mets Trivia:
- *A met to the vagina in the anterior wall upper 1/3 is "always" (90%) upper genital tract.*
- *A met to the vagina in the posterior wall lower 1/3 is "always" (90%) from the GI tract.*

Cystic Vaginal / Cervical Masses:

Nabothian Cysts – These are usually on the cervix and you see them all the time. They are the result of inflammation causing epithelium plugging of mucous glands.

Gartner Ducts Cysts – These are the result of **incomplete regression of the Wolffian ducts**. They are classically located along the anterior lateral wall of the upper vagina. If they are located at the level of the urethra, that **can cause mass effect on the urethra** (and symptoms).

Bartholin Cysts – These are the result of obstruction of the Bartholin glands (mucin-secreting glands from the urogenital sinus). They are found below the pubic symphysis (helps distinguish them from Gartner duct).

Skene Gland Cysts – Cysts in these periurethral glands, can cause recurrent UTIs and urethral obstruction.

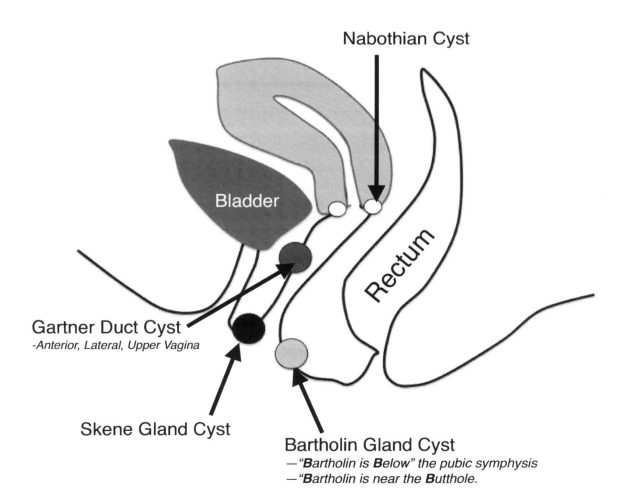

Nabothian Cyst

Bladder

Rectum

Gartner Duct Cyst
-*Anterior, Lateral, Upper Vagina*

Skene Gland Cyst

Bartholin Gland Cyst
—*"Bartholin is **Below**" the pubic symphysis*
—*"Bartholin is near the **B**utthole.*

SECTION 4:
Ovary / Adnexa

Before we begin, a few general tips (1) never biopsy or recommend biopsy of an ovary, (2) on CT if you can't find the ovary, follow the gonadal vein, and (3) hemorrhage in a cystic mass usually means it's benign.

A quick note on ovarian size; ovarian volume can be considered normal up until 15 ml (some say 20 ml). The post menopausal ovary should NOT be larger than 6 cc.

Let's talk about ovulation - *to help understand the normal variation in the ovary.*

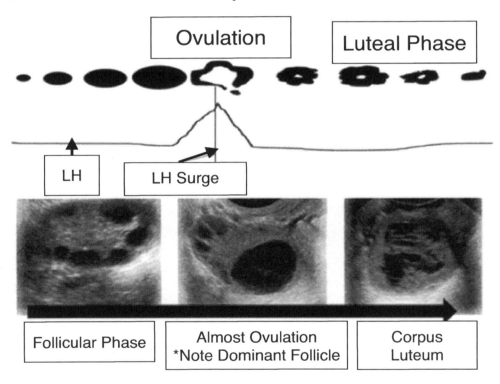

Follicles seen during the early menstrual cycle are typically small (< 5 mm in diameter). By day 10 of the cycle, there is usually one follicle that has emerged as the dominant follicle. By mid cycle, this dominant follicle has gotten pretty big (around 20 mm). Its size isn't surprising because it contains a mature ovum. The LH surge causes the dominant follicle to rupture, releasing the egg. The follicle then regresses in size, forming a Corpus Luteum. A small amount of fluid can be seen in the cul-de-sac. Occasionally, a follicle bleeds and re-expands (hemorrhagic cyst) – more on this later.

Cumulus Oophorus

This is a piece of anatomy trivia. It is a collection of cells in a mature dominant follicle that protrudes into the follicular cavity, and **signals imminent ovulation** (its absence means nothing).

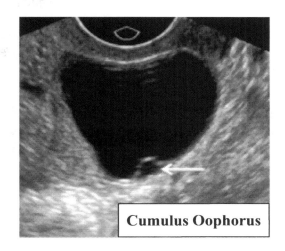

Cumulus Oophorus

Fertility Meds

 Medications such as a Clomiphene Citrate (Clomid), force the maturation of multiple bilateral ovarian cysts. It is not uncommon for the ovaries of women taking this drug to have multiple follicles measuring more than 20 mm in diameter by mid cycle.

Theca Lutein Cysts – this is a type of functional cyst (more on that below), related to overstimulation from b-HCG. What you see are large cysts (~ 2-3 cm) and the **ovary has a typical multilocular cystic "spoke-wheel" appearance**.

Think about 3 things:

•Multifetal pregnancy,
•**Gestational trophoblastic disease (moles)**,
•Ovarian **Hyperstimulation syndrome**.

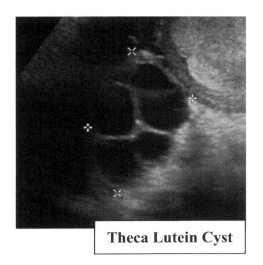

Theca Lutein Cyst

Ovarian Hyperstimulation Syndrome – This is a complication associated with fertility therapy (occurs in like 5%). They will show you the ovaries with **theca lutein cysts**, then ascites, and **pleural effusions**. They may also have pericardial effusions. Complications include increased risk for ovarian torsion (big ovaries) and hypovolemic shock.

THIS vs THAT: Old vs Young

Premenstrual:

- The ovaries of a pediatric patient stay small until around age 8-9.

- Ovaries may contain small follicles.

Premenopausal:

- A piece of trivia; premenopausal ovaries **may be HOT on PET** (depending on the menstrual cycle).

- This is why you do a PET in the first week of the menstrual cycle.

Postmenopausal *(> one year after menses stops):*

- Considered **abnormal if** it exceeds the upper limit of normal, or is **twice the size of the other ovary (even if no mass is present).**

- Small cysts (< 3 cm) are seen in around 20% of post menopausal women.

- In general, postmenopausal ovaries are atrophic, lack follicles, and can be difficult to find with ultrasound.

- The ovarian volume will decrease from around 8cc at age 40, to around 1cc at age 70.

- The **maximum ovarian volume in a post menopausal woman is 6 ml.**

- Unlike premenopausal ovaries, **post menopausal ovaries should NOT be hot on PET.**

⚕ Simple Cyst in ⚕ Postmenopausal Woman
WTF Do I Do Now?

If the cyst is simple, regardless of age it's almost certainly benign.

Having said that, the rules are (per SRU 2010):

- Premenopausal
  - < = 5cm = No Followup
  - > 5cm and < 7 cm = Yearly US Followup
- Postmenopausal
  - < 1cm = *"Meaningless!"*
  - > 1cm and < = 7 cm = Yearly US Followup
- Any Age
  - > 7 cm = Surgical Eval (maybe MRI)

If it's first seen on another modality (CT), I would get an Ultrasound first to confirm it's totally cystic - without suspicious features like papillary projections, nodules, thick septations, etc.... Then follow the rules as above.

Smokey this is not `Nam, this is bowling. There are rules...

- THE SINISTER SIX -

In most clinical practices, the overwhelming majority of ovarian masses are benign (don't worry, I'll talk about cancer, too).

- Physiologic and functioning follicles
- Corpora lutea
- Hemorrhagic cysts
- Endometriomas
- Benign cystic teratomas (dermoids)
- Polycystic ovaries

Functioning Ovarian Cysts: Functioning cysts (follicles) are affected by the menstrual cycle (as I detailed eloquently above). These cysts are benign and usually 25 mm or less in diameter. They will usually change / disappear in 6 weeks. If a cyst persists and either does not change or increases in size, it is considered a nonfunctioning cyst (not under hormonal control).

Simple cysts that are > 7 cm in size may need further evaluation with MR (or surgical evaluation). Just because it's hard to evaluate them completely on US when they are that big, and you risk torsion with a cyst that size.

Corpus Luteum: The normal corpus luteum arises from a dominant follicle (as I detailed eloquently above). These things can be large (up to 5-6 cm) with a variable appearance (solid hypoechoic, anechoic, thin-walled, thick-walled, cyst with debris). The most common appearance is solid and hypoechoic with a "ring of fire" (intense peripheral blood flow).

THIS *vs* THAT: Corpus Luteum *vs* Ectopic Pregnancy

They both can have that "ring of fire" appearance, but please don't be an idiot about this. Most ectopic pregnancies occur in the tube (the corpus luteum is an ovarian structure). If you are really lucky, a "hint" is that the corpus luteum should move with the ovary, where an ectopic will move separate from the ovary (you can push the ectopic away from it). Also, the tubal ring of an ectopic pregnancy is usually more echogenic when compared to the ovarian parenchyma. Whereas, the wall of the corpus luteum is usually less echogenic. A specific (but not sensitive) finding in ectopic pregnancy is a RI of <0.4 or >0.7.

Ectopic	Corpus Luteum
RI < 0.4, or > 0.7	RI 0.4 – 0.7
THICK Echogenic Rim	Thin Echogenic Rim
"Ring of Fire"	"Ring of Fire"
Moves Separate from the Ovary	Moves with the Ovary

Endometrioma:

This targets young women during their reproductive years and can cause chronic pelvic pain associated with menstruation. The traditional clinical history of endometriosis is the triad of infertility, dysmenorrhea, and dyspareunia.

The classic appearance is **rounded mass with homogeneous low level internal echoes and increased through transmission (seen in 95% of cases)**. Fluid-fluid levels and internal septations can also be seen. It can look a lot like a hemorrhagic cyst (sometimes). As a general rule, the more unusual or varied the echogenicity and the more ovoid or irregular the shape, the more likely the mass is an endometrioma. Additionally, and of more practical value, they are not going to change on follow up (hemorrhagic cysts are). In about 30% of cases you can get small echogenic foci adhering to the walls (this helps make the endometrioma diagnosis more likely). Obviously, you want to differentiate this from a true wall nodule.

> **Q:** What is the most sensitive imaging feature on MRI for the diagnosis of malignancy in an endometrioma ?
>
> **A:** An enhancing mural nodule

The complications of endometriosis (bowel obstruction, infertility, etc...) are due to a fibrotic reaction associated with the implant. The most common location for solid endometriosis is the uterosacral ligaments.

Do Endometriomas Ever Become Cancer? About 1% of endometriomas undergo malignant transformation (usually endometrioid or **clear cell carcinoma**). How do you tell which one is which??? Malignancy is very rare in endometriomas smaller than 6 cm. They usually have to be bigger than 9 cm. Additionally, the majority of women with carcinoma in an endometrioma are older than 45 years. So **risk factors for turning into cancer: (a) older than 45, (b) bigger than 6-9 cm.**

Pregnancy Trivia: There is a thing called a ***"decidualized endometrioma."*** This is a vocab word used to describe a solid nodule with blood flow in an endometrioma of a pregnant girl. Obviously this is still gonna get followed up - but is a mimic of malignancy. The thing never to forget is that if the patient is NOT pregnant and you see a solid nodule with blood flow - that is malignant degeneration - period - no hesitation, next question.

Endometrioma on MRI: Will be T1 bright (from the blood). Fat saturation will not suppress the signal (showing you it's not a teratoma). Will be T2 dark! (from iron in the endometrioma). The shading sign is a buzzword for endometriomas on MR imaging. On T2 you should look for "shading." **The shading sign describes T2 shortening (getting dark) of a lesion that is T1 bright.**

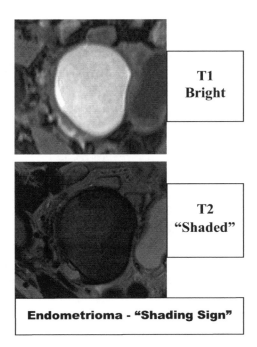

T1 Bright

T2 "Shaded"

Endometrioma - "Shading Sign"

Hemorrhagic Cysts:

As mentioned on prior pages, sometimes a ruptured follicle bleeds internally and re-expands. The result is a homogenous mass with **enhanced through transmission** *(tumor won't do that)* with a very similar look to an endometrioma. A lacy **"fishnet appearance"** is sometimes seen and is considered classic. Doppler flow will be absent. The traditional way to tell the difference between a hemorrhagic cyst vs endometrioma, is that the **hemorrhagic cyst will go away in 1-2 menstrual cycles** (so repeat in 6-12 weeks).

Hemorrhagic Cyst on MRI – Will be T1 bright (from the blood). Fat saturation will not suppress the signal (showing you it's not a teratoma). The lesion should NOT enhance.

Hemorrhagic cysts in old ladies? Postmenopausal women may occasionally ovulate, so you don't necessarily need to freak out (follow up in 6-12 weeks). Now, late postmenopausal women should NEVER have a hemorrhagic cyst and if you are shown something that looks like a hemorrhagic cyst in a 70 year old – it's cancer till proven otherwise.

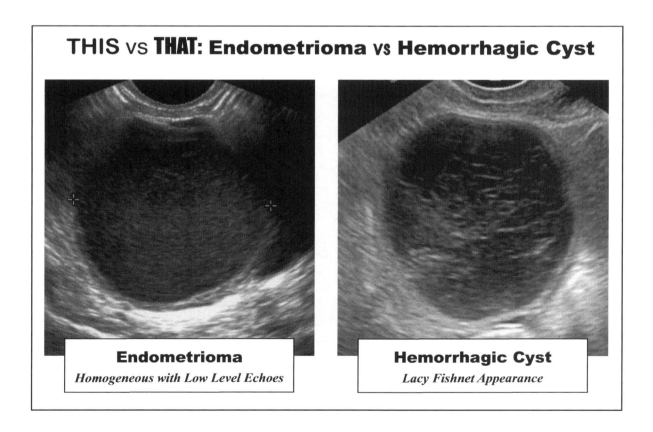

THIS vs THAT: Endometrioma vs Hemorrhagic Cyst

Endometrioma
Homogeneous with Low Level Echoes

Hemorrhagic Cyst
Lacy Fishnet Appearance

Dermoid:

These things typically occur in young women (20s-30s), and are the most common ovarian neoplasm in patients younger than 20. The "Tip of the Iceberg Sign" is a classic buzzword and refers to absorption of most of the US beam at the top of the mass. The typical ultrasound appearance is that of a cystic mass, with a hyperechoic solid mural nodule, (Rokitansky nodule or dermoid plug). Septations are seen in about 10%.

Dermoid on MRI: Will be bright on T1 (from the fat). There will be fat suppression (not true of hemorrhagic cysts, and endometriomas).

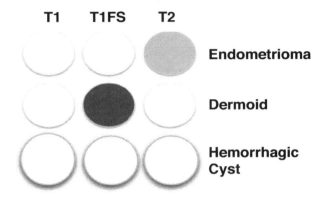

Do Dermoids Ever Become Cancer? About 1% of dermoids can undergo malignant transformation (**almost always to squamous cell CA**). Again, risk factors are size (usually larger than 10cm), and age (usually older than 50).

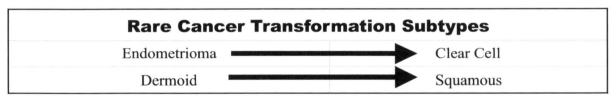

Rare Cancer Transformation Subtypes	
Endometrioma ⟶	Clear Cell
Dermoid ⟶	Squamous

Dermoid Gamesmanship = Gross Fat containing ovarian mass on CT

Dermoid Gamesmanship = The Old Tooth Trick - shown on plain film, CT, or even as susceptibility (dark stuff) on MR. Remember Dermoids are basically teratomas, and teratomas grow all kinds of gross shit including teeth, hair, finger nails etc… The tooth is obviously the classic one.

Polycystic Ovarian Syndrome:

—Typically an overweight girl with infertility, acne, and a mustache.

The imaging criteria is:

- **Ten or more peripheral simple cysts** *(typically small < 5 mm)*
- Usually Characteristic *'string-of-pearls'* appearance.
- **Ovaries are typically enlarged (> 10 cc),**
  although in 30% of patients the ovaries have a normal volume

SECTION 5:
Ovarian Cancer

Ovarian cancers often present as complex cystic and solid masses. They are typically intra-ovarian (most extra-ovarian masses are benign). The role of imaging is not to come down hard on histology (although the exam may ask this of you), but instead to distinguish benign from malignant and let the surgeon handle it from there.

Think Cancer if:

- Unilateral (or bilateral) complex cystic adnexal masses with thick (> 3 mm) septations, and papillary projections (nodule with blood flow).
- Solid adnexal masses with variable necrosis

Knee Jerks:

- Multiple thin or thick septations = Call the Surgeon
- Nodule with Flow = Call the Surgeon
- Solid Nodules Without Flow =
  - Get an MR to make sure it's not a dermoid plug,
  - If it's not a dermoid, then call the surgeon

Serous Ovarian / Cystadenocarcinoma / Cystadenoma

Serous tumors are the **most common type of ovarian malignancy**. About 60% of serous tumors are benign, and about 15% are considered borderline (the rest are malignant). They favor women of childbearing age, with the malignant ones tending to occur in older women. They typically are unilocular with few septations. They are frequently bilateral (especially when malignant). Papillary projections are a common finding, and are suggestive of malignancy. If you see ascites, they have mets (70% have peritoneal involvement at the time of diagnosis).

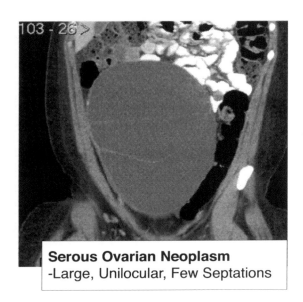

Serous Ovarian Neoplasm
-Large, Unilocular, Few Septations

Mucinous Ovarian Cystadenocarcinoma

Often a large mass. They are **typically multi-loculated** (although septa are often thin). **Papillary projections are less common** than with serous tumors. You can see low level echos (from mucin). These dudes can get Pseudomyxoma peritonei with scalloping along solid organs. Smoking is a known risk factor (especially for mucinous types).

| THIS vs **THAT**: Serous vs Mucinous ||
Serous:	Mucinous:
Unilocular (fewer septations)	Multi-locular (more septations)
Papillary Projections Common	Papillary Projections Less Common

Endometrioid Ovarian Cancer:

This is the second most common ovarian cancer (serous number one, mucinous number three). These things are bilateral about 15% of the time.

What to know:

- 25% of women will have concomitant endometrial cancer, with the endometrial cancer as the primary (ovary is met).
- Endometriomas can turn into endometrioid cancer
- 15% are bilateral

> **Gamesmanship: Ovarian Mass + Endometrial Thickening**
>
> This is a way to show both Endometrioid CA (which often has both ovarian and endometrial CA), and Granulosa-Theca Cell Tumor (which produce estrogen - and cause endometrial hyperplasia)

B.F.M's - for Adults

It's useful to have a differential for a **B.F.M.** (**B**ig **F**ucking **M**ass) in an adult and a child. I discuss the child version of this on page 58. For adults think about 3 main things:

(1) Ovarian Masses - Mucinous and Serous
(2) Desmoids - *Remember Gardner Syndrome*
(3) Sarcomas

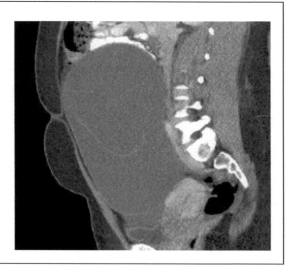

Fibroma / Fibrothecoma:

The ovarian fibroma is a benign ovarian tumor, most commonly seen in middle aged women. The fibrothecoma / thecoma spectrum has similar histology. It's **very similar to a fibroid**. On ultrasound it's going to be hypoechoic and solid. On MRI it's going to be T1 and T2 dark, with a **band of T2 dark signal around the tumor on all planes. Calcifications are rare.**

Similar or Related Conditions:

- **Meigs Syndrome:** This is the triad of ascites, pleural effusion, and a benign ovarian tumor (most commonly fibroma).

•**Fibromatosis:** This is a zebra. You have tumor-like enlargement of the ovaries due to ovarian fibrosis. It typically hits girls around the age of 25. It's associated with omental fibrosis and sclerosing peritonitis. You are going to get dark T1 and T2 signal. **The buzzword for that T2 signal is "black garland sign. "** The condition is benign, and sometimes managed with surgical removal of the ovaries.

- **Brenner Tumor:** Epithelial tumor of the ovary seen in women in their 50s-70s. It's fibrous and T2 dark. Unlike Fibromas, calcifications are common (80%). They are also sometimes referred to as *"Ovarian Transitional Cell Carcinoma"* for the purpose of fucking with you.

—

Struma Ovarii:

These things are actually a subtype of ovarian teratoma. On imaging you are looking for a multilocular, predominantly cystic mass with an INTENSELY enhancing solid component. On MRI - the give away is very low T2 signal in the "cystic" areas which is actually the thick colloid. These tumors contain THYROID TISSUE, and even though it's very rare (like 5%), I would expect that the question stem will lead you to this diagnosis by telling you the patient is hyperthyroid or in a thyroid storm.

Metastatic Disease to the Ovary

Around 10% of malignant ovarian tumors are mets. The primary is most commonly from colon, gastric, breast, lung, and contralateral ovary. The most common look is bilateral solid tumors.

Krukenburg Tumor

– This is a metastatic tumor to the ovaries from the GI tract (usually stomach).

SECTION 6:
Random Ovarian Path

-Ovarian Torsion

Rotation of the ovarian vascular pedicle (partial or complete) can result in obstruction to venous outflow and arterial inflow. Torsion is typically associated with a cyst or tumor (anything that makes it heavy, so it flops over on itself).

 <u>Critical Point</u> = The most constant finding in ovarian torsion is a large ovary.

Features:

- Unilateral enlarged ovary (greater than 4 cm)
- **Mass on the ovary**
- Peripheral Cysts
- Free Fluid
- Lack of arterial or venous flow

The Ovary is Not a Testicle: The ovary has a dual blood supply. Just because you have flow, does NOT mean there isn't a torsion. You can torse and de-torse. In other words, big ovary + pain = torsion. *Clinical correlation recommended.*

-Hydrosalpinx

Thin (or thick in chronic states) elongated tubular structure in the pelvis.

 The buzzword is **"cogwheel appearance,"** referring to the normal longitudinal folds of a fallopian tube becoming thickened. Another buzzword is **"string sign"** referring to the incomplete septae. The **"waist sign"** describes a tubular mass with indentations of its opposing walls (this is suppose to help differentiate hydrosalpinx from an ovarian mass).

There are a variety of causes, the most common is being a skank, infidel, or free spirit (PID). Additional causes include endometriosis, tubal cancer, post hysterectomy (without salpingectomy / oophorectomy), and tubal ligation. Rare and late complication is tubal torsion.

- Pelvic Inflammatory Disease (PID) *A plague upon the "dirty, slovenly, untidy woman"*

Infection or inflammation of the upper female genital tract. It's usually secondary to the cultural behaviors of trollops and strumpets (collectors of Gonorrhea / Chlamydia). As a hint, the question writer could describe the patient as "sexually disreputable. "

On ultrasound you are gonna see a **Hydrosalpinx**. The margin of the uterus may become ill defined ("indefinite uterus" – is a buzzword). Later on you can end up with tubo-ovarian abscess or pelvic abscess. You can even get bowel or urinary tract inflammatory changes.

- Paraovarian Cyst

This is a congenital remnant that arises from the Wolffian duct. They are more common than you think with some texts claiming these account for 10-20% of adnexal masses. They are classically round or oval, simple in appearance, and **do NOT distort the adjacent ovary** (key finding). They can indent the ovary and mimic an exophytic cyst, but a good sonographer can use the transducer to separate the two structures.

- Ovarian Vein Thrombophlebitis

This is seen most commonly in **postpartum women**, often presenting with acute pelvic pain and <u>fever</u>. For whatever reason, **80% of the time it's on the right**. It's most likely to be shown on CT (could be ultrasound) with a tubular structure with an enhancing wall and low-attenuation thrombus in the expected location of the ovarian vein. A dreaded sequela is pulmonary embolus.

- Peritoneal Inclusion Cyst

This is an inflammatory cyst of the peritoneal cavity that occurs when adhesions envelop an ovary. Adhesions can be thought of as diseased peritoneum. Whereas the normal peritoneum can absorb fluid, adhesions cannot. So, you end up with normal secretions from an active ovary confined by adhesions and resulting in an expanding pelvic mass. The classic history is patient with prior pelvic surgery (they have to tell you that, to clue you in on the presence of adhesions), now with pain.

They could get tricky and say history of PID or endometriosis (some kind of inflammatory process to piss off the peritoneum). In that case, it is likely they would show an ultrasound (or MR) with a complex fluid collection occupying pelvic recesses and containing the ovary. It's not uncommon to have septations, loculations, and particulate matter within the contained fluid.

Key Features:

- Lack of walls. "Passive shape" that conforms to and is defined by surrounding structures.

- Entrapment of an ovary. Ovary will be either in the collection, or at the periphery.

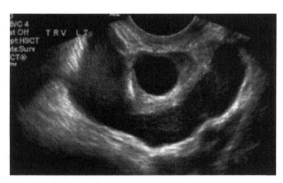

Peritoneal Inclusion Cyst -
Adhesions around an Ovary

Classic Vignette: A woman of reproductive age with a history of endometriosis, <u>pelvic surgery</u>, and pelvic inflammatory disease. Accompanied by images (most likely ultrasound, less likely CT or MR) or a fluid-filled mass that conforms to the shape of the pelvis and surrounds an ovary.

- Gestational Trophoblastic Disease

Think about this with marked elevation of B-hCG. They will actually trend betas for tumor activity. Apparently, elevated B-hCG makes you vomit – so hyperemesis is often part of the given history. Other pieces of trivia is that moles are more common in ages over 40, and prior moles makes you more likely to get another mole.

Hydatidiform Mole

This is the most common form, and the benign form of the disease. There are two subtypes:

- *Complete Mole* (classic mole) (70%): This one involves the entire placenta. There will be no fetus. The worthless trivia is that the karyotype is diploid. A total zebra scenario is that you have a normal fetus, with a complete mole twin pregnancy (if you see that in the wild, write it up). The pathogenesis is fertilization of an egg that has lost its chromosomes (46XX).

  First Trimester US: Classically shows the uterus to be filled with an echogenic, solid, highly vascular mass, often described as **"snowstorm"** in appearance.

  Second Trimester US: Vesicles that make up the mole enlarge into individual cysts (2-30 mm) and produce your **"bunch of grapes"** appearance.

- *Partial Mole* (30%): This one involves only a portion of the placenta. You do have a fetus, but it's all jacked up (triploid in karyotype). The pathogenesis is fertilization of an ovum by two sperm (69XXY). Mercifully, it's lethal to the fetus.

  US: The placenta will be enlarged, and have areas of multiple, diffuse anechoic lesions. You may see fetal parts.

Remember I mentioned that **Theca Lutein cysts are seen in molar pregnancies**.
Theca Lutein Cyst Trivia: Most commonly bilateral and seen in the second trimester

Invasive Mole

This refers to invasion of molar tissue into the myometrium. You typically see it after the treatment of a hydatidiform mole (about 10% of cases). US may show echogenic tissue in the myometrium. However, MRI is way better at demonstrating muscle invasive. MRI is going to demonstrate focal myometrial masses, dilated vessels, and areas of hemorrhage and necrosis.

Choriocarcinoma (the guacamole has gone bad)

This is a very aggressive malignancy that forms only trophoblasts (no villous structure). The typical attacking pattern of choriocarcinoma is to spread locally (into the myometrium and parametrium) then to spread hematogenous to any site in the body. It's very vascular and bleeds like stink. The classic clinical scenario is serum β-hCG levels that rise in the 8 to 10 weeks following evacuation of molar pregnancy. On ultrasound, choriocarcinoma (at any site) results in a highly echogenic solid mass. Treatment = methotrexate.

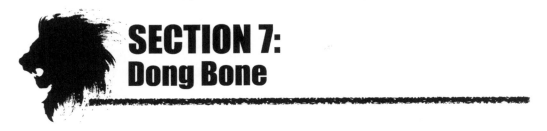

SECTION 7: Dong Bone

Could also be referred to as the *"Penis."*

Anatomy of this thing in cross section:

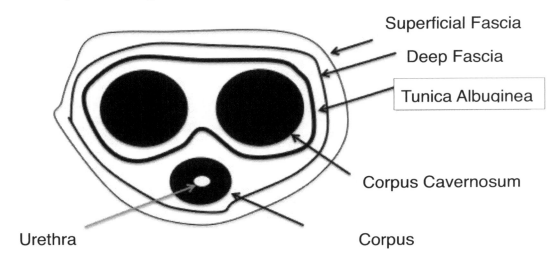

Superficial Fascia

Deep Fascia

Tunica Albuginea

Corpus Cavernosum

Urethra

Corpus

Fractured Penis: This is one of the most tragic situations that can occur in medicine. There are several potential mechanisms of injury. Anecdotally, it seems to be most common in older men participating in extra-marital relations with strippers named "Whisper." There is at least one article stating "impotence" is protective - which makes sense if you think about the pathophysiology.

They can show it on ultrasound (look for hematoma) or MRI.

Key Trivia: **Defined by fracture of the corpus cavernosum and its surrounding sheath, the tunica albuginea** (black line outlining the dong bone).

Cartooned T1 axial through the Dong Bone (Penis): Interruption of the black line (tunica albuginea) - arrow. It's helpful to look for hemorrhage (T1 bright) in the corpus cavernosum (the primary stabilizing strut of this battering ram).

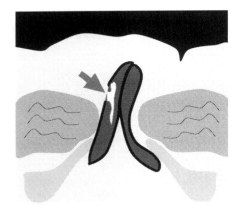

Stigmata of this injury can include a sub optimal angulation (Peyronie disease) from fibrous scar formation.

SECTION 8:
The People's Prostate

Cancer: Biopsy of the prostate is a terrible terrible situation, worse than anything you can imagine in 1000 years of hell. MRI of the prostate (instead of biopsy) is probably a little better although many sites use an endorectal coil...my God this endorectal coil! You can use prostate MRI for high risk screening (high or rising PSA with negative biopsy), or to stage (look for extracapsular extension).

First, let's talk about prostate anatomy: Anatomists like to use "zones" to describe locations, and it actually helps with pathology. The anterior fibromuscular gland is dark on T1 and T2. The central and transitional zones (together called the *"central gland"*) are brighter than the anterior muscular zone, but less bright than the peripheral zone on T2. In other words the **peripheral zone is the most T2 bright**.

Adenocarcinoma:
• Peripheral Zone: 70%
• Transition Zone: 20%
• Central Zone: 10%

Central "Gland"

Anterior Fibromuscular Zone

Transitional Zone

Central Zone

Median Lobe

TZ
CZ
PZ

Base

Midgland

CZ
PZ

Apex

PZ

Peripheral Zone
-70% of prostate cancer is here
-70% of gland mass

Dark Stuff = Central Gland
(this is where BPH nodules live)

Bright Stuff = Peripheral Zone
(this is where cancer lives)

Don't Confuse "Zones" and "Glands"

Vocab interposition is classic multiple choice fuckery.

Prostate Cancer Continued:

MRI finding for Prostate CA: **Cancer is dark on T2** (background is high) , restricts on diffusion (low on ADC), and enhances early and washes out (type 3 curve - just like a breast cancer).

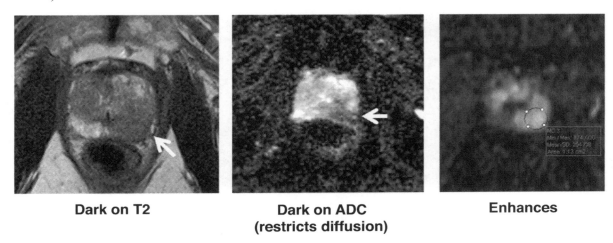

| Dark on T2 | Dark on ADC (restricts diffusion) | Enhances |

Bone scan is the money for prostate mets (vertebral body mets).

Trivia: PSA can be useful when considering risk of bone mets. There is at least 1 paper that says a PSA < 20 has a high predictive value in ruling OUT skeletal mets. In other words, PSA tends to be high when disease is aggressive enough to go to the bones.

Staging: The main thing to know is stage II vs stage III, as extra capsular extension is the most important factor governing treatment.

Stage II	Stage III
Confined by capsule (T2)	Extension through capsule (T3a)
Abutment of the capsule without bulging	Bulging of the capsule, or frank extension through it

Seminal vesicles (T3b) and the nerve bundle are also right behind the prostate and can get invaded (urologists love to hear about that).

Benign prostatic hyperplasia (BPH): Obviously this is super common, and makes old men pee a lot. Volume of 30cc is one definition. **Most commonly involves the transitional zone** (cancer is rare in the transitional zone – 10%). The central gland enlarges with age. The **median lobe** component is the one that hypertrophies and sticks up into the bladder. It can cause outlet obstruction, bladder wall thickening (detrusor hypertrophy), and development of bladder diverticulum.

 The IVP buzzword is "J shaped", "Fishhook", or "Hockey stick" shaped ureter - as the distal ureter curves around the enlarged prostate.

With regard to the BPH nodules you see on MRI, they are usually:
- In the Transitional Zone (Central Gland)
- T2 Heterogenous
- Can Restrict Diffusion
- May enhance and washout

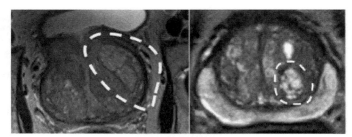

BPH Nodules
-Bright / Heterogenous Shit in the Central Gland-

Post Biopsy Changes: Classically T1 bright stuff in the gland. It's subacute blood.

The People's Prostate Pathology Summary Chart So You Can More Easily Smell What the Prostate is Cooking			
	T2	**ADC**	**Enhancement**
Peripheral Zone Tumor	Dark	Dark	Early Enhancement, Early Washout
Peripheral Zone Hemorrhage *Typically Post Biopsy	Dark (sometimes T1 bright)	Dark (less dark)	None
Central Gland / Transitional Zone Tumor	Dark "Charcoal"	Dark	Early Enhancement, Early Washout
BPH	Dark "Well Defined"	Less Dark	Can Enhance

SECTION 9:
Miscellaneous Male

It is best to first think about lower pelvic cysts in a male as either midline or lateral.

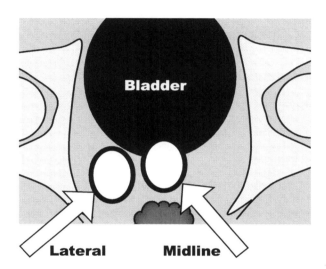

Male Pelvic Cysts	
Midline	**Lateral**
Prostatic Utricle	Seminal Vesicle Cyst
Mullerian Duct Cyst	Diverticulosis of the ampulla of vas deferens
Ejaculatory Duct Cysts	

LATERAL:

Seminal Vesicle Cyst:

The classic look is a **unilateral cyst that is lateral to the prostate.** If they get large they can look midline, but if they show you a large one you won't be able to tell it from a utricle cyst. They can be congenital or acquired.

Congenital Trivia:
- Associated with renal agenesis
- Associated with vas deferens agenesis
- Associated with ectopic ureter insertion
- **Associated with polycystic kidney disease**

Acquired Trivia:
- Obstruction often from prostatic hypertrophy, or chronic infection/scarring
- Classic history is prior prostate surgery

MIDLINE:

Prostatic Utricle Cyst:
Things to Know

- This represents a focal dilation in the prostatic urethra (remnant of the Mullerian duct) - as such they communicate with the urethra and can cause "dribbling" (both on and off the basketball court).
- Hypospadias is the most common associated condition - which makes sense given the relationship with the urethra.
- *Other Associations*: Prune Belly Syndrome, Downs, Unilateral Renal Agenesis, and my personal favorite - the Imperforate Anus
- The tendency towards superinfection is also explained by the communication with the urethra.
- A sneaky trick would be to show it on a RUG, where a prostate utricle cyst would look like a focal out-pouching from the prostatic urethra.

Mullerian Duct Cyst
Things to Know

- This represents a failed regression of the caudal ends of the Mullerian ducts (male equivalent of the vagina / cervix).
- Does not communicate with the urethra and does not have the same associations as utricle cyst.

THIS vs THAT:

Utricle Cyst	Mullerian Cyst
Pear Shaped and Usually Smaller	Tear Drop Shaped
Will NOT extend above the base of the prostate	Will extend above the base of the prostate
Communicates with the Urethra (Utricle) , therefore could opacify on a RUG	Does NOT communicate with the Urethra, should not opacify on a RUG

Both have a tiny risk (mostly case reports) of malignancy (various types: endometrial, clear cell, squamous).

Prostate Abscess: This can cause a thick walled, septated, heterogenous, cystic lesion anywhere in the prostate. It is usually bacterial (E. coli). When chronic it can have a more "swiss cheese" appearance referred to as "cavitary prostatitis." Usually this is imaged via transrectal ultrasound - because it gives you (the urologist) the option to do an image guided drain.

- The Painful Scrotum -

Torsion of the Testicle:

Results from the testis and spermatic cord twisting within the serosal space leading to ischemia.
If it was 1950 you'd call in your nuclear medicine tech for scintigraphy. Now you just get a Doppler ultrasound.

The grey scale findings are fairly straight forward. The testicle is going to be darker (hypo-echoic) and asymmetrically enlarged - at least in the chronic setting. If it's chronic then it will shrink up.

The doppler findings are somewhat complex. The most obviously / basic look would be to show you absent arterial flow. This would be the equivalent of an underhand slow pitch. The curve ball would be to show you preserved arterial flow BUT with increased resistance and a decreased diastolic flow (or reversed diastolic flow).

 That is correct my friends. Arterial flow does NOT need not be absent for torsion to be present (depending on the duration and severity). This leads the way for some seriously fuckery if the test writer wants to be an asshole.

The best way to think about it is like this: **Testicle = Brain.**

Just like the brain requires continuous diastolic flow (the thing is never off), so does the testicle.

So when you look at the waveform for a rule out torsion case you need to remember that torsion has three possible patterns:

1 - Classic Absence of Arterial Flow
2 - High resistance Arterial Flow (with decreased or reversed diastolic flow)
3 - Monophasic Arterial Waveform (loss of the normal dicrotic notch)

Fuckery: We are talking about testicular artery wave forms here. The normal cremasteric artery will not have diastolic flow (think about that think as the artery to a muscle) - it's normally high resistance.

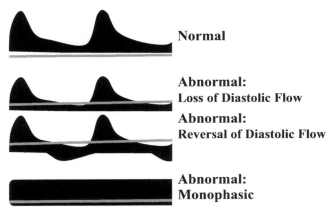

Normal

Abnormal:
Loss of Diastolic Flow

Abnormal:
Reversal of Diastolic Flow

Abnormal:
Monophasic

- *Cause:* The "bell-clapper deformity," which describes an abnormal high attachment of the tunical vaginalis, increases mobility and predisposes to torsion. It is usually a bilateral finding, so the contralateral side also gets an orchiopexy.

- *Viability:* The viability is related to the degree of torsion (how many spins), and how long it has been spun. As a general rule, the surgeons try and get them in the OR before 6 hours.

High Flow States / Hyperemia:

If torsion demonstrates decreased flow, it is useful to have an idea about what can demonstrate increased flow (decreased R.I. or increased diastolic flow)

Two things worth thinking about in this scenario: (1) Epididymo-orchitis (2) Detorsion.

The distinction between these two will be the clinical scenario.
Orchitis is painful. Detorsion is pain free.

Epididymitis: Inflammation of the epididymis, and the most common cause of acute onset scrotal pain in adults. In high-school / college age men (likely sexually active men) the typical cause is chlamydia or gonorrhea. In married men (not likely to be sexually active) it is more likely to be e-coli, due to a urinary tract source. The epididymal head is the most affected. Increased size and hyperemia are your ultrasound findings. You can have infection of the epididymis alone or infection of the epididymis and testicle (isolated orchitis is rare).

Typical Spread : Tail ⟶ Body ⟶ Head

Gamesmanship: Could be asked as "where is the most common location" ? = Tail (because in most cases it starts there).

Orchitis: Typically progresses from epididymitis (isolated basically only occurs from mumps). It looks like asymmetric hyperemia.

Typical: (1) Epididymitis ⟶ (2) Epididymitis + Orchitis

Mumps: Straight to Orchitis

Impending Infarct: The swelling of the testicle can become so severe that it compromises venous flow. In this case you will see loss of diastolic flow (or reversal) - similar to the atypical torsion patterns. This is reported as a sign of "impending infarct."

Testicular Trauma: The big distinction is rupture vs fracture. Surgical intervention is required if there is testicular rupture. Intratesticular fracture, and hematomas (small) do not get surgery.

- *Rupture:* Disrupted tunica albuginea, heterogenous testicle, poorly defined testicular outline

- *Fracture:* Intact tunica albuginea, linear hypoechoic band across the parenchyma of the testicle, well defined testicular outline.

- Random Path-

Epidermoid Cyst: This is a benign mass of the testicle (no malignant potential), with an Aunt Minnie **"onion skin"** look, - alternating hypoechoic and hyperechoic rings. It's relatively non-vascular relative to the rest of the testicle.

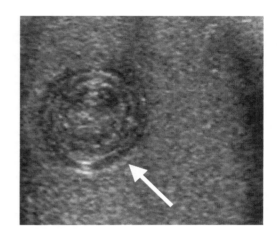

Tubular Ectasia of the Rete Testis: This is a common benign finding, resulting from obliteration (complete or partial) of the efferent ducts. It's usually bilateral - and in older men. The location of the cystic dilation is next to the mediastinum testis. Think about this as a normal variant. It requires no follow up or further evaluation.

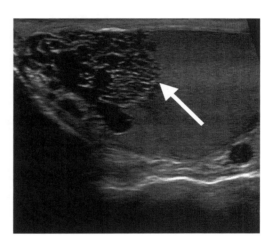

Calcified Vas Deferens: You see this all the time in bad **diabetics.**

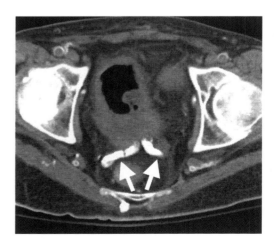

SECTION 10:
Testicular Cancer

Testicle Cancer in the pediatric setting is discussed in the pediatric chapter. This discussion will focus of the adult subtypes (with some overlap).

In general, hypoechoic solid intratesticular masses should be thought of as cancer until proven otherwise. Doppler flow can be helpful only when it is absent (can suggest hematoma - in the right clinical setting). If it's extratesticular and cystic, it's probably benign. The step 1 trivia is that cryptorchidism increases the risk of cancer (in both testicles), and is not reduced by orchiopexy. Most testicular tumors met via the lymphatics (retroperitoneal nodes at the level of the renal hilum). The testable exception is choriocarcinoma, which mets via the blood. Most testicular cancers are germ cell subtypes (95%) - with seminomas making up about half of those.

Risk Factors: Cryptorchidism (for both testicles), Gonadal Dysgenesis, Klinefelters, Trauma, Orchitis, and testicular microlithiasis (maybe).

Testicular Microlithiasis: This appears as multiple small echogenic foci within the testes. Testicular microlithiasis is usually an incidental finding in scrotal US examinations performed for unrelated reasons. It might have a relationship with Germ Cell Tumors (controversial). Follow-up in 6 months, then yearly is probably the recommendation - although this recommendation is controversial.

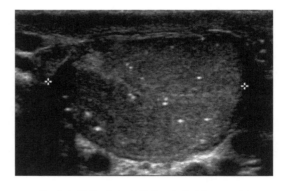

Seminoma: This is the most common testicular tumor, and has the best prognosis as they are very radiosensitive. They are much more common (9x) in white people. The classic age is around 25. It usually looks like a homogenous hypoechoic round mass, which classically replaces the entire testicle. On MRI they are usually homogeneously T2 dark (non-seminomatous GCTs are often higher in signal).

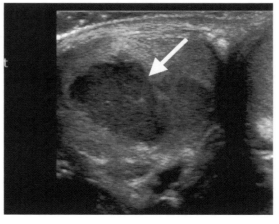

Non-Seminomatous Germ Cell Tumors: Basically this is not a seminoma. We are talking about mixed germ cell tumors, teratomas, yolk sac tumors, and choriocarcinoma. They typically occur at a young age relative to seminomas (think teenager). They are more heterogeneous and have larger calcifications.

Testicular Lymphoma: Just be aware that lymphoma can "hide" in the testes because of the blood testes barrier. Immunosuppressed patients are at increased risk for developing extranodal/ testicular lymphoma. Almost all testicular lymphomas are non-hodgkin B-cell subtypes. On US, the normal homogeneous echogenic testicular tissue is replaced focally or diffusely with hypoechoic vascular lymphomatous tissue.

 Buzzword = multiple hypoechoic masses of the testicle.

Burned-Out Testicular Tumor - If you see large, dense calcifications with shadowing in the testicle of an old man this is probably what you should be thinking. The idea is that you've had spontaneous regression of a germ cell testicular neoplasm, that is now calcified. An important pearl is that there can still be viable tumor in there. Management is somewhat controversial and unlikely to be asked (most people pull them out).

Staging Pearl

Testicular mets should spread to the para-aortic, aortic, caval region (N1-N3). It's an embryology thing.

If you have mets to the pelvic, external iliac, and inguinal nodes - this is considered "non-regional" i.e. M1 disease. The exception is some kind of inguinal or scrotum surgery was done before the cancer manifested - but I wouldn't expect them to get that fancy on the test.

High Yield Testicle Tumor Trivia
Seminoma is the most common and has the best prognosis (it melts with radiation)
Multiple hypoechoic masses = Lymphoma
Homogenous and Microcalcifications = Seminoma
Cystic Elements and Macrocalcifications = Mixed Germ Cell Tumor / Teratoma
Most testicular tumors met via the lymphatics (choriocarcinoma mets via the blood - and tends to bleed like stink)
Gynecomastia can be seen with Sertoli Leydig Tumors
Sertoli Cell Tumors are also seen with Peutz-Jeghers

Elevated Beta hCG	Elevated AFP
Seminoma	Mixed Germ Cell (Non-S)
Choriocarcinoma (Non-S)	Yolk Sac (Non-S)

 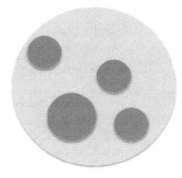 

Seminoma　　　　**Lymphoma**　　　　**Mixed Germ Cell / Teratoma**

 = *Macrocalcification*

SECTION 11:
Male Infertility

Causes: Can be thought of as Obstructive vs Non-Obstructive

- Obstructive: Congenital bilateral absence of the vas deferens (seen in Cystic Fibrosis), ejaculatory duct obstruction, prostatic cysts. **Think about associated renal anomalies (Zinner Syndrome).**

- Non-Obstructive: Varicocele, Cryptorchidism, Anabolic Steroid Use, Erectile Dysfunction.

Varicocele: This is **the most common correctable cause of infertility**. They can be unilateral or bilateral. Unilateral is much more common on the left. Isolated **right sided should make you think retroperitoneal process** compressing the right gonadal vein.

Cryptorchidism: Undescended testes. The testicle is usually found in the inguinal canal. The testicle has an increased risk of cancer (actually they both will – which is weird). It's **most commonly seen in premature kids** (20%).

Major complication association for cryptorchidism:
- Malignant degeneration - of both the undescended and contralateral testicle
- Infertility
- Torsion
- Bowel Incarceration - related to the association of indirect inguinal hernia

Gamesmanship: A good distractor would be "orchitis." It's a pathology that involves the balls, so it's not totally far fetched. Obviously they can get orchitis… but not at a higher rate. It's not a reported association - so don't fall for that.

Zebras and Syndromes Associated With Male Infertility:

- *Pituitary Adenoma* making prolactin
- *Kallman Syndrome* (can't smell + infertile)
- *Klinefelter Syndrome* (tall + gynecomastia + infertile)
- *Zinner Syndrome* (renal agenesis + ipsilateral seminal vesicle cyst)

SECTION 12: OB

- Early Pregnancy -

Vocab:

- Menstrual Age: Embryologic Age + 14 days
- Embryo: 0-10 weeks (menstrual age)
- Fetus: > 10 weeks (menstrual age)
- Threatened Abortion – Bleeding with closed cervix
- Inevitable Abortion – Cervical dilation and/or placental and/or fetal tissue hanging out
- Incomplete Abortion – Residual products in the uterus
- Complete Abortion – All products out
- Missed Abortion – Fetus is dead, but still in the uterus.

Intradecidual Sign: This is the early gestational sac. When seen covered by echogenic decidua is very characteristic of early pregnancy. You can see it around 4.5 weeks. You want to see the thin echogenic line of the uterine cavity pass by (not stop at) the sac to avoid calling a little bit of fluid in the canal a sac.

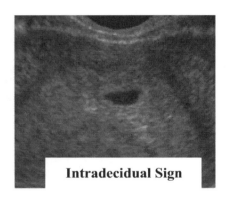

Intradecidual Sign

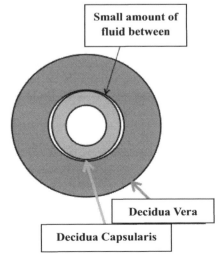

Small amount of fluid between

Decidua Vera

Decidua Capsularis

Double Decidual Sac Sign

Double Decidual Sac Sign:

This is another positive sign of early pregnancy.

It's produced by visualizing the layers of decidua.

Yolk Sac: This is the first structure visible within the GS. The classic teaching was you should always see it when the GS measures 8mm in diameter. The thing should be oval or round, fluid filled, and smaller than 6 mm.

The yolk sac is located in the chorionic cavity, and hooked up to the umbilicus of the embryo by the vitelline duct.

Yolk Sac Gone Bad: The yolk sac shouldn't be too big (> 6 mm), shouldn't be too small (< 3 mm), and shouldn't be solid or calcified.

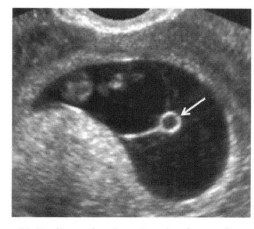

Yolk Sac - in the chorionic cavity

The Amnion: The membranes of the amniotic sac and chorionic space typically remain separated by a thin layer of fluid, until about 14-16 weeks at which point fusion is normal. If the amnion gets disrupted before 10 weeks the fetus might cross into the chorionic cavity and get tangled up in the fibrous bands. This is the etiology of **amniotic band syndrome**, which can be terrible (decapitation, limb amputation, etc…).

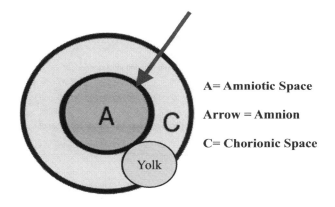

A= Amniotic Space

Arrow = Amnion

C= Chorionic Space

Double Bleb Sign: This is the earliest visualization of the embryo. This is two fluid filled sacs (yolk and amniotic) with the flat embryo in the middle.

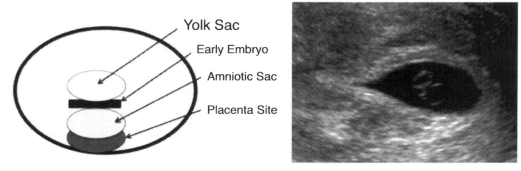

Double Bleb Sign

Crown Rump Length – This is typically used to estimate gestational age, and is more accurate than menstrual history. *Embryo is normally visible at 6 weeks.

Anembryonic Pregnancy – A gestational sac without an embryo. When you see this, the choices are (a) very early pregnancy, or (b) non-viable pregnancy. The classic teaching was you should see the yolk sac at 8 mm (on TV). Just remember that a large sac (> 8-10 mm) without a yolk sac, and a distorted contour is pretty reliable for a non-viable pregnancy.

Pseudogestational Sac – This is not the same thing as an anembryonic pregnancy. This is seen in the presence of an ectopic pregnancy. What you are seeing is a little bit of blood in the uterine cavity with surrounding bright decidual endometrium (charged up from the pregnancy hormones).

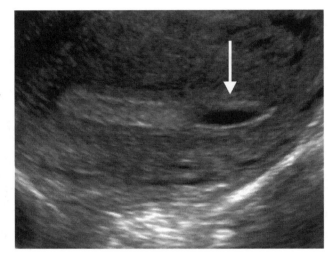

Subchorionic Hemorrhage: These are very common. The thing to know is that the percentage of placental detachment is the prognostic factor most strongly associated with fetal demise; hematoma greater than 2/3 the circumference of the chorion has a 2x increased risk of abortion. Other trivia: women older than 35 have worse outcomes with these.

Implantation Bleeding: This is a nonspecific term referring to a small subchorionic hemorrhage that occurs at the attachment of the chorion to the endometrium.

Criteria for Fetal Demise:

Diagnostic of Pregnancy Failure	Suspicious for Pregnancy Failure
Crown–rump length of ≥7 mm and no heartbeat	No embryo ≥6 wk after last menstrual period
Mean sac diameter of ≥25 mm and no embryo	Mean sac diameter of 16–24 mm and no embryo
No embryo with heartbeat ≥2 wk after a scan that showed a gestational sac without a yolk sac	No embryo with heartbeat 13 days after a scan that showed a gestational sac without a yolk sac
No embryo with heartbeat ≥11 days after a scan that showed a gestational sac with a yolk sac	No embryo with heartbeat 10 days after a scan that showed a gestational sac with a yolk sac

Pregnancy of Unknown Location:

This is the vocabulary used when neither a normal IUP or ectopic pregnancy is identified in the setting of a positive b-hCG. Typically this just means it is a very very early pregnancy, but you can't say that with certainty. In these cases you have three possibilities:

1 - Normal Early Pregnancy

2 - Occult Ectopic

3 - Complete Miscarriage

The management is follow up (serial b-hCG) and repeat US —- assuming the patient is hemodynamically stable.

- Ectopic -

High Risk for Ectopic: Hx of PID, Tubal Surgery, Endometriosis, Ovulation Induction, Previous Ectopic, Use of an IUD.

The majority of ectopic pregnancies (nearly 95%) occur in the fallopian tube (usually the ampulla). A small percentage (around 2%) are "interstitial" developing in the portion of the tube which passes through the uterine wall. These interstitials are high risk, as they can grow large before rupture and cause a catastrophic hemorrhage. It is also possible (although very rare) to have implantation sites in the abdominal cavity, ovary, and cervix.

Always start down the ectopic pathway with a positive BhCG. At around 1500-2000 mIU/L you should see a gestational sac. *At around 5000 mIU/L you should see a yolk sac.* As a general rule, a normal doubling time makes ectopic less likely.

Tubal Ring Sign: An echogenic ring, which surrounds an un-ruptured ectopic pregnancy. This is an excellent sign of ectopic pregnancy – and has been described as 95% specific.

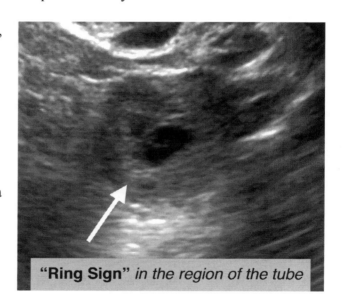

"Ring Sign" *in the region of the tube*

Heterotopic Pregnancy: This is a baby in the uterus and a baby in the tube (or other ectopic location). This is pretty rare, and typically only seen in women taking ovulation drugs, or with prior bad PID.

The Big 3 to Remember with Ectopics (positive B-hCG)

(1) Live Pregnancy / Yolk Sac outside the uterus = Slam Dunk

(2) Nothing in the uterus + anything on the adnexa (other than corpus luteum) = 75-85% PPV for ectopic
   a. A moderate volume of free fluid increases this to 97% PPV

(3) Nothing in the uterus + moderate free fluid = 70% PPV
   a. More risk if the fluid is echogenic

Fetal Biometry and Fetal Growth:

In the second and third trimesters, four standard measurements of fetal growth are made (Biparietal, Head Circumference, Abdominal Circumference, and Femur Length). The testable trivia seems to include what level you make the measurement, and what is and is not included (see chart).

Fetal Measurement For Growth			
	Measurement Made	**NOT including**	**Trivia**
Biparietal Diameter "BPD"	Recorded at the level of the thalamus from the outermost edge of the near skull to the inner table of the far skull		Affected by the shape of the fetal skull (false large from brachycephaly, false small from dolichocephaly)
Head Circumference	Recorded at the same slice as BPD	Does NOT include the skin	Affected less by head shape
Abdominal Circumference	Recorded at the level of the junction of the umbilical vein and left portal vein	Does NOT include the subcutaneous soft tissues	
Femur Length	Longest dimension of the femoral shaft	Femoral epiphysis is NOT included	

Estimated Fetal Weight: This is calculated by the machine based or either (1) BPD and AC, or (2) AC and FL.

Gestational Age (GA): Ultrasound estimates of gestation age are the most accurate in early pregnancy (and become less precise in the later portions). Age in the first trimester is made from crown rump length. Second and third trimester estimates for age are typically done using BPD, HC, AC, and FL – and referred to as a "composite GA."

Gestation Age (Less Good Later in the Pregnancy)	
First Trimester – Crown Rump Length	Accurate to 0.5 weeks
2nd and 3rd Trimester – "Composite GA"	Accurate to 1.2 weeks (between 12 and 18 weeks)
	Accurate to 3.1 weeks (between 36 and 42 weeks)

Intrauterine Growth Restriction:

*Baby is smaller than expected

Readings Suggestive of IUGR:

- Estimated Fetal Weights Below 10th percentile
- Femur Length / Abdominal Circumference Ratio (F /AC) > 23.5
- Umbilical Artery Systolic / Diastolic Ratio > 4.0

Not All is lost: If the kid is measuring small, he might just be a little guy. If he has normal Doppler studies – most of the time they are ok.

Maybe All is lost: If the kid is measuring small, suggesting IUGR, and he has oligohydramnios (AFI < 5) or polyhydramnios, he/she is probably toast.

Trivia: Most common cause for developing oligohydramnios during the 3rd trimester = Fetal Growth Restriction associated with Placental Insufficiency.

THIS vs THAT: Symmetric vs Asymmetric:

- **Asymmetric:** Think about this as a restriction of weight followed by length. It is the more common of the two types. The head will be normal in size, with the body being small. Some people call this "**head sparing,**" as the body tries to protect the brain. You **see this mainly in the third trimester**, as a result of extrinsic factors.

- The classic scenario would be normal growth for the first two trimesters, with a normal head / small body (small abdominal circumference) in the third trimester - with a mom having chronic high BP / pre-eclampsia.

- There are a bunch of causes. I recommend remembering these three: **High BP, Severe Malnutrition, Ehler-Danlos.**

- **Symmetric:** This is a global growth restriction, that **does NOT spare the head**. This is **seen throughout the pregnancy** (including the first trimester). The head and body are both small. This has a **much worse prognosis**, as the brain doesn't develop normally.

- There are also a bunch of causes. I recommend remembering these: **TORCH infection, Fetal Alcohol Syndrome / Drug Abuse, Chromosomal Abnormalities, and Anemia.**

Normal Kid
-Normal Sized Head
-Normal Sized Body

Symmetric IUGR
-**S**mall Head
-**S**kinny Body
-**S**ame Throughout Pregnancy
-**S**yphilis (*Among other TORCHs*)
-**S**cotch Whiskey (*Fetal EtOH*)
-**S**ome Extra Chromosomes

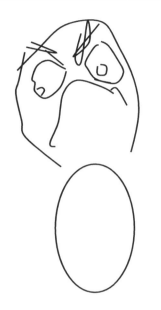

Asymmetric IUGR
-**A**bdomen is small
-**A**ching Belly (*Malnutrition*)
-**A**bnormally High BP
-"**A**lastic" skin (*Ehler Danlos*)
-**A**symmetric Time Interval (*primarily seen in 3rd trimester*)

Umbilical Artery Systolic / Diastolic Ratio:

The resistance in the umbilical artery should progressively decrease with gestational age. **The general rule is 2-3 at 32 weeks**. The ratio should not be more than 3 at 34 weeks. An elevated S/D ratio means there is high resistance. High resistance patterns are seen in pre-eclampsia and IUGR. Worse than an elevated ratio, is absent or reversed diastolic flow – this is associated with a very poor prognosis.

The way I remember this: I think about the kid starting out as a clump of cells/mashed up soup.

Early on he/she is basically just a "muscle." Then as he/she gets closer and closer to viable age he/she becomes more like a "brain." Once you think about it like that - muscle vs brain, it's much easier to understand why the diastolic flow goes up (S/D ratio goes down).

Remember the brain is always on, so it needs continuous flow. Muscles are only on when you need to perform amazing feats of strength. So more brain = more diastolic flow. This also explains why absent or reversed diastolic flow is so devastatingly bad. In fact, the evil socialist health care systems in Europe use carotid ultrasound as a cheap brain death test (no diastolic flow in the ICA = brain dead). Coincidently, the absence of diastolic flow in the ICA is also used in many American Radiology Departments as hiring criteria for the QA Officer.

Biophysical Profile: This thing was developed to look for acute and chronic hypoxia. Points are assigned (2 for normal , 0 for abnormal). A score of 8-10 is considered normal. To call something abnormal, technically you have to be watching for 30 mins.

Components of Biophysical Profile		
Amniotic Fluid	At least 1 pocket measuring > 2 cm in a vertical plane	Assess Chronic Hypoxia
Fetal Movement	3 discrete movements	Assess Acute Hypoxia
Fetal Tone	1 episode of fetal extension from flexion	Assess Acute Hypoxia
Fetal Breathing	1 episode of "Breathing motion" lasting 30 sec	Assess Acute Hypoxia
Non-stress Test	2 or more fetal heart rate accelerations of at least 15 beats per minute for 30 seconds or longer	Assess Acute Hypoxia

- Macrosomia -

Babies that are too big (above the 90th percentile). **Maternal diabetes** (usually gestational, but could be type 2 as well), is the most common cause. As a point of trivia, type 1 diabetic mothers can also have babies that are small secondary to hypoxia from microvascular disease of the placenta. The big issue with being too big is **complications during delivery** (shoulder dystocia, brachial plexus injury) and **after delivery** (neonatal hypoglycemia, meconium

Erb's Palsy:

Injury to the upper trunk of the brachial plexus (C5-C6), most commonly seen in shoulder dystocia (which **kids with macrosomia are at higher risk for** aspiration).

If you see an aplastic or hypoplastic humeral head / glenoid in a kid, you should immediately think about an Erbs Palsy.

Clinical Correlation Recommended.

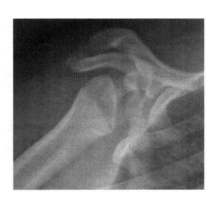

- Amniotic Fluid -

Early on, the fluid in the amnion and chorionic spaces is the result of filtrate from the membranes. After 16 weeks, the fluid is made by the fetus (urine). The balance of too much (polyhydramnios) and too little (oligohydramnios) is maintained by swallowing of the urine and renal function. In other words, if you have too little fluid you should think kidneys aren't working. If you have too much fluid you should think swallow or other GI problems. Having said that, a common cause of too much fluid is high maternal sugars (gestational diabetes). Fine particulate in the fluid is normal, especially in the third trimester.

Amniotic Fluid Index: Made by measuring the vertical height of the deepest fluid pocket in each quadrant of the uterus, then summing the 4 measurements.

Normal is 5-20.

Oligohydramnios is defined as AFI < 5 cm.

Polyhydramnios is defined as AFI > 20 cm , or a single fluid pocket > 8 cm.

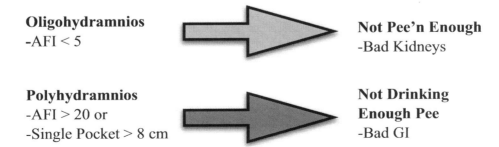

Oligohydramnios
-AFI < 5
→
Not Pee'n Enough
-Bad Kidneys

Polyhydramnios
-AFI > 20 or
-Single Pocket > 8 cm
→
Not Drinking Enough Pee
-Bad GI

- Normal Development -

I'm going to briefly touch on what I think is testable trivia regarding normal development.

Brain: Choroid plexus is large and echogenic. There should be less than 3 mm of separation of the choroid plexus from the medial wall of the lateral ventricle (if more it's ventriculomegaly). The cisterna magna should be between 2 mm-11 mm (too small think Chiari II, too large think Dandy Walker).

Face / Neck: The "fulcrum" of the upper lip is normal, and should not be called a cleft lip.

Lungs: The lungs are normally homogeneously echogenic, and similar in appearance to the liver.

Heart: The only thing to know is that papillary muscle can calcify "Echogenic Foci in the ventricle," and although this is common and can mean nothing – it's also associated with an increased risk of Downs (look hard for other things).

Abdominal: If you only see one artery adjacent to the bladder, you have yourself a two vessel cord. Bowel should be less than 6mm in diameter. Bowel can be moderately echogenic in the 2nd and 3rd trimester but **should never be more than bone**. The adrenals are huge in newborns, and are said to be 20x their relative adult size.

🔥 Two Vessel Cord - Gamesmanship 🔥

There are two main ways to show a two vessel cord. The first one is a single vessel running lateral to the bladder down by the cord insertion. The second is to show the cord in cross section with two vessels.

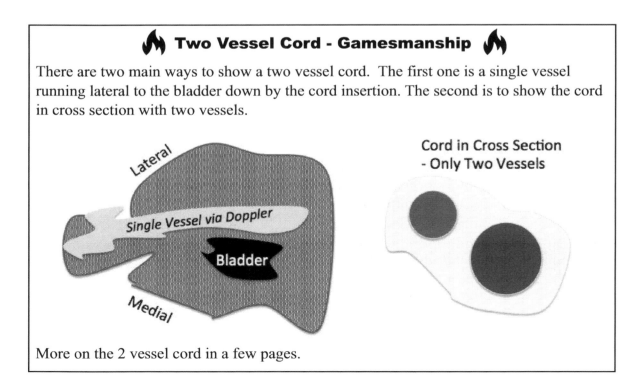

More on the 2 vessel cord in a few pages.

Classic Normal Pictures
THAT LOOK SCARY

Cystic Rhombencephalon:

The normal rhombencephalon is present as a cystic structure in the posterior fossa around 6-8 weeks.

Don't call it a Dandy-Walker malformation, for sure that will be a distractor.

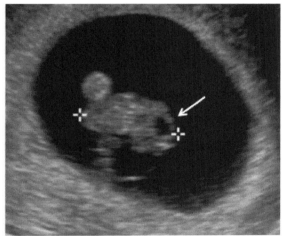

Normal Cystic Rhombencephalon (6-8 weeks)

Physiologic Midgut Herniation:

The midgut normally herniates into the umbilical cord around 9-11 weeks.

Don't call it an omphalocele, for sure that will be a distractor.

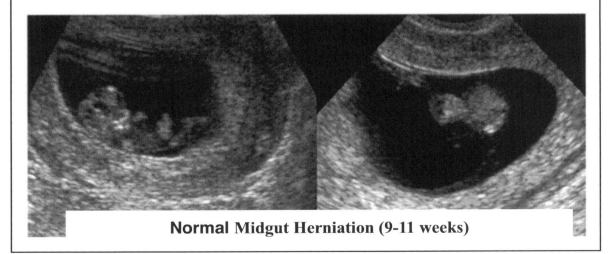

Normal Midgut Herniation (9-11 weeks)

SECTION 13:
Placenta and Cord

http://www.womenshealthmag.com/mom/placenta-recipes
My opinion: Use two cups of strawberries in the smoothie.

Normal: You can first start to see the placenta around 8 weeks (focal thickening along the periphery of the gestational sac). It should be shaped like a disc around 12 weeks. The normal sonographic appearance is "granular" with a smooth cover (the chorion). Underneath the basal surface there is a normal retroplacental complex of decidual and myometrial veins.

Normal Placental Aging: As the placenta ages it gets hypoechoic areas, septations, and randomly distributed calcifications.

Venous Lakes: These are an incidental finding of no significance. They look like focal hypoechoic areas under the chorionic membrane (or within the placenta). You can sometimes see slow flow in them.

Variant Placental Morphology:

Bilobed Placenta	Two near equal sized lobes - connected by a thin strip.	Increased risk of type 2 vasa previa (vessel cross the internal os), post partum hemorrhage from retained placental tissue, and velamentous insertion of the cord	
Succenturiate Lobe	One or more small accessory lobes	Increased risk of type 2 vasa previa, post partum hemorrhage from retained placental tissue	
Circumvallate Placenta	Rolled placental edges with smaller chorionic plate	High risk for placental abruption and IUGR	

THIS vs THAT: Placental Thickness	
Too Thin (< 1 cm)	**Too Thick (> 4cm)**
Placental Insufficiency, Maternal Hypertension, Maternal DM, Trisomy 13, Trisomy 18, Toxemia of Pregnancy	Fetal Hydrops, Maternal DM, Severe Maternal Anemia, Congenital Fetal Cancer, Congenital Infection, <u>Placental Abruption</u>

Placental Abruption: — PAINFUL

This is a premature separation of the placenta from the myometrium. The step 1 history was always "mother doing cocaine," but it also occurs in the setting of hypertension. Technically, subchorionic hemorrhage (marginal abruption) is in the category – as previously discussed. Retroplacental Abruption is the really bad one. The hematoma will appear as anechoic or mixed echogenicity beneath the placenta (often extending beneath the chorion).

 Buzzword is "disruption of the retroplacental complex."

THIS vs THAT: Placental Abruption vs Myometrial Contraction / Fibroid	
Placental Abruption will **disrupt** the retroplacental complex of blood vessels	Myometrial Contractions / Fibroids will **displace** the retroplacental complex

Placenta Previa: — PAINLESS

This is a low implantation of the placenta that covers part of or all of the internal cervical os. A practical pearl is that you need to have an empty bladder when you look for this (full bladder creates a false positive). Several subtypes - as seen in my awesome little chart below.

 Buzzword is "painless vaginal bleeding in the third trimester."

Low-Lying	**Marginal**	**Complete**	**Central**
Margin is within <u>2 cm</u> of the internal cervical os	Extends to the edge of the internal cervical os (but doesn't cover it)	Covers the internal os	Centered over the internal os

Placenta Creta:

This is an abnormal insertion of the placenta, which invades the myometrium. The severity is graded with fancy sounding Latin names. The risk factors include prior C-section, placenta previa, and advanced maternal age. The sonographic appearance varies depending on the severity, but generally speaking you are looking for a "moth-eaten" or "Swiss cheese" appearance of the placenta, with vascular channels extending from the placenta into the myometrium (with turbulent flow on Doppler). Thinning of the myometrium (less than 1mm) is another sign. This can be serious business, with life threatening bleeding sometimes requiring hysterectomy.

Placenta Accreta	Most common (75%) and mildest form. The villi attach to the myometrium, without invading.
Placenta Increta	Villi partially invade the myometrium
Placenta Percreta	The really bad one. Villi penetrate through the myometrium or beyond the serosa. Sometimes there is invasion of the bladder or bowel.

Risk factors are <u>prior c-section</u>, and <u>placenta previa</u>.

	"Ad" = To	*"In" = Into*	*"Per" = Through*
Normal	**Accreta**	**Increta**	**Percreta**

Endometrium

Myometrium

Serosa

Placenta Chorioangioma:

This is basically a **hamartoma** of the placenta, and is the most common benign tumor of the placenta. These are usually well-circumscribed hypoechoic masses **near the cord insertion.** Flow within the mass pulsating at the fetal heart rate is diagnostic (they are perfused by the fetal circulation). They almost always mean nothing, but if they are large (> 4 cm) and multiple ("choriangiomatosis") they can sequester platelets, and cause a high output failure (hydrops).

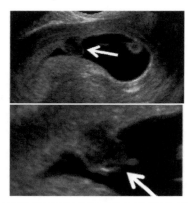

THIS vs THAT: Placental Chorioangioma vs Placental Hematoma	
Chrorioangioma has pulsating Doppler flow	Hematoma does NOT

306

- Umbilical Cord -

Normal Cord: Should have 3 vessels (2 arteries, 1 vein).

Two Vessel Cord: This is a normal variant – seen in about 1% of pregnancies. Usually the left artery is the one missing. This tends to occur more in twin pregnancies and maternal diabetes. There is an increased association with chromosomal anomalies and various fetal malformations (so look closely). Having said that, in isolation it doesn't mean much.

Velamentous Cord Insertion:

This is the term for when the cord inserts into the fetal membranes outside the placental margin, and then has to travel back through the membranes to the placenta (between the amnion and the chorion). It's more common with twins, and increases the risk of intra-uterine growth restriction and growth discordance among twins.

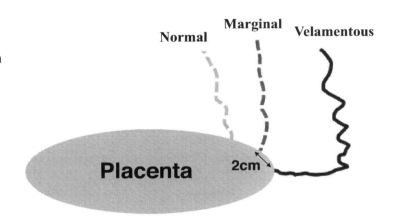

Marginal Cord Insertion:

This is basically almost a velamentous insertion (cord is within 2 cm of the placental margin). It's also seen more in twin pregnancies.

Vasa Previa: Fetal vessels that cross (or almost cross) the internal cervical os. It's seen more in twin pregnancies, and variant placental morphologies. There are two types:

• Type 1: Fetal vessels connect to a velamentous cord insertion within the main placental body

• Type 2: Fetal vessels connect to a bilobed placenta or succenturiate lobe.

Nuchal Cord: This is the term used to describe a cord wrapped around the neck of the fetus. Obviously this can cause problems during delivery.

Umbilical Cord Cyst: These are common (seen about 3% of the time) and are usually single (but can be multiple). As a point of completely irrelevant trivia, you can divide these into false and true cysts. True cysts are less common, but have fancy names so they are more likely to be tested. Just know that the omphalomesenteric duct cyst is usually peripheral, and the allantoic cyst is usually central. If the cysts persist into the 2nd or 3rd trimester then they might be associated with trisomy 18 and 13. You should look close for other problems.

SECTION 14:
Congenital Fetal

- DOWNS -

Ultrasound Findings Concerning for Down Syndrome	
Congenital Heart Disease	More than half of fetuses (or feti, if you prefer) with Downs have congenital heart issues, - most commonly AV canal and VSD
Duodenal Atresia	Most common intra abdominal pathology associated with Downs (hard to see before 22 weeks)
Short Femur Length	Not Specific
Echogenic Bowel	Not Specific (can be seen with obstruction, infection, CF, ischemia, and lots of other stuff)
Choroid Plexus Cyst	Not Specific, and actually seen more with Trisomy 18. It should prompt a close survey for other findings (normal if in isolation)
Nuchal Translucency	Translucency > 3mm in the first trimester,
Nuchal Fold Thickness	Thickness > 6mm in the second trimester- nonspecific and can also be seen with Turners
Echogenic Focus in Cardiac Ventricle	Not Specific, but increased risk of Downs x 4

Nuchal Lucency: Measured between 9-12 weeks, this anechoic area between the neck/ occiput and the skin **should be less than 3 mm**.

Measurements > 3 mm are associated with Downs (trisomy 21) or other chromosomal abnormalities.

Positioning of the neck is critical to avoid false positives. The ideal positioning is a neutral neck, with the nasal bone visualized, and the head in the mid-sagittal position. A well delineated skin edge.

Maternal blood sample also analyzed for free **Beta hCG** and **pregnancy associated plasma protein-A (PAPP-A).**

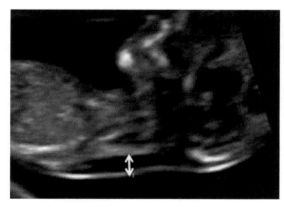

- OTHER HORRIBLE SHIT THAT CAN HAPPEN -

Amniotic Band Syndrome:

The fetus needs to stay in the amniotic cavity, and stay the hell out of the chorionic cavity. If the amnion gets disrupted and the fetus wanders / floats into the chorionic cavity he/she can get caught in the sticky fibrous septa. All kinds of terrible can result ranging from decapitation, to arm/leg amputation.

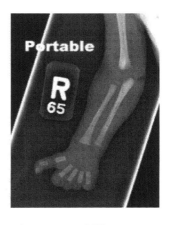

-Amputated Fingers

Losing fingers like this is terrible - it's much better to cut them off in a more manly way. For example, drunken chainsaw lumberjack work or trying to do that thing with the knife that the cyborg did in the Movies Aliens (youtube "Aliens: Bishop's Knife Trick"). Not to mention, unless you are Jean Jacque Machado (youtube "Heart of the champion documentary") your chances of becoming a world champion in Jiu Jitsu are going to be significantly deceased.

This is most likely to be shown in one of two ways:

(1) X-ray of a hand or baby gram showing fingers amputated or a hand/arm amputated – with the remaining exam normal, or

(2) Fetal ultrasound with the bands entangling the arms or legs of a fetus.

Hydrops:

Fetal hydrops is bad news. This can be from immune or non-immune causes. The most common cause is probably Rh sensitization from prior pregnancy. Some other causes include; TORCHS, Turners, Twin Related Stuff, and Alpha Thalassemia. Ultrasound diagnosis is made by the presence of two of the following: **pleural effusion, ascites, pericardial effusion**, and Subcutaneous Edema. A sneaky trick is to instead show you a thickened placenta (> 4-5cm) *"placentomegaly" - they call it,* although I think it's much more likely to show a pleural effusion and pericardial effusion.

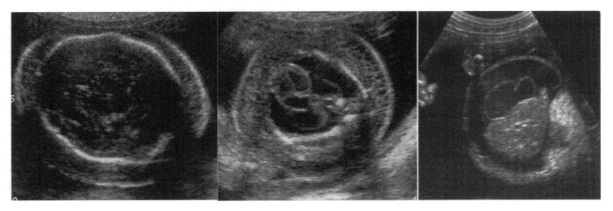

Hydrops - Body Wall Edema, Pleural Effusion, Ascites

- Chiari II / Open Neural Tube Defect

I think at least some general idea of the mechanism for this pathology is helpful for understanding the ultrasound findings. There are a bunch of purposed mechanisms, and of course they all think they are right. I don't give a shit which one is the "real mechanism," I just picked the one that helps me understand the findings.

So this is the one I like: You have a hole in your back from a neural tube defect (Step 1 trivia = not enough folate). The hole in your back ("myelomeningocele") lets CSF drip out. So you end up with a low volume of CSF. The CSF volume needs to be at a certain pressure to distend the ventricular system. If it's under distended then the hindbrain structures drop into a caudal position. This caudal herniation of the cerebellar vermis, brainstem, and 4th ventricle is the hallmark of Chiari II.

This caudal herniation of the cerebellum into the foramen magnum obliterate the normal contour of the vermis, creating the contour of a **banana**.

If you can think about a normal pressure in the developing ventricular system being necessary for the brain to stretch into a normal shape, then it isn't a far stretch to think about this normal pressure being needed to shape the skull correctly, too. The low pressure and abnormal distention of the developing brain results in incomplete stretching of the postal (front part) skull. The result is a "**lemon** shaped" rostral skull. The key point (testable) is that this lemon shape goes away in the 3rd trimester. So it's only present in the 2nd trimester. The way I remember this is that the problem was from a lack of volume. Once the brain grows big enough (even if there isn't enough CSF distention) it still gets big enough to put a normal curve on that rostral skull. So they "grow" out of it.

Testable Trivia:
- Both banana and lemon signs are classic for the Chiari II / Spina Bifida Path
- The banana sign is present in both 2nd and 3rd trimesters
- The lemon sign is only in the 2nd trimester (you grow out of it).
- The banana sign is more sensitive and specific
- The lemon sign is less sensitive and specific; it can also be seen in Dandy Walker, Absent Corpus Callosum, Encephaloceles, etc... Having said that if you see it on the test it's Chiari 2 + Open NTD.
- Hydrocephalus is also seen with Chiari II + Open NTD - but only later in gestation, and only when it's severe.

Open Neural Tube Defect

Low CSF Pressure During Development

Chiari II

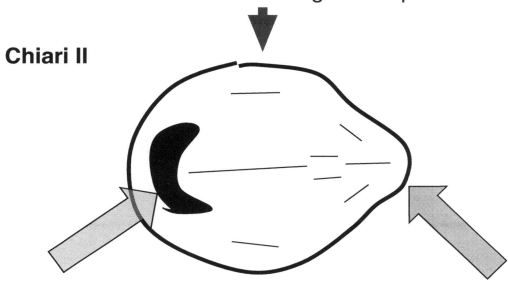

Banana
-Loss of the normal bilobed shaped of the cerebellum

Lemon
-Flat / Concave Frontal Bones

This is what it's supposed to look like

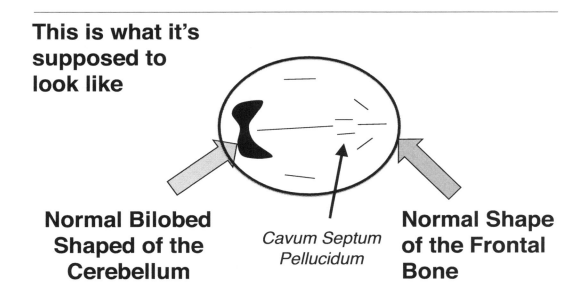

Normal Bilobed Shaped of the Cerebellum

Cavum Septum Pellucidum

Normal Shape of the Frontal Bone

Ventriculomegaly - There are multiple causes including hydrocephalus (both communicating and non-communicating), and cerebral atrophy. Obviously this is bad, and frequently associated with anomalies.

Things to know:
- Aqueductal Stenosis is the most common cause of non-communicating hydrocephalus in a neonate
- Ventricular atrium diameter > 10 mm = too big
- "Dangling choroid" hanging off the wall more than 3 mm = too big

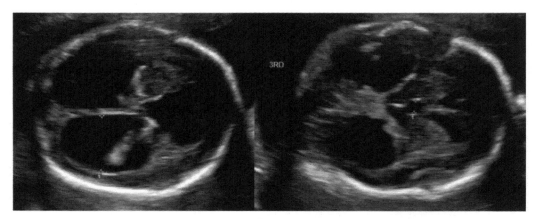

Ventriculomegaly - Shows dangling choroid

Choroid Plexus Cyst –

This is one of those incidental findings that in isolation means nothing. Having said that, the incidence of this finding is increased in trisomy 18, trisomy 21, Turner's Syndrome, and Klinefelter Syndrome.

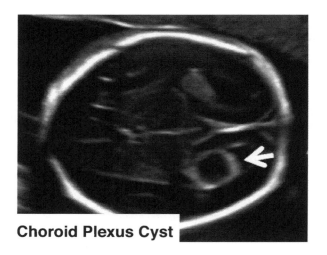

Choroid Plexus Cyst

Facial Clefts – This is the most common fetal facial anomaly. About 30% of the time you are dealing with chromosome anomalies. Around 80% of babies with cleft lips have cerebral palsy. You can see cleft lips, but cleft palate (in isolation) is very hard to see.

Cystic Hygroma – If they show you a complex cystic mass in the posterior neck, in the antenatal period, this is the answer. The follow-up is the association with Turners and Downs.

Anencephaly - This is the most common neural tube defect. You have total **absence of the cranial vault and brain above the level of the orbits**. Obviously this is not compatible with life.

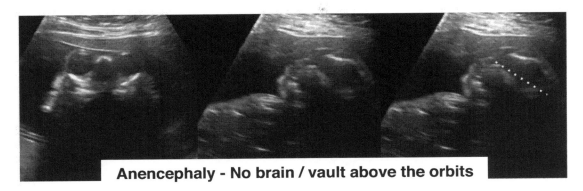

Anencephaly - No brain / vault above the orbits

Congenital Diaphragmatic Hernia – Abdominal contents push into the chest. Nearly all are on the left (85%). The things to know is that it (1) causes a high mortality because of its association with **pulmonary hypoplasia**, and (2) that all the kids are **malrotated** (it messes with normal gut rotation). If they show this it will either be (a) a newborn chest x-ray, or (b) a 3rd trimester MRI.

Echogenic Intracardiac Focus (EIF) - This is a calcification seen in a papillary muscle (usually in the left ventricle). You see them all the time, they don't mean that much but are seen at a higher rate Trisomy 21 (12%) and Trisomy 13. So you are supposed to look for more features.

Highest Yield Trivia:

- It occurs in the normal general population - around 5%,

- It occurs more in Downs patients - around 12%.

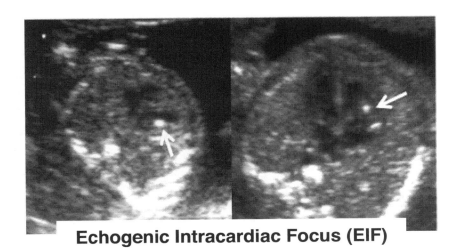

Echogenic Intracardiac Focus (EIF)

Abnormal Heart Rate: Tachycardia is defined as a rate > 180 bpm. Bradycardia is defined as a rate < 100 bpm.

Double Bubble:

This is described in detail in the Peds Chapter.

Just realize this can be shown with antenatal ultrasound or MRI. It's still duodenal atresia.

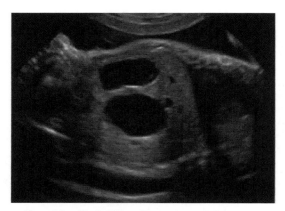
Double Bubble - Duodenal Atresia

Echogenic Bowel: This can be a normal variant but can also be associated with significant badness. Normally bowel is isoechoic to the liver. If it's equal to the iliac crest bone then it's too bright. The DDx includes CF, Downs and other Trisomies, Viral Infections, and Bowel Atresia.

Sacrococcygeal Teratoma: This is the most common tumor of the fetus or infant. These solid or cystic masses are typically large and found either on prenatal imaging or birth. They can cause mass effect on the GI system, hip dislocation, nerve compression causing incontinence, and high output cardiac failure. Additionally, they may cause issues with premature delivery, dystocia, and hemorrhage of the tumor. They are usually benign (80%). Those presenting in older infants tend to have a higher malignant potential. The location of the mass is either external to the pelvis (47%), internal to the pelvis (9%), or dumbell'd both inside and outside (34%).

Autosomal Recessive Polycystic Kidney Disease - The classic look is massively enlarged bilateral kidneys with oligohydramnios. Additional details in the Peds chapter.

Posterior Urethral Valves: The classic look is bilateral hydro on either fetal US or 3rd Trimester MRI.

Short Femur: A short femur (below the 5th percentile) can make you think of a skeletal dysplasia.

SECTION 15: Maternal Disorders

Incompetent Cervix: When shortened, the cervix is associated with a high risk of premature delivery. You call it short when the endocervical canal is < 2.5 cm in length.

Hydronephrosis: occurs in 80% of pregnancies (mechanical compression of the ureters is likely the cause). It tends to affect the right more than the left (dextrorotation of the pregnant uterus).

Things That Grow During Pregnancy:
• Babies
• Splenic Artery Aneurysms
• Renal AMLs
• Fibroids

Fibroids: Fibroids tend to grow in early pregnancy secondary to elevated estrogen. Progesterone will have the opposite effect, inhibiting growth, in later pregnancy. Stretching of the uterus may affect the arterial blood supply and promote infarcts and cystic degeneration.

Uterine Rupture: You see this most commonly in the **3rd trimester at the site of prior c-section**. Other risk factors worth knowing are the unicornuate uterus, prior uterine curettage, "trapped uterus" (persistent retroflexion from adhesions), and interstitial implantation.

HELLP Syndrome: **H**emolysis, **E**levated **L**iver Enzymes, **L**ow **P**latelets. This is the most severe form of pre-eclampsia, and favors young primigravid women in their 3rd trimester. It's bad news and 20-40% end up with DIC. If they are going to show this, it will be as a subcapsular hepatic hematoma in pregnant (or recently pregnant) women.

Peripartum Cardiomyopathy: This is a dilated cardiomyopathy that is seen in the last month of pregnancy to 5 months postpartum. The cardiac MRI findings include a global depressed function, and non-vascular territory subepicardial late Gd enhancement – corresponding to cellular lymphocytic infiltration.

Sheehan Syndrome: This is pituitary apoplexy seen in postpartum female who suffer from large volume hemorrhage (causing acute hypotension). The pituitary grows during pregnancy, and if you have an acute hypotensive episode you can stroke it out (it bleeds). The look on MR is variable depending on the time period, acute it will probably be **T1 bright** (if they show a picture). Ring enhancement around an empty sella is a late look.

Ovarian Vein Thrombophlebitis: This can be a cause of postpartum fever. Risk factors include C-section and endometritis. The right side is affected five times more often than the left. They could show you an enlarged ovary and a thrombosed adjacent ovarian vein.

Retained Products of Conception: The typical clinical story is continued bleeding after delivery (or induced abortion). The most common appearance is an echogenic mass within the uterine cavity. The presence or absence of flow is variable, you can have lots or you can have none. A sneaky way to show this is irregular thickening of the endometrium (>10mm) with some reflective structures and shadowing – representing the fetal parts. You can also think about RPOC when the endometrial thickness is > 5 mm following dilation and curettage. Testable associations include: medical termination of pregnancy (abortion), second trimester miscarriage, and placenta accreta.

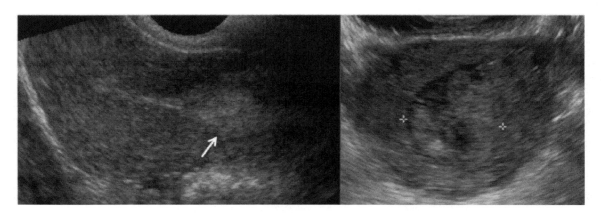

Retained Products of Conception

Endometritis - Broadly speaking, it is an inflammation or infection of the endometrium. The history will be (if you are given one) fever, and uterine tenderness and recent c-section (or prolonged labor). On ultrasound you will see a thickened, heterogenous endometrium, with or without fluid / air.

SECTION 16:
Multiple Gestations

Placentation Terminology: So you can have monozygotic twins (identical) or dizygotic twins (not-identical). The dizygotics are always dichorionic and diamniotic. The placenta of the monozygotics is more variable and depends on the timing of fertilized ovum splitting (before 8 days = diamniotic, after 8 days = monoamniotic). As a point of trivia, a late splitting (after 13 days) can cause a conjoined twin. As a general rule, the later the split the worse things do (monoamniotics have more bad outcomes – they get all tangled up, and the conjoined ones have even more problems).

| Monochorionic Monoamniotic | Monochorionic Diamniotic | Dichorionic Diamniotic Fused Placenta | Dichorionic Diamniotic Separate Placentas |

THIS vs THAT: Monochorionic vs Dichorionic

Membrane Thickness: To differentiate the different types, some people use a method classifying thin and thick membranes. Thick = "easy to see" 1-2 mm, Thin = "hard to see." Thick is supposed to be 4 layers (dichorionic). Thin is supposed to be 2 layers (monochorionic). Obviously this method is very subjective.

Twin-Peak Sign: A beak-like tongue between the two membranes of dichorionic diamniotic fetuses. This **excludes a monochorionic pregnancy**.

T Sign: Think about this as basically the absence of the twin peak sign. You don't see chorion between membrane layers. **T sign = monochorionic pregnancy**.

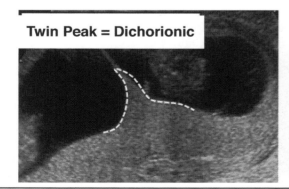

Twin Peak = Dichorionic

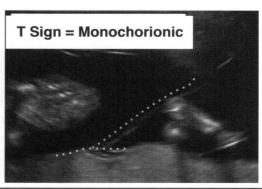

T Sign = Monochorionic

Twin Growth – You can use normal growth charts in the first and second trimester (but not the third). The femur length tends to work best for twin age in later pregnancy. More than 15% difference in fetal weight or abdominal circumference between twins is considered significant.

Twin- Twin Transfusion - This occurs in monochorionic twins when a vascular communication exists in the placenta. You end up with one greedy fat twin who takes all the blood and nutrients, and one skinny wimpy looking kid who gets the scraps. The somewhat counter intuitive part is that the skinny kid actually does better, and the fat one usually gets hydrops and dies. You are going to have unequal fluid in the amniotic sacs, with the donor (skinny) twin having severe oligohydramnios and is sometimes **(*buzzword)** **"stuck to the wall of the uterus,"** or **"shrink wrapped."** The fat twin floats freely in his polyhydramniotic sac. The donor (skinny) twin will also have a high resistance umbilical artery.

Twin Reversed Arterial Perfusion Syndrome – You can get intraplacental shunting that results in a "pump twin" who will pump blood to the other twin. The other twin will not develop a heart and is typically referred to as an "acardiac twin." The acardiac twin will be wrecked (totally deformed upper body). The "pump twin" is usually normal, and does ok as long as the strain on his/her heart isn't too much. If the acardiac twin is really big (> 70% estimated fetal weight of the co-twin) then the strain will usually kill the pump twin. They could show this as a Doppler ultrasound demonstrating umbilical artery flow toward the acardiac twin, or umbilical vein flow away from the acardiac twin (opposite of normal flow).

One Dead Twin – At any point during the pregnancy one of the twins can die. It's a bigger problem (for the surviving twin) if it occurs later in the pregnancy. **"Fetus Papyraceous"** is a fancy sounding Latin word for a pressed flat dead fetus.

"Twin-Embolization Syndrome" is when you have embolized, necrotic, dead baby being transferred to the living fetus *(soylent green is people!)*. This can result in DIC, tissue ischemia, and infarct. By the way, a testable point is that this transfer can only occur in a monochorionic pregnancy.

6
ENDOCRINE
PROMETHEUS LIONHART, M.D.

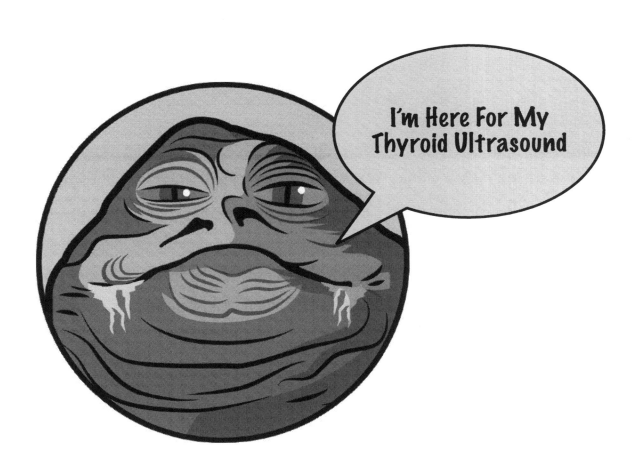

SECTION 1:
Adrenal

Anatomy: The adrenal glands are paired retroperitoneal glands that sit on each kidney. The right gland is triangular in shape, and the left gland tends to be more crescent shaped. If the kidney is congenitally absent the glands will be more flat, straight, discoid, or *"pancake"* in appearance. Each gland gets arterial blood from three arteries (superior from the inferior phrenic, middle from the aorta, and inferior from the renal artery). The venous drainage is via just one main vein (on the right into the IVC, on the left into the left renal vein).

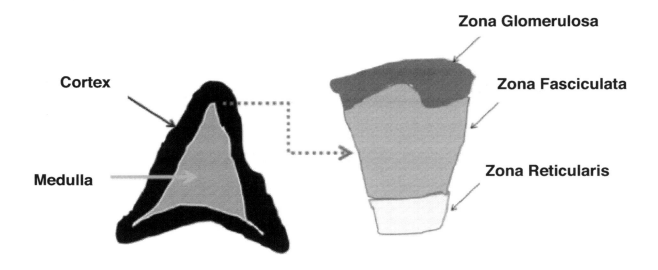

Step 1 Trivia: There are 4 zones to the adrenal, each of which makes different stuff.

- *Zona Glomerulosa*: Makes Aldosterone – prolonged stimulation here leads to hypertrophy.
- *Zona Fasciculata:* Makes Cortisol
- *Zona Reticularis* – Makes Androgens
- *Medulla* – Makes Catecholamines

Adrenal Ultrasound Cases - Gamesmanship

If you get shown an adrenal case on ultrasound, then you are almost certainly dealing with a peds case. What that means is that your choices are narrowed down to: (a) normal, (b) neuroblastoma, (c) hemorrhage, and (d) hyperplasia.

Normal: In babies, the cortex is hypoechoic, and the medulla is hyperechoic. This gives the adrenal a **triple stripe appearance (dark cortex, bright medulla, dark cortex).**

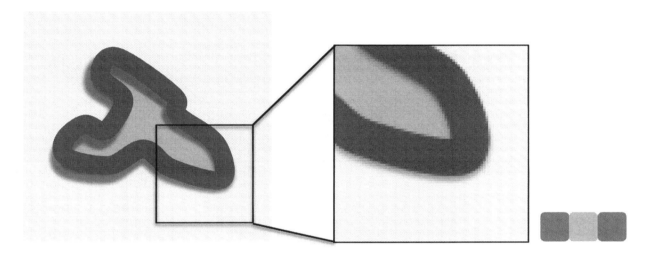

Normal Adrenal - Hypoechoic Cortex, Hyperechoic Medulla, Hypoechoic Cortex
- like an Oreo, with a cream filling.

Neuroblastoma:

I talk about this a ton in the peds chapter. To rehash the important parts, they form in the adrenal medulla (usually), and typically look like an enlarged gland with a **hyperechoic** component. Having said that they can have cystic components and look like hemorrhage. For the purpose of multiple choice I'd go with hyperechoic.

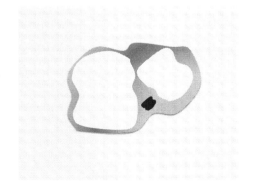

Hemorrhage:

This occurs most commonly in the setting of trauma or stress (neonates). What this typically looks like on ultrasound is an enlarged gland with an anechoic component. With time, the clot changes and it can be more and more echogenic. So basically, it can look like anything but for the purpose of multiple choice I'd go with anechoic.

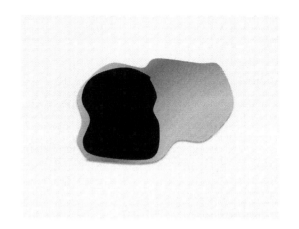

Second order path type trivia/knowledge:

- **Stress:** It's classically seen after a breech birth, but can also be seen with fetal distress, and congenital syphilis. Imaging features change based on the timing of hemorrhage. Calcification is often the end result (that could be shown on CT or MR). It should be avascular. This can occur bilaterally, but favors the right side (75%).

    o *Classic Next Step*: Serial ultrasounds (or MRI) can differentiate it from a cystic neuroblastoma. The hemorrhage will get smaller (cancer will not).

    o *So which is it?* Serial ultrasound or MRI? - If forced to pick you want <u>serial ultrasounds</u>. It's cheaper and doesn't require sedation.

- **Trauma:** This is going to be an adult (in the setting of trauma). Most likely it will be shown on CT. It's more common on the right.

 Waterhouse-Friderichsen Syndrome – Hemorrhage of the adrenal in the setting of fulminant meningitis (from Neisseria Meningitidis).

Hyperplasia:

What this typically looks like on ultrasound is a "big adrenal" that "looks like a brain." *So what does "big" mean?* Most sources will say longer than 20mm, and a limb that is thicker than 4 mm (although this is debated - and will likely not be asked). For the purpose of multiple choice I would say that <u>if they stick calibers on it, then it is too big</u>. So what does *"looks like a brain"* mean? That means the surface is wrinkled, like it has gyri and sulci.

Cerebriform Pattern

Second order path type trivia/knowledge:

- **21-Hydroxylase Deficiency:** Congenital adrenal hypertrophy is caused **by 21-hydroxylase deficiency** in > 90% of cases. It will manifest clinically as either **genital ambiguity (girls)** or some salt losing pathology (boys). The salt losing can actually be life threatening. The look on imaging is adrenal limb width greater than 4mm. In some cases you lose the central hyperechoic stripe (the whole thing looks like cortex).

  - I say "Genital ambiguity", you say 21-Hydroxylase Deficiency

- **Too much cortisol** from overproduction of ACTH - which results in bilateral adrenal gland hyperplasia. If someone wanted to be a real asshole they could get into the weeds with vocabulary. For example, the "Disease" vs "Syndrome" **THIS** vs **THAT:**

  - **Cushing Disease:** This is an overproduction of ACTH by a **pituitary adenoma**, resulting in too much cortisol. This is actually the most common cause of excess cortisol (75%).

  - **Cushing Syndrome:** The "syndrome" is basically a variety of causes resulting in common symptoms. So you can have overproduction of ACTH by an ACTH secreting tumor (classic step 1 example is the small cell lung tumor), or overproduction of ACTH via an adrenal adenoma (these cases will not have hyperplasia), or you can have straight up primary adrenal hyperplasia. You could even get the "syndrome" by taking chronic high dose steroids. Any way you end up with a fat moon face and big gross lines all over you belly counts as "syndrome."

—Summary / Rapid Review —

Normal:

- Triple Stripe
    - Hypoechoic Cortex,
    - Hyperechoic Medulla,
    - Hypoechoic Cortex
- Smooth Surface

Hyperplasia:

- Big (longer than 20mm)
- Looks like a brain (wrinkled surface)
- Can sometimes lose the central bright layer

- "Genital ambiguity", = 21-OH Deficiency

Hemorrhage:

- Big with an anechoic (or echogenic) component
- Gets smaller over time

- Seen with "stress" or trauma

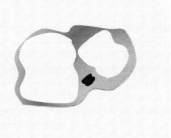

Neuroblastoma:

- Big with an echogenic (or anechoic) component
- Does NOT gets smaller over time

Adrenal Adenoma:

These things are easily the most common tumor in the adrenal gland. Up to 8% of people have them. Proving it is an adenoma is an annoying (testable) problem.

- Non-Contrast: Less than 10 HU

- Contrast: Two options:

Absolute Washout

$$\frac{\text{Enhanced CT - Delayed CT}}{\text{Enhanced CT - Unenhanced CT}} \times 100 \qquad \text{Greater than 60\% = Adenoma}$$

Relative Washout

$$\frac{\text{Enhanced CT - Delayed CT}}{\text{Enhanced CT}} \times 100 \qquad \text{Greater than 40\% = Adenoma}$$

- Hypervascular mets (usually renal, less likely HCC) can mimic adenoma washout. Portal venous HU values > 120 should make you think about a met.

- Along those lines Pheochromocytomas can also exhibit washout. The trick is the same, if you are getting <u>HU measurements > 120</u> on arterial or portal venous phase you <u>can NOT call the thing an adenoma</u>.

- MRI: Look for drop out on in and out of phase T1.

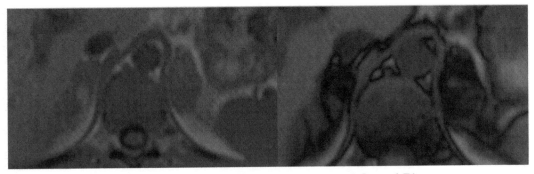

Adrenal Adenoma -*Signal drop out in and Out of Phase*

Adrenal Adenoma Continued

- Real Life = Mass in Adrenal = Adenoma

- Multiple Choice = Mass in the Adrenal = Possible Fuckery

- Although most adenomas are not functional, Cushings (too much cortisol) and Conn's (too much aldosterone) can present as functional adenoma.

 Tips / Tricks:

- Adenoma are usually homogeneous. If they are showing you hemorrhage (in the absence of trauma), calcifications, or necrosis you should start thinking about other things.

- Adenomas are usually small (less than 3 cm). The bigger the mass, the more likely it is to be a cancer. *How big?* Most people will say more than 4 cm = 70% chance cancer, and more than 6 cm = 85% chance cancer. The exceptions are bulk fat (myelolipomas) or biochemical catecholamines in the question stem (pheo) - those can be big.

- Bilateral Small = Probably adenoma

- Bilateral Large = Pheo or Met (Lung cancer)

- Portal Venous Phase HU > 120 = Probably a met (RCC, HCC) or pheo.

"Collision Tumors" - Two different tumors that smash together to look like one mass. Usually one of them is an adenoma. Remember adenoma should be homogenous and small. If you see heterogenous morphology consider that you could have two tumors. FDG PET and MRI can both usually tell if the tumor is actually a collision of two different tumors - those would be the appropriate next steps.

Conn's Syndrome - Syndrome of excessive aldosterone production. This is **most commonly caused by a benign adenoma** (70%). Cortical-carcinoma can also do it, but that is much more rare and usually accompanied by hypercortisolism.

Pheochromocytoma

Uncommon in real life (common on multiple choice tests). They are usually large at presentation (larger than 3 cm). It's usually a heterogeneous mass on CT. On MRI they are **T2 bright**. Both MIBG and Octreotide could be used (but MIBG is better since Octreotide also uptakes in the kidney). Could also be suggested by using the hyper enhancement washout trick (remember <u>HU measurements > 120</u> on arterial or portal venous phase you <u>can NOT call the thing an adenoma</u>.)

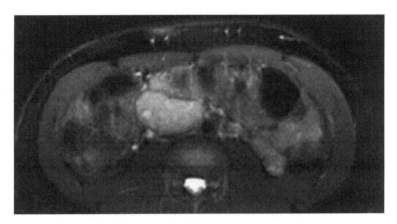

Pheo at the Organ of Zuckerkandl - T2 Bright

- **"Rule of 10s"**

  - 10% are extra adrenal (organ of Zuckerkandl – usually at the IMA), 10% are bilateral, 10% are in children, 10% are hereditary, 10% are NOT active (no HTN).

- **"Syndromes"**

  - Associated syndromes: First think **Von Hippel Lindau**, then think **MEN IIa and IIb.** Other things less likely to be tested include NF-1, Sturge Weber, and TS.

- **"Carney Triad"**

  - Extra-Adrenal Pheo, GIST, and Pulmonary Chondroma (hamartoma).
  - *Don't confuse this with the Carney Complex (Cardiac Myxoma, and Skin Pigmentation).*

Other Misc Adrenal Masses:

Myelolipoma

Benign tumor that **contains bulk fat**. About ¼ have calcifications. If they are big (> 4 cm) they can bleed, and present with a retroperitoneal hemorrhage. Another piece of trivia is the association with endocrine disorders (Cushings, Congenital Adrenal Hyperplasia, Conns).

Don't get it twisted, these tumors are NOT functional, they just happen to have associated disorders about 5-10% of the time.

Cyst – You can get cysts in your adrenal. They are often unilateral, and can be any size. The really big ones can bleed. They have a thin wall, and do NOT enhance.

Mets: Think **breast, lung, and melanoma**. They have no specific imaging findings and look like lipid poor adenomas. If the dude has a known primary (especially lung, breast, or melanoma), and it's not an adenoma then it's probably a met.

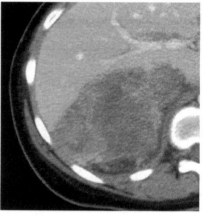

Myelolipoma - Bulk Fat Hyperechoic on US

Cortical Carcinoma:

These are **large** (4 cm -10 cm), may be functional (Cushings), and **calcify in about 20% of cases**.

They are bad news and often met everywhere (direct invasion often first).

As a pearl, an adrenal carcinoma is not likely to be less than 5 cm and often has central necrosis.

Adrenal Cortical Carcinoma
-Direct invasion of the liver

Calcifications:

This is often the result of prior trauma or infection (TB). Certain tumors (cortical carcinoma, neuroblastoma) can have calcifications. Melanoma mets are known to calcify.

 **Wolman Disease:** - This is a **total Aunt Minnie** (and massive zebra / unicorn). **Bilateral enlarged calcified adrenals.** It's a fat metabolism error thing that kills ("booka" - Ali G) before the first year of life.

SECTION 2: Syndromes

MEN: "**M**ultiple **E**ndocrine **N**eoplasia"

There are three of these stupid things, and people who write multiple choice tests love to ask questions about them.

- **MEN 1:** Parathyroid Hyperplasia (90%), Pituitary Adenoma, Pancreatic Tumor (Gastrinoma most commonly)

- **MEN 2:** Medullary Thyroid Cancer (100%), Parathyroid hyperplasia, Pheochromocytoma (33%)

- **MEN 2b:** Medullary Thyroid Cancer (80%), Pheochromocytoma (50%), Mucosal Neuroma, Marfanoid Body Habitus

---

MEN Mnemonics

MEN I *(3 Ps)*
- **P**ituitary, **P**arathyroid, **P**ancreas

MEN IIa *(1M,2Ps)*
Medullary Thyroid Ca,
Pheochromocytoma, **P**arathyroid

MEN IIb *(2Ms,1P)*
- **M**edullary Thyroid Ca, **M**arfanoid Habitus /mucosal neuroma,
Pheochromocytoma

Carcinoid Syndrome:

Flushing, diarrhea, pain, right heart failure from serotonin manufactured by the carcinoid tumor. The syndrome **does not occur until the lesion mets to the liver** (normally the liver metabolizes the serotonin). The typical primary location for the carcinoid tumor is the GI tract (70%). The **most common primary location is the distal ileum** *(older literature says appendix)*. The actual syndrome only occurs in 10% of cases - and is actually very rare (in real life - not on tests).

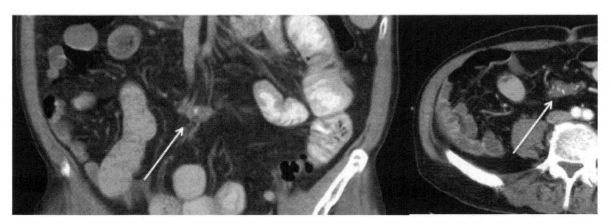

Carcinoid *-Classic Mesenteric Involvement*

Trivia: GI carcinoids are associated with other GI tumors (GI adenocarcinoma).

Trivia: Urine Test for Carcinoid = 5-HIAA (5-hydroxyindoleacetic acid)

Trivia: Nukes Test of Choice: ^{111}In-Octreotide (Octreoscan)

Trivia: MIBG is also positive - but less than 25% of the time (like 15%). Gallium is positive, but super non-specific.

Trivia: Systemic serotonin degrades the heart valves (right sided), and classically causes tricuspid regurgitation

SECTION 3:
Thyroid

Anatomy: The thyroid gland is a butterfly shaped gland, with two lobes connected by an isthmus. The thyroid descends from the foramen cecum at the anterior midline base of the tongue along the thyroglossal duct. The posterior nodular extension of the thyroid (Zuckerkandl tubercle) helps give a location of the recurrent laryngeal nerve (which is medial to it).

Thyroid Nodules: Usually evaluated with ultrasound. Nodules are super super common and almost never cancer. This doesn't stop Radiologists from imaging them, and sticking needles into them. Ultrasound guided FNA of colloid nodules is a major cash cow for many body divisions, that on very rare occasions will actually find a cancer. Qualities that make them more suspicious include: more solid (cystic more benign), calcifications (especially microcalcifications). **Microcalcifications are supposed to be the buzzword for papillary thyroid cancer**. "Comet Tail" artifact is seen in Colloid Nodules. "Cold Nodules" on I-123 scans are still usually benign but have cancer about 15% of the time, so they actually deserve workup.

Colloid Nodules: These are super super common. Suspicious features include microcalcifications, increased vascularity, solid size (larger than 1.5 cm), and being cold on a nuclear uptake exam. As above, **Comet tail artifact is the buzzword**.

Thyroid Adenoma: These look just like solid colloid nodules on ultrasound. They can be hyper functioning (hot on uptake scan). Usually if you have a hyper-functioning nodule (toxic adenoma), your background thyroid will be colder than normal (which makes sense).

Goiter – Thyroid that is too big. In North America it's gonna be a multi-nodular goiter or Graves. In Africa it's low iodine. You can get compressive symptoms if it mashes the esophagus or trachea. These are often asymmetric - with one lobe bigger than the other.

Subacute Thyroiditis / De Quervains Thyroiditis: The classic clinical scenario is a female with a painful gland after an upper respiratory infection. There is a similar subtype that happens in pregnant women, although this is typically painless. You get hyperthyroidism (from spilling the hormone) and then later hypothyroidism. As you get over your cold, the gland recovers to normal function. Radiotracer uptake will be decreased during the acute phase.

Acute Suppurative Thyroiditis: This is an actual bacterial infection of the thyroid. It is possible to develop a thyroid abscess in this situation. A unique scenario (highly testable) is that **in kids this infection may start in a 4th branchial cleft anomaly** (usually on the left), travel via a pyriform fistula and then infect the thyroid. Honestly, that is probably too much for the exam – but could show up on a certification exam under neuro.

Thyroglossal Duct Cyst (TGDC): The most common congenital neck cyst in Pediatrics. This can occur anywhere between the foramen cecum (the base of the tongue) and the thyroid gland (or below). It looks like a thin walled cyst.

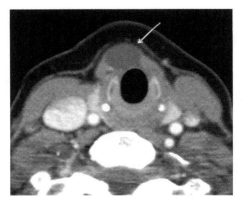

Thyroglossal Duct Cyst - *Midline*

Why Care?
- They can get infected
- They can have ectopic thyroid tissue
- Rarely, that ectopic tissue can get papillary thyroid cancer (if you see an enhancing nodule)

TGDC - Location Fuckery

These are the general numbers to think about:

Suprahyoid = 25%
At the Hyoid = 30%
Infrahyoid = 45%

So, where is the most common location?

Well, it depends on how they ask. If all things are equal the answer is Infrahyoid (which seems counterintuitive based on the embryology but is non the less true).

BUT - if *"at or above the hyoid"* is a choice - then that is actually the right answer (25+30 > 45). As always, read every choice carefully.

Ectopic and Lingual Thyroid: Similar to a thyroglossal duct cyst, this can be found anywhere from the base of the tongue through the central neck. The **most common location (90%) is the tongue base ("Lingual Thyroid")**. It will look hyperdense because of its iodine content (just like a normally located thyroid gland). If you find this, make sure you check for a normal thyroid (sometimes this is the only thyroid the dude has). As a point of trivia, the rate of malignant transformation is rare (3%).

Reidels Thyroiditis:

This is one of those IgG4 associated diseases (others include orbital pseudotumor, retroperitoneal fibrosis, sclerosing cholangitis). You see it in women in their 40s-70s. The thyroid is replaced by fibrous tissue and diffusely enlarges causing compression of adjacent structures (dysphagia, stridor, vocal cord palsy). On US there will be decreased vascularity. On an uptake scan you are going to have decreased values. A sneak trick would be to show you a MR (it's gonna be dark on all sequences - like a fibroma).

Graves – Autoimmune disease that causes hyperthyroidism (most common cause). It's primarily from an antibody directed at the TSH receptor. The actual TSH level will be low. The gland will be enlarged and "inferno hot" on Doppler.

- *Graves Orbitopathy*: Spares the tendon insertions, doesn't hurt (unlike pseudotumor). Also has increased intra-orbital fat.

- *Nuclear Medicine:* Increased uptake of I-123 %RAIU usually 50-80%. Visualization of pyramidal lobe is accentuated.

Hashimotos – The **most common cause of goitrous hypothyroidism** (in the US). It is an autoimmune disease that causes hyper then hypo thyroidism (as the gland burns out later). It's usually hypo – when it's seen. It has an **increased risk of primary thyroid lymphoma**. Step 1 trivia; associated with autoantibodies to thyroid peroxidase (TPO) and anti-thyroglobulin.

On Ultrasound:
There are two classic findings:

(a) Heterogeneous "giraffe skin" appearance,

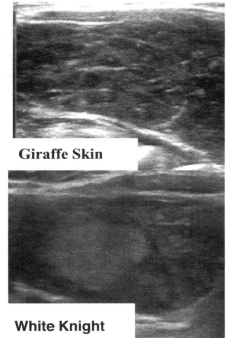

Giraffe Skin

(b) White Knights – uniform hyperechoic nodules – which are actually regenerative nodules.

White Knight

Level 6 Nodes - "Delphian Nodes"

- These are the nodes around the thyroid in the front of the neck.
- You can commonly see them enlarged with Hashimotos.
- However, for the purpose of multiple choice tests, a sick looking level 6 node - or "Delphian Node" is a laryngeal cancer met.

Thyroid Cancer: You can get lots of cancers in your thyroid. There are 4 main subtypes of primary thyroid cancer. Additionally you can get mets to the thyroid or lymphoma in your thyroid – this is super rare and I'm not going to talk about it.

Papillary	The **Most Common** Subtype. *"Papillary is Popular"*	**Microcalcifications is the buzzword and key finding (seen in the cancer and nodes).**	Mets via the lymphatics. Has an overall excellent prognosis, and responds well to I-131.
Follicular	The second most common subtype.		**Mets hematogenously** to bones, lung, liver, etc.. Survival is still ok, (less good than papillary). Does respond to I-131.
Medullary	Uncommon	**Association with MEN II syndrome.** *Calcitonin production is a buzzword.*	Tendency towards local invasion, lymph nodes, and hematogenous spread. **Does NOT respond to I-131.**
Anaplastic	Uncommon	Seen in **Elderly**. Seen in people who have had **radiation treatment**.	Rapid growth, with primary lymphatic spread. **Does NOT respond to I-131.**
Hurthle Cell *(variant of Follicular)*	Uncommon	Seen more in Elderly.	**Does not take up I-131 as well as normal follicular.** *FDG-PET is the way to go for surveillance.*

Metastasis: The buzzword is going to be **microcalcifications in a node** (with papillary). The nodes are typically hyperechoic compared to regular nodes, hyperenhancing on CT, and T1 bright on MR. Remember that thyroid cancer is hypervascular, and it can bleed like stink when it mets to the brain. If there are **mets to the lungs, the classic pattern is "miliary."** The additional pearl with regard to lung mets is that they can be occult on cross sectional imaging, and only seen on whole body scintigraphy. For the purpose of multiple choice tests *pulmonary fibrosis is a risk of treating with I-131 if you have diffuse lung mets.*

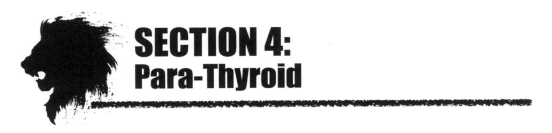

SECTION 4:
Para-Thyroid

Anatomy: There are normally 4 parathyroid glands located posterior to the thyroid. The step 1 trivia is that the superior 2 are from the 4th branchial pouch, and the inferior 2 are from the 3rd branchial pouch. The inferior two are more likely to be in an ectopic location.

Parathyroid Adenoma: This is by far the **most common cause of hyperparathyroidism** (90%). On ultrasound these things look like hypoechoic beans posterior to the thyroid. A 4D-CT can be used to demonstrate early wash-in and delayed wash-out. Nuclear medicine can use two techniques (1) the single-tracer, dual-phase Sestamibi, or (2) the dual tracer Sestamibi + I-123 (or Pertechnetate). These are discussed in detail in the nukes section.

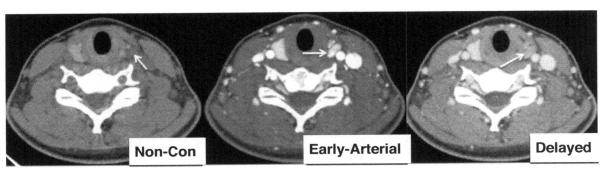

Parathyroid Adenoma - 4D CT shows early enhancement, and delayed washout

Parathyroid Carcinoma: This is pretty uncommon, and only makes up about 1% of the causes of hyperparathyroidism. It looks exactly like an adenoma on imaging. The only way you can tell on imaging is if they show you cervical adenopathy or invasion of adjacent structures.

High Yield Parathyroid Trivia:

Q: What are the causes of hyperparathyroidism?
A: *Hyperfunctioning Adenoma (85-90%),*
Multi-Gland Hyperplasia (8-10%), Cancer (1-3%).

Q: What factors does sestamibi parathyroid imaging depend on ?
A: Mitochondrial density and blood flow

Blank for Scribbles and Notes:

7

THORACIC

PROMETHEUS LIONHART, M.D.

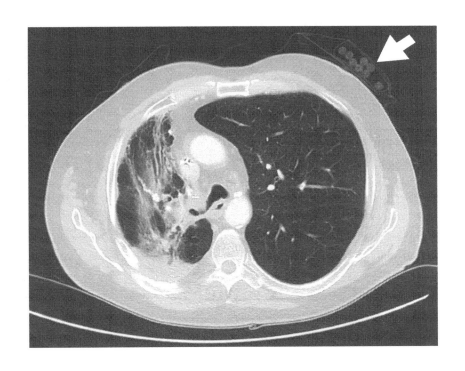

SECTION 1:
Anatomy and Atelectasis

The Lateral CXR "The Radiologists View"

THIS vs THAT:
Right Ribs vs Left Ribs

By convention, lateral CXRs are taken in the left lateral position (left side against the x-ray film/cassette). Therefore, the left ribs will not be magnified (right ribs will be magnified). Right ribs also project more posteriorly. Another strategy is to follow the diaphragm over the stomach bubble (usually left sided).

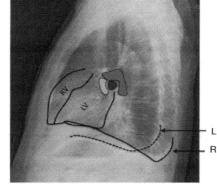

L Costophrenic Angle

R Costophrenic Angle

Normal Hilum on Lateral:

If you put your finger in the *"Dark Hole"* – which is the *left upper lobe bronchus*, in front of it will be the right PA, and overtop of it will be the left PA. The posterior wall of the bronchus intermedius runs through the black hole, and can be thickened by edema.

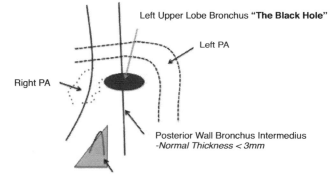

Left Upper Lobe Bronchus **"The Black Hole"**

Left PA

Right PA

Posterior Wall Bronchus Intermedius
-*Normal Thickness < 3mm*

Normal Hilum on Frontal:

This is the right hilar anatomy on the frontal view. Of course it never looks that nice in the real world. Ben Felson used to say the right interlobar artery reminded him of a woman's leg... but then again most things did.

The <u>left hilar point should always be around 1cm higher than the right</u>

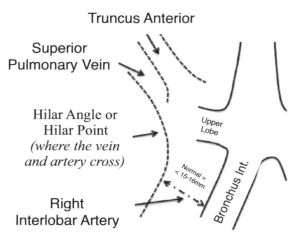

Truncus Anterior

Superior Pulmonary Vein

Hilar Angle or Hilar Point *(where the vein and artery cross)*

Upper Lobe

Normal = < 15-16mm

Right Interlobar Artery

Bronchus Int.

338

Retrotracheal Triangle (Raider Triangle).

This is a triangle which sits on the aortic arch and is bordered anteriorly by the back wall of the trachea, and posteriorly by the upper thoracic vertebral bodies. Many things can obliterate this, but for the purpose of multiple choice tests an opacity in the Raider Triangle is an **Aberrant right subclavian arter**y.

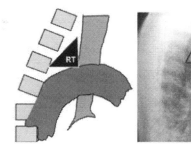

Heart Valves on CXR: This is high yield. I like to use a two intersecting line method on both the frontal and lateral chest to answer these kinds of questions.

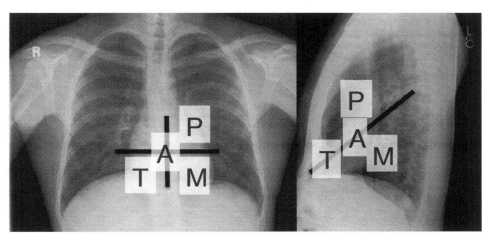

- Notice the Pulmonic is the Most Superior

- Notice the Tricuspid is the Most Anterior

- Notice the Aortic is in front of the Mitral on the Lateral

A few other sneaky tricks include knowing that the pointy parts of the mechanical valves (*Carpentier-Edwards aortic valve*) point out (towards the direction of blood flow). Know that the mitral valve is larger than the aortic valve (so if you see two metallic rings, the larger is the mitral). Know that a pacemaker wire going through a valve makes it the tricuspid valve (lead terminates in the right ventricle).

Fissures:

Notice the right major fissure is anterior to the left.

A = Horizontal (Minor) Fissure,
B = Right Major (Oblique),
C = Left Oblique

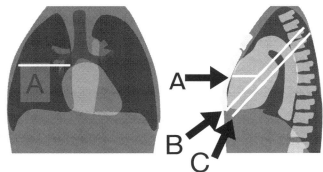

Azygos Lobe Fissure – This is considered variant anatomy. These things happen when the azygos vein is displaced laterally during development. The result is a deep fissure in the right upper lobe. It's not actually an accessory lobe but rather a variant of the right upper lobe. If they show you one, I suspect the question will revolve around the pleura. Something like *"how many layers of pleura?"* The answer is 4.

Segmental Anatomy

The tertiary bronchi are grouped into bronchopulmonary segments.

On the right, there are 10 segments (3 upper, 2 middle, and 5 lower).

On the left, there are only 8 (4 upper lobe / lingula, and 4 lower lobe).

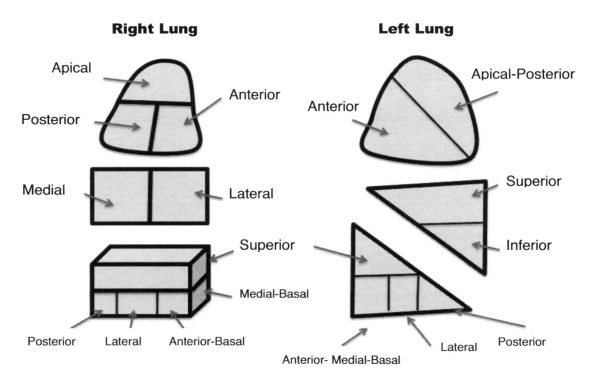

Varient Airway Anatomy:

Normal For Comparison

Pig Bronchus (Tracheal Bronchus):	**Cardiac Bronchus:**
Bronchus that comes right off the trachea (prior to bifurcation into right and left mainstem).	Bronchus that comes off bronchus intermedius, opposite to the origin of the right upper lobe bronchus In, contrast to the Pig Bronchus this thing is often blind ending - and supposedly represents the only <u>true supernumerary bronchus</u>
Means nothing clinically, but occasionally people can get some air trapping or <u>recurrent infections</u> from impaired ventilation.	Similar to the pig bronchus, it means nothing clinically, but occasionally people can get <u>recurrent infections</u>
Trigger: Recurrent RUL Pneumonia in kid.	

Mediastinal Anatomy

The mediastinum is classically divided into 4 sections, superior, anterior, middle, and posterior. The borders of these areas make good trivia questions.

- *Superior* – The inferior border is the oblique plane from the sternal-manubrial junction.

- *Anterior* – The posterior border is the pericardium

- *Middle* - The heart, pericardium, and bifurcation of the trachea are all included. On lateral CXR, people sometimes say posterior to the trachea, and anterior to the vertebral bodies (or 1cm posterior to the vertebral bodies).

- *Posterior* – From the back of the heart to the spine. Contains the esophagus, thoracic duct, and descending aorta.

Mediastinal Variant Anatomy

Pulmonary Veins: Pulmonary vein anatomy is highly variable. You typically have 4 total (2 right – upper and lower, 2 left – upper and lower). The **most common anatomic variation is a separate vein draining the right middle lobe** (seen 30% of the time). Who cares??? Two people (1) People who write multiple choice tests, (2) Electrophysiologists prior to ablations.

Proximal Interruption of the Pulmonary Artery: Basically you have congenital absence of the right (or left) PA with the more distal pulmonary vasculature present. It's also called unilateral absence of the PA, but that is confusing because the distal pulmonary vasculature is present.

How it could be shown:
- Classically with volume loss of one hemi-thorax (could be on CXR or CT), then a contrast CT shot through the heart with only one PA. Normally, you might think one PA is just volume averaging - but once you've been shown volume loss on one side your suspicion for this should be raised.

Trivia:
- It's seen on the opposite side of the aortic arch (Absent right PA with left-sided aortic arch, Absent left PA with right-sided aortic arch).
- Associated with PDA
- Interrupted left PA is associated with TOF and Truncus

Patterns of Atelectasis:

Atelectasis (incomplete lung expansion) exists on a scale of severity; ranging from the tiny horizontal "plate-like" / "discoid" subsegmental to complete collapse of the lung (lobar).

The degree of collapse depends on the location of obstruction (peripheral vs central).

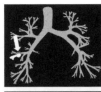

There are some described vocabulary words for the different subtypes of atelectasis - and those words, the supposed mechanisms, and the attributed causes are all potentially testable.

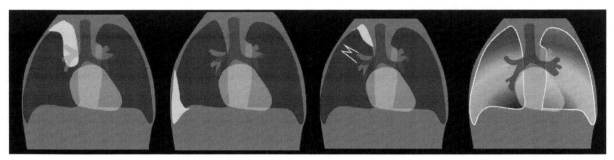

Obstructive (Absorptive)	**Compressive** (Relaxation / Passive)	**Fibrotic** (Cicatrization)	**Adhesive**
• Result of complete obstruction of an airway • No new air can enter and any air that is already there is eventually <u>absorbed</u> leaving a collapsed section of lung • **Causes:** Obstructing neoplasms, mucous plugging in asthmatics or critically ill patients, and foreign body aspiration.	• Results from direct mass effect on the lung • **Causes:** Most classically seen adjacent to a <u>pleural effusion</u>. Could also be seen from adjacent compression of lung from a mass, hiatal hernia, or a large bleb — anything directly pushing on the lung.	• Results from scarring / fibrosis which fails to allow the lung to collapse completely. • **Causes:** Most classic is <u>TB</u>, but scarring from radiation, other infections, or really any other cause of fibrosis can do this.	• Results from loss of surface tension / inadequate pleural adherence of the alveolar walls - from a surfactant deficiency. • Alveoli become unstable and collapse. • **Causes:** RDS (premature infants), ARDS (more diffuse pattern), and in the setting of pulmonary embolism (loss of blood flow / lack of CO_2 disrupts integrity of surfactant).

Another easily testable topic related to atelectasis are the primary and **secondary signs**. The big 3 ones being **shadow**, **silhouette,** and **shift**. Just like any normal person would, when I think of the word "**shadow**," I immediately think of either Lamont Cranston (hypnotist and master detective) , or Carl Jung's "Phenomenology of the Self." I'm sure you do too. However, in the case of atelectasis "**shadow**" refers to the **shadow** made by the opacified (collapsed lung). This is the direct sign, and is the most obvious (more on the next page). The **silhouette** refers to the loss of interface between this opacity and the adjacent normal structures. This is useful in localization (more on the next page). The **shift** refers to the movement of structures as they are "pulled" towards the site of volume loss. Remember, space occupying things (tumors, pneumonia, pleural effusion, cavitary lesions, etc...) push things away. Atelectasis is a volume losing process - so it pulls (examples - pulling the right hilar point above the left, pulling the left hilar point below the right, shifting the mediastinum, etc...).

- Lobar Patterns -

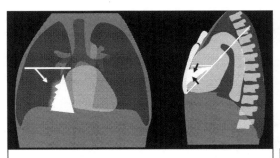
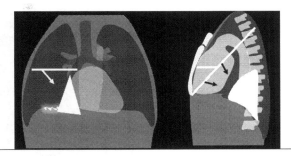

Right Middle Lobe:
- Classic look is increased density at the right heart border with <u>loss of that border</u> (shadow and silhouette)
- The lateral will show anterior density over the heart (as the RML is anterior)

Right Middle Lobe Syndrome:
Chronic collapse of the RML is classically described with MAI infection in an elderly women who is too proper too cough (Lady Windermere syndrome). On CT you'd see additional findings of small nodules and bronchiectasis - with additional involvement of the Lingula.

Right Lower Lobe:
- Classic look is increased density at the right heart border similar to collapse of the RML.
- The critical distinction is the right heart border. You <u>should NOT lose the border of the right heart with RLL collapse</u>. In fact it should be easier to see from compensatory hyper-expansion of the RML.
- In some cases, the mediastinal vessels are pulled to the right creating a triangle of opacity to the right of the trachea **(Superior Triangle Sign)**

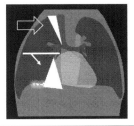

Right Lower Lobe + Right Middle Lobe:

- Uncommon Combination and a Sneaky Move
- The trick is a <u>loss of visualization of the right hemidiaphragm and right heart border</u>

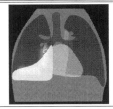

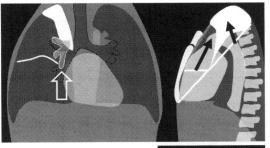

Right Upper Lobe:
- Closes like a fan attached at the Hilum
- Horizontal Fissure may bow upward
- Hilum may elevate
- The lateral will again show this hilar attachment with the lobe collapsing from both the anterior and posterior directions.
- The top half of the oblique fissure will be pulled anterior.

S Sign of Golden:
Refers to a reverse "S" shape that the minor fissure in cases of RUL collapse resulting from a central obstructing mass.

- Lobar Patterns Continued-

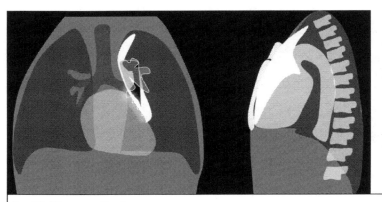

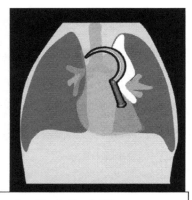

Left Upper Lobe:

- This is different than the right upper lobe (which collapsed like a fan making a dense wedge shaped opacity.
- The LUL tends to be more subtle with a subtle increased density medially. There won't be any well defined borders
- A hint may be non-visualization of the aortic knob.

- Sometimes (if you are lucky) you can get some non-specific peaking of the diaphragm from upward traction

Luftsichel Sign:

"Air Sickle" - appearance from the lucent stripe appearance of the hyper inflated superior (apical) segment of the lower lobe pinned between the medial edge of the collapsed segment and the aortic arch

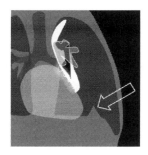

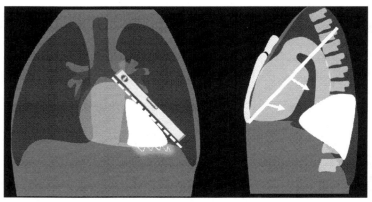

Cartoon Level demonstrating the "flat" appearance of the left heart / hilum.

Left Lower Lobe:

- Can Be sneaky on a frontal only (opacity is hidden behind the heart)
- The lateral makes it more obvious with a posteriorly directed triangular opacity

The **Flat Waist Sign** - has been used as a description of the flattened appearance of the contours of the hilum and heart border.

SECTION 2:
Localization - 1970s Style

This was a known thing done on the old oral boards, so the idea is not new. They show you a mass on a frontal radiograph and tell you to localize it (anterior, middle, posterior, or pulmonary). Here are the common tactics you can use to get this right.

Posterior Junction Line is ABOVE the clavicles

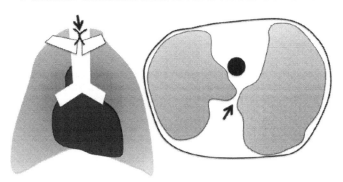

Cervicothoracic Sign – This takes advantage of the posterior junction line, which demonstrates that *things above the clavicles are in the posterior mediastinum.*

Hilum Overlay Sign: Mass at the level of the hilum arising from the hilum will obliterate the silhouette of the pulmonary vessels. If you can see the edge of the vessels through the mass, then the mass is not in the hilum (so it is either anterior or posterior).

THIS vs THAT:
Pulmonary vs Mediastinal Origin:

The easiest trick is if they show you air bronchograms. Only a pulmonary mass will have air bronchograms. The harder trick is the angle with the lung. The mass will make an acute angle with the lung if it's within the lung. The mass will make an obtuse margin with the lung if it's in the mediastinum.

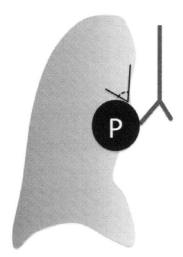

Pulmonary Origin
-makes an acute angle with the lung

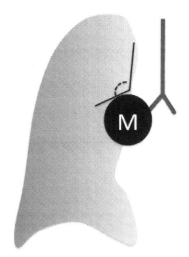

Mediastinal Origin
-makes an obtuse angle with the lung

SECTION 3:
Infection

Bacterial Infection		
Strep Pneumo	Lobar Consolidation	Favors lower lobes. Can be severe in sickle cell patients post splenectomy. The **most common cause of pneumonia in AIDS patient**.
Staph A.	**Bronchopneumonia** – patchy opacities	Often bilateral, and can make abscess. Can be spread via the blood in endocarditis patients
Anthrax	Hemorrhagic lymphadenitis, mediastinitis, and hemothorax	Classic Look: **Mediastinal widening** with pleural effusion in the setting of bio-terrorism
Klebsiella	Buzzword: "**Bulging Fissure**" from exuberant inflammation. More likely to have pleural effusions, empyema, and cavity than conventional pneumonia.	Alcoholic and Nursing Home Patients. Step 1 Buzzword was "currant jelly sputum"
H. Flu	Usually bronchitis, sometimes bilateral lower lobe bronchopneumonia	Seen in **COPDers**, and people without a spleen
Pseudomonas	Patchy opacities, with abscess formation	ICUers on a ventilator (also CF and Primary Ciliary Dyskinesia). Pleural effusions are common, but usually small
Legionella	Peripheral and sublobar airspace opacity	Seen in **COPDers**, and around crappy air conditioners. Only cavitates in immunosuppressed patients. X-ray tends to lag behind resolution of symptoms.
Aspiration	Anaerobes, with airspace opacities. They can cavitate, and abscess is not uncommon	Posterior lobes if supine when aspirating, Basal Lower lobes in upright aspiration May favor the right side, just like an ET tube. The most common complication is empyema (which can get a bronchopleural fistula).
Actinomycosis	Airspace in peripheral lower lobes. Can be aggressive and cause rib osteomyelitis/ invade adjacent chest wall.	Classic story is dental procedure gone bad, leading to mandible osteo, leading to aspiration.
Mycoplasma	Fine reticular pattern on CXR, Patchy airspace opacity with tree-in-bud	

Immunocompromised

Post Bone Marrow Transplant: You see pulmonary infections in nearly 50% of people after bone marrow transplant, and this is often listed as the most common cause of death in this population. Findings are segregated into: early neutropenic, early, and late – and often tested as such.

Post Bone Marrow Transplant Graft vs Host	
Acute (20-100 Days)	Chronic (> 100 days)
Favors extrapulmonary systems (skin, liver, GI tract)	Lymphocytic Infiltration of the airways and obliterative bronchiolitis.

Post Bone Marrow Transplant (Pulmonary Findings)		
Early Neutropenic (0-30 days)	**Early (30-90)**	**Late > 90**
Pulmonary Edema, Hemorrhage, Drug Induced Lung Injury	PCP, CMV	Bronchiolitis Obliterans, Cryptogenic Organizing Pneumonia
Fungal Pneumonia (invasive aspergillosis)		

AIDS Related Pulmonary Infection:

Questions related to AIDS and pulmonary infection are typically written in one of two ways (1) with regard to the CD4 count, and (2) by showing you a very characteristic infection.

PCP: This is the most classic AIDS infection. This is the one they are most likely to show you. **Ground glass opacity** is the dominant finding, and is seen bilaterally in the perihilar regions with sparing of the lung periphery. Cysts, which are usually thin-walled, can occur in the ground glass opacities about 30% of the time.

Buzzwords:

- Most common airspace opacity = Strep Pneumonia
- If they show you a CT with ground glass = PCP
- "Flame-Shaped" Perihilar opacity = Kaposi Sarcoma
- Persistent Opacities = Lymphoma
- Lung Cysts = LIP
- Lungs Cysts + Ground Glass + Pneumothorax = PCP
- Hypervascular Lymph Nodes = Castleman or Kaposi

Infections in AIDS by CD4		CT Pattern – With AIDS	
> 200	Bacterial Infections, TB	Focal Airspace Opacity	Bacterial Infection (**Strep Pneumonia**) is **the most common**. DDx should include TB if low CD4. If it's a chronic opacity think Lymphoma or Kaposi.
< 200	PCP, Atypical Mycobacterial	Multi-Focal Airspace Opacity	Bacterial, or Fungal
< 100	CMV, Disseminated Fungal, Mycobacterial	Ground Glass	**PCP** (if that's not a choice it could be CMV if CD4 is < 100).

TB

You can think about TB as either:
(a) Primary, (b) Primary Progressive, (c) Latent or (d) Post Primary / Reactivation.

- **Primary:** Essentially you inhaled the bug, and it causes necrosis. Your body attacks and forms a granuloma (Ghon Focus). You can end up with nodal expansion (which is bulky in kids, and less common in adults), this can calcify and you get a "Ranke Complex. " The bulky nodes can actually cause compression leading to atelectasis (which is often lobar). If the node ruptures you can end up with either (a) endobronchial spread or (b) hematogenous spread – depending on if the rupture is into the bronchus or a vessel. This hematogenous spread manifests as a miliary pattern. **Cavitation in the primary setting is NOT common.** Effusions can be seen but are more common in adults (uncommon in kids).

- **Primary Progressive**: This term refers to local progression of parenchymal disease with the **development of cavitation** (at the initial site of infection / or hematogenous spread). This primary progression is uncommon – with the main risk factor being **HIV**. Other risk factors are all the things that make you immunosuppressed – transplant patients, people on steroids. The ones you might not think about is jejunoileal bypass, subtotal gastrectomy, and silicosis. This form is **similar in course to post primary disease**.

- **Latent:** This is a positive PPD, with a negative CXR, and no symptoms. If you got the TB vaccine, you are considered latent by the US health care system/industry if your PPD converts. This scenario buys you 9 months of INH and maybe some nice drug induced hepatitis.

- **Post Primary (reactivation):** This happens about 5% of the time, and describes an endogenous reactivation of a latent infection. The classic location is in the apical and posterior upper lobe and superior lower lobe (more oxygen, less lymphatics). In primary infection you tend to have healing. In post primary infection you tend to have progression. The **development of a cavit**y is the thing to look for when you want to call this. Arteries near the cavity can get all pseudoaneursym'd up – "Rasmussen Aneurysm" they call it – in the setting of a TB cavity.

> **Immune Reconstitution Inflammatory Syndrome:**
> The story will be a patient with TB and AIDS started on highly active anti-retroviral therapy (HAART) and now doing worse. The therapy is steroids.

> **Pleural Involvement with TB:** This can occur at any time after initial infection. In primary TB development of a pleural effusion can be seen around 3-6 months after infection – hypersensitivity response. This pleural fluid is usually culture negative (usually in this case is like 60%). You have to actually biopsy the pleura to increase your diagnostic yield. You don't see pleural effusions as much with post primary disease, but when you do, the fluid is usually culture positive.

High Yield Factoids Regarding TB:
- Primary = No Cavity, Post Primary / Primary Progressive = Cavity
- Ghon Lesion = Calcified TB Granuloma ; sequela of primary TB
- Ranke Complex = Calcified TB Granuloma + Calcified Hilar Node ; Healed primary TB
- Bulky Hilar and Paratracheal Adenopathy = Kids
- Location for Reactivation TB = Posterior / Apical upper lobes, Superior Lower Lobes
- Miliary Spread when? – Hematogenous dissemination (usually in the setting of reactivation), but can be in primary progressive TB as well
- Reactive TB Pattern (Cavitation) seen in HIV patient when the CD4 is > 200
- Primary Progressive Pattern (Adenopathy, Consolidation, Miliary Spread) in HIV is CD4 < 200
- TB does NOT usually cause a lobar pattern in HIV

Non Tuberculous Mycobacteria:

Not all mycobacterium is TB. The two non-TB forms worth knowing are mycobacterium avium-intracellulare complex (MAC) and Mycobacterium Kansasii. I find that grouping these things into 4 buckets is most useful for understanding and remembering them.

- **Cavitary** ("Classic") – This one is usually caused by MAC. It favors an old white man with COPD (or other chronic lung disease), and it looks like reactivation TB. So you have an upper lobe cavitary lesion with adjacent nodules (suggesting endobronchial spread).

- **Bronchiectatic** ("Non-Classic") – This is the so-called "**Lady Windermere**" disease (everyone knows it's just not lady-like to cough). They often do not cough, and are asymptomatic. This favors an old white lady. You see tree-in-bud opacities and cylindric bronchiectasis in the right middle lobe and lingula.

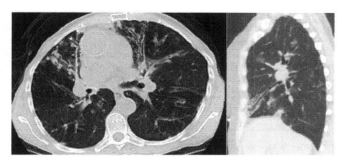

Lady Windermere - MAC
-Bronchiectasis with tree-in-bud funk in the right middle lobe and lingula

- **HIV Patients** – You see this with low CD4s (< 100). The idea is that it's a GI infection disseminated in the blood. You get a big spleen and liver. It frequently is mixed with other pulmonary infections (PCP, etc...) given the low CD4 – so the lungs can look like anything. Mediastinal lymphadenopathy is the most common manifestation.

- **Hypersensitivity Pneumonitis** – This is the so-called "**hot-tub lung**." Where you get aerosolized bugs (which exist in natural sea water and in fresh water). The lungs look like ill-defined, **ground glass centrilobular nodules**.

Non Tuberculous Mycobacteria - Rapid Review		
Cavitary Type	Old White Male Smoker	Looks like reactivation TB
Non-Classic *(Lady Windermere)*	Old Lady	Middle Lobe and Lingula, bronchiectasis and tree in bud.
HIV	Low CD4 (< 100)	Mediastinal Lymphadenopathy
Hypersensitivity *(Hot Tub Lung)*	History of hot tub use	Ground glass centrilobular nodules

Fungal

Aspergillus: So this can cause a variable appearance and the trivia surrounding that variability comes in three flavors: (1) normal immune, (2) immune suppressed, or (3) Hyper-immune.

- *Normal Immune:* This is the situation when aspergillus makes a fungus ball "Aspergilloma" in an existing cavity. The way this is asked is pretty much always the same. They will show you a fungus ball, and they want you to call it invasive. Don't fall for that. This is not the same thing as invasive. They can be totally normal people who have a cavity from trauma, or prior infection ect…

- *Immune Suppressed (AIDS, or Transplant Patient):* This is when you get your **invasive aspergillus.** This is going to be shown one of two ways. (1) A **halo sign** – consolidative nodule/mass with a ground glass halo. The halo of ground glass is actually the invasive component. (2) **Air Crescent sign** – a thin crescent of air within the consolidative mass. This actually represents healing, as the necrotic lung separates from the parenchyma. The timing is usually about 2-3 weeks after treatment. Lastly, they could show you some peripheral wedge shaped infarcts in the setting of some halo signs.

- *Hyper-Immune:* This is your asthmatic with **ABPA**. Allergic Broncho-Pulmonary Aspergillosis. This is "Always" seen in patients with **long standing asthma** (sometimes CF). You classically have upper lobe central saccular bronchiectasis with mucoid impaction (<u>finger-in-glove</u>).

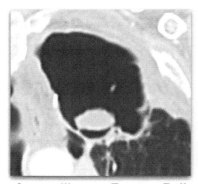 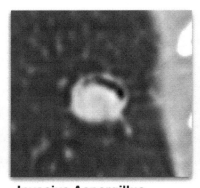 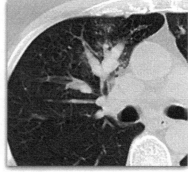

Aspergilloma - Fungus Ball
- Normal immune system

Invasive Aspergillus
- Air Crescent Sign
- Dude has AIDS

ABPA
- Finger in Glove; think asthma

Mucormycosis – This aggressive fungal infection almost always occurs in impaired patients (AIDS, Steroids, Bad Diabetics Etc..). You usually think about mucor eating some fat diabetic's face off, but it can also occur in the lungs. Think about this when you have <u>invasion of the mediastinum, pleura, and chest wall.</u>

Viral

CMV – This can be seen in two classic scenarios: (1) Reactivation of the latent virus after prolonged immunosuppression (post bone marrow transplant), and (2) Infusing of CMV positive marrow or in other blood products. The timing for bone marrow patients is "early" between 30-90 days. The radiographic appearance is multiple nodules, ground glass or consolidative.

Random Viral Trivia		
Measles	Multifocal ground glass opacities with small nodular opacities	Pneumonia can be before or after the skin lesions. Complications higher in pregnant and immunocompromised
Influenza	Coalescent lower lobe opacity. Pleural effusion is rare.	
SARS	Lower lobe predominant ground glass opacities	
Varicella	Multiple peripheral nodular opacities. They form small round calcific lung nodules in the healed version.	Most commonly causes Chickenpox in kids. The pneumonia more commonly occurs in immunocompromised adults (with AIDS or lymphoma).
Ebstein Barr	Uncommonly affects the lung. Can cause lymph node enlargement	Most common radiographic abnormality is a big spleen.

Septic Emboli

There are a variety of ways you can throw infectious material into the lungs via the bloodstream (pulmonary arteries).

Some common sources would include; infected tricupsid valves, infection in the body, infected catheters, infected teeth…etc…

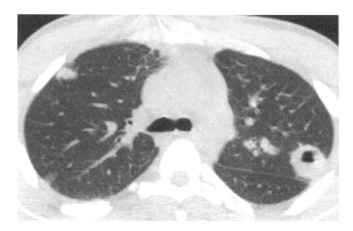

Septic Emboli - Multiple round opacities, one with cavitation

Septic Emboli Trivia:
* It's lower lobe predominant (more blood flow)
* You get peripheral nodular densities and wedge shaped densities (can infarct).
* They can **cavitate**, and likely will be cavitated if they show you a CT image.
* The **feeding vessel sign** – nodule with a big vessel going into it can be shown (also seen with hematogenous mets).
* Empyema and pneumothorax are both known complications.

Lemierre Syndrome:

This is an eponym referring to **jugular vein thrombosis with septic emboli** classically seen after an oropharyngeal infection or recent ENT surgery.

High Yield Trivia
Q: What is the bacterial agent responsible in the majority of cases?
A:"**Fusobacterium Necrophorum**."

CAVITY Mnemonic For Lung Cavity:

Cancer (usually squamous cell)

Auto-immune (Wegeners, Rheumatoid / Caplan Syndrome)

Vascular – Septic Emboli / Bland Emboli

Infection - TB

Trauma - Pneumatoceles

Young – "Congenital" – CCAMs, Sequestrations

SECTION 4:
Cancer

Lung Cancer Risk Factors: include; being over 30 (under 30 is super rare), exposures to bad stuff (arsenic, nickel, uranium, asbestos, chromium, beryllium, radon), having lung fibrosis, COPD (even if you didn't smoke), and family history. <u>Diffuse fibrosis supposedly gives you 10x the risk.</u>

Screening:

Recently, the US preventive services task force has approved lung cancer screening with low dose CT for asymptomatic adults aged 55-80 who have a 30 pack-year history and currently smoke (or have quit within the past 15 years).

Some trivia related to the screening program:
- Shockingly, it is backed up by evidence (which is extremely rare in medical screening programs), and legit improves outcomes (also rare in medicine).
- The follow up recommendations are NOT the same as the Fleischner Society Recommendations. So nodules found on a CT done for any reason other than official lung cancer screening will follow Fleischner and not the LUNG RADS recommendations used with the screening program.
- Dose on the screening CTs is supposed to be low - **recommended below CTDI$_{vol}$ 3 mGy**
- "Growth" is considered 1.5mm or more in one year
- LUNG RADS scoring is based off the most suspicious nodule. You don't give multiple ratings for multiple nodules.
- Endobronchial "lesions" (mucus) are treated as 4a - and given a 3 month follow up.
- A treated remote (> 5 years) lung cancer patient must still meet the normal screening criteria to be enrolled in the program.

Lung Rads Overview (Abbreviated Version)		
Category 0	Shitty test that you can't read, or you need priors	Repeat or get priors
Category 1	Negative, < 1% chance of cancer. Either no nodules or granulomas.	1 year follow up
Category 2	Benign < 1 % chance of cancer. Baseline exam - nodules smaller than 6mm. Subsequent exam - no new nodules larger than 4mm. Ground glass nodule smaller than 20mm.	1 year follow up
Category 3	Probably Benign, 1-2% chance of cancer. Baseline nodule 6-8mm. Subsequent exam new nodule > 4mm. Ground glass > 20mm.	6 month follow up
Category 4a	Suspicious, 5-15% chance of cancer, Baseline 8-15mm. New nodule 6-8mm	3 month follow up vs PET
Category 4b	Suspicious, > 15% chance of cancer, > 15mm at baseline New nodule > 8mm	PET vs Tissue Sampling
Category 4X	> 15 % chance of cancer Worsening of category 3 or 4 nodules (growth or new spiculation)	PET vs Tissue Sampling

Nodules (incidental discover):

As discussed on the prior page, nodules discovered incidentally on non-screening scans are treated different for followup. These nodules are the captives of the dreaded Fleischner Society recommendations.

Few Pearls:
- Fleischner guidelines only apply for patients older than 35
- They do NOT apply to patients with known or suspected cancer
- They do NOT apply to patients who are immunocompromised
- Measurements are reported as the average diameter (short + long / 2) obtained in the same plane.
- Risk stratification for followup (low, intermediate, high) is based on multiple risk factors (smoking, cancer history, family history, age, uranium / random / asbestos exposure and nodules characteristics / size).
- Follow up is based off the arbitrary guess of a cancer risk > 1%
- Perifissural nodules (discussed later) - do not need a follow up, even if they are > 6mm in size. This is NOT the case with LUNG-RADS - which recommends they should be treated the same as any other solid nodule.
- Nodule characterization should be performed on thin-slice CT images ≤1.5 mm. This is done to look for a small solid component hiding behind partial volume effect in a ground glass nodule.
- Multiple nodules (> 5) makes malignancy statistically less likely.

Behold the recommendations.

Notice how the nodules are stratified based on number and risk.

Risk is determined based on the characteristics of the nodule (spiculated, etc..), and the characteristics of the patient (exposure to uranium, etc...).

This is different than the LUNG-RADS algorithm.

Fleischner Society Overview for SOLID nodules (Abbreviated Version)			
< 6 mm	Single	Low Risk	No follow up
		High Risk	12 month Repeat
	Multiple	Low Risk	No follow up
		High Risk	12 month Repeat
6 - 8 mm	Single	Low Risk	6-12 month follow up
		High Risk	6-12 month follow up
	Multiple	Low Risk	3-6 month follow up
		High Risk	3-6 month follow up
> 8 mm	Single	Low and High	PET or Biopsy
	Multiple	Low Risk	3-6 month follow up
		High Risk	3-6 month follow up

Ground Glass nodule follow up recommendations are variable. Most people will not follow up nodules smaller than 6mm. If they are greater than 6mm people will either do 6 month or 1 year (depends on who you ask). Follow up is persistent for 5 years, because of the slow growth of the potential adenocarcinoma in situ.

Part Solid nodules are slightly different. Smaller than 6mm still gets ignored. However, the ones larger than 6mm get a 3 month follow up - with interval widening but persisting up to 5 years. Regular solid nodules typically get set free after 2 years of stability.

Nodules
- Types and Trivia -

Solitary Pulmonary Nodule: A SPN is defined as a round or oval lesion measuring less than 3cm in diameter (more than 3cm = mass). Technically to be "solitary" it needs to be surrounded by lung parenchyma, with no associated adenopathy, or pleural effusion. So, you can have numerous "solitary" nodules in the lungs.

There are 4 classic "benign calcification" patterns:

Solid, Laminated, Central, and Popcorn.

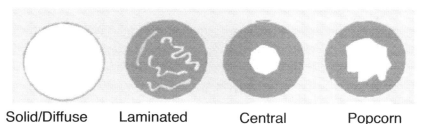

Solid/Diffuse   Laminated   Central   Popcorn

Anything else is considered suspicious. <u>Eccentric patterns are considered the most suspicious.</u> Some notable (testable) exceptions include when you see popcorn and central calcifications in the setting of a GI cancer. Solid calcifications can also be bad in the setting of osteosarcoma.

Eccentric

Makes You Think B9
Presence of Fat
Rapid Doubling Time (less than 1 month)
Slow Doubling Time (longer than 16 months) *Stable at two years = B9

Make You Think Cancer
Spiculated Margins "Corona Radiata Sign"
Air Bronchogram through the nodules (usually Adenocarcinoma in situ)
Partially solid lesions with ground glass component

Solid and Ground Glass Components: A **part solid lesion with a ground glass component is the most suspicious morphology you can have**. Non-solids (only ground glass) is intermediate. Totally solid is actually the least likely morphology to be cancer.

PET for SPN: You can use PET for SPNs larger than 1 cm. Lung Cancer is supposed to be HOT (SUV > 2.5). Having said that, infectious and granulomatous nodules can also be hot. If you are dealing with a ground glass nodule it's more likely to be:

Solid Nodule (> 1cm in size):
HOT = Cancer, COLD = Not Cancer
Ground Glass Nodules:
HOT = Infection , COLD = Cancer

SPN / Cancer Trivia:

- Lung Cancer is 1.5 x more likely in the Right Lung
- 70% of Lung Cancer is in the Upper Lobes
- Exception to the rule is pulmonary fibrosis - where peripheral basilar cancer is more common.
- SPN in the setting of head and neck CA is more likely to be a primary bronchogenic carcinoma rather than a metastasis (they have similar risk factors).
- Lung Cancer is very rare under 40 (unless the patient has AIDS)
- Air Bronchograms are 5x more common in malignant SPN
- Air Bronchograms are found in 50% of BACs
- Just because a nodule gets smaller doesn't mean it is benign. Especially if the nodule increases

Nodules
- Types and Trivia Continued -

Nodule Volume / Size Change:

Most people will call nodule "growth" at 1.5 mm per year. Anything smaller than that can easily be attributed to technical factors.

This growth, in particular the concept of *"doubling time"* makes up the basis of differentiated benign vs malignant. With out this concept you would be forced into follow nodules forever. The trivia worth knowing is that lung cancers doubling times range from 20 days to 400 days.

Any nodule that doubles in size in less than 20 days is almost certainly benign (statistically infectious or inflammatory). The same is true with doubling times greater than 400 days.

The notable difference is the ground glass or part solid nodule vs the solid nodule. Ground glass and part solid nodules are more characteristic of the adenocarcinoma in situ (formerly BAC) and they tend to grow slower. This is why the follow up term for GGN and Part solid nodules in 5 years, vs 2 years for a pure solid nodule.

Perifissural Nodule (PFNs) / Intrapulmonary Lymph Node:

Typical morphological features would include well circumscribed, smoothly marginated, triangular, oval, or polygonal nodules which either contact the fissure or pleural surface directly.

They technically don't have to contact a pleural surface, as long as they are within 15 mm (some people say 20mm).

Spiculated or Round nodules are not typical for PFNs. These two guys should be treated like "regular" nodules.

Trivia:
- PFNs are probably lymph nodes
- They are almost certainly benign and treated as such by the Fleischner society
- LUNG-RADS defies all logic and reason by continuing to treat them like regular nodules. I assume this is deliberate to justify an exotic vacation (meeting) to update the recommendations in a year or two.
- Interval growth does NOT mean these things are full of cancer - lymph nodes normally fluctuate in size. s
- Size greater than 6mm still doesn't justify follow up per Fleischner.

Lung Cancer

Type	Location	Features and Trivia	
Non Small Cell **Squamous**	Central	• Strong Association with Smoking • Cavitation is Classic • Prognosis is relatively good (tend to met late)	Paraneoplastic Syndromes can be associated with ectopic Parathyroid Hormone
Non Small Cell **Large Cell**	Peripheral	• Usually large (> 4cm) • Prognosis Suck — this is the subtype of Cancer that killed comedy legend Andy Kaufman in his 30s.	
Non Small Cell **Adenocarcinoma**	Peripheral	• Most common subtype • Favors the upper lobe • Most common subtype to present as a solitary pulmonary nodule • Known association with pulmonary fibrosis	
Small Cell	Central	• May only present with central lymphadenopathy • Terrible Horrible Incredibly Shitty Prognosis • Paraneoplastic Syndromes can be associated with SIADH and ACTH	Also associated with the mythical Paraneoplastic Syndrome of **Lambert Eaton**. They get proximal weakness from abnormal release of acetylcholine at the neuromuscular junction. The clinical presentation often comes before the cancer diagnosis.
Carcinoid	Endobronchial (usually)	• Carcinoids usually have a central endobronchial location (although they can rarely be found in the pulmonary parenchyma- presented as a nodule or mass in an older patient). • Pulmonary carcinoid tends to be slow growing and locally invasive (only met to nodes about 10% of the time). No surprise they can cause obstructive symptoms. They can also cause hemoptysis because they are highly vascular. • It's rare to see them in the trachea (< 1%) • No association with smoking (**maybe an association with the atypical sub-type) • An octreotide scan can be used to localize a carcinoid tumor. PET will have a false negative in around 25% of cases (they can be cold on PET). • Rarely they can cause a carcinoid syndrome with flushing etc… The valvular degradation that occurs tends to be on the left side (mitral and aortic), as opposed to the GI carcinoid syndrome which targets the right side (tricuspid and pulmonic).	
Adenoid **Cystic** **(Cylindroma)**	Endobronchial	• This is the most common bronchial gland tumor. • It is NOT associated with smoking. • They are usually in the main or lobar bronchus. • 20x more likely to be in the trachea (relative to carcinoid).	

 *Memory Aid — *"LA is on the Coast"* - **L**arge and **A**deno favor peripheral locations

The Artist Formerly Known as BAC (Now Adenocarcinoma In-Situ Spectrum)		

Why change the name? Well it's a simple reason. Academic Radiologists need to be on committees to get promoted. Committees need an excuse to go on vacation ("International Meetings" they call them). Name changes happen…

Pre-invasive lesions	Atypical Adenomatous Hyperplasia of Lung (**AAH**):	The smaller (< 5mm) and more mild pre-invasive sub-type. Usually a pure ground glass nodule.
	Adenocarcinoma in situ (**ACIS**):	Typically larger than AAH but < 3 cm. Although features overlap with AAH, they tend to be more part-solid (rather than pure ground glass)
Minimally Invasive Adenocarcinoma (MIA)		These are also < 3 cm. The distinction is that there is < 5 mm of stromal invasion (> 5 mm will be called a lepidic predominant adenocarcinoma).
Invasive Mucinous Adenocarcinoma		This is what most people used to call BAC (bronchoalveolar carcinoma).

To make this simple, just think about it on a spectrum with the small pre-invasive lesions on one end and the invasive adenocarcinoma on the other. That same spectrum follows a relative increase in the density of the nodule. This is why a growing consolidate component inside a previously existing ground glass nodule is such a suspicious feature.

Key Concept: The larger the solid component of the "part solid" nodule gets the more likely it is to be malignant. **Partially solid nodules are more likely to be cancer than ground glass nodules.**

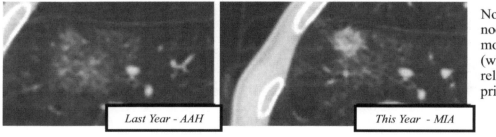

Notice the nodule getting more dense (white) relative to the prior year.

Last Year - AAH   *This Year - MIA*

Trivia: These Adenocarcinoma subtypes are **classically cold on PET.**

Superior Sulcus / Pancoast Tumors: Some people make a big deal about only using the word "pancoast" when the tumor causes the associated syndrome (shoulder pain, C8-T2 radiculopathy, and Horner Syndrome). In my experience most everyone just calls apical tumors "pancoast" with no regard to symptoms. Having said that, I would remember "shoulder pain" as a possible hint in the question header. These things are typically non-small cell cancers.

Staging = MRI is the tool of choice (you need to look at that brachial plexus).

General Contraindication to Surgical Resection (may vary by institution): invasion of the vertebral body (> 50%), invasion of the spinal canal, involvement in the upper brachial plexus (C8 or higher), diaphragm paralysis (infers phrenic nerve C3-5 involvement), distal mets.

Staging:

Lung cancer staging used to be different for small cell vs non-small cell (NSCLC) . In 2013 the 7th edition of the TNM made them the same. Below is a chart describing the staging based on tumor size. For a solid lesion, the size is defined as maximum diameter in any of the three orthogonal planes - measured on lung window. If the lesion is subsolid, then you define the T classification by the diameter of the solid component only (NOT the ground glass part).

Lung Cancer Staging (8th edition)			
T1	Tumor is < 3cm		
T2	Tumor is 3-5 cm	Irregardless of size the tumor • Invades the visceral pleura • **Invades the main bronchus** • Causes obstruction (atelectasis or pneumonia) that extends to the hilum	
T3	Tumor is 5-7 cm	Irregardless of size the tumor • Invades the chest wall • Invades the pericardium • Invades the phrenic nerve (diaphragm paralysis) • Has one or more satellite nodule in the **same lung** lobe	Pancoast (Superior Sulcus) Tumor that is limited to involvement of T1 and T2 nerve roots
T4	Tumor > 7cm	Irregardless of size the tumor • Invades the mediastinal fat or great vessels • Invades the diaphragm • Involves the carina • Has one or more satellite nodule in **another lobe** in the same long	Pancoast (Superior Sulcus) Tumor that involves level C8 or higher

Multiple Lesions:

The handling of multiple lung lesion is complicated. Deciding if lesions are going to be treated as synchronous primaries or a single lung cancer with metastatic disease often requires a discussion at tumor board (after imaging, and path results).

If the lesions are decided to be separate primaries each cancer will be staged separately within the TNM system and given an overall stage. If the lesions are decided to be metastatic their distribution will alter the stage.

Vocab:

Synchronous = Two or more primary carcinomas which coexist at the time of diagnosis.

Metachronous = A cancer that develops consequently (some time interval) after the first primary.

  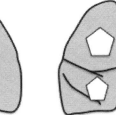   

T3 (two in same lobe)   **T4** (two in different lobes, but still the same lung)   **M1a** (two in different lungs)

Lung Cancer Staging Continued (Nodal Disease):

Nodes		
N1	Ipsilateral within the lung up to the hilar nodes.	N1 is a worse prognosis than N0 (no nodes) but the management is not changed.
N2	Ipsilateral mediastinal or subcarinal nodes	In many cases NOT Resectable Only those with microscopic disease (negative mediastinoscopy) will benefit from resection
N3	Contralateral mediastinal or contralateral hilum. Or Scalene or Supraclavicular nodes.	NOT Resectable

First it is important to point out that CT is unreliable for nodal staging. PET-CT is far superior, regardless of the size threshold that is chosen. This is why PET is pretty much always done of lung cancer patients prior to surgical evaluation.

For the purpose of multiple choice (and real life) the most important anatomy boundary to consider is the distinction between level 1 nodes (which at N3) and level 2 nodes (which are N2).

In some cases, this can literally make the difference between resectable disease or not. The border is the lower level of the clavicles / upper border of the manubrium (above this is level 1).

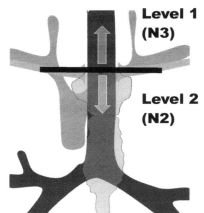
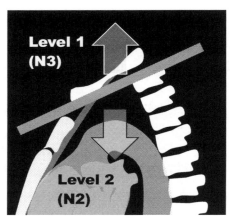

Level 1 (N3)

Level 2 (N2)

Typical Contraindications to Lobectomy / Resection

The big issues (things that make lobectomy impossible) are going to be:
- Growth of the tumor through a fissure
- Invasion of the Pulmonary Vasculature
- Invasion of the main bronchus
- Invasion of both the upper and lower lobe bronchi.

> Stage 3B implies N3 or T4 disease

Other findings that will make the tumor NOT resectable:
- N2*(usually) or N3 Nodal Disease — typically corresponding to a **Stage 3B** cancer
- Multi-lobar Disease
- Malignant Pleural Effusion

Lung Cancer Treatment

Wedge Resection vs Lobectomy: This is on the fringe of what should be considered fair game, and I'm certain the decision varies by institution and the size and composition (percentage of brass) of the surgeon's testicles. In general, if a stage 1A or 1B cancer is peripheral and less than 2cm they can consider a wedge resection. The advantage to doing this over a lobectomy is preserving pulmonary reserve. If the tumor is larger than 3cm then lobectomy seems to (in general) be a better option.

Bronchopleural Fistula:

This is an uncommon complication of pneumonectomy, that has a characteristic look and therefore easy to test.

So normally after a pneumonectomy the space will fill with fluid. If you see it filling with air than this is the dead give away.

If you are a weirdo, you could confirm the diagnosis with a xenon nuclear medicine ventilation study, which will show xenon in the pneumonectomy space. The major risk factor is ischemia to the bronchi (disrupted blood supply from aggressive lymph node dissection, or using a long bronchial stump).

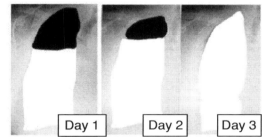

Normal - Become More **Fluid** Filled

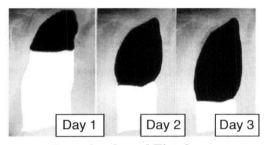

Bronchopleural Fistula
- Become More **Air** Filled

Radiation Changes - The appearance of radiation pneumonitis is variable and based on the volume of lung involved, how much/long radiation was given, and if chemotherapy was administered as well.

Rib Fractures - Ribs within the treatment field are susceptible to degradation and fracture.

RFA/MWA Pearl - It is normal to see bubbles in the lesion immediately after treatment.

Radiation Changes	
Early *(within 1-3 months)*	**Late**
Homogenous or patchy ground glass opacities.	Dense consolidation, traction bronchiectasis, and volume loss.

Recurrent Disease - Recurrence rates are relatively high (especially in the first 2 years). From a practical stand point, I always focus my attention towards the periphery of the radiation bed, regional nodes, and/or the bronchial stump. A useful concept is to focus on morphology - radiation scarring is usually not round. If you see something with a round morphology - especially if it is growing over time, that is highly suspicious.

Other findings concerning for recurrence:
- Enhancing solid tissue along the resection line (or bronchial stump) which is enlarging over time.
- New enlarged mediastinal nodes with a short axis greater than 1 cm
- New pleural effusion (that persists on follow ups)

- Mimics and Other Cancers -

Pulmonary Hamartoma – This is not a cancer, but to the uninitiated can look scary. It is usually described as is an Aunt Minnie because it will have **macroscopic fat and "popcorn" calcifications.** It is the most common benign lung mass. It's usually incidental, but can cause symptoms if it's endobronchial (rare – like 2%).

Technically the fat is only seen in 60%, but for sure if the exam shows it, it will have fat. These **can be hot on PET**, they are still benign.

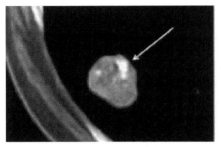

Pulmonary Hamartoma
- Popcorn Calcifications
- Fat Density

Mets – Metastatic disease to the lungs can be thought of in 3 categories; direct invasion, hematogenous, lymphangitic:

• **Direct Invasion:** This is seen with cancer of the mediastinum, pleura, or chest wall. The most common situation is an esophageal carcinoma, lymphoma, or malignant germ cell tumor. More rarely you are going to have mets to the pleura then invading the lung. Even more rarely you can have malignant mesothelioma, which can invade the lung. It should be obvious.

• **Hematogenous Mets:** The most common manifestation of hematogenous mets to the lung is the pulmonary nodule (usually multiple, in a **random distribution**, and **favoring the lower lobes** which have greater blood volume). The nodules tend to be smoother than the primary neoplasm. The main culprits are breast, kidney, thyroid, colon, and head & neck squamous cells. Obviously the squamous mets can cavitate. **"Cannonball Mets" are classically from renal cell or choriocarcinoma** (testicle).

> **Feeding Vessel Sign:** A prominent pulmonary vessel heading into a nodule. This supposedly means it's from a hematogenous origin. It's nonspecific – but if you see it the answer is (1) mets , or (2) septic emboli.

• **Lymphangitic Carcinomatosis (LC):** The most common cause of unilateral LC is actually bronchogenic carcinoma lung cancer invading the lymphatics. The most common extrathoracic culprits are breast, stomach, pancreas, and prostate. The finding is nodular thickening of the interlobular septa and subpleural interstitium. Unlike interstitial fibrosis, this thickening classically does NOT distort the pulmonary lobule.

Kaposi Sarcoma: This is the most common lung tumor is AIDS patients (Lymphoma is number two). The tracheobronchial mucosa and perihilar lung are favored. The buzzword is "flame shaped." A bloody pleural effusion is common (50%).

Key Points:
- Most common lung tumor in AIDS (requires CD4 < 200)
- Most common hepatic neoplasm in AIDS
- Buzzword = Flame Shaped Opacities
- Slow Growth, with asymptomatic patients (despite lungs looking terrible)
- Thallium Positive, Gallium Negative

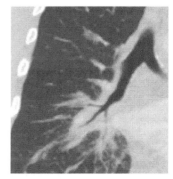

Kaposi Sacroma
- "Flame Shaped" Hilar Opacities

Lymphoma – There are basically 4 flavors of pulmonary lymphoma; primary, secondary, AIDS related, or PTLD. Radiographic patterns are variable and can be lymphangitic spread (uncommon), parahilar airspace opacities, and/or mediastinal adenopathy.

• **Primary:** This is rare, and usually non-Hodgkin in subtype. You define it as the lack of extrathoracic involvement for 3 months. Almost always (80%) we are talking about a low grade MALToma.

• **Secondary:** Here we are talking about pulmonary involvement of a systemic lymphoma. This is much much much more common than primary lung lymphoma. The thing to see is that NHL is much more common, but if you have HL it is more likely to involve the lungs. With HL you gets nodes and parenchyma, in NHL you might just get parenchyma.

Secondary NHL	Secondary HL
80-90% of lymphoma cases	10-20% of lymphoma cases
45% have intrathoracic disease at presentation	85% have intrathoracic disease at presentation
25% have pulmonary parenchymal disease	40% have pulmonary parenchymal disease
Pulmonary involvement frequently occurs in the absence of mediastinal disease	Lung involvement almost always associated with intrathoracic lymph node enlargement

• **PTLD:** This is seen after solid organ or stem cell transplant. **This usually occurs within a year of transplant** (late presentations > 1 year have a more aggressive course). This is a B-Cell lymphoma, with a relationship with EB Virus. You can have both nodal and extra nodal disease. The typical look is well-defined pulmonary nodules / mass, patchy airspace consolidation, halo sign, and interlobular septal thickening.

• **AIDS related pulmonary lymphoma (ARL) -** This is the second most common lung tumor in AIDS patients (Kaposi's is first). Almost exclusively a high grade NHL. There is a relationship with EBV. It is seen in patients with a **CD4 < 100.** The presentation is still variable with multiple peripheral nodules ranging from 1 cm-5 cm being considered the most common manifestation. Extranodal locations (CNS, bone marrow, lung, liver, bowel) is common. **AIDS patient with lung nodules, pleural effusion, and lymphadenopathy = Lymphoma.**

Nukes Cross Over Blitz

• Thallium is a potassium analog. Things with a functional Na/**K**/ATP pump tend to be alive. Hence anything this is "alive" will be thallium positive.

• Gallium is an Iron analog. Iron is an inflammatory marker (acute phase reactant) hence things that are "smoldering" tend to be gallium negative, and things that are inflamed - infection, active sarcoid, most cancers - tend to be Gallium hot.

Kaposi Sarcoma	Lymphoma
Thallium [201] Positive	Thallium [201] Positive
Gallium[67] Negative	Gallium[67] Positive

• In general, it is safe to say "Lymphoma is HOT on Gallium." Where things can get sneaky is the subtype. Hodgkin is nearly always Gallium Avid. Certain Non-Hodgkin subtypes can be Gallium cold. As such (and because it's not 1970) PET is usually used for staging and not Gallium.

SECTION 5:
Congenital

Sequestration, CCAMs, and a bunch of other congenital path is discussed in detail in the Peds chapter (starting on page 61). Here are some other randos.

Poland Syndrome –

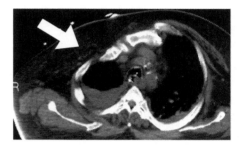

Unilateral absence of a pectoral muscle. It can cause a unilateral hyper-lucent chest. They can have limb issues (small weird arms / hands).

Bronchial Atresia – This most commonly involves the apical-posterior segment of the left upper lobe. The usual look is a blind ending bronchus, filled with mucus ("**finger in glove**"), with the **distal lung hyper-inflated** – from collateral drift and air trapping.

AVM - They can occur sporadically. For the purpose of multiple choice when you see them think about HHT (Hereditary Hemorrhagic Telangiectasia / Osler Weber Rendu). Pulmonary AVMs are most commonly found in the lower lobes (more blood flow), and can be a source of right to left shunt (**worry about stroke and brain abscess**). The rule of **treating once the afferent vessel is 3 mm** is based on some tiny little abstract and not powered at all. Having said that, it's quoted all the time, and a frequent source of trivia that is easily tested.

Persistent Left SVC - This is the most common congenital venous anomaly of the chest. It usually only matters when the medicine guys drop a line in it on the floor and it causes a confusing post CXR (line is in a left paramedian location). It usually **drains into the coronary sinus**. In a minority of cases (like 5%) it will drain into the left atrium, and cause right to left shunt physiology (very mild though). This is typically shown on an axial CT at the level of the AP window, or with a pacemaker (or line) going into the right heart from the left.

Swyer-James - This is the classic **unilateral lucent lung**. It typically occurs after a viral lung infection in childhood resulting in **post infectious obliterative bronchiolitis** (from constrictive bronchiolitis). The *size of the affected lobe is smaller* than a normal lobe (it's not hyper-expanded).

 Horseshoe Lung: Rare as fuck. Defined by fusion of the posterior basilar segments of the lower lobes behind the heart.

The most likely testable points are:
(1) *What is it ?* and
(2) *What is the association ?* Most common = Scimitar syndrome

SECTION 6:
Cystic Lung

Pulmonary Langerhans Cell Histiocytosis (LCH) – This cystic lung disease classically effects **smokers, who are young (20s-30s).** The disease starts out with centrilobular nodules with an upper lobe predominance. These nodules eventually cavitate into cysts which are thin walled to start, and then some become more thick walled. Late in the disease you are primarily seeing cysts. The buzzword is **bizarre shaped**, which occurs when 2 or more cysts merge together. In about half the cases this spontaneously resolves (especially if you stop smoking). Another piece of trivia is that LCH spares the costophrenic angles.

What Spares the Costophrenic Angles???
(1) LCH and (2)Hypersensitivity Pneumonitis

Lymphangiomyomatosis (LAM) – This cystic lung disease can occur in **child bearing aged women** or in association with **tuberous sclerosis (a trick is to show the kidneys with multiple AMLs first)**. The cysts are **thin walled** with a uniform distribution. There is an **association with chylothorax** (which is HIGH YIELD Trivia). The pathophysiology is that it is estrogen dependent (why it strongly favors women). This is usually progressive despite attempts at hormonal therapy (tamoxifen).

 Birt Hogg Dube (BHD)

This is a **total zebra**. This cystic lung disease has **thin walled "oval" shaped cysts**. There is an association with renal findings (bilateral oncocytomas, and chromophobe RCCs). They also have a bunch of gross skin stuff.

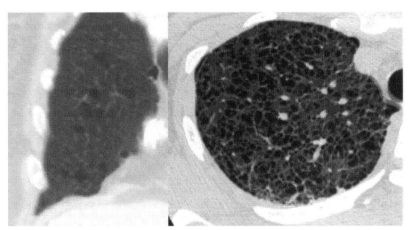

Birt-Hogg-Dube
-Oval Cysts

LAM
-Multiple Thin Walled Round Cysts

LCH	LAM
Cysts and Nodules	Cysts (no nodules)
Smoker	Women, Pts with Tuberous Sclerosis
Upper and Mid Lungs	Diffuse
Thicker Cysts (Bizarre)	Thin Round Cysts

LCH	Bizarre Shape	Thick Wall
LAM	Round	Thin Wall
BHD	Oval	Thin Wall

Lymphocytic Interstitial Pneumonitis (LIP) – This is a benign lymphoproliferative disorder, with infiltration of the lungs. It has an association with autoimmune diseases (**SLE, RA, Sjogrens**). **The big one to know is Sjogrens which is concomitant in 25% of LIP cases.** The other one to know is **HIV** – which is the LIP in a younger patient *(children, – LIP in HIV positive adults is rare).* There is also an association with Castlemans. The appearance of LIP varies depending on the underlying cause. **The cystic lung disease is usually thin walled, "deep within the lung parenchyma," and seen predominantly with Sjogrens**. The dominant feature described as ground glass or nodules is seen more in the other causes and is far beyond the scope of the exam.

When I say LIP... You say Sjogrens & HIV
When I say LIP in a kid... You say HIV

Pneumocystis Pneumonia (PCP) – This is the most common opportunistic infection in AIDS.

 The typical buzzword is **ground glass appearance, predominantly in the hilar and mid lung zones**.

Pneumatoceles are present in 30% of cases. In patients receiving aerosolized prophylaxis, a cystic form is more common, which **may have bilateral thin walled upper lung predominant cysts. Gallium ^{67} scan will show diffuse uptake** (Thallium will be negative).

When I say AIDS + Ground Glass Lungs.... You say PCP

Emphysema

The textbook definition is "permanent enlargement of the airspaces distal to the terminal bronchioles accompanied by destruction of the alveolar wall without clear fibrosis." What you need to know are (1) the CXR findings and (2) the different types.

CXR Findings: Until it's really really bad, CXR doesn't have direct signs, but instead has indirect signs. **Flattening of the hemidiaphrams** is regarded as the most reliable sign. The AP diameter increases. The retrosternal clear space becomes larger. There is a paucity of, or pruning of the blood vessels.

Types:

- *Centri-lobular*: By far the **most common type**. Common in asymptomatic elderly patients. It has an apical to basal gradient – **favoring the upper zones** of each lobe. It appears as focal lucencies, located centrally within the secondary pulmonary lobule, often with a central dot representing the central bronchovascular bundle. This **central dot sign is a buzzword**. This is the **type of emphysema dominant in smokers.**

- *Pan-lobular:* In contradistinction to centrilobular this one favors the lower lobes. It also has a more uniform distribution across parts of the secondary pulmonary lobule. The association is with **alpha 1 antitrypsin**. A piece of trivia is the **"Ritalin Lung"** from IV Ritalin use can also cause a pan-lobular appearance ("Ritalin keeps you from 'trypsn' out"). *If they show this it will be in the coronal view on CT to demonstrate the **lower lobe predominance**.* Patient's will present in their 60s and 70s (unless they smoke – then they present in their 30s). **Smoking accelerates the process**.

- *Para-septal*: This one is found adjacent to the pleura and septal lines with a peripheral distribution within the secondary pulmonary lobule. The affected lung is almost always sub-pleural, and demonstrates small focal lucencies up to 10 mm in size. This looks like honeycombing but is less than 3 bubbles thick.

Trivia:

- Saber Sheath Trachea – Diffuse coronal narrowing of the trachea, sparing the extrathroacic portion. This is said to be pathognomonic for COPD.

- If the Main PA is larger than the Aorta COPD patients have a worse outcome (pulmonary HTN can be caused by emphysema).

- Surgery to remove bad lung "volume reduction" is sometimes done

Vanishing Lung Syndrome: This is an idiopathic cause of giant bullous emphysema, resulting from avascular necrosis of the lung parenchyma and hyperinflation. It favors the bilateral upper lobes, and is **defined as bullous disease occupying at least one-third of a hemithorax**. The most common demographic is a young man. About 20% of these guys have alpha-1 antitrypsin deficiency.

Compensatory Emphysema (Postpneumonectomy Syndrome): There is no obstructive process here. Instead you have hyper-expansion of one lung to compensate for the absence of the other one.

Honeycomb Lung: When I say honeycombing you should say UIP. However, this is seen with a variety of causes of end stage fibrotic lung processes. The cysts are tightly clustered (2-3 rows thick) and subpleural. The walls are often thick.

SECTION 7:
Pneumoconiosis

As a general rule, these are inhaled so they tend to be upper lobe predominant. You can have centrilobular nodules (which makes sense for inhalation), or often perilymphatic nodules – which makes a little less sense, but is critical to remember * especially with silicosis and CWP.

Asbestos Exposure: The term "Asbestosis" refers to the changes of pulmonary fibrosis – NOT actual exposure to the disease. The look is very **similar to UIP**, with the presence of **parietal pleural thickening** being the "most important feature" to distinguish between IPF and Asbestosis. Obviously, the history of working in a ship yard or finding asbestos bodies in a bronchoalveolar lavage is helpful.

Things to know about Asbestos:
* "Asbestosis" = the lung fibrosis associated with exposure, NOT actual exposure
* Interstitial pattern looks like UIP + parietal pleural thickening
* There is a 20 year latency between initial exposure and development of lung cancer or pleural mesothelioma
* There is an association with extrapulmonary cancer including: Peritoneal mesothelioma, GI cancer, Renal Cancer, Laryngeal Cancer, and Leukemia
* Benign pleural effusions are the "earliest pleural-based phenomenon" associated with exposure – still with a lag time of around 5 years

---

Benign Asbestosis Related Changes:

Pleural effusion is the earliest and most common. Pleural plaques may develop around 20-30 years, with calcifications occurring around 40 years. These plaques tend to spare the apices and Costophrenic angles. *Round atelectasis – which is associated with pleural findings is sometimes called the "asbestos pseudotumor."*

Malignant Mesothelioma

The most common cancer of the pleura. About 80% of them have had asbestos exposure, and development is NOT dose-dependent. The lag time is around 30-40 years from exposure. The **buzzword pleural rind** is worth knowing. **Pleural thickening along the lateral lung (from old rib fractures or whatever is common), but when you see thickening that wraps all the way around the lung - especially along the medial surface of the pleura (near the heart) you need to immediately think of mesothelioma. Extension into the fissure is highly suggestive.** This shit believes in nothing Lebowski with a known tendency is for direct invasion.

Silicosis: This is seen in miners, and quarry workers. You can have simple silicosis, which is going to be multiple nodular opacities favoring the upper lobes, with egg shell calcifications of the hilar nodes. You also get perilymphatic nodules. The complicated type is called **progressive massive fibrosis (PMF). This is the formation of large masses in the upper lobes with radiating strands.** You can see this with both silicosis and coal workers pneumoconiosis (something similar also can happen with Talcosis). These masses can sometimes cavitate – but you should always raise the suspicion of TB when you see this (especially in the setting of silicosis).

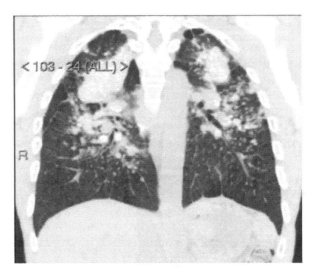

Progressive Massive Fibrosis
-Large Apical Masses with Radiating Strands

Silicotuberculosis: Silicosis actually raises your risk of TB by about 3 fold. If you see *cavitation in the setting of silicosis you have to think about TB*.

MRI : Cancer vs PMF	
Cancer = T2 Bright	PMF = T2 Dark

Coal Workers Pneumoconiosis: This is the result of exposure to "washed coal." Just like silicosis there are simple and complicated forms. There is also an increased risk of TB (just like silicosis). The simple form was multiple nodular opacities, with calcifications showing a central nodular dot. The small nodule pattern tends to have a perilymphatic distribution. The complicated form gives you a progressive massive fibrosis that is similar to that seen in silicosis.

Additional Inhalational Diseases - Not Worthy of a Full Discussion		
Berylliosis	Metal used in aircraft and space industries	Generalized granulomatous disease with hilar adenopathy and upper lobe predominant reticular opacities.
Silo Filler's Disease	Nitrogen Dioxide	Pulmonary Edema Pattern. Recovery is typically within 5 weeks.
Talcosis	Filler in tablets, sometimes injected (along with drugs) in IV drug users.	Hyperdense micronodules, with conglomerate masses (similar to PMF). Ground glass opacities

SECTION 8:
ILDs

Don't Be Scared Homie

Everyone seems to be afraid of interstitial lung diseases. The concept is actually not that complicated, it's just complicated relative to the rest of chest radiology (which overall isn't that complicated). The trick is to ask yourself two main questions: (1) Acute or Chronic ? – as this narrows the differential considerably, and (2) What is the primary finding ? – as this will narrow the differential further. Now, since we are training for the artificial scenario of a multiple choice test (and not the view box), I'll try and keep the focus on superficial trivia, and associations. Remember when you are reading to continue to ask yourself "how can this material be written into a question?"

Vocab: Like most of radiology, the bulk of understanding the pathology is knowing the right words to use (plus, a big vocabulary makes you sound smart).

- **Consolidation** = Density that obscures underlying vessels
- **Ground Glass Opacity** = Density that does **NOT** obscure underlying vessels
- **Secondary Pulmonary Lobule** = The basic unit of pulmonary structure and function. It is the smallest part of the lung that is surrounded by connective tissue. In the middle runs a terminal bronchial with an accompanying artery. Around the periphery runs the vein and lymphatics.

Anatomy of the Secondary Pulmonary Lobule

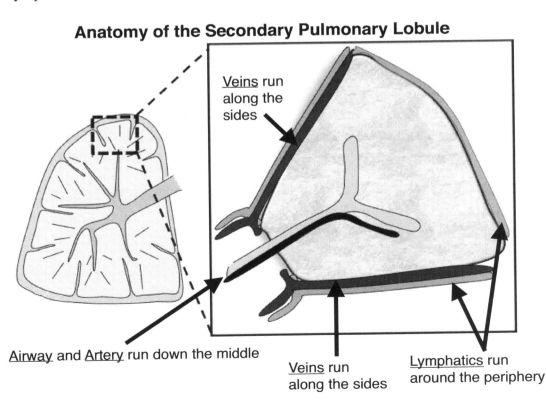

Veins run along the sides

Airway and Artery run down the middle

Veins run along the sides

Lymphatics run around the periphery

Nodule Vocabulary (Random, Perilymphatic, Centrilobular)

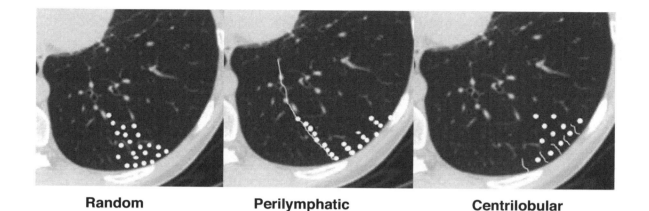

| Random | Perilymphatic | Centrilobular |

Telling them apart can be done by first asking if they abut the pleura?

If the answer is no they are centrilobular.

If the answer is yes, then ask do they follow a peribronchovascular pattern,

if the answer is no then they are random, if the answer if yes then they are perilymphatic.

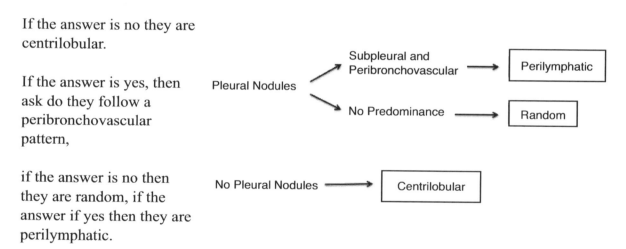

Nodule Pattern	Key DDx
Perilymphatic	•Sarcoid (90%), •Lymphangitic Spread of CA •Silicosis
Random	•Miliary TB •Mets •Fungal
Centrilobular	•Infection •RB-ILD •Hypersensitivity Pneumonitis *(if ground glass)*

Patterns

Interlobular Septal Thickening: Reticular abnormality, that outlines the lobules' characteristic shape and size (about 2 cm). It's usually from **pulmonary edema** (*usually symmetric and smooth*), or **lymphangitic spread of neoplasm** (*often asymmetric and nodular*). **Kerley B Lines are the plain film equivalent.**

Honeycombing: Cystic areas of lung destruction in a subpleural location. This is a hallmark of UIP. Paraseptal emphysema is a mimic, but the distinction is made by how many rows of bubbles.

- One Row of Bubbles = Paraseptal Emphysema.

- Two-Three Rows of Bubbles = Honey- combing.

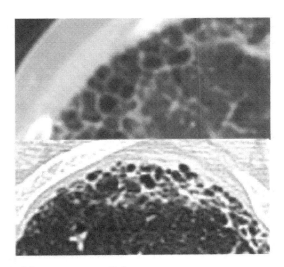

Honeycombing - *Two examples*

Pathology

Idiopathic Interstitial Pneumonias – These are NOT diseases, but instead lung reactions to lung injury. They occur in a variety of patterns and variable degrees of inflammation and fibrosis. The causes include: idiopathic, collage vascular disease, medications, and inhalation.

For practical purposes the answer is either (a) UIP or (b) Not UIP. Not UIP will get better with steroids. UIP will not. UIP has a dismal prognosis (similar to lung cancer). Not UIP often does ok. The exam will likely not make it this simple, and will instead focus on buzzwords, patterns, and associations (which I will now discuss).

UIP (Usual Interstitial Pneumonia) - This is the *most common* Interstitial Lung Disease. When the cause is idiopathic it is called IPF. On CXR the lung volume is reduced (duh, it's fibrosis). *Reticular pattern in the posterior costophrenic angle is supposedly the first finding on CXR.*

 Buzzwords include:

- **Apical to basal gradient** (it's worse in the lower lobes)
- **Traction bronchiectasis**, and honeycombing
- **Honeycombing** is found 70% of the time, and people expect you to knee jerk UIP when that term is uttered
- Histologic Buzzword = Heterogeneous. ***"The histology was heterogeneous"*** = **UIP**

It's important to know that basically any end stage lung disease (be it from sarcoid, RA, Scleroderma, or other collagen vascular disease) has a similar look once the disease has ruined the lungs. *Technically honeycombing is uncommon in end stage sarcoid – but the rest of the lung looks jacked up.*

The prognosis is terrible (similar to lung cancer).

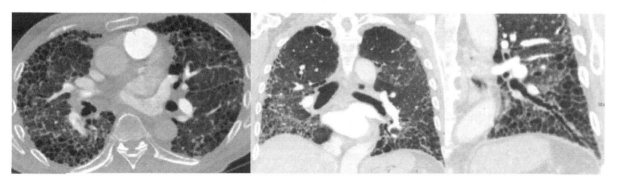

UIP- Honeycombing, Traction Bronchiectasis, Apical-to-Basal Gradient

---

Fibrosis and Cancer Go Together Like Tacos and Tuesdays

Pulmonary fibrosis is a risk factor for lung cancer
(especially if these patients are dumb enough to also smoke).

Cancer in the Fibrotic Lung Trivia:
- Favors the lower lobes
- Favors the interface between the fibrotic cysts and normal lung
- Progressive wall thickening or a developing nodule within a cyst is suspicious for cancer (enlarging pericystic nodules are dodgy as fuck - hide your kids / hide your wife)
- NELSON Lung Cancer Screening Trial showed cystic lesions were a common miss

NSIP (Nonspecific Interstitial Pneumonia)

Less Common than UIP. Even though the name infers that its non-specific, it's actually is a specific entity. Histologically it is homogenous inflammation or fibrosis (UIP was heterogeneous). It is a common pattern in collagen vascular disease, and drug reactions.

It comes in 2 flavors (cellular or fibrotic):

- Ground Glass Alone = Cellular
- Ground Glass + Reticulation = Cellular or Fibrotic
- Reticulation + Traction Bronchiectasis = Fibrotic NSIP
- Honeycombing – uncommon and usually minimal in extent

 Trivia: NSIP is the most common Interstitial Lung Disease in Scleroderma

The disease has a lower lobe, posterior, peripheral predominance with sparing of the immediate subpleural lung seen in up to 50% of cases. This finding of **immediate subpleural sparing is said to be highly suggestive**. Ground glass is the NSIP equivalent of honeycombing.

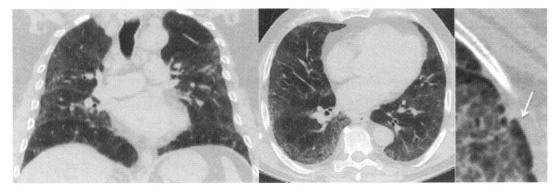

NSIP - *Peripheral Ground Glass with Subpleural Sparing*

UIP	NSIP
Apical to Basal Gradient	Gradient is less obvious (but still more in lower lobes)
Heterogeneous Histology	Homogenous Histology
Honeycombing	Ground Glass
Traction Bronchiectasis	Micronodules

RB-ILD and DIP:

I'm going to discuss these two together because some people feel they are a spectrum. For sure they are **both smoking related diseases**.

- RB-ILD – Apical Centrilobular ground glass nodules
- DIP – More diffuse GGO, with patchy or subpleural distribution

RB-ILD: This tends to be more upper lobe predominant (note that DIP tends to be more lower lobe predominant). Localized centrilobular ground glass nodules. The pathology tends to involve the entire cross section of lung.

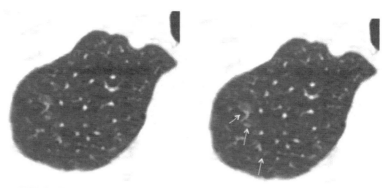

RB-ILD- Apical Centrilobular ground glass nodules + Smoking History

Respiratory Brochiolitis + Symptoms = RB-ILD.

DIP: Desquamative interstitial pneumonia is thought of as the end spectrum of RB-ILD, and generally seen in 50 year old heavy smokers. Extras from 1984 comedy classic "Revenge of the Nerds" seem to enjoy going to radiology conferences to voice their disapproval of the term "<u>D</u>IP" because the pathology is not <u>d</u>esquamation of alveolar epithelium but instead represents a filling of alveolar spaces with macrophages. Could these same weirdos be writing the questions ? The dark side clouds everything. Impossible to see the future is.

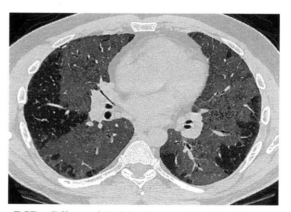

DIP - Bilateral Fairly Symmetric Basilar Predominant Ground Glass

Just think <u>peripheral lower lobe predominant ground glass, with small cystic spaces</u>.

You can see consolidations - but they are usually associated with cryptogenic pneumonia. You can see fibrosis - but it is rare (like 5-10%) - I would not expect that on the exam.

Sarcoid:

This is a multi-system disease that creates "non-caseating granulomas." The classic age is between 20-40. Along those lines, if the header to the question describes an African American female in her 20s-30s the answer is probably sarcoid. The lungs are by far the most common organ affected (90%).

> **CXR can be used to "Stage" Sarcoid**
>
> Stage 0 = Normal
> Stage 1 = Hilar / Mediastinal Nodes Only
> Stage 2 = Nodes + Parenchyma Disease
> Stage 3 = Parenchymal Disease
> Stage 4 = End Stage (Fibrosis)

Misc Trivia to know:
- Elevated angiotensin-converting enzyme (ACE)
- Hypercalcemia

Mediastinal lymph nodes are seen in 60-90% of patients (classically in a 1-2-3 pattern of bilateral hila and right paratracheal). They have **perilymphatic nodules**, with an **upper lobe predominance**. Late changes include, upper lobe fibrosis, and traction bronchiectasis (honeycombing is rare). Aspergillomas are common in the cavities of patients with end stage sarcoid.

- ***1-2-3 Sign*** - *bilateral hila and right paratracheal*
- ***Lambda Sign*** – *same as 1-2-3, but on Gallium Scan*
- ***CT Galaxy Sign*** – *upper lobe masses (conglomerate of nodules) with satellite nodules*

CHF:

CHF is obviously not an ILD. However, it can sorta look like one on Chest X-Ray so I opted to lump it in here. Congestive heart failure occurs because of cardiac failure, fluid overload, high resistance in the circulation, or some combination of the three. There are three phases of CHF, and these lend themselves to testable trivia.

Stages of CHF		
Stage 1 " Redistribution"	Wedge Pressure 13-18	Cephalization of vessels, Big heart, Big Vascular Pedicle
Stage 2 " Interstitial Edema"	Wedge Pressure 18-25	Kerley Lines, Peribronchial Cuffing, Less distinct contour of Central Vessels
Stage 3 "Alveolar Edema"	Wedge Pressure > 25	Airspace "fluffy" opacity, Pleural effusion

Swan Ganz Pulmonary Wedge Pressures are an indirect measurement of left atrial pressure. They can help prove a cardiogenic etiology to pulmonary edema.

Right Heart Failure:

This is less common than left heart failure, which ironically is the most common cause. Left heart failure causes pulmonary venous HTN which causes pulmonary arterial HTN, which causes right heart failure. Some other less common causes of right heart failure include chronic PE and right-sided valve issues (tricuspid regurg). The imaging features of right heart failure include dilation of the azygos vein, dilation of the right atrium, dilation of the SVC, ascites, big liver, and contrast reflux into the hepatic veins on CTPA.

SECTION 9:
Transplant

Lung transplants are done for end-stage pulmonary disease (fibrosis, COPD, etc..). The complications lend themselves easily to multiple choice test questions, and are therefore high yield. The best way to think about the complications is based on time.

Immediate Complications (< 24 hours)	
Donor-Recipient Size Mismatch	Mismatch up to 25% is ok. You can have a compressed lung (by the hyperexpanded emphysematous lung). Imaging is usually atelectasis.
Hyperacute Rejection	Secondary to HLA and ABO antigens. It's rapid and often fatal. Imaging shows massive homogenous infiltration
Early Complications (24 hours – 1 week)	
Reperfusion Injury	Peaks at day 4 as a non-cardiogenic edema related to ischemia-reperfusion. Typically improves by day 7.
Air Leak / Persistent Pneumothorax	Defined as a continuous leak for more than 7 days.
Intermediate Complication (8 days – 2 months)	
Acute Rejection	Ground Glass opacities and intralobular septal thickening. (No ground glass = no rejection). Improves with steroids.
Bronchial Anastomotic Complications	Leaks occur in the first month, stenosis can develop later (2-4 months).

Late Complications (2-4 months)	
CMV Infection	**The most common opportunistic infection.** Ground glass, tree-in-bud. Rare before 2 weeks.
Later Complications (> 4 months)	
Chronic Rejection	Bronchiolitis Obliterans; **Affects 50% at 5 years.** Brochiectasis, bronchial wall thickening, air trapping.
Cryptogenic Organizing Pneumonia	Occurs with chronic rejection (but more commonly with acute rejection). Responds to steroids.
PTLD	Typically seen within the first year. EBV in 90%.
Upper Lobe Fibrosis	Associated with chronic rejection

Chronic Rejection / Bronchiolitis Obliterans Syndrome: This is the major late complication, that affects at least half of the transplants at 5 years (most commonly at 6 months). The term bronchiolitis obliterans is often used interchangeably with chronic rejection. The findings on CT include bronchiectasis, bronchial wall thickening, air trapping, and interlobular septal thickening. Just think **air trapping on expiration seen at or after 6 months = chronic rejection.**

Recurrence of Primary Disease after Transplant: For the purpose of multiple choice tests know that sarcoidosis is the **most common recurrent primary disease (around 35%).** Lots of other things can recur.

Lung Cancer after Transplant: Just remember that the native lung is still diseased, and can get cancer. The highest rate is with pulmonary fibrosis, and the most common risk factor is heavy tobacco use.

—

SECTION 10:
Alveolar

Pulmonary Alveolar Proteinosis (PAP): For the purpose of multiple choice, this is an Aunt Minnie - always shown as crazy paving lung (interlobular septal thickening with ground glass). This can be primary (90%), or secondary (10%). The secondary causes worth knowing are cancer or inhalation (silico-proteinosis).

Trivia Worth Knowing:
*   They are at increased risk of **Nocardia infections**, and can have nocardia brain abscesses.
*   **Smoking is strongly associated with the disease**.
*   When seen in children (presenting before age 1) there is a known association with alymphoplasia.
*   Can progress to pulmonary fibrosis (30%).
*   Treatment is bronchoalveolar lavage

<u>Crazy Paving</u> – Interlobular septal thickening and ground glass. This isn't always PAP, in fact in real life that it is usually NOT PAP. There is a differential that includes common things like edema, hemorrhage, BAC, Acute Interstitial Pneumonia.

Just know that for the purpose of multiple choice tests, the answer is almost always PAP.

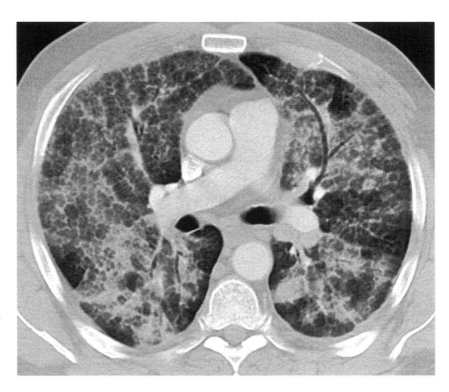

Lipoid Pneumonia – There are actually two types; endogenous and exogenous.

- **Exogenous:** A certain percentage of elderly people become absolutely obsessed with their bowel movements. If you did Family Medicine addressing this psychopathology would steal a certain amount of hours out of your life per week. Lipoid pneumonia is seen in **old people who like to drink/aspirate mineral oil** (as a laxative). It can also be seen with the aspiration of vegetable oil or other animal oils. The look on plain film is an area of lung opacification that is chronic or slowly increases with time. The look on CT is a dead give away and the most likely way this will be shown is with **low attenuation / fat density in the consolidation**. Having said that this is also in the crazy paving differential.

- *Acute Exogenous Lipoid Pneumonia* – This is seen in children who accidentally poison themselves with hydrocarbons, or idiots trying to perform fire-eating or flame blowing.

- **Endogenous** – This is actually more common than the exogenous type, and results from post obstructive processes (cancer) causing build up of lipid laden macrophages.

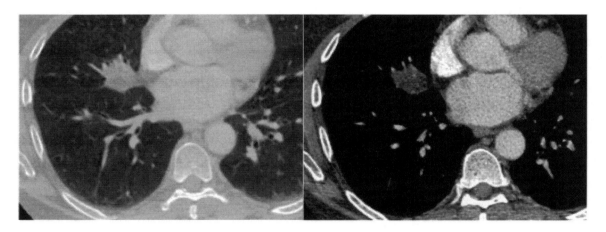

Lipoid Pneumonia - *Fat Density in the Consolidation*

Gamesmanship: "Why are you showing me the lung on that window?"

 Obviously pulmonary pathology is best shown on a lung window. So anytime the test writer is showing you a pulmonary pathology on a non-lung window, that should cue you to think about some different things.

(1): Is the finding in the mediastinum or ribs?
(2): If it's clearly a lung finding then what window are they using?
- Soft tissue window is classically used to show fat in a lesion - think hamartoma or lipoid pneumonia.
- Bone window might be used to show a diffuse process such as pulmonary microlithiasis.

Organizing Pneumonia *(cryptogenic / cause not known "COP")*

This used to be called BOOP, which was a lot more fun to say. There are lots of different causes; idiopathic, infection, drugs (amiodarone), collagen vascular disease, fumes, etc... These guys respond well to steroids, and have an excellent prognosis.

Patchy air space consolidation or GGO (90%), in a **peripheral** or peri-bronchial distribution. Opacities tend to be irregular in shape. Findings of fibrosis are typically absent.

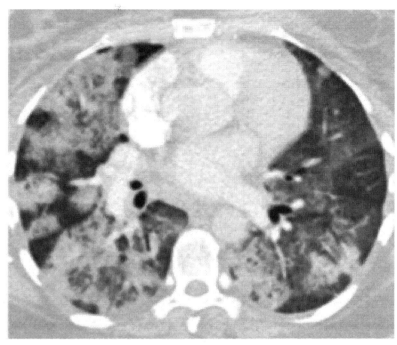

Cryptogenic Organizing Pneumonia-
Reverse Halo Sign

Reverse Halo (Atoll) Sign is the classic sign: Consolidation around a ground glass center.

Chronic Eosinophilic Pneumonia:

Can be idiopathic or associated with a known antigen. Peripheral eosinophilia (blood test) is usually present. An asthma history is found in about 50% of cases. It looks exactly look COP. When you say COP you should say this one too (some people think it's the same disease as COP).

CT Findings: Peripheral GGO or consolidation. Upper lobes tend to be favored.

Hypersensitivity Pneumonitis:

This is actually common. It's caused by inhaled organic antigens. It has acute, subacute, and chronic stages. Most of the time it's imaged in the subacute stage.

•**Subacute:** Patchy ground glass opacities. <u>Ill-defined Centrilobular ground glass nodules</u> (80%). Often has mosaic perfusion, and air trapping.

•**Chronic:** *Looks like UIP + Air trapping*. You are gonna have traction bronchiectasis and air trapping.

 Buzzword is "headcheese" because it's a mix of everything (Ground Glass, Consolidation, Air-Trapping, and Normal Lung)

THIS vs **THAT:** Halo Signs	
Halo	**Reverse (Atoll)**
-Nodule with ground glass around it -Represents hemorrhage / invasion into surrounding tissues	Central ground glass with rim of consolidation
- **Invasive Aspergillosis (Classic)** - Other Fungus - Hemorrhagic Mets - Adenocarcinoma in Situ (BAC) - Wegeners	- **COP (Classic)** - TB - Pulmonary Infarct - Invasive Fungal and Wegeners ** *these can also be seen with regular Halo*

SECTION 11:
Airways

Anatomy The basic anatomy of the trachea is a bunch of anterior horseshoes of cartilage, with a posterior floppy membrane. This membrane can bow inward on expiratory CT (and this is normal). The transverse diameter should be no more than 2.5 cm (same as the transverse diameter of an adjacent vertebral body).

Tracheal Disease Game Plan: Three big questions to ask yourself.
(1) Does it involve the posterior membrane ? (2) is it focal or diffuse ? and
(3) is there calcification ?

Relapsing Polychondritis: **Spares the posterior membrane.** **Diffuse** thickening of the trachea. No calcifications. Characterized by recurrent episodes of cartilage inflammation, and recurrent pneumonia.

Post Intubation Stenosis: **Focal** Subglottic **circumferential** stenosis, with an hourglass configuration.

Wegener's: **Circumferential** thickening, which can be **focal or long segment**. No calcifications. Subglottic involvement is common.

Tracheobronchopathia Osteochondroplastica (TBO):

Spares the posterior membrane. You have development of **cartilaginous and osseous nodules** within the submucosa of the tracheal and bronchial walls.

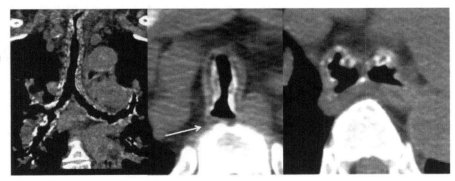

TBO - Note the sparing of the posterior membrane (arrow)

Amyloidosis: **Irregular** focal or short segment thickening, which can involve the posterior membrane. Calcifications are common.

Spares the Posterior Membrane		Does NOT Spare the Posterior Membrane	
Relapsing Polychondritis	Recurrent episodes of cartilage inflammation (ears, nose, joints, laryngeal and thyroid cartilage). Recurrent pneumonia is the most common cause of death.	**Amyloid**	Often confined to the trachea and main bronchi. Calcifications are common.
		Post Intubation	Focal Subglottic
Tracheobronchopathia Osteochondroplastica (TBO):	Development of cartilaginous and osseous nodules. Typically occurs in men older than 50.	**Wegeners**	C-ANCA +, Sub-glottic trachea is the most common location.

Saber-Sheath Trachea: Defined as a coronal diameter of less than two thirds the sagittal diameter.

I say "saber-sheath trachea," you say COPD.

Trivia: The main bronchi will be normal in size.
The tracheal wall will be normal in thickness.

Tracheal Tumors

Tumors of the trachea are not common in the real world.

Squamous Cell	**Most Common.** Associated with smoking, Often multifocal (10%), favors the **lower trachea** / proximal bronchus
Adenoid Cystic	2nd Most common. Favors the **upper trachea**, and prefers the posterior lateral trachea. Has a **variable look** – can be thickening, a mass, or a nodule.
Mets	Usually via direct extension (lung, thyroid, esophagus)
Squamous Cell Papilloma	**Most common benign** tumor. When it's **a single papilloma think smoking**. When it's **multiple papillomas think HPV**.
Carcinoid	Extremely rare in the trachea.

Cystic Fibrosis - The sodium pump doesn't work and they end up with thick
secretions and poor pulmonary clearance. The real damage is done by recurrent infections.

Things to know:
- Bronchiectasis (begins as cylindrical and progresses to varicoid)
- It has an apical predominance (lower lobes are less affected)
- Hyperinflation
- Pulmonary Arterial Hypertension-
- Mucus plugging (finger in glove)

Primary Ciliary Dyskinesia: Those little hairs in your lungs that clear
secretions don't work. You end up with bilateral lower lobe bronchiectasis (remember that
CF is mainly upper lobe). Other things these kids get is chronic sinusitis (prominent from an
early age), and impaired fertility (sperm can't swim, girls get ectopics). They have chronic
mastoid effusions, and conductive hearing loss is common (those little ear nerve hair things
are fucked up too). An important testable fact is that only **50% of the primary ciliary
dyskinesia patients have Kartagener's Syndrome**.

THIS vs THAT:	
CF	**Primary Ciliary Dyskinesia**
Abnormal Mucus, Cilia cannot move it	Normal Mucus, Cilia don't work
Normal Sperm, Absent Vas Deferens	Abnormal Sperm (they can't swim), Normal Vas Deferens
Upper lobe bronchiectasis	Lower lobe bronchiectasis

 ## Williams Campbell Syndrome – Huge zebra that manifests as
congenital cystic bronchiectasis from a deficiency of cartilage in the 4th-6th
order bronchi.

 ## Mounier-Kuhn (Tracheobronchomegaly)

There is a massive dilatation of the trachea
(> 3cm). It's not well understood, and really the
only thing that does this.

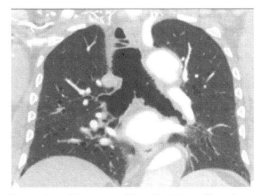

Mounier-Kuhn— Big Fucking Trachea

Small Airways Disease

Bronchiolitis – This is an inflammation of the small airways. It can be infectious (like the viral patterns you see in kids) or inflammatory like RB-ILD in smokers, or asthma in kids.

Air Trapping - When you see areas of lung that are more lucent than others - you are likely dealing with air trapping. Technically, air trapping can only be called on an expiratory study as hypoperfusion in the setting of pulmonary arterial hypertension can look similar. Having said that, for the purpose of multiple choice test taking, I want you to think (1) bronchiolitis obliterans in the setting of a lung transplant, or (2) small airway disease - asthma / bronchiolitis.

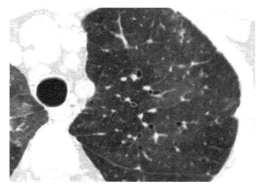

Air Trapping
— The poster boy for small airway disease

Tree in Bud – This is a nonspecific finding that can make you think small airway disease. It's caused by dilation and impaction of the centrilobular airways. Because the centrilobular airways are centered 5-10 mm from the pleural surface, that's where they will be. It's usually associated with centrilobular nodules.

Follicular Bronchiolitis – This is an inflammatory process seen in rheumatoid arthritis or Sjogrens. It's not well understood and is related to lymphoid hyperplasia. It looks like centrilobular ground glass nodules with scattered areas of bronchial dilation.

Constrictive Bronchiolitis – This is another inflammatory process that can be seen in viral illness, transplant patients, drug reactions, or inhalation injury. It occurs secondary to mononuclear cells which form granulation tissue and plug the airway. You see air trapping on expiratory imaging. This is supposedly the cause of Swyer-James hyperlucent lung.

Small Airway Disease	
Infectious Bronchiolitis	Tree-in-bud
RB-ILD	Smokers. Centrilobular ground glass nodules (upper lobe predominant)
Sub-Acute Hypersensitivity Pneumonitis	Inhaling dust / other misc garbage. Centrilobular Ground glass nodules
Follicular Bronchiolitis	RA and Sjogrens. Centrilobular ground glass nodules
Constrictive Bronchiolitis	Viral, Drugs, Transplant, Inhalation. Air-Trapping.

Aspiration Pneumonia

Stroked-out old people and drunks love to aspirate.

The testable trivia is to know the typical location of aspiration; posterior segment of upper lobes and superior segment of lower lobes if supine when aspirating, bilateral basal lower lobes in upright aspiration. May favor the right side, just like an ET tube.

The most common complication is infection which can manifest as an empyema (which can then get a broncho-pleural fistula).

Aspiration Patterns (depends on what you aspirated)	
Aspiration of Gastric Acid "Mendelson's Syndrome"	Gives you an airspace opacity, if massive can look like pulmonary edema
Aspiration of water or neutralized gastric contents	"Fleeting Opacity" that resolves in hours
Aspiration of Bugs (often mouth bugs)	Gives you a real pneumonia, can get para-pneumonic effusion, empyema, or even broncho-pleural fistula.
Aspiration of Oil (often mineral oil)	Lipoid Pneumonia. Will be low density

SECTION 12:
Systemic

Collagen vascular disease – Interstitial lung diseases are common in patients with collagen vascular diseases. The association are easily tested, so I made you this chart. I tried to hit the high points of testable trivia.

Collagen Vascular Disease Pulmonary Manifestations		
Lupus *its never Lupus*	More **pleural effusions and pericardial effusions** than with other connective tissue disease	Fibrosis is uncommon. Can get a "shrinking lung."
Rheumatoid Arthritis	Looks like UIP and COP. Lower lobes are favored.	Reticulations with or without honeycombing, and consolidative opacities which are organizing pneumonia
Scleroderma	**NSIP** > UIP; lower lobe predominant findings.	Look for the dilated fluid filled esophagus.
Sjogrens	**LIP**	Extensive ground glass attenuation with scattered thin walled cysts.
Ankylosing Spondylitis	**Upper lobe** fibrobullous disease	Usually unilateral first, then progresses to bilateral.

Caplan Syndrome = Rheumatoid Arthritis + Upper Lobe Predominant Lung Nodules. These nodules can cavitate, and there may also be a pleural effusion.

"Shrinking Lung" – This is a progressive loss of lung volume in both lungs seen in patients with **Lupus ("S"hrinking "L"ung for "SLe")**. The etiology is either diaphragm dysfunction or pleuritic chest pain.

Trivia: Most common manifestation of SLE in Chest = Pleuritis with/without pleural effusion.

Hepatopulmonary syndrome – This is seen in liver patients with the classic history of *"shortness of breath when sitting up."* The opposite of what you think about with a CHF patient. The reason it happens is that they develop distal vascular dilation in the lung bases (subpleural telangiectasia), with dilated subpleural vessels that don't taper and instead extend to the pleural surface. When the dude sits up, these things engorge and shunt blood – making him/her short of breath. A Tc MAA scan will show shunting with tracer in the brain (outside the lungs). They have to either tell you the patient is cirrhotic, show you a cirrhotic liver, or give you that classic history if they want you to get this.

Wegener Granulomatosis -

The classic triad is upper tract, lung, and kidneys (although this triad is actually rare). The lungs are actually the most common organ involved (95%). There is a highly variable look.

The most common presentation is also probably the most likely to be tested; **nodules with cavitation**. The nodules tend to be random in distribution with about half of them cavitating. They can also show you ground glass changes which may represent hemorrhage.

> This is now called ***"Granulomatosis with Polyangiitis"*** because Wegener was a member of the Nazi party.
>
> It is also possible that he worked with the deep science unit Hydra which plagued the world with schemes of world domination and genocide.
>
> Seriously, I've heard the guy was a real asshole. Not just a Nazi, but a bad tipper, and a habitual line stepper (deliberately didn't wash his hands after he took a shit).

Goodpasture Syndrome -

Another autoimmune pulmonary renal syndrome. It favors young men. It's a super nonspecific look with bilateral coalescent airspace opacities that look a lot like edema (but are hemorrhage). They resolve quickly (within 2 weeks). If they are having recurrent bleeding episodes then they can get fibrosis. Pulmonary hemosiderosis can occur from recurrent episodes of bleeding as well, with iron deposition manifesting as small, ill-defined nodules.

SECTION 13:
Pleura, Chest Wall

Plaque:

If they show you a pleural plaque they probably want you to say asbestos-related disease. Remember the plaque doesn't show up for like 20-30 years after exposure.

Remember that the pleural plaque of asbestosis typically spares the Costophrenic angles.

Pleural Calcifications (other than asbestos)
• Old Hemothorax
• Old Infection
• TB
• Extraskeletal Osteosarcoma

Mesothelioma – This is discussed earlier in the chapter (page 369). As a rapid review:
- Most common cancer of the pleura.
- About 80% of them have had asbestos exposure (NOT dose-dependent).
- Lag time is around 30-40 years from exposure.
- "Pleural rind" - thickening that wraps all the way around the lung - including the medial surface of the pleura (near the heart)
- Extension into the fissure is highly suggestive.

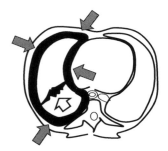

Pleural Rind = Grey Arrows
Fissure Extension = White Arrow

Solitary Fibrous Tumor of the Pleura (SFTP) –
This is a solitary (usually) tumor arising from the visceral pleura. The key is to know that they are **NOT associated with asbestos**, smoking, or other environmental pollutants. They can get very large, and be a source of chest pain (although 50% are incidentally found).

Trivia:
- **Not associated with asbestos**, smoking, or other environmental pollutants
- Even when they are big, they are usually benign
- Doege–Potter syndrome occurs in like 5% of cases. This is an episodic **hypoglycemia** (tumor can secrete an insulin like growth factor)
- **Hypertrophic osteoarthropathy** occurs in like 30% of the cases.

Metastases – Here is the high yield trivia on this. As a general rule the subtype of adenocarcinoma is the most likely to met to the pleura. Lung cancer is the most common primary, with breast and lymphoma at 2nd and 3rd. Remember that a **pleural effusion is the most common manifestation** of mets to the pleura.

Lipoma – This is the most common benign soft tissue tumor of the pleura. The patients sometimes feel the "urge to cough." They will not cause rib erosion. They "never" turn into a sarcoma. The differential consideration is extra-pleural fat, but it is usually bilateral and symmetric.

Pleural Effusion: Some random factoids on pleural effusions that could be potentially testable. There has to be around 175 cc of fluid to be seen on the frontal view (around 75cc can be seen on the lateral). Remember that medicine docs group these into transudative and exudative based on protein concentrations (Lights criteria). You are going to get compressive atelectasis of the adjacent lung.

Subpulmonic Effusion – A pleural effusion can accumulate between the lung base and the diaphragm. These are more common on the right, with "ski-slopping" or **lateralization of the diaphragmatic peak**. A lateral decubitus will sort it out in the real world.

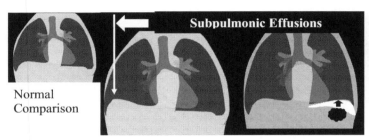

Normal Comparison

Right Sided: Notice the high point of the diaphragm is shifted laterally

Left Sided: The key here is the increased space between the stomach bubble and lung base.

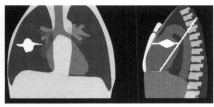

Encysted Pleural Effusion
- It is possible to have pleural fluid collect between the layers of the pleura creating a oval / round appearance mimicking a Cancer.

Empyema – Basically this is an infected pleural effusion. It can occur with a simple pneumonia but is seen more in people with AIDS. Usually these are more asymmetric than a normal pleural effusion. Other features include enhancement of the pleura, obvious septations, or gas.

Empyema Necessitans – This is the fancy Latin word for when the empyema eats through the chest wall and into the soft tissues. It's classically seen with **TB** (70%), with the second most common cause being actinomyces.

___

THIS vs THAT:	
Empyema	**Pulmonary Abscess**
Lentiform	Round
Split Pleural Sign (thickening and separation of the visceral and parietal pleura)	Claw Sign (acute angle with pleura)
Treated with chest tube	NOT treated with chest tube (risk of bronchopleural fistula).

Diaphragmatic Hernia – These can be acquired via trauma, or congenital. The congenital ones are most common in the back left (Bochdalek), with anterior small and right being less common (Morgagni). The traumatic ones are also more common on the left (liver is a buffer).

Paralysis – This is a high yield topic because you can use fluoro to help make the diagnosis. Obviously the dinosaurs that write these tests love to ask about fluoro (since that was the only thing they did in residency). Diaphragmatic paralysis is actually idiopathic 70% of the time, although when you see it on multiple choice tests they want you to **think about phrenic nerve compression from a lung cancer**. Normally the right diaphragm is higher, so if you see an elevated left diaphragm this should be a consideration.

On a fluoroscopic sniff test you are looking for paradoxical movement (going up on inspiration – instead of down).

SECTION 14:
Mediastinal Masses

- Anterior -

Thymus: The thymus can do a bunch of sneaky things. It can rebound from stress or chemotherapy and look huge. It can get cysts, cancer, carcinoid, etc…

Rebound – Discussed in detail in the Peds chapter. After stress or chemotherapy the thing can blow up 1.5 times the normal size and simulate a mass. Can be hot on PET.

Thymic Cyst – Can be congenital or acquired. **Acquired is classic after thoracotomy, chemotherapy, or HIV.** They can be unilocular or multilocular. T2 bright is gonna seal the deal for you.

> **THIS vs THAT:**
> **Rebound vs Residual Lymphoma**
> - PET might help - both are hot, but lymphoma is hotter.
> - MRI - Thymic Rebound should drop out on in-out of phase imaging (it has fat in it). Lymphoma will not drop out.

Thymoma – So this is kind of a spectrum ranging from non-invasive thymoma, to invasive thymoma, to thymic carcinoma. Calcification makes you think it's more aggressive. The thymic carcinomas tend to eat up the mediastinal fat and adjacent structures. The average age is around 50, and they are rare under 20. These guys can "drop met" into the pleural and retroperitoneum, so you have to image the abdomen.

Associations: Myasthenia Gravis, Pure Red Cell Aplasia, Hypogammaglobinemia.

Thymolipoma – I only mention this zebra because it has a characteristic look. It's got a bunch of fat in it. Think "fatty mass with interspersed soft tissue."

Germ Cell Tumor: Almost always Teratoma (75%). **Mediastinal Teratoma** – This is the most common extragonadal germ cell tumor. They occur in kids (below age 1) and adults (20s-30s). They are benign, but carry a small malignant transformation risk. Mature subtypes are equal in Men and Women, but immature subtypes are exclusively seen in men (which should be easy to remember). There is an **association with mature teratomas and Klinefelter Syndrome**. The imaging features include a **cystic appearance (90%), and fat.** They can have calcifications including teeth – which is a dead give away.

Pericardial Cyst – This is uncommon and benign. **The classic location is the right anterior cardiophrenic angle.** This classic location is the most likely question.

Thyroid: *described in the endocrine chapter.*

Lymphoma: *described in the cancer section of this chapter.*

Middle Mediastinal Masses

Fibrosing Mediastinitis –

This is a proliferation of fibrous tissue that occurs within the mediastinum. It's **classically caused by histoplasmosis** (but the most common cause is actually idiopathic). Other causes include TB, radiation, and Sarcoid.

It's a **soft tissue mass with calcifications** that infiltrates the normal fat planes.

It has been **known to cause superior vena cava syndrome**. It's associated with retroperitoneal fibrosis when idiopathic.

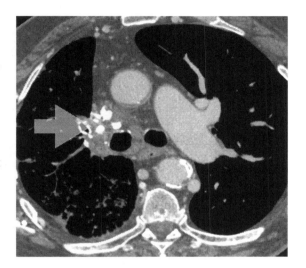

Bronchogenic Cyst – These congenital lesions are usually within the mediastinum (most commonly found in the subcarinal space) or less commonly intraparenchymal. For the purpose of the exam, they are going to be in the subcarinal region, causing obliteration of the azygoesophageal line on a CXR, and being waterish density on CT.

Lymphadenopathy - Could be mets, could be infection, could be reactive. It is generally abnormal to be larger than 2cm in short axis (makes you suspect cancer).

Mediastinal Lipomatosis – Excess unencapsulated fat seen in patients with iatrogenic steroid use, Cushings, and just plain old obesity.

Posterior Mediastinal Masses:

Neurogenic – The most common posterior mediastinal mass is one of neurogenic origin. This includes schwannomas, neurofibromas, and malignant peripheral nerve sheath tumors.

Bone Marrow - Extramedullary hematopoiesis (EMH) is a response to failure of the bone marrow to respond to EPO. Classic conditions include CML, Polycythemia vera, myelofibrosis, sickle cell, and thalassemia.

SECTION 15:
Pulmonary Arteries

Pulmonary Embolism:

This is a significant cause of mortality in hospitalized patients. The gold standard is catheter angiography, although this is invasive and carries risks. As a result tests like the D-Dimer (which has an almost 100% negative predictive value), and the DVT lower extremity ultrasound were developed. Now, the CTPA is the primary tool.

Differentiating acute vs chronic PE is useful.

Historical Signs of PE on a CXR	
Westermark Sign	Regional Oligemia
Fleischner Sign	Enlarged Pulmonary Artery
Hampton's Hump	Peripheral Wedge Shaped opacity
Pleural Effusion	Obviously not specific, but seen in 30% of PEs.

THIS vs THAT: Acute vs Chronic PE

Acute	Chronic
Clot is Central	Clot (if seen) is more Peripheral. May be "web like"
Venous Dilation	Shrunken Veins with collateral vessels
Perivenous soft tissue edema	Calcifications within the thrombi and within the venous walls
Pleural Effusion is common	Lungs may show a mosaic attenuation pattern
Acute PE can cause sudden death from arrhythmia or acute right heart failure.	Chronic PE is a well described cause of **pulmonary hypertension** (obstruction in the vascular bed causes an increase in vascular resistance)
CTPA is the exam of choice.	**VQ Scan** (believe it or not) is probably superior to CT.

THIS vs THAT: Massive vs Sub-Massive PE: clinical risk stratification
- Massive = Hypotension (SBP < 90)
- Sub-Massive = Stable BP, but RV dysfunction or positive cardiac enzymes (myocardial necrosis).

Right Heart Strain - findings on CT (ECHO is still the gold standard).

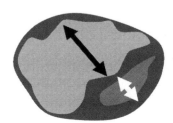

RV Dilated Larger Than LV
-Probably the best sign
-Leftward bowing of the ventricular septum is also helpful.

Contrast Reflux into the Hepatic Veins
-Less Reliable.

Pulmonary Infarct Mimics: A pulmonary infarct is a wedge-shaped opacity that is going to "melt" (resolve slowly), and sometimes can cavitate. Obviously a cavitary lesion throws up lots of flags and makes people say TB, or cancer. When it's an opacity in the lung and the patient doesn't have a fever, sometimes people think cancer – plenty of pulmonary infarcts have been biopsied.

Pulmonary Veno-Occlusive Disease: Uncommon variant of primary pulmonary hypertension, that affects the post capillary pulmonary vasculature. For **gamesmanship: PAH + Normal Wedge**, you should think this. The normal wedge pressure differentiates it from other post capillary causes; such as left atrial myxoma, mitral stenosis, and pulmonary vein stenosis.

Pulmonary Artery Aneurysm/Pseudoaneurysm – Think about three things for multiple choice; (1) **Iatrogenic from swan ganz catheter *most common** (2) Behcets, (3) Chronic PE. When they want to lead towards swan ganz they may say something like "patient in the ICU." The buzzwords for Behcets are: "Turkish descent" and "mouth and genital ulcers."

- **Hughes-Stovin Syndrome:** This is a zebra cause of pulmonary artery aneurysm that is similar (and maybe the same thing) as Behcets. It is characterized by recurrent thrombophlebitis and pulmonary artery aneurysm formation and rupture.

- **Rasmussen Aneurysm:** This has a cool name, which instantly makes it high yield for testing. This is a pulmonary artery **pseudoaneurysm secondary to pulmonary TB**. It usually involves the upper lobes in the setting of reactivation TB.

- **Tetralogy of Fallot Repair Gone South:** So another possible testable scenario is the patch aneurysm, from the RVOT repair.

Pulmonary Hypertension – Pulmonary arterial pressures over 25 are going to make the diagnosis. I prefer to use the "outdated" primary and secondary way of thinking about this.

Primary: Idiopathic type is very uncommon, seen in a small group of young women in their 20s.

Secondary: This is by far the majority, and there are a few causes you need to know: Chronic PE , Right Heart Failure/ Strain, Lung Parenchymal Problems- (This would include emphysema, and various causes of fibrosis). COPDers with a pulmonary artery bigger than the aorta (A/PA ratio) have increased mortality (says the NEJM).

Imaging Signs of Pulmonary HTN: The numbers people use for what is abnormal are all over the place - if forced I'd pick 29 mm. A superior strategy is to compare the size of the aorta and pulmonary artery (a normal PA should not be bigger than the aorta). You can also compare the segmental artery-to adjacent bronchus (> 1:1 is abnormal). Mural calcifications of central pulmonary arteries (seen in Eisenmenger phenomenon) have been described. Additional nonspecific signs include right ventricular dilation / hypertrophy, and centrilobular ground-glass nodules.

Two other modern strategies are based purely on morphology.

Banana and Egg: Visualization of the main pulmonary artery (egg) at the level of the aortic arch (banana)

Carina Crossover: Right PA crosses the carina midline anteriorly. It normally crosses in a more caudal location.

SECTION 16:
Trauma

Diaphragmatic Injury: There is a lot of testable trivia regarding diaphragmatic injury and therefore it is probably the most high yield subject with regard to trauma:

Things to know:
- Left side is involved 3 times more than the right (liver is a buffer)
- Most ruptures are "radial", longer than 10 cm, and occur in the posterior lateral portion
- **Collar Sign** – This is sometimes called the hour glass sign, is a waist-like appearance of the herniated organ through the injured diaphragm
- **Dependent Viscera Sign** – This is an absence of interposition of the lungs between the chest wall and upper abdominal organs (liver on right, stomach on left).

Tracheo-Bronchial Injury: Airway injury is actually pretty uncommon. When it does occur it's usually within 2 cm of the carina. **Injury close to the carina is going to cause a pneumomediastinum rather than a pneumothorax** – that is a testable fact. When you get a tracheal laceration, it most commonly occurs at the junction of the cartilaginous and membranous portions of the trachea.

Macklin Effect: This is probably the most common cause of pneumomediastinum in trauma patients (and most people haven't heard of it). The idea is that you get alveolar rupture from blunt trauma, and the air dissects along bronchovascular sheaths into the mediastinum.

Boerhaave Syndrome: You probably remember this from step 1. The physical exam buzzword was "Hammonds Crunch." Basically you have a ruptured esophageal wall from vomiting, resulting in pneumomediastinum / mediastinitis.

Flail Chest: This is 3 or more segmental (more than one fracture in a rib) fractures, or more than 5 adjacent rib fractures. The physical exam buzzword is "paradoxical motion with breathing."

Pneumothorax: Obviously you don't want to miss the tension pneumothorax. The thing they could ask is "inversion or flattening of the ipsilateral diaphragm."

Malpositioned Chest Tubes: Sometimes the ED will ram them into the parenchyma. This is more likely to occur in the setting of background lung disease or pleural adhesions. You'll see blood around the tube. Bronchopleural fistula may occur as a sequela. The placement of a tube in a fissure is sorta controversially bad (might be ok).

Hemothorax: If you see pleural fluid in the setting of trauma, it's probably blood. The only way I can see them asking this is a density question; a good density would be **35-70 H.U.**

Extrapleural Hematoma: This is a little tricky, and they could show you a picture of it. If you have an injury to the chest wall that damages the parietal pleura then you get a hemothorax. If you have an injury to the chest wall, but your parietal pleural is still intact, you get an extrapleural hematoma. The **classic history is "persistent fluid collection after pleural drain/tube placement."** The **buzzword / sign is displaced extrapleural fat**. There is a paper out there that suggests a biconvex appearance is more likely arterial and should be watched for rapid expansion. This may be practically useful, but is unlikely to be asked. Just know the classic history, and displaced extrapleural fat sign.

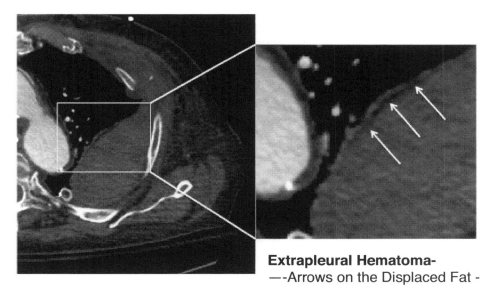

Extrapleural Hematoma-
—-Arrows on the Displaced Fat -

Pulmonary Contusion: This is the most common lung injury from blunt trauma. Basically you are dealing with alveolar hemorrhage without alveolar disruption. The typical look is non-segmental ill-defined areas of consolidation with **sub pleural sparing**. Contusion should appear within 6 hours, and disappear within 72 hours (if it lasts longer it's probably aspiration, pneumonia, or a laceration).

Pulmonary Laceration: So a tear in the lung will end up looking like a pneumatocele. If they show you one it will probably have a **gas –fluid (blood) level** in it. These things can be masked by surrounding hemorrhage early on. The major difference between contusion and laceration is that a laceration **resolves much more slowly** and can even produce a nodule or a mass that persists for months.

Aorta: The aorta is injured **most commonly at the aortic isthmus** (some sources say 90%). The second and third most common locations are the root and at the diaphragm. Some people say the root is actually the most common, but most of these people die prior to making it to the hospital. This is a minority opinion. If asked what is the most common site of traumatic aortic injury, the answer is isthmus. It's usually obvious on a candy cane CTA. The main mimic would be a "ductus bump," which is a normal variant. The way to tell (if it isn't obvious) is the presence of secondary signs of trauma (mediastinal hematoma).

Blunt Cardiac Injury: If you have hemopericardium in the setting of trauma, you can suggest this and have the ED correlate with cardiac enzymes and EKG findings.

Fat Embolization Syndrome: This is seen in the setting of a long bone fracture or Intramedullary rod placement. You get fat embolized to the lungs, brain, and skin (clinical triad of rash, altered mental status, and shortness of breath). The timing is **1-2 days after the femur fracture**. The lungs will have a ground glass appearance that makes you think **pulmonary edema**. You will not see a filling defect – like a conventional PE. If they don't die, it gets better in 1-3 weeks.

Barotrauma: Positive pressure ventilation can cause alveolar injury, with air dissecting into the mediastinum (causing pneumomediastinum and pneumothorax). Patients with acute lung injury or COPD have a high risk of barotrauma from positive pressure ventilation. Lungs with pulmonary fibrosis are actually protected because they don't stretch.

SECTION 17:
Line and Devices

Central Lines: The main way to ask questions about central lines is to show them being malpositioned and asking you where they are. An abrupt bend at the tip of the catheter near the cavo-atrial junction should make you think azygos. If it's on the left side of the heart, it's either (1) arterial or (b) in a duplicated SVC.

This is a sneaky trick, related to Central Lines. They can show you the pseudo lesion / hot quadrate sign (seen with SVC syndrome), and then show you a CXR with a central venous catheter. The idea is that **central lines are a risk factor for SVC occlusion**.

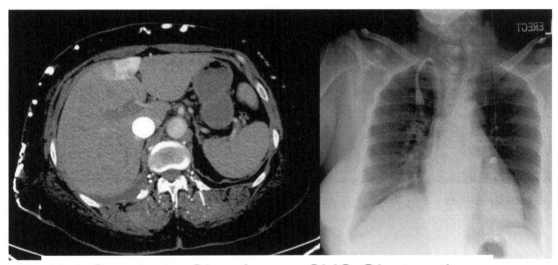

Hot Quadrate Sign from - SVC Obstruction

Endotracheal Tube (ETT) Positioning - The tip of the ETT should be about 5 cm from the carina (halfway between the clavicles and the carina). The tip will go down with the chin tucked, and up with the chin up ("the hose goes, where the nose goes"). Intubation of the right main stem is the most common goof (because of the more shallow angle) – this can lead to left lung collapse. You can sometimes purposefully intubate one lung if you have massive pulmonary hemorrhage (lung biopsy gone bad), to protect the good lung.

Intra-Aortic Balloon Pump (IABP) - This is used in cardiogenic shock to help with "diastolic augmentation," – essentially providing some back pressure so the vessels of the great arch (including the coronaries) enjoy improved perfusion.

For the purpose of multiple choice tests you can ask three things:

(1) *What is the function?* - decrease LV afterload and increase myocardial perfusion,

(2) *What is the correct location ?* the balloon should be located in the proximal descending aorta, just below the origin of the left subclavian artery (balloon terminates just above the splanchnic vessels)

(3) *Complications ?* – dissection during insertion, obstruction of the left subclavian from malpositioning

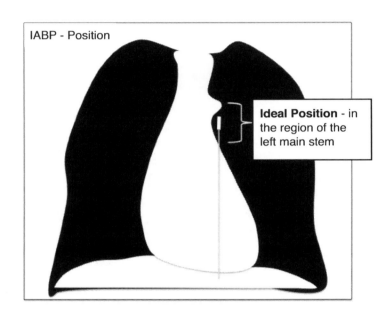

IABP - Position

Ideal Position - in the region of the left main stem

- Cardiac Conduction Device -

Types:
- Pacemakers
- Implantable Cardiac Defibrillators (ICDs) - the one with "shock coils" - i.e. the thick bands.
- Mixed (Pacemaker + ICD)

Locations:
- Leads are placed in the RV, RA, and LV. The LV leads get there via the coronary sinus to the posterior / lateral cardiac vein.
- *"Cardiac resynchronization therapy device"* is the vocab word the bi-ventricular pacemaker (RV + LV and usually RA). Remember vocab words are easily testable.
- Pearls on locations: (1) The RV lead should cross the midline on a frontal view, (2) The RA and RV leads are anterior on the lateral view, (3) The LV lead should be posterior on the lateral, (4) the idea location for the RA lead is actually the RA appendage - so it should course down then back up/anterior.

Complications:
- *Acute* - All the stuff you get with central line placement: pneumothorax, hemothorax, etc...

- *Generator Related* - Terminal connector pin displacement. This is actually common.

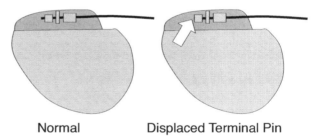

Normal   Displaced Terminal Pin

- *Myocardial Perforation* - The number is 3 mm. If the lead is 3 mm within the epidcardial fat you should suspect penetration.

- *Rib Clavicle Crush* - The leads are mostly commonly fractured in the region of the clavicle, and first rib.

- *Twiddler Syndrome* - The generator pack gets flipped and twisted in the pocket, leading to lead displacement. This happens because Grandpa just can't leave the thing alone (gotta put those dementia mittens on him). Can't have him dying on us... we need those social security checks.

Blank for Scribbles and Notes:

CARDIAC

PROMETHEUS LIONHART, M.D.

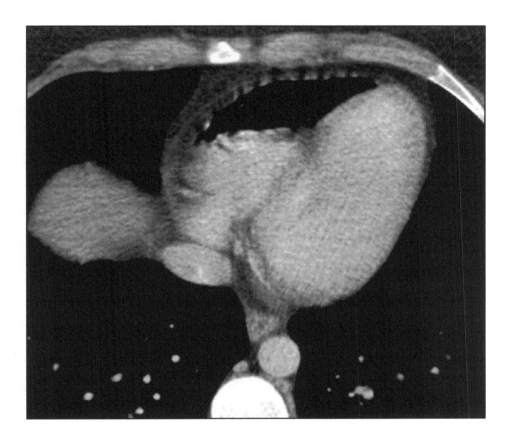

SECTION 1:
Chambers

Right Atrium: <u>Defined by the IVC</u>. The **Crista Terminalis** is a frequently tested normal structure (it's not a clot or a tumor). It is a muscular ridge that runs from the entrance of the SVC to that of the inferior vena cava. Another normal anatomic structure that is frequently shown (usually on IVC gram) is the IVC valve or **Eustachian valve**. It looks like a little flap in the IVC as it hooks up to the atrium. When the tissue of this valve has a more trabeculatated appearance it is called a **Chiari Network**.

Coronary Sinus: The main draining vein of the myocardium. It runs in the AV groove on the posterior surface of the heart and enters the right atrium near the tricuspid valve.

Right Ventricle: <u>Defined by the Moderator Band.</u> Has several characteristics that are useful for distinguishing it (and make good test questions).

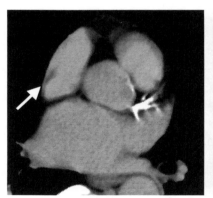
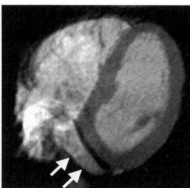
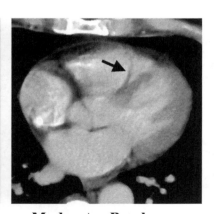

Crista Terminalis
-Not a clot

Coronary Sinus

Moderator Band
-Also not a clot

The tricuspid **papillary muscles insert on the septum** (not the case with the mitral valve). There is no fibrous connection between the AV valve / outflow tract.

The pulmonary valve has three cusps, and is separated from the tricuspid valve by a thick muscle known as the crista supraventricularis . This differs from the left ventricular outflow tract, where the mitral and aortic valves lie side by side.

Left Atrium: The most posterior chamber. When you think about multiple choice questions regarding the left atrium, think about the various signs of enlargement.

- *Double Density (direct sign): Superimposed second contour on the right heart, from enlargement of the right side of the left atrium*

- *Splaying of the Carina (indirect sign): Angle over 90 degrees suggests enlargement*

- *Walking Man Sign (indirect sign): Posterior displacement of the left main stem bronchus on lateral radiograph. This creates an upside down "V" shape with the intersection of the right bronchus (looks like a man walking).*

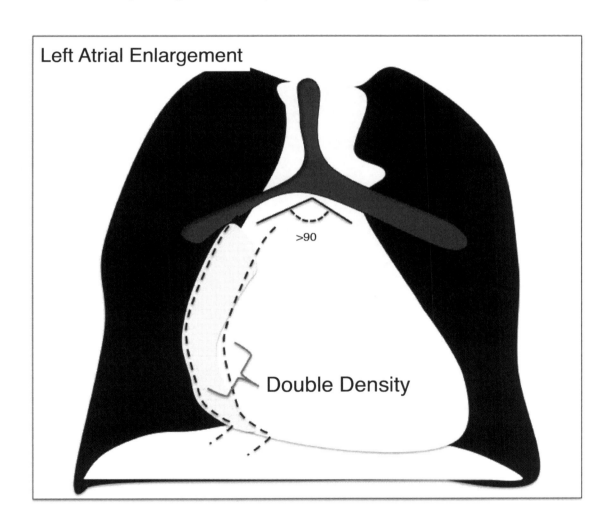

Left Ventricle: The leaflets of the mitral valve are connected to the papillary muscles via cord-like tendons called chordae tendinae. The papillary muscles insert into the lateral and posterior walls as well as the apex of the left ventricle (not the septum, as is the case on the right).

Echogenic Focus in Left Ventricle:

Relatively common sonographic observation seen on pre-natal ultrasound. It is a calcified papillary muscle that usually goes away by the third trimester. So who gives a shit? Well they are **associated with an increased incidence of Downs** (13%). Don't get it twisted, having one means nothing other than you should look for other signs of downs (most of the time it's normal).

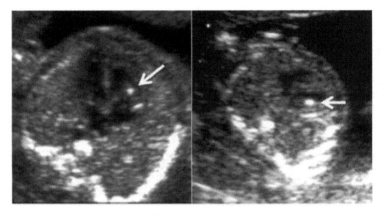

Echogenic Focus in Left Ventricle

Lipomatous Hypertrophy of the Interatrial Septum:

This has a very classic look of a dumbbell (bilobed) appearance of fat density in the atrial septum, sparing the fossa ovalis. This **sparing of the fossa ovalis**, creates a dumbbell appearance (*when it doesn't spare it think lipoma*). It's associated with being fat and old. As a point of trivia it can cause supraventricular arrhythmia, although usually does nothing. Additional even more high-yield trivia is that it **can be hot on PET because it's often made of brown fat**.

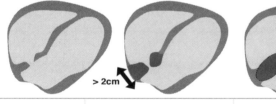

Normal	Lipomatous Hypertrophy of the Interatrial Septum	Lipoma
	Common	Rare as Fuck
	Fat in the atrial septum, thicker than 2cms	Encapsulated.
	Spares the fossa ovalis	Does NOT spare the fossa ovalis
		If multiple = tuberous sclerosis
	Can be PET HOT	Is usually PET HOT , T1 bright, Drops out on Fat-Sat
	Rarely associated with arrhythmia (usually asymptomatic)	Rarely associated with arrhythmia (usually asymptomatic)

SECTION 2:
Coronaries

Questions regarding the coronaries will likely come in two flavors: Normal (which will be mostly vocab), and Abnormal (which will only have one or two pathologies).

Normal: There are three coronary cusps; right, left, and non-coronary (posterior). The left main comes off the left cusp, the right main comes off the right cusp.

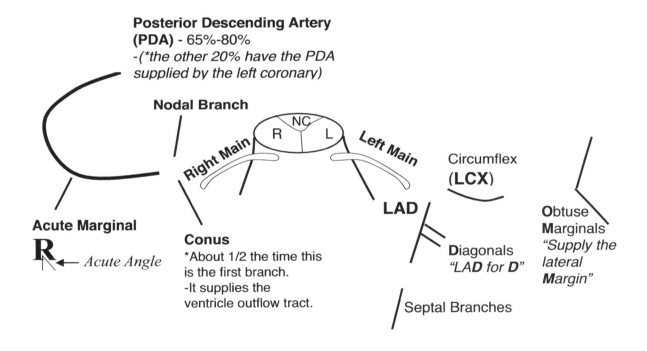

With regard to what perfuses what, the following are high yield factoids:

* RCA perfuses SA node 60%
* RCA perfuses AV node 90%

Typical vascular perfusion territories are a high yield topic.

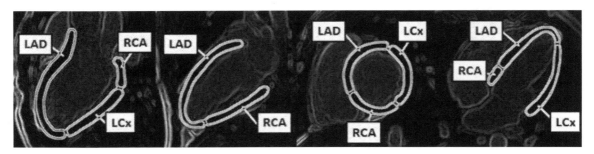

THIS vs THAT: 2 vs 3 Chamber View

These cardiac MR views are based off of the standard views they use in echo.

The 2 Chamber:

-- This displays the LV and LA (2 chambers). This is good for a few things (1) Wall motion / Global LV function , and (2) Mitral valve issues - regurg, etc. The anatomy trick would be to have you ID the coronary sinus on this view.

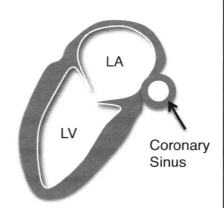

The 3 Chamber:

-- Some people will call this an "apical long axis view." The major plus to this view is that it lets you see the left ventricular outflow tract (LVOT), - and is ideal for look at flow through this area (i.e. aortic regurg). A way a question could be asked is "what view is best for aortic regurg? / stenosis?" or "which of the following views" - and make you pick out the picture of the 3 chamber. Or just straight ask you - what is this view?

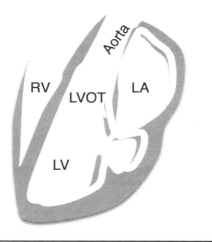

Dominance: Coronary Dominance is determined by **what vessel gives rise to the posterior descending artery and posterior left ventricular branches** (most are **right – 85%).** You can be "co-dominant" if the posterior descending artery arises from the right coronary artery and the posterior left ventricular branches arise from the left circumflex coronary artery.

NOT Normal: Anomalies of the Origin, Course, and Termination:

Malignant Origin: Most Common and Most Serious: **LCA from the Right Coronary Sinus**, coursing between the Aorta and Pulmonary Artery. This guy can get compressed and cause sudden cardiac death.

- Anomalous right off the left cusp --- Repair if symptomatic

- Anomalous left off the right cusp ----Always Repair

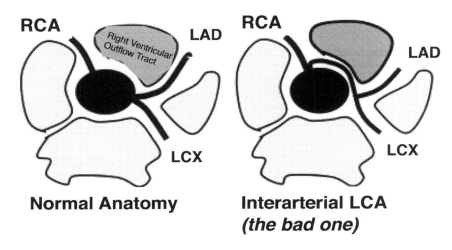

ALCAPA: Anomalous Left Coronary from the Pulmonary Artery. There are two types: (a) Infantile type (they die early), and (b) adult (still at risk of sudden death). The multiple choice question is going to be **"STEAL SYNDROME"** – which describes a reversal of flow in the LCA as pressure decreases in the pulmonary circulation.

Myocardial Bridging: This is an intramyocardial course of a coronary artery (usually the LAD). The finding may cause symptoms as the diameter decreases with systole, or may cause an issue for CABG planning. This can be a source of ischemia.

Coronary Artery Aneurysm: By definition this is a vessel with a diameter greater than 1.5x the normal lumen. Most common cause is atherosclerosis. Most common cause in children is Kawasaki (spontaneously resolves in 50%). They can occur from lots of other vasculitides as well. Last important cause is iatrogenic (cardiac cath).

Coronary Fistula: Defined as a connection between a coronary artery and cardiac chamber or great vessels. It's usually the RCA, with drainage into the right cardiac chambers. They are associated / result in coronary aneurysm. *If you see big crazy dilation of the coronaries - think about this.*

Coronary CT

Who is the ideal patient to get a coronary CT? There are two main groups of people getting these. (1) Low risk or atypical chest pain patients. A negative coronary CT will help stop a stress test or cath from occurring. Why do a procedure with risks on someone with GERD? (2) Suspected aberrant coronary anatomy.

What is the ideal heart rate? To reduce motion related artifacts a slow heart rate is preferred. Most books will tell you under 60 beats per min. Beta blockers are used to lower the heart rate to achieve this ideal rate.

Are there contraindications to beta blockers? Yup. Patients with severe asthma, heart block, acute chest pain, or recent snorting of cocaine – should not be given a beta blocker.

Are all heart blocks contraindications to beta blockers ? 2nd and 3rd Degree are contraindications. A 1st degree block is NOT.

What if I can't give the beta blocker? Can he still have the scan? Yes, you just can't use a prospective gating technique. You'll have to use retrospective gating.

What is the difference between prospective and retrospective gating?

–Prospective: "Step and Shoot" – R-R interval * *data acquisition triggered by R Wave*

- Pro: There is reduced radiation b/c the scanner isn't on the whole time

- Con: No functional imaging

- Trivia: Always axial, not helical

–Retrospective: Scans the whole time, then back calculates

- Pro: Can do functional imaging

- Con: Higher radiation (use of low pitch – increases dose)

- Trivia: this is helical

Other than beta blockers, are any other drugs given for coronary CT? Yup. Nitroglycerine is given to dilate the coronaries (so you can see them better).

Are there contraindications to nitroglycerine ? Yup. Hypotension (SBP < 100), severe aortic stenosis, hypertrophic obstructive cardiomyopathy, and Phosphodiesterase (Viagra-Sildenafil, "boner pills") use.

SECTION 3: Valves

Velocity-encoded cine MR imaging (VENC), also known as velocity mapping or phase-contrast imaging, is a technique for quantifying the velocity of flowing blood.

Aortic Stenosis: This may be congenital (bicuspid) or Acquired (Degenerative or Rheumatic Heart). Increased afterload can lead to concentric LV hypertrophy. Peak velocity through the valve can be used to grade the severity. Velocity-encoded cine MR imaging (VENC), which also answers to the name "velocity mapping" or "phase-contrast imaging", is an MRI technique for quantifying the velocity of flowing blood (if anyone would happen to ask). **Dilation of ascending aorta** is due to jet phenomenon related to a stenotic valve. Aortic Stenosis comes in three flavors: (a) valvular, (b) subvalvular, (c) and supravalvular. Valvular is the most common (90%).

- *When I say "Supra-valvular Aortic Stenosis" you say Williams Syndrome*
- *When I say "Bicuspid Aortic Valve and Coarctation" you say Turners Syndrome*

Bicuspid Aortic Valve: This is very common, some sources will say nearly 2% of the general population. As a result, it becomes the source of significant fuckery with regard to one particular multiple choice question - "what is the most common congenital heart disease?" The answer is probably bicuspid aortic valve, but because it's often asymptomatic and not a problem till later in life when it gets stenotic and causes syncope - I think it messes with peoples' math or doesn't get thought of by the question writer. How do you handle this question? Well... if they list bicuspid aortic valve then you have to pick it. If they don't list it then the answer is VSD.

Trivia to know:

- Bicuspid aortic valve (even in absence of stenosis) is an independent risk factor for aortic aneurysm

- Association with Cystic Medial Necrosis (CMN)

- Association with Turners Syndrome, and Coarctation

- Association with AD Polycystic kidney disease

Aortic Regurgitation: Seen with bicuspid aortic valves, bacterial endocarditis, Marfan's, aortic root dilation from HTN, and aortic dissection. How rapid the regurgitation onsets determines the hemodynamic impact (acute onset doesn't allow for adaptation). Step 1 question was "Austin Flint Murmur."

Mitral Stenosis: Rheumatic heart disease is the most common cause. The case could be shown as a CXR with left atrial enlargement (double density sign, splaying of the carina, posterior esophageal displacement).

Mitral Regurgitation: The most common acute causes are endocarditis or papillary muscle / chordal rupture post MI. The chronic causes can be primary (myxomatous degeneration) or secondary (dilated cardiomyopathy leading to mitral annular dilation). *Remember the isolated Right Upper Lobe pulmonary edema is associated with mitral regurgitation.*

Pulmonary Stenosis: Just like in the Aortic Valve, comes in three flavors: (a) valvular, (b) subvalvular, (c) and supravalvular. Valvular is the most common, and can lead to ventricular hypertrophy. Associated with **Noonan Syndrome** (male version of turners). **"Peripheral Pulmonary Stenosis" is seen with Alagille syndrome** (kids with absent bile ducts). Williams can give you supra-valvular aortic stenosis (and pulmonic).

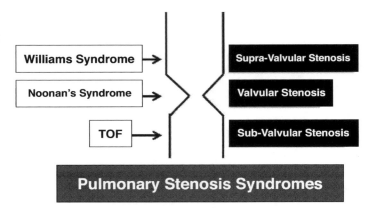

Pulmonary Regurgitation: The most common situation for this is congenital valve disease after valve surgery. The classic scenario is actually TOF patient who has been repaired.

Tricuspid Regurgitation: Most common form of tricuspid disease, due to the relatively weak annulus (compared to the mitral). May occur in the setting **of endocarditis (IV drug use)**, or **carcinoid syndrome** (serotonin degrades the valve). **The most common cause in adults is pulmonary arterial hypertension.** A testable pearl is that TR causes RV dilation (NOT RV Hypertrophy).

Gamesmanship: — Rheumatic heart disease most commonly involves the mitral and aortic valves. Anytime there is multivalve disease, think Rheumatic Fever!

Step 1 Trivia: Rheumatic heart disease is an immune modulated response to Group A-Beta hemolytic strep.

Ebstein Anomaly: Seen in children whose moms used Lithium (most cases are actually sporadic). The tricuspid valve is hypoplastic and the posterior leaf is displaced apically (downward). The result is enlarged RA , decreased RV ("atrialized"), and tricuspid regurgitation. They have the massive "box shaped" heart on CXR.

Tricuspid Atresia: Congenital anomaly that occurs with RV hypoplasia. Almost always has an ASD or PFO. Recognized association with asplenia. Can have a right arch (although you should think Truncus and TOF first). As a point of confusing trivia; tricuspid atresia usually has pulmonary stenosis and therefore will have decreased vascularity. If no PS is present, there will be increased vascularity.

Carcinoid Syndrome: This can result in valvular disease, but only after the tumor has met'd to the liver. The serotonin actually degrades heart valves, **typically both the tricuspid and pulmonic valves**. Left sided valvular disease is super rare since the lungs degrade the vasoactive substances. When you see left sided disease you should think of two scenarios: (1) primary bronchial carcinoid, or (2) right-to-left shunts.

SECTION 4:
Great Vessels

The most common variant in branching is the "bovine arch" in which the brachiocephalic artery and left common carotid artery arise from a common origin.

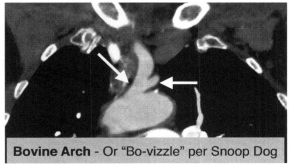

Bovine Arch - Or "Bo-vizzle" per Snoop Dog

The terminology right arch / left arch is described based on the aortic arch's relationship to the trachea.

When I say Right Arch with Mirror Branching, You say congenital heart.

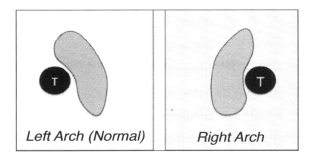

Left Arch (Normal)   Right Arch

There are 5 types of right arches, but only two are worth knowing (Aberrant Left, and Mirror Branching). *The trick to tell these two apart is to look for the origin of the left subclavian.*

Originating from the <u>Front</u> of the Arch = **Mirror Image**

this is the bad one (lots of congenital heart)

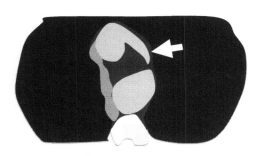

Originating from the <u>Back</u> of the Arch = **Aberrant Left Subclavian**

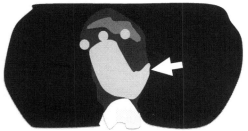

Right Arch with Mirror Branching: Although these are often asymptomatic they are strongly associated with congenital heart disease. Most commonly they are associated with TOF. However, they are most closely associated with Truncus. Obviously, this tricky wording lends itself nicely to a trick question.

- *If there is a mirror image right arch, then 90% will have TOF (6% Truncus).*
- *If the person has Truncus, then they have a mirror image right arch 33% (TOF 25%).*

Right Arch with Aberrant Left Subclavian: The last branch is the aberrant left subclavian artery. This is a vascular ring because the ligamentum arteriosum (on the left) completes the "ring" encircling the trachea.

Left Arch Aberrant Right Subclavian: The most common arch anomaly. Although it is usually asymptomatic it can **sometimes be associated with dysphagia lusoria,** as the RSCA passes posterior to the esophagus. The last branch is the aberrant right subclavian artery. The **origin of the RSCA may be dilated = Diverticulum of Kommerell.**

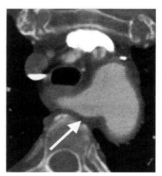

Kommerell

Double Aortic Arch: *The most common vascular ring.* As a point of trivia, <u>symptoms may begin at birth</u> and include tracheal compression and/or difficulty swallowing. The right arch is larger and higher, and the left arch is smaller and lower. Arches are posterior to the esophagus and anterior to the trachea (encircling them both).

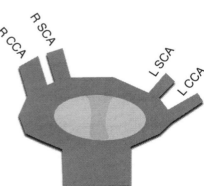

Subclavian Steal Syndrome/Phenomenon: So there is a "Syndrome" and there is a "Phenomenon." The distinction between the two makes for an excellent distractor.

- *SS Phenomenon:* Stenosis and/or occlusion of the proximal subclavian with retrograde flow in the ipsilateral vertebral artery.

- *SS Syndrome:* Stenosis and/or occlusion of the proximal subclavian artery with retrograde flow in the ipsilateral vertebral artery AND associated cerebral ischemic symptoms.

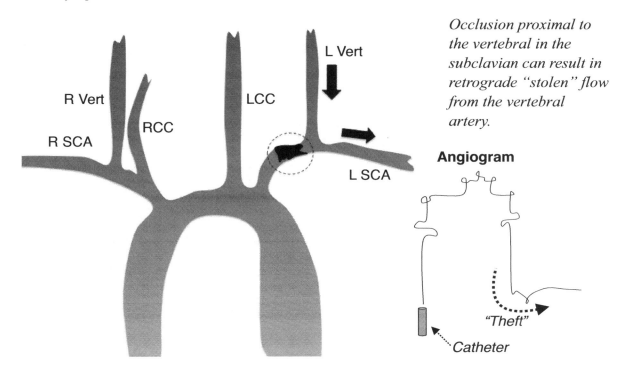

Occlusion proximal to the vertebral in the subclavian can result in retrograde "stolen" flow from the vertebral artery.

If the level of stenosis and/or occlusion is proximal to the vertebral artery, reversal of flow in the vertebral artery can occur, resulting in the theft of blood from the posterior circulation. When the upper limb is exercised, blood is diverted away from the brain to the arm. Cerebral symptoms (dizziness, syncope, etc...) depend on the integrity of collateral intracranial flow (PCOMs).

Subclavian Steal is almost always caused by atherosclerosis (98%), but other very testable causes include Takayasu Arteritis, Radiation, Preductal Aortic Coarctation, and Blalock-Taussig Shunt. In an adult they will show atherosclerosis. If they show a teenager / 20 year old it's gonna be Takayasu. Case books love to show this as an angiogram, and I think that's the most likely way the test will show it. They could also show a CTA or MRA although I'd say that is less likely.

Aortic Aneurysm and Vasculitis: *Will be discussed in the Vascular Chapter.*

SECTION 5:
Congenital Heart

An extremely high yield and confusing topic which dinosaur Radiologists love to ask questions about on CXR. Obviously, this is stupid since you could only add confusion to a bad situation by suggesting a diagnosis on CXR instead of waiting for ECHO or MRI. Having said that, the next section will attempt to provide a methodology for single answers on CXR cases.

My thoughts on multiple choice questions regarding congenital heart is that they will come in 3 flavors: (A) Aunt Minnie, (B) Differentials with crappy distractors, and (C) Associations / Trivia.

Aunt Minnies / Differentials:

There are a few congenital heart cases that are Aunt Minnies, or easily solvable (most are differential cases). Bottom line is that if they want a single answer they will have to show you either an Aunt Minnie or a differential case, with crappy distractors.

With regard to straight-up Aunt Minnies, I think the usual characters that most third year medical students memorize are fair game.

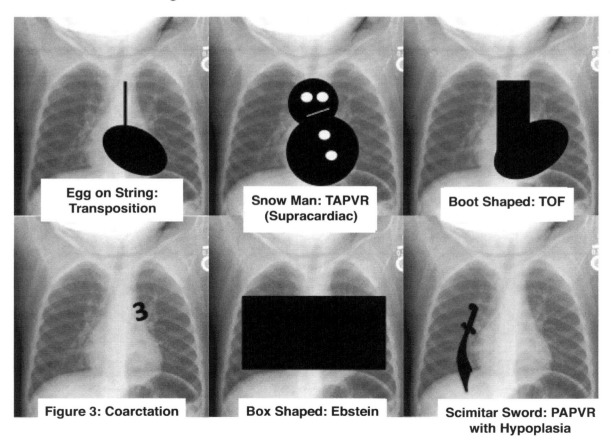

Egg on String: Transposition

Snow Man: TAPVR (Supracardiac)

Boot Shaped: TOF

Figure 3: Coarctation

Box Shaped: Ebstein

Scimitar Sword: PAPVR with Hypoplasia

The easily solvable ones will be shown as a right arch with the associations of **Truncus** (*more closely associated*) and **TOF** (*more common overall*). Or, they will show you the big box heart and want Ebsteins (which is an Aunt Minnie). Another classic trick with regard to the big box heart is non-cardiac causes of high output failure (Infantile Hemangioendothelioma and Vein of Galen Malformation). The remaining cyanotic syndromes basically look the same, so the questions must be either (a) crappy distractors (none of the others are cyanotic, etc...), or (b) trivia (which is more likely).

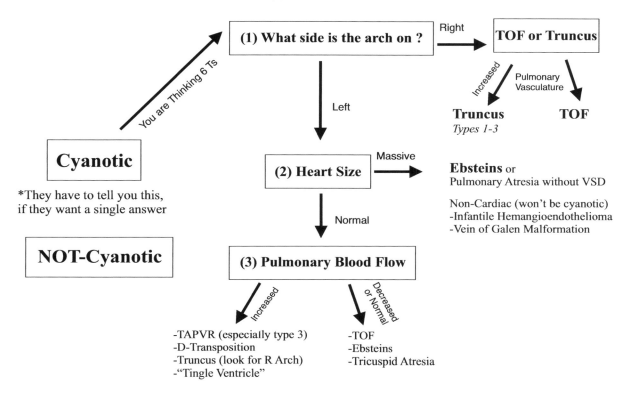

With regard to identifying bad distractors I think the easiest way is the cyanotic vs not cyanotic disorders. They literally must tell you the kid is cyanotic, otherwise there is no way to know.

Cyanotic	Not Cyanotic
TOF	ASD
TAPVR	VSD
Transposition	PDA
Truncus	PAPVR
Tricuspid Atresia	Aortic Coarctation (adult type – post ductal)

419

There are a few other key differentials that may make it easier to weed out bad distractors, or get "which of the following do NOT" questions.

CHF in Newborn	Survival dependent on admixture - Cyanotics	Small Heart DDx
TAPVR (Infracardiac type "III")	TAPVR (has PFO)	**Adrenal Insufficiency (Addisons)**
Congenital Aortic or Mitral Stenosis	Transposition	Cachectic State
Left Sided Hypoplastic Heart	TOF (has VSD)	Constrictive Pericarditis
Cor Triatriatum	Tricuspid Atresia (has VSD)	
Infantile (pre-ductal) Coarctation	Hypoplastic Left	

Trivia and Associations:

VSD: The **most common congenital heart disease.** There are several types with Membranous (*just below the aortic valve*) being the most common (70%). **Outlet subtypes (infundibulum) must be repaired** as the right coronary cusp prolapses into the defect. On CXR we are very nonspecific (big heart, increased vasculature, small aortic knob). They could ask or try and show **splaying of the carina** (from big left atrium). About 70% of the small ones close spontaneously.

PDA: The PDA normally closes around 24 hours after birth (functionally) , and anatomically around 1 month. A PDA should make you say three things (1) **Prematurity**, (2) **Maternal Rubella**, (3) **Cyanotic Heart Disease**. CXR is nonspecific (big heart, increased pulmonary vasculature, large aortic arch "ductus bump"). You can close it or keep it open with meds.

ASD: Several types with the Secundum being the most common (50-70%). The larger subtype is the Primum, (results from an endocardial cushion defect), is more likely to be symptomatic. Only Secundums may close without treatment (Primum, AV Canal, Sinus Venosus will not). Primums are not amendable to device closure because of proximity to AV valve tissue. On CXR, if it's small it will show nothing, if it's large it will be super nonspecific (big heart, increased vasculature, and small aortic knob). It's more common in female.

- When I say hand/thumb defects + ASD, you say Holt Oram
- When I say ostium primum ASD (or endocardial cushion defect), you say Downs
- When I say Sinus Venosus ASD, you say PAPVR

AV Canal: Also referred to as an endocardial cushion defect. They happen secondary to deficient development of a portion of the atrial septum, a portion of the inter-ventricular septum, and the AV valves. **Strong association with Downs**. You can't use closure devices on these dudes either. Surgical approach and management is complex and beyond the scope of this text.

Trivia: Of all the congenital heart stuff with Downs patients - AV Canal is the most common

Unroofed Coronary Sinus: This is a rare ASD which occurs secondary to a fenestrated (as in the cartoon) or totally unroofed coronary sinus. The most important clinical is that you can get paradoxical emboli and chronic right heart volume overload.

Trivia: STRONG association with a persistent left SVC.

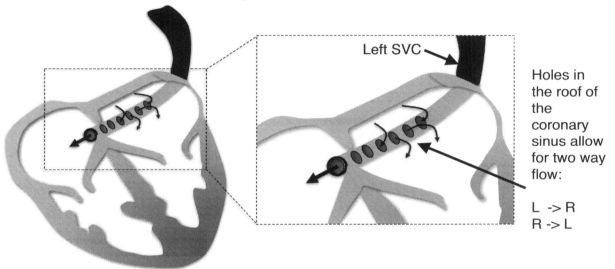

Left SVC

Holes in the roof of the coronary sinus allow for two way flow:

L -> R
R -> L

PAPVR: Partial anomalous pulmonary venous return, is defined as one (or more) of the four pulmonary veins draining into the right atrium. It is often of mild or no physiologic consequence. It is often **associated with ASDs (secondum and sinus venosus types)**.

* *When I say Right Sided PAPVR, you say Sinus Venosus ASD*

   o *RUL: SVC association with sinus venosus type ASD*

* *When I say Right Sided PAPVR + Pulmonary Hypoplasia, you say Scimitar Syndrome*

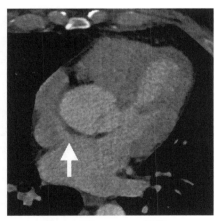

Sinus Venosus ASD

ASD Subtypes:

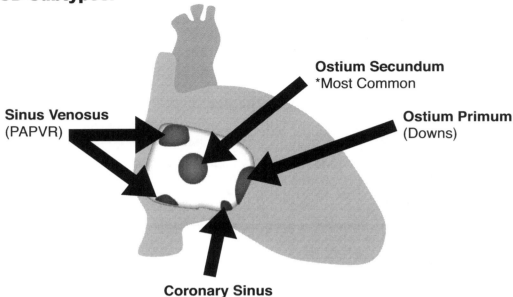

Sinus Venosus
(PAPVR)

Ostium Secundum
*Most Common

Ostium Primum
(Downs)

Coronary Sinus

TAPVR: A cyanotic heart disease characterized by all of the pulmonary venous system draining to the right side of the heart. A large PFO or less commonly ASD is required for survival (this is a high yield and testable point). There are 3 types, but only two are likely to be tested (cardiac type II just doesn't have good testable features). All 3 types will cause increased pulmonary vasculature, but type 3 is famous for a full on pulmonary edema look in the newborn.

- Type 1: Supracardiac:

    o Most Common Type

    o Veins drain above the heart, **gives a snowman appearance**.

- Type 2: Cardiac

    o Second Most Common Type

- Type 3: Infracardiac

    o Veins drain below the diaphragm (hepatic veins or IVC)

    o **Obstruction on the way through the diaphragm is common and causes a full on pulmonary edema look**

Key Points on TAPVR:

- Supracardiac Type = Snowman

- Infracardiac Type = Pulmonary Edema in Newborn

- Large PFO (or ASD) needed to survive

- Asplenia – 50% of asplenia patients have congenital heart disease. Of those nearly 100% have TAPVR, (85% have additional endocardial cushion defects).

422

Transposition: This is the most common cause of cyanosis during the first 24 hours. It is seen most commonly in infants of diabetic mothers. The basic idea is that the aorta arises from the right ventricle and the pulmonary trunk from the left ventricle (*ventriculararterial discordance*).

Which one is the Right Ventricle ? You have to find the moderator band (that defines the RV)

Just like TAPVR survival depends on an ASD, VSD, or PDA (*most commonly VSD*). There are two flavors: D & L. The D type only has a PDA connecting the two systems. Where as the L type is "Lucky" enough to be compatible with **Life.**

D-Transposition: Classic radiographic appearance is the "egg on a string". Occurs from discordance between the ventricles and the vessels. The intra-atrial baffle (Mustard or Senning procedure) is performed to fix them

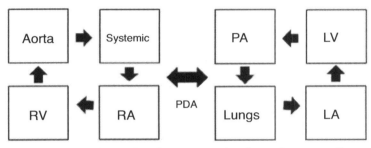

In D-Transposition, the ductus may be the only connection between the two systems, which would otherwise be separate (and not compatible with life)

L-Transposition: The L type is "Lucky" enough to be congenitally corrected. This occurs from a "double discordance" where the atrium hooks up with the wrong ventricle and the ventricle hooks up with the wrong vessel.

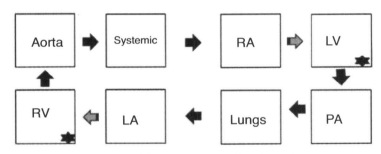

In L-Transposition of the great vessels - there is an inversion of the ventricles, leading to a "congenital correction." No PDA is needed.

A **corrected D-transposition** has a very characteristic appearance, lending itself to an Aunt Minnie-type question.

The PA is draped overtop the Aorta, which occurs after a surgeon has performed the *"LeCompte Maneuver"* -- sounds French so must be high yield.

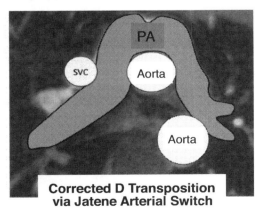

Corrected D Transposition via Jatene Arterial Switch

Tetralogy of Fallot (TOF): The *most common cyanotic heart disease*. Describes 4 major findings; (1) VSD, (2) RVOT Obstruction – often from valvular obstruction, (3) Overriding Aorta, (4) RV hypertrophy (develops after birth). The degree of severity in symptoms is related to how bad the RVOT obstruction is. If it's mild you might even have a "pink tet" that presents in early adulthood. This is called a pentalogy of Fallot if there is an ASD. Very likely to have a right arch.

Surgically it's usually fixed with primary repair. The various shunt procedures (Blalock-Taussig being the most famous) are only done if the kid is inoperable or to bridge until primary repair.

Trivia: The most common complication following surgery is pulmonary regurgitation.

Truncus Arteriosus: Cyanotic anomaly where there is a single trunk supplying both the pulmonary and systemic circulation, not a separate aorta and pulmonary trunk. It almost always has a VSD, and is closely associated with a right arch. **Associated with CATCH-22 genetics (DiGeorge Syndrome).**

—

Coarctation:

- There are two subtypes (as shown in the chart)

- Strong Association with **Turners Syndrome** (15-20%).

- **Bicuspid Aortic valve** is the most common associated defect (80%).

- They have more **berry aneurysms**.

- **Figure 3 sign** (appearance of CXR).

- **Rib Notching**: most often involves 4th - 8th ribs. It does NOT involve the 1st and 2nd because those are fed by the costocervical trunk.

THIS vs THAT: Coarctation of the Aortic (Narrowing the of the Aortic Lumen)	
Infantile	**Adult**
Presents with heart failure within the first week of life.	Leg Claudication BP differences between arms and legs.
Pre-Ductal (Before the left Subclavian A.)	Post-Ductal (Distal to left Subclavian A.)
Aortic Arch = Hypoplastic	Aortic Arch = Normal Diameter
	Collateral Formation is More Likely

—

Hypoplastic Left Heart: Left ventricle and aorta are hypoplastic. They present with pulmonary edema. **Must have an ASD** or large PFO. They also typically have a large PDA to put blood in their arch. Strongly associated with aortic coarctation and endocardial fibroelastosis.

Cor Triatriatum Sinistrum:

This is a very rare situation where you have an **abnormal pulmonary vein draining into the left atrium** (*sinistrum meaning left*) with an unnecessary fibromuscular membrane that causes a sub division of the left atrium. This **creates the appearance of a tri-atrium heart**. This can be a cause of unexplained pulmonary hypertension in the peds setting. Basically it acts like mitral stenosis, and can cause **pulmonary edema**. The outcomes are often bad (fatal within two years), depending on surgical intervention and associated badness.

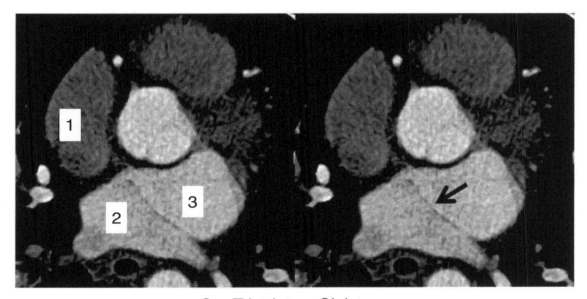

Cor Triatriatum Sinistrum

SECTION 6:
Ischemic Heart

Imaging regarding ischemic heart disease is going to fall into two modalities; cardiac MR, and Nuclear. Cardiac MRI currently offers the most complete evaluation of ischemic heart disease.

Myocardial infarction typically is initiated by rupture of an unstable coronary atherosclerotic plaque, leading to abrupt arterial occlusion. The **wave front of necrosis always starts subendocardial and progresses to the subepicardium.** The ischemic necrosis will affect not just the myocardium but also blood vessels. The destruction of small capillaries will not allow contrast to the area of injury. This is termed "microvascular obstruction" and manifests as islands of dark signal in an ocean of delayed enhancement. The presence of microvascular obstruction is an independent predictor of death and adverse LV remodeling.

Testable Vocab:

* *Stunned Myocardium:* After an Acute Injury (ischemia or reperfusion injury), dysfunction of myocardium persists even after restoration of blood flow (can last days to weeks). A perfusion study will be normal, but the contractility is crap.

* *Hibernating Myocardium:* This is a more chronic process, and the result of severe CAD causing chronic hypoperfusion. You will have areas of **decreased perfusion and decreased contractility** even when resting. Don't get it twisted, **this is not an infarct. On an FDG PET, this tissue will take up tracer more intensely than normal myocardium, and will also demonstrate redistribution of thallium**. This is reversible with revascularization.

* *Scar:* This is dead myocardium. It will not squeeze normally, so you'll have abnormal wall motion. It's <u>not a zombie</u>. It will NOT come back to life with revascularization.

Stunned	Hibernating	Infarct / Scar
Wall Motion Abnormal	Wall Motion Abnormal	Wall Motion Abnormal
Normal Perfusion (Thallium or Sestamibi)	Abnormal Fixed Perfusion	Abnormal Fixed Perfusion
	Will Redistribute with Delayed Thallium and will take up FDG	Will NOT Redistribute with Delayed Thallium, will NOT take up FDG
Associated with acute MI	Associated with chronic high grade CAD	Associated the chronic prior MI

Delayed imaging: It works for two reasons: (1) Increased volume of contrast material distribution in acute myocardial infarction (and inflammatory conditions) (2) Scarred myocardium washes out more slowly. It is **done using an inversion recovery technique** to null normal myocardium, followed by a gradient echo. T1 shortening from the Gd looks bright ("Bright is Dead").

Why stress imaging is done: Because coronary arteries can auto-regulate, a stenosis of 85% can be asymptomatic in a resting state. So demand is increased (by exercise or drugs) making a 45% stenosis significant. An inotropic stress agent (dobutamine) is used for wall motion, and a vasodilator (adenosine) is used for perfusion analysis.

Typical Sequence Pattern / Technique - with approximate times in minutes:

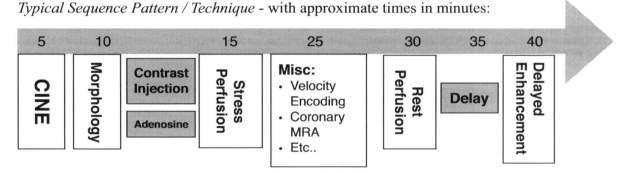

MRI in Acute MI: Cardiac MRI can be done in the first 24 hours post MI (if the patient is stable). Late gadolinium enhancement will reflect size and distribution of necrosis. Characteristic pattern is a **zone of enhancement that extends from the subendocardium toward the epicardium in a vascular distribution**. Microvascular obstruction will present as islands of dark signal in the enhanced tissue (as described above), and this represents an acute and subacute finding . **Microvascular obstruction is NOT seen in chronic disease** as these areas will all turn to scar eventually.

In the acute setting (1 week) injured myocardium will have increased T2 signal, which can be used to estimate the area at risk *(T2 Bright – Enhanced = Salvageable Tissue).*

THIS vs THAT: Acute vs Chronic MI:

- Both have delayed enhancement
- If the infarct was transmural and chronic you may have thinned myocardium
- Acute will have normal thickness (chronic can too but shouldn't for the purposes of MC tests.
- T2 signal from edema may be increased in the acute setting. Chronic is T2 Dark (scar)
- You won't see Microvascular Obstruction in Chronic

> *How do you diagnose Myocardial Infarction with Contrast Enhanced MR?*
>
> (1) Delayed Enhancement follows a vascular distribution,
>
> (2) The enhancement extends from the endocardium to the epicardium

Microvascular Obstruction: Islands of dark tissue in an ocean of late Gd enhancement. These indicate microvascular obliteration in the setting of an acute infarct. The Gd is unable to get to these regions even after the restoration of epicardial blood flow. Microvascular obstruction is a **poor prognostic finding**, associated with lack of functional recovery.

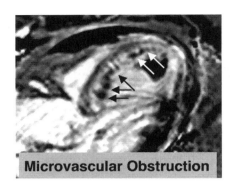

Microvascular Obstruction

Key Point: It's **NOT seen in chronic infarct.**

Trivia: Microvascular obstruction is best seen on first pass imaging (25 seconds)

Ventricular Aneurysm: This is rare (5%), but can occur as the result of MI. The question is always true vs false:

- *True:* Mouth is wider than body. Myocardium is intact. Usually anterior-lateral wall.

- *False:* Mouth is narrow compared to body. Myocardium is NOT intact (pericardial adhesions contain the rupture). Usually posterior-lateral wall. Higher risk of rupture.

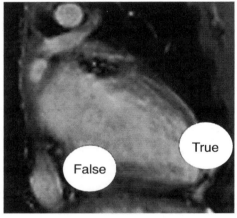

False Aneurysms are Usually Posterior Lateral
True Aneurysms are Usually Anterior Lateral

Viability - You can grade this based on % of transmural thickness involved in the infarct.

- <25%: likely to improve with PCI
- 25-50%: may improve
- 50-100%: unlikely to recover function

What is the timing on the bad sequelae of an MI?

Dressler Syndrome (effusion)	4-6 weeks
Papillary Muscle Rupture	2-7 Days
Ventricular Pseudoaneurysm	3-7 Days
Ventricular Aneurysm	Months – Requires remodeling and thinning.
Myocardial Rupture	Within 3 Days (50% of the time)

SECTION 7:
Non-Ischemic Heart

Dilated Cardiomyopathy: Defined as dilatation with an end diastolic diameter greater than 55mm, with a decreased EF. Can be idiopathic, ischemic, or from a whole list of other random crap (Alcohol, Doxorubicin, Cyclosporine, Chagas, etc…). The ischemic variety may show subendocardial enhancement. The **idiopathic variety will show** either no enhancement or **linear mid-myocardial enhancement**. There is often an association with mitral regurgitation due to dilation of the mitral ring.

Restrictive Cardiomyopathy: Basically anything that causes a decrease in diastolic function. Can be the result of myocardium replaced by fibrotic tissue (endocardial fibroelastosis), infiltration of the myocardium (Amyloidosis), or damage by iron (hemochromatosis). **The most common cause is actually amyloid.**

> • **Restrictive** = Myocardial Process
> • **Constrictive** = Pericardial Process

- *Amyloidosis:* Deposits in the myocardium causes abnormal diastolic function with biatrial enlargement, concentric thickening of the left ventricle and reduced systolic function of usually both ventricles. Seen in 50% of cases of systemic amyloid. Has a terrible prognosis. You can sometimes see late Gd enhancement over the entire subendocardial circumference.

    Amyloid Classic Scenario: A **long TI is needed** (like 350 milliseconds, normal would be like 200). TI will be so long that the blood pool may be darker than the myocardium. **Buzzword "difficult to suppress myocardium".**

- *Eosinophilic Cardiomyopathy (Loeffler):* **Bilateral Ventricular thrombus** is the classic phrase / buzzword. You will need a long TI to show the thrombus.

Constrictive Pericarditis: Historically this used to be TB or Viral. Now the most common cause is iatrogenic secondary to CABG or radiation. On CT the pericardium is too thick (> 0.4 cm), and if it's calcified that is diagnostic. Calcification is usually largest over the AV groove. "Sigmoidization" is seen on SSFP cine imaging: The ventricular septum moves toward the left ventricle in a wavy pattern during early diastole (**"Diastolic Bounce"**). This "bounce" will be most pronounced during inspiration - indicating ventricular interdependence.

THIS vs THAT: Constrictive vs Restrictive Cardiomyopathy:

- Pericardium is usually thickened in constrictive
- Diastolic septal bounce is seen in constrictive (Sigmoidization of the septum).

Myocarditis: Inflammation of the heart can come from lots of causes (*often viral i.e. Coxsackie virus*). The late Gd enhancement follows a non-vascular distribution preferring the **lateral free wall.** The **pattern will be epicardial or mid wall (NOT subendocardial).**

Myocarditis
-Mid Wall Late Gd Enhancement

Sarcoidosis: Cardiac involvement is seen in 5% of Sarcoidosis cases, and is associated with an increased risk of death. Signal in both T2 and early Gd (as well as late Gd) will be increased. Late Gd pattern may be middle and epicardial in a non-coronary distribution. **Focal wall thickening from edema can mimic hypertrophic cardiomyopathy. It often involves the septum.** The RV and papillaries are RARELY affected.

Takotsubo Cardiomyopathy – A takotsubo is a Japanese Octopus trap, which looks like a pot with a narrow mouth and large round base. The octopus will go into the pot, but then can't turn around and get out (sorta like medical school). A condition with Chest pain and EKG changes seen in post menopausal women after they either break up with their boyfriend , win the lottery, or some other stressful event has been described with the shape of the ventricle looking like a takotsubo. There is **transient akinesia or dyskinesia of the left ventricular apex without coronary stenosis. Ballooning of the left ventricular apex is a buzzword.** No delayed enhancement.

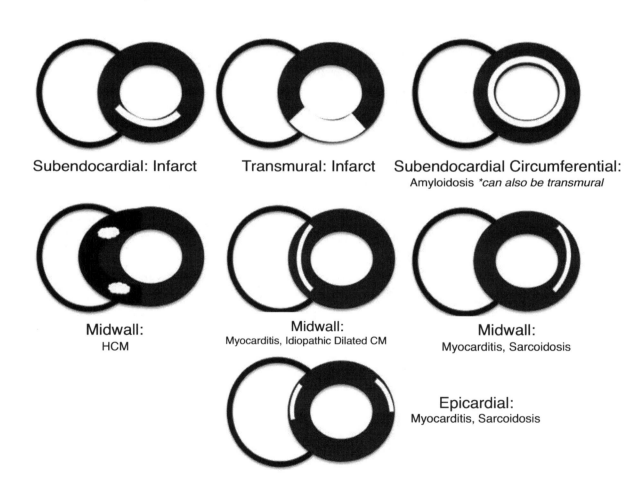

Subendocardial: Infarct   Transmural: Infarct   Subendocardial Circumferential:
Amyloidosis *can also be transmural*

Midwall:
HCM

Midwall:
Myocarditis, Idiopathic Dilated CM

Midwall:
Myocarditis, Sarcoidosis

Epicardial:
Myocarditis, Sarcoidosis

SECTION 8:
Genetics

(ARVC): Characterized by fibrofatty degeneration of the RV leading to arrhythmia and sudden death. Features include dilated RV with reduced function and **fibrofatty replacement of the myocardium**, and normal LV. People use this major/minor criteria system that includes a bunch of EKG changes that no radiologist could possibly understand (if they are stupid enough to ask just say left bundle branch block). Watch out for the use of fat sat to demonstrate the fat in the RV wall.

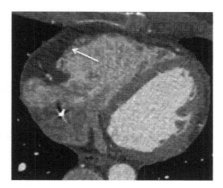

ARVC - Dilated RV, with Fat in the Wall

Hypertrophic Cardiomyopathy: Abnormal hypertrophy (from disarray of myofibrils) of the myocardium that compromises diastole. There are multiple types but the one they are going to show is asymmetric hypertrophy of the intraventricular septum. The condition is a cause of sudden death. There is a subgroup which is associated with LVOT obstruction ("hypertrophic obstructive cardiomyopathy"). Venturi forces may pull the anterior leaflet of the mitral valve into the LVOT (**SAM** – Systolic Anterior Motion of the Mitral Valve). Patchy midwall **delayed enhancement of the hypertrophied muscle** may be seen, as **is an independent risk factor for sudden death.**

Noncompaction:

Left ventricular noncompaction is an uncommon congenital cardiomyopathy that is the result of loosely packed myocardium. The left ventricle has a spongy appearance with increased trabeculations and deep intertrabecular recesses.

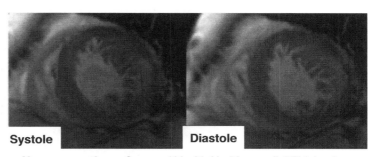

Systole   Diastole

Noncompaction - *Spongy LV with No Myocardial Thickening*

As you might expect, these guys get heart failure at a young age. Diagnosis is based of a ratio of non compacted end-diastolic myocardium to compacted end-diastolic myocardium of more than 2.3:1.

Muscular Dystrophy: Becker (mild one) and Duchenne (severe one) are X-linked neuromuscular conditions. They have biventricular replacement of myocardium with connective tissue and fat (delayed Gd enhancement in the midwall). They often have dilated cardiomyopathy. Just think **kid with dilated heart and midwall enhancement**.

SECTION 9:
Tumors

Mets: Thirty times more common than a primary malignancy. The **pericardium is the most common site** affected (by far). The most common manifestation is a pericardial effusion (second most common is a pericardial lymph node). Melanoma may involve the myocardium.

Trivia: Most common met to the heart is lung cancer (pericardium and epicardium)

Angiosarcoma: Most common primary malignant tumor of the heart in adults. They like the RA and tend to involve the pericardium. They often cause right sided failure and/or tamponade. They are bulky and heterogenous. Buzzword is "sun-ray" appearance which describes enhancement appearance of the diffuse subtype as it grows along the perivascular spaces associated with the epicardial vessels.

Left Atrial Myxoma: Most common primary cardiac tumor in adults (rare in children). They are associated with MEN syndromes, and Blue Nevi (Carney Complex). They are most often **attached to the interatrial septum.** They may be calcified. They may prolapse through the mitral valve. They **will enhance with Gd** (important discriminator from a thrombus).

THIS vs THAT:
Tumor vs Thrombus:

Cardiac MRI is the way to tell.
- Tumor will enhance
- Thrombus will NOT enhance.

Rhabdomyoma: Most common fetal cardiac tumor. It is a hamartoma. They prefer the **left ventricle**. Associated with **tuberous sclerosis**. Most tumors will regress spontaneously (those NOT associated with TS are actually less likely to regress).

Fibroma: Second most common cardiac tumor in childhood. They like the IV septum, and are dark / dark on T1/T2. They enhance very brightly on perfusion and late Gd.

Fibroelastoma: Most common neoplasm to involve the **cardiac valves** (80% aortic or mitral). They are highly mobile on SSFP Cine. Systemic emboli are common (especially if they are on the left side).

Cardiac Tumors / Mimics

Myxoma	Fibroelastoma	Rhabdomyoma	Angiosarcoma	Metastatic Disease	Thrombus
Most common primary cardiac tumor (adult)	2nd most common primary cardiac tumor (adult)	Most common primary cardiac tumor (**infants**)	The most common primary **MALIGNANT** tumor	Much more common than Primary tumors	Most common intra-cardiac "mass"
Adult (30-60) with **distal emboli** and **fainting spells**. Younger people are likely syndromic (Carney Complex)	Adult (50-60) - usually an incidental finding. If they are symptomatic its from emboli (stroke / TIA)	Infant with **tuberous sclerosis**		Lung cancer is the most common. Melanoma goes to the heart with the greatest percentage *(but prevalence is less than lung)*	
Arise from the intra-atrial septum, usually growing into the **left atrium**	Involves the **cardiac valves** - aortic is most common — usually the aortic side of the aortic cusp.	Favor the **ventricular myocardium**	Favors the **right atrium**	Favors the **pericardium**	Favors the **left atrial appendage** (A-Fib), Left Ventricular Apex (post MI)
About 1/4 have calcification	Most are small - less than 1cm.	They tend to be multiple	Pericardial thickening = invasion		
"Ball with stalk attached to the inter-atrial septum" Dynamic imaging will show mobility / prolapse of the "ball".	*Discriminator:* **Vegetations tend to involve the valve free edges. Fibroelastoma does NOT do that.**	*Discriminator:* Fibroma is T2 dark **Rhabdomyoma is T2 Bright** *Fibroma is the 2nd most common tumor in this age group	Large heterogenous mass	Pericardial nodularity and effusion	*Discriminator:* **Thrombus won't enhance.** Tumors will.

433

SECTION 10:
Pericardium

The pericardium is composed of two layers (visceral and parietal), with about 50cc of fluid normally between the layers.

Pericardial Effusion:

Basically more than 50cc between the pericardial layers. This can be from lots and lots of causes – renal failure (uremia) is probably the most common. For the purpose of multiple choice tests you should think about Lupus, and Dressler Syndrome (inflammatory effusion post MI).

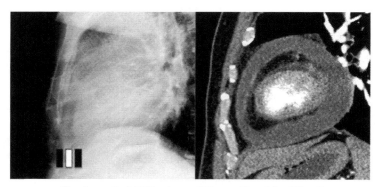

Pericardial Effusion: *"Oreo Cookie Sign"*

On CXR they could show this 3 ways: (1) Normal Heart on Comparison, Now Really Big Heart (2) Giant Water Bottle Heart, (3) Lateral CXR with two lucent lines (epicardial and pericardial fat) and a central opaque line (pericardial fluid) – the so called **"oreo cookie sign."**

Cardiac Tamponade: Pericardial effusion can cause elevated pressure in the pericardium and result in compromised filling of the cardiac chambers (atria first, then ventricles). This can occur with as little as 100cc of fluid, as the **rate of accumulation is the key factor** (chronic slow filling gives the pericardium a chance to stretch). The question is likely related to **short-axis imaging during deep inspiration showing flattening or inversion of the intraventricular septum toward the LV**, a consequence of augmented RV filing. Another indirect sign that can be shown on CT is reflux of contrast into the IVC and azygos system.

Pericardial Cysts: Totally benign incidental finding. Usually seen on the right cardiophrenic sulcus. They do not communicate with the pericardium. Rarely they can get infected or hemorrhage. **They will show you an ROI measuring water density along the right cardiophrenic sulcus, and this will be the answer**.

Congenital / Acquired Absence: Even though you can have total absence of the pericardium - the most common situation is **partial absence of the pericardium over the left atrium and adjacent pulmonary artery**. When the left pericardium is absent the heart shifts towards the left. They could show you a CT or MRI with the heart contacting the left chest wall, and want you to infer partial absence. Another piece of trivia is that cardiac herniation and volvulus can occur in patients who undergo extrapleural pneumonectomy (herniation can only occur if the lung has also been removed).

Trivia: The left atrial appendage is the most at risk to become strangulated.

SECTION 11:
Surgeries

Palliative Surgery for the Hypoplastic Left Heart: Surgery for Hypoplasts is not curative, and is instead designed to extend the life (prolong the suffering) of the child. It is done in a 3 stage process, to protect the lungs and avoid right heart overload:

(1) Norwood or Sano – within days of birth

(2) Glenn – at 3- 6 months

(3) Fontan at 1 ½ to 5 years

(1a) Norwood: The goal of the surgery is to create an unobstructed outflow tract from the systemic ventricle. So the tiny native aorta is anastomosed to the pulmonary trunk, and the arch is augmentented with a graft (or by other methods). The ASD is enlarged to create non restrictive atrial flow. A Blalock-Taussig Shunt (see below) is used between the right Subclavian and right PA. The ductus is removed as well to prevent over shunting to the lungs. Apparently, when this goes bad it's usually from issues related to damage of the coronary arteries or **over shunting of blood to the lungs (causing pulmonary edema)**. As a point of trivia, sometimes the thymus is partially removed to get access.

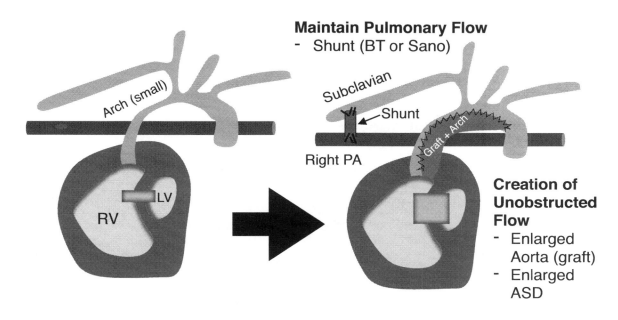

Maintain Pulmonary Flow
- Shunt (BT or Sano)

Creation of Unobstructed Flow
- Enlarged Aorta (graft)
- Enlarged ASD

435

(1b) Sano: Same as the Norwood, but instead of using a Blalock-Taussig shunt a conduit is made connecting the right ventricle to the pulmonary artery. The disadvantage of the BT Shunt is that it undergoes a steal phenomenon (diverted to low pressure pulmonary system).

(2a) Classic Glenn: Shunt between the SVC and right pulmonary artery (end-to-end), with the additional step of sewing the proximal end of the Right PA closed with the goal of reducing right ventricular work, by diverting all venous return straight to the lung (right lung).

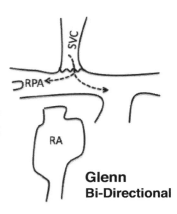

Glenn Bi-Directional

(2b) Bi-Directional Glenn: Shunt between the SVC and the right pulmonary artery (**end-to-side**). The RPA is left open, letting blood flow to both lungs. This procedure can be used to address right sided heart problems in general, and is also step two in the palliative hypoplastic series. If it's being used as step two the previously placed Blalock-Taussig Shunt or Sano shunt will come down as the Glenn will be doing its job of putting blood in the lungs.

(3) Fontan Operation: Used for Hypoplastic Hearts. The old school Fontan consisted of a classic Glenn (SVC to RPA), closure of the ASD, and then placing a shunt between the Right atrium to the Left PA. The idea is to let blood return from systemic circulation to the lungs by passive flow (no pump), and turn the right ventricle (the only one the kid has) into a functional left ventricle. There are numerous complications including right atriomegaly with resulting arrhythmias, and plastic bronchitis (they cough up "casts of the bronchus" that look like plastic).

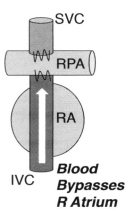

Blood Bypasses R Atrium

Other Surgeries:

Classic Blalock-Taussig Shunt: Originally developed for use with TOF. **Shunt is created between the Subclavian artery and the pulmonary artery**. It is constructed on the **opposite side** of the arch. It's apparently technically difficult and often distorts the anatomy of the pulmonary artery.

High Yield Point:
Glenn = Vein to Artery *(SVC to Pulmonary Artery)*
Blalock-Taussig = Artery to Artery *(Subclavian Artery to Pulmonary Artery)*

Modified Blalock-Taussig Shunt: This is a gortex shunt between the Subclavian artery and pulmonary artery, and is performed on the **SAME SIDE as the arch**. It's easier to do than the original.

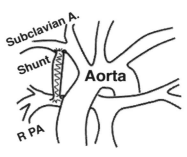

BT- Shunt

Pulmonary Artery Banding: Done to reduce pulmonary artery pressure (goal is 1/3 of systemic pressure). Most common indication is CHF in infancy with anticipated delayed repair. The **single ventricle is the most common lesion requiring banding**.

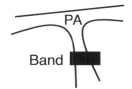

Atrial Switch: Mustard and Senning procedures are used to correct transposition of the great arteries by creating a baffle within the atria in order to switch back the blood flow at the level of inflow. The result is the right ventricle becomes the systemic ventricle, and the left ventricle pumps to the lungs. This is usually done in the first year of life.

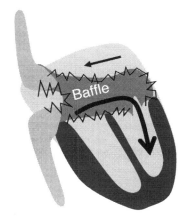

- **Senning:** Baffle is created from the right atrial wall and atrial septal tissue WITHOUT use of extrinsic material

- **Mustard:** Involves the resection of the atrial septum and creation of a baffle using pericardium (or synthetic material).

Rastelli Operation: This is the most commonly used operation for transposition, pulmonary outflow obstruction, and VSD. The procedure involves the placement of a baffle within the right ventricle diverting flow from the VSD to the aorta (essentially using the VSD as part of the LVOT). The pulmonary valve is oversewn and the conduit is inserted between the RV and the PA. The primary advantage of this procedure is the left ventricle becomes the systemic ventricle. The primary limitation of this procedure is that the child will be committed to multiple additional surgeries because the conduit wears out and must be replaced.

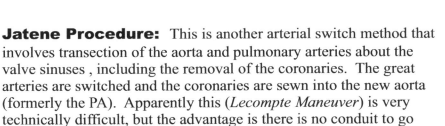

Jatene Procedure: This is another arterial switch method that involves transection of the aorta and pulmonary arteries about the valve sinuses , including the removal of the coronaries. The great arteries are switched and the coronaries are sewn into the new aorta (formerly the PA). Apparently this (*Lecompte Maneuver*) is very technically difficult, but the advantage is there is no conduit to go bad, and the LV is the systemic ventricle.

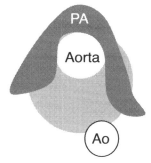

Ross Procedure: Performed for Diseased Aortic Valves in Children. Replaces the aortic valve with the patient's pulmonary valve and replaces the pulmonary valve with a cryopreserved pulmonary valve homograft. Follow-up studies have shown interval growth of the aortic valve graft in children and infants.

Bentall Procedure:

Operation involving composite graft replacement of the aortic valve, aortic root and ascending aorta, with re-implantation of the coronary arteries into the graft. This operation is used to treat combined aortic valve and ascending aorta disease, including lesions associated with Marfan syndrome.

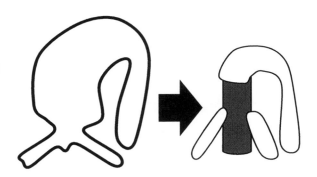

Summary - Most Common Surgery / Key Points

Glenn	Blalock Taussig	Fontan
Vein to Artery *(SVC to Pulmonary Artery)*	Artery to Artery *(Subclavian Artery to Pulmonary Artery)*	*It's complicated with multiple versions - steps are unlikely to be tested*
Primary Purpose: Take systemic blood directly to the pulmonary circulation (it bypasses the right heart).	Primary Purpose: Increase pulmonary blood flow	Primary Purpose: Bypass the right ventricle / direct systemic circulation into the PAs.
Most Testable Complications: -SVC Syndrome **-PA Aneurysms**	Most Testable Complications: -Stenosis at the shunt's pulmonary insertion site	Most Testable Complications: -Enlarged Right Artium causing arrhythmia **-Plastic Bronchitis**

THIS vs THAT: Heart Transplant Types

Orthotopic Heart Transplant: All of the heart is removed, except the circular part of the left atrium (the part with the pulmonary veins). The donor heart is trimmed to fit to the left atrium.

Heterotopic Heart Transplant: The recipient heart remains in place, and the donor heart is added on top. This basically creates a double heart. The advantages of this are (1) it gives the native heart a chance to recover , and (2) gives you a backup if the donor is rejected.

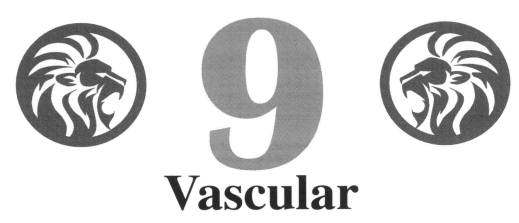

9
Vascular

PROMETHEUS LIONHART, M.D.

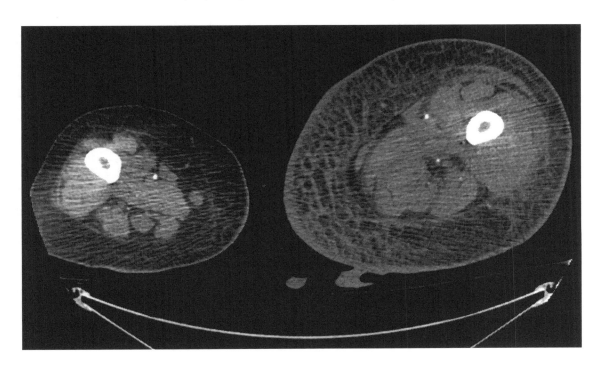

SECTION 1:
Anatomy

Aorta: The thoracic aorta is divided anatomically into four regions; the root, the ascending aorta, the transverse aorta (arch), and the descending aorta. The "root" is defined as the portion of the aorta extending from the aortic valve annulus to the sino-tubular junction. The diameter of the thoracic aorta is largest at the aortic root and gradually decreases *(average size is 3.6 cm at the root, 2.4 cm in the distal descending).*

- *Sinuses of Valsalva:* There are 3 outpouchings (right, left, posterior) above the annulus that terminate at the ST Junction. The right and left coronaries come off the right and left sinuses. The posterior cusp is sometimes called the "non-coronary cusp."

- *Isthmus:* The segment of the aorta between the origin of the left Subclavian and the ligamentum arteriosum.

- *Ductus bump:* Just distal to the isthmus is a contour bulge along the lesser curvature, which is a normal structure (not a pseudoaneurysm).

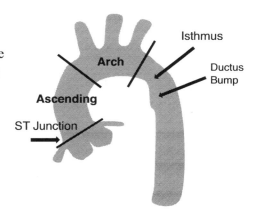

Aortic Arch Variants: There are 4 common variations: Normal (75%), Bovine Arch (15%) – common origin of brachiocephalic artery and left common carotid artery, left common carotid coming off the brachiocephalic proper (10%), and in 5% of people the left vertebral artery originates separately from the arch. Branching with regards to right arch, left arch and double arch was discussed in more detail in the cardiac chapter.

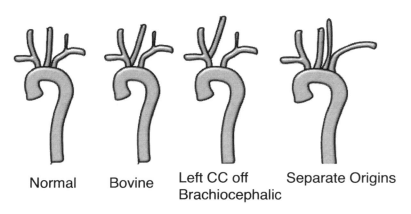

Adamkiewicz:

The thoracic aorta puts off multiple important feeders including the great anterior medullary artery (Artery of Adamkiewicz) which serves as a dominate feeder of the spinal cord.

This thing usually comes off on the **left side (70%) between T9-T12.**

"Beware of the Hairpin Turn"
-The classic angiographic appearance of the artery is the "hairpin turn" as its anastomosis with the anterior spinal artery.

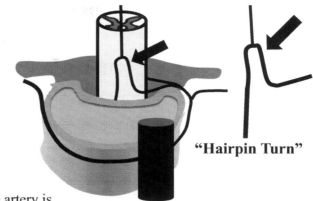

"Hairpin Turn"

Mesenteric Branches:

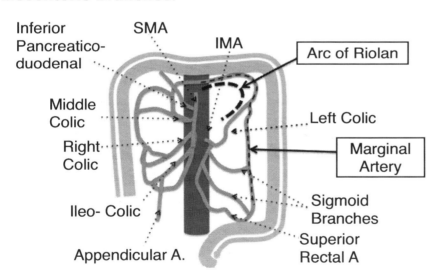

The anatomy of the SMA and IMA is high yield, and can be shown on a MIP coronal CT, or Angiogram. I think that knowing the inferior pancreaticoduodenal comes off the SMA first, and that the left colic (from IMA) to the middle colic (from SMA) make up the Arc of Riolan are probably the highest yield facts.

Celiac Branches:

The classic branches of the celiac axis are the common hepatic, left gastric, and the splenic arteries.

The "common" hepatic artery becomes the "proper" hepatic artery after the GDA.

This "traditional anatomy" is actually only seen in 55% of people.

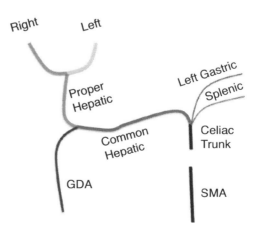

Celiac Anatomy - Remember this can be shown with an angiogram, CTA, or MRA.

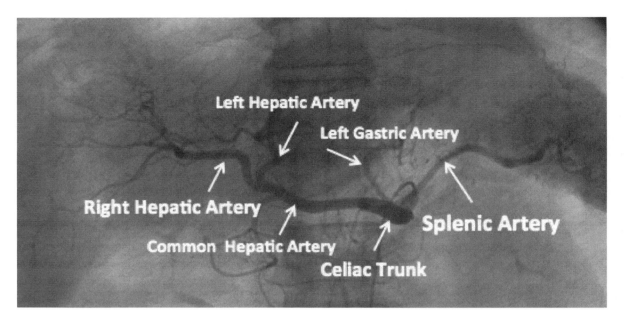

Variant Hepatic Artery Anatomy – The right hepatic artery and left hepatic arteries may be "replaced" (originate from a vessel other than the proper hepatic) or duplicated - which anatomist called "accessory." This distinction of "replaced" vs "accessory" would make a great multiple choice question.

Trivia to know:

- Replaced = Different Origin, usually off the left gastric or SMA

- Accessory = Duplication of the Vessel, with the spare coming off the left gastric or SMA

- If you see a **vessel in the fissure of the ligamentum venosum** (where there is not normally a vessel), it's probably an accessory or **replaced left hepatic artery arising from the left gastric artery**.

- **The proper right hepatic artery is anterior to the right portal vein, whereas the replaced right hepatic artery is posterior to the main portal vein**. This positioning of the replaced right increases the risk of injury in pancreatic surgeries.

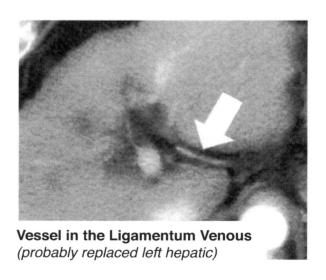

Vessel in the Ligamentum Venous
(probably replaced left hepatic)

Iliac Anatomy: The branches of the internal iliac are high yield, with the most likely question being "which branches are from the posterior or anterior divisions?" A *useful mnemonic is "I Love Sex," Illiolumbar, Lateral Sacral, Superior Gluteal, for the posterior division.*

My trick for remembering that the mnemonic is for posterior and not anterior is to think of that super religious girl I knew in college — *I Like Sex in the butt / posterior*.

I don't think they will actually show a picture, it's way more likely to be a written question.

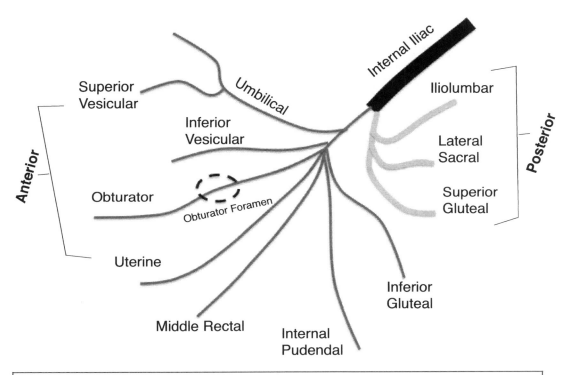

Anterior Division	Posterior Division
Umbilical	Iliolumbar
Superior Vesicular (off umbilical)	Lateral Sacral
Inferior Vesicular	Superior Gluteal
Uterine (if you have a uterus)	*Inferior Gluteal *** sometimes*
Middle Rectal	
Internal Pudendal	
Inferior Gluteal	
Obturator	

Trivia: The ovarian arteries arise from the anterior-medial aorta 80-90% of time.

Persistent Sciatic Artery – An anatomic variant, which is a **continuation of the internal iliac**. It passes posterior to the femur in the thigh and then will anastomose with the distal vasculature. Complications worth knowing include aneurysm formation and early atherosclerosis in the vessel. The classic vascular surgery boards question is "external iliac is acutely occluded, but there is still a strong pulse in the foot", the answer is the patient has a persistent sciatic.

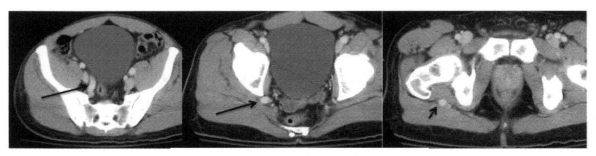

Persistent Sciatic Artery

Mesenteric Arterial Collateral Pathways:

Celiac to SMA: The conventional collateral pathway is Celiac -> Common Hepatic -> GDA -> Superior Pancreatic Duodenal -> Inferior Pancreatic Duodenal -> SMA.

Arc of Buhler: This is a variant anatomy (seen in like 4% of people), that represents a collateral pathway from the celiac to the SMA. The arch is independent of the GDA and inferior pancreatic arteries. This rare collateral can have an even more rare aneurysm, which occurs in association with stenosis of the celiac axis.

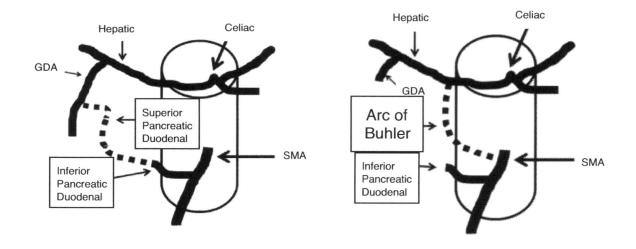

SMA to IMA: The conventional collateral pathway is SMA -> Middle Colic -> Left Branch of the Middle Colic -> Arc of Riolan (as below) -> Left Colic - > IMA.

Arc of Riolan – Also referred to as the meandering mesenteric artery. Classically a **connection between the middle colic of the SMA and the left colic of the IMA.**

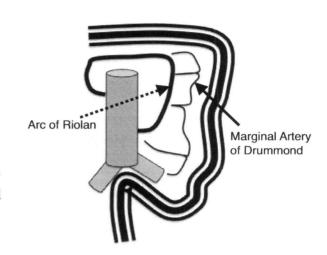

Marginal Artery of Drummond – This is another **SMA to IMA connection.** The anastomosis of the terminal branches of the ileocolic, right colic and middle colic arteries of the SMA, and of the left colic and sigmoid branches of the IMA, form a **continuous arterial circle or arcade along the inner border of the colon.**

IMA to Iliacs: The conventional collateral pathway is IMA -> Superior Rectal -> Inferior Rectal -> Internal Pudendal -> Anterior branch of internal iliac.

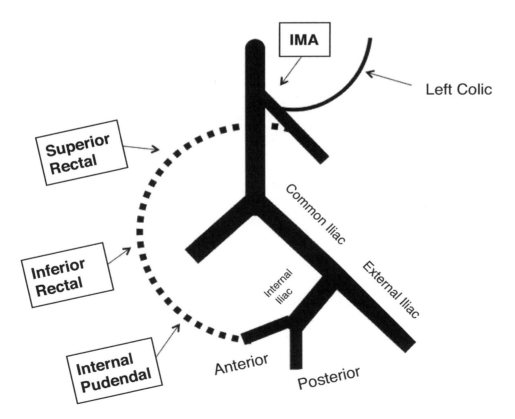

Winslow Pathway – This is a collateral pathway that is seen in the setting of aorto-iliac occlusive disease. The pathway apparently can be inadvertently cut during transverse abdominal surgery. The pathway runs from subclavian arteries -> internal thoracic (mammary) arteries -> superior epigastric arteries -> inferior epigastric arteries -> external iliac arteries.

Corona Mortis – Classically described as a vascular connection between the **obturator and external iliac.** Some authors describe additional anastomotic pathways, but you should basically think of it as any vessel **coursing over the superior pubic rim**, regardless of the anastomotic connection. The "crown of death" is significant because it can (a) be **injured in pelvic trauma** or (b) be **injured during surgery – and is notoriously difficult to ligate.** Some authors report that it causes 6-8% of deaths in pelvic trauma. The last piece of trivia is that it could hypothetically cause a type 2 endoleak.

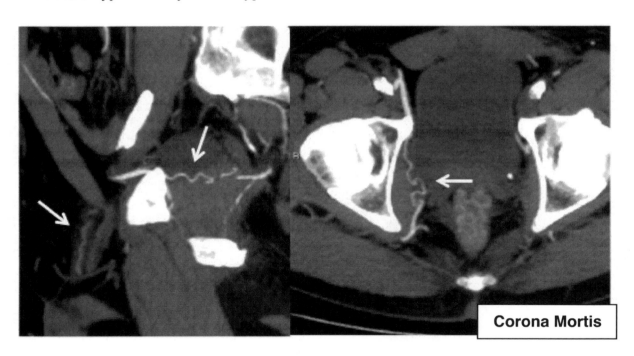

Corona Mortis

Upper Extremity Anatomy:

The scalene muscles make a triangle in the neck. If you have ever had the pleasure of reading a brachial plexus MRI finding this anatomy in a sagittal plane is the best place to start (in my opinion). The relationship to notice (because it's testable) is that the subclavian vein runs anterior to the triangle, and the subclavian artery runs in the triangle (with the brachial plexus).

Trivia to Remember: The subclavian artery runs posterior to the subclavian vein.

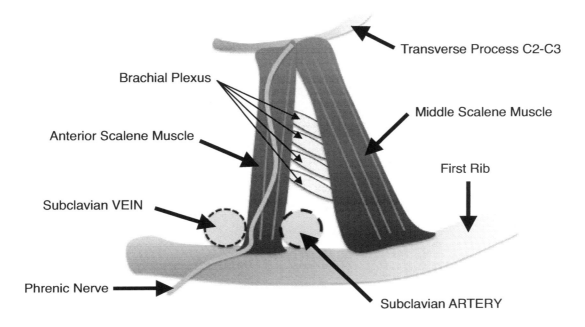

The subclavian artery has several major branches: the vertebral , the internal thoracic, the thyrocervical trunk, the costocervical trunk, and the dorsal scapular.

As the subclavian artery progresses down the arm, anatomists decided to change it's name a few times. This name changing makes for great multiple choice fodder.

The highest yield thing you can know with regard to upper extremity vascular anatomy is when stuff becomes stuff:

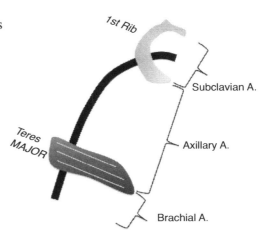

- **Axillary Artery:** Begins at the first rib
- **Brachial Artery:** Begins at the lower border of the teres <u>major</u> (major NOT minor!)
- **Brachial Artery:** Bifurcates to the ulnar and radial

Upper Extremity Normal Variants:

- Anterior Interosseous Branch (Median Artery) persists and supplies the deep palmar arch of the hand.

- **"High Origin of the Radial Artery"** – Radial artery comes off either the axillary or high brachial artery (remember it normally comes off at the level of the radial head).

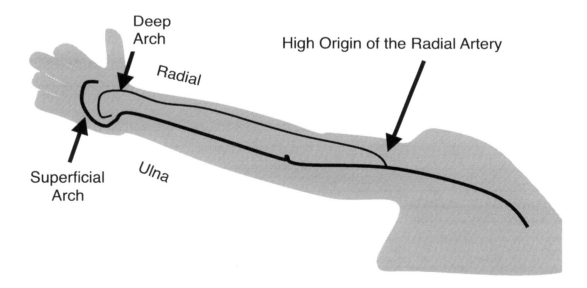

Lower Extremity Anatomy:

Every medical student knows the aorta bifurcates into the right and left common iliac arteries, which subsequently bifurcate into the external and internal iliac arteries. The nomenclature pearl for **the external iliac is that it becomes the common femoral once it gives off the inferior epigastric** *(at the inguinal ligament).*

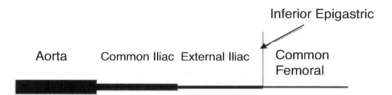

Once the inferior epigastric comes off (level of the inguinal ligament) you are dealing with the common femoral artery(CFA). The CFA divides into the deep femoral (profunda) and superficial femoral. The deep femoral courses lateral and posterior. The superficial femoral passes anterior and medial into the flexor muscle compartment (ADDuctor / Hunter's Canal). At the point the vessel emerges from the canal it is then the popliteal artery. At the level of the distal border of the popliteus muscle the popliteal artery divides into the **anterior tibialis (the first branch)** and the tibioperoneal trunk. The anterior tibialis courses anterior and lateral, then it <u>transverses the interosseous membrane</u>, running down the front of the anterior tibia and terminating as the dorsalis pedis. The tibioperoneal trunk bifurcates into the posterior tibialis and fibular (peroneal) arteries. A common quiz is "what is the most medial artery in the leg?" , with the answer being the posterior tibial (felt at the medial malleolus). Notice how lateral the AT is - you can imagine it running across the interosseous membrane, just like it's suppose to.

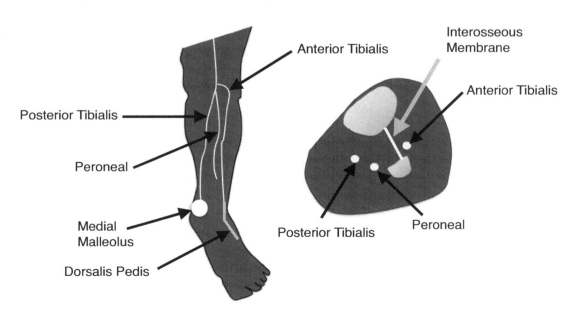

Mesenteric Venous Collaterals:

Gastric Varices: As described in more detail in the GI chapter, portal hypertension shunts blood away from the liver and into the systemic venous system. Spontaneous portal-systemic collaterals develop to decompress the system. The thing to know is that **most gastric varices are formed by the left gastric (coronary vein)** . That is the one they always show big and dilated on an angiogram. Isolated gastric varices are secondary to splenic vein thrombosis. Gastric Varices (80-85%) drain into the inferior phrenic and then into the left renal vein, forming a gastro-renal shunt.

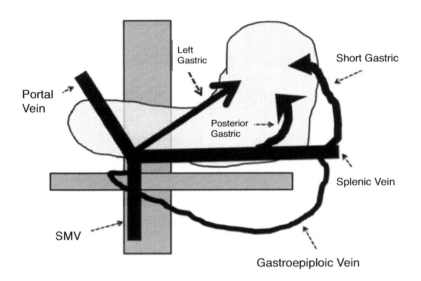

Splenorenal Shunt: Another feature of portal hypertension, this is an abnormal collateral between the splenic vein and renal vein. This is actually a desirable shunt because it is **not associated with GI bleeding**. However, **enlarged shunts are associated with hepatic encephalopathy** (discussed in greater detail in the BRTO section of the IR chapter). A common way to show this is an enlarged left renal vein and dilatation of the inferior vena cava at the level of the left renal vein.

Caval Variants

Left Sided SVC – The most common congenital venous anomaly in the chest. In a few rare cases these can actually result in a right to left shunt. They are only seen in isolation in 10% of cases (the other 90% it's "duplicated"). The location and appearance is a total **Aunt Minnie**.

Trivia to know:

• Most commonly associated CHD is the ASD

• Associated with an unroofed coronary sinus

• <u>Nearly always (92% of the time) it drains into the coronary sinus</u>

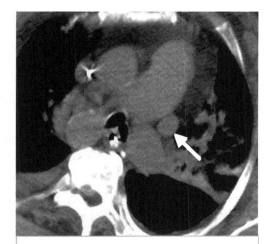

Left Sided SVC - *When you see that son of a bitch right there, that thing can only be one of two things - a lymph node or a duplicated SVC.*

Duplicated SVC – The above discussed "Left Sided SVC" almost never occurs in isolation. Instead, there is almost always a "normal" right sided SVC, in addition to the left sided SVC. It is in this case (which is the majority of cases of left sided SVC) that the terminology "duplicated SVC" is used. It is so common that people will use the terms duplicated and left sided interchangeably. But, technically to be duplicated you need a right sided and left sided SVC (even if the right one is a little small - which is often the case in the setting of a left SVC).

Duplicated IVC - There are two main points worth knowing about this: (1) that the appearance is an **Aunt Minnie**, and (2) it's **associated with Renal stuff**. Renal associations include horseshoe and crossed fused ectopic kidneys.

Also these dudes often have circumaortic renal collars (see below).

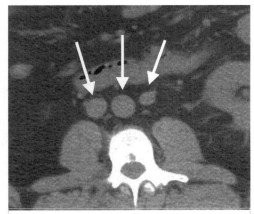

Duplicated IVC *(IVCs are the bread, Aorta is the cheese or peanut butter… or bacon)*

Circumaortic Venous Collar – Very common variant with an additional left renal vein that passes posterior to the aorta. It only matters in two situations (a) renal transplant, (b) IVC filter placement. The classic question is that the **anterior limb is superior**, and the posterior limb is inferior.

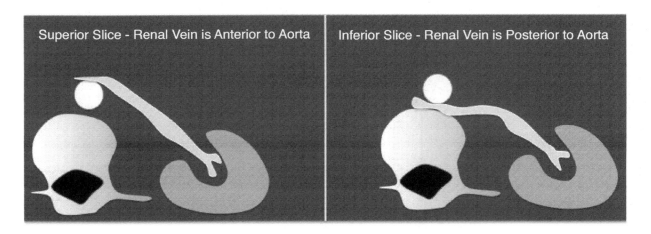

Azygos Continuation – This is also known as absence of the hepatic segment of the IVC. In this case, the hepatic veins drain directly into the right atrium. Often the IVC is duplicated in these patients, with the left IVC terminating in the left renal vein , which then crosses over to join the right IVC.

The first thing you should think when I say azygous continuation is **polysplenia** (reversed IVC/Aorta is more commonly associated with asplenia).

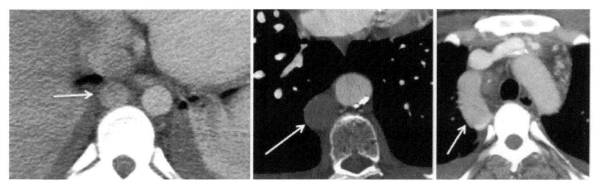

Azygos Continuation - *No IVC in the Liver, Dilated Azygos in the Chest*

SECTION 2:
Acute Aortic Syndromes

There are 3 "acute aortic syndromes" , aortic dissection, intramural hematoma, and penetrating ulcer. Lets take these one at a time and talk about the trivia.

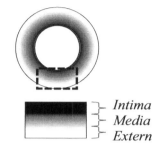

Intima
Media
Externa

Anatomy Review:

Remember vessels have 3 layers: Intima, Media, and that other one no one gives a shit about.

Penetrating Ulcer:

This is an ulceration of an atheromatous plaque that has eroded the inner elastic layer of the aortic wall. When it reaches the media it produces a hematoma within the media.

- **#1 Risk Factor = Atherosclerosis**
  (Delicious Burger King and Tasty Cigarettes)

- **Classic Scenario:** Elderly patient with hypertension and atherosclerosis usually involving the descending thoracic aorta

- **Genesis:** Eating like a pig and smoking results in atherosclerosis. Nasty atherosclerotic plaque erodes through the intima. Hematoma forms in the media (intra-mural hematoma). With severe disease can eventually progress to a pseudo aneurysm (and maybe even rupture)

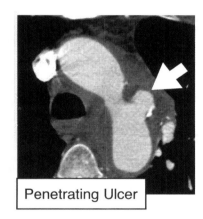

Penetrating Ulcer

- **Pearl:** Look for a gap in the intimal calcifications (that's how you know it's truly penetrated through the intima, and not just some funky contour abnormality).

- **Classification:** All 3 AASs can be classified as type A or B Stanford, based on their locations before (type A) or after the takeoff the of the left subclavian (type B).

- **These things often result in a saccular morphology around the arch.** In general, sac like aneurysm above the diaphragm is related to penetrating ulcer. Sac like aneurysm below the diaphragm is gonna be septic ("mycotic").

453

Relationship between Penetrating Ulcer and Dissection:

—*Controversial (which usually means it won't be tested)* – famous last words

If forced to answer questions on this relationship, I would go with the following:
- Penetrating Ulcers are caused by atherosclerosis (this is a fact)
- Penetrating Ulcer can lead to Dissection (this is probably true in some cases)
- Atherosclerosis does NOT cause Dissection (which is confusing, may or may not be true, and is unlikely to be tested). What is true is that the presence of dense calcified plaque can stop extension of a dissection tear.
- Dissections often occur in the aortic root – where you have the highest flow pressures
- Penetrating Ulcers nearly never occur in the root – as these flow pressures prevent atherosclerosis (wash those cheeseburger crumbs away).

Treatment of Penetrating Ulcer ?

- "Medical" = Similar to Type B Dissections. If they do get treated (grafted etc...) they tend to do WORSE than dissections (on average)

- Q: When are they Surgical ?
- A: Hemodynamic instability, Pain, Rupture, Distal Emboli, Rapid Enlargement

Dissection

- The most common cause of acute aortic syndrome (70%)
- **Hypertension** is the main factor – leads to an intimal tear resulting in two lumens
- Marfans, Turners, and other Connective Tissue Diseases increase risk

Classic Testable Scenarios:
- Pregnancy — known to increase risk
- Cocaine Use in a young otherwise healthy person
- Patient with "Hypertension" and a sub-sternal "Tearing Sensation."

Chicken vs Egg: Some people say that hypertensive pressures kill the vasa vasorum (the little vessels inside the vessel walls) leading to development of intramural hematoma which then ruptures into the intima. This is the "inside out" thinking. Other people think the hypertensive forces tear the inner layer directly ("outside in" thinking).
Honestly... who gives a shit? Not even sure why I mentioned that.

Dissection Continued...

There are two general ways to classify these things:
(1) Time: Acute (< 2 weeks), or Chronic
(2) Location:

- **Stanford A:** Account for 75% of dissections and involves the ascending aorta and arch <u>proximal to the take-off of the left subclavian</u>. These guys need to be <u>treated surgically.</u>

- **Stanford B:** Occur <u>distal to the take-off of the left subclavian</u> and are <u>treated medically </u>unless there are complications (organ ischemia etc...)

THIS vs THAT:		Floating Viscera Sign:
True Lumen	**False Lumen**	
Continuity with undissected portion of aorta	"CobWeb Sign" – slender linear areas of low attenuation	This is a classic angiographic sign of abdominal aortic dissection.
Smaller cross sectional areas (with higher velocity blood)	**Larger** cross section area (slower more turbulent flow)	It is shown as opacification of abdominal aortic branch vessels during aortography (catheter placed in the aortic true lumen), with the branch vessels— (celiac axis, superior mesenteric artery, and right renal artery) arising out of nowhere.
Surrounded by calcifications (if present) 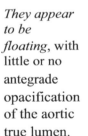	**Beak Sign** - acute angle at edge of lumen - seen on axial plane	*They appear to be floating*, with little or no antegrade opacification of the aortic true lumen. 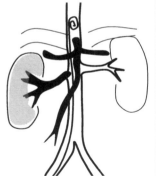
Usually contains the origin of celiac trunk, SMA, and **RIGHT** renal artery	Usually contains the origin of **LEFT** renal artery	
	Surrounds true lumen in Type A Dissection	

***just remember false is left (like left handed people are evil, or false) – then everything else is true.*

Dissection Flap in the Abdomen - Vocab Trivia:

- **Static** = dissection flap in the feeding artery (usually treated by stenting)
- **Dynamic** = dissection flap dangling in front of ostium (usually treated with fenestration).

It can be hard to tell these apart. If asked I'd expect them to just use the vocab words.

THIS vs THAT: Aneurysm with Mural Thrombus vs Thrombosed Dissection
- The dissection should spiral, the thrombus tends to drop straight down
- Intimal Calcs – the dissection will displace them.

Intramural Hematoma

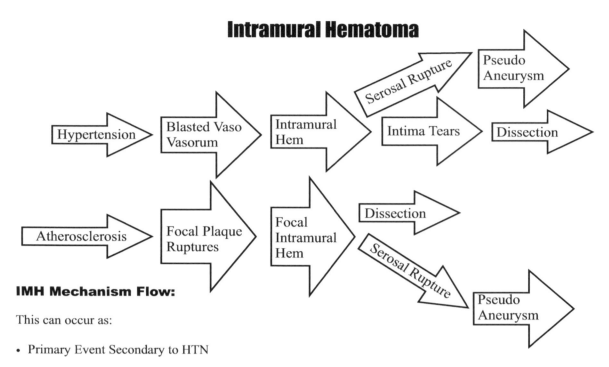

IMH Mechanism Flow:

This can occur as:

- Primary Event Secondary to HTN

- Secondary Event usually From Atherosclerosis, but also as a Focal Hematoma on the road to dissection

For the purpose of multiple choice – the cause is HTN

Ways this can be shown:

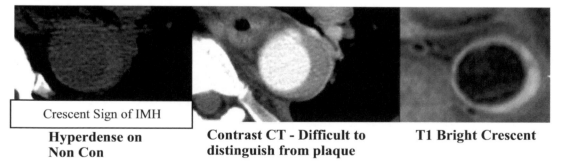

Crescent Sign of IMH

Hyperdense on Non Con **Contrast CT - Difficult to distinguish from plaque** **T1 Bright Crescent**

Treatment:
- Also uses the Stanford A vs B idea
- Some people will say Type A = Surgery, Type B medical
- This is controversial and unlikely to be tested

Predictors of Shitty Outcome:
- Most of these will spontaneously regress. These are the things that make that less likely:
  - Hematoma Thickness Greater than 2 cm
  - Association with aneurysmal dilation of the aorta – 5 cm or more
  - Progression to dissection or penetrating ulcer
  - IMH + Penetrating Ulcer has a worse outcome compared to IMH + Dissection

SECTION 3:
Aneurysm, Misc...

THIS vs THAT: Aneurysm vs Pseudo-aneurysm – The distinction between a true and false aneurysm lends itself well to multiple choice testing. A true aneurysm is an enlargement of the lumen of the vessel to 1.5 times its normal diameter. True = 3 layers are intact. In a false (pseudo) aneurysm all 3 layers are NOT intact, and it is essentially a contained rupture. The risk of actual rupture is obviously higher with false aneurysm. It can sometimes be difficult to tell, but as a general rule fusiform aneurysms are true, and saccular aneurysms might be false. Classic causes of pseudoaneurysm include trauma, cardiologists (groin sticks), infection (mycotic), pancreatitis, and some vasculitides. On ultrasound they could show you the classic yin/yang sign, with "to and fro" flow on pulsed Doppler. The yin/yang sign can be seen in saccular true aneurysms, so you shouldn't call it on that alone (unless that's all they give you). To and Fro flow within the aneurysm neck + clinical history is the best way to tell them apart.

SVC Syndrome - Occurs secondary to complete or near complete obstruction of flow in the SVC from external compression (lymphoma, lung cancer) or intravascular obstruction (Central venous catheter, or pacemaker wire with thrombus). A less common but testable cause is fibrosing mediastinitis (just think histoplasmosis). The dude is gonna have face, neck, and bilateral arm swelling.

Traumatic Pseudoaneurysm –

Again a pseudoaneurysm is basically a contained rupture. The most common place to see this (in a living patient) is the **aortic isthmus (90%)**. This is supposedly the result of tethering from the ligamentum arteriosum. The second and third most common sites are the ascending aorta and diaphragmatic hiatus - respectively. Ascending aortic injury is actually probably number one, it just kills them in the field so you don't see it. They could show you a CXR with a wide mediastinum, deviation of the NG Tube to the right, depressed left main bronchus, or left apical cap and want you to suspect acute injury.

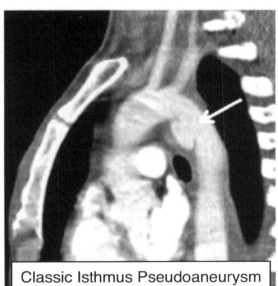

Classic Isthmus Pseudoaneurysm

Ascending Aortic Calcifications - There are only a few causes of ascending aortic calcifications, as atherosclerosis typically spares the ascending aorta. **Takayasu and Syphilis** should come to mind. The real-life significance is the clamping of the aorta may be difficult during CABG.

Aneurysm - Defined as enlargement of the artery to 1.5 times its expected diameter (> 4 cm Ascending and Transverse, > 3.5 cm Descending, > 3.0 cm Abdominal). Atherosclerosis is the most common overall cause. Medial degeneration is the most common cause in the ascending aorta. Patients with connective tissue (Marfans, Ehlers Danlos) diseases tend to involve the aortic root. *When I say cystic medial necrosis you should think Marfans.* Aneurysms may develop in any segment of the aorta, but most involve the infra-renal abdominal aorta. This varies based on risk factors, rate of growth, etc... but a general rule is surgical repair for aneurysms at 6cm in the chest (5.5 cm with collagen vascular disease) and 5 cm in the abdomen.

Sinus of Valsalva Aneurysm – Aneurysms of the valsalva sinus (aortic sinus) are rare in real life, but have been known to show up on multiple choice tests. Factoids worth knowing are that they are more common in Asian Men, and **typically involve the right sinus**. They can be congenital or acquired (infectious). VSD is the most common associated cardiac anomaly. Rupture can lead to cardiac tamponade. Surgical repair with Bentall procedure.

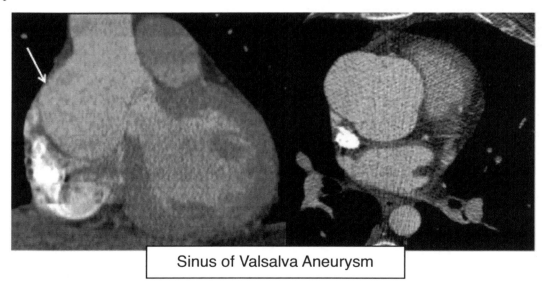

Sinus of Valsalva Aneurysm

Endoleaks - There are 5 types, and type 2 is the most common. These are discussed in detail in the IR chapter.

Rupture / Impending Rupture- Peri-aortic stranding, rapid enlargement (10 mm or more per year), or pain are warning signs of impending rupture. A retroperitoneal hematoma adjacent to an AAA is the most common imaging finding of actual rupture. The most common indicator for elective repair is the maximum diameter of the aneurysm , "Sac Size Matters," with treatment usually around 6 cm (5.5 cm in patients with collagen vascular disease). A thick, circumferential mural thrombus is thought to be protective against rupture. Enlargement of the patent lumen can indicate lysis of thrombus and predispose to rupture.

Findings of Impending Rupture	
Draped Aorta Sign	Posterior wall of the aorta drapes over the vertebral column.
Increased Aneurysm Size	10 mm or more increased per year
Focal Discontinuity in Circumferential Wall Calcifications	
Hyperdense Crescent Sign	Well-defined peripheral crescent of increased attenuation. One of the most specific manifestations of impending rupture.

Mycotic Aneurysm – These are most often **saccular** and most often **pseudoaneurysms**. They are prone to rupture. They most often occur via hematogenous seeding in the setting of septicemia (**endocarditis**). They can occur from direct seeding via a psoas abscess or vertebral osteomyelitis (but this is less common). **Most occur in the thoracic or supra-renal aorta** (most atherosclerotic aortic aneurysms are infra-renal). Typical findings include saccular shape, lobular contours, peri-aortic inflammation, abscess, and peri-aortic gas. They tend to expand faster than atherosclerotic aneurysms. In general small, asymptomatic, and unruptured.

 Gamesmanship - If you see a saccular aneurysm of the aorta (especially the abdominal aorta) you have to lead with infection.

NF 1 – One of the more common neurological genetic disorders, which you usually think about causing all the skin stuff (Café au lait spots and freckling), and bilateral optic gliomas. Although uncommon, vascular findings also occur in this disorder. **Aneurysms and stenoses are sometimes seen in the aorta and larger arteries**, while dysplastic features are found in smaller vessels. **Renal artery stenosis can occur, leading to renovascular hypertension** (found in 5% of children with NF). **The classic look is orificial renal artery stenosis presenting with hypertension in a teenager or child.** The mechanism is actually Dysplasia of the arterial wall itself (less common from peri-arterial neurofibroma).

Marfan Syndrome – Genetic disorder caused by mutations of the fibrillin gene (step 1 question). There are lots of systemic manifestations including ectopic lens, being tall, pectus deformity, scoliosis, long fingers etc... Vascular findings can be grouped into aneurysm, dissection, and pulmonary artery dilation:

- *Aneurysm:* Dilation with Marfans is classically described as **"Annuloaortic ectasia"**, with dilatation of the aortic root. The dilation usually begins with the aortic sinuses, and then progresses into the sinotubular junction, ultimately involving the aortic annulus. **Dilatation of the aortic root leads to aortic valve insufficiency**. Severe aortic regurgitation occurs that may progress to aortic root dissection or rupture. The mechanism for all this nonsense is that disruption of the media elastic fibers causes aortic stiffening, and predisposes to aneurysm and dissection. The buzzword for the Marfans ascending aneurysm is **"tulip bulb."** They are usually repaired earlier than normal aneurysm (typically around 5.5 cm).

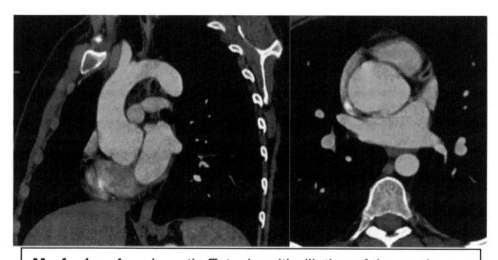

Marfan's - *Annuloaortic Ectasia*, with dilation of the aortic root

- *Dissection:* Recurrent dissections are common, and even "triple barreled dissection" can be seen (dissections on both sides of a true channel).

- *Pulmonary Artery Enlargement:* Just like dilation of the aorta, pulmonary artery enlargement favors the root.

Loeys Dietz Syndrome - Despite the name, this is actually not a Puerto Rican DJ. Instead think of this as the really shitty version of Marfans. They have a terrible prognosis, and rupture their aortas all the time. **Vessels are very tortuous** (twisty). They also have crazy wide eyes (hypertelorism).

Ehlers-Danlos - This one is a disorder in collagen, with lots of different subtypes. They have the stretchy skin, hypermobile joints, blood vessel fragility with bleeding diatheses. Invasive diagnostic studies such as conventional angiography and **other percutaneous procedures should be avoided** because of the excessive risk of arterial dissection. Imaging characteristics of aortic aneurysms in Ehlers-Danlos syndrome **resemble those in Marfan syndrome, often involving the aortic root.** Aneurysms of the abdominal visceral arteries are common as well.

Syphilitic (Luetic) Aneurysm – This is super rare and only seen in patients with untreated tertiary syphilis. There is classically a saccular appearance and it involves the ascending aorta as well as the aortic arch. Classic description **"saccular asymmetric aortic aneurysm with involvement of the aortic root branches. "** Often heavily calcified **"tree bark" intimal calcifications.** Coronary artery narrowing (at the ostium) is seen 30% of the time. Aortic valve insufficiency is also common.

Aortoenteric Fistula - These come in two flavors: (a) Primary, and (b) Secondary.

* **Primary:** Very, very, very rare. Refers to an A-E fistula without history of instrumentation. They are only seen in the setting of aneurysm and atherosclerosis.

* **Secondary:** Much more common. They are **seen after surgery** with or without stent graft placement.

The question is usually what part of the bowel is involved, and the answer is **3rd and 4th portions of the duodenum.** The second most likely question is A-E fistula vs perigraft infection (without fistula)? The answer to that is unless you see contrast from the aorta into the bowel lumen (usually duodenum), you can't tell. Both of them have ectopic perigraft gas > 4 weeks post repair, both have perigraft fluid and edema, both lose the fat place between the bowel and aorta (tethering of the duodenum to the anterior wall of the aorta), both can have pseudoaneurysm formation.

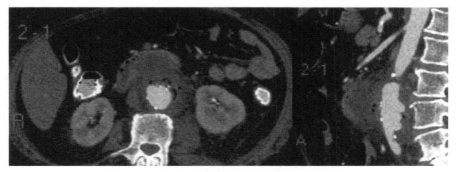

Aortoenteric Fistula - *Primary Type*

Inflammatory Aneurysms -   Most are **symptomatic**, more common in **young men**, and associated with increased risk of rupture regardless of their size. Unlike patients with atherosclerotic AAA, most with the inflammatory variant have an **elevated ESR**. Their etiology is not well understood but may be related to periaortic retroperitoneal fibrosis or other autoimmune disorders (SLE, Giant Cell, RA). **Smoking is apparently a strong risk factor**, and smoking cessation is the first step in medical therapy. **In 1/3 of cases hydronephrosis or renal failure** is present at the time of diagnosis because the inflammatory process usually involves the ureters. Imaging findings include a thickened wall and inflammatory or fibrotic changes in the periaortic regions. Often there is asymmetrical thickening of the aorta with sparing of the posterior wall (helps differentiate it from vasculitis).

Leriche Syndrome - Refers to complete occlusion of the aorta distal to the renal arteries (most often at the aortic bifurcation). It is often secondary to bad atherosclerosis. There can be large collaterals.

Clinical Triad:

- Limp Dick (impotence)
- Ass claudication
- Absence femoral pulses

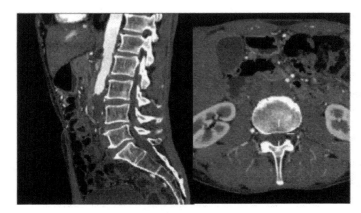

Leriche Syndrome - *Complete occlusion of the aortal distal to the renal arteries*

Mid Aortic Syndrome - Refers to progressive narrowing of the abdominal aorta and its major branches. Compared to Leriche, this is higher, and longer in segment. It's also a total freaking zebra. It tends to affect children / young adults. This thing is characterized by progressive narrowing of the aorta. It is **NOT secondary to arteritis or atherosclerosis** but instead the result of some intrauterine insult (maybe) with fragmentation of the elastic media.

This also has a clinical triad:

- **HTN (most common presenting symptom)**
- Claudication
- Renal failure

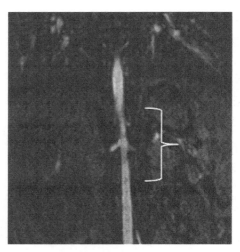

Mid Aortic Syndrome - *Narrow aorta without arteritis or atherosclerosis*

Aortic Coarctation -

- There are two subtypes (as shown in the chart)

- Strong Association with **Turners Syndrome** (15-20%).

- **Bicuspid Aortic valve** is the most common associated defect (80%).

- They have more **berry aneurysms**.

- **Figure 3 sign** (appearance of CXR).

- **Rib Notching**: most often involves 4th - 8th ribs. It does NOT involve the 1st and 2nd because those are fed by the costocervical trunk.

THIS vs THAT: Coarctation of the Aortic (Narrowing the of the Aortic Lumen)	
Infantile	**Adult**
Presents with heart failure within the first week of life.	Leg Claudication BP differences between arms and legs.
Pre-Ductal (Before the left Subclavian A.)	Post-Ductal (Distal to left Subclavian A.)
Aortic Arch = Hypoplastic	Aortic Arch = Normal Diameter
	Collateral Formation is More Likely

Pseudocoarctation - This is a favorite of multiple choice writers. You will have elongation with narrowing and kinking of the aorta. It really looks like a coarctation, BUT there is **NO pressure gradient, collateral formation, or rib notching** - that is the most likely question. The second most likely question is the area of aneurysmal dilation may occur distal to the areas of narrowing in pseudocoarctation, and they may become progressively dilated and should therefore be followed.

Thoracic Outlet Syndrome – Congenital or acquired compression of the Subclavian vessels (artery and vein), and brachial plexus nerves as they pass through the thoracic inlet. *It is a spectrum: **Nerve (95%)** >>>>>> **Subclavian Vein** >> **Subclavian Artery**.* With symptoms varying depending on what is compressed. **Compression by the anterior scalene muscle is the most common cause.** However, cervical rib, muscular hypertrophy, fibrous bands, Pagets, tumor etc… can all cause symptoms. Treatment is usually surgical removal of the rib / muscle. The classic way to show this is arms up and arms down angiography (occlusion occurs with arms up).

Paget Schroetter – This is **essentially thoracic outlet syndrome, with development of a venous thrombus in the Subclavian vein**. It's sometimes called "effort thrombosis" because it's associated with athletes (pitchers, weightlifters) who are raising their arms a lot. They will use catheter directed lysis on these dudes, and surgical release of the offending agent as above. Stenting isn't usually done (and can only be done after surgery to avoid getting the stent crushed).

Pulmonary Artery Aneurysm/Pseudoaneurysm – Think about three things for multiple choice; (1) **Iatrogenic from Swan Ganz catheter *most common** (2) Behcets, (3) Chronic PE. When they want to lead Swan Ganz they may say something like "patient in the ICU." The buzzwords for Behcets are: "Turkish descent", and "mouth and genital ulcers."

- **Hughes-Stovin Syndrome:** This is a zebra cause of pulmonary artery aneurysm that is similar (and maybe the same thing) as Behcets. It is characterized by recurrent thrombophlebitis and pulmonary artery aneurysm formation and rupture.

- **Rasmussen Aneurysm:** This has a cool name, which instantly makes it high yield for testing. This is a pulmonary artery **pseudoaneurysm secondary to pulmonary TB**. It usually involves the upper lobes in the setting of reactivation TB.

- **Tetralogy of Fallot Repair Gone South:** So another possible testable scenario is the patch aneurysm, from the RVOT repair.

Splenic Artery Aneurysm: The most common visceral arterial aneurysm (3rd most common abdominal - behind aorta and iliac).

Etiology of these things depends on who you ask. Some source will say arteriosclerosis is the most important cause. However, it seems that most sources will say that arteriosclerosis less important and things like *portal hypertension* and a *history of multiple pregnancy* are more important. **More common in pregnancy, and more likely to rupture in pregnancy.**

Classic Scenarios
- High Risk For Rupture -
- Liver Transplantation
- Portal Hypertension
- Pregnancy

Most are located in the distal artery. False aneurysms are associated with pancreatitis.

An important mimic is the islet cell pancreatic tumor (which is hypervascular). Don't be a dumb ass and try to biopsy the aneurysm. If you are forced to choose *which ones to treat* I guess I'd go with: anything over 2 cm, any pseudoaneurysm, and any in a women planning on getting pregnant.

Median Arcuate Ligament Syndrome (Dunbar Syndrome) : This is compression of the celiac artery by the median arcuate ligament (fibrous band that connects the diaphragm). Most people actually have some degree of compression, but it's not a syndrome until there are symptoms (abdominal pain, weight loss). Typical age is 20-40 years old. The buzzword is **"hooked appearance."** It's classically shown on angiography and they will want you to know that it gets **worse with expiration**. It can actually lead to the development of pancreaticoduodenal collaterals and aneurysm formation. It's treated surgically.

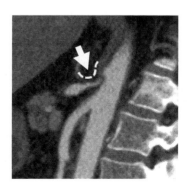

Median Arcuate Ligament

SECTION 4:
Mesenteric Ischemia

This can be broadly classified as acute or chronic.

Chronic: Significant Stenosis of 2 out of 3 main mesenteric vessels + symptoms ("food fear") , LUQ pain after eating, pain out of proportion to exam). Some practical pearls are that you can have bad disease and no symptoms if you have good collaterals. Alternatively if you have bad one-vessel disease you can have symptoms if you have crappy collaterals. Remember that the *splenic flexure ("Griffith's Point") is the most common* because it's the watershed of the SMA and IMA.

Acute: This comes from 4 main causes. Arterial, Venous, Non-occlussive, and Strangulation.

- **Arterial:** Occlusive emboli (usually more distal, at branch points), or Thrombus (usually closer to the ostium). Vasculitis can also cause it. The SMA is most commonly affected. Bowel typically has a **thinner wall** (no arterial inflow), and is **NOT typically dilated**. After reperfusion the bowel wall will become thick, with a target appearance.

- **Venous: Dilation with wall thickening** *(8-9mm, with < 5mm being normal)* is more common. Fat stranding and ascites are especially common findings in venous occlusion.

- **Non-Occlusive**: Seen in patients in shock or on pressors. This is the most difficult to diagnose on CT. The involved bowel segments are often thickened. Enhancement is variable. *Look for delayed filling of the portal vein at 70 seconds.*

- **Strangulation:** This is almost always secondary to a closed loop obstruction. This is basically a mixed arterial and venous picture, with **congested dilated bowel**. Hemorrhage may be seen in the bowel wall. The lumen is often fluid-filled.

Mesenteric Ischemia			
Arterial	**Venous**	**Strangulation**	**Non-Occlusive**
Thin Bowel Wall (thick after reperfusion)	Thick Bowel Wall	Thick Bowel Wall	Thick Bowel Wall
Diminished Enhancement	Variable	Variable	Variable
Bowel *Not Dilated*	Moderate Dilation	Severe Dilation (and fluid filled)	Bowel *Not Dilated*
Mesentery *Not Hazy* (until it infarcts)	<u>Hazy</u> with Ascites	<u>Hazy</u> with Ascites, and "whirl sign" with closed loop.	Mesentery *Not Hazy* (until it infarcts)

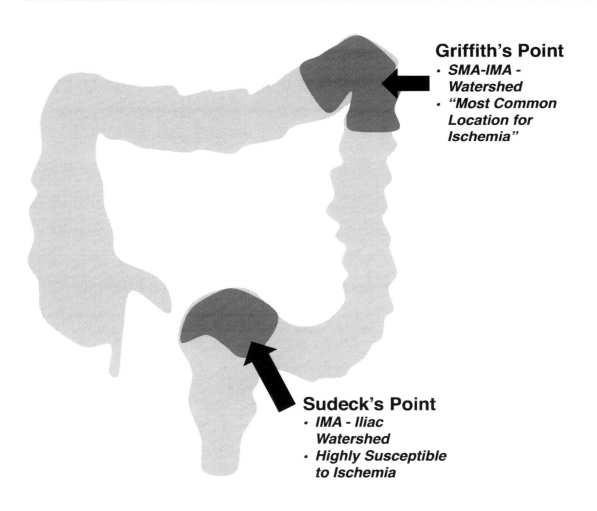

Griffith's Point
- *SMA-IMA - Watershed*
- *"Most Common Location for Ischemia"*

Sudeck's Point
- *IMA - Iliac Watershed*
- *Highly Susceptible to Ischemia*

SECTION 5:
Misc, So on and So Forth, Etc.. Etc..

This is my general algorithm if I see angry (thick walled) bowel

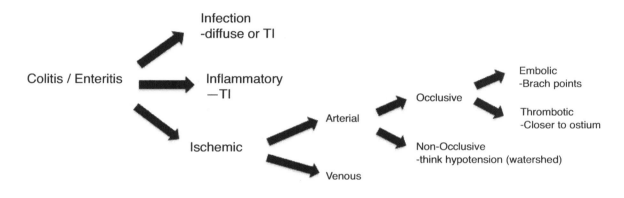

Colonic Angiodysplasia – This is the second most common cause of colonic arterial bleeding (diverticulosis being number one). This is primarily **right sided** with angiography demonstrating a cluster of small arteries during the arterial phase (along the antimesenteric border of the colon), with *early opacification of dilated draining veins* that persists late into the venous phase. There is an **association with aortic stenosis which carries the eponym Heyde Syndrome** (which instantly makes it high yield for multiple choice).

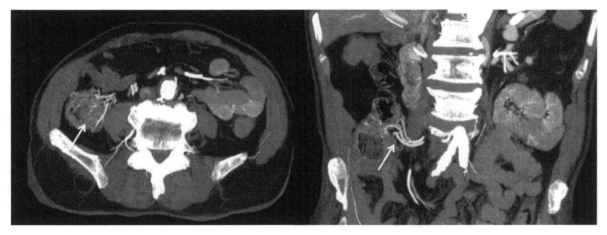

Colonic Angiodysplasia

Osler Weber Rendu (Hereditary Hemorrhagic Telangiectasia) – This is an AD multi-system disorder characterized by multiple AVMs. On step 1 they used to show you the tongue / mouth with the telangiectasis and a history of recurrent bloody nose. Now, they will likely show multiple hepatic AVMs or multiple pulmonary AVMs. Extensive shunting in the liver can actually cause biliary necrosis and bile leak. They can have high output cardiac failure. **Most die from stroke or brain abscess.**

 Gamesmanship "Next Step" - If the syndrome is suspected, these guys need CT of the Lung & Liver (with contrast), plus a Brain MR / MRA

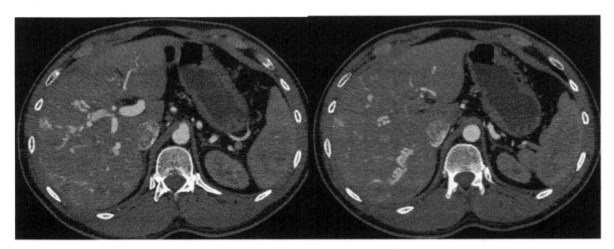

Osler Weber Rendu (Hereditary Hemorrhagic Telangiectasia)

Renal Artery Stenosis – Narrowing of the renal artery most commonly occurs secondary to atherosclerosis (75%). This type of narrowing is usually near the ostium, and can be stented. FMD is the second most common cause and typically has a beaded appearance sparing the ostium (should not be stented). Additional more rare causes include PAN, Takayasu, NF-1, and Radiation.

FMD (Fibromuscular Dysplasia) – A non-atherosclerotic vascular disease, primarily affecting the renal arteries of young white women.

Things to know:

- Renovascular HTN in Young Women = FMD

- Renal arteries are the most commonly involved (carotid #2, iliac #3)

- There are 3 types, but just remember medial is the most common (95%)

- They are predisposed to spontaneous dissection

 - Buzzword = String of Beads

- Treatment = Angioplasty WITHOUT stenting.

Nutcracker Syndrome – Smashing of the left renal vein as it slides under the SMA, with resulting abdominal pain (left flank) and hematuria. The left renal vein gets smashed a lot, but it's not a syndrome without symptoms. Since the left gonadal vein drains into the left renal vein, it can also cause left testicle pain in men, and LLQ pain in women.

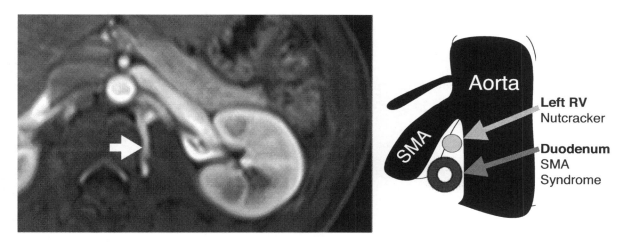

Nutcracker: Renal Vein, Smashed by SMA.
Note the prominent venous collateral (arrow)

SAM (Segmental Arterial Mediolysis) – Targets the splanchnic arteries in the elderly, and the coronaries in young adults. Not a true vasculitis, with no significant inflammation. It's complicated but essentially the media of the vessel turns to crap, and you get a bunch of aneurysms. The aneurysms are often multiple. The way this is shown is **multiple abdominal splanchnic artery saccular aneurysms, dissections, and occlusion** – *this is the disease hallmark. Can also be shown as spontaneous intra-abdominal hemorrhage.*

> WTF is a
> ***"Splanchnic"*** Artery ?
>
> Typically the splanchnic circulation of the GI tract refers to the Celiac, SMA, and IMA.

Pelvic Congestion Syndrome – This is a controversial entity, sometimes grouped in the fibromyalgia spectrum. Patients often have "chronic abdominal pain." They also often wear a lot of rings and drink orange soda. The classic demographic is a depressed, multiparous, pre-menopausal women with chronic pelvic pain. Venous obstruction at the left renal vein (nutcracker compression) or incompetent ovarian vein valves leads to **multiple dilated parauterine veins**. This very "real" diagnosis can be treated by your local Interventional Radiologist via ovarian vein embolization.

Testicular Varicocele – Abnormal dilation of veins in the pampiniform plexus. Most cases are idiopathic and **most (98%) are found on the left side** *(left vein is longer, and drains into renal vein at right angle)*. They can also occur on the left, secondary to the above mentioned "nutcracker syndrome." They **can cause infertility**. "Non-decompressible" is a buzzword for badness. Some sources state that neoplasm is actually the most likely cause of **non-decompressible varicocele** in men over 40 years of age; (left renal malignancy invading the renal vein). Right-sided varicocele can be a sign of malignancy as well. When it's new, and on the right side (in an adult), you should raise concern for a pelvic or abdominal malignancy. New right-sided varicocele in an adult should make you think renal cell carcinoma, retroperitoneal fibrosis, or adhesions.

Non-Decompressible = Bad

Right = Bad

Left = Ok

Bilateral = Ok (probably)

 Gamesmanship - This diagnosis is the classic next step question of all next step questions because you need to recognize when this common diagnosis is associated with something bad.

• Isolated Right Varicocele = Get an ABD CT (or MR, or US)

• Non-decompressible Varicocele = Get an ABD CT (or MR, or US)

• Bilateral Decompressible Varicoceles = Might need treatment if infertile etc.., but doesn't need additional cancer hunting imaging.

• Isolated Left Varicocele = Might need treatment if infertile etc.., but doesn't need additional cancer hunting imaging.

Uterine AVM – This can present with life threatening massive genital bleeding. Rarely they can present with CHF. They come in two flavors (a) Congenital, and (b) Acquired. **Acquired occurs after D&C**, abortion, or multiple pregnancies. They are most likely to show this on color Doppler with serpiginous structures in the myometrium with low resistance high velocity patterns. This one needs embolization. Could look similar to retained products of conception (clinical history will be different, and *RPOC is usually centered in the endometrium rather than the myometrium*).

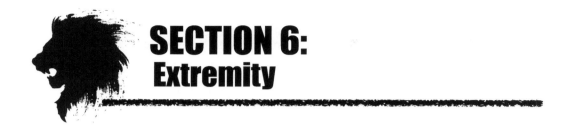

SECTION 6: Extremity

May Thurner – A syndrome resulting in DVT of the left common iliac vein. The pathology is **compression of the left common iliac vein by the right common iliac artery**. Treatment is thrombolysis and stenting. *If they show you a swollen left leg, this is probably the answer.*

Popliteal Aneurysm – This is the most common peripheral arterial aneurysm (2nd most common overall, to the aorta). The main issue with these things is distal thromboembolism, which can be limb threatening. There is a strong and frequently tested association with AAA.

- *30-50% of patients with popliteal aneurysms have a AAA*

- *10% of patients with AAA have popliteal aneurysms*

- *50-70% of popliteal aneurysms are bilateral*

The **most dreaded complication of a popliteal artery aneurysm is an acute limb** from thrombosis and distal embolization of thrombus pooling in the aneurysm.

Popliteal Entrapment – Symptomatic compression or occlusion of the popliteal artery due to the developmental relationship with the **medial head of the gastrocnemius** (less commonly the popliteus). Medial deviation of the popliteal artery is supposedly diagnostic. This usually occurs in young men (<30). These patients may have *normal pulses that decrease with plantar flexion or dorsiflexion of the foot.* They will show you either a MRA or conventional angiogram in rest and then stress (dorsi / plantar flexion) to show the artery occluding.

Hypothenar Hammer – Caused by blunt trauma (history of working with a jack-hammer) to the ulnar artery and superficial palmar arch. The impact occurs against the hook of the hamate. Arterial wall damage leads to aneurysm formation with or without thrombosis of the vessel. Emboli may form, causing distal obstruction of digits (this can cause confusion with the main DDx Buergers). Look for **corkscrew configuration of the superficial palmar arch, occlusion of the ulnar artery, or pseudoaneurysm of the ulnar artery**.

Peripheral Vascular Malformations - About 40% of vascular malformations involve the extremities (the other 40% are head and neck, and 20% is thorax). Different than hemangiomas, vascular malformations generally increase proportionally as the child grows. This dude Jackson classified vascular malformation as either low flow or high flow. Low flow would include venous, lymphatic, capillary, and mixes of the like. **High flow has an arterial component.** Treatment is basically determined by high or low flow.

Klippel-Trenaunay Syndrome (KTS) - This is often combined with **Parkes-Weber which is a true high flow AV malformation.** KTS has a triad of port wine nevi, bony or soft tissue hypertrophy (localized gigantism), and a venous malformation. A persistent sciatic vein is often associated. The marginal vein of Servelle (some superficial vein in the lateral calf and thigh) is pathognomonic (it's basically a great saphenous on the wrong side).

Additional trivia: 20% have GI involvement and can bleed, if the system is big enough it can eat your platelets (**Kasabach Merritt**). Basically, **if you see a MRA/MRV of the leg with a bunch of superficial vessels (and no deep drainage) you should think about this thing**.

- *KTS* = Low Flow (venous)

- *Parkes Weber* = High Flow (arterial)

- *"Klippel Trenaunay Weber"* = Something people say when they (a) don't know what they are talking about, or (b) don't know what kind of malformation it is and want to use a blanket term.

ABIs – So basic familiarity with the so called "Ankle to Brachial Index" can occasionally come in handy, with regard to peripheral arterial disease. This is basically a ratio of systolic pressure in the leg over systolic blood pressure in the arm. Diabetics can sometimes have unreliable numbers (usually high), because dense vascular calcifications won't let the vessels compress.

Opinions vary on what the various cut off numbers mean. Most people will agree that you can safely deploy the phrase "peripheral arterial disease" if the resting ABI is less than 0.90

You can also deploy the following generalizations: 0.5-0.3 = claudication, < 0.3 = rest pain

**More on page 515

Intimal Hyperplasia – "The bane of endovascular intervention." This is not a true disease but a response to blood vessel wall damage. Basically this is an exuberant healing response that leads to intimal thickening which can lead to stenosis. You hear it talked about the most in IR after they have revascularized a limb. Re-Stenosis that occurs 3-12 months after angioplasty is probably from intimal hyperplasia. It's sneaky to treat and

often resists balloon dilation and/ or reoccurs. If you put a bare stent in place it may grow through the cracks and happen anyway. If you put a covered stent in, it may still occur at the edges of the stent. The take home point is that it's a pain in the ass, and if they show an angiogram with a stent in place, that now appears to be losing flow, this is probably the answer.

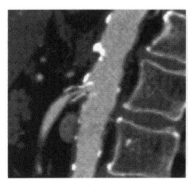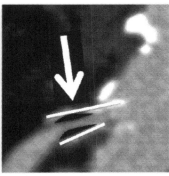

Intimal Hyperplasia
-dark stuff growing along the inside of the stent walls

Cystic Adventitial Disease – This uncommon disorder classically **affects the popliteal artery, of young men**. Basically you have one or **multiple mucoid-filled cysts** developing in the outer media and adventitia. As the cysts grow, they compress the artery.

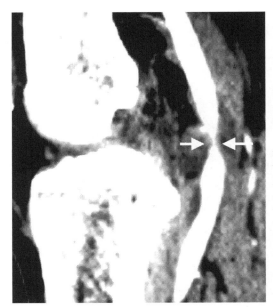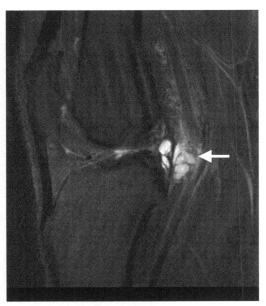

MIP CTA showing Vascular Narrowing

Fluid sensitive MR showing a bunch of cysts around the vessel, extrinsically narrowing it

SECTION 7:
Vasculitis

Basically all vasculitis looks the same, with wall thickening, occlusions, dilations, and aneurysm formation. The trick to telling them apart is the age of the patient, the gender / race, and the vessels affected. Classically, they are broken up into large vessel, medium vessel, small vessel ANCA +, and small vessel ANCA negative.

Large:

Takayasu - "The pulseless disease." This vasculitis loves **young Asian girls** (usually 15-30 years old). If they mention the word "Asian," this is likely to be the answer. Also, if they show you a **vasculitis involving the aorta** this is likely the answer. In the acute phase there will be both **wall thickening and wall enhancement**. There can be occlusion of the major aortic branches, or dilation of the aorta and its branches. The aortic valve is often involved (can cause stenosis or AI). In the late phase there is classically diffuse narrowing distally. The pulmonary arteries are commonly involved, with the typical appearance of peripheral pruning.

If anyone was a big enough jerk to ask, there are 5 types with variable involvement of the aorta and its branches. Which type is which is beyond the scope of the exam, just know type 3 is most common - involves arch and abdominal aorta.

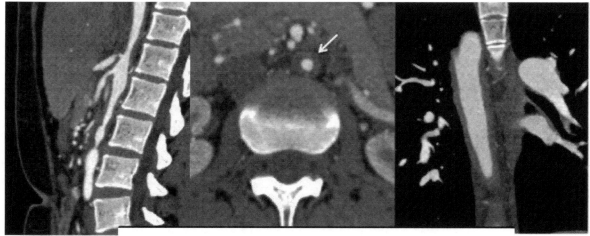

Takayasu *- Wall Thickening Involving the Aorta*

Giant Cell (GCA) – The most common primary system vasculitis. This vasculitis loves **old men** (usually 70-80)** *although there are a few papers that will say this is slightly more common in women.* This vasculitis involves the aorta and its major branches particularly those of the external carotid (**temporal artery**). This can be shown in two ways: (1) an ultrasound of the temporal artery, demonstrating wall thickening, or (2) CTA / MRA or even angiogram of the armpit area (Subclavian/ Axillary/ Brachial), demonstrating wall thickening, occlusions, dilations, and aneurysm. Think about it as the **part of the body that would be compressed by crutches** (old men need crutches).

Trivia worth knowing:

• ESR and CRP are markedly elevated,

• Disease responds to steroids.

• "Gold Standard" for diagnosis is temporal artery biopsy (although it's often negative).

• Clinical connection between GCA and <u>polymyalgia rheumatica</u>, (they might be different phases of the same disease). History might be "morning stillness in shoulders and hips."

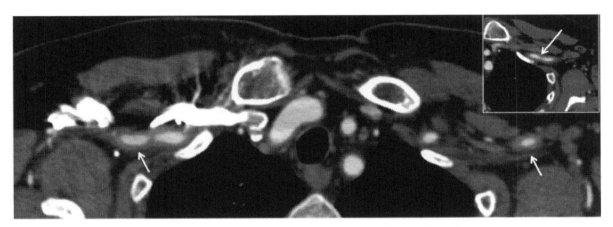

Giant Cell - *"Armpit"* Vessel Thickening

 **Cogan Syndrome** – Total Zebra probably not even worth mentioning. It is a large vessel vasculitis that targets children and young adults. It likes the eyes and ears causing optic neuritis, uveitis, and audiovestibular symptoms resembling Menieres. They can also get aortitis, and those that do have a worse prognosis.

Basically, **kid with eye and ear symptoms + or – aortitis.**

Medium

PAN (Polyarteritis Nodosa) – This is one of two vasculitides (*the other being Buergers*) that is more common in men. **PAN is more common in a MAN**. This can effect a lot of places with the big 3 being Renal (90%), Cardiac (70%), and GI (50-70%). Typically we are talking about **microaneurysm formation**, primarily at branch points, followed by infarction. I would expect this to be shown either as a CTA or angiogram of the **kidneys with microaneurysms**, or a kidney with areas of infarct (multiple wedge shaped areas).

Trivia to know is the **association with Hep B.**

Also, as a point of trivia the micro-aneurysm formation in the kidney can also be seen in patients who abuse Crystal Meth (sometimes called a "speed kidney").

Kawasaki Disease – Probably the most common vasculitis in children (HSP also common). Think about this as a cause of coronary vessel aneurysm. A **calcified coronary artery aneurysm shown on CXR is a very rare aunt Minnie.**

-Coronary Artery Aneurysms > 8mm are "Giant" and prone to badness including MI

-Coronary Artery Aneurysms < 8mm may regress

Clinical Trivia:

"Fever for 5 Days"

- Strawberry Tongue
- Neck Lymph Nodes
- Rash of Palms of Hands / Soles of Feet
- Sore Throat Diarrhea

- "Etiology Unknown"

Small Vessel Disease (ANCA +)

Wegeners - I think about upper respiratory tract (sinuses), lower respiratory tract (lungs), and kidneys. cANCA is (+) 90% of the time. Ways this is shown are the **nasal perforation** (like a cocaine addict) and the **cavitary lung lesions**.

Churg Strauss – This is a necrotizing pulmonary vasculitis which is in the spectrum of Eosinophilic lung disease. They always have asthma and eosinophilia. **Transient peripheral lung consolidation** or ground glass regions is the most frequent feature. Cavitation is rare (this should make you think Wegeners instead). They are pANCA (+) 75% if the time.

Microscopic Polyangiitis – Affects the kidneys and lungs. Diffuse pulmonary hemorrhage is seen in about 1/3 of the cases. It is pANCA (+) 80% of the time.

As I've previously mentioned, you aren't supposed to say "Wegener" - because apparently he ate his boogers, and was a Nazi. He also could not (more likely deliberately chose not to) correctly pronounce the word "Gyro." No matter how many times people corrected him. Dude- it is "YEE-roh."

Wegener was truly one of histories greatest assholes.

So we don't say his name. Instead say "Granulomatosis with polyangiitis."

You know who else was a Nazi?? Henry Ford. No one ever talks about that… Google it - he wrote a book called *"The International Jew, the World's Foremost Problem,"* and got an award from Hitler.

Small Vessel Disease (ANCA -)

HSP (Henoch-Schonlein Purpura) – The most common vasculitis in children (usually age 4-11). Although it is a systemic disease, GI symptoms are most common (painful bloody diarrhea). It is a common lead point for intussusception. They could show this two classic ways: (1) ultrasound with a **doughnut sign for intussusception**, or (2) as a ultrasound of the **scrotum showing massive skin edema**. A less likely (but also possible) way to show this case would be multi-focal bowel wall thickening, or a plain film with thumbprinting.

Behcets – Classic history is mouth ulcers and genital ulcers in someone with Turkish descent. It can cause thickening of the aorta, but for the purpose of multiple choice test I expect the question will be **pulmonary artery aneurysm**.

Buergers – This vasculitis is strongly associated with **smokers**. It affects both small and medium vessels in the arms and legs (more common in legs). Although it is more commonly seen in the legs, it is more commonly tested with a hand angiogram. The characteristic features are extensive arterial occlusive disease with the development of corkscrew collateral vessels. It usually affects more than one limb. **Buzzword = Auto-amputation**.

Gamesmanship Hand Angiograms:

If they are showing you a hand angiogram, it's going to be either Buergers of Hypothenar Hammer Syndrome (HHS).

My strategy centers around the ulnar artery.

(1) Ulnar artery involved = HHS. The most helpful finding is a pseudo-aneurysm off the ulnar artery - this is a slam dunk for HHS.

(2) Ulnar artery looks ok - then look at the fingers - if they are out, go with Buergers. It sure would be nice to see some "corkscrew collaterals" - to make it a sure thing.

Be careful, because the fingers can be out with HHS as well (distal emboli), but the ulnar artery should be fucked.   Look at that ulnar artery first.

Location - Location

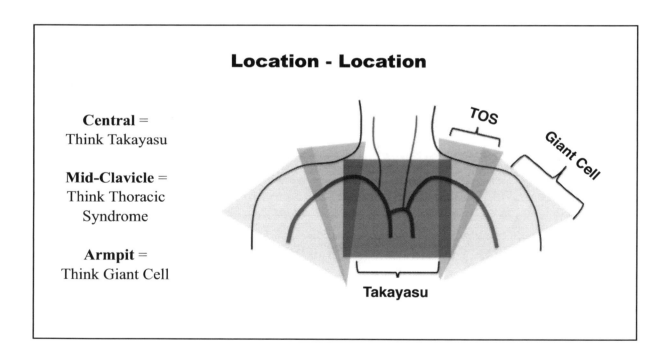

Central = Think Takayasu

Mid-Clavicle = Think Thoracic Syndrome

Armpit = Think Giant Cell

TOS

Giant Cell

Takayasu

Large Vessel	
Takayasu	Young Asian Female – thickened aneurysmal aorta
Giant Cell	Old Person with involvement of the "crutches" / armpit region (Subclavian, axillary, brachial).
Cogan Syndrome	Kid with eye and ear symptoms + Aortitis
Medium Vessel	
PAN	PAN is more common in a MAN (M > F). Renal Microaneurysm (similar to speed kidney). Associated with Hep B.
Kawasaki	Coronary Artery Aneurysm
Small Vessel (ANCA +)	
Wegeners	Nasal Septum Erosions, Cavitary Lung Lesions
Churg Strauss	Transient peripheral lung consolidations.
Microscopic Polyangiitis	Diffuse pulmonary hemorrhage
Small Vessel (ANCA -)	
HSP	Kids. Intussusception. Massive scrotal edema.
Behcets	Pulmonary artery aneurysm
Buergers	Male smoker. Hand angiogram shows finger occlusions.

SECTION 8:
Carotid Doppler

There are a couple of high yield topics regarding carotid Doppler.

Stenosis: They will show you an elevated velocity (normal is < 125cm/s). They may also show you the ICA/CCA ratio (normal is < 2), or the ICA end diastolic velocity (< 40 cm/s is normal).

<u>Here are the rules:</u>

• Less that 50% stenosis will not alter the peak systolic velocity

• 50-69% Stenosis: ICA PSV 125-230 cm/s , ICA/CCA PSV ratio: 2.0-4.0 , ICA EDV 40-100

• >70 % Stenosis: ICA PSV > 230 cm/s, ICA/CCA PSV ratio: > 4.0 , ICA EDV >100

Proximal Stenosis: OK here is the trick; they will show a tardus parvus waveform. **If they show it unilateral, it is stenosis of the innominate. If it's bilateral then it's aortic stenosis.**

Subclavian Steal: This is discussed in greater detail in the cardiac chapter, but this time lets show it on ultrasound.   As a refresher, we are talking about stenosis and/or occlusion of the proximal subclavian artery with retrograde flow in the ipsilateral vertebral artery.

How will they show it? They are going to show two things: (1) Retrograde flow in the left vertebral, and (2) a stenosis of the subclavian artery with a high velocity.

How they can get really sneaky? They can show this thing called "early steal." Steal is apparently a spectrum, which starts with mid-systolic deceleration with antegrade late-systolic velocities. Some people think the "early steal" waveform looks like a rabbit.

Early Steal

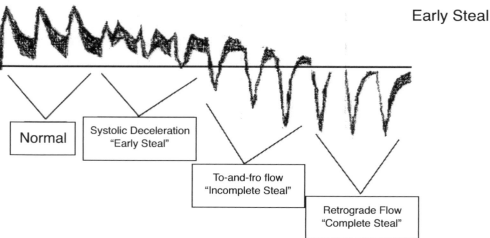

Normal

Systolic Deceleration "Early Steal"

To-and-fro flow "Incomplete Steal"

Retrograde Flow "Complete Steal"

THIS vs THAT: Gamesmanship Internal Carotid vs External Carotid

This really lends itself well to multiple choice test questions. The big point to understand is that the brain is always on. You need blood flow to the brain all the time, which means diastolic flow needs to be present all the time, and thus continuous color flow throughout the cardiac cycle. The external carotid feeds face muscles... they only need to be on when you eat and talk.

Internal Carotid	External Carotid
Low Resistance	High Resistance
Low Systolic Velocity	High Systolic Velocity
Diastolic velocity does not return to baseline	Diastolic velocity approaches zero baseline
Continuous color flow is seen throughout the cardiac cycle	Color flow is intermittent during the cardiac cycle

Temporal Tap – It is a technique Sonographers use to tell the external carotid from the internal carotid. You tap the temporal artery on the forehead and look for ripples in the spectrum. The tech will usually write "TT" on the strip - when they do this.

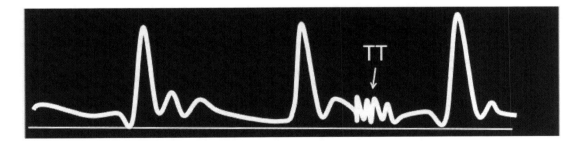

*You can also **look for branches** to tell the external carotid vs the internal.*

Aortic Regurgitation: - Just like aortic stenosis they are going to show you bilateral CCAs. In this case you are going to get **reversal of diastolic flow**.

Brain Death – Apparently in the ever-feuding monarchies of Europe, ultrasound can be used for brain death studies. **A loss of diastolic flow suggests cessation of cerebral blood flow.**

Aneurysms - In case someone asks you, distal formation of an aneurysm (such as one in the skull) cannot be detected by ultrasound, because proximal flow remains normal.

Intra-Aortic Balloon Pump - Remember these guys are positioned so that the superior balloon is 2 cm distal to the take off of the left subclavian artery, and the inferior aspect of the balloon is just above the renals (you don't want it occluding importing stuff when it inflates). When the balloon does inflate it will displace the blood in this segment of the aorta - smashing it superior and inferior to the balloon. The balloon will inflate during early diastole (right after the aortic valve closes) because this is when the maximum amount of blood is available for displacement.

What does this do to the internal carotid (ICA) waveform? You are going to see an extra bump or "augmentation" as the balloon inflates and displaces blood superior.

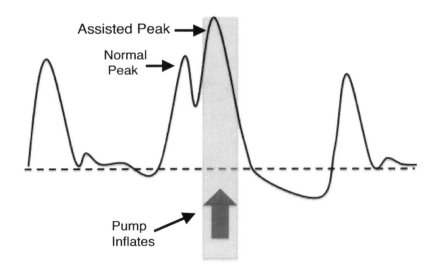

Which wave would you measure to evaluate the velocity?
The first one (the one that is not assisted).

Doppler Evaluation in the LVAD

Bro… WTF is a "LVAD" ?

The Left Ventricular Assist Device is a surgically implanted device that helps pump blood from the left ventricle to the aorta. It's done in the setting of severe heart failure, typically as a bridge to cardiac transplantation, or in those who are simply too evil to die of natural causes (Dick Cheney) and require an intermediate step while the Darth Vader suit is prepped.

Testable Doppler Changes:

LVAD Waveforms will lose the normal high resistance spiked look of the ICA, CCA, Vertebral Arteries. Instead they are mostly flat, with a **tardus parvus** look. The flow is continuous through systole and diastole. The little spikes you see during systole are from the small amount of residual LV function.

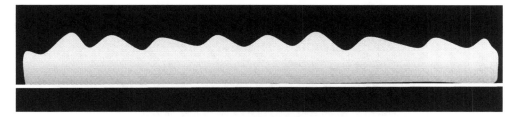

ICA - LVAD Patient

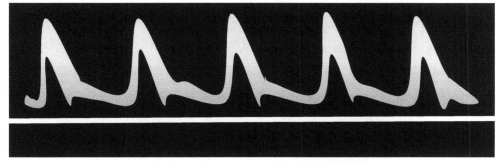

ICA - Normal Patient

Classic Carotid Doppler Cases

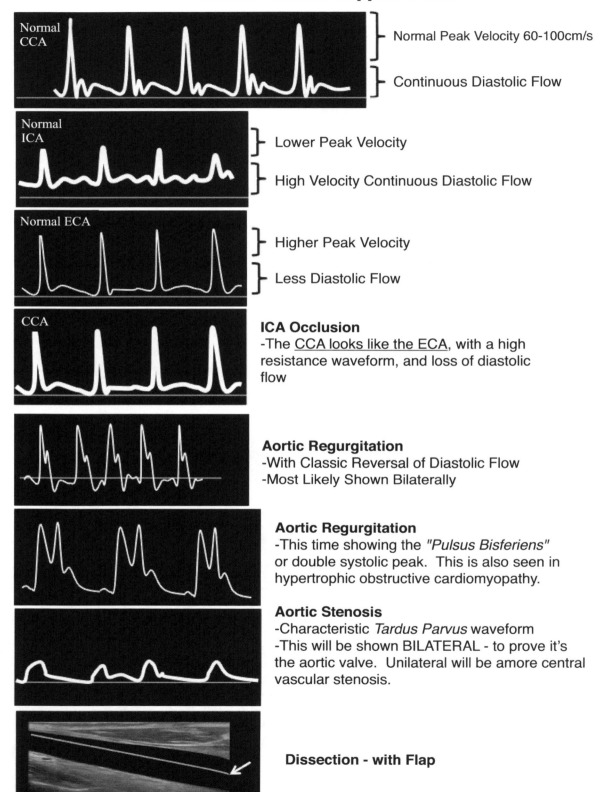

Normal CCA — Normal Peak Velocity 60-100cm/s · Continuous Diastolic Flow

Normal ICA — Lower Peak Velocity · High Velocity Continuous Diastolic Flow

Normal ECA — Higher Peak Velocity · Less Diastolic Flow

CCA

ICA Occlusion
-The <u>CCA looks like the ECA</u>, with a high resistance waveform, and loss of diastolic flow

Aortic Regurgitation
-With Classic Reversal of Diastolic Flow
-Most Likely Shown Bilaterally

Aortic Regurgitation
-This time showing the *"Pulsus Bisferiens"* or double systolic peak. This is also seen in hypertrophic obstructive cardiomyopathy.

Aortic Stenosis
-Characteristic *Tardus Parvus* waveform
-This will be shown BILATERAL - to prove it's the aortic valve. Unilateral will be amore central vascular stenosis.

Dissection - with Flap

10
Interventional

PROMETHEUS LIONHART, M.D.

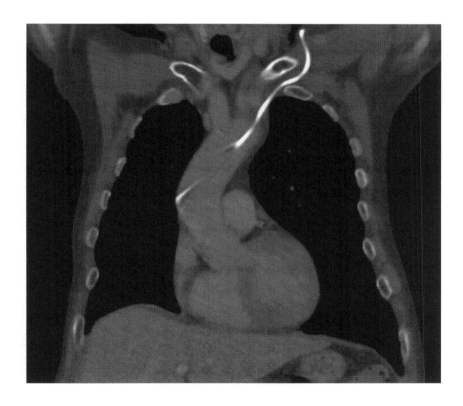

SECTION 1:
Instruments of Intervention

Puncture Needles:

- The smaller the "gauge" number, the bigger the needle. It's totally counterintuitive. For example, an 8G Needle is much bigger than a 16G Needle. *This is the opposite of a "French," which is used to describe the size of a catheter or dilator. The larger the French, the larger the catheter.*

- The Gauge "**G**" refers to the OUTER diameter of the needle.

Wires:

Just some general terminology:

- 0.039 inch = 1mm
- 0.035 inch is the usual size for general purposes
- 0.018 and 0.014 are considered microwires
- "Glide Wires" are hydrophilic coated wires that allow for easier passage of occlusions, stenosis, small or tortuous vessels.

> **Puncture Needle** sizes are designated by the **OUTER** diameter
>
> **Catheter and Dilator** sizes are designated by the **OUTER** diameter
>
> **Sheaths** are designated by their **INNER** lumen size, (the maximum capacity of a diameter they can accommodate)

Catheters – General

- 3 French = 1 mm (6 French = 2 mm, 9 French = 3 mm) **Diameter in mm = Fr / 3**
- Important trivia to understand is that the French size is the external diameter of a catheter (not the caliber of the internal lumen).
- *The standard 0.035 wire will fit through a 4F catheter (or larger)*

Sheaths

- Sheaths are used during cases that require exchange of multiple catheters. The sheath allows you to change your catheters / wires without losing access.
- They are sized according to the largest catheter they will accommodate.
- The outer diameter of a vascular sheath is usually 1.5F to 2F larger than the inner lumen.

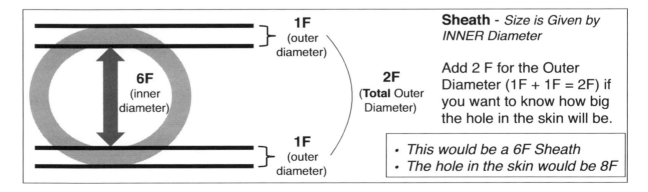

	Sheath - *Size is Given by INNER Diameter*
1F (outer diameter) / 6F (inner diameter) / 1F (outer diameter) — 2F (Total Outer Diameter)	Add 2 F for the Outer Diameter (1F + 1F = 2F) if you want to know how big the hole in the skin will be. • This would be a 6F Sheath • The hole in the skin would be 8F

Gamesmanship — *Various Forms of Fuckery That Can Be Performed ~*

There are a few classic ways this can be asked. You can get all these questions right if you understand the following trivia:

- 3 French = 1 mm, so 1 French = 0.3 mm
- Puncture Needles, Guide Wires, and Dilators are designated with sizes that describe their OUTER diameters.
- Sheaths are designated with sizes that describe their INNER diameter
- The rubber part of the sheath is about 2F (0.6 mm) thick, so the hole in the skin is about 0.6mm bigger than the size of the sheath.
- Wire DIAMETERs are given in INCHES (example "0.035 wire" is 0.035 inches thick)
- Wire LENGTHS is typically given in CENTIMETERS (example "180 wire" is 180 cm long)

Example Quiz 1: *What is the size of a puncture hole in mm of a 6 French sheath?*

Diameter in mm = Fr / 3
2.7 mm = (6 + 2) / 3

Answer = 2.7 mm

> - 6 French Describes the Inner Diameter
> - Add 2 French for the thickness of the rubber
> - Total is 8 French

Example Quiz 2: *What is the size of a puncture hole in mm of a 6 French sheath, placed coaxially into a short access sheath ?*

**This is some second level fuckery.

6 French sheath is being placed inside of another sheath
6 French sheath is actually 8 French Big (remember you add 2F for the rubber wall). So you need a sheath that can accommodate an 8 French Diameter. Remember that sheaths are named for what they can accommodate, so you need an 8 French Sheath. 8 French sheath is actually 10 French Big (remember you add 2F for the rubber wall).

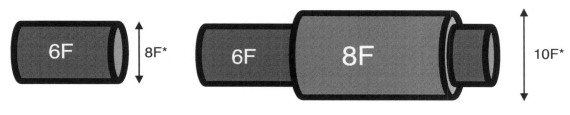

Diameter in mm = Fr / 3
3.3 mm = (8 + 2) / 3

Answer = 3.3 mm

> - 8 French Describes the Inner Diameter
> - Add 2 French for the thickness of the rubber
> - Total is 10 French

Puncture Needles - The Legend Continues:

Some Conversions:

- 16G needle has an outer diameter of 1.65 mm, = 5 F catheter;

- 20G needle has an outer diameter of 0.97 mm, = 3 F catheter.

Some Needle Wire Rules:

Old School Seldinger Technique:

- 18G needle will accept a 0.038 inch guidewire

- 19G needle will allow a 0.035 inch guidewire

> **Remember 0.035 is probably the most common wire used. Thus the 19G is the standard needle in many IR suites.*

Micro Puncture Style:

- Initial puncture is performed with a 21G (rather than a typical 18G or 19G) needle.

- <u>21G needle will allow a 0.018 inch guidewire</u>

- After you have that tiny wire in, you can exchange a few dilators up to a standard 4F-5F system with the popular 0.035 wire.

Micro Puncture is Good when….	*Micro Puncture is Bad when….*
• *Access is tough (example = a fucking antegrade femoral puncture)* • *You suck ("lack experience")* • *Anatomically sensitive areas (internal jugular, dialysis access)*	• *Scarred Up Groins* • *Big Fat People* • *When you try and upsize, sometimes that flimsy 0.018 won't give enough support for antegrade passage of a dilator.*

Guidewires - The Legend Continues to Continue:

There are two main flavors of guidewires:

(1) Non-Steerable - These are used as supportive rails for catheters. These are NOT for negotiating stenosis or selecting branches

(2) Steerable - These have different shaped tips that can be turned or flipped into tight spots. Within this category is the "hydrophilic" coated which are used to fit into the tightest spots.

Hydrophilic Guidewires - *"Slippery when wet"*. They are sticky when dry, and super slippery when wet. At most academic institutions dropping one of these slippery strings on the floor will result in "not meeting the milestone" and "additional training" (weekend PICC workups).

- *Next Step Questions:* Could revolve around the need to "wipe the wire with a wet sponge each time it is used."

- *Next Step Questions:* Pretty much any situation where you can't get into a tight spot. This could be a stenotic vessel, or even an abscess cavity.

Length - Here is the testable trivia regarding wire length.

- Remember *Diameter* is in *INCHES*, Length is in CENTIMETERS

- 180 cm is the standard length

- 260 cm is the long one. These are used if you are working in the upper extremity (from a groin access), working in the visceral circulation and need to exchange catheters, using a guide cath that is longer than 90 cm, through-and-through situation ("body flossing").

- Minimal guidewire length = length of catheter + length of the guidewire in the patient.

Floppy Tips - A lot of wires have pointy ends and soft floppy ends. The floppy ends are usually available in different sizes. The testable point is that **the shorter the floppy part the greater the chance of vessel dissection.** For example, a 1 cm floppy tip has a greater risk of dissection compared to a 6 cm floppy tip. The practical tip is to choose a wire with a long floppy tip (unless you are trying to squeeze into a really tight spot).

Guidewires - The Legend Continues to Continue to Continue

Stiffness: I feel like there are two primary ways to ask questions about stiffness:

(1) Your classic *"right tool for the right job"* questions.
Unfortunately, these are often *"read my mind, and understand my prejudices"* questions. The following are probably the clearest scenarios:

- Bentson (floppy tip) = Classic guidewire test for acute thrombus lysability

- Lunderquist (super stiff) = "The coat hanger." This thing is pretty much only for aortic stent grafting.

- Hydrophilic = Trying to get into a tight spot. Yes a Bentson is also an option, but this is more likely the "read my mind" choice.

(2) *Which is "Stiffer ?"* or *Which is "Less Stiff ?"* types of question. Basically just have a general idea of the progression. A second-order style question would be *"Which is more or less likely to cause dissection?"* Remember the rule is "more stiff = more dissection."

Less ——————————————————————————→ More Stiff

"Noodle Like"	Normal	Supportive	Stiff	Hulk Smash !!
Bentson	Hydrophilic	Stiff Hydrophilic	Flexfinder	Lunderquist
	Standard 0.035 J or Straight	"Heavy Duty" J or Straight	Amplatzer Stiff or Extra Stiff	Backup Meier
			0.018 Platinum Plus	
			V18 - *shapeable tip*	

Trivia: Stiff guidewires should NEVER be steered through even the mildest of curves. You should always introduce them through a catheter (that was originally placed over a conventional guidewire).

J Tip Terminology: A "J Shaped" Tip supposedly has the advantages of not digging up plaque and of missing branch vessels. Often you will see a number associated with the J (example 3 mm, 5 mm, 10 mm, 15 mm etc...). *This number refers to the radius of the curve.* Small curves miss small branch vessels, larger curves miss larger branch vessels. The classic example is the 15mm curve that can be used to avoid the profunda femoris during the dreaded arterial antegrade stick.

Catheters - The Legend Continues
— Fuckery with Numbers

If you look at a "buyers guide" or the packaging of an angiographic catheter you may (if you look hard enough) find 3 different numbers. I think it would be easy to write a question asking you to ID the numbers, or asking what size sheath or wire you can use with the catheter.

The three numbers that you are going to see on the package are: the outer diameter size (in French), the inner diameter size (in INCHES), and the length (in CENTIMETERS).

Example Question 1: *What size is this catheter?*

VANDELAY INDUSTRIES
FINE ANGIOGRAPHIC CATHETERS

4, 110, 0.035

Answer = 4F

Remember that the outer diameter of a catheter defines it's size (unlike the sheath which is defined by the inner diameter), and that these sizes are given in French. 4F catheters are very commonly used. 110 and 0.035 are not catheter sizes available for humans existing outside of middle earth.

Remember that length of the catheter is given in centimeters. The standard lengths vary from about 45 cm to 125 centimeters.

Lastly the inner diameter of a catheter is given in inches and will pair up with the size wire. For example, the largest wire a 0.035 catheter will accommodate is a 0.035.

Example Question 2: *What size sheath and guidewire can you use with this catheter?*

VANDELAY INDUSTRIES
FINE ANGIOGRAPHIC CATHETERS

4, 110, 0.035

Answer =
- **4F Sheath or Larger**
- **0.035 wire or Smaller**
a 0.038 wire would NOT fit

It's a 4F sheath because sheaths are defined by their INNER diameter. So a 4F snake can crawl through a 4F tube. Obviously a bigger tube (5F, 6F, etc...) will also have enough room for a 4F snake.

It's a 0.035 wire because the inner diameter measurements are given in inches, just like the guidewires. In this case the tube is the catheter and the wire is the snake. So a bigger snake (any wire thicker than 0.035) wouldn't fit.

Catheters - Selective vs Non-Selective

Just like Guidewires can be grouped into "steerable" or "non-steerable" , catheters can be grouped into "non-selective (flush) catheters" and "selective catheters".

- *Non-Selective Catheters:* These things are used to inject contrast into medium and large shaped vessels. This is why you"ll hear them called "flush catheters."

- *Selective Catheters:* These things come in a bunch of different shapes/angles with the goal of "selecting" a branch vessel (as the name would imply).

Non-Selective Catheters

Pigtail: For larger vessels this is the main workhorse. It's called a "pigtail" because the distal end curls up as you retract the wire. This curled morphology keeps it out of small branch vessels. The catheter has both side and end holes.

> *Q:* What might happen if you consistently inject through the pigtail like a pussy?

> *A:* All the contrast will go out the proximal side holes and not the tip. Eventually, if you keep flushing like a pansy you will end up with a clot on the tip.

> *Q:* What should you do prior to giving it the full on alpha male injection ?

> *A:* Give a small test injection to make sure you aren't in or up against a small branch vessel. Pigtails are for use in medium to large vessels.

> *Q:* What if the pigtail fails to form as you retract the wire?

> *A:* Push the catheter forward while twisting.

Straight Catheter: This one doesn't curl up as you retract the wire. Otherwise, it's the same as a pigtail with side holes and an end hole. The utility of this catheter is for smaller vessels (with the caveat that they still need decent flow).

The *classic location is the iliac.*

Catheters - Selective vs Non-Selective cont...

Selective Catheters

Selective catheters come in two main flavors: (1) end hole only, or (2) side + end holes (*that's what she said*).

End Hole Only	Side + End Holes *"Girl who went to catholic school"*
Hand Injection Only *high flow injection can displace the catheter, or cause dissection*	Works fine with Pump Injected runs *(can handle a rapid bolus without displacing)*
Utility = Diagnostic Angiograms and Embolization Procedures	Utility = Classic would be a SMA Angiogram
	NEVER use with Embolotherapy. The fucking coils can get trapped in the sideholes or the particulate matter/mush may go out a side hole and go crush the wrong vessel. *"Non-targeted"* they call it.

I think the above chart is probably good enough to get most reasonable selective catheter questions correct. Unfortunately, it's also possible that you could be asked a *"read my mind, understand my prejudices"* type of question in the form of *"which catheter would you use?"*

This is how I would guess - if forced.

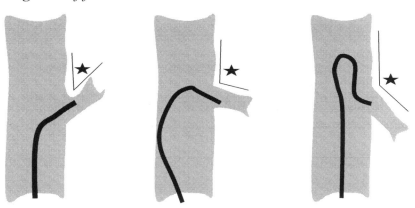

Acute Angle (< 60)	Angle of 60-120	Obtuse Angle (> 120)
Example = Aortic Arch Vessels	Example = Renals, *Maybe SMA and Celiac*	Example = Celiac, SMA, IMA
"Angled Tip Catheter"	"Curved Catheter"	"Recurved"
-Berenstein or *Headhunter*	*"RDC" Renal Double Curve, or a "Cobra"*	*Sidewinder (also called a Simmons), or a "Sos Omni"*

WTF is a "Recurve" ?

For whatever reason Academic Angio guys tend to spaz if residents don't understand why a *"recurve"* is different than a regular curved catheter.

Basically any curved catheter has a "**p**rimary" curve and a "**s**econdary" curve. On a regular curved cath both are in the same direction. However, on a recurved cath the primary goes one way, and the secondary goes the other.

These catheters are good for vessels with an obtuse angle. You pull the catheter back to drop into them.

I trained under a guy who was always very impressed with himself when he could perform a basic catheter maneuver like this. After dropping into the IMA he would sometimes slowly turn to one of the female techs and say *"that's why I'm the king."*

I was really afraid he was going to break his own arm, jerking himself off that hard.

That guy (or someone like him) is probably writing questions for the IR section (guessing / not confirmed - but makes me smile to think so).

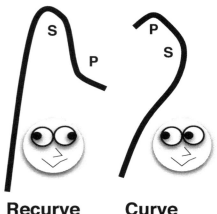

Recurve   Curve

Vocab

"Co-Axial Systems" - Basically one catheter inside another catheter/sheath. The most basic example would be a catheter inside the lumen of an arterial sheath.

"Guide Catheters" - These are large catheters meant to guide up to the desired vessel. Then you can swap them for something more conventional for distal catheterization.

"Introducer Guide" - This is another name for a *long sheath*. The assholes are trying to trick you.

"Microcatheter" - These are little (2-3 French). They are the weapon of choice for tiny vessels (example "super-selection" of peripheral or hepatic branches).

"Vascular Sheath" - It's a sheath (plastic tube) + hemostatic valve + side-arm for flushing

Flow Rate

"Give me 20 for 30" — typical angio lingo for a run at 20cc/sec for a total of 30 seconds.

How do you decide what the correct flow rate is ? For the purpose of multiple choice, I'll just say memorize the chart below. In real life you have to consider a bunch of factors: catheter size, catheter pressure tolerance, flow dynamics, vessel size, volume of the distal arterial bed (hand arteries can tolerate less blood displacement compared to something like the spleen), and interest in the venous system (a common concern in mesenteric angiography - hence the relatively increased volumes in the SMA, IMA, and Celiac on the chart).

Bigger Artery = Higher Rate. You want to try and displace 1/3 of the blood per second to get an adequate picture.

Typical Rates / Volumes			
Rate 1-2mL/sec Volume 4-10 mL	**Rate 4-8mL/sec Volume 8-15 mL**	**Rate 5-7mL/sec Volume 30-40 mL**	**Rate 20-30mL/sec Volume 30-40 mL**
Bronchial Artery Intercostal Artery	Carotid Subclavian Renal Femoral IMA	Celiac SMA	Aorta, Aortic Arch, IVC, Pulmonary Artery
	IMA are typically given a higher volume (15-30 mL)		*Abdominal Aorta has a slightly lower rate (15-20 mL/sec) as it is smaller than the Thoracic Aorta*

Maximum Flow Rates:

These are determined by the INTERNAL diameter, length, and number of size holes. In general, *each French size gives you about 8ml/s*.

These are the numbers I would guess if forced to on multiple choice. In the real world its (a) written on the package and (b) a range of numbers

3F = 8 ml/s, 4F = 16 ml/s, 5F = 24 ml/s.

Catheter Flushing

Double Flush Technique - This is used in situations where even the smallest thrombus or air bubble is going to fuck with someone's golf game (neuro IR / cerebral angiograms). The technique is to (1) aspirate the catheter until you get blood in the catheter, then (2) you attach a new clean saline filled syringe and flush.

Single Flush Technique - This is used everywhere else (below the clavicles). The technique is to (1) aspirate until you get about 1 drop of blood in a saline filled syringe, and (2) tilt the syringe 45 degrees and flush with saline only.

What if you accidentally mixed the blood in with the saline?

Discard the syringe and double flush

What if you are unable to aspirate any blood ?

Hopefully you are just jammed against a side wall. Try pulling back or manipulating the catheter. If that doesn't work then you have to assume you have a clot. In that case your options are to (1) pull out and clear the clot outside the patient, or (2) blow the clot inside the patient - you would only do this if you are embolizing that location anyway (and a few other situations that are beyond the scope of this exam).

SECTION 2:
Vascular Access

Arterial Access

General "Next Step" Scenarios:

- *You meet resistance as you thread the guidewire.* Next Step = STOP! *"Resistance"* is an angio buzzword for something bad. Pull the wire out and confirm pulsatile flow. Reposition the needle if necessary.

- *The wire will not advance beyond the top of the needle even after you pull the wire back and have normal pulsatile flow.* Next Step = Flatten the needle against the skin. You are assuming the need to negotiate by a plaque.

- *The wire stops after a short distance.* Next Step = Look under fluoro to confirm correct anatomic pathway. If it is normal then you could put a 4F sheath in and inject some contrast. After that monkeying around with a hydrophilic wire is the conventional answer.

Femoral Artery Access - This is the most common arterial access route.
Anatomy review = the external iliac becomes the CFA after it gives off the inferior epigastric.

The ideal location is over the femoral head (which gives you something to compress against), distal to the inguinal ligament / epigastric artery and proximal to the common femoral bifurcation.

- If you stick too high (above inguinal ligament): You risk retroperitoneal bleed
- If you stick too low, you risk AV Fistula
- If you stick at the bifurcation: You risk occluding branching vessels with your sheath.

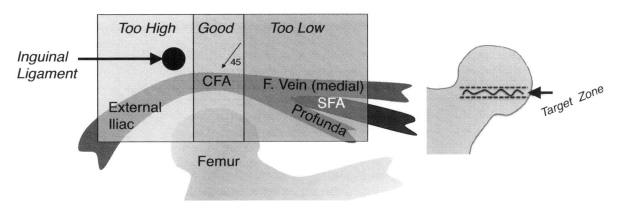

Brachial Access - Possible situations when you might want to do this:

- Femoral Artery is dead / unaccessible.

- The patient's abdominal pannus, vagina, or ballsack is really stinky.

- Upper limb angioplasty is needed

Special Testable Facts/Trivia:

- Holding pressure is often difficult. Even a small hematoma can lead to **medial brachial fascial compartment syndrome** (cold fingers, weakness) – and is a surgical emergency which may require fasciotomy.

- The **risk of stroke is higher** (relative to femoral access), if the catheter has to pass across the great vessels / arch.

- A sheath larger than a 7F may require a surgical cut down.

- The vessel is smaller and thus more prone to spasm. Some people like to give prophylactic "GTN" - glyceryl trinitrate, to prevent spasm.

Which arm ?

- Left Side if headed south (abdominal aorta or lower extremity).

- Right Side if headed north (thoracic aorta or cerebral vessels).

- All things equal = Left side (it's usually non-dominant, and avoids the most cerebral vessels).

- Blood pressure difference greater than 20 Systolic suggest a stenosis (choose the other arm).

Radial Access - This is also a thing. There are two pieces of trivia that I think are the most testable about this access type.

(1) **Bedrest is not required after compression**.

(2) You need to **perform an "Allen Test" prior to puncture.** The "Allen Test" confirms collateral flow via the ulnar artery to the hand (just in case you occlude the radial artery). The test is done by manually compressing the radial and ulnar arteries. A pulse ox placed on the middle finger should confirm desaturation. Then you release the ulnar artery and saturation should improve, proving the ulnar artery is feeding the hand.

Translumbar Aortic Puncture - This was more commonly performed in the dark ages / Cretaceous period. You still see them occasionally done during the full-on thrash that is the typical type 2 endoleak repair.

Trivia:

- The patient has to lay on his/her stomach (for hours!) during these horrible thrashes

- Hematoma of the psoas happens pretty much every case, but is rarely symptomatic.

- Known supraceliac aortic aneurysm is a contraindication

- Typically "high" access - around the endplate of T12 - is done. Although you can technically go "low" - around L3.

- The patient "Self compresses" after the procedure by rolling over onto his/her back.

- Complaining about a "mild backache" occurs with literally every one of these cases because they all get a psoas hematoma.

Pre Procedure Trivia: Prior to an arterial stick you have to know some anticoagulation trivia.

- Stop the heparin 2 hours prior to procedure (PTT 1.2x of control or less; normal 25-35 sec)
- INR of 1.5 is the number I'd pick if asked (technically this is in flux)
- Stop Coumadin at least 5-7 days prior (vitamin K 25-50 mg IM 4 hours prior, or FFP/ Cryo)
- Platelet count should be > 50K (some texts say 75)
- Stop ASA/Plavix 5 days prior (according to SIR)
- Per the ACR - diagnostic angiography, routine angioplasty, and thrombolysis are considered "clean procedures." Therefore, antibiotic prophylaxis is unnecessary.

Post Procedure Trivia: By the book, you want 15 minutes of compression. You can typically pull a sheath with an ACT of <150-180. Heparin can get turned back on 2 hours post (assuming no complications). Groin check and palpate pulses should be on the post procedure nursing orders.

Closure Devices: Never used if there is a question of infection at the access site.

Venous Access:

PICC lines: Use the non-dominant arm. The preference is basilic > brachial > cephalic. You don't place these in patients with CRF, on dialysis, or maybe going to be on dialysis.

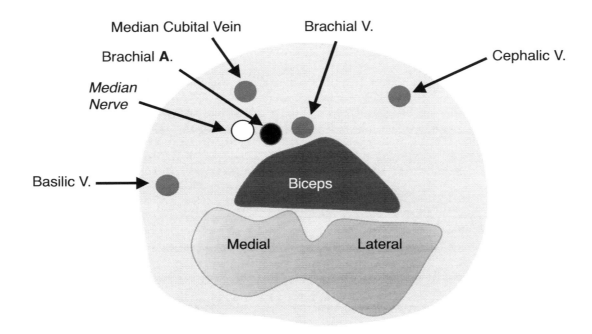

Central Lines/Port: The right IJ is preferred. External jugular veins can be used. Subclavian access is contraindicated in patients with a contraindication to PICC lines. Don't place any tunneled lines/ports in septic patients (they get temporary lines).

National Kidney Foundation-Dialysis Outcome Quality Initiative (NKF-KDOQI): Order of preference for access: RIJ > LIJ > REJ > LEJ. *"Fistula First Breakthrough Initiative"*: is the reason you don't place PICCs in dialysis patients.

What is the preferred access site for a dialysis catheter? The right IJ is the preferred access, because it is the shortest route to the preferred location (the cavoatrial junction). It will thrombose less than the subclavian (and even if it does, you don't lose drainage from the arm – like you would with a subclavian). Femoral approach is less desirable because the groin is a dirty dirty place.

Bleeding

The word *"hypotension"* in the clinical vignette after an arterial access should make you think about high sticks / retroperitoneal bleeds.

Things that won't help:

- Yelling "Mother Fucker!!" - trust me, I've tried this

Things that might help:

- Placing an angioplasty balloon across the site of the bleeding (or inflow) vessel.

> **Applying Pressure**
> *- Where dat hole be?*
>
> The hole in the skin and the hole in the artery don't typically line up.
>
> - *Antegrade Puncture* = Below the skin entry point
> - *Antegrade Puncture on a Fatty* = Well Below the skin entry point
> - *Retrograde Puncture* = Above the skin entry

Pseudoaneurysm Treatment: As described in the vascular chapter, you can get a pseudoaneurysm after a visit to the cardiology cath lab (or other rare causes). A lot of the time, small ones (< 2 cm) will undergo spontaneous thrombosis. The ones that will typically respond to interventional therapy are those with long narrow necks, and small defects. There are 3 main options for repair: (1) open surgery, (2) direct ultrasound compression, or (3) thrombin injection.

Direct Compression	Direct compression of the neck (if possible avoid compression of the sac). Enough pressure should be applied to stop flow in the neck.	Painful for the Patient (and the Radiologist), can take 20 mins to an hour. Don't compress if it's above the inguinal ligament.
Thrombin Injection	Needle into apex of cavity *(aim towards the inflow defect)* - inject 0.5-1.0 ml (500-**1000 units**). Do NOT aspirate blood into syringe - will clot.	***Contraindications:*** Local infection , Rapid Enlargement, Distal Limb Ischemia, Large Neck (risk for propagation), Pseudoaneurysm cavity size < 1cm.
Surgery	May be needed if thrombin injection fails, there is infection, there is tissue breakdown, or the aneurysm neck is too wide.	

Pseudoaneurysm Treatment Cont:

Which option do you pick? For the purpose of multiple choice I would suggest the following:

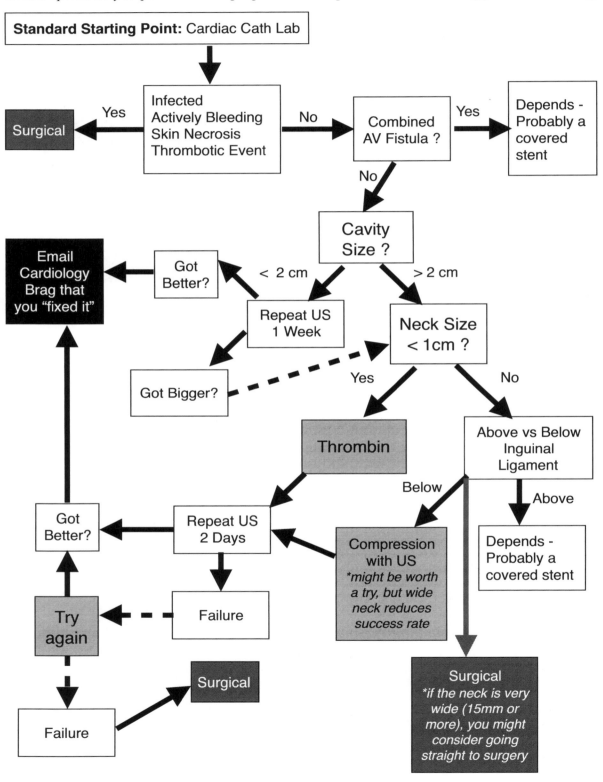

Pseudoaneurysm Treatment Cont:

*This algorithm on the prior page assumes the Test Writer agrees that **Thrombin is superior to Compression** (it hurts less, and probably has a higher success rate). Most modernly trained guys will think like this. However, some conservative strategies favor trying to compress all the ones below the Inguinal ligament first - then trying thrombin second line. Simply read the test writers mind to know his / her bias prior to answering.*

Thrombin Injection - Where do you stick the needle ?

The needle should be placed in the apex of the cavity *(tip directed towards the inflow defect).*

Ultrasound Compression - Where do you compress ?

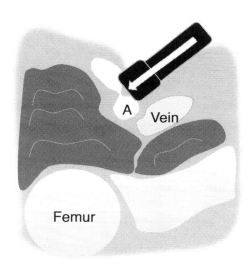

Orthogonal plane to the neck of the pseudoaneurysm. Pressure is directed to obliterate flow in the neck / sac.

Trivia - Seriously Watch the Wording Carefully:

- Anticoagulation has no effect on thrombin injection treatment - primary success**
- Anticoagulation does* increase the risk of recurrence (10%?) after thrombin injection treatment
- Anticoagulation is NOT a contraindication to attempting direct compression, although it DOES reduce success rate and most people will tell you to stop them prior to the procedure (if possible).
- Failure to respond to thrombin = Occult vascular issue (big puncture site laceration, infection)
- Untreated Pseudoaneurysm for greater than 30 days tend to resist compression and thrombin therapy to variable degrees. They do best if treated within 2 weeks.
- Attempted compression of a Pseudoaneurysm above the inguinal ligament can cause a RP bleed. It is still safe to try and thrombin inject.

SECTION 3:
PTA and Stents

General Tips/Trivia regarding angioplasty: The balloon should be big enough to take out the stenosis and stretch the artery (slightly). The ideal balloon dilation is about 10-20% over the normal artery diameter. Most IR guys/gals will claim success if the residual stenosis is less than 30%. Obviously you want the patient anticoagulated, to avoid thrombosis after intimal injury. The typical rule is 1-3 months of anti-platelets (aspirin, clopidogrel) following a stent.

"Primary Stenting": This is angioplasty first, then stent placement. You want to optimize your result. Stenting after angioplasty usually gives a better result than just angioplasty alone (with a few exceptions – notably FMD – to which stenting adds very little). An important idea is that a stent can't do anything a balloon can't. In other words, the stent won't open it any more than the balloon will, it just prevents recoil.

Balloon Expanding vs Self Expanding: Stents come in two basic flavors, balloon expandable or self expandable. Location determines the choice.

Self Expandable stents are good for areas that might get compressed (superficial locations).

• Classic Examples = Cervical Carotid or SFA.

Balloon Expandable stents are good for more precise deployment

• Classic Example = Renal ostium

Closed vs Open Cell Stents - Vascular stent designs may be categorized as (a) closed-cell - where every stent segment is connected by a link (less flexible, with better radial force) or (b) open-cell in which some stent segment connections are deliberately absent (flexible/conforms to tortuous vessels, less radial force).

Nitinol (magic?): Nitinol is said to have a "thermal memory." It is soft at room temperature, but can become more rigid at body temperature. This is exploited for self-expanding stents.

Drug Eluting Stents – These things have been used for CAD for a while. The purpose of the "drug" is to retard neointimal hyperplasia.

Balloon Selection - Balloons should be 10-20% larger than the adjacent normal (non-stenotic) vessel diameter. A sneaky move would be to try and get you to measure a post-stenotic dilation.

A rough guessing guide (if forced):

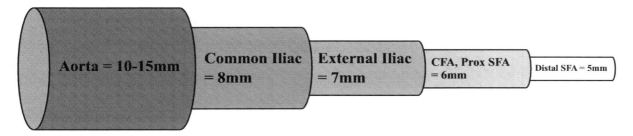

Aorta = 10-15mm   **Common Iliac = 8mm**   **External Iliac = 7mm**   **CFA, Prox SFA = 6mm**   Distal SFA = 5mm

****Popliteal would be 4 mm*

As a general rule, larger balloons allow for more dilating force but the risk of exploding the vessel or creating a dissection is also increased.

Stent Selection - Stents should be 1-2 cm longer than the stenosis and 1-2 mm wider than the unstenosed vessel lumen

Special Situations -

(1) **You have more than 30% residual stenosis (failed you have).** The first thing to do (if possible) is to measure a pressure gradient. If there is no gradient across the lesion, you can still stop and claim victory. If there is a gradient you might be dealing with *elastic recoil* (the lesion disappeared with inflation, but reappeared after deflation). The next step in this case is to place a stent.

(2) **You can't make the waist go away with balloon inflation.** Switch balloons to either a higher pressure rated balloon, or a "cutting balloon."

(3) **You caused a distal embolization.** First do an angiographic run. If the limb / distal vessels look fine then you don't need to intervene. If you threatened the limb, then obtain ipsilateral access and go after the clot ("aspiration").

(4) **You exploded the vessel ("Extravasation").** This is why you always leave the balloon on the wire after angioplasty. If you see extravasation get that balloon back in there quickly, and perform a low pressure insufflation proximal to the rupture to create tamponade. You may need to call vascular surgery ("the real doctors").

(5) What if you are trying to cross a tight stenosis and you see something like this ?

This is the classic *"spiral"* of a *dissecting wire.*

SECTION 4:
Stent Grafts

"EVAR" = EndoVascular abdominal aortic Aneurysm Repair. These include the bifurcated iliac systems and unilateral aortic + iliac systems.

"TEVAR" = Thoracic EndoVascular aortic Aneurysm Repair.

THIS vs THAT: Endografts vs Open Repair:

- 30 Day Mortality is LESS for Endovascular Repair (like 30% less)
- Long Term Aneurysm Related Mortality (and total mortality) is the SAME for open vs endovascular repair
- Graft Related Complications and Re-interventions are HIGHER with Endovascular Repair

---

Indications for EVAR:

(1) AAA larger than 5 cm (or more than 2x the size of the normal aorta)

(2) AAA growing "rapidly" (more than 0.5 cm in 6 months)

Anatomy Criteria for EVAR:

- Proximal landing zone must be:

  - 10 mm long,

  - Non- aneurysmal (less than 3.2 cm),

  - Angled less than 60 degrees.

10 mm Long
< 3.2 cm Wide
< 60 Degree of Tortuosity

Device Deployment:

Tortuosity and Vessel Size are issues for device deployment. The general rules are that you have problems if:

- Iliac vessels have an angulation > 90 degrees (especially if heavily calcified)

- Iliac artery diameters < 7 mm (may need a cut down and the placement of a temporary conduit).

Absolute Contraindication to Infrarenal EVAR:

• Landing sites that won't allow for aneurysm exclusion

• Covering a critical artery (IMA in the setting of known SMA and Celiac occlusion, Accessory renals that are feeding a horseshoe kidney, dominant lumbar arteries feeding the cord).

Dealing with the Renals.

There are several anatomy vocab words that are worth knowing for aneurysms near the renals.

• *"Para-Renal"* - which is an umbrella term for aneurysms near the renals

• *"Juxta-Renal"* - Aneurysm that has a "short neck" (proximal landing zone < 1 cm) or one that encroaches on the renals.

• *"Supra-Renal"* - Aneurysm that involves the renals and extends into the mesenterics.

• *"Crawford Type 4 Thoracoabdominal Aortic Aneurysm"* - Aneurysm that extends from the 12th intercostal space to the iliac bifurcation with involvement of the origins of the renal, superior mesenteric, and celiac arteries.

Treating these types of aneurysms requires all kinds of fancy stuff; snorkels, chimney technique, etc… All is beyond the scope of the exam. Just know that it can be done, but it's not easy.

Complications:

The most feared/dreaded (testable) complication of an aortic stent graft is paraplegia secondary to cord ischemia. You see this most commonly when there is extensive coverage of the aorta (specifically T9-T12 Adamkiewicz territory), or a previous AAA repair. "Beware of the hair pinned turn" - famously refers to the morphology of Adamkiewicz on angiogram.

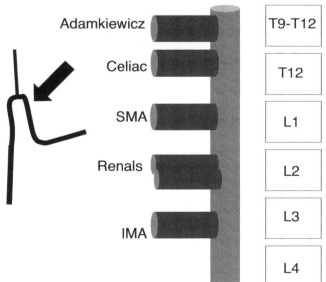

Symptoms of possible / developing paraplegia post procedure. **Next Step = CSF drainage.**

AAA pre/ post Endograft

After an aneurysm has been treated with an endograft, things can still go south. There are 5 described types of endoleaks that lend themselves easily to multiple choice questions.

- **Type 1:** Leak at the top (A) or the bottom (B) of the graft. They are typically high pressure and require intervention (or the sac will keep growing).
- **Type 2:** Filling of the sac via a feeder artery. This is the **MOST COMMON** type, and is usually seen after repair of an abdominal aneurysm. The most likely culprits are the IMA or a Lumbar artery. The majority spontaneously resolve, but some may require treatment. Typically, you follow the sac size and if it grows you treat it.
- **Type 3:** This is a defect/fracture in the graft. It is usually the result of pieces not overlapping.
- **Type 4:** This is from porosity of the graft. (*"4 is from the Pore"*). It's of historic significance, and doesn't happen with modern grafts.
- **Type 5:** This is endotension. It's not a true leak and it may be due to pulsation of the graft wall. Some people don't believe in these, but I've seen them. They are real.

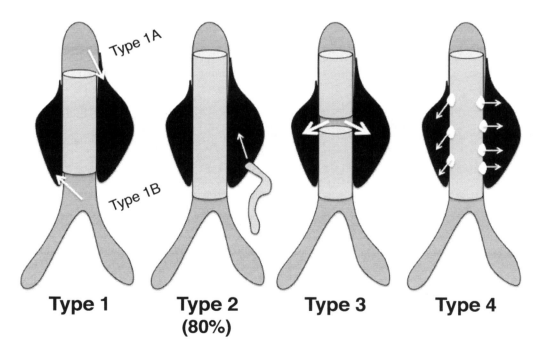

Treatment: *The endoleaks that must be emergently treated are the high flow ones - Type 1 and Type 3.* Most IR guys / vascular surgeons (real doctors) will watch a Type 2 for at least a year (as long as it's not enlarging). Most Type 4s will resolve within 48 hours of device implantation.

SECTION 5:
Embolization

There's a bunch of reasons you might want to do this. The big ones are probably stopping a bleed and killing a tumor.

Which agent do you want? Unfortunately just like picking a catheter these types of questions tend to fall into the mind reading category.

In general you are going to choose the agent based on the desired outcome, and the need to minimize risk. The most classic thinking goes something like this:

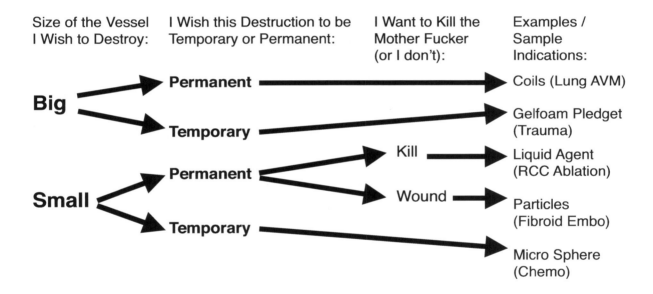

Another way to think / groups the agent is the general class. I think this is the most helpful to talk about them in an introductory sense. After I introduce them, we will revisit what to pick based on a multiple choose vignette.

Mechanical	Particulate	Liquid Agents
Coils	PVA - Particles *(permanent)*	Sclerosants
Vascular Plugs *(Amplatzer)*	Gelfoam *(temporary)*	Non-Sclerosants
	Autologous Blood Clot *(temporary)*	

Mechanical Agents:

Coils:

These are typically used to permanently occlude a large vessel. They come in all kinds of different sizes and shapes. You can deploy them with a "push" via a coaxial system, or if you don't need exact precision you can "chase" them with a saline bolus.

It gets complicated and beyond the scope of the exam (probably), but there are a variety of strategies for keeping these in place. Just know you can pack these things behind an Amplatzer, or you can use scaffolding techniques to hook small coils to a large one

<table>
<tr><td>THIS vs THAT:
Coils vs Micro-Coils

Coils: Deployed via standard 4-7F catheter

Micro: Deployed via Micro-Catheter. If you try and deploy them through a standard cath they can ball up inside the thing and clog it.</td></tr>
</table>

 Buzzword "Accurate Deployment" = Detachable Coil

Trivia: Remember never deploy these with a side-hole + end-hole catheter. You want end-hole only for accurate deployment.

Trivia: Never pack coils directly into an arterial pseudoaneurysm sac - *more on this later in the chapter.*

Amplatzer Vascular Plug (AVP)

This is a self expanding wire mesh that is made of Nitinol (thermal memory James Bond shit). You mount this bomb on the end of a delivery device/wire. When deployed it shrinks in length and expands in width.

Best Use = High Flow Situations, when you want to kill a single large vessel. If you are thinking to yourself - I'm gonna need a bunch of coils to take that beast down the answer is probably an amplatzer plug.

Particulate Agents:

These are grouped into:

- *Temporary:* Gelfoam, Autologous Blood Clot

- *Permanent:* PVA Particles

Best Use = Situations where you want to block multiple vessels. Classic examples would be fibroids and malignant tumors.

THIS *vs* THAT:
Gelfoam Powder vs
Gelfoam Pledgets/Sheets

Powder causes occlusion at the capillary level **(tissue necrosis)**

Pledgets/Sheets cause occlusion at the arteriole or larger level (tissue infarct is uncommon)

You are Doing it Wrong / Avoiding Reflux = An easy way to ask this would simply be "When do you stop deploying the agent?"

The classic teaching is to stop embolization when the flow becomes "to and fro." If you continue to pile the particulate agent in until you get total occlusion you risk refluxing the agent into a place you don't want it to go.

THIS vs THAT: Coils vs PVA Particles

In many cases if you can use coils, you can also use appropriately sized particles.

Size is one way to pick. Coils are good for medium to small arteries. PVA is good for multiple small arteries or capillaries.

Smaller particles (less than 300 microns) are going to risk tissue necrosis in many cases - so if you want to preserve the tissue, that's probably the wrong answer.

Another tip for picking between the two is the need for repeat Access. The classic example is the bronchial artery embolization. These things tend to re-bleed. So you should NEVER ever use coils (this will block you from re-accessing).

Bronchial artery embolization = Particles (> 325 micrometers).

Next Step ?

Q: What do you do after placement of an occlusion balloon in the setting of particle embolization ?

A: Test injection to confirm adequate occlusion.

Liquid Agents:

These are grouped into:

- *Sclerosants:* Absolute Alcohol (the one that hurts) and Sodium Dodecyl Sulfate (SDS)

- *Non-Sclerosants:* Onyx (Ethylene–Vinyl Alcohol Copolymer) , Ethiodol

Sclerosants:

As would be expected, the sclerosant agents work by producing near immediate thrombosis / irreversible endothelial destruction. As a result, non-targeted embolization can be fairly devastating. There are three main strategies for not causing a major fuck up (i.e. burning a hole in the dude's stomach, infarcting his bowel, etc...).

(1) Knowing the anatomy really well through careful mapping

(2) Frequent intermittent angiograms during the embolization procedure

(3) Use of Balloon Occlusion to protect non-target sites.

Next Step ?

Q: What do you do prior to deflating the occlusion balloon?

A: Aggressively aspirate (with a 60 cc syringe) to make sure all the poison is out of there.

Non-Sclerosants:

Onyx: Typically used for neuro procedures, hypervascular spine tumors, shit like that. It drys slowly (outside in) and allows for a slower, more controlled delivery.

Ethiodol: This is an oil that blocks vessels at the arteriole level (same as the really small PVA particles). For some reason, hepatomas love this stuff, and it will preferentially flow to the hepatoma. It is also unique in that it is radio-opaque, which helps decrease non-targeted embolization and lets you track tumor size on follow up.

Single Best Answer Classic Scenario

- Autologous Blood Clot = Post-Traumatic High-Flow Priapism (or Priapism induced by the female Brazilian olympic volleyball team)

- Varicocele (Spermatic Vein) = Coils

- Uterine Fibroid embolization (Bilateral Uterine Artery) = PVA or microspheres 500–1000 μm

- Generic Trauma = Gel Foam in many cases.

- Diffuse Splenic Trauma (Proximal embolization) = Amplatzer plug in the splenic artery proximal to the short gastric arteries. **Discussed in detail later in the chapter.

- Pulmonary AVM = Coils

- Hemoptysis (Bronchial artery embolization) = PVA Particles (> 325 μm).

- Hyper-vascular Spinal Tumor = Onyx

- Total Renal Embolization = Absolute ethanol

- Partial or Selective Renal Embolization = Glue (bucrylate–ethiodized oil)

- Segmental Renal Artery Aneurysm = Coils

- Main Renal Artery Aneurysm = Covered Stent (or coils after bare metal stent)

- Peripartum hemorrhage = Gel Foam

- Upper GI Bleed = Endoscopy First (if that fail then in most cases coils)

- Lower GI Bleed = Usually Microcoils

LARGE Vessel - Permanent	small Vessel - Permanent
Coils	Particles
	Liquid Sclerosants
Amplatz Occluder	Thrombin
LARGE Vessel - Temporary	Ethiodol
	small Vessel - Temporary
Gelfoam Pledget / Sheet	Microspheres
Autologous Clot	Gelfoam Powder

Post Embolization Syndrome:

Pain, nausea, vomiting, and low grade fever – is basically an expected finding. You don't need to order blood cultures - without other factors to make you consider infection. There is a *rule of 3 days* - it starts within the first 3 days, and goes away within 3 days of starting.

The vignette is most classic for a large fibroid embolization, but it's actually common after a solid organ (e.g. liver) - the tumor just needs to be big. Some texts suggest prophylactic use of anti-pyrexial and antiemetic meds prior to the procedure.

SECTION 6:
Acute Limb - Curse of the Baconator

"Threatened Limb" - Acute limb ischemia can be secondary to thrombotic or embolic events. Frequent sites for emboli to lodge are the common femoral bifurcation and the popliteal trifurcation. You can also get more distal emboli resulting in the so called *blue toe syndrome*.

As crazy as this may sound to a Radiologist, physical exam is actually used to separate patients into 3 categories: viable, threatened, or irreversible. This chart (or something similar) is how most people triage.

Category		Capillary Return	Muscle Paralysis	Sensory Loss	Arterial Doppler	Venous Doppler
1 - Viable	Not Threatened	Intact	None	None	+	+
2a - Threatened	Salvageable	Intact/Slow	None	Partial	-	+
2b - Threatened	Salvageable if immediate intervention	Slow/Absent	Partial	Partial	-	+
3 - Irreversible	NOT Salvageable *Amputation	Absent	Complete	Complete	-	-

Know who you can and can't treat

"Critical Limb Ischemia" – This is described as rest pain for two weeks (or ulceration, or gangrene).

General Idea on Treatment: An important point to realize is that lysis of a clot only re-establishes the baseline (which was likely bad to start with). So after you do lysis, consider additional therapy (angioplasty, surgery, stenting, etc...). If there is combined inflow and outflow disease, you should treat the inflow first (they just do better).

Surgery vs Thrombolysis: If it has been occluded for less than 14 days, thrombolysis is superior, if more than 14 days, (surgery is superior).

ACR Appropriate: Embolism Above / Below the Common Femoral Artery

- Isolated suprainguinal embolism probably should be removed surgically.
- Fragmented distal emboli should have endovascular thrombolytic therapy

Ankle – Brachial Index (ABI):

Calculation: Opinions actually vary on this - most people do it by dividing the higher of either the dorsalis pedis or posterior tibial systolic pressure (at the ankle) by the higher of either the right or left arm systolic pressure.

What it means: Opinions also vary on what the various cut off numbers mean. Most people will agree that you can safely deploy the phrase "peripheral arterial disease" if the resting ABI is less than 0.90

Ulcer Location Trivia (dinosaur IR guys love this - it really gets their dicks hard):

- Medial Ankle = Venous Stasis
- Dorsum of Foot = Ischemic or Infected ulcer
- Plantar (Sole) Surface of Foot = Neurotrophic Ulcer

Who are Rutherford and Fontaine? These are "useful" categories and classifications of signs and symptoms of peripheral arterial disease.

False Numbers? Arterial calcifications (common in diabetics) make compression difficult and can lead to a false elevation of the ABI.

Post-Operative Bypass Vocabulary:

- **Primary Patency** – Uninterrupted patency of the graft with no procedure done on the graft itself (repair of distal vessels, or vessels at either anastomosis does not count as loss of primary patency).

- **Assisted Primary Patency** – Patency is never lost, but is maintained by prophylactic interventions (stricture angioplasty etc..).

- **Secondary Patency** – Graft patency is lost, but then restored with intervention (thrombectomy, thrombolysis, etc..).

"Where to Access ? "

One simple way to ask a threatened leg treatment question is to ask for the best route of access per lesion. Again, like many IR questions, this falls into the "depends on who you ask", and/or "read my mind" category. If forced to choose, this is how I would guess:

Lesion	Access
Iliac	First Choice - Ipsilateral CFA. If that is down also (which it often is), I'd pick the contralateral CFA
CFA	Contralateral CFA
SFA	Ipsilateral CFA
Fem-Pop Graft	Ipsilateral CFA
Fem-Fem Cross-Over	First Choice - Direct Stick. Second choice-inflow CFA

If you are presented with other scenarios, the rule most people use is "shortest, most direct approach."

When would you use the contralateral CFA ? There are two general situations:

1. The Ipsilateral CFA is occluded.

2. The patient is very very fat. Even fatter than your normal acute leg patient. These are the guys/gals who got the milkshake (instead of the diet coke) with the baconator. As a point of gamesmanship, if the question header specifically mentions that the patient is obese they are likely leading you towards contralateral access.

 *Gamesmanship:* Watch out for "retrograde" vs "antegrade" access terminology in the distractors. The nomenclature for a downward (towards the toe) access is "antegrade." The terminology is based on the directions of the arterial flow.

•*Antegrade* access = towards the toes.

•*Retrograde* access = towards the heart.

General Procedural Trivia / Possible "Next Steps"

There are a whole bunch of ways to do this. In the most generic terms, you jam the catheter into the proximal clot and infuse TPA directly into the mother fucker. Every 6-8 hours you check to see if you are making progress. People call that "check angiography."

What if you can't cross the clot with a wire? If they spell that out in the vignette, they are trying to tell you that this clot is organized and probably won't clear with thrombolysis.

What if there is no clearing of the clot during a "check angiogram"? If they specifically state this, they are describing *"lytic stagnation,"* which for most reasonable people is an indication to stop the procedure.

The patient develops "confusion"? Neuro symptoms in a patient getting TPA should make you think head bleed. Next step would be non-con CT head.

The patient develops "tachycardia and hypotension"? This in the setting of TPA means the patient is bleeding out. Next step would be (1) go to the bedside and look at the site. Assuming he/she isn't floating in a lake of their own blood (2) CT abdomen/pelvis and probably stopping the TPA.

End Point? Most people will continue treating till the clot clears. Although continuing past 48 hours is typically bad form.

- - -

Venous Treatment

Varicose Vein Treatment: Just know that "tumescent anesthesia" (lots of diluted subcutaneous lidocaine) is provided for ablation of veins. Veins are ablated using an endoluminal heat source. A contraindication to catheter-based vein ablation is DVT (they need those superficial veins).

Post Thrombotic Syndrome (PTS): This is basically pain and stuff (venous ulcers) after a DVT. Risk factors include being old (>65), a more proximal DVT, recurrent or persistent DVT, and being fat. Catheter-directed intrathrombus lysis of iliofemoral DVT is done to prevent post thrombotic syndrome. This is not needed as much with femoropopliteal DVT as it will recanalize more frequently and have less severe post thrombotic syndrome.

SECTION 7:
Filters

An IVC filter is used in the following situations:

• Proven PE while on adequate anticoagulation

• Contraindication to anticoagulation with clot in the femoral or iliac veins

• Needing to come off anticoagulation – complications. There are a few additional indications that are less firm (basically, we think he/she might get a DVT and we can't anti-coagulate).

Vocab:

• *Permanent Filters:* Do Not Come Out
• *Retrievable Filters:* Can Come Out, But Do Not Have To
• *Temporary Filter:* Come out, and have a component sticking outside the body to aide in retrieval

Position *(before submission)*:

> *Why Not Leave Them In?*
>
> Depending on who bought you lunch (gave you a free pen), thrombosis rates vary.
>
> In general (for the purpose of multiple choice) about *10% of the permanent filters thrombose within 5 years*.

The device is usually placed infrarenal with a few exceptions (see below chart).

Why isn't it always just positioned suprarenal? A supra-renal filter has a theoretic increased risk of renal vein thrombosis. There is zero evidence behind this - like most things in medicine.

Indication	Filter Placement	Rationale
Pregnancy	Supra-renal	To avoid compression
Clot in the Renals or Gonadals	Supra-renal	Get above the clot
Duplicated IVCs	Either bilateral iliac, or supra-renal (above the bifurcation)	Gotta block them both
Circumaortic Left Renal	Below the lowest renal	Risk of clot by passing filter via the renals

MEGA-Cava: If the IVC is less than 28 mm, then any filter can be placed. If it's bigger than that, you might need to place a bird's nest type of filter which can be used up to 40 mm. You can also just place bilateral iliac filters.

Complications/Risks:

- *Malposition:* The tip of the filter should be positioned at the level of the renal vein. If it's not, honestly it's not a big deal
- *Migration:* The filter can migrate to another part of the IVC, the heart, or even the pulmonary outflow tract. If it goes to the heart, you need surgery. If it's just superior, you need to snare it out.
- *Thrombosis:* Although the incidence of PE is decreased, the **risk of DVT is increased**. Caval thrombosis is also increased, and you should know that clot in the filter is a contraindication to removal (you need to lyse it, before you remove it).
- *IVC Perforation:* A strut going through the caval wall is common and doesn't mean anything. However, aortic penetration, ureteral perforation, duodenal perforation, or lumbar vessel laceration can occur (rarely) from a strut hanging out of the cava – this is a bigger problem.
- *Device Infection:* A relative contraindication to IVC filter placement is bacteremia.

Random Trivia:

- A "Gunther Tulip" has a superior end hook for retrieval
- A "Simon-Nitinol" has a low profile (7F) and can be placed in smaller veins (like an arm vein).
- All filters are MRI compatible

Prior to placing the Filter:

You need to do an angiographic run. Where I trained, the classic pimping question for residents on service was to "name the 4 reasons you do an angiogram prior to filter placement!" The only answer that would not result in "additional training" (more weekend PICC workups) was:

1. Confirm patency of the IVC

2. Measure the size of the IVC

3. Confirm that you are dealing with 1 IVC

4. Document the position of the renal veins

Positioning the Filter:

Renals on an IVC Gram: There are two ways to show the renals on an IVC Gram. There is the nice way where they opacify normally and it's obvious, and there is the sneaky way where you see the *"steaming effect"* of unopacified blood allowing you to infer the position.

Obviously the sneaky way is more likely to show up on the exam.

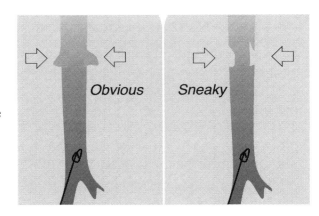

The Tip: For standard anatomy, the standard answer for a cone shaped filter is to put the apex at the level of the renals. Some people think the high flow in this location helps any clot that might get stuck in the filter dissolve.

What if there is clot in the IVC? The filter should be positioned above the most cranial extension of the clot. As mentioned in my glorious IVC Filter position chart, if the clot extends beyond the renals you need a suprarenal filter.

What if you fuck up the deployment (severe tilt, legs won't open, etc…) ? If it's retrievable, you may be able to snare it and restart. If it's permanent you are kind of hosed. Some people will try and stick a second filter above the retarded one.

Filter Removal:

The longer these things stay in, the more likely they will thrombose. Prior to removal you should perform an angiogram of the IVC. The main reason to do this is to evaluate for clot.

- More than 1 cm³ of clot = Filter Stays In

- Less than 1 cm³ of clot = Filter Comes Out

You snare the filter but when you pull on it you meet resistance ? In the real world, people will yank that mother fucker out of there. The IVC is the Rodney Dangerfield of vessels - no respect. For multiple choice? Stop and assume that it can't be retrieved.

Angiogram should also be done after removal of the filter to make sure you didn't rip a hole in the IVC. ***If you did rip a hole in it -*** *Next Step* - Angioplasty balloon with low pressure insufflation to to create tamponade. If that doesn't work, most people would try a covered stent graft. If you created a ***wall injury/dissection ?*** Again - answers will vary, but the classic answer is systemic anticoagulation.

SECTION 8:
Dialysis - the fucking fistulogram

Generally speaking there are two types of "permanent" access options for dialysis; (1) the arterio-venous fistula and (2) the arterio-venous graft.

AV Fistula - This is a subcutaneous anastomosis between an artery and adjacent native vein (for example the radial artery to the cephalic vein). All things equal, the preferred access (over the graft).

AV Graft - This is also a subcutaneous anastomosis between an artery and adjacent native vein. Except this time the distance between the vessels is bridged with a synthetic tube graft.

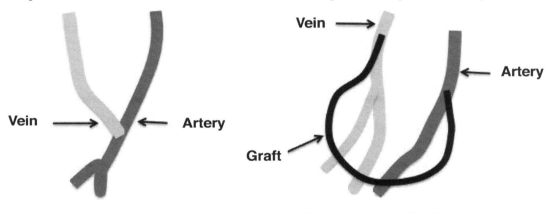

Arteriovenous Fistula   **Arteriovenous Graft**

What are the pros and cons of each types?

Pros of AV Graft:

- Ready for use in 2 weeks
- Easier to declot (clot is usually confined to the synthetic graft)

Pros of AV Fistula:

- Lasts Longer & More Durable
- Much less prone to development of venous neointimal hyperplasia at or downstream from the artery-vein anastomosis.
- Fewer infections

Cons of AV Graft:

-Less overall longevity
-Promotes hyperplasia of the venous intima at or downstream from the graft vein anastomosis, resulting in stenosis and eventual obstruction
-More infections (foreign graft material)

Cons of AV Fistula:

-Needs 3-4 Months to "Mature" (vein to enlarge enough for dialysis)

Why do grafts/fistulas need treatment (politics and greed) ? The primary reason is "slow flows." It's important to understand that nephrologists get paid per session of dialysis. If they can do a session in 1 hour or 4 hours they make the same amount of money. Therefore they want them running fast. So, really "slow-flow" is referring to slow cash flow in the direction of the nephrologist's pocket.

For the purpose of multiple choice I'd go with:

< 600 cc/min for graft = diagnostic fistulogram

< 500 cc/min for fistula = diagnostic fistulogram

Having said that, you may find different numbers different places - the whole issue is controversial based on the real motivation people have for treating these. Some texts say a fistula can maintain patency with rates as low as 80 cc/min, and grafts can maintain patency with rates as low as 450 cc/min. Also remember medicare won't pay for two treatments within 90 days, so make sure you treat on day 91.

Why do grafts/fistulas need treatment (actual pathophysiology)? Its a violation of nature to have a AF Fistula / Graft pulsating in your arm. Your body won't tolerate it forever. Neointimal hyperpasia develops causing an ever-worsening stenosis. If they don't get treated, they will eventually thrombose. All fistulas/grafts must die.

"Working it Up"

The only thing worse then actually doing a fistulogram is having to talk with and examine the patient prior to the procedure. Nearly all the IR texts and any program worth its snuff will "work them up" starting with physical exam.

Patient arrives in the IR department for "slow flows." *Next Step = Physical Exam*

This is the buzzword orientated algorithm that I would suggest for dealing with physical exam / history related fistula/graft questions:

LOOK	"Arm Swelling"	Central Venous Stenosis
	"Chest Wall Collaterals"	
	"Breast Swelling"	
LOOK	"Discolored Hand"	Dialysis-Associated **Steal Syndrome** (DASS)
	"Pale Colored Hand"	
	"Pallor of the Hand"	
LISTEN	"High-Pitched Bruit"	Localized Stenosis
	"Bruit in Systole Only"	
	"Discontinuous Bruit"	
FEEL	"Water Hammer Pulse"	Pre Stenosis
	"Diminished Pulse"	Post Stenosis

What is normal? A normal graft has an *easily compressible pulse*, a *low-pitched bruit* that is present *in both systole + diastole*, and a *thrill* that is palpable with compression *only at the arterial anastomosis*.

Localizing a Stenosis - *Classic Example - Straight Forearm Graft:*

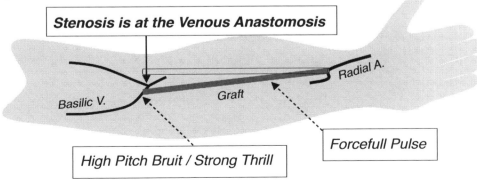

Stenosis is at the Venous Anastomosis

Basilic V.

Graft

Radial A.

Forcefull Pulse

High Pitch Bruit / Strong Thrill

GRAFTS:

Where is the problem (usually) in grafts? The most common site of obstruction is venous outflow (usually at or just distal to the graft-to-vein anastomosis). This is usually secondary to intimal hyperplasia.

What about the normal thrill and bruit in a graft ? There should be a thrill at the arterial anastomosis, and a low pitched bruit should be audible throughout the graft.

What if the bruit is high pitched? High Pitch = Stenosis, Low Pitch = Normal

What are you thinking if I tell you the dude has a swollen arm and chest ? This is classic for central venous stenosis.

FISTULAS:

Where is the problem (usually) in fistulas? It's more variable - you are less likely to be asked this. If you are forced - I'd say venous outflow stenosis - typically junta-anastomotic or runoff vein (AV anastomosis stenosis is uncommon).

If you fix a stenotic area - they are good to go right ? Nope - they reoccur about 75% of the time within 6 months.

What about the "thrill" in the fistula, is this a helpful finding? Yes - there should be a continuous thrill at the anastomosis. If it is present only with systole then you are dealing with a stenosis. Also, if you can localize a thrill somewhere else in the venous outflow - that is probably a stenosis.

What if the fistula is very "pulsatile" ? This indicates a more central stenosis - the fistula should be only slightly pulsatile.

Should there be a bruit ? A low pitched bruit in the outflow vein is an expected finding.

"Steal Syndrome" –The classic story is "**cold painful fingers**" during dialysis, relieved by manual compression of the fistula. Too much blood going to the fistula leaves the hand ischemic. The issue is usually a stenosis in the native artery distal to the fistula. *Fixing this is typically surgical* (DRIL = Distal Revascularization and Interval Ligation of Extremity, or Flow Reduction Banding).

ACCESS and TREATMENT:

Contraindications ? Infection is the only absolute one. If you fuck with an infected fistula or graft the patient could get endocarditis. If you don't fuck with it, the patient will probably still get endocarditis but infectious disease will have to blame it on someone else at the QA meeting.

What if it's "Fresh" ? A "relative contraindication" is a new graft or fistula. "New" to most people means less than 30 days. Significant stenosis prior to 30 days strongly suggests a surgical fuck up ("technical problem" they call it). Not to mention that a new dilating anastomosis is high risk for rupture. Those grafts are doomed to never reach long-term patency.

Access less than 30 days old with stenosis. *Next Step = Send them back to the surgeon.*

What about "long segments" ? You will read some places that stenotic segments **longer than 7 cm** respond poorly to treatment. Some people even consider this a **"relative contraindication."** If the question writer actually spells out the length of the stenosis greater than 7 cm he/she probably wants you to say send them back to surgery. In reality there are plenty of stubborn IR guys that will try and treat multiple long lesions because there is no better way than to prove one's manhood.

What about a contrast allergy? You can use CO_2 for runs.

What direction do you access the graft ? Access is typically directed towards the venous anastomosis - unless you are thinking arterial is the problem (which is much less common). Remember the lingo "antegrade" and "retrograde" refers to the direction of blood flow. *Antegrade is the typical route for venous problems*, and retrograde is the typical route for arterial inflow issues.

How do you typically look at the arterial anastomosis ? The move most places teach is to obstruct the venous outflow (with a clamp, blood pressure cuff, angioplasty balloon, finger - or whatever) which allows the contrast to reflux into the artery.

What are the moves for angioplasty of a narrow spot ? Give them heparin (3000-5000 units). Exchange your catheter for a 5 or 6 F sheath over a standard 0.035-inch guidewire. Dilate the narrow spot with a 6-8 mm balloon with multiple prolonged inflations. Remember to never take that balloon off the wire when you are doing diagnostic runs - as you might need to rapidly put it back if you caused a tear.

When do you place a stent ? There are two main reasons (1) you are getting bad elastic recoil, or (2) you have recurrent stenosis within 3 months of angioplasty.

Does Nitro have a role? You can use a vasodilator (like nitroglycerin) to distinguish between spasm and stenosis. The spasm should improve. The stenosis will be fixed.

What is considered a Successful Treatment? (1) Improved Symptoms (arm swelling better, etc..), or (2) less than 30% residual stenosis.

What about Aneurysms ? Small ones get monitored for size increase, but the classic teaching is that these are *managed surgically.*

General Vascular Access Trivia: Remember that PICC lines should not be put in dialysis (or possible dialysis – CKD 4 or 5) patients because they might need that arm for a fistula.

SECTION 9:
TIPS & BRTO

TIPS (Transjugular Intrahepatic Portosystemic Shunt) -

What is this portal hypertension? The portal vein gives you 70-80% of your blood flow to the liver. The pressure difference between the portal vein and IVC ("*PSG*", portosystemic gradient) is normally 3-6 mm Hg. Portal HTN is defined as pressure in the portal vein > 10mm Hg or PSG > 5 mm Hg. The most common cause is EtOH (in North America).

What does portal hypertension look like? On ultrasound we are talking about an enlarged portal vein (>1.3-1.5 cm), and enlarged splenic vein (>1.2 cm), big spleen, ascites, portosystemic collaterals (umbilical vein patency), and reversed flow in the portal vein.

Who gets a TIPS ? Accepted indications include:

- Variceal hemorrhage that is refractory to endoscopic treatment

- Refractory ascites.

- Budd Chiari (thrombosis of the hepatic veins) ** *most authors will include this*

Preprocedural steps for TIPS? You need two things. (1) An ECHO to evaluate for heart failure (right or left). (2) Cross sectional imaging to confirm patency of the portal vein.

How is a TIPS done? The real answer is do an IR fellowship.

First thing you do is measure the right heart pressure. If it is elevated (10-12 mmHg) you stop (absolute contraindication). A normal right heart pressure is around 5 mmHg.

If it is normal, you proceed with the procedure. Access the jugular vein on the right, go down the IVC to the hepatic veins, opacify the veins, do a wedge pressure (don't blow the capsule off), use CO_2 to opacify the portal system. Then stick "Crotch to Crotch" from the hepatic veins to the portal vein (usually right to right). Then put a *covered stent* in and balloon it up. Lastly check pressures and make you sure you didn't over do it (usually want a gradient around 9-12 — **"less than 12"**).

Which direction do you turn the catheter when you are moving from the right hepatic vein, to the right portal vein?

You want to turn anterior.

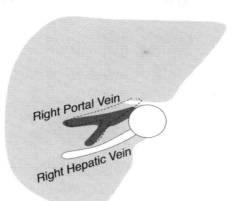

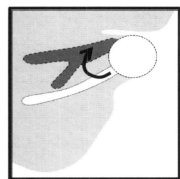

Keeping Score

While you are busy pretending you are a surgeon, why not pretend that you are a medicine doctor also? For the purpose of multiple choice, anything that resembles "Real Doctor" work is always high yield. *"Score Calculation"* is the poster child for the kind of fringe knowledge board examiners have traditionally loved to ask (this was definitely true for the old oral boards). The two highest yield scores are the MELD and the Childs-Pugh.

What is this "MELD" Score ? This was initially developed to predict three month mortality in TIPS patients. Now it's used to help prioritize which drunk driving, Hep C infected, Alcoholic should get a transplant first. MELD is based on liver and renal function - calculated from bilirubin, INR, creatinine. MELD scores greater than 18 are at higher risk of early death after an elective TIPS.

What about this "Childs-Pugh" Score ? This is the "old one," which was previously used to determine transplant urgency prior to the MELD. It works for TIPS outcomes, too, but is *"less accurate"* than a MELD. This score assesses the severity of liver disease by looking at the bilirubin, albumin, PT, ascites, and hepatic encephalopathy. The trivia to know is that *class B & C are risk factors of variceal hemorrhage.*

MELD	Child Pugh
Bilirubin	Bilirubin
INR	PT
creatinine	Albumin
– – –	Ascites, Hepatic Encephalopathy
Greater than 18 = High Risk Death	Class B and C are High Risk

Trivia = "Simplest prognostic measure" = Serum Bilirubin. > 3 mg/dL is associated with an increase in 30-day mortality after TIPS.

What are the contraindications for TIPS? Some sources will say there is no "absolute" contraindication. Others (most) will say <u>severe heart failure</u> (<u>right</u> or left), - but especially right. That the whole reason you check the right heart pressure at the beginning of the procedure. If you are forced to pick a contraindication and right heart failure is not an option, I would choose biliary sepsis, or isolated gastric varices with splenic vein occlusion. Accepted (by most) "relative" contraindications include cavernous transformation of the portal vein, and severe hepatic encephalopathy.

The main acute post procedural complications of TIPS include: Cardiac decompensation (elevated right heart filling pressures), accelerated liver failure, and worsening hepatic encephalopathy.

Evaluation of a "Normal TIPS"

Because the stent decompresses the portal system, you want to see flow directed into the stent. Flow should reverse in the right and left portal vein and flow directly into the stent. Flow in the stent is typically 90-190 cm/s.

Stenosis / Malfunction:

- Elevated maximum velocities (> 200 cm/s) across a narrowed segment.
- Low portal vein velocity (< 30 cm/s is abnormal).
- A temporal increase (or decrease) in shunt velocity by more than 50 cm/s is also considered direct evidence.
- "Flow Conversion" with a change of flow in a portal vein branch from towards the stent to away from the stent.
- An indirect sign of malfunction is new or increased ascites.

TIPS Follow-Up

These things tend to fail (50% primary patent within 1 year for a bare metal stent), so they need tight follow up.

Worsening Ascites, Bleeding, Etc (things that make you think the TIPS isn't working)

> *Next Step = Venogram with pressures*

> PSG >12 mmHg. *Next Step = Treat the stenosis (angioplasty + balloon)*

Trivia: The stenosis usually occurs in the hepatic vein, or within the TIPS tract.

Addressing Hepatic Encephalopathy – Dropping the gradient too low increases the risk of HE. If the TIPS is too open you may need to tighten it down with another stent.

What is an alternative to TIPS for treatment of refractory ascites? There is a rarely indicated thing called a "peritoneovenous shunt." This stupid thing has a high rate of infection and thrombosis, and can even lead to DIC. It's designed to allow drainage of the ascites through a tunneled line all the way up to the systemic circulation (jugular).

—

BRTO (Balloon-Occluded Retrograde Transverse Obliteration).

TIPS and BRTO are brother and sister procedures. Where the TIPS takes blood and steers it away from the liver (to try and help the side effects of portal hypertension), the BRTO does the opposite - driving more blood into the liver (to try and help with the side effects of extra hepatic shunting). The inverted indications and consequences are highly testable:

TIPS	BRTO
Treat Esophageal Varices	Treat Gastric Varices
Place a shunt to <u>divert blood around liver</u>	Embolize collaterals to <u>drive blood into liver</u>
Complication is worsening hepatic encephalopathy	Complication is worsening esophageal varices and worsening ascites
Improves esophageal varices and ascites	Improves hepatic encephalopathy

"The Moves": The general idea is that you access the portosystemic gastrorenal shunt from the left renal via a transjugular or transfemoral approach. A balloon is used to occlude the outlet of either the gastrorenal or gastro-caval shunt. Following balloon occlusion, a venogram is performed. A sclerosing agent is used to take the vessels out. After 30-50 minutes you aspirate the remaining sclerosing agent and let down the balloons.

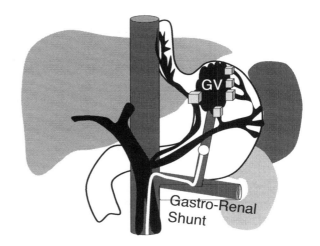

Trivia: The most common side effect of BRTO is gross hematuria.

SECTION 10:
Hepatic & Biliary Intervention

Biliary Duct Anatomy Trivia:

The ductal anatomy mimics the segmental anatomy. The simple version is at the hilum. There are two main hepatic ducts (right and left) which join to make the common hepatic duct. The right hepatic duct is made of the horizontal right posterior (segment 6 & 7) and vertical right anterior (segment 5 & 8). The left duct has a horizontal course and drains segment 2 and 4.

For whatever reason, IR guys love to grill residents about ductal variants (of which there are many). There was a dinosaur GI guy where I trained who also obsessed over this stuff. Apparently, obscure anatomic trivia tickles a psychopathology common to Academic Radiologists. As a result, I would know the 2 most common variants. The right posterior segment branch draining into the left hepatic duct is the most common. The second most common is trifurcation of the intrahepatic radicles.

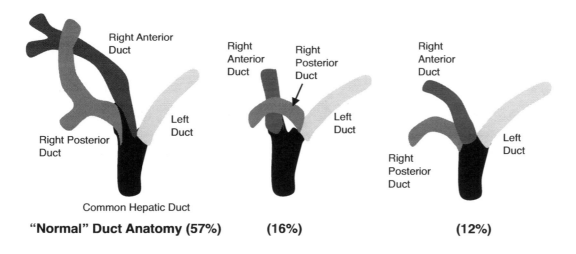

"Normal" Duct Anatomy (57%)   (16%)   (12%)

Biliary Drainage:

The role of **PTC** (Percutaneous Transhepatic Cholangiogram) and **PTBD** (Percutaneous Transhepatic Biliary Drainage) is centered around situations when ERCP and endoscopy have failed or are not possible (Roux-en-Y).

Things to do before the procedure:

• Check the coags - correct them if necessary (vitamin K, FFP, etc…).

• Most institutions give prophylactic antibiotics (ascending cholangitis is bad).

Approaches:

There are two approaches: right lateral mid axillary for the right system, or subxyphoid for the left system. Realistically, diagnostic cholangiogram and PTBD is usually done from the right. The left is more technically challenging (although better tolerated by the patient because the tube isn't in-between ribs) and usually there is a hilar stricture that won't allow the left and right system to communicate.

"The Moves" - Right-Sided Approach

Line up on the patient's right flank / mid axillary line. Find the 10th rib. Don't go higher than the 10th rib - always below (avoiding the pleura can save you a ton of headaches). Prior to jamming the needle in, most reasonable people put metal forceps (or other metal tool) over the target and fluoro to confirm you are over the liver and below the pleural reflection.

> When I say "Below the 10th Rib," I mean caudal to the 10th rib, not actually under the rib. Always puncture at the TOP EDGE OF A RIB to avoid the intercostal artery (which runs under the rib).

Now the fun begins. The basic idea is to pretend the patient is a voodoo doll of the Attending (or childhood tormentor) that you hate the most. Proceed to blindly and randomly jam a chiba needle in and inject slowly under fluoro as you pull back (but not all the way out). Obviously less sticks is better and it's ideal to do in less than 5 (most places will still consider less than 15 ok). Once you get into a duct the system will opacify. You then can pick your target (posterior is best for best drainage). You stick again, wire in, and place the catheter into the duodenum.

A non-dilated system can be very difficult and there is an old school trick where you stick the gallbladder (on purpose) and retrograde fill the system. The problem with that is you have to keep a drain in the gallbladder as well.

> **In the Duct?**
>
> • *Ducts* = Flow Towards the Hilum
> • *Vein* = Flow Cranially towards the Heart
> • *Artery* = Flow Towards the Periphery

The Moves" - Left Sided Approach

This time you use a sub-sternal / subxyphoid approach with ultrasound. Most people aim for the anterior inferior peripheral ducts. Otherwise the moves are pretty much the same.

Catheter / Stent Choice - Bare Bones of Trivia:

Most stent placement is preceded by a period of biliary decompression with an internal-external drain. Plastic stents are cheaper but have a short patency period. Metal stents will stay patent longer but can't be removed. Metal stents are not usually used in benign disease unless the patient has a long life expectancy.

Internal-External drains are the standard for crossing lesions. They have superior stability to a straight drain or pigtail. They offer the advantage of possible conversion to an internal only drain (save those bile-salts).

Some testable trivia is that many centers will manually punch some additional side holes in the proximal portion of the tube to make sure that drainage is adequate.

The key is to NOT position any side holes outside the liver (proximal to the liver parenchyma).

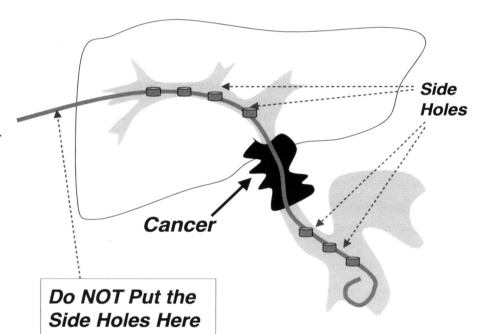

Side Holes

Cancer

Do NOT Put the Side Holes Here

"Next Step" - Testable Scenarios / Trivia:

- There is extensive ascites. *Next Step* = Drain it prior to doing the PTC.

- There is a small amount of ascites. *Next Step* = Opinions are like assholes (everyone has one), so you'll hear different things for this. I think most people would look to make sure the liver still abuts the peritoneum at the puncture site. If it does, then they will do a right sided approach. If it doesn't then they will use ultrasound and go substernal on the left.

- Right Approach with no filling of the left ducts. *Next Step* = Slowly and carefully roll the patient on their side (right side up). The right ducts are dependent - so this is actually fairly common. Now obviously if there is a known obstruction you don't need to roll them. The rolling is to prove it's not a real obstruction.

- You do your contrast run and the patient instantly goes into a full rigor. *Next Step* = Look around the room for the person you are going to blame for injecting too forcefully. "Rigor" is a multiple choice buzzword for cholangitis. Yes… full on biliary sepsis can happen instantly with a forceful injection. This is actually pretty easy to do if the patient has strictures or an obstructive neoplastic process. In those cases you will want to have your Scapegoat / "Not Me" (tech, med student, resident, fellow, drug rep, non-english-speaking international observer) do the injection. For the purpose of multiple choice some good next step options would be: aggressive resuscitation, place a drain, and inform the primary team / ICU that the Scapegoat gave the patient biliary sepsis.

> **Forceful Injection = ICU Visit for Cholangitis**
>
> **Buzzword = "Rigors after Injection"**

- You encounter (or expect stones). *Next Step* = Dilute contrast to 200-250 mg/ml to avoid obscuring filling defects.

- You can't cross the obstruction with a wire. *Next Step* = Place a pigtail drain and let the system cool down for like 48 hours. Try again when there is less edema.

Cholecystostomy:

This is done when you have a super sick patient you can't take to the OR, but the patient has a toxic gallbladder. In cases of acalculous cholecystitis (with no other source of sepsis), 60% of the time cholecystostomy is very helpful. It's a "temporizing measure." You have to give pre-procedure antibiotics. There are two approaches:

- *Transperitoneal* – This is preferred by many because it's a direct approach, and avoids hitting the liver. The major draw back is the wire / catheter often buckles and you lose access (and spill bile everywhere). This is typically not the first choice. However in patients with liver disease or coagulopathy it may be preferred (depending on who you ask). *If the question writer specifically states (or infers) that the patient has an increased risk of bleeding this is probably the right choice.* Otherwise, if forced to choose, pick the Transhepatic route

- *Transhepatic* – The major plus here is that when you cross the liver it stabilizes the wire and **minimizes the chance of a bile leak**. This is the route most people choose.

    o *Trivia* = Typically you go through *segments 5 and 6* on your way to the gallbladder

    o *Trivia* = This route transverse the "bare area" / upper one third of the gallbladder (hypothetically).

Important Trivia:

- Prior to the procedure, make sure the bowel isn't interposed in front of the liver/ gallbladder. If a multiple choice writer wanted to be sneaky he/she could tell you the patient has *"Chilaiditi Syndrome"* - which just means that they have bowel in front of their liver. Some sources will list this as a contraindication to PC.

- Even if the procedure instantly resolves all symptoms, you need to leave the tube in for 2-6 weeks (until the tract matures), otherwise you are going to get a bile leak.

- After that *"at least 2 week"* period you should *perform a cholangiogram* to confirm that the cystic duct is patent before you pull the tube.

- Most places will *clamp the tube for 48 hours prior to removal.* This helps confirm satisfactory internal drainage.

Managing Bile Leak – Bile leak is bad as it can lead to massive biliary ascites and chemical peritonitis. Most people will try and place a tube within the bile ducts to divert bile from the location of the leak (this usually works).

General Biopsy Pearls

There are two primary techniques for sampling tissue:

(1) Fine Needle Aspiration — *Cytology*

(2) Cutting Needle ("Core") — *Biopsy*

Fine Needle Aspiration:

This is for situations when you only need a few cells. It is typically performed through a 21 or 22G Chiba needle. Vacuum aspiration with a 20 cc syringe is applied as you pass the needle back and forth through the target.

Trivia: Apply "gentle" suction as you remove the needle. If you suck too hard a tiny sample could get lost in the syringe. If you forget to apply suction the sample will stay in the patient.

The needle is small so the risks are small.

Cutting / Core Needle

This is for situations when you need a larger sample. There are lots of devices but the most basic mechanism involves a needle with two parts; an outer shaft for cutting, and an inner stylet.

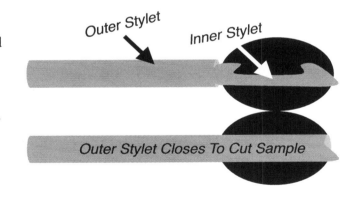

Trivia: For the purpose of multiple choice, the target is "cut" where the outer shaft is advanced.

Trivia: The general rule is pick the shortest length needle that will reach the target.

Trivia: "Automated Systems" fire both the inner and outer components to take the sample. The key point is that with these systems the sample is taken from tissue 10-20 mm in front of the needle.

Conventional Liver Biopsy -

You can do targeted approaches (for a specific lesion) or you can do non-targeted approaches (sampling). General pearls include: trying to cross the capsule only once, <u>biopsy the subcapsular masses through an area of uninvolved liver, and avoid the diaphragm.</u>

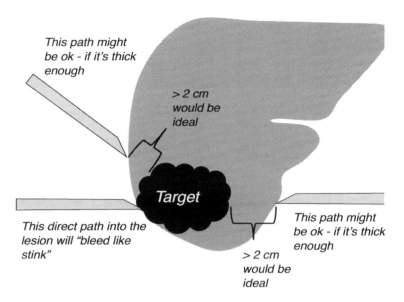

If given the choice, you want to biopsy peripheral lesions through 2-3 cm of normal liver prior to hitting the target.

This is done to avoid a blood bath.

Next Step: There is ascites = Drain it prior to doing the biopsy

Trivia: Mild shoulder pain (referred pain) is common after liver biopsy.

Trivia: Prolonged Shoulder Pain (> 5 mins) = Possible Bleed *"Kehr Sign"*.

Next Step: Prolonged Shoulder Pain (> 5 mins) = Re-evaluation with ultrasound. Always look behind the liver (Morrison's pouch) to see if blood is accumulating. Bleeding after liver biopsy occurs more from biopsy of malignant lesions (compared to diffuse disease).

Contraindications: Uncorrectable coagulopathy, thrombocytopenia (< 50,000), infections in the right upper quadrant – are contraindications for a conventional biopsy.

Trivia: Biopsy of carcinoid mets is controversial and death by carcinoid crisis has occurred after biopsy.

Next Step: Massive ascites or severe coagulopathy = *Transjugular approach*

Transjugular Liver Biopsy

The rationale is that the liver capsule is never punctured, so bleeding is less of a risk. Obviously this is a non-targeted biopsy for the diagnosis of infectious, metabolic, and sometimes neoplastic processes (classic example = grading chronic hep C).

Specific Indications:

- <u>**Severe Coagulopathy**</u>
- Massive ascites
- Failure of prior percutaneous liver biopsy
- Massive obesity *("Fat Even By West Virginia Standards")*
- Patients on mechanical ventilation
- Need for additive vascular procedures like TIPS

Procedural Trivia:

The general technique is to access the hepatic veins via the IVC (*via the right jugular vein*). Most people will tell you to biopsy through the *right hepatic vein* while angling the sheath anterior. The reason this is done is to get the biggest bite of tissue, and avoid capsular perforation (which was the entire point of this pain in the ass procedure).

Trivia: Right Sided Jugular Route is the superior route (better than left IJ, or femoral)

Trivia: Biopsy via the Right Hepatic Vein by angling anterior. Never perform an anterior biopsy from the middle hepatic vein.

Trivia: This procedure has the added benefit of allowing you to measure hepatic venous pressures - which can guide therapy or assess varix bleeding risk.

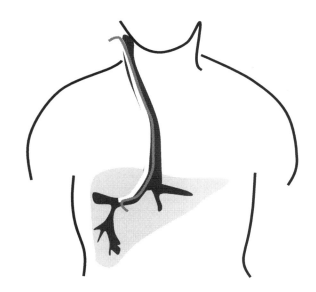

Hepatic / Splenic Trauma –

Embolization is a potential method for dealing with significant trauma to the hepatic or splenic arteries. Opinions on the exact role of angiography vary between institutions, so "read my mind" questions are likely.

I think the most likely type of indication question might actually be *who does NOT go to angio?*

The most accepted contraindication in a bleeding patient is probably a very busted-up unstable dude who needs to go straight to the OR for emergent laparotomy.

> **Indications**
> *agreed upon by most:*
>
> - Continuous hemorrhage (active extrav) in a patient who is borderline stable post resuscitation
>
> - Early ongoing bleeding after a surgical attempt to gain primary hemostasis
>
> - Rebleeding after successful initial embolization
>
> - Post traumatic pseudo-aneurysm and AVFs (even if they aren't currently bleeding).

 Tools and Strategy - Hepatic Considerations:

- Gelfoam, pledgets, particles, and/or microcoils are typically used.

- Massive non-selective hepatic artery embolization is usually avoided to reduce the risk of large volume tissue necrosis.

- *What's the main issue with tissue necrosis?* Hepatic abscess development (which is fairly common in a major liver injury anyway).

- *Trivia:* Coils should NOT be placed in the pseudoaneurysm sac. This can lead to a late rupture. The strategy is to occlude the distal and proximal parent vessels. You'll want to perform "completion angiography" to prove the thing is occluded prior to catheter removal.

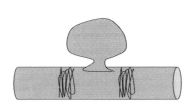

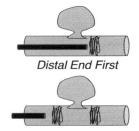
Distal End First

"Sandwich Technique" to exclude arterial pseudo aneurysm

Then Pull Back

- Hepatic surface is bleeding from more than one spot. Next Step = Gelfoam or particles.

- Hepatic Pseudoaneurysms can be treated at the site of injury (with the sandwich technique) because they are not end arteries (no collaterals). Plus the liver has a dual blood supply.

Tools and Strategy Continued - Spleen Considerations:

- Splenic laceration (without active extravasation) is NOT considered an indication to angio (by most people). Remember to use your mind reading powers to confirm the question writer agrees.

- The spleen does not have a dual blood supply, and is considered an "end organ" unlike the liver. So if you go nuts embolizing it you can infarct the whole fucking thing.

- Focal Splenic Abnormality. *Next Step* = Selective Embolization treatment

- Multiple Bleeding Sites. *Next Step* = Use a proximal embolization strategy, and drop an Amplatzer plug into the splenic artery proximal to the short gastric arteries. The idea is to maintain perfusion but reduce the pressure to the spleen (slower blood will clot), with the benefit of preserved collateral supply and less infarction risk.

- *Trivia:* Even with this proximal embolization strategy the patient usually does not require vaccination post embolization, as a lot of functional tissue should remain.

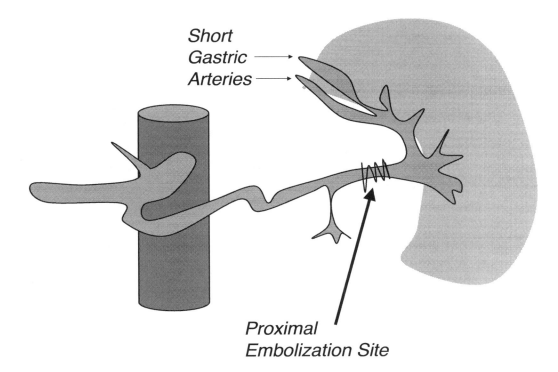

Short Gastric Arteries

Proximal Embolization Site

HCC Treatment:

You will read in some sources that transplant is the only way to "cure" an HCC. Others will say transplant, resection, or ablation are "curative" if the tumor is small enough. Arterial embolization (TACE) is typically used in situations where the tumor burden is advanced and the patient cannot undergo surgery.

> **ACR Appropriate: Liver Transplant**
>
> — Transplantation should be considered ONLY in patients < 65 years of age with limited tumor burden (1 tumor ≤ 5 cm or up to 3 tumors < 3 cm).

Transarterial Chemoembolization (TACE) – Most people will consider this first line for palliative therapy in advanced cases. The mechanism relies on HCC's preference for arterial blood. High concentration of chemotherapy within Lipiodol (iodized oil transport agent) is directly delivered into the hepatic arterial system. The tumor will preferentially take up the oil resulting in a prolonged targeted chemotherapy. The Lipiodol is usually followed up with particle embolization, with the goal of slowing down the washout of the agent.

Absolute Contraindication = Decompensated (acute on chronic) Liver failure.

Trivia: Some sources will list portal vein thrombosis as a contraindication (because of the risk of liver infarct). Others say portal vein thrombosis is fine as long as an adjustment is made to limit the degree of embolization and you can document sufficient hepatic collateral flow. Simply read the mind of the question writer to know which camp they are in.

Trivia = TACE in Patients with a biliary stent, prior sphinctertomy, or post Whipple are all high risk for biliary abscess.

Trivia = *"Sterile cholecystitis" or "chemical cholecystitis"* are buzzwords that when used in the setting of TACE should lead you to believe that the agent was injected into the *right hepatic artery prior to the takeoff of the cystic artery* (artery to the gallbladder) .

Trivia = TACE will prolong survival better than systemic chemo

Trivia: Unfortunately, repeat TACEs can result in a ton of angio time and therefore a ton of radiation. Patient do sometimes get *skins burns* (usually *on their left back* because of the RAO camera angle).

RFA: Tumor is destroyed by heating the tissue to 60 degrees C (140 F). Any focal or nodular peripheral enhancement in the ablation lesion should be considered residual / recurrent disease. Sometimes, on the immediate post treatment study you can have some reactive peripheral hyperemia – but this should decrease on residual studies. Important trivia is that RF ablation is indicated in patients with HCC and colorectal mets (who can't get surgery).

TACE + RFA: As a point of trivia, it has been shown that TACE + RFA for HCC lesions larger than 3cm, will improve survival (more so than either treatment alone). This is still not curative.

Yttrium-90 Radioembolization - An alternative to TACE is using radioactive embolic materials (Y-90). The primary testable trivia regarding Y-90 therapy is understanding the pre-therapy work up. There are basically two things to know:

> (1) *Lung Shunt Fraction* - You give Tc-99 MAA to the hepatic artery to determine how much pulmonary shunting occurs. A shunt fraction that would give 30 Gy in a single treatment is too much (Y-90 is contraindicated).

What is this Yttrium ?

Yttrium-90 is a high-energy beta emitter with a mean energy of 0.93MeV. It has no primary gamma emission. Yttrium-90 has a half-life of 64 hours. After administration, 94% of the radiation is delivered over 11 days (4 half-lives). The maximum range of irradiation from each bead is 1.1 cm.

> (2) *The take off of the right gastric.* The fear is that you get non-targeted poisoning of the stomach, leading to a non-healing gastric ulcer. To help prevent reflux of the Y-90 (poison) into places you don't want (basically anywhere that's not liver) prophylactic embolization of the right gastric and the GDA is performed. The right gastric origin is highly variable, and can come off the proper hepatic or the left hepatic.

Trivia Review:

- Shunt Fraction > 30 Gy to the Lungs = No Y-90

- Before you give the poison, embo the right gastric (which has a variable take off) and GDA - so you don't put a hole in the stomach.

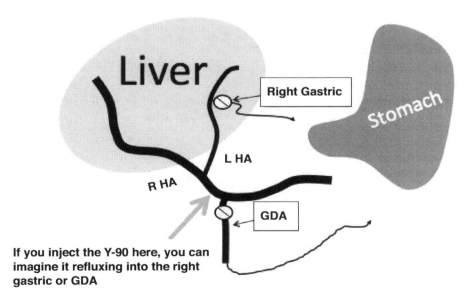

If you inject the Y-90 here, you can imagine it refluxing into the right gastric or GDA

Generalized Tumor Treatment Trivia (Regardless of the Organ)

RFA

- Tumors need to be less than 4 cm or you can't "cure" them. You can still do RFA on tumors bigger than 4 cm but the buzzword you want for this is "debulking".

> - Cure = < 4 cm
> - Debulk = > 4 cm

- You always need a burn margin of 0.5-1.0 cm around the tumor. So your target is the tumor + another 1 cm of healthy organ.

- A key structure (something you don't want to burn up) that is within 1 cm of the lesion is considered by most to be a contraindication to RFA. Some people won't cook lesions near the *vascular hilum*, or near the gallbladder. Be on the look out for *bowel*. It is possible to cook bowel adjacent to a superficial lesion. If they are asking you if a lesion is appropriate for RFA and it's superficial look for adjacent bowel - that is probably the trick.

- RFA requires the application of a "Grounding pad" on the patient's leg. Blankets should be jammed between the arms/body and between legs to prevent closed circuit arcs/burns.

- *"Hot Withdrawal"* supposedly can reduce the risk of tumor seeding. Basically you leave the cooker on as you remove the probe to burn the tract.

- *"Heat Sink"* - this is a phenomenon described exclusively with RFA. Lesions that are near blood vessels 3mm or larger may be difficult to treat (without getting fancy) because the moving blood removes heat away from the lesion.

- You can overcook the turkey. Temperatures at 100 C or greater tend to carbonize the tissue near the probe, reducing electrical conductance (resulting in suboptimal treatment). Around 60 C is the usual target.

- ***"Post Ablation Syndrome"*** - Just like a tumor embolization you can get a low grade fever and body aches. The larger the tumor, the more likely the syndrome (just like embolization).

  - Low Grade Fever and Body Aches Post Ablation. *Next Step* = Supportive Care

  - Persistent Fever x 2-3 weeks post ablation. *Next Step* = Infection workup.

Microwave

Similar to RFA is that it cooks tumors. The testable differences are that it can generate more power, can cook a bigger lesion, requires less ablation time, it's less susceptible to heat sink effect, and it does NOT require a ground pad.

Cryoablation

Instead of burning the tumors, this technique uses extreme cold in cycles with thawing. The freeze-thaw cycles fuck the cells up pretty good. The cold gun is generated by the compressing argon gas. I actually knew a guy who constructed a similar device shortly after an industrial accident left him unable to survive outside of subzero environments.

Trivia = Thawing is what actually kills the cancer cells

Trivia = If you are planning on treating immediately after biopsy, most sources will advise you to place the probes first, then biopsy, then treat. If you try and place the probes you make a bloody mess then you might not get accurate probe placement. Just don't biopsy the probe. Seriously, if you crack the probe and the high pressure gas leaks out - shit is gonna explode (better have your medical student ready as a shield).

Trivia: It hurts less than RFA - so patients need less sedation

Trivia: The risk of bleeding is higher than with RFA - because you aren't ablating the small vessels

Treatment Response

RFA Treatment Response:

Size:

- Week 1-4: It's ok for the lesion to get bigger. This is a reactive change related to edema, tissue evolution, etc…

- Month 3: The lesion should be the same size (or smaller) than the pre-treatment study.

- Month 6: The lesion should be smaller than pre-treatment.

Contrast Enhancement:

- Central or Peripheral Enhancement is NEVER normal in the lesion post treatment.

- You can have "benign peri-ablational enhancement" - around the periphery of the ablation zone. This should be smooth, uniform, and concentric. It should NOT be scattered, nodular, or eccentric (those are all words that mean residual tumor).

Time Interval

- Multiphase CT (or MR) at 1 month. If residual disease is present at this time, *Next Step =* Repeat treatment (assuming no contraindications)

- Additional follow up is typically at 3-6 months intervals.

TACE Treatment Response

On follow up CT, you need to have pre and post contrast imaging including washout. The iodized oil is going to be dense on the pre-contrast. The more dense oil is in the tumor the better outcome is likely to be. The necrotic tissue should not enhance. If there is enhancement and/or washout in or around the tumor, then you have viable tumor that needs additional treatment.   Beam hardening from the iodized oil can cause a problem.

"Zone of Ablation" is the preferred nomenclature for the post-ablation region on imaging.

Also, Dude, "Chinaman" is not the preferred nomenclature. Asian-American

Cryoablation Treatment Response

Post therapy study is typically performed at 3 months, with additional follow ups at 6 months and 12 months.

A good result should be lower in density relative to the adjacent kidney. On MR, a good result is typically T2 dark and T1 iso or hyper.

Size: Just like RFA, ablated lesions can initially appear that they grew in size relative to the pre-treatment study. With time they should progressively shrink (usually faster than with RFA). An increase in size (after the baseline post treatment) should be considered recurrent tumor.

Enhancement: Any nodular enhancement (>10HU change from pre-contrast run) after treatment should be considered cancer.

Vocab

"Residual tumor" or *"Incomplete Treatment"* = Vocab words used when you see focal enhancement in the tumor ablation zone of a patient for their <u>first post therapy study</u>.

"Recurrent tumor" = Word used when you see focal enhancement in the tumor ablation zone that is <u>new from the first post therapy study</u>.

SECTION 11:
Luminal GI

G Tubes:

A "G- Tube" is a gastric tube, placed directly into the stomach. They are primarily used as an attempt to prolong the suffering of stroked out Alzheimer Patients with stage 4 sacral decubitus ulcers.

Traditional method (Radiographically Inserted Gastrostomy - RIG): The basic idea is that you put an NG tube down and pump air into the stomach until it smushes flat against the anterior abdominal wall. Then you spear it and secure it with 4 "T-Tacks" to tack the stomach to the abdominal wall in the gastric body. Then spear it again, wire in and dilate up to the size you want. Typically, the T-Tacks are removed in 3-6 weeks. Other things that you can do is give a cup of barium the night before to outline the colon.

If the patient has ascites. *Next Step* = Drain that first.

The Ideal Target:

Left of Midline *(lateral to the rectus muscle to avoid inferior epigastric)*

Mid to Distal Body

Equal distance from the greater and less curves - *to avoid arteries*

Anatomy Trivia: The cardia of the stomach is actually the most posterior portion.

There is another method often called a *"PIG"* because of the *P*erioral route. In that version you stab the stomach and tread a wire up the esophagus. Then you grab the wire, slip the tube over it, and advance the tube over the wire into the stomach all the way out the stabbed hole. Then it's back to the nursing home for Grandma.

Honestly, it's probably best to do it with a scope, but since we are Radiologists my official statement is that only a Radiologist can do this procedure well.

Esophageal Stents

Probably the most common indication for one of these is esophageal cancer palliation. These are usually placed by GI, but that doesn't mean you won't get asked about them.

In the real world, most people don't even size these things. The overwhelming majority of lesions can be covered by one stent. Having said that, for the purpose of multiple choice you need a stent with *a length at least 2 cm longer than the lesion on each side*. You do the procedure through the mouth. I imagine it would be great fun to try and place a stent through the nose - if you really hated the person. You give them some oral contrast to outline the lesion. An amplatz wire is dropped down into the stomach. The stent (usually self expanding) is deployed over the wire.

Post Angioplasty? Most people don't angioplasty after deployment of the stent. However, if the tumor is bulky and near the carina, some sources will suggest doing a pre-stent angioplasty test up to 20 mm to see if this invokes coughing / stridor. The concern is that a large tumor may get displaced against the carina and cause a respiratory emergency. If the patient doesn't cough from the test you are safe to deploy the stent (probably).

Upper 1/3 Cancer: Most esophageal cancers are in the lower 1/3. If the question specifically tells you it's higher up (or shows you), they may be leading you towards a *"don't cover the larynx dumbass!"* question. The way to avoid this is to have endoscopy do the case so they can identify the cords. If that isn't an option then placing a smaller device might be an alternative.

Stent Drops into the Stomach: Most people will just leave the motherfucker alone. However, if the patient is symptomatic, endoscopic removal is the textbook answer.

Stent Occludes. *Next Step* = Esophagram. The most common cause is food impaction - which sometimes can be cleared with a soda. If that fails, the next step is endoscopy. If it's not food but instead tumor overgrowth, sometimes you can place a second stent. It depends on a lot of factors and asking that would be horse shit.

Gamesmanship:

- Acute obstruction is likely food

- Worsening symptoms over time is likely tumor.

GI Bleed

You can split GI bleeds into two categories upper (proximal to ligament of Treitz) and lower.

Upper GI:

Some testable trivia is that 85% of upper GI bleeds are from the left gastric, and often *if a source cannot be identified, the left gastric is taken down prophylactically.* If the source of bleeding is from a *duodenal ulcer, embolization of the GDA* is often performed. About 10% of the time, an upper GI bleed can have bright red blood per rectum.

"Pseudo-Vein" Sign – This is a sign of active GI bleeding, with the appearance of a vein created by contrast pooling in a gastric rugae or mucosal intestinal fold. If you aren't sure if it's an actual vein, the "pseudo-vein" will persist beyond the venous phase of injection.

Dieulafoy's Lesion - This is a monster artery in the submucosa of the stomach which pulsates until it causes a teeny tiny tear (not a primary ulcer). These tears can bleed like stink. It's typically found in the lesser curvature. It's not exactly an AVM, more like angiodysplasia. Sometimes you can treat it with clips via endoscopy. Sometimes it needs endovascular embolization.

> *When I say pancreatic arcade bleeding aneurysm, you say celiac artery stenosis.*

There is a known association with celiac artery compression (median arcuate ligament) and the dilation of pancreatic duodenal arcades with pseudoaneurysm formation.

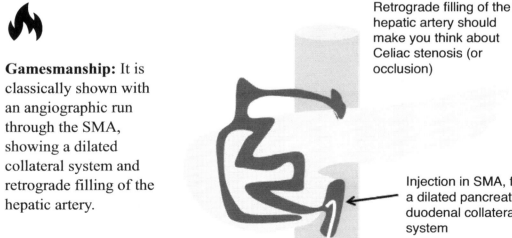

Gamesmanship: It is classically shown with an angiographic run through the SMA, showing a dilated collateral system and retrograde filling of the hepatic artery.

Retrograde filling of the hepatic artery should make you think about Celiac stenosis (or occlusion)

Injection in SMA, fills a dilated pancreatic duodenal collateral system

Upper GI Bleed "Next Step" Algorithm

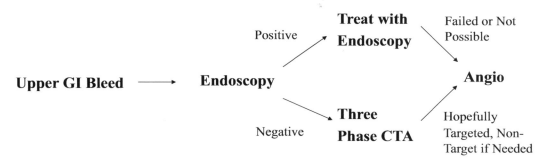

Lower GI:

The work-up for lower GI bleeds is different than upper GI bleeds. With the usual caveat that algorithms vary wildly from center to center, this is a general way to try and answer next step type questions regarding the workup.

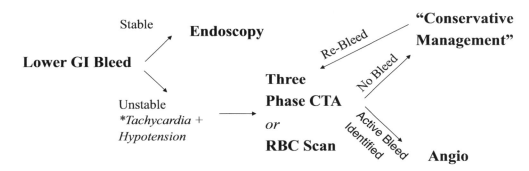

ACR Appropriateness specifically states that in a STABLE patient with lower GI bleeding that endoscopy is first line.

ACR Appropriate:
Intermittent / Obscure GI Bleeding

— GI Bleeding that continues (or recurs) despite negative upper endoscopy and colonoscopy is described as *"obscure GI bleeding."* The actual culprit is often from the small bowel (arteriovenous malformation).

— There is no clear consensus on the optimal study to interrogate the small bowel.

— ACR Appropriateness Criteria rank CT angiography and capsule endoscopy as the most appropriate choices in this situation. Tc-99m RBC scan is considered as a "reasonable alternative" for localization - but only in the setting of active bleeding. Remember GI bleed scan only works if there is active bleeding.

High Yield Trivia is that **nuclear scintigraphy (RBC bleeding scan) is more sensitive than angiography**.

Bleed Scan = 0.1 mL/min
CTA = 0.4 ml/min
Angiography = 1.0 mL/min

Causes with Angiographic Buzzwords:

 •Angiodysplasia - Right Sided Finding. *"Early Draining Vein."* Embolization of angiodysplasia rarely stops a re-bleed and these often need surgery.

 •Diverticulosis - Left Sided Finding (usually). More commonly venous. If arterial, *"filling the diverticulum first"* is classic.

 •Meckles - Usually shown on Meckles scan (^{99m}Tc-Na-pertechnetate). The feeding artery (vitelline) has a classic look with *"extension beyond the mesenteric border,"* *"no side branches"* and *"a corkscrew appearance"* of the terminal portion.

Technical Aspects / Trivia:

You will want runs of all 3 vessels (SMA, Celiac, IMA). Some old school guys will say to start with the IMA because contrast in the bladder will obscure that territory as the procedure continues. That's not really an issue anymore with modern DSA and starting with the SMA will typically be the highest yield. You have to sub select each vessel. Runs in the aorta are not good enough and that would never be the right answer.

What if you don't see bleeding? You can try **"provocative angiography"** - which is not nearly as interesting as it sounds. This basically involves squirting some vasodilator (nitro 100-200 mcg) or thrombolytic drug (tPA 4 mg) into the suspected artery to see if you can make it bleed for you.

What if you do see it bleeding? Administer some street justice. Anyone who trained in the last 30 years is going to prefer microcoils and PVA particles. Old guys might use gel-foam. Alcohol should not be used for lower GI bleeds (causes bowel necrosis).

Microcoils: Good because you can see them. Good because you can place them precisely. Bad because they deploy right where you drop them. So you need to go right up next to that bleed to avoid a large bowel infarct.

Trivia = Inability to advance the micro-catheter peripherally is the most common cause of microcoil embo failure

I say "non-selective embolization of bowel with microcoils," you say "bowel infarct"

PVA: Good because they are "flow directed." So you don't need to be as peripheral compared to the microcoils. Bad because you have less control.

Trivia: Particles must be 300-500 microns. Particles that are smaller will/could cause bowel infarct.

But Prometheus my Geriatric Attending says to use Vasopressin?
Between me and you this argument was settled in 1986 by a lady named Gomes. Her study showed coils stopped GI bleeds 86% of the time, compared to 52% for vasopressin and the shit we have today is way better making the disparity even greater. Having said that, some Dinosaurs still do it.

For the purpose of multiple choice this is what I would know:

- Vasopressin works as a vasoconstrictor

- Vasopressin does not require superselection. You can put it right into the main trunk of the artery.

- Vasopressin sucks because the re-bleed rates are high (once the drug wears off)

- Vasopressin can actually cause non-occlusive mesenteric ischemia (NOMI)

- Vasopressin should not be used with large artery bleeding (i.e. splenic pseudoaneurysm), bleeding at sites with dual blood supply (classic example is pyloroduodenal bleed), severe coronary artery disease, severe hypertension, dysrhythmias, and after an embolotherapy treatment (risk of bowel infarct).

Post Embolization: You need to do angiography post embolization to look for collateral flow (if there is a dual supply). The classic example is: after performing an embolization of the GDA (for duodenal ulcer), you need to do a run of the SMA to look at the inferior pancreaticoduodenal (collateral to the GDA). You might have to take that one out too, but obviously that would increase the risk of bowel infarct.

Trivia - Risk of bowel infarct is way lower for upper GI bleeds (because of the extensive collateral supply), relative to bleeds distal to the ligament of Trietz.

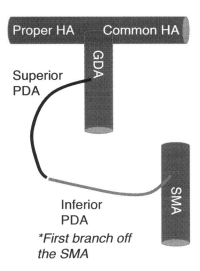

SECTION 12:
Abscess Drainage

General Tactics:

In general, there are two methods, you can use a trocar or you can use the seldinger technique (wire guided).

- *Trocar:* You nail it with a spinal needle first. Then adjacent to the needle (in tandem) you place a catheter.
- *Seldinger:* One stick with a needle, then wire in, dilate up and place a catheter.

Drain Size: The grosser and thicker stuff will need a bigger tube. If forced I'd go with:

- 6-8 F for clear fluid

- 8-10 F for thin pus

- 10-12 F for thick pus

- 12F+ for collections with debris or in collections that smell like a Zombie farted.

Drain Type: You pretty much always use a pigtail. I wouldn't guess anything else.

 Trivia / Gamesmanship

- Any "next step" question that offers to *turn doppler on prior to sticking it* with a needle is always the right answer. Trying to trick you into core needling a pseudoaneurysm is the oldest trick in the book.

- Decompressing the urinary bladder prior to a pelvic abscess drainage is often a good idea.

- Collection has pus. Next step = aspirate all of it (as much as possible) prior to leaving the drain

- You can't advance into the cavity because it's too fibrous/thick walled. *Next Step ?* I'd try a hydrophilic coated

- Family medicine want you to put a 3 way on that 12 F drain. Next step = don't do that. You are reducing the functional lumen to 6F.

552

Trivia / Gamesmanship Continued

- Family medicine wants you to hold off on antibiotics till after you drain this unstable septic shock patient's abscess. Next step = don't do that. Antimicrobial therapy should never be withheld because some knuckle head is worried about sterilizing cultures. (1) Cultures almost never change management from the coverage they were on anyway, (2) the trauma of doing the drainage will seed the bloodstream with bacteria and make the sepsis worse.

- Family medicine wants to know how many cc to flush this complex (but small) abscess with? Remember that *"flushing"* and *"irrigation"* are different. Flushing is done to keep the tube from clogging with viscous poop. Irrigation is when you are washing out the cavity (the solution to pollution is dilution) for complete cavity drainage. Going nuts with the irrigation can actually cause a bacteremia. The vignette could say something like "waxing and waning fever corresponding to flush schedule." The next step would be to train the nurses / family medicine to limit the volume to less than the size of the cavity.

- You irrigate the abscess with 20 cc of fluid but when you aspirate back you only get 5ccs. Next Step? Stop irrigating it! You have a big problem. The fluid (which is dirty) is being washed into a location that is not able to be sucked back out by the tube. So you are creating a new pocket of infection that isn't being drained.

- Catheter started out draining but now is stopped. Next Step = (1) confirm that it is in the correct location and not kinked - might need imaging if not obvious at bedside, then (2) try flushing it or clearing an obstruction with a guidewire. If the catheter is clogged for real then you'll need to exchange it - probably for a larger size. If the tract is mature (older than a week) you can probably get a hydrophilic guidewire through the tract into the collection to do an easy exchange.

- Remove the catheter when: (1) drainage is less than 10cc / day, (2) the collection is resolved by imaging (CT, Ultrasound, etc…), and (3) there is no fistula.

- Persistent Fever > 48 Hours post drainage. The patient should get better pretty quickly after you drain the abscess. If they aren't getting better it implies one of two things (1) you did a shitty job draining it, or (2) they have another abscess somewhere else. Either way they need more imaging and probably another drain.

- The drainage amount spikes. This is a bad sign. In a normal situation the drainage should slower taper to nothing and then once you confirm the abscess has resolved you pull the drain. Spikes in volume (especially on multiple choice exams) suggest the formation of a fistula. Next step is going to be more imaging, possibly with fluoro to demonstrate the fistula (urine, bowel, pancreatic duct, bile duct, etc…).

Pelvic Abscess Drainage - *tubo-ovarian abscess, diverticular abscess, or peri-appendiceal*

General Ideas for Choosing the Correct Route:

(1) All things equal, pick the shortest route

(2) Avoid bowel, solid organs, blood vessels *(inferior epigastrics are classic)*, nerves

(3) Try not to contaminate sterile areas

(4) Choose the most dependent position possible *(usually posterior or lateral)* to facilitate drainage

Routes

Most abscesses in the pelvis are layering in a dependent position so anterior routes are typically not easy. In general there are 4 routes; transabdominal, transgluteal, transvaginal, and transrectal. I'm gonna try and cover the pros/cons and testable trivia for each route.

Transabdominal - The pull of gravity tends to cause infection to layer in the more posterior spaces. As a result transabdominal approaches tend to be long, and therefore violate one of the 4 general ideas. If you are shown an abscess where this would be the best, shortest route then remember to watch out for the inferior epigastrics. For sure there will be an option to stick the trocar right through one of them. Make sure you ID them before you choose your answer.

Transgluteal - The transgluteal approach is done for a variety of posterior targets. The patient is positioned prone for targeting.

Avoid the sciatic nerve and gluteal arteries by:

• Access through the sacrospinous ligament

• Medial as possible

• Inferior to the piriformis

Disadvantages: Legit risk of artery/ nerve injury. Prone to catheter kinking. Gotta use CT (radiation).

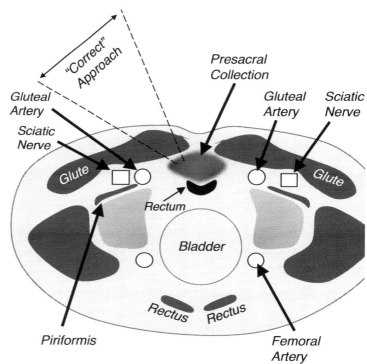

Endoluminal Routes: There is a subset of perverts who prefer to biopsy and drain things through the vagina (tuna purse) and/or the rectum…. Not that there's anything wrong with that. Well actually the primary disadvantage of both of these "endoluminal routes" is catheter stability. Many catheters are literally pooped out within 3-4 days. Although advocates for these routes will argue that (a) they are more fun to do, and (b) most collections resolve within 3 days.

Transvaginal: Biopsy and/or drainage through the vagina (pink taco) has the advantage of providing a very short safe route that can be guided by transvaginal ultrasound, allowing for no radiation and very accurate placement. This was the classic in office route for drainage of infected gynecologic fluid collections (PID related). The procedure is done in the lithotomy position. Catheter size is traditionally limited to 12F (or smaller). You should never do this to a patient under the age of 14 - not even Jared from Subway would try that.

Although controversial, it is possible (and well described in the literature) to drain / biopsy adnexa cysts through the vagina (twinkle cave).

Vaginal prep / cleansing prior to the procedure is controversial and unlikely to be tested.

Transrectal: Of the three routes (gluteal, vaginal, rectal) transrectal is supposedly the least painful - although in my literature review the psychological pain was not discussed (this kinda thing would really fuck with my machismo). Essentially this route offers all the advantages of the transvaginal route (ultrasound guidance, very short / safe route) plus the added advantage of pre-sacral access. Depending on what you read, people will argue this is first line (over trans-gluteal) for pre-sacral collection but that is highly variable.

Choosing between transgluteal and trans-rectal for a pre-sacral collection would be the worst "read my mind" question ever. If forced into that scenario I would set aside the psychologic trauma to the alpha male ego and use (1) the size of the collection - *do you think that will drain before he/she poops the catheter out ?*, and (2) is the transgluteal route safe - *are the vessels nerves obviously in the way?*

Prep with a cleansing enema is not controversial and is endorsed pretty much everywhere.

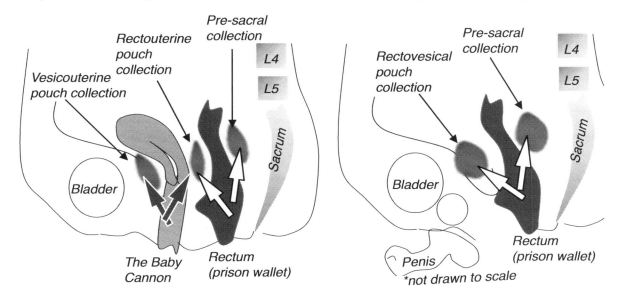

555

Diverticular Abscess

There are a few pearls / special considerations that we should discuss regarding the diverticular abscess.

Size: The typical threshold for a diverticular abscess to be drained is 2 cm. Anything smaller than that will be more trouble than it is worth.

Tube Choice: Remember the grosser and thicker stuff will need a bigger tube. Diverticular abscesses form because of a perforated diverticulum. Thus, you can come to the logical conclusion that you need a tube capable of draining shit. For the purpose of multiple choice, anything smaller than 10F is probable NOT the right answer.

Gas: If the abscess is gas producing (they would have to tell you the bulb suction fills rapidly with gas), the correct ***next step*** is to treat the collection like a pleural drain in a patient with an air leak (i.e. put on water seal).

Liver Abscess

Lots of etiologies for these, but don't forget to think about the appendix or diverticulitis. The draining of these things is somewhat controversial with some authors feeling the risk of peritoneal spread out weighs the benefits and reserving the drainage for patient's with a poor prognosis. Other authors say that everyone and their brother should get one, and consider it first line treatment.

A pearl to draining these things is to not cross the pleura (you'll give the dude an empyema). If there is a biliary fistula, prolonged drainage will usually fix it (biliary drainage or surgery is rarely needed).

Trivia: Biopsy / Aspiration of Echinococcal cysts can cause anaphylaxis. Surgical removal of the presumed echinococcal cysts should be discussed with surgery before attempting the procedure in IR (you want to be able to blame it on them, if shit goes bad).

Renal Abscess

Renal abscess is usually secondary to ascending infection or hematogenous spread. The term *"perinephric abscess"* is used when they perforate into the retroperitoneal space. When they are small (< 3-5 cm) they will resolve on their own with the help of IV antibiotics.

Indications for aspiration or drainage include a large (> 3-5 cm), symptomatic focal fluid collection that does not respond to antibiotic therapy alone.

The strategy is to use ultrasound and stick a pig tail catheter in the thing. After a few days if the thing is not completely drained you can address that by upsizing the tube. If you create or notice a urine leak, you'll need to place a PCN. There are really only relative contraindication – bleeding risk etc…, and the procedure is generally well tolerated with a low complication rate.

Perirenal Lymphocele

This is seen in the setting of a transplant. When they are small you typically just watch them. However, on occasion they get big enough to cause local mass effect on the ureter leading to hydronephrosis. You can totally aspirate them, but they tend to recur and repeated aspiration runs the risk of infecting the collection. For multiple choice I would say do this: Aspirate the fluid and check the creatinine. If it's the same as serum it's probably a lymphocele (*if it's more then it's a urinoma*). Either way you are going to drain them with a catheter. However, if it's a lymphocele you might sclerose the cavity (alcohol, doxy, povidine-iodine).

Urinomas (that are persistent) of any size are drained.

Pancreas Drainage

Remember that necrotizing pancreatitis is bad, but infected necrotizing pancreatitis is a death sentence. So, be careful draining something that is NOT infected already (otherwise you might make it infected). If you aren't sure if it's infected, consider aspirating some for culture (but not placing a tube).

Indications: General indications include infected collections or collections causing mass effect (bowel or biliary obstruction).

Progression to surgery: If you can get 75% reduction in 10 days, the drain is good enough. If not, the surgeons can use the tract for a video-assisted retroperitoneal debridement (which still avoids open debridement).

Pancreatic Cutaneous Fistula: Other than pancreatic pseudocysts, most pancreatic collections are either brown or grayish. When the fluid is clear, you should think about pancreatic fluid, and send a sample for amylase to confirm. If this lasts more than 30 days then you have yourself a *"persistent pancreatic fistula."* Nice job idiot... you could have just left it alone. That will teach you to let those medicine docs pressure you into doing stuff that's not indicated. It may be possible to treat that with octreotide (synthetic somatostatin) to inhibit pancreatic fluid, although in these cases extended drainage is usually needed.

SECTION 13:
Urinary Intervention

Percutaneous Nephrostomy (PCN) –

There are 3 main reasons you might subject someone to this:

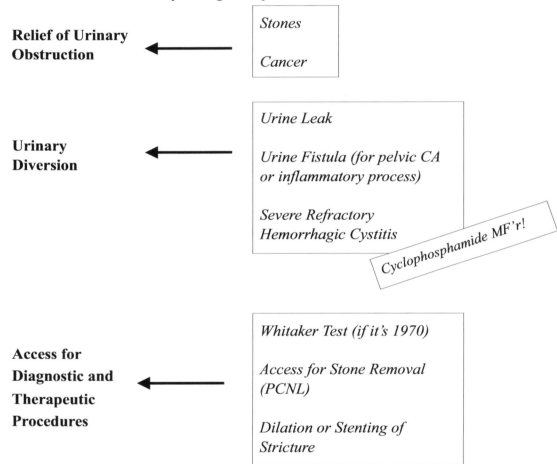

Relief of Urinary Obstruction ← | *Stones*

 Cancer |

Urinary Diversion ← | *Urine Leak*

 Urine Fistula (for pelvic CA or inflammatory process)

 Severe Refractory Hemorrhagic Cystitis |

Cyclophosphamide MF'r!

Access for Diagnostic and Therapeutic Procedures ← | *Whitaker Test (if it's 1970)*

 Access for Stone Removal (PCNL)

 Dilation or Stenting of Stricture |

PCN Contraindications (Absolute):

Severe Coagulopathy →
- *INR Should be less than 1.5*
- *PLT > 50K*

Technically Not Possible →
- *Approach would cross colon, spleen, or liver*

Technical Stuff:

- Prior to the procedure, it would be ideal if you normalized the potassium (dialysis). Certainly anything about 7 should be corrected prior to the procedure.

- Hold anti-platelet drugs for at least 5 days prior to the procedure.

- The lower pole of a posteriorly oriented calyx is ideal. The reason you use a posterior lateral (30 degrees) approach is to attack along **Brodel's Avascular Zone** (area between the arterial bifurcation).

  30 Degrees off sagittal (towards the back)

- Skin entry site should be 10 cm lateral to the midline (not beyond the posterior axillary line). You don't want to go too medial unless you want to try and dilate through the paraspinal muscles. You don't want to go too lateral or you risk nailing the colon.

- Choosing a lower target minimizes the chance of pneumothorax. Additional benefit of the posterior calyces approach is that the guidewire takes a less angled approach (compared to an anterior calyces approach).

- Direct stick into the collecting system without passing through renal parenchyma is NOT a good move (high risk of urine leak).

- Dilated System = Single Stick: Ultrasound and stick your ideal target (low and posterior), then use fluoro to wire in, dilate up, and then place the tube. Alternatively you can do the whole thing under CT.

- Non-Dilated System = Get your partner to do it (these blow). If forced to do = Double Stick. Ultrasound and stick anything you can. Opacify the system. Then stick a second time under fluoro in an ideal position (low and posterior), then wire in, dilate up, and then place the tube. Alternatively you can do the whole thing under CT.

- The posterior calyces (your target) will be seen "end on" if you use contrast. The anterior ones should be more lateral. If you use air, you should just fill the posterior ones (which will be non-dependent with the patient on their belly. Air is useful to confirm.

- You place the drain and get frank pus back. *Next Step* = Aspirate the system

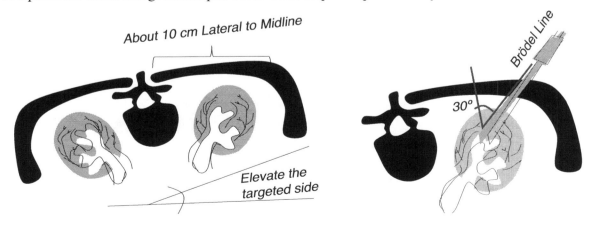

About 10 cm Lateral to Midline

Elevate the targeted side

Brödel Line

30°

Special Situations:

Nephrostomy on Transplant - The test writer will likely write the question in a way to make you think it's crazy to try one of these. Transplant is NOT a contraindication. In fact it's technically easier than a posterior / native kidney.

Testable Transplant Trivia:

• Anterolateral Calyx Should be Targeted (*instead of posterior*)

• Entry site should be LATERAL to the transplant to avoid entering the peritoneum

• Middle to Upper Pole (*instead of a lower pole*)

Percutaneous Nephrostolithotomy – This is done to remove stones in conjunction with urology. The idea is very similar with a few differences. The most testable difference is that the **site is often the upper pole (instead of lower pole) to make stone access easier.** The tube / hole is bigger and there is more risk of bleeding.

"Tube Fell Out" - The trick to handling these scenarios is the "freshness" of the tube. If the tract is "fresh, " which usually means less than 1 week old, then you have to start all over with a fresh stick. If the tract is "mature," which usually means older than 1 week, you can try and re-access it with a non-traumatic wire.

Catheter Maintenance: Exchange is required every 2-3 months because of the crystallization of urine in the tube. Some hospitals / departments will do exchanges more frequently than 2 months and that is because of how well this pays… uh I mean they do it for excellent patient care.

"Encrusted Tube" - If this thing gets totally gross it can be very difficult to exchange in the normal fashion. The most likely "next step" is to use a hydrophilic wire along the side of the tube (same tract) to maintain access.

Ureteral Occlusion - Sometimes urology will request that you just kill the ureters all together. This might be done for fistula, urine leak, or intractable hemorrhagic cystitis. There are a bunch of ways to do it. The most common is probably a sandwich strategy with coils. The sandwich is made by placing large coils in the proximal and distal ends of the "nest", and small coils in the middle. Big Coils = Bread, Small Coils = Bacon.

Nephroureteral Stent (NUS)

This is used when the patient needs long-term drainage. It's way better than having a bag of piss strapped to your back.

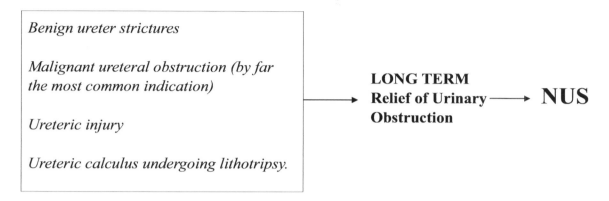

Benign ureter strictures

Malignant ureteral obstruction (by far the most common indication)

Ureteric injury

Ureteric calculus undergoing lithotripsy.

LONG TERM Relief of Urinary Obstruction ⟶ **NUS**

Technically they can be placed in a retrograde (bladder up) or an antegrade (kidney down) fashion. You are going to use the antegrade strategy if (a) you've got a nephrostomy tube, or (b) retrograde failed.

Can you go straight from Nephrostomy to NUS ? Yes, as long as you didn't fuck them up too bad getting access. If they are bleeding everywhere or they are uroseptic you should wait. Let them cool down, then bring them back to covert to the NUS.

Who should NOT get a NUS ? Anyone who doesn't have a bladder that works (outlet obstruction, neurogenic bladder, bladder tumors, etc..). It makes no sense to divert the urine into a bladder that can't empty.

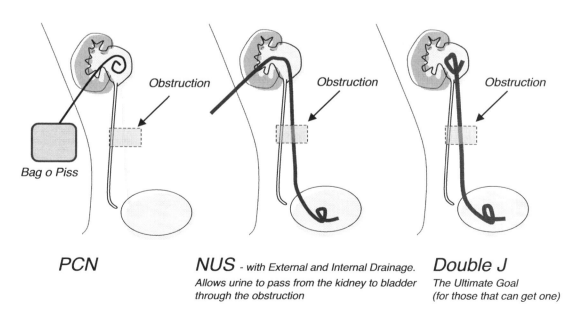

PCN

NUS - *with External and Internal Drainage.*
Allows urine to pass from the kidney to bladder through the obstruction

Double J
*The Ultimate Goal
(for those that can get one)*

Internal NUS - Double J:

Internal NUS - Double J: This is the ultimate goal for the patient. The testable stipulation is that this will require the ability to do retrograde exchanges (via the bladder).

"The Safety" - A safety PCN – is often left in place after the deployment of a double J PCN. The point is to make sure the stent is going to work.

The typical protocol:

1. Place the double J and the safety

2. Cap the safety - so that the internal NUS is draining the patient

3. Bring the patient back in 24-48 hour and "squirt the tube" (antegrade nephrostogram). The system should be non-obstructed.

4. If it's working then you pull the safety.

5. If it's NOT working you uncap the safety and just leave it as a PCN.

—

Suprapubic Cystostomy –

Done to either (a) acutely decompress the bladder or (b) decompress long-term outflow obstruction *(neurogenic bladder, obstructing prostate cancer, urethral destruction, etc..)*

The best way to do it is with ultrasound in the fluoro suite. The target is midline just above the pubic symphysis at the junction of the mid and lower thirds of the anterior bladder wall. You chose this target because:

• The low stick avoids bowel and the peritoneal cavity

• The low 1/3 and mid 1/3 junction avoids the trigone (which will cause spasm).

• The vertical midline is chosen to avoid the inferior epigastric.

Use ultrasound and stick it, confirm position with contrast, wire in and then dilate up. Use a small tube for temporary stuff and a larger tube for more long-term stuff. You can always upsize to a foley once the tract is mature. A 16F foley is ideal for long-term drainage.

Contraindications:

• Buncha Pelvic Surgeries – Extensive scar
• Being a Big Fat Pig/Cow
• Coagulopathy
• Inability to distend bladder
• Inability to displace overlying small bowel

Weapon of Choice

Let's do a rapid review of urinary diversion options.

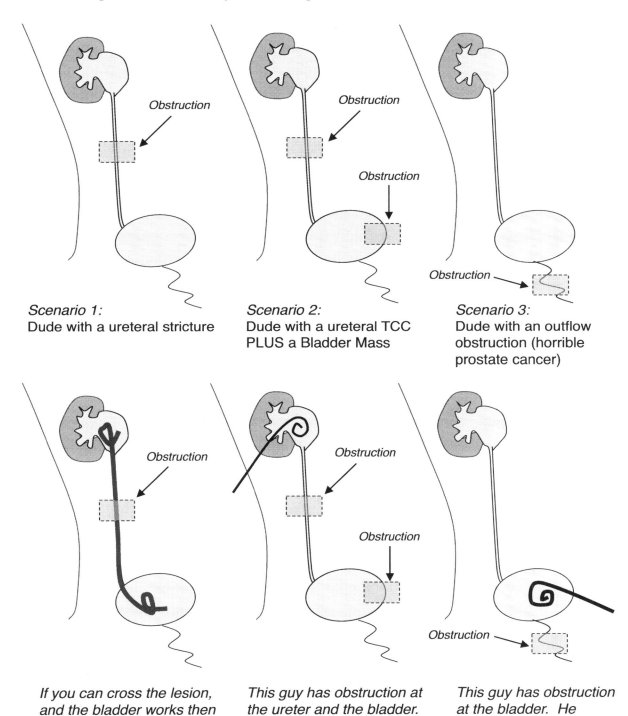

Scenario 1:
Dude with a ureteral stricture

Scenario 2:
Dude with a ureteral TCC PLUS a Bladder Mass

Scenario 3:
Dude with an outflow obstruction (horrible prostate cancer)

*If you can cross the lesion, and the bladder works then internal **Double J** NUS is idea*

*This guy has obstruction at the ureter and the bladder. The only option is to divert at the level of the kidney. He gets a **PCN**.*

*This guy has obstruction at the bladder. He doesn't need to cross the ureter. He gets a **Cystostomy***

Renal Biopsy – This can be done for two primary reasons:

(1) renal failure or (2) cancer biopsy.

Non-Focal: The renal failure workup "non-focal biopsy" is typically done with a 14 - 18 gauge cutting needle , with the patient either prone or on their side (target kidney up). The most obvious testable fact is that **you want tissue from cortex** (lower pole if possible) to maximize the yield of glomeruli on the specimen and minimize complications by avoiding the renal sinus. The complication rate is relatively low, although small AV fistulas and pseudo-aneurysms are relatively common (most spontaneously resolve). Some hematuria is expected. In a high risk for bleeding situation a transjugular approach can be done but that requires knowing what you are doing.

Focal: It used to be thought that focal biopsy should NEVER be done because of the dreaded risk of upstaging the lesion and seeding the track. This has been shown to be very rare (<0.01%). Having said that I think it's still the teaching at least in the setting of pediatric renal masses. This procedure is probably better done with CT. The patient is placed in whatever position is best, but the lateral decubitus with the **lesion side down** is "preferred" , as it stabilizes the kidney from respiratory motion, and bowel interposition. Just like with ultrasound, not crossing the renal sinus is the way to go. Just put the needle in the tumor. If it's cystic and solid make sure you hit the solid part. Some texts recommend both fine needle and core biopsy. The core biopsy is going to give a higher yield. A testable pearl is that if lymphoma is thought likely, a dedicated aspirate should be sent for flow cytometry. As with any renal procedure hematuria is expected (not gross – just a little). Renal colic from blood clots is rare.

ACR Appropriate / SIR Practice Guidelines: Renal Biopsy

— Renal Bx is a procedure with "significant bleeding risk, difficult to detect or control."

— SIR guidelines recommend holding aspirin for 5 days prior to the procedure.

— *Why 5 Days ?* Aspirin irreversibly inhibits platelet function and since platelet lifespan is about 8-10 days, patients with normal marrow will replenish 30-50% of their platelets within 5 days of withholding the willow bark (aspirin).

Renal RFA: Radiofrequency ablation (RFA) is an alternative to partial nephrectomy and laparoscopic nephrectomy. It can be used for benign tumors like AMLs, renal AVMs, and even for RCCs. Angiomyolipomas (AMLs) are treated at 4cm because of the bleeding risk. Sort of a general rule is that things that are superficial you can burn with RFA. Things that are closer to the collecting system it may be better to freeze (cryoablation) to avoid scaring the collecting system and making a stricture. Pyeloperfusion techniques (cold D5W irrigating the ureter) can be done to protect it if you really wanted to RFA. If anyone would ask, RFA has no effect on GFR (it won't lower the GFR).

Things that make you think recurrent/residual disease after therapy:
(1) Any increase in the size beyond the acute initial increase,
(2) Areas of "nodular" or "crescentic" enhancement, or
(3) A new or enlarging bright T2 signal.

There is a paper in AJR (2009) that says that lesions that are < 3cm will appear larger in 1-2 months and lesions >3cm do not grow larger – when successfully treated. So, smaller lesions may initially get bigger but after that – any increase in size should be considered tumor recurrence.

——

Renal Arteriography:
You should always do a non-selective aortogram first to see how many arteries feed the kidney, where they are , etc. Sometimes the aortogram will show you an obvious ostial problem which you can then select down on and address. Otherwise, you need to do selective angiography and look at each vessel. **LAO is the projection of choice for looking at the renals**. Sometimes the stenosis is further out, in fact branch artery stenosis is a cause of hypertension in kids.

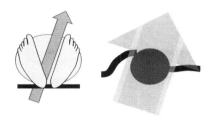

LAO Minimizes Angiographic Overlap from the Aorta

Angioplasty of Renal Arteries: Used to treat hypertension caused by atherosclerosis (usually ostial) or FMD. Risks include thrombosis, and vessel spasm. Calcium channel blockers can be given to decrease the risk of spasm. Heparin should be on board to reduce thrombosis risk. Most people take daily aspirin the day before and every day after for 6 months, to reduce the risk of restenosis.

- *Indications for angioplasty = Renal Vascular HTN or Azotemia*
- *Atherosclerosis at the Ostium = Angioplasty + Stent*
- *FMD - usually mid vessel = Angioplasty Alone*

But Prometheus!?! - I was reading the New England Journal...

The NEJM is run by a bunch of family medicine doctors who hate all procedures. They published a thing called the **CORAL trial** in 2014, that showed no added benefit from angio + stenting in the setting of renal vascular stenosis compared to high quality medical therapy.

This remains controversial and several prominent IR guys still like to stent, especially if they can measure a pressure gradient in the renal artery. For the purpose of multiple choice, if "high quality medical therapy" is a choice for treated RAS related hypertension, that is probably the right answer — otherwise, pick angio + stent.

Renal Hemorrhage:

Trauma to the kidney (usually iatrogenic from biopsy or diversion procedure) can typically be embolized. The renal arteries are "end arteries," which means that collaterals are not an issue. It also means that infarction is a legit issue so if you want to salvage the kidney you need to try and get super selective. Having said that, don't be an idiot and fuck around trying to get super selective while the patient is bleeding to death. Remember most people have two of these things, plus in a worst case scenario there is always dialysis. Bottom line: if you get into trouble and the patient is crashing, just trash the whole thing.

Next Step: Arterial trauma from the nephrostomy tube placement. Bleeding source is occult on angio. *Next step ?* Remover the nephrostomy tube (over a guidewire), then look again. Often the catheter tamponades the bleed, making it tougher to see.

Gamesmanship: Oral boards guys used to be sticklers for the phrase *"over a wire."* In other words if you just said "I'd remove the PCN" they would ding you. You have to say "I'd remove the PCN *over a wire.*" The only reason I bring this up is the use of possible distractors / fuckery.

Maybe something like this:

Q: The highly skilled Interventionalist grants the Fellow the great privilege of performing a fresh stick nephrostomy. The clumsy, good for nothing Fellow manages to place the tube, but now there is a large volume of bright red blood in the tube and the Patient's blood pressure is dropping rapidly. You start fluids and perform an emergent renal arteriography. The source of bleeding is not seen. *What is the best next step?*

A: Remove the PCN and repeat another angio run
B: Kick the fellow in the shin for using too much fluoro time
C: Call Urology and admit you need help from a "real doctor"
D: Remove the PCN *over a wire* and repeat another angio run. ←

> *Just like a Midget using a urinal… you gotta stay on your toes.*
>
> **Read all the choices!**

Renal Aneurysms

"Look, man. I only need to know one thing: where they are" - Private Vasquez

- *Small Segmental Arteries* = coils

- *Main Renal Artery* = Covered Stent to exclude the aneurysm. Alternatively, you could place a bare metal stent across the aneurysm and then pump detachable coils into the sac.

SECTION 14:
Pulmonary Intervention

Pleural Drainage – Most everyone has done a few thoracenteses as a resident. I just want to touch on a few testable points.

- Remember that you go *"above the rib"* to avoid the neurovascular bundle.

- If you pull off too much fluid too fast you can possibly get pulmonary edema from re-expansion (this is uncommon).

- If it's malignant you might end up with a trapped lung (lung won't expand fully). A "vacu-thorax" - in the setting of a trapped lung, does not mean anything, and does not need immediate treatment even if it's big. If you really need to fix it, you'll need a surgical pleurectomy / decortication. Pleurodesis (which can be done to patients with recurrent pleural effusions), does NOT help in the setting of trapped lung.

- Pneumothorax is rare but is probably the most common complication (obviously it's more common when done blind).

Additional Trivia related to Chest Tubes:

- Continuous air bubbles in the Pleur-evac chamber represent an air leak, either from the drainage tubing or from the lung itself. In the setting of multiple choice - think about a bronchopleural fistula.

- INR should generally be < 1.5 prior to placement of a chest tube.

- In the paravertebral region, the intercostal vessels tend to course off of the ribs and are therefore more prone to injury if this route is chosen for chest tube placement

Lung Abscess: Just remember that you can drain an empyema (pus in the pleural space), but you should NOT drain a lung abscess because you can create a bronchopleural fistula (some people still do it).

Lung Biopsy – The most

common complication is pneumothorax, which occurs about 25% of the time (most either resolve spontaneously or can be aspirated), with about 5% needing a chest tube. The second most common complication (usually self-limiting) is hemoptysis.

The testable pearls include:

- The lower lung zones are more affected by respiratory motion,

- The lingula is the most affected by cardiac motion,

- Avoid vessels greater than 5 mm,

- Try and avoid crossing a fissure (they almost always get a pneumothorax),

- Areas lateral to and just distal to the tip of a biopsy gun will be affected by "shock wave injury", so realize vessels can still bleed from that.

Reducing the Risk of Pneumothorax - Post Biopsy

Enter the lung at 90 degrees to pleural surface

Avoid interlobar fissures

Put the patient puncture side DOWN after the procedure

No talking or deep breathing after the procedure (at least 2 hours)

If the patient is a cougher, consider postponing the procedure - or giving empiric anti-tussive meds

When to Place a Chest Tube? - Post Biopsy

Pneumothorax is symptomatic

Pneumothorax continues to enlarge on serial radiographs

Many people will attempt to aspirate the air if the pneumothorax is > 2cm (even if the patient is not symptomatic)

Pneumothorax chest tubes often 10 French Pigtail Catheters which require: 18G needle / 0.035 Amplatz wire

---

Lung RFA – Radiofrequency ablation of lung tumors can be performed on lesions between 1.5cm and 5.2cm in diameter. The most common complication is pneumothorax (more rare things like pneumonia, pseudoaneurysm, bronchopleural fistula, and nerve injury have been reported). The effectiveness of RFA is similar to external beam radiation with regard to primary lung cancer. The major advantage of lung RFA is that it has a limited effect on pulmonary function, and can be performed without concern to prior therapy.

Imaging (CT and PET) should be performed as a follow up of therapy. Things that make you think residual /recurrent disease: nodular peripheral enhancement measuring more than 10 mm, central enhancement (any is bad) , growth of the RFA zone after 3 months (after 6 months is considered definite), increased metabolic activity after 2 months, residual activity centrally (at the burned tumor).

Thoracic Angio:

This section is going to focus on the two main flavors of pulmonary angio; *pulmonary artery* (done for massive PE and pulmonary AVM treatment) and *bronchial artery* (done for hemoptysis).

Pulmonary Artery

The primary indications for pulmonary arteriography is diagnosis and treatment of massive PE or pulmonary AVM.

Technical Trivia:

The "Grollman" catheter, which is a preshaped 7F, is the classic tool. You get it in the right ventricle (usually from the femoral vein) and then turn it 180 degrees so the pigtail is pointing up, then advance it into the outflow tract. Some people will say that a **known LBBB is high risk**, and these patients should get prophylactic pacing (because the wire can give you a RBBB, and RBBB + LBBB = asystole). An important thing to know is that patients with chronic PE often have pulmonary hypertension. Severe pulmonary hypertension needs to be evaluated before you inject a bunch of contrast. **Pressures should always be measured before injecting contrast** because you may want to reduce your contrast burden. Oh, one last thing about angio… never ever let someone talk you into injecting contrast through a swan-ganz catheter. It's a TERRIBLE idea and the stupid catheter will blow apart at the hub. I would never ever do that….

Next Step: Cardiac dysrhythmias (v-tach) during procedure. *Next Step ?* Re-position the catheter / wire.

Pulmonary Embolism – Patients with PE should be treated with medical therapy (anticoagulation with Coumadin, Heparin, or various newer agents), allowing the emboli to spontaneously undergo lysis. In patients who can't get anticoagulation (for whatever reason), an IVC filter should be placed. The use of transcatheter therapy is typically reserved for unstable patients with massive PE.

Massive PE? Just think lotta PE with hypotension.

In those situations, catheter directed thrombolysis, thromboaspiration, mechanical clot fragmentation, and stent placement have all been used to address large clots.

Pulmonary Angiography
Relative Contraindications

Pulmonary HTN with elevated right heart pressures (greater than 70 systolic and 20 end diastolic).

If you need to proceed anyway - they get low osmolar contrast agents injected in the right or left PA (NOT the main PA).

Left Bundle Branch Block - The catheter in the right heart can cause a right block, leading to a total block.

If you need to proceed anyway - they get prophylactic pacing.

Pulmonary AVM – They can occur sporadically. For the purpose of multiple choice when you see them think about HHT (Hereditary Hemorrhagic Telangiectasia / Osler Weber Rendu). Pulmonary AVMs are most commonly found in the lower lobes (more blood flow) and can be a source of right to left shunt (**worry about stroke and brain abscess**). The rule of **treating once the afferent (feeding) artery is 3mm** is based on some tiny little abstract and not powered at all. Having said that, it's quoted all the time and a frequent source of trivia that is easily tested. The primary technical goal is to crush the feeding artery (usually with coils) as close to the sac as possible. You don't want that think reperfusing from adjacent branches. Pleurisy (self limited) after treatment seems to pretty much always happen.

Key Trivia:

- HHT Association

- Brain Abscess / Stroke - via paradoxical emboli

- Treat once the afferent (feeding) artery is **3mm**

- Coils in the feeding vessel, as close as possible to the sac

Special Situation - Rasmussen Aneurysm

This is an aneurysm associated with chronic pulmonary infection, classically TB. The trick on this is the history of hemoptysis (which normally makes you think bronchial artery).

"It's a Trap!" - *Admiral Gial Ackbar*

Next Step Strategy to avoid the trap:

Patient blah blah blah hemoptysis….. *Next Step?* Bronchial Artery Angio

- Bronchial Artery Angio is negative, still bleeding. Oh, and his PPD is positive. *Next Step ?* Pulmonary Artery angio to look for Rasmussen Aneurysms

- Rasmussen Aneurysm identified. *Next Step ?* Coil embolization (yes coils for hemoptysis - this is the exception to the rule).

Bronchial Artery

The primary indication for pulmonary arteriography is diagnosis and treatment of massive hemoptysis.

Hemoptysis – Massive hemoptysis (> 300 cc) can equal death. Bronchial artery embolization is first line treatment (bronchial artery is the culprit 90% of the time). Unique to the lung, active extravasation is NOT typically seen with the active bleed. Instead you see tortuous, enlarged bronchial arteries. The main thing to worry about is cord infarct. For multiple choice the most likely bad actor is the *"hairpin-shaped"* anterior medullary artery (Adamkiewicz). Embolizing that thing or anywhere that can reflux into that thing is an obvious contraindication. If present, those bad boys typically arise from the right intercostal bronchial trunk.

Particles (> 325 micrometers) are used (<u>coils should be avoided</u> - because if it re-bleeds you just jailed yourself out).

The vast majority (90%) of bronchial arteries are located within the lucency formed by the left main bronchus. This is right around the T5-T6 Level

There is a ton of vascular variation but the pattern of an intercostobronchial trunk on the right and two bronchial arteries on the left is most common (about 40%)

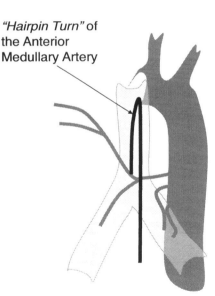

"Hairpin Turn" of the Anterior Medullary Artery

In the lower thoracic / upper lumbar region the primary feeding artery of the anterior spinal cord is the legendary anterior radiculomedullary artery (artery of Adamkiewicz). This vessel most commonly originates from a left sided posterior intercostal artery (typically between T9-T12) , which branches from the aorta. The distal portion of this artery, as it merges with the anterior spinal artery, creates the classic (and testable) *"hairpin"* turn.

It is worth noting that Adamkiewicz can originate from the right bronchus (like 5%).

Occlusion of Central Veins (SVC Syndrome) –

Yes - I know this really isn't a pulmonary thing, but it is in the chest so I'm going to talk about it here.

Acute vs Chronic SVC Occlusion:

- Acute = No Collaterals
- Acute = Emergency

- Chronic = Has Collaterals
- Chronic = Not an Emergency

There are a variety of ways to address occlusion of the SVC. The goal is to return in line flow from at least one jugular vein down through the SVC. Most commonly thrombolysis is the initial step, although this is rarely definitive. The offending agent (often a catheter) should be removed if possible. If the process is non-malignant, often angioplasty alone is enough to get the job done (post lysis).

Technical Trivia:

- Malignant causes: you should do lysis, then angioplasty, then stent.

- Non-malignant causes: may still need a stent if the angioplasty doesn't remove the gradient (if the collateral veins are still present).

- Self-expanding stents should NOT be used, as they tend to migrate.

- The last pearl on this one is not to forget that the pericardium extends to the bottom part of the SVC and that if you tear that you are going to end up with hemopericardium and possible tamponade.

SECTION 15:
Reproductive Intervention

Uterine Artery Embolization (UAE):

This has been around a long time and can be used for bleeding or for the bulk symptoms of fibroids.

Patient Selection (not all fibroids were created equal):

- Submucosal does the best. Intramural does the second best. Serosal does the third best (it sucks).
- Smaller lesions do better than larger lesions.
- "Cellular" Fibroids, which are densely packed smooth muscle (without much connective tissue) and high T2 signal tend to respond well to embolization
- Intracavitary Fibroids – Less than 3 cm. Next Step = GYN referral for hysteroscopic resection
- Intracavitary Fibroids – Less than 3 cm , with failed hysteroscopic resection = IR Embo
- Large Serosal Fibroid, patient wants to be pregnant, no history of prior myomectomy = GYN referral for myomectomy
- Pedunculated Serosal Fibroid = GYN referral for resection
- Broad Ligament Fibroid = Refer to voodoo priest (these don't do well with UAE and are technically challenging to operate on).

PreTreatment Considerations / Trivia

- Remember fibroids are hormone responsive. They grow with estrogen (and really grow during pregnancy). Gonadotropin-releasing medications are often prescribed to control fibroids by blocking all that fancy hormone axis stuff.
- The testable trivia is to delay embolization for 3 months if someone is on the drugs because they actually shrink the uterine arteries which makes them a pain in the ass to catheterize.
- The EMMY trial showed that hospital stays with UAE are shorter than hysterectomy
- The incidence of premature menopause is around 5%
- DVT / PE is a known risk of the procedure (once pelvic vein compression from large fibroid releases – sometimes the big PE flies up). The risk is about 5%.

Contraindications: <u>Pregnancy</u>, Uterine/Cervical <u>Cancer</u>, Active Pelvic Infection, Prior Pelvic Radiation, Connective Tissue Disease, Prior Surgery with Adhesions (relative)

Treatment Trivia
- Remember the uterine artery is off the anterior division of the internal iliac
- Regardless of the fibroid location, bilateral uterine artery embolization is necessary to prevent recruitment of new vessels
- In most cases, branches of the ovarian artery feed the fibroids via collaterals with the main uterine artery
- Occlusion of small feeding arteries cause fibroid infarction (and hopefully shrinkage). Embolic material is typically PVA or embospheres for fibroids (targeting the pre-capillary level). For postpartum hemorrhage / vaginal bleeding, gel foam or glue is typically used.
- Treatment of adenomyosis with UAE is done exactly the same way, and is an effective treatment for symptomatic relief (although symptoms recur in about 50% of the cases around 2 years post treatment).
- Fibroids should reduce volume 40-60% after the procedure.

Post Embolization Syndrome: I mentioned this earlier but just wanted to remind you that it's classically described with fibroid embolization. Remember you don't need to order blood cultures - without other factors to make you consider infection. The low-grade fever should go away after 3 days. Some texts suggest prophylactic use of anti-pyrexial and antiemetic meds prior to the procedure.

- 3 Days or less with low grade fever = Do nothing
- More than 3 Days with fever = "Work it up" , cultures, antibiotics, etc…

Hysterosalpingogram (HSG):

I'm 100% certain no one went into radiology to do these things. You do it like a GYN exam. Prep the personal area with betadine, drape the patient, put the speculum in and find the cervix. There are various methods and tools for cannulating and maintaining cannulation of the cervix (vacuum cups, tenaculums, balloons). Insertion of any of these devices is made easier with a catheter and wire. Once the cervix and endometrial cavity have been accessed, the contrast is inserted and pictures are obtained.

Contraindications: Pregnancy, Active Pelvic Infection, Recent Uterine or Tubal Pregnancy.

Trivia:

- The ideal time for the procedure is the proliferative phase (day 7-14), as this is the time the endometrium is thinnest (improves visualization, minimizes pregnancy risk).

  > - Rag Week 0-7
  > - **Proliferative 7-14**
  > - Secretory 14-21

- It's not uncommon for a previously closed tube to be open on repeat exam (sedative, narcotics, tubal spasm – can make a false positive).

- Air bubbles can cause a false positive filling defect.

- **Intravasation** – The backflow of injected contrast into the venous or lymphatic system, used to be an issue during the Jurassic period (when oil based contrast could cause a fat embolus). Now it means nothing other than you may be injecting too hard, or the intrauterine pressure is increased because of obstruction.

- *The reported risk of peritonitis is 1%.*

Fallopian Tube Recanalization (FTR):

Tubal factors (usually PID / Chlamydia) are responsible for about 30% of the cases in female infertility ~ depending on what part of the country you are from sometimes much more (*insert joke about your hometown here*). Tubal obstruction comes in two flavors; proximal / interstitial, or distal. The distal ones get treated with surgery. The proximal ones can be treated with an endoscope or by poking it with a wire under fluoro.

Things to know:

- You should schedule it in the follicular/proliferative phase (just like a HSP) - day 6-12ish.
- You repeat the HSG first to confirm the tube is still clogged. If clogged you try and unclog it with a wire (*"selective salpingography"*).
- Hydrophilic 0.035 or 0.018 guidewire (plus / minus microcatheter) is the typical poking tool
- Repeat the HSG when you are done to prove you did something
- Contraindications are the same as HSG (active infection and pregnancy)

Pelvic Congestion Syndrome

– Women have mystery pelvic pain. This is a real (maybe) cause of it. They blame dilated ovarian and periuterine veins in this case, and give it a name ending in the word "syndrome" to make it sound legit. The symptoms of this "syndrome" include pelvic pain, dyspareunia, menstrual abnormalities, vulvar varices, and lower extremity varicose veins. The symptoms are most severe at the end of the day, and with standing.

Diagnosis ? Clinical symptoms + a gonadal vein diameter of 10 mm (normal is 5 mm).

Treatment ? GnRH agonists sometimes help these patients, since estrogen is a vasodilator. But the best results for treatment of this "syndrome" are sclerosing the parauterine venous plexus, and coils/plugs in the ovarian and internal iliac veins (performed by your local Interventional Radiologist). This is often staged, starting with ovarian veins plugged first, and then (if unsuccessful) iliac veins plugged second.

Trivia: Most optimal results occur when the entire length of both gonadal veins are embolized.

Complications ? Complications are rare but the one you worry about is thrombosis of the parent vein (iliac or renal), and possible thrombus migration (pulmonary embolism).

Will it get better on its own ? The symptoms will classically improve after menopause.

Varicocele

- They are usually left-sided (90%), or bilateral (10%). Isolated right-sided varicoceles should prompt an evaluation for cancer (next step = CT Abd).

When do you treat them? There are three indications: (1) infertility, (2) testicular atrophy in a kid, (3) pain.

Anatomy Trivia (regarding varicoceles): Remember that multiple venous collaterals "pampiniform plexus" or "spermatic venous plexus" drain the testicles. Those things come together around the level of the femoral head, forming the internal spermatic vein. The left internal spermatic vein drains into the left renal vein, and the right internal spermatic vein drains into the IVC. Common variants include: multiple veins on the right terminating into the IVC or renal vein, or one right-sided vein draining into the renal vein (instead of the IVC).

Why Varicoceles Happen: The "primary factor" is right angle entry of the left spermatic vein into the high pressure left renal vein. Nut-cracker syndrome (compression of the left renal vein between the SMA and aorta) on the left is another cause (probably more likely asked).

Basic Idea: You get into the renal vein and look for reflux into the gonadal vein (internal spermatic) which is abnormal but confirms the problem. You then get deep into the gonadal vein, and embolize close to the varicocele (often with foam), then drop coils on the way back, and often an Amplatzer or other occlusion device at the origin.

SECTION 16:
Misc Topics

Vertebroplasty

There is a paper in the NEJM that says this doesn't work. Having said that, NEJM doesn't like any procedures. They're run by family medicine doctors. They are equally amoral to the person that will do any non-indicated procedure. Regardless of the actual legitimacy, it's a big cash cow and several prominent Radiologists have made their names on it… so it will be tested on as if it's totally legit and without controversy.

Trivia to Know:

- Indications = Acute to subacute fracture with pain refractory to medical therapy or an unstable fracture with associated risk if further collapse occurs.
- Contraindications = Fractures with associated spinal canal compression or improving pain without augmentation.
- There is a risk of developing a new vertebral fracture in about 25% of cases. The literature says you should *"counsel patients on the need for additional treatments prior to undergoing vertebroplasty."*.
- The cement can embolize to the lungs.
- Risk of local neurologic complications are about 5%.

Lymphangiogram:

1950 called and they want to stage this cancer. Prior to CT, MRI, and US injecting dye into the toes was actually a way to help stage malignancy (mets to lymph nodes, lymphoma, etc..).

Another slightly more modern application is to use this process as the first step in the embolization of the thoracic duct. Why would you take down the thoracic duct? If it's leaking chylous pleural effusions - status post get hacked to pieces by a good for nothing Surgery Resident.

Technical Trivia:

This is done by first injecting about 0.5 cc methylene blue dye in between the toes bilaterally. You then wait half an hour until the blue lymphatic channels are visualized. You then cut down over the lymphatic channels and cannulate with a 27 or 30 gauge lymphangiography needle. An injection with lipiodol is done (maximum 20 ml if no leak). If you inject too much there is a risk of oil pneumonitis. You take spot films in a serial fashion until the cisterna chyli (the sac at the bottom of the thoracic duct) is opacified. At that point you could puncture it directly and superselect the thoracic duct to embolize it, typically with coils.

Standing Waves:

Standing waves are an angiographic phenomenon (usually) that results in a ringed layering of contrast that sorta looks like FMD. A common trick is to try and make you pick between FMD and Standing Waves.

Obviously it's bullshit because in real life standing waves typically resolve prior to a second run through the same vessel, and even if they stayed around they tend to shift position between each run (up or down). FMD on the other hand is an actual physical irregularity of the vessel wall so it's fixed between runs and doesn't go away.

Morphology should be your strategy for multiple choice:

Standing waves are very symmetric and evenly spaced.

FMD is more irregular and asymmetric.

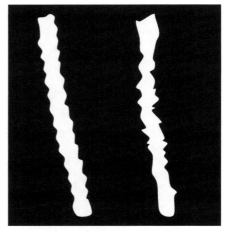

Standing Waves   FMD

"The Lingo"

"Give me a 10 x 6 Balloon" - This means a 10 mm diameter x 6 cm length balloon

"Give me 20 for 30" - This means do an angio run at 20 cc/sec for a total of 30 mL.

"Squirted" - An Angiogram — Oh really? A splenic lac with active extrav? Let's call IR right away and get him squirted.

"Thrash" - A difficult case

"Hot Mess" - I have an admit for you. This lady is a hot mess.

"That poor lady" - A way of feigning sympathy.

"Sick as Stink" - also, "sick AND stinks" be careful not to mess this up.

Artery of Interest	C Arm Angulation	Misc
Aortic Arch	70 Degrees LAO	"Candy Cane"
Innominate (Right Subclavian & Right Common Carotid)	RAO	In the LAO the right subclavian and right common carotid overlap
Left Subclavian	LAO	——
Mesenteric Vessels	Lateral to Steep RAO	——
Left Renal	LAO	Same side as renal
Right Renal	RAO or LAO - depending on who you ask.	This is controversial - a lot of sources will say you can get away with LAO.
Left Iliac Bifurcation	RAO	Opposite side common
Right Iliac Bifurcation	LAO	Opposite side common
Left Common Femoral Bifurcation	LAO	Ipsilateral Oblique
Right Common Femoral Bifurcation	RAO	Ipsilateral Oblique

The Confusing Oblique Views

Normally, views are defined by the direction of the x-ray beam.
However, in Angio it gets a little squirrely. The sidedness refers to the side of the I.I.

RAO: The imaging intensifier is on the right side of the patient.

A reasonable person might call this LPO - but they would be wrong.

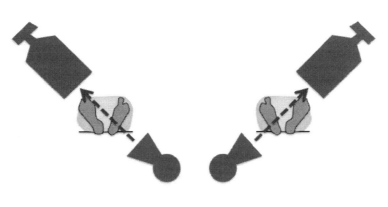

LAO: The imaging intensifier is on the left side of the patient.

A reasonable person might call this RPO - but they would be wrong.

Superficial or Deep? - Understanding Geometry

Sometimes it's difficult to tell if you are superficial or deep to the lesion you are trying to put a needle in under fluoro. You can problem solve by tilting the I.I. towards the patient's head or towards the patient's feet.

If you tilt towards the head, a superficial needle will be shorter but a deep needle will look longer.

If you tilt towards the feet, a superficial needle will be longer but a deep needle will look shorter.

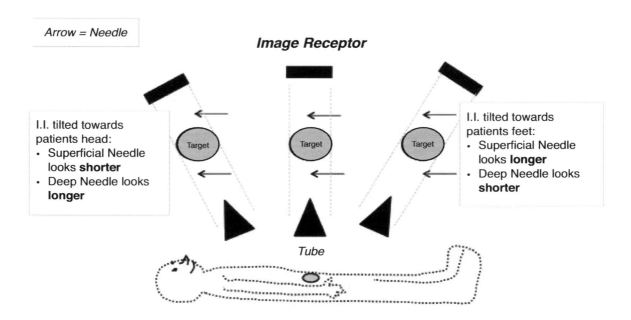

Air Embolus

Classic Clinical Buzzwords: "Sudden onset shortness of breath" "Whoosh sound" or "Sucking sound" during central catheter insertion.

Next Step: *"Durant's maneuver"* = left-lateral decubitus + head-down positioning. Other verbiage = "right side up" or "left side down", "trendelenburg"

Next Next Step: 100% Oxygen

Medications:

Anti-Coagulation Issues:

- Remember that Platelets Replace Platelets.
- Cryoprecipitate is used to correct deficiencies of fibrinogen.
- Heparin: The half life is around 1.5 hours. Protamine Sulfate can be used as a more rapid Heparin Antidote.
- Protamine can cause a sudden fall in BP, Bradycardia, and flushing
- Coumadin: Vitamin K can be given for Coumadin but that takes a while *(25-50mg IM 4 hours prior to procedure)*, more rapid reversal is done with factors (cryoprecipitate).
- Remember that patients with "HIT" (Heparin Induced Thrombocytopenia) are at increased risk of clotting – not bleeding. If they need to be anti-coagulated then they should get a thrombin inhibitor instead (remember those end in "rudin" and "gatran").
- The Life Span of a Platelet is 8-10 days
- IV Desmopressin can increase factor 8 - may be helpful of hemophilia

Medication	Mechanism	Trivia
Aspirin	Inhibits thromboxane A_2 from arachidonic acid by an irreversible acetylation	Irreversible - works the life of the platelet (8-12 days).
Heparin	Binds antithrombin 3 - and increases its activity.	Monitored by PTT. Can be reversed with protamine sulfate
Plavix (Clopidogrel)	Inhibits the binding of ADP to its receptors - leads to inhibition of GP IIb/IIIa	——
Coumadin	Inhibits vitamin K dependent factors (2,7,9,10)	Monitored by INR. Delay in onset of activity (8-12 hours). Action can be antagonized by vitamin K - but this takes time (4 hours). For immediate reversal give factors (cryopercipitate)
Thrombolytic Agents (TPA)	Act directly or indirectly to convert plasminogen to plasmin (cleaves fibrin)	TPA has a very short biologic half life - between 2-10 mins.

ACR Appropriate: / SIR Practice Guide: Pre-Procedure Hold

— For procedures with a MODERATE risk of bleeding (liver or lung biopsy, abscess drain placement, vertebral augmentation, tunneled central line placement)

— INR should be corrected to < 1.5 prior to the procedure.
— Aspirin need not be held,
— Clopidogrel (plavix) should be held for 5 days.
— Platelet count should be more than 50,000.

Sedation Related:

- "Conscious Sedation" is considered "moderate sedation", and the patient should be able to respond briskly to stimuli (verbal commands, or light touch). No airway intervention should be needed.
- Flumazenil is the antidote for Versed (Midazolam).
- Narcan is the antidote for Opioids (Morphine, Fentanyl).

Local Anesthesia (Lidocaine)

- Maximum Dose is 4-5 mg/kg
- A dirty trick would be to say - "Lido with Epi" - in which case it is 7 mg/kg
- Some basic scrub nurse math:
  - 1% Plain Epi - 10 mg per 1 mL
  - So 1 mg per 0.1 mL
  - And we said Maximum Dose is 5 mg/kg, so it would be equal to 0.5 mL / kg
- Remember that small doses in the right spot can cause a serious reaction.
  - 150 mg in the thecal sac can cause total spine anesthesia and the need for a ventilator.
  - Direct arterial injection can cause immediate seizures.
  - Tinnitus and dizziness are the earliest signs of toxicity.
- Local anesthesia agents have a low potential for allergy - although it can still occur, it's usually a bogus allergy once a real history is taken. Most "allergies" to lidocaine are actually vaso-vagal, or other CV side effects from epinephrine mixed with lidocaine
- There are elaborate mechanisms for testing for a true allergy, or reaction to methylparaben (a preservative).
- So what if the allergy is real? or you can't prove it's false? - Some texts describe using an antihistamine such as diphenydramine (which can have anesthetic properties).

Green, Steven M., Steven G. Rothrock, and Julie Gorchynski. "Validation of diphenhydramine as a dermal local anesthetic." Annals of emergency medicine 23.6 (1994): 1284-1289.

	Indications	**Contraindications**
Angiography	Numerous; usually diagnosis of and treatment of vascular disease	Only one absolute which is an unstable patient with multisystem dysfunction (unless angio is life saving). There are numerous relatives including inability to lay flat, uncooperative patient, and connective tissue diseases
Ascending Venography	Diagnosis of DVT, Evaluate Venous malformation or tumor encasement.	Contrast Reaction Pregnancy Severely compromised cardiopulmonary status
Descending Venography	Evaluation of post-thrombotic syndrome; valvular incompetence and damage following DVT	
Venography (Non-inclusive)	Thoracic Outlet Syndrome, Venous Access, Pacer Placement, Eval for fistula	
IVC Filter	Can't get anticoagulation, Failed anticoagulation (clot progression), Massive PE requiring lysis, Chronic PE treated with thromboendarterectomy. Trauma high risk DVT	Total thrombosis of IVC IVC too big or too small *Sepsis is NOT a contraindication, including septic thrombophlebitis*
Fistulography	Making the nephrologist money ("slow flows" they call it).	Absolute: Right to left cardiopulmonary shunt, Uncorrectable coagulopathy, fistula infection. Relative is significant cardiopulmonary disease (a declot invariably causes PE)

	Indications	**Contraindications**
TIPS	Variceal bleeding refractory to endoscopy. Refractory ascites.	Absolute: Heart Failure (especially right heart failure). Severe encephalopathy. Rapidly progressing liver failure.
Percutaneous Transhepatic Cholangiography (PTC)	Performed prior to percutaneous biliary interventions, Choledochojejunostomy patients (liver transplant) with suspected obstruction	Absolute: Uncorrectable Coagulopathy, Plavix or other anti-platelet agent Relative: Large Volume Ascites (consider para and left sided approach)
Percutaneous Biliary Drainage	Basically CBD obstruction (with failed ERCP), cholangitis, bile duct injury/leak.	No absolute contraindications Relative: Large Volume Ascites (consider para and left sided approach), Coagulopathy
Percutaneous Cholecystosomy	Cholecystitis in patients who are not surgical candidates, Unexplained sepsis when other sources excluded, Access to biliary tree required and other methods failed	No absolute contraindications Relative: Large Volume Ascites (consider para and left sided approach), Coagulopathy
Percutaneous Nephrostomy	Obstructive Uropathy (**Not hydronephrosis**), Urinary diversion (leak, fistula), Access for percutaneous intervention	Uncorrectable coagulopathy, Contrast Reactions

New Shit Has Come to Light:

Made in the USA
San Bernardino, CA
11 February 2019